Books by Robert P. Swierenga

Quantification in American History:

Theory and Research (EDITOR) *1970*

Pioneers and Profits: Land Speculation on the Iowa Frontier *1968*

QUANTIFICATION IN AMERICAN HISTORY:

Theory and Research

QUANTIFICATION IN AMERICAN HISTORY:

Theory and Research

EDITED BY

Robert P. Swierenga

NEW YORK

Atheneum

1970

To my Mother and Father

Preface

QUANTIFICATION IN HISTORY is a development so recent that many are unaware of the current state of research and the potential problems and rewards of the new methodology. Indeed, few historians as yet have ventured into the seemingly dark and forbidding world of numbers and algebraic formulas. Of the nearly 300 essays submitted to the *Journal of American History* in 1969 for consideration for publication, fewer than 3 per cent, according to the editor, "employed quantification to substantiate their conclusions."[1]

The primary aim of this anthology is to stimulate interest among historians in the quantitative work being done in American history. The book offers a selection of seminal articles that examine the theoretical implications and practical applications of statistical and computer-aided techniques in the field of American history. All of these studies were written by scholars within the last decade and most have appeared in professional journals. The book is designed for historiography and historical methods courses. It illustrates the wide variety of quantitative techniques adopted by pioneering historians in the areas of content analysis, legislative and judicial behavior, popular voting analysis, economic history, and socio-cultural developments. The time span of the articles ranges from the colonial period to the twentieth century.

Two things this book does not attempt are to teach quantitative methods and to disparage traditional approaches to history. To master correlation and regression techniques, factor analysis, scaling, and significance tests, one must turn to other sources. Methodological explanations are frequently included in the various articles, but these are merely designed to make the method intelligible to the general reader. Secondly, the book does not try to persuade historians to desert traditional methods for new ones. There are many doors to historical

---

[1] The comment is in the annual report of the editor, Martin Ridge, to the Board of Editors for the year 1968–1969, *Journal of American History,* LVI (Sept., 1969), 462. This is the same ratio of quantitative articles that the editor received the previous year, 1967–1968, the first time this statistic was reported (*ibid.,* LV [Sept., 1968], 468).

truth and a healthy discipline is one in which various viewpoints and methods complement one another.

Several debts were incurred in preparing this volume. My colleagues at Kent State University, August Meier and John T. Hubbell, gave unstintingly of their time to offer technical and editorial advice. The Kent State University Library extended many courtesies, especially in the Interlibrary Loan department. I am grateful to the editorial staff of Atheneum Publishers for many valuable suggestions and trenchant criticism which greatly strengthened the finished product. Finally, I am indebted to my wife, Joan, for advice and encouragement and her assistance as a typist.

Contents

INTRODUCTION

American History and the
Quantitative Method

*Historians deal with a universe not of absolutes but of
probabilities, and for a world conceived in these terms
statistics are the appropriate tool.*
                                WILLIAM O. AYDELOTTE [1]

*As an humanist, I am bound to reply that almost all
important questions are important precisely because they
are not susceptible to quantitative answers.*
                                ARTHUR SCHLESINGER, JR.[2]

IN NO PERIOD of human history have there been greater advances in
science and technology than in the past twenty-five years. Physical and biological scientists have charted the course, but inevitably scholars in the social
and behavioral sciences have also been swept into the vortex of the new
developments. Anthropology, economics, geography, political science, psychology, and sociology all increasingly bear the marks of a mathematical method
and quantification of their theories and findings. All human activity—economic,
social, political, and cultural—is being subjected to mathematical analysis in
the pattern of the biological sciences. For convincing evidence, one need only
consult such works as John von Neumann's *The Computer and the Brain*
(1958), Donald Fink's *Computers and the Human Mind* (1966), John Loehlin's

[1] William O. Aydelotte, "Notes on Historical Generalization," in Louis Gottschalk
(ed.), *Generalization in the Writing of History* (Chicago, 1963), 175.
[2] Arthur Schlesinger, Jr., "The Humanist Looks at Empirical Social Research,"
American Sociological Review, XXVII (Dec., 1962), 770.

Computer Models of Human Personality (1968), and Nicholas Rashevsky's
Looking at History Through Mathematics (1968).

Whether desired or not, the influence of the mathematical approach on the
study of history is inescapable, and indeed the impact has been so great that
within the past decade a fascinating field has sprung up called quantitative
history. Acolytes of the new approach maintain a standing committee within the
American Historical Association to collect basic quantitative data,[3] boast a
journal *qua* newsletter with a circulation list of nearly 2000 scholars which
serves as a clearing house to report research in progress,[4] and assemble in annual conferences, workshops, and symposia.[5] Votaries of quantification have
produced an apologia,[6] a textbook on statistical methods in history,[7] and a fifty-
page annotated bibliographical guide to sources in quantitative historical research.[8] All of this adds up to a rather remarkable accomplishment for a period
of less than ten years. Nevertheless, history remains far behind other disciplines
in the humanities in the application of mathematics and computers to research
problems.[9]

I

Although the use of social statistics, econometrics, and digital computers
is of recent origin, quantification—"the numerical summary of comparable
data," to use William O. Aydelotte's phrase [10]—is not an entirely new technique

[3] The nine-man committee, formed in 1962, was originally called the "Ad Hoc
Committee to Collect the Basic Quantitative Data of American Political History." A
second history committee, numbering only six men, was formed in 1964 under the
auspices of the Mathematics Social Science Board (a joint product of the Social
Science Research Council and the Institute for Advanced Study in the Behavioral
Sciences) to educate historians in the use of quantitative techniques. See note 5 below.
[4] The journal, edited and published at the University of Pittsburgh, is the *Historical
Methods Newsletter: Quantitative Analysis of Social, Economic, and Political Development* (Dec., 1967–   ). Since 1969, *HMN* is partially republished in Social
Science Information. Another journal serving historians is *Computers and the
Humanities* (Sept., 1966–   ), published at Queens College of the City University
of New York.
[5] Economic historians have held annual conferences at Purdue University since
1960. More recently, political behavioralists have convened annually at various universities in New York, specifically at Cortland in 1968 and Brockport in 1969. Since
1965, the Inter-University Consortium for Political Research at Ann Arbor has
sponsored annual summer training programs in social research methods. The Mathematics Social Science Board during the years 1967–1969 conducted an annual "Conference on Applications of Quantitative Methods to Political, Social and Economic
History." Finally, in 1964 and 1965, International Business Machines sponsored six
regional conferences in which 1200 academicians were introduced to the role of
computers in humanistic research. These conferences are only the major ones and by
no means exhaust the list of such meetings.
[6] William O. Aydelotte, "Quantification in History," *American Historical Review*,
LXXI (Apr., 1966), 803–25.
[7] Richard Jensen and Charles M. Dollar, *Quantitative Historical Research* (New
York, 1970).
[8] Richard Jensen and Charles M. Dollar, "Guide to Resources of Value in
Quantitative Historical Research," mimeograph, 1969.
[9] Samuel P. Hays, "Computers and Historical Research," in Edmund A. Bowles,
(ed.), *Computers in Humanistic Research, Readings and Perspectives* (Englewood
Cliffs, 1967), 72. As of Nov., 1969, the "Directory of Scholars Active" in *Computers
and the Humanities* (IV, 125–41) has listed 33 historians engaged in computerized
projects, compared to 329 scholars in the language and literature category and 45 in
music.
[10] "Quantification in History," 805.

in historical method.[11] At the turn of the century, Frederick Jackson Turner, Orin G. Libby, A. Lawrence Lowell, and Henry Adams, among others, were pioneering in the quantitative approach to historical research. In 1897 Turner called for a "detailed study of the correlations between party votes, by precincts, wards, etc., soils, nationalities and state-origins of the voter, assessment rolls, denominational groups, illiteracy, etc." This type of micro-analysis, he insisted, would indicate "what kind of people tend to be Whigs, what Democrats, or Abolitionists, or Prohibitionists, etc." [12] Turner's gifted student Orin Libby similarly issued a plea for Congressional roll-call analysis and for "carefully prepared maps showing the exact location of every vote for and against each measure." Libby himself charted the geographical distribution of votes of the thirteen states on the ratification of the Constitution, and the partisan factions in Washington's administrations based on Congressional voting patterns.[13] In 1904 Turner reiterated his support of quantified history, declaring "that no satisfactory understanding of the evolution of this American people is possible without calling into cooperation many sciences and methods hitherto little used by the American historian. . . . The method of the statistician as well as that of the critic of evidence is absolutely essential." [14]

A. Lawrence Lowell of Harvard University, meanwhile, followed up Libby's suggestion of roll-call analysis. Intrigued by the strong partisanship in America since the 1830's, Lowell decided to measure party influence on legislation by tabulating every non-unanimous division in seven selected sessions of the English House of Commons, five Congresses, and seven legislative terms in five selected states. The Commons was included for comparative purposes. "It is difficult to form an accurate estimate of the extent of party influence without thorough statistics," Lowell declared in justification of his tedious project. Although he was swamped by raw data and handicapped by inadequate methodological tools, his time-series graphs of party cohesion indexes were indeed a remarkable achievement in quantification.[15] Lowell's colleague Henry Adams

[11] This section relies heavily on the following works: Edward N. Saveth, "The Conceptualization of American History," in Saveth (ed.), *American History and the Social Sciences* (Glencoe, 1964), 3–22; Aydelotte, "Quantification in History," 803–25; Aydelotte, "Notes on Historical Generalization," and David Potter, "Explicit Data and Implicit Assumptions in Historical Study," in Gottschalk, *Generalization in the Writing of History,* 144–94; Robert F. Berkhofer, Jr., *A Behavioral Approach to Historical Analysis* (New York, 1969), especially chapters 12–13; and Allan G. Bogue, "United States: The 'New' Political History," *Journal of Contemporary History,* III (Jan., 1968), 5–27.
[12] Quoted in Joseph Schafer, "The Microscopic Method Applied to History," *Minnesota History Bulletin,* IV (Feb., 1921), 19.
[13] Orin G. Libby, "A Plea for the Study of Votes in Congress," *American Historical Association, Report, 1896* (Washington, 1897), I, 332. Libby's substantive contributions are *Geographical Distribution of the Vote of the Thirteen States on the Federal Constitution* (Madison, 1894), and "Political Factions in Washington's Administrations," *Quarterly Journal of the University of North Dakota,* III (July, 1913), 291–318.
[14] Frederick Jackson Turner, *The Significance of Sections in American History* (New York, 1932), 20. The quoted section was written in 1904.
[15] A. Lawrence Lowell, "The Influence of Party upon Legislation in England and America," *American Historical Association, Report, 1901* (2 vols., Washington, 1902), I, 321–542. The quote is on page 321. Lowell tabulated every non-unanimous roll call (more than 90 per cent of both parties voting on the same side) in the British Commons' sessions of 1836, 1850, 1860, 1870, 1881, 1894, and 1899; both sessions of the 29th (1849), 38th (1862), 55th (1896), and 56th (1898) Congresses; and the

also showed a marked interest in the then primitive field of statistics, and much earlier, George Bancroft, called the "father of American historical writing," had served as first president of the American Geographical and Statistical Society.[16]

This early interest in quantification, however, failed to spark a sustained effort among historians in the new direction. Perhaps, as Allan G. Bogue has suggested, it was "because of the inadequate statistical methods of the pioneers." [17] The tools themselves were also blunt, however, as Libby and Lowell learned to their dismay. Data-processing machinery was primitive and Herman Hollerith's ingenious punched-card electrical tabulating machine, developed in the 1880's for the United States Census Bureau to automate the 1890 census, seemed to hold little immediate promise for historians.[18]

Not until the early 1930's were data cards used in a large-scale historical study. In 1933 a young agricultural economist, William G. Murray of Iowa State University, transcribed to tabulating-machine cards detailed coded information from some 26,000 land mortgages in Story County, Iowa, from 1854 to 1932.[19] Murray's significant study has remained a landmark in machine manipulation of historical data. The first historians to follow Murray's method were Merle Curti in his demographic study of a Wisconsin frontier community, 1850–1880, and Bernard and Lotte Bailyn in their analysis of shipping registers in colonial Massachusetts. Both books appeared in 1959 with appended essays explaining and praising the new methods.[20] Three years later, Sam B. Warner, Jr., published *Streetcar Suburbs,* a study of the process of suburban development in Boston based on a punch-card analysis of some 28,000 building permits issued between 1872 and 1901.[21] William I. Davisson utilized the same technique and 26,000 punch cards to analyze inventories of colonial estates in Essex County, Massachusetts.[22] Stephan Thernstrom's computerized reconstruction of the demographic and social structure of Boston from 1880 to the present is

---

legislatures of Massachusetts (1899), New York (1894, 1899), Pennsylvania (1895, 1899), Ohio (1900), and Illinois (1899).

[16] Edward N. Saveth (ed.), *Henry Adams* (New York, 1963), xxii, 54, 66, 165–71; I. L. Bernard and Jessie Bernard, *Origins of American Sociology* (New York, 1943), 763. Edward N. Saveth argues for Bancroft's rightful title in "Historical Understanding in Democratic America," in Saveth (ed.), *Understanding the American Past* (Boston, 1954), 2.

[17] Allan G. Bogue, " 'New' Political History," 5. One of Lowell's students followed his example. See Hannah G. Roach, "Sectionalism in Congress (1870 to 1890)," *American Political Science Review,* XIX (Aug., 1925), 500–26.

[18] F. J. Rex, Jr., "Herman Hollerith, the First 'Statistical Engineer,' " *Computers and Automation,* X (1961), 10–13.

[19] William G. Murray, *An Economic Analysis of Farm Mortgages in Story County, Iowa, 1854–1931* (Iowa Agricultural Experiment Station, Research Bulletin No. 156 [Ames, 1933]), 361–424.

[20] Merle Curti, *et al., The Making of an American Community: A Case Study of Democracy in a Frontier County* (Stanford, 1959), esp. Appendix I ("Analysis of Census Data"); and Bernard Bailyn and Lotte Bailyn, *Massachusetts Shipping, 1697–1714: A Statistical Study* (Cambridge, 1959), esp. 135–41 ("A Note on Procedure"). Curti's study involved some 17,000 data cards and Bailyn's 4,725.

[21] Sam B. Warner, Jr., *Streetcar Suburbs: The Process of Growth in Boston, 1870–1900* (Cambridge, 1962).

[22] William I. Davisson, "Essex County Price Trends: Money and Markets in 17th Century Massachusetts," *Essex Institute Historical Collections,* CIII (Apr., 1967), 144–85; "Essex County Wealth Trends: Wealth and Economic Growth in 17th Century Massachusetts," *ibid.,* (Oct., 1967), 291–342.

equally ambitious.[23] All of these efforts are dwarfed, however, by the $500,000 data-collection project of the Inter-University Consortium for Political Research at Ann Arbor, launched in 1964 in conjunction with the Survey Research Center of the University of Michigan and the ad hoc committee of the American Historical Association. The Consortium, now supported by more than 130 colleges, universities, and data archives, plans to build a vast historical data archive of basic election returns, demographic facts, and Congressional roll calls; to disseminate the information widely in machine-readable form; and to train scholars in quantitative methods of data analysis.[24]

II

While historians are not loath to use punch cards and counter sorters (at least since the 1950's), they seem to be less eager to master social statistics or the digital computer. William Aydelotte's scalogram analysis of voting patterns in the British House of Commons in the 1840's, which appeared in January 1963, is the first published work by an historian involving computerized research and a statistical method.[25] Aydelotte's tool, the Guttman scalogram, was primitive by contemporary statistical standards, but among historians he was truly in the vanguard. In 1965 a member of the AHA Committee on Quantitative Data estimated somewhat generously that not more than two dozen historians of faculty rank had a knowledge of statistics through multiple correlation and regression analysis. The number is probably no larger than three or four dozen today, provided one excludes economic historians.[26]

Use of the electronic computer is hardly more common. An informal survey of computerized research projects in the humanities conducted by the American Council of Learned Societies in 1965 turned up the names of only thirty historians among the more than 200 respondents. Most of the historians were involved in roll-call analyses of legislative bodies and multiple biography studies of leadership groups (elites), although there was also a smattering of studies

[23] Stephan Thernstrom, "The Historian and the Computer," in Bowles, *Computers in Humanistic Research,* 6, and "Notes on the Historical Study of Social Mobility," *Comparative Studies in History and Theory,* X (Jan., 1968), 162–72.

[24] Jerome M. Clubb, "The Inter-University Consortium for Political Research; Progress and Prospects," *Historical Methods Newsletter,* II (June, 1969), 1–5; William E. Miller and Philip E. Converse, "The Inter-University Consortium for Political Research," *International Social Science Journal,* XVI (1964), 70–76; Inter-University Consortium for Political Research, *Biennial Report, 1966–1968,* 51–100, esp. 61–64. County-level election returns from 1824 are available for more than 90 per cent of all elections, state and national. Also at hand are historical census data abstracted from the published U.S. Census Reports from 1790, amounting to the equivalent of two million data cards. Congressional roll-call records are nearly complete from 1863 for both houses of Congress. The entire initial project is slated for completion in 1970 after which additional bodies of information will be added to the data repository.

[25] William O. Aydelotte, "Voting Patterns in the British House of Commons in the 1840's," *Comparative Studies in Society and History,* V (Jan., 1963), 134–63.

[26] Hays, "Computers and Historical Research," in Bowles, *Computers in Humanistic Research,* 71; Bogue, " 'New' Political History," 10. Economic historians frequently hold degrees in economics rather than history and are conversant with calculus and statistics. The situation regarding historians may soon change. In the summer of 1968, for example, 28 pre- and post-doctoral historians from major universities participated in the training program of the Inter-University Consortium for Political Research with a course on "Quantitative Methods for Historical Data," *Historical Methods Newsletter,* II (Dec., 1968), 6.

in content analysis, social mobility, economic history, demography, and voting statistics.[27] Since the inception in 1964 of the ACLS post-doctoral program of grants and fellowships for computer-oriented research in the humanities, only 8 historians have been among the 44 recipients of awards.[28] Until 1966 when two articles appeared, Aydelotte's essay stood alone as a published example of computer-aided historical research.[29] Since the mid-1960's, however, a growing number of historians have taken cram courses in machine languages such as FORTRAN and PL/I offered by congenial computer departments, and a burgeoning list of publications and "research in progress" attests to the fruitful results of the reorientation, especially among younger scholars.[30]

III

What is this electronic marvel, the computer, that services a growing band of scholars on more than 800 college and university campuses in the United States? [31] Basically, the digital computer is a glorified adding machine, capable of performing at a rate of a million or billion times faster than human beings and with absolute accuracy. Mechanical counting devices date back to the abacus invented in 3000 B.C., and in the more recent past to the ingenious calculating machines of Blaise Pascal (1642) and Gottfried Leibnitz (1694).[32]

[27] Edmund A. Bowles (comp.), "Computerized Research in the Humanities: A Survey," *ACLS Newsletter, Special Supplement* (June, 1966), 10–16.

[28] *ACLS Newsletter*, XV (Apr., 1964), 16; XVI (Mar., 1965), 18; XVI (May, 1965), 7–31; XVII (Mar., 1966), 14–15; XVIII (Mar., 1967), 16; XIX (Jan., 1968), 8; XX (Mar., 1969), 29–30; XX (Apr., 1969), 24–25.

[29] Robert P. Swierenga, "Land Speculator 'Profits' Reconsidered: Central Iowa as a Test Case," *Journal of Economic History*, XXVII (Mar., 1966), 1–28; and Glenn M. Linden, " 'Radicals' and Economic Policies: The Senate, 1861–1873," *Journal of Southern History*, XXXII (May, 1966), 189–99. The next year several major books and articles appeared: Thomas B. Alexander, *Sectional Stress and Party Strength: A Computer Analysis of Roll-Call Voting Patterns in the United States House of Representatives, 1836–1860* (Nashville, 1967); Theodore K. Rabb, *Enterprise and Empire: Merchant and Gentry Investments in the Expansion of England, 1575–1630* (Cambridge, 1967); Glenn M. Linden, " 'Radicals' and Economic Policies: The House of Representatives, 1861–1873," *Civil War History*, XIII (Mar., 1967), 51–65; Allan G. Bogue, "Bloc and Party in the United States Senate, 1861–1863," *ibid.*, XIII (Sept., 1967), 221–41; Jerome M. Clubb and Howard W. Allen, "Party Loyalty in the Progressive Years: The Senate, 1909–1915," *Journal of Politics*, XXIX (Aug., 1967), 567–84.

[30] The "Directory of Scholars Active," updated semi-annually and published in *Computers and the Humanities,* as of Nov., 1969, lists 92 scholars in the social sciences of which 33 are historians. *CHum's* annual bibliography of quantitative studies is growing. The 1966 bibliography included 74 books and articles, with 37 added for 1967 and 48 for 1968. For the "Social Science" section of the Directory see *Computers and the Humanities,* I (May, 1967), 228–40; II (Nov., 1967), 89–92; II (May, 1968), 246–49; III (Nov., 1968), 113–17; III (May, 1969), 313–19; IV (Nov., 1969), 125–41. The bibliography for history is in I (Mar., 1967), 145–49; II (Mar., 1968), 169–70; III (Mar., 1969), 219–21. "Research in Progress" as reported periodically in the *Historical Methods Newsletter* since 1968, contained as of Dec., 1969, summaries of 34 computerized historical projects in progress.

[31] Edmund A. Bowles (ed.), *Computers in Humanistic Research,* v.

[32] For this and the following paragraph, I have relied heavily on Harold Borko, "History and Development of Computers," in Borko (ed.), *Computer Applications in the Behavioral Sciences* (Englewood Cliffs, 1962), chap. 3; Jeremy Bernstein, *The Analytical Engine: Computers—Past, Present and Future* (New York, 1963); and Saul Rosen, "Electronic Computers: A Historical Survey," *Computing Surveys*, I (Mar., 1969), 7–36.

But the true forerunner of the modern automatic computer is the "Difference Engine" of Charles Babbage, conceived in 1812 and partially built in the 1820's with the aid of $75,000 from the British government. The Difference Engine and Babbage's more advanced "Analytic Engine" were designed not only to calculate tables of squares and polynomial functions but also to print out the results—a great advance in automation. Unfortunately, neither of Babbage's computers became operational. He lacked sufficient funds despite the initial governmental support; machine-tool technology was too primitive to mass produce precision parts; and above all, neither government nor business felt a real urgency for automatic computation.

Babbage's death in 1871 virtually halted computer development until the military exigencies of the Second World War promoted further research. In the interim, the only major advance was the mechanical analog calculator built in 1931 by Vannevar Bush at the Massachusetts Institute of Technology. This machine, which can be thought of as an automated slide-rule, was used extensively during the war to compute artillery firing tables. But, as is true of all analog calculators, there were inherent limits in its flexibility and accuracy.

The digital computer, which counts rather than measures, obviates these difficulties and therefore has become the model of most present computers. Howard W. Aitken, a graduate student in physics at Harvard University, began work in 1939 on the first modern digital computer, the Mark I, in collaboration with the International Business Machines Company. This primitive machine became operational in 1944, and utilized electrical relays rather than the more efficient vacuum tubes or transistors which were subsequently developed. The Mark I was updated two years later by the first generation of electronic computers such as ENIAC and EDVAC, built in connection with university projects sponsored by government, military, and research organizations.

John von Neumann, one of the greatest mathematicians and theoretical physicists of the twentieth century, played a key role in the engineering revolution leading to the more sophisticated computers. Von Neumann, a fellow of the Institute for Advanced Study at Princeton University and subsequently a physicist at the Los Alamos nuclear research laboratory, began to devote his time to the computer field in 1944, the same year that he published his definitive treatise on Game Theory. During the next few years, von Neumann formulated the now standard methods of translating mathematic procedures into machine "language" instructions for the computer, and even more important, he standardized the internal circuitry and execution cycle of computers.[33]

Following the war, computers invaded the commercial world, beginning with UNIVAC I in 1950. The word that characterizes their subsequent history is "proliferation"—in computer installations, users, and uses. In 1959, the second generation computers arrived, characterized by transistorized "super" marvels such as the IBM series 7090. Since 1965, most new computers such as the IBM system 360 belong to a third generation which features integrated circuit technology and multiprocessor, multiprogramming systems.

---

[33] The best brief biographical sketch is S. Ulam *et al.*, "John Von Neumann, 1903–1957," *Perspectives in American History*, II (1968), 235–69. See also Von Neumann and Oskar Morgenstern, *Theory of Games and Economic Behavior* (Princeton, 1944), and Von Neumann, *The Computer and the Brain* (Princeton, 1958).

For the historian, the computer revolution opens a wide vista, "a research in new dimensions," as Edmund A. Bowles recently noted.[34] The incredible speed and accuracy of computers permit scholars to broaden their data base, attempt more complex and comprehensive analyses, and increase the reliability of the resulting generalizations. Computers played a key role in eight of the essays included in this book, those by Allan G. Bogue, Robert R. Dykstra and Harlan Hahn, Robert W. Fogel, Ivor S. Francis, Richard Jensen, Richard L. Merritt, Robert P. Swierenga, and Roger E. Wyman. In several instances, the authors attest to the tremendous boon, if not the indispensability, of the computer in their research. An additional bonus of computerized methods is that the scholar is impelled to begin with the basic but neglected step of defining terms explicitly and formulating his problem with clarity and logic.

Computerized history is not without its problems, both practical and theoretical. In the first place, the initial input effort is often extremely costly. Preparing data for computer manipulation requires key punching as well as the preliminary abstracting and classifying of non-aggregated data such as census, tax, and land records. Some knowledge of statistics and computer languages is also necessary to communicate with the electronic wizard. Little has been said within the profession as to the optimum level of competence. One can identify at least three types of users: (1) the entrepreneur who hires proficient programmers, (2) the dependent user who leans on the consulting staff of the computer center but struggles to master the machine himself by a process of trial and error, and (3) the expert investigator who has acquired a basic understanding of the design and logic of computers and has learned the computer language most compatible with his research needs.[35] Most historical quantifiers fall into the second category, those who try to obtain computer skills on the job. At the very least, a rudimentary knowledge of a programming language is necessary, if only to assess the data contained in the "print out" and to converse with the skilled programmers and avoid the GIGO effect ("Garbage In, Garbage Out").[36] Better yet is to undertake a comprehensive instructional

[34] Edmund A. Bowles, "Toward a Research in New Dimensions," in Bowles, *Computers in Humanistic Research,* 8–15, and Bowles, "The Humanities and the Computer: Some Current Research Problems," *Computers and Automation,* XV (Apr., 1966), 24–27. On the promising uses of computerized research in history, see also Samuel P. Hays, "Computers and Historical Research" and Stephan Thernstrom, "The Historian and the Computer," in Bowles, *Computers in Humanistic Research,* 62–81; Harold Borko, "Computer Functions and Applications," in Borko, *Computer Applications in the Behavioral Sciences,* chap. 4; Thomas J. Condon, "Goals for Humanistic Research with Computers," *ACLS Newsletter,* XVIII (Apr., 1967), 1–7; Vern L. Bulloch, "The Computer and the Historian—Some Tentative Beginnings," *Computers and the Humanities,* I (Jan., 1967), 61–64; Charles M. Dollar, "Innovation in Historical Research: A Computer Approach," *ibid.,* III (Jan., 1969), 139–51; Jerome M. Clubb and Howard W. Allen, "Computers and Historical Studies," *Journal of American History,* LIV (Dec., 1967), 599–607; Marshall Smelser and William I. Davisson, "The Historian and the Computer: A Simple Introduction to Complex Computation," *Essex Institute Historical Collections,* CIV (Apr., 1968), 109–26.
[35] See Smelser and Davisson, "The Historian and the Computer," 114–16; Hugh F. Cline, "Computer Instruction for Scholars in the Humanities," *Computers and the Humanities,* III (Sept., 1968), 31–40.
[36] The GIGO effect, J. H. Hexter facetiously noted, "is now available by computer to some who hitherto relied on their own resources to achieve it. Although this technological improvement will most certainly increase the GNP of GIGO, it is

program, a path trodden by an increasing number of students and faculty. As Judith S. Rose recently observed: "We are living in an age of computers and most of us will sooner or later find them impinging on our professional lives, whether as users, advisors to users, evaluators of the efforts of users, or merely as readers of professional literature." [37] Edmund Bowles' prediction is stronger: "Within a short time . . . a knowledge of data processing will be part of the 'common baggage' of research tools and techniques required of every graduate student in the humanities. . . . The time will come when students will be as fluent in programming as in writing English compositions." [38]

IV

Apart from the primary gains of speed, accuracy, and ease in handling large quantities of data, the use of computers often results in a significant secondary gain—the intellectual reorientation of the user. In the first place, historians typically pose specific questions and then search for sources containing the answers. In computer-assisted research, however, the reverse technique is best. First one collects the total universe of relevant data and then he asks questions. "The facts must be assembled to answer every conceivable question which may ever be asked of a given universe," Marshall Smelser and William I. Davisson insist. "After all," they add, "what is a collection of historical data but a collec-tion of answers waiting to be questioned? If the questions are unanswerable the answers are unknowable" (5).

Secondly, and more important, historians need to generalize far more than they do at present if they wish to say anything meaningful. Generalizations, as Professor Aydelotte reminds us, are "implicitly quantitative in character." Com-puters prompt generalization. Therefore, to exploit the machine, one must systematize procedures, formulate reasonable hypotheses based on theory, break large problems into their component parts, convert implicitly quantitative information into explicit numbers and scales, and, in general, follow the scientific method. Computers may thus lead to the fulfillment of Lee Benson's dream—"a genuinely scientific historiography." Historians will make increas-ingly systematic cumulative studies, which collectively can produce refined data that permit scholars to discover and demonstrate general laws of human be-havior.

But the goal of science is more than the discovery of explanatory generaliza-tions. To achieve the objective of science one must aim for predictability as well as explanation. Waiting in the wings, therefore, is the most controversial and innovative usage of computers and quantitative methods, that of predictive

---

doubtful whether it will significantly affect its proportionate share of TSO (Total Scholarly Output)." Hexter, "Some American Observations," *Journal of Contempo-rary History,* II (Jan., 1967), 18.

[37] Judith S. Rose's review of Thomas H. Crowley, *Understanding Computers* (New York, 1967), in *Historical Methods Newsletter,* II (Dec., 1968), 13–14.

[38] Edmund A. Bowles, "Computers: The Tool of the Future," in Rutgers, The State University—IBM, *Conference on the Use of Computers in Humanistic Research, December 4, 1964* (New Brunswick, 1965), 6–7. This prediction is reiterated in Bowles, "Humanities and the Computer," 27.

history. If psychologists, sociologists, and political scientists can sample individuals and groups of people, test and refine their theory, and arrive at rudimentary forecasts of behavior, historians willing to collaborate with these sister scientists may also be able to make at least short-range predictions about the course of events. Although history never repeats itself, comparisons with analogous periods in the past can certainly aid in interpreting the present and pointing the way to the future. S. Sidney Ulmer, for example, successfully predicted the Supreme Court alignment on civil rights cases for six consecutive terms (1955–1961), based on a scale analysis of behavior patterns in the previous terms (11). The historical pattern of high rates of homicide and assault in the American South, which seems to be a product of the colonial status of the South and a consequent paranoiac "siege mentality," according to Sheldon Hackney (18), may help explain the present propensity to violence among Afro-Americans who likewise are alienated and feel a deep sense of grievance and persecution. Another testable hypothesis is the assumption of modern social reformers that educational programs such as pre-school training can help overcome the results of cultural deprivation on ghetto children. An historical case study of educational innovations in earlier periods of rapid advance such as the Jacksonian era or the Progressive period might allow one to test this unproven assumption.[39]

In the internecine battles among historians over quantification, the victory has gone to the quantifiers. How could it have been otherwise, one defender of the traditional approach confesses somewhat abjectly. "It is not easy even for the most jealous obscurantist to argue that historical problems which hinge on the question 'how many?' are better solved by answers like 'lots,' or 'quite a few,' or 'not many,' or 'a mere handful,' than by 80, 45, 20 or 2 per cent." [40] The principal value of quantification in historical method, however, is not the greater accuracy but, as Professor Aydelotte holds (1), the greater ease in verifying general statements. As we have already noted, many historical generalizations are implicitly quantitative in character, whether this is clearly stated or not. The value of the quantitative approach is that it substitutes an examined generalization for an unexamined one, and thus helps to compensate for the selective screening process of the human mind. Not all historical problems are amenable to numerical analysis but statistical tests can be applied to many problems heretofore overlooked or considered purely qualitative.

That statistical presentations prove nothing in themselves is of course a truism. A graph or table is only a convenient restatement of the facts. Nonetheless, quantitative data are useful in determining the extent to which a general statement holds up under testing. Statistics are the appropriate tool in a world of probabilities, Professor Aydelotte has observed, and "once we stop asking whether a given statement is true and inquire instead how far it is true the argument reaches a new level not only of reliability but also of significance." [41] For, correctly speaking, a generalization is never proved, it merely remains a useful explanatory hypothesis until disproved. Statistics provide an indispensable tool in the testing or disproving process. Of course, quantification can never

[39] This is Vern Bulloch's suggestion in "The Computer and the Historian," 63.
[40] J. H. Hexter, "Some American Observations," 11.
[41] William O. Aydelotte, "Notes on Historical Generalization," 175–76.

substitute for a carefully contrived set of hypotheses. Robert Berkhofer is at least partially correct in his observation that "counting far too often replaces cerebration in the recent adoption of social science fads by historians." [42]

How "significant" the fruits are from the application of quantitative techniques in history is a moot question at this early stage of development. From Arthur Schlesinger's perspective, the findings of the past decade are mere trivia. Human events in their larger context, he insists, are too complex to be susceptible to quantification. Despite Schlesinger's caveat, significant beginnings have been made in various aspects of quantitative history—in the application of content-analysis methods to historical documents, in roll-call studies of political group behavior, in multivariate factoring of electoral patterns, in the macro- and micro-analysis of American economic growth, and in the social dimensions of violence, mobility, and leadership elites. We now have a clearer picture of the development of American nationalism in the late colonial period (7), the role of Republican radicals in the Civil War Senate (9), the partisan concerns of state politicos in the Jacksonian era (10), the ecological parameters of racism during Reconstruction (13), the impact of transcontinental railroads on economic growth (16), the profitability of frontier land speculation (17), and the mobility gains of urban workers during the industrial revolution (19).

These innovative pieces of research are obviously only small advances in knowledge when measured against the weighty demands of humanist critics. But the methods thus far have been fairly simple. Greater results can be expected from the second generation of quantitative historians now emerging from graduate seminars. Many of these scholars have mastered inferential as well as descriptive statistics, are conversant with computers and mathematical models, and have surmounted the traditional insistence on individual research in favor of joint projects with an interdisciplinary flair.

In the final analysis, however, quantitative history has its limitations. Historical information is often limited and nothing can be gained by imposing a method unsuited for the sparse evidence. More important, men and events are complex and not always predictable. "Exceptional people and facts and major breaks in continuity are exogenous variables," Jean Marczewski has observed, which the researcher "can deal with only by borrowing from qualitative history." A mass of numerical data may be coherent in itself, but purposeless until new ideas come to mind which raise challenging questions. "There can therefore be no opposition, nor even competition, between quantitative and qualitative history," Marczewski concludes. "They represent nothing more than two distinct but complementary approaches, both equally indispensable to historical research." [43]

[42] Robert Berkhofer, *Behavioral Approach to Historical Analysis,* 315. Nor can statistics overcome the basic problem of data verification. See the timely warning of Robert M. Zemsky, "Numbers and History: The Dilemma of Measurement," *Computers and the Humanities,* III (Sept., 1969), 31–40.
[43] Jean Marczewski, "Quantitative History," *Journal of Contemporary History,* III (Apr., 1968), 190. J. H. Hexter also views the polarization as a false *Methodenstreit* ("Some American Observations," 19).

PART I

Quantification, Scientific History, and the Computer

S INCE THE EARLY YEARS of the twentieth century historians have carried on a continual debate concerning the "social science approach" to their craft.[1] Behavioralist reformers insist that scientific explanation—the testing of general laws in the study of specific events—is the appropriate model of historical research. The vast majority of historians, however, prefer their individual modes and goals of research rather than any monolithic social scientific ideal. There is no "One Saving Methodological Truth," J. H. Hexter asserts. "The notion that in recent years all the Good Things in history came to it by way of quantification and the social sciences is not false in fact, . . . it is wrong in theory."[2]

In recent years, William O. Aydelotte, Lee Benson, Allan G. Bogue, and Samuel P. Hays, among others, have sought to encourage the quantitative approach to history. They have also been directly involved in the data collection project of the Inter-University Consortium for Political Research at Ann Arbor. With the ready accessibility of the Consortium data in machine-readable form, political historians have made significant contributions to the quest for behavioral laws. Benson and Bogue also bring to their work a background in the more analytic and statistical field of economic history, having trained together in Professor Paul W. Gates' famed inter-disciplinary seminar at Cornell University. In the 1950's, Aydelotte, Bogue, and Hays comprised a behavioral triumvirate within the history faculty in the University of Iowa. Led by Aydelotte, the department chairman and seminal figure, this group and their graduate students, notably Robert R. Dykstra, Samuel T. McSeveney, and Joel H. Silbey, were among the initiators of the "new" political history. Although now dispersed, the so-called "Iowa school" continues to carry on the message of quantitative history.[3]

---

[1] An account of the dialogue, with extensive documentation, is John Higham, *History: The Development of Historical Studies in the United States* (Englewood Cliffs, 1965), esp. chap. 4. Other valuable contributions are Louis Gottschalk (ed.), *Generalization in the Writing of History* (Chicago, 1963); *Theory and Practice in Historical Study: A Report of the Committee on Historiography* (Social Science Research Council Bulletin 54 [New York, 1946]); *The Social Sciences in Historical Study: A Report of the Committee on Historiography* (Social Science Research Council Bulletin 64 [New York, 1954]).

[2] J. H. Hexter, "Some American Observations [on Quantitative History]," *Journal of Contemporary History*, II (Jan., 1967), 17–18.

[3] For a discussion of the research results of the "Iowa School," see in addition to Bogue's essay (4): Dwight W. Hoover, "Political Behavioralism in American History: A Case Study," Indiana Academy of the Social Sciences, *Proceedings, Third Series*, II (1967), 144–60, and Joel W. Silbey, "The Civil War Synthesis in American Political History," *Civil War History*, X (June, 1964), 130–40. Aydelotte blazed the quantitative trail with a number of articles, including: "Voting Patterns in the British House of Commons in the 1840's," *Comparative Studies in Society and History*, V (Jan., 1963), 134–63; "Parties and Issues in Early Victorian England," *Journal of British Studies*, V (May, 1966), 95–101; "The County Gentlemen and the Repeal of the Corn Laws," *English Historical Review*, LXXXII (Jan., 1967), 47–60; "The Conservative and Radical Interpretations of Early Victorian Social Legislation," *Victorian Studies*, XI (1967), 225–36; "The Disintegration of the Conservative Party

Although they share a common background, the leading behavioralists discussed here differ in their ideological commitment to scientific history. Benson and Hays especially have stated the charges against conventional history [4] and Benson confidently predicts that past human behavior will be studied scientifically within fifteen years by a "significant proportion" of American historians (2).[5] Aydelotte (1) and Bogue (4), in contrast, consider quantitative techniques simply as additional aids in scholarly research. Biography and institutional studies also remain necessary and useful. Both men likewise recognize limits in the application of quantitative methods to historical problems. As Bogue declared in one of his well-turned phrases: "The quantifier may build some dams and breakwaters in what Matthew Arnold unfairly termed 'that huge Mississippi of falsehood called history,' but there are rapids he will not tame, tributaries he cannot explore, and quicksands he still cannot plumb by quantification."

Even Bogue's irenic imagery would fail to satisfy some critics of quantitative and computerized history.[6] Building dams and breakwaters of any consequence implies a major body of water. But historians who prefer to call themselves "humanists" insist that major problems in history cannot be studied quantitatively. "Almost all important questions are important precisely because they are *not* susceptible to quantitative answers," Arthur Schlesinger, Jr., asserted to a gathering of sociologists some years ago (3). Professor Schlesinger seems to have overlooked the fact, however, that historians cannot avoid problems of measurement simply by restricting their data to non-numerical words or concepts. As sociologist Philip Hauser reminded Schlesinger, "the humanist-historian in his effort to explain an event is actually working with a dependent and a series of independent variables; and he is after all skillfully or clumsily using a nominal scale of measurement." The explanation of the humanist, Professor Hauser continued, "is as much subject to the question of sampling, of reliability,

in the Eighteen-Forties: A Study of Political Attitudes," paper presented to the Conference on Applications of Quantitative Methods to Political, Social, and Economic History, Chicago, June, 1969.

[4] Frederick Jackson Turner, Charles Beard, and Arthur Schlesinger, Jr., among others have been the objects of Benson's trenchant critiques: *Turner and Beard: American Historical Writing Reconsidered* (Glencoe, 1960); *The Concept of Jacksonian Democracy: New York as a Test Case* (Princeton, 1961). For Hays, see "New Possibilities for American Political History: The Social Analysis of Political Life," in Seymour Martin Lipset and Richard Hofstadter, *Sociology and History: Methods* (New York, 1968), 181–227.

[5] Benson's methodological essays are, "Research Problems in American Political Historiography," in Mirra Komarovsky (ed.), *Common Frontiers of the Social Sciences* (Glencoe, 1957), 113–83, and "An Approach to the Scientific Study of Past Public Opinion," *Public Opinion Quarterly,* XXXI (Winter, 1967–1968), 522–62.

[6] For discussion of the adverse reaction of historians to computer-assisted historical research, see Vern L. Bulloch, "The Computer and the Historian—Some Tentative Beginnings," *Computers and the Humanities,* I (Jan., 1967), 61; Charles M. Dollar, "Innovation in Historical Research: A Computer Approach," *ibid.,* III (Jan., 1969), 139–40; Thomas J. Condon, "The Computer and the Humanist," *ACLS Newsletter,* XVII (Apr., 1966), 1–2; Jerome Clubb and Howard W. Allen, "Computers and Historical Studies," *Journal of American History,* LIV (Dec., 1967), 606–7; Marshall Smelser and William I. Davisson, "The Historian and the Computer: A Simple Introduction to Complex Computation," *Essex Institute Historical Collections,* CIV (Apr., 1968), 109–11; Warren E. Miller and Philip E. Converse, "The Inter-University Consortium for Political Research," *International Social Science Journal,* XVI (1964), 70–71; J. H. Hexter, "Some American Observations," 5–23.

of validity and of precision as is the explanation of the researcher who uses admittedly statistical methods." In the final analysis, concluded Hauser, both quantitative and qualitative techniques involve the same steps. Both map the real world to be explained against a set of symbols, verbal or numerical, which are manipulated and arranged "to achieve order of a type constituting explanation or predictability." [7] The problem, therefore, is one of method rather than of the nature of the data.

Since careful method is the key to sound historical research, computers can be an invaluable ally whenever the symbols under study are numeric or can be converted into numerals. Marshall Smelser and William I. Davisson (5) and Stephan Thernstrom (6) illustrate this point in light of their own research excursions into economic and social history. Computers aid historical scholarship in several ways, the authors note. The electronic machines can digest mountains of facts in microseconds, thus obviating the need for small samples, and they force users to make their assumptions explicit by asking precise questions.

[7] Philip M. Hauser, "Schlesinger on Humanism and Empirical Research," *American Sociological Review*, XXVIII (Feb., 1963), 98. See also the comments by George C. Homans, *ibid.*, 99–100.

I

WILLIAM O. AYDELOTTE

Quantification in History

Few advocates of quantification in history present a more reasoned, moderate, and balanced apologia than William O. Aydelotte. This essay, in print only a few years and already considered a classic, is a perceptive analysis of the potentialities and pitfalls in the use of quantitative methods and materials in historical research. The author meets directly the brunt of the arguments of the critics—that quantitative work has often been methodologically sloppy and that quantification theoretically is neither feasible, valid, nor useful in the study of history. Whether or not one agrees with Aydelotte's moderate reply, the value to the profession of the quantifiers' publication efforts ultimately will determine the future of the new methodology.

OVER THE PAST GENERATION a number of historians have recognized that counting, when circumstances permit it, may assist in the explanation of a limited class of historical problems. The historical monographs in which quantitative methods have been used are already sufficiently numerous so that a review of them would require an article by itself. The purpose here is not to survey this literature but, instead, to raise several general questions related to it. Professional opinion regarding the value of quantification for history has been rather less than unanimous, and discussion of the subject has occasionally been acrimonious. There have also been a few misunderstandings. I wish to consider here what is involved in trying to apply quantitative methods to history, what kinds of results may be expected, and what difficulties lie in the way. Though I

William O. Aydelotte, "Quantification in History," *American Historical Review*, LXXI (Apr., 1966), 803–25. Reprinted with permission of the author.

shall say something about the advantages of quantification, I am also, in a sense, concerned to speak against it and to make clear the problems it presents. My own approach to the subject is conservative and skeptical, and at times I feel that the current fad for quantification has been pushed too far. In any case, the exploration of the limitations of a method is an effective device for revealing its characteristic features.

The principal value of quantification for the study of history, stated in the simplest terms, is that it provides a means of verifying general statements. Some historians, of course, disclaim any intention of making such statements and insist that the business of a historian is not to generalize but to tell a story. Such a view can hardly be seriously entertained as a description of the objectives of all historians, for it manifestly does not apply to the work of a number of eminent members of the profession. One might question, indeed, whether any historian can avoid generalizing altogether.[1] It is an idle task, however, to attempt a formal prescription of a historian's duties. If some wish to emphasize narrative more than others, there is no reason why they should not. History is what historians do, and they do different things. It would be presumptuous to dismiss any of their objectives as being in some fashion improper. The day of a single methodology in history, if it ever existed, is at any rate now gone. In a discipline where there are at present so much upheaval, reassessment of methods and values, and introduction of new approaches, it seems better to say that anything historians do is useful if it can be shown to be useful.

For historians who do wish to generalize, however, quantitative methods can offer certain advantages. Generalizations are implicitly quantitative in character, even though this may not always be clearly brought out. As Lee Benson says, historians who use words like "typical," "representative," "significant," "widespread," "growing," or "intense" are making quantitative statements whether or not they present figures to justify their assertions. Unfortunately, not all historians seem to realize the need to check general statements. Benson complains, in the same passage, of "the impressionistic approach long dominant in American historiography," [2] and I have occasionally been bothered by this kind of thing in my own field. Historians justly pride themselves on their techniques of verification, which have become in some areas highly sophisticated. It seems fair to say, however, that these techniques have more often been applied to individual bits of information than to broader statements. Some writers, after a precise description of a few cases, will proceed to generalize blithely about the motives of large groups of men even though the evidence to support their views is often not presented and, indeed, would be hard to come by, for the motives of most men are obscure and not easy to discern. To an uncritical audience several concrete illustrations may carry more conviction than a statistical table. Yet to support an argument by only a few examples, though it may be a

---

[1] The eleven contributors to a recent volume of essays on this subject, as the editor states in his summary: "all agree that the historian willy-nilly uses generalizations at different levels and of different kinds." (*Generalization in the Writing of History*, ed. Louis Gottschalk [Chicago, 1963], 208; see also, on this point, Alfred Cobban, *The Social Interpretation of the French Revolution* [Cambridge, Eng., 1964], 5–7.)
[2] Lee Benson, "Research Problems in American Political Historiography," in *Common Frontiers of the Social Sciences*, ed. Mirra Komarovsky (Glencoe, Ill., 1957), 117.

persuasive rhetorical device, is not logically adequate. There are exceptions to most historical generalizations, and, if the citation of occasional instances were accepted as proof, it would be possible to prove almost anything.

Quantitative methods, the numerical summary of comparable data, make it possible, in some cases, to avoid these pitfalls. The condensation of data by such means, when it is clearly legitimate, constitutes a saving of time and a convenience in that it makes the information easier to describe and to handle. It also helps to ensure a greater degree of accuracy. Memory is selective, and general impressions are notoriously untrustworthy. When the data are so numerous that they cannot all be kept clearly in mind at once, the investigator is likely to remember best the cases that fit his own preconceptions or his pet hypotheses. An orderly presentation of the evidence in quantitative form helps the student to escape the tricks that his memory plays upon him. Quantitative analyses are, of course, gratuitous when the number of cases is small, when the student is concerned with only a few men or, perhaps, one man, and when the general tenor of the materials can be immediately grasped. As the data become more numerous, however, a systematic arrangement of them becomes the more desirable. There are, indeed, some questions, of which examples will be given presently, which could hardly be attacked without the use of methods of this kind.

A quantitative presentation of the available information can help to direct the student's attention to the questions most worth investigating. Since it brings the whole of the evidence, on the point it covers, into intelligible focus, the general character of the findings can be more readily perceived and relationships and differences emerge that could not so easily have been observed without this reduction of the data. Such an analysis reveals what events or issues were of special interest, in the sense of involving change through time or departure from the norm, and hence might particularly repay investigation. It can, in this manner, help in defining or restating the historical problem to be studied.

Beyond this, a quantitative analysis offers a systematic means of testing hypotheses. It establishes how many examples there are to support each side of the argument and thus reveals not only the main features of the evidence but also, more important, the exceptions to them, the nuances, the degree to which the emerging generalizations need to be qualified. Measurement locates the defect in the original hypothesis and registers "the departure from theory with an authority and finesse that no qualitative technique can duplicate." A quantitative discrepancy between theory and observation is obtrusive. "No crisis is . . . so hard to suppress as one that derives from a quantitative anomaly that has resisted all the usual efforts at reconciliation." [3]

The general overview of the whole evidence obtained by quantitative means can also be a powerful stimulus toward the reformulation of one's ideas. When anomalies occur, the student can direct his attention to the cases that do not fit the original theory, try to find out why they are exceptional, and, by rearrangements of the data, test alternative hypotheses that may account for a larger proportion of the evidence. Such manipulations of the data would take an

---

[3] Thomas S. Kuhn, "The Function of Measurement in Modern Physical Science," in *Quantification: A History of the Meaning of Measurement in the Natural and Social Sciences,* ed. Harry Woolf (Indianapolis, 1961), 50, 52.

immense amount of time to do by hand, but, ordinarily, they can readily be performed by machines. I advise my students, if they are working with fifty cases or more, to punch the information. This is easily done, and, once it is done, there is no great difficulty about trying additional correlations. By the same token a quantitative analysis can even, in some cases, point the way to the formulation of new hypotheses that will make the findings more intelligible.

The case for quantification might be made in still a different way by saying that it is a method of reasoning, one that involves number. As one of my colleagues at the University of Iowa has put it, quantification adds, to whatever factual or historical premises may have been established, the premises of mathematics as well. "Arithmetic is a vast treasure house of additional premises, or, what amounts to the same thing, of patterns of deductive inference. Quantification is the key to the treasure." [4]

The advantages of this approach have been appreciated by a number of present-day historians. G. Kitson Clark suggests as appropriate advice to someone who wishes to generalize about a group or a class: "do not guess, try to count, and if you can not count admit that you are guessing." [5] Lawrence Stone writes: "Owing to the obstinate perversity of human nature, it would no doubt be possible in England of 1958 to find, if one tried, declining manual labourers and rising landed gentry. To have any validity at all, conclusions about social movements must have a statistical basis." [6]

Applications of quantitative techniques to historical materials have, in some cases, materially advanced the discussion of major problems. Monographs on the composition of the British House of Commons, which are now fairly numerous and cover a span of six centuries, have brought to light significant continuities and changes in the social structure of the British political elite. Crane Brinton, in his well-known quantitative study of the members of the Jacobin Clubs, reached the conclusion that the Jacobins represented "a complete cross-section of their community" and that: "The Jacobins of 1794 were not a class, and their enemies the 'aristocrats' were not a class; the Terror was not chiefly then a phase of the class-struggle, but even more a civil war, a religious war." [7] Donald Greer, on the basis of a quantitative analysis of the victims of the Terror, argued that the lower classes, by the definitions he used, supplied 70 per cent of the victims and the upper classes less than 30 per cent and that: "The split in society was perpendicular, not horizontal. The Terror was an intra-class, not an inter-class, war." [8] From the researches of Brinton, Greer, and others, crude class theories about the French Revolution have received a setback. Revisions have also been made in accepted views about American history. Richard P. McCormick published in the *American Historical Review* a set of tables, drawn from readily available election statistics, on the basis of which he was able to show that the great popular turnout of 1824 was a myth and that: "In the 1824 election not a single one of the eighteen states in

[4] Gustav Bergmann, *Philosophy of Science* (Madison, Wis., 1957), 69.
[5] G. Kitson Clark, *The Making of Victorian England* (London, 1962), 14.
[6] Lawrence Stone, letter to editor, *Encounter*, XI (July 1958), 73.
[7] Clarence Crane Brinton, *The Jacobins: An Essay in the New History* (New York, 1930), 70–72.
[8] Donald Greer, *The Incidence of the Terror during the French Revolution: A Statistical Interpretation* (Cambridge, Mass., 1935), 97–98.

which the electors were chosen by popular vote attained the percentage of voter participation that had been reached before 1824." His finding contradicts the assertion he quotes from a standard text that, in the period before 1824, "only small numbers of citizens seem to have bothered to go to the polls." It contrasts also with Charles and Mary Beard's colorful statement that, by 1824, "the roaring flood of the new democracy was now foaming perilously near the crest . . ." and with Arthur M. Schlesinger, Jr.'s reference to the "immense popular vote" received by Jackson in 1824.[9] Albert Ludwig Kohlmeier, using statistical data on canal and riverboat traffic, was able to show when and how rapidly the trade of the Old Northwest shifted away from the South and to the Northeast.[10] Stephan Thernstrom, by a quantitative analysis based largely on census records, exploded various familiar hypotheses about social mobility in a Massachusetts town in the later nineteenth century.[11] Quantitative presentations have formed the basis for substantial generalizations by an impressive group of additional historians including Thomas B. Alexander, Bernard and Lotte Bailyn, Allan G. Bogue, Jean Delumeau, Robert W. Fogel, Frank L. Owsley, Lawrence Stone, Charles Tilly, Sylvia L. Thrupp, and Sam B. Warner, Jr.[12] This list of examples could be considerably extended.

These results have often been achieved by fairly simple methods; for much historical research the quantitative procedures required are not complex. Historians do not ordinarily need to deal with problems of statistical inference in which an attempt is made to ascertain the characteristics of a large population by inspection of relatively small samples. Their work is usually limited to the easier task of descriptive statistics in which the object is to portray the characteristics of a group, all members of which have been studied, and to correlate some of these characteristics with each other. The computations needed for this are not ambitious. All that is generally required are a few totals, a few percentages, and a few correlations in which the relationship between

[9] Richard P. McCormick, "New Perspectives on Jacksonian Politics," *American Historical Review*, LXV (Jan. 1960), 288–301, esp. 289–91; Richard Hofstadter *et al.*, *The American Republic* (2 vols., New York, 1959), I, 391; Charles A. and Mary R. Beard, *The Rise of American Civilization* (new ed., 2 vols., New York, 1931), I, 550; Arthur M. Schlesinger, Jr., *The Age of Jackson* (Boston, 1945), 36.
[10] Albert Ludwig Kohlmeier, *The Old North-West as the Keystone of the Arch of American Federal Union: A Study in Commerce and Politics* (Bloomington, Ind., 1938).
[11] Stephan Thernstrom, *Poverty and Progress: Social Mobility in a Nineteenth Century City* (Cambridge, Mass., 1964).
[12] Thomas B. Alexander *et al.*, "Who Were the Alabama Whigs?" *Alabama Review*, XVI (No. 1, 1963), 5–19; Thomas B. Alexander and Peggy J. Duckworth, "Alabama Black Belt Whigs during Secession: A New Viewpoint," *ibid.*, XVII (No. 3, 1964), 181–97; Bernard and Lotte Bailyn, *Massachusetts Shipping, 1697–1714: A Statistical Study* (Cambridge, Mass., 1959); Allan G. Bogue, *From Prairie to Corn Belt: Farming on the Illinois and Iowa Prairies in the Nineteenth Century* (Chicago, 1963); Jean Delumeau, *L'alun de Rome, xvᵉ–xixᵉ siècle* (Paris, 1962), and *Le mouvement du port de Saint-Malo à la fin du xviiᵉ siécle, 1681–1700* (Rennes, 1962); Robert William Fogel, *Railroads and American Economic Growth: Essays in Econometric History* (Baltimore, 1964); Frank Lawrence Owsley, *Plain Folk of the Old South* (Baton Rouge, La., 1949); Lawrence Stone, "The Educational Revolution in England, 1560–1640," *Past and Present*, XXVIII (July 1964), 41–80, and *The Crisis of the Aristocracy, 1558–1641* (Oxford, Eng., 1965); Charles Tilly, *The Vendée* (Cambridge, Mass., 1964); Sylvia L. Thrupp, *The Merchant Class of Medieval London, 1300–1500* (Chicago, 1948); Sam B. Warner, Jr., *Streetcar Suburbs: The Process of Growth in Boston, 1870–1900* (Cambridge, Mass., 1962).

certain variables is examined while other variables are controlled. This is a simple matter mathematically, although the research may be laborious, and it is simple mechanically as well. Even so modest a use of quantitative methods can sometimes produce results of great interest and can be used to test historical generalizations of some scope on which there has heretofore been scholarly disagreement. Since only a limited amount of such research has been done, much gold is still near the surface. It may turn out, however, that richer veins lie deeper. Though it has proved extremely useful to classify, arrange, and summarize the available information, it may be even more rewarding—to judge from some of the ventures that have already been made—to attempt more complex methods of descriptive statistical analysis by the use, for example, of mathematical models or of scaling techniques.[13]

Although substantial and interesting work has been done along these lines, much more could be attempted. Historians who have used quantitative methods have been timid in their application of them and have come nowhere near exploiting their full potentialities. Also, many historians who deal with problems for which such methods might be helpful have not tried to use them at all. Economic history is, perhaps, an exception. This field is naturally suited to quantitative research since many of the original data come in quantified form, the problems and hypotheses tend to assume a quantified shape, and, in the field of economics, theoretical analysis is more advanced. In political and social history, however, opportunities have been missed. Though the area of historical research to which these methods can be applied may be limited, it has certainly not yet been fully explored.

Furthermore, much hostility to quantitative methods still remains among some members of the historical profession. Despite what might seem the obvious advantages of these methods for certain kinds of problems, despite their notably successful application in many historical projects, and despite their long acceptance as a matter of course in several related disciplines, some historians still object to them vociferously and consider them altogether inappropriate for historical research. Questions have been raised regarding: (1) the value of the work that has been done; (2) the feasibility of this approach in view of the admittedly limited materials available to historians; (3) the reliability of the results obtained by these techniques; and (4) the usefulness or significance of the results. These objections are not wholly without foundation. It would be pointless to deny either the limitations of the method or the lapses of some of its practitioners. To concede this, however, is not to tell the whole story.

(1) Certainly the ventures of historians into this kind of research have not been uniformly fortunate. Some of these studies, far from revolutionizing

---

[13] On the use of models, see the review of the work of Harold Hotelling and others and the further discussion of this problem in Donald E. Stokes, "Spatial Models of Party Competition," *American Political Science Review,* LVII (June 1963), 368–77. On scaling techniques, see Duncan MacRae, Jr., *Dimensions of Congressional Voting: A Statistical Study of the House of Representatives in the Eighty-first Congress* (Berkeley, Calif., 1958), and "Intraparty Divisions and Cabinet Coalitions in the Fourth French Republic," *Comparative Studies in Society and History,* V (Jan. 1963), 164–211; William O. Aydelotte, "Voting Patterns in the British House of Commons in the 1840s," *ibid.,* 134–63.

historical thought, have themselves not stood the test of time and have been shown to contain imperfections of method, which, to some extent, vitiate their conclusions. It would be unfair to mention individual monographs without a more extended discussion of their arguments than is possible in this paper. I shall have occasion to describe some of the statistical solecisms committed by a few workers in my own field in separate articles on special topics. In general, it has been contended, sometimes plausibly, that a number of the pioneers in quantitative historical research overlooked certain elementary precautions. They did not, it is said, always appreciate or remember that a sample that is small and, hence, biased or unrepresentative may distort the results, that percentages should be figured in terms of what is hypothesized to be the independent variable, that a conscientious search should be made for all possible relevant variables (though it is unlikely that they can all be found), that failure to make such a search may produce spurious correlations, or that refinements of technique cannot compensate for the inaccuracy or incompleteness of the original data. Doubtless the application of quantitative techniques to history has not paid off as well as might have been expected because of the statistical naïveté of a few of those who first tried it. To say this, however, is not to disparage quantitative methods. On the contrary, these are exactly the errors that an experienced statistician would not commit, and they arise not from an overemphasis but from an underemphasis on accepted statistical procedures. It may not be unreasonable to expect that simple technical errors of this kind will occur less frequently in the future as a new generation of historians becomes more alert to what is needed for this type of work.

(2) A more serious objection is that quantitative techniques may not be feasible at all in history, or can be used only within narrow limits, because of the complexity of historical materials and the restrictions on historical knowledge. It is difficult to get accurate information, for the sources may prove inconsistent or unreliable. Also the task of correctly recording so great a mass of data is more arduous than is likely to be believed by anyone who has not tried it; the natural proclivity of almost all men to error, to incorrect observation, has been repeatedly shown by experiment. Beyond this, however, there are formidable problems of taxonomy. A given body of data can generally be classified in any of many different ways, and skill and experience are needed to choose the categories that will prove most useful. Unfortunately it may not become apparent which these are until one is well into the research and it is too late to change. It is also no easy matter to make the categories precise and clearly distinguishable from one another. The existing vocabulary of social history is inexact, and many of the terms in common usage are too vague to permit unequivocal classification of the data. To give one example, problems of this kind have, according to a recent review article, bedeviled research on the supposed conflict of the aristocracy and the bourgeoisie during the French Revolution. The ambiguities in the definitions of these terms have had the result that:

> the central doctrine of the class struggle between bourgeois and aristocrats can now only be accepted as an act of faith; for no two people can agree on who the bourgeois and the aristocrats were; no one can formulate (and few even try to formulate) a criterion for

distinguishing between them that can be followed consistently, and every argument is thus liable to be at variance with easily ascertainable facts.[14]

Similar problems arise, of course, in the social history of other countries. If a historian tries to distribute a group of men among conventional categories of this kind, borderline cases may necessitate so many subjective judgments that the resulting classifications will not be worth much. No amount of *expertise* in the manipulation of the figures will make adequate correction for imprecision in the original data or for categories that do not adequately measure what it is claimed that they measure. A quantitative approach does not of itself ensure accuracy. Jeremy Bentham's "felicific calculus" was set forth in quantitative terms, but it is not generally regarded as a precise conceptual scheme. There is a danger, in this kind of work, of a spurious precision—giving the results, to several decimal places, of calculations based on incorrect original assumptions. If the classifications used at the start are worthless, the computations based upon them will be equally so, no matter how many times they are passed through the computer, and the situation will develop which is known in the trade as "GIGO": "garbage in and garbage out."

Furthermore, historical information is restricted. Historians who seek to use quantitative methods are, in comparison to those working with contemporary affairs, at a disadvantage. It is difficult—and the difficulty generally increases with the remoteness of the period studied—to obtain relevant data for a large enough sample of the group or "population" under consideration to make a quantitative presentation useful and effective. It is feasible, for example, to study the composition of the British House of Commons in recent centuries, though the task becomes harder as one goes back in time, but it might be less rewarding to attempt an analysis of the personnel of Justinian's army.

Even some of the historians who have made conspicuously successful use of these methods complain frequently about the inadequacy of the sources with which they had to work. Brinton found the membership lists of the Jacobin Clubs incomplete, a problem heightened by the considerable turnover in membership, while the occupations of some Jacobins were not listed and the occupations of others were described in ambiguous terms. He insists that part of his information does not "have even the relative accuracy possible in a study of contemporary demography." [15] Greer speaks of "the impossibility of determining with any degree of exactitude the total death roll of the Terror." [16] Owsley found that the tax lists for many large areas of the South had not survived, while the census reports, besides being less accurate as a rule than the tax lists, were seriously incomplete except for the latter part of the ante bellum period.[17] Warner found rich statistical materials surviving for nineteenth-century Boston, but noted that city, state, and federal counts did not agree with each other and added the warning that: "The presence of substantial errors in the census

[14] Betty Behrens, " 'Straight History' and 'History in Depth': The Experience of Writers on Eighteenth-Century France," *Historical Journal*, VIII (No. 1, 1965), 125; see Greer's comments on the ambiguities of his own categories, in *Incidence of the Terror*, 88–96; for a more extended discussion of these problems, see Cobban, *Social Interpretation of the French Revolution*, Chaps. III, VI, VIII–XIV.

[15] Brinton, *Jacobins*, 48–51, 57–58.

[16] Greer, *Incidence of the Terror*, 37.

[17] Owsley, *Plain Folk of the Old South*, 150–51.

requires the local historian to use census data with the same sophistication he would use any other source. The past tendency to check writings of individuals against other sources but to accept statistics as prima facie fact must be abandoned." [18]

Even in cases of groups for which quantitative methods can to some extent be used, it is not always possible to employ tests of sufficient refinement to verify what appear to be the most significant hypotheses. Benson, in his discussion of Beard's interpretation of the battle over the Constitution, has suggested that "we are likely to progress further if we group men, not according to their 'economic interests,' " but according to various other things including, for example, "their values, their beliefs, their symbols, their sense of identity." [19] Yet it may not be easy to obtain this kind of information for all or most members of a population of any size removed at some distance in time. It could, perhaps, be found for a few individuals on whom detailed information can be gathered from their correspondence and papers, but in statistics arguing from a few not necessarily representative examples is the great heresy. Doubtless more can be done than has always been realized, and, in another book, Benson has applied imagination and ingenuity to available materials, to draw impressive and persuasive inferences on some of these difficult matters.[20] It can scarcely be denied, however, that these are obdurate questions, and anyone who tries to solve them has his work cut out for him; ingenuity can carry only a limited distance. For many groups in the past the kind of information needed to make such tests, much of it at least, has long since disappeared and is now irretrievable.

Clearly, formal statistical presentations are feasible only for a limited range of historical problems. The available information may be insufficient or may contain ambiguities that make it difficult to summarize in intelligible categories. Nothing is to be gained by pretending otherwise or by attempting to force the use of these methods beyond where evidence will carry. Frank Knight once observed that the dictum attributed to Lord Kelvin—"If you cannot measure, your knowledge is meagre and unsatisfactory"—has in practice been translated into the injunction: "If you cannot measure, measure anyhow." [21] This, of course, would be a counsel of darkness. Whether quantitative methods will be helpful on a given problem is a matter not of rule but of the strategy of research.

Though these difficulties are substantial, it would be a gross distortion to regard them as insuperable. Taxonomic problems vary in incidence, and it is mistaken to suppose that all subjects are equally difficult to quantify. Social categories may be tricky, but other kinds of information, such as votes in a legislative body, can be tabulated with some assurance. Economic and demographic data have been handled quantitatively with success for some time.

---

[18] Warner, *Streetcar Suburbs*, 173–74.

[19] Lee Benson, *Turner and Beard: American Historical Writing Reconsidered* (Glencoe, Ill., 1960), 169–70.

[20] *Id., The Concept of Jacksonian Democracy: New York as a Test Case* (Princeton, N.J., 1961), Chaps. XII–XIV.

[21] Kuhn, "Measurement," 31, 34; remarks by Frank H. Knight in *Eleven Twenty-Six: A Decade of Social Science Research,* ed. Louis Wirth (Chicago, 1940), 169. The quotation ascribed to Kelvin appears on the façade of the Social Science Building at the University of Chicago. Kuhn has been unable to find these exact words in Kelvin's writings, though Kelvin expressed the idea more than once in slightly different language.

Even in the study of social history it has sometimes proved possible, as it has in scientific investigation,[22] to advance the argument by jettisoning subjective definitions and adopting objective ones, by disregarding earlier concepts that were too vaguely defined to admit of measurement, and by concentrating instead on categories that could be unmistakably specified—not "aristocrats," but peers and their sons; not "gentry," but men included by John Burke in his reference work *The Landed Gentry of Great Britain and Ireland;* not "business-men," but men engaged in certain ways in certain types of business. Whether these more sharply defined categories correspond accurately to the old catego-ries is a question that cannot be answered since the old ones are so indefinite that they cannot be said to correspond accurately to anything. One cannot, by using the new categories, effectively test propositions couched in terms of the old ones. Such propositions cannot, indeed, be tested at all, for an imprecise or slipshod formulation is impregnable; a statement that has no exact meaning cannot be disproved. What is feasible, however, is to study a group or an entity that might be conjectured to correspond somewhat to the old and loosely defined concept but that at least has the virtue that it can be identified. The investigator must, of course, assume the burden of showing that his new categories are viable and useful. The great step forward is to take the objective or unequivocal definition as the norm, as describing the entity that will be subjected to analysis, and to demote the subjective or vague concept to a subordinate position, to appreciate that, though it may serve as a useful starting point in the formulation of an operational definition, it may also contain variables that are difficult to measure or even to identify and that it cannot, therefore, be handled in any conclusive fashion. By this procedure one at least knows where one stands, and the problems of social measurement may become less intractable.

Nor is the argument about limitations on historical knowledge really convinc-ing. No doubt much valuable information has been lost. It is clear enough, however, that historical materials that lend themselves to quantitative research, even if they do not cover everything, are enormously abundant. Some great storehouses of information such as census records and tax records are still relatively unused, except by a few pioneers. Other rich sources such as recorded votes in legislative bodies have been used only in a desultory and sporadic fashion, and much more could be done with them. Ample materials exist for collective biographies of groups of prominent individuals, and in some cases obscure ones too; for the economic and demographic characterization of constituencies; and for ascertaining the relationship of the facts unearthed in such investigations to political choice.[23] Evidence is particularly rich for social and political history, two areas in which quantitative methods have not been extensively attempted.

Furthermore, it has proved possible, again and again, to describe in quantita-

[22] See the discussion of the development of the concept "degree of heat" in Kuhn, "Measurement," 58–59.
[23] An extended account of the work that has been done and that might be attempted along this line in American history has been given by Samuel P. Hays in "New Possibilities for American Political History: The Social Analysis of Political Life," a paper presented at the Annual Meeting of the American Historical Associa-tion in December 1964;- see also *id.,* "Archival Sources for American Political History," *American Archivist,* XXVIII (Jan. 1965), 17–30.

tive terms things that were formerly thought to fall beyond the reach of this net. Matters that seemed to an earlier generation unquantifiable can sometimes be caught and measured by a change in approach or by reaching a clearer perspective concerning what it may be most profitable to measure. This applies, for example, to the study of attitudes, a field in which notable advances have been made over the last several decades. David Hume, speaking through the mouth of Philo, a man of "careless scepticism," argued that "controversies concerning the degrees of any quality or circumstance" can never "reach a reasonable certainty or precision." Thus, he says, it is impossible to settle how great a general Hannibal was or "what epithet of praise Livy or Thucydides is entitled to . . . because the degrees of these qualities are not, like quantity or number, susceptible of any exact mensuration, which may be the standard in the controversy." [24] Even if we cannot measure qualities of excellence, however, we can perfectly well measure opinions about them, which are all we have to go on anyway, and this is done all the time with questionnaires. Similarly, ways have been found to measure degrees of liberalism and conservatism by indexes in which men have come to place some reliance, or degrees of attachment to a particular cause or principle, or degrees of interest or apathy regarding political questions, or even degrees of patient welfare in a hospital. It has been possible to do this last by a set of objective tests that fit into a cumulative scale and that have turned out to be reliable and consistent.[25]

Recent quantitative research in history contains several examples of a tour de force of this kind, attempts—fairly convincing attempts—to measure what previously seemed impossible to measure. One is the effort of Alfred H. Conrad and John R. Meyer to appraise the profitability of slavery and the efficiency of the slave labor market in the American South before the Civil War. It would be difficult to summarize here their complex and rather technical analysis, but it is interesting that their conclusions tell strongly against the long-standing though not wholly unchallenged view that the system of slavery was being undermined because of its unprofitability and because of the impossibility of maintaining and allocating a slave labor force. They found, on the contrary, that "slavery was apparently about as remunerative as alternative employments to which slave capital might have been put" and that: "Slavery was profitable to the whole South, the continuing demand for labor in the Cotton Belt ensuring returns to the breeding operation on the less productive land in the seaboard and border states." [26] Another example is the attempt by McCormick to describe, for the period in which he does research, the relation between the economic status of members of the electorate and their political choice. This topic, though important, is difficult for historians to study since the rich and poor in an electorate are generally buried in the anonymity of mass figures, and it is now virtually impossible to distinguish who voted for whom. McCormick, however, in attacking the problem, was able to take advantage of the dual franchise existing in North Carolina in the years 1836–1856, when only adult

[24] David Hume, *Dialogues concerning Natural Religion* (London, 1779), Pt. XII.
[25] Myrtle Kitchell Aydelotte, *An Investigation of the Relation between Nursing Activity and Patient Welfare* (Iowa City, Iowa, 1960), 41–123.
[26] Alfred H. Conrad and John R. Meyer, *The Economics of Slavery and Other Studies in Econometric History* (Chicago, 1964), 66, 82.

freemen who owned fifty acres of land within the county could vote for a member of the state senate while all freemen, including the above, who had paid county or state taxes, could vote for governor. By comparing, county by county, the size of the vote cast for governor with the comparable vote for state senators it was possible to determine the proportion of the electorate that could not meet the fifty-acre requirement. Then, by examining the distribution of each class of the electorate between the two major parties, McCormick was able to reach some conclusions on the relation of economic status to party affiliation. His finding, one of considerable interest, was that "the economic distinction implicit in the dual suffrage system had no substantial significance as a factor in determining party alignments in these North Carolina elections." [27]

In any case, the complexity and the limited scope of historical information are not arguments against quantification in particular. These limitations exist no matter what techniques are used. They arise from the insufficiency of the evidence and not from the peculiarities of the method. The obstacles to quantitative generalizations apply with equal force to nonquantitative ones, and what cannot be done with statistics cannot be done without them, either. No serious student of methodology would contend that a disciplined approach can overcome the inherent frailties in the data. But it hardly follows that, when the sources are suspect or the facts incomplete, an impressionistic, subjective approach can surmount these difficulties. Problems due to inadequacy of the data may be brought out more sharply and may become more apparent in a formal and systematic investigation, but they cannot in any circumstances be evaded.

(3) The objection is also sometimes made that the general conclusions of a quantitative investigation are not proved by the figures. This is, of course, true, and no one who knows anything about statistical theory would argue otherwise. To expect finality for the broader conclusions of a quantitative investigation is to misconstrue the nature of the approach. On this point some misunderstanding apparently exists for, in everyday speech, reckless claims are sometimes made as to what "statistics prove." Actually the range of statistical proof is limited. A statistical table is nothing more than a convenient arrangement of the evidence, and it proves only what it contains: that there was, for example, a relationship or, more usual, a partial relationship between two variables. Theories that attempt to account for such a relationship, in the sense of fitting the findings into a wider conceptual scheme, are not proved by the figures. They are merely propositions that appear to explain what is known in a plausible fashion and that do not conflict with any relevant evidence that can, after a conscientious search, be uncovered. This is not to say that they are nonsense, for they may be supported by persuasive arguments. Yet since, notoriously, different arguments have proved persuasive to different audiences, the broader inferences from a quantitative investigation can scarcely be accepted as final. Thus it is possible, if the information is available, to establish how people voted, but it is

[27] Richard P. McCormick, "Suffrage Classes and Party Alignments: A Study in Voter Behavior," *Mississippi Valley Historical Review*, XLVI (Dec. 1959), 398–403; for a review of other attempts to measure what cannot be measured directly and a discussion of the problems involved, see Robert William Fogel, "Reappraisals in American Economic History—Discussion," *American Economic Review*, LIV (May 1964), 377–89.

much more difficult to say why they voted as they did. There might, of course, even be some difference of opinion on how they voted: for example, the accuracy of the records or of the tabulations made from them might be challenged. Yet such a disagreement is clearly on a lower level than a disagreement about men's motives, and there is a greater likelihood that it could be resolved through collecting and arranging the relevant data by acceptable procedures. In regard to more general explanatory propositions, however, a statistical inquiry, like any other method of verification, can only disprove. If the hypothesis does not fit the evidence, it may be rejected; in this sense a quantitative finding can indeed be conclusive. "Once we recognize that the Jacksonians won either by narrow majorities before 1837 or by narrow pluralities after that date, or frequently failed to win by any margin, it will surely become apparent that there is no basis for explanations that tell why they were the 'popular party.' " [28] The absence of unfavorable findings does not, however, prove an explanatory generalization for there may be some other explanation, and it is also possible that adverse evidence may be discovered later. Strictly speaking, a generalization of this kind is never proved and remains on probation indefinitely.[29]

Hence there is always, in quantitative research of any scope, a gap between observation and theory. To bridge this gap it may be necessary to resort to assumptions that are not demonstrated by the evidence. Some recent presentations of this kind depend not only on the figures but also on the use of hypotheses that are designed to show either what the figures measure or what their relevance is to certain general questions. The gap cannot always be bridged. Interesting findings may be obtained that are difficult to explain in the sense of devising an acceptable theory that will account for them. An example from my own research is a cumulative scale, derived through Louis Guttman's technique of scalogram analysis, that ties together votes in the House of Commons on a number of different subjects in a way consistent with the hypothesis that they all measure a single variable. Yet the nature of this variable, this larger issue that subsumes many smaller ones, has proved difficult to determine. Though the existence of the scale can be demonstrated with about as much certainty as can ever be obtained in historical research, the characterization of it can be, for the present, only tentative and hypothetical.[30] Comparable dilemmas have sometimes been encountered in other fields.[31]

The hypotheses used to connect observation and theory are, no matter how plausible they at first appear, always open to challenge. The broader conclusions of a quantitative presentation may be vulnerable regardless of the accuracy of the mathematics or the reliability of the original data, and questions may be raised about them that cannot be answered by a resort to numbers. A critic may accept the findings, but then point out that the conclusions based upon them

[28] Benson, *Concept of Jacksonian Democracy,* 289–90.
[29] For a further discussion of this point, see W. I. B. Beveridge, *The Art of Scientific Investigation* (rev. ed., New York, 1957), 115–22.
[30] Aydelotte, "Voting Patterns," 148–51.
[31] "In spite of the great social and scientific usefulness of psychological tests it must be acknowledged that for the most part we have had very inadequate ideas as to what it is that they actually measure." (Joy Paul Guilford, *Psychometric Methods* [2d ed., New York, 1954], 470.)

follow only if certain assumptions are made, and go on to question these assumptions. Some of the large modern quantitative studies have been criticized exactly on this ground: that the chain of argument, the series of connecting hypotheses, was too long and too tenuous to make the conclusions convincing.[32]

By the same token, a quantitative investigation may not and often will not settle an argument. It may settle certain disputed points about the evidence. The discussion of larger questions of historical interpretation, however, concerns not merely what the facts were but also what may be inferred from them, and on this level controversy may continue.[33] A quantitative finding may be open to more than one interpretation: in some cases it can be used to support either of two alternative and mutually exclusive theoretical schemes.[34] It can also happen that quantitative results that appear to disprove an accepted theory will simply be "explained away." This procedure can be quite legitimate, since it may prove possible to achieve a reformulation of the earlier view, which preserves some of the original insights, but does not conflict with the new evidence. If contradictory findings continue to accumulate, however, it may eventually be more satisfactory to abandon the earlier position altogether.

Quantitative procedures by no means preclude, nor indeed can they possibly eliminate, the use of value judgments, speculations, intelligent guesses, or "the imagination and intuitive feel which the historian, and for that matter the social scientist, should bring to his subject." [35] What is gained by attempting such exactitude as the circumstances allow is not finality but reasonable credibility, not the elimination of subjective factors but the minimizing of their role. No greater claim than this would be asserted by responsible social scientists or statisticians.

[32] Nathan Glazer, " 'The American Soldier' as Science: Can Sociology Fulfil Its Ambitions?" *Commentary,* VIII (Nov. 1949), 487–96; C. Wright Mills, *The Sociological Imagination* (New York, 1959), 72.

[33] Greer based his conclusions on a calculation of what percentage each social or occupational group constituted of the total number of victims of the Terror. If he had argued from percentages figured in the other direction—designed to show what proportion of each of the various divisions of French society was executed in the Terror—the picture would have looked somewhat different. This is because, as Greer points out, the "proportional incidence" of the Terror was "almost directly inverse to its absolute incidence"; in proportion to their total numbers, "the nobles, the clergy, and the rich suffered far more than the lower classes." (Greer, *Incidence of the Terror,* 105–109.) This aspect of the findings has been made the ground for a sharp critique of Greer's book by Richard Louie who argues that Greer's own data contradict his principal conclusion and show "with 95 per cent confidence that the Terror was an 'inter-class war.' " (Richard Louie, "The Incidence of the Terror: A Critique of a Statistical Interpretation," *French Historical Studies,* III [Spring 1964], 379–89.) Neither way of presenting the figures is "right" in any ultimate sense; it is a matter of what question one wishes to answer and what features of the evidence it is most useful, for this purpose, to bring out.

[34] In case this appears puzzling, it may be helpful to summarize the hypothetical illustration given by Hans Zeisel. If Company A increases its sales volume in a year from one to two million dollars and Company B, a bigger outfit to begin with, increases its sales in the same period from four to seven million dollars, then one could argue either that Company B did better since its net increase was three times that of A, or that Company A did better since it increased its sales 100 per cent in comparison to B's 75 per cent. Which alternative is preferred depends not on the figures but on what causal assumptions are implied in making the comparison and on what kinds of questions the investigator wishes to test. (Hans Zeisel, *Say It with Figures* [4th ed., New York, 1957], 8–13.)

[35] James Cornford, "The Transformation of Conservatism in the Late Nineteenth Century," *Victorian Studies,* VII (Sept. 1963), 40.

These points, though they are elementary, are not always understood or remembered. Quantitative findings are impressive in appearance and may, by their psychological impact, numb or blunt the critical abilities of the reader. It does occasionally seem to happen that a statistical presentation wins acceptance not through intellectual persuasion but through a kind of hypnosis. There is, however, no magic about quantitative evidence. It may be more conveniently arranged and, on the points it covers, more complete than other forms of documentation. Its significance, however, depends on what can be inferred from it, and such inferences, like all other inferences, may be fallible.

This disadvantage is not, of course, peculiar to quantitative procedures. On the contrary, quantitative evidence stands, in this respect, on a level with all other kinds of evidence, and arguing from it is subject to the same rules and the same hazards. The danger of false reasoning from good evidence occurs in any kind of research. It is not only in the field of statistics that men may agree on the facts but disagree on the inferences to be drawn from them.

(4) Questions have been raised not merely regarding the feasibility and reliability of quantitative research in history but also regarding its usefulness. It is sometimes argued that quantitative findings, even if they can be trusted, tend to be trivial, inconsequential, and uninteresting. This is because any system of classification, such as is needed for such work, uses only a small part of the available information and leaves out the full richness of reality. Hence the ordinary statistical categories are too crude and threadbare to explain the complicated chains of events with which history is concerned. The problems in which historians are most interested are so complex that they elude these methods. One critic holds that: "almost all important questions are important precisely because they are not susceptible to quantitative answers." [36]

It is true, of course, that any quantitative procedure involves using only selected classes of data. It is seldom possible to include everything, or to come anywhere near this. Hence, statistical tables, though they seem impressive, may also present an appearance of bleakness or barrenness which can act as an impediment to thought. Often they will not stimulate the imagination as the detailed recital of an individual case will do. Indeed, it is useful, when one comes to an impasse in interpreting the figures, to turn to the consideration of individuals about whom much is known. Such individuals may not be representative, and one cannot generalize from them to the whole group; a study of them may, however, yield suggestions or leads, fresh hypotheses that can be tested, which will make the evidence as a whole more intelligible. It is always necessary, when working with the figures, to remember that they do not tell the whole story, that many elements of the situation are not reflected in them, and that what they do not cover may turn out to be more important than what they include. To interpret the quantitative evidence it is generally necessary to have recourse to the more conventional sources of historical information: memoirs and biographies, congressional debates, private papers, and the like.

The charge that quantification abstracts and uses only limited parts of the available information, however, is not an objection to this method specifically. On the contrary, any generalization abstracts. A generalization is a comparison

[36] Arthur M. Schlesinger, Jr., "The Humanist Looks at Empirical Social Research," *American Sociological Review,* XXVII (Dec. 1962), 770.

of a number of cases, not in terms of all the attributes of each, but in terms of certain selected attributes in respect to which the cases are comparable. This problem is not peculiar to quantification; it arises in any research in which a conscientious effort is made to substantiate general statements.

The objection that the findings of quantitative studies are not significant sometimes takes other forms. It has been alleged, for example, that this kind of research is destructive and not constructive and that: "the recent use of quantitative methods to test historical generalization has resulted in the whole-sale destruction of categories that previously held sway in the historian's vocabulary without supplanting them with new generalizations of comparable significance." [37] As an objection to quantification, however, this argument has no weight for it applies equally to any form of verification. All verification is in this sense negative. The argument fails to distinguish between the two quite different activities involved in research: getting ideas and testing them. Quantitative inquiries are generally directed to testing hypotheses formulated in advance. It has frequently been observed that, in work of this kind, a flat-footed empiricism is not likely to rise above a fairly low conceptual level and that systematic thought will progress more rapidly when it is directed by some adequate general hypothesis. The point should not be pushed too far for it occasionally happens that important relationships are not anticipated, but emerge as windfalls after the inquiry is completed. Also, in an area in which little work has been done, the original investigations must often be to some extent exploratory. It would be pedantic to insist on a full-fledged hypothesis in every case.[38] Nevertheless, the criticism that quantitative methods destroy and do not create is clearly based on a mistaken notion of the usual role of hypothesis in research. Hypotheses and generalizations are not simple inductions that emerge of their own accord from the evidence; they have, as is now better understood, different and more complex origins.[39]

Nor does a negative finding necessarily represent a dead end. If a generalization is wrong, it is useful to have it disproved; the disproof constitutes an advance in knowledge. As J. H. Hexter observes: "it may be worth saying that violent destruction is not necessarily of itself worthless and futile. Even though it leaves doubts about the right road for London, it helps if someone rips up, however violently, a 'To London' sign on the Dover cliffs pointing south." [40] A negative finding can be, in some cases, as valuable as a positive finding, depending on what theoretical inferences follow from it. Furthermore, to blame the quantitative method for disproving bad hypotheses is to blame the doctor instead of the disease. What is at fault is the mistaken opinion, not the technique that reveals when we have gone astray. The remedy is not to abandon

---

[37] Richard Hofstadter, "History and the Social Sciences," in *Varieties of History: From Voltaire to the Present,* ed. Fritz Stern (New York, 1956), 415, n. 14.

[38] Patricia L. Kendall and Paul F. Lazarsfeld, "Problems of Survey Analysis," in *Continuities in Social Research: Studies in the Scope and Method of "The American Soldier,"* ed. Robert K. Merton and Paul F. Lazarsfeld (Glencoe, Ill., 1950), 133, 137–42, 161; L. H. C. Tippett, *Statistics* (London, 1943), 139–40.

[39] I have discussed this point at greater length in "Notes on the Problem of Historical Generalization," in *Generalization in the Writing of History,* ed. Gottschalk, 163–72.

[40] J. H. Hexter, "Storm over the Gentry," in *Reappraisals in History,* ed. *id.* (Evanston, Ill., 1961), 138.

the technique but to try to develop a new theory that fits the evidence better.

It is also sometimes argued that quantitative methods only prove the obvious, that they merely demonstrate, by an unnecessarily cumbersome apparatus, what everyone already knew.[41] It is admitted that they can occasionally be used to disprove certain crude generalizations that still appear in the textbooks. Yet, it is said, the crudity of such generalizations is already widely appreciated, and, on the whole, they are not accepted by sophisticated historians. In other words, quantitative techniques are useful only when historians have made fools of themselves. Their function is to clear away rubbish. However, if there is no rubbish, if scholarship in a field has been reasonably careful and responsible, a quantitative analysis is unlikely to reveal anything that is not already fairly well understood.

This criticism, also, is not well taken. Even if research merely confirms in a more conclusive fashion what some people already believe, it is good to have this additional assurance and to establish this belief on a more solid foundation. Also, on many questions that can be studied by quantitative methods, the answer is by no means a matter of course. More often there is evidence pointing in both directions, and both sides of the argument have been supported with some plausibility by different individuals. In such cases, it is useful to establish which of two contradictory statements comes closer to describing the total evidence and just how close it comes. It might be added that, in disputes of this kind, either answer will be "obvious" in the sense of being already familiar, even though the two alternative answers exclude each other. Furthermore, the results of quantitative investigations have frequently told directly against interpretations that had been widely accepted. Several examples have already been given; another is Fogel's attempt to appraise the role of the railroads in American economic growth, which resulted in the conclusions, disheartening to some enthusiasts, that even in the absence of railroads the prairies would have been settled and exploited, that the combination of wagon and water transportation could have provided a relatively good substitute for the railroad, and that "no single innovation was vital for economic growth during the nineteenth century."[42]

Whether the results of a quantitative investigation are important or trivial is and can only be a matter of opinion. The presumption of significance is based not on a demonstration of fact but on a judgment of value. This applies, incidentally, even to the so-called "tests of significance" commonly used in statistics. Properly speaking, they are evaluations of probability, and, while probability can be mathematically determined, the degree of it that will be regarded as acceptable in any study is a question not of mathematics but of the investigator's preference. A quantitative study, it might be said, is significant if the investigator thinks it is and can persuade others to share his view. Speaking simply on this basis, it seems difficult to support the assertion that the topics open to quantitative investigation are of no consequence. Far from this being the case, an intelligent use of the method opens up a host of new, potentially interesting questions that could be approached in no other way. Some of these possibilities and some of the studies conducted along these lines have already

[41] Mills, *Sociological Imagination*, 53–55, 75.
[42] Fogel, *Railroads and American Economic Growth*, 219, 234.

been discussed. Perhaps it is enough to say here that the substantive weight of the findings of the limited number of historians who have attempted quantitative research is already impressive enough to render the accusation of triviality something less than plausible.

It seems reasonable to argue, furthermore, that the significance of a project of research does not depend on whether it is quantitative or not. Quantitative presentations vary greatly in value. They may be significant or trivial, interesting or uninteresting, and it is incorrect to suppose that they are all on the same level in these respects. What gives them such worth as they may have are the importance of the problem, the abundance, reliability, and relevance of the available evidence, and, above all, the intelligence with which the work is executed.

In fact, what is most needed in research of this kind is not the automatic application of certain techniques but, rather, qualities of logic and imagination. The main problems here, as in all research, are not technical and mechanical but intellectual and analytical. It is not easy to make the figures "talk" or to show their bearing on significant problems, and nothing is drearier than a presentation that merely summarizes the evidence. I am disturbed by students who want to do quantitative research and who seem to expect that this will solve their problems and that the application of a method will save them the trouble of thinking. This expectation is erroneous. Quantitative techniques, though they may play a crucial role in demolishing previous theories, are usually not adequate, by themselves, to establish general alternative hypotheses. They are nothing more than a means of deploying the evidence, although they perform this limited service wonderfully well. Once this subordinate and ancillary work has been done, however, the basic problems of historical interpretation still remain to be dealt with; they are not to be resolved by a gimmick. The greatest hazard in quantitative research is not that of neglecting techniques but that of becoming too much absorbed in them. This danger is particularly threatening now because of the rapid development of mechanical facilities for the processing of data. It is only too easy to become absorbed in the gadgets and to forget the ideas. The refinement and sophistication of methods, though desirable in themselves, can become a kind of escapism, an evasion or postponement of the intellectual tasks that must ultimately be faced.

In general, the discussion of quantification in history has involved much talking at cross-purposes. Many of the common objections to this approach seem to arise from a misconception of its function. They appear to assume that claims have been made for it that no responsible statistician would make. No one well versed in this line of work would argue that all historical materials can be quantified, that the figures provide any final demonstration of the broader inferences derived from them, or that the figures tell the whole story. Such assertions are clearly improper. If they are not made, however, as by informed workers in this line they are not, much of the current offensive against quantitative techniques fails. The central point around which discussion of the subject has in part revolved is not an intellectual issue but a problem of communication.

The use of quantitative methods for history presents substantial difficulties not always appreciated by enthusiasts or neophytes. Those who have employed them are likely to be less starry-eyed about their possibilities than those who have merely commended them without trying them. Indeed, quantitative projects may be more glamorous in the planning stage than they are after the results have been gathered; the findings sometimes turn out to be flatter and less revolutionary than had been hoped.

Though the difficulties are real enough, however, it is not clear that they constitute objections specifically to a quantitative approach, or that they can be resolved by dispensing with it. The standard objections are misconceived or placed out of context when presented as grounds for rejecting these methods altogether. Properly understood, these reservations serve not to discredit quantification but to mark the boundaries of what it can accomplish. Indeed, the apparent disadvantages of quantitative research, the impediments to generalization that it presents, are actually advantages for they call attention to limits in knowledge or to flaws in reasoning that might not otherwise be perceived or fully appreciated. When all reservations have been made, quantification has still shown itself, in the light of the considerable experience we now have, to be a powerful tool in historical analysis. It helps to make the work both easier and more reliable, and, in some cases, it provides a means of dealing with questions that could not be attacked in any other way. Those wrestling with problems for which this approach is appropriate can ill afford to dispense with it. In the general intellectual twilight in which historians are condemned to spend their lives, even some small effort to render the darkness less opaque may be advantageous.

2

LEE BENSON

Quantification, Scientific History, and Scholarly Innovation

Among behavioral historians, none is more insistent on a "genuinely scientific historiography" than Lee Benson. Benson, one of the leading iconoclasts in the American scholarly community, demands that historians use explicit theory, social science methods, and, whenever possible, the electronic computer in order to fulfill their main task— to discover or develop general laws of human behavior. Like Henry T. Buckle, his counterpart of a century ago, Benson insists that past human behavior can be studied scientifically, provided however that scholars first collect, systematize, and widely disseminate the basic data, and master the techniques needed to manipulate the information. Only then can powerful concepts and theories be developed and tested. This article urges historians to break free from former restraints, enter the quantitative maelstrom, and join in the scientific quest for behavioral law in the moral world.

THE CURRENT STATE of historiography is deplorable, lamented Henry Buckle in 1857, in the "General Introduction" to his *History of Civilization in England:*

> In all the other great fields of inquiry, the necessity of generalization is universally admitted, and noble efforts are being made to rise from

Lee Benson, "Quantification, Scientific History, and Scholarly Innovation," American Historical Association *Newsletter,* IV (June, 1966), 11–16. Reprinted with permission of the author.

particular facts in order to discover the laws by which those facts are governed. So far, however, is this from being the usual course of historians, that among them a strange idea prevails, that their business is merely to relate events, which they may occasionally enliven by such moral and political reflections as seem likely to be useful.[1]

Distressed by the course historians usually took, Buckle demanded radical changes in direction. His lengthy "General Introduction," in effect, constituted a revolutionary manifesto proclaiming the coming triumph of the new science of history. Certain that scientific historians would discover "the principles which govern the character and destiny of nations," Buckle predicted that:

> . . . before another century has elapsed, the chain of evidence will be complete, and it will be as rare to find an historian who denies the undeviating regularity of the moral world [i.e., human events], as it now is to find a philosopher who denies the regularity of the material [i.e., physical] world.[2]

Another century has elapsed. Buckle's prediction has not been fulfilled. Far from accepting his dictum, the great majority of Western historians today would undoubtedly deny that their business is to discover or develop general laws of human behavior. Thus we clearly should regard the scientific revolution so triumphantly proclaimed by Buckle as abortive—an unsuccessful rebellion inspired by illogical positivist delusions of historiographic grandeur. Or should we? Are the returns all in? Was Buckle more premature than deluded?

Buckle *was* more premature than deluded in my judgment. If we dispense with his non-essential, nineteenth-century notions of science (e.g., mechanical inductionism, undeviating regularities), the prediction does not seem absurd that two decades from now, say by 1984 (*sic*), a significant proportion of American historians will have accepted Buckle's two basic propositions: 1) past human behavior can be studied scientifically; 2) the main business of historians is to participate in the overall scholarly enterprise of discovering and developing general laws of human behavior.

Apart from naive and perversely wilful optimism untutored by experience, does any reasoned basis exist for this prediction about American historiography in 1984? I think so and propose to support the argument by examining Buckle's explanation for the low state of historiography in the 1850's:

> . . . whoever now attempts to generalize historical phenomena, must collect the facts, as well as conduct the generalization. He finds nothing ready to his hand. He must be the mason as well as the architect; he must not only scheme the edifice, but likewise excavate the quarry. *The necessity of performing this double labour* [emphasis added] entails upon the philosopher such enormous drudgery, that the limits of an entire life are unequal to the task; and history, instead of being ripe, as it ought to be, for complete and exhaustive generalizations, is still in so crude and informal a state, that not the most

[1] Henry T. Buckle, *History of Civilization in England* (New York: D. Appleton and Company, 1892, from the second London edition), 1:3.
[2] *Ibid.*, 1:4, 24.

determined and protracted industry will enable any one to comprehend the really important actions of mankind during even so short a
period as two successive centuries.[3]

Buckle's predicted triumph of scientific history derived from his assumption
that the "double labour" barrier to generalization would soon be demolished.
Inspired by similar and successful work in other disciplines, historians, he
anticipated, would undertake *systematic and cumulative* studies which, collectively, would produce the data necessary "to comprehend the really important
actions of mankind." Moreover, given the requisite data ready to hand, historians would rapidly adopt statistical methods calculated to make most effective
use of those data.[4] As a result, philosophically-minded historians would have
greatly increased power to discover and demonstrate general laws of human
behavior, and "before another century has elapsed, the chain of evidence will be
complete. . . ."

My argument, woefully oversimplified and sketchy in deference to space
limitations, claims that Buckle perceptively identified some conditions necessary
for a genuinely scientific historiography. Writing in the 1850's, a "solitary
student" strongly shaped by Victorian radical individualism,[5] he understandably
failed to recognize that for those conditions to obtain, major organizational and
technological innovations had first to be made. The argument can most economically proceed by restricting attention to American political historiography and
advancing this admittedly partial hypothesis: Given the hard job assigned
American political historians (reconstruction and explanation of the highly
complex behavior of great numbers and varieties of human beings unavailable
for direct interview, observation, or experiment), their relative lack of scientific
achievement to date stems largely from the combined effects of two factors: 1)
the primitive social institutions which, until very recently, have governed their
social relations; 2) the primitive technology which, until very recently, has
restricted their research operations.

By primitive social institutions and relationships, I mean that although
political historians in theory comprise a "company of scholars" banded together
to advance knowledge, in practice they operate in something like a Hobbesian
state of nature, a war of "every man, against every man," each distrusting the
other and all desiring power. Atomistic institutions and relationships have
created conditions highly unfavorable to developing the advanced professional
culture needed to generate and nurture talented individuals. Is the metaphor
overdrawn? Somewhat. Universities, historical associations, councils of learned
societies such as the SSRC and the ACLS, research libraries and depositories, *et
al.* have long existed and long provided useful services and some kind of
socialization. But when we calculate the extent to which these institutions have
satisfied the requisites for an advanced professional culture, we can reasonably
say that they have not yet enabled American political historians to move much

---

[3] *Ibid.*, 1:166–67.
[4] See *ibid.*, 1:24–25, for Buckle's eulogy to "statistics; a branch of knowledge
which, though still in its infancy, has already thrown more light on the study of
human nature than all the sciences put together."
[5] See Giles St. Aubyn, *A Victorian Eminence: The Life and Works of Henry
Thomas Buckle* (London: Barrie, 1958), *passim.*

beyond the primitive stage of every researcher his own raw-data gatherer. And as Buckle emphasized so eloquently, research at that primitive level of social existence proves either so exhausting to individual researchers that it limits their capacity to perform the hard intellectual work required to develop powerful concepts, theories, and methods, or so dull that it tends strongly to lead gifted scholars to flee from systematic, empirical research to impressionistic, non-empirical speculation, informed no doubt by intelligence and intuition, but characterized by merely haphazard scatterings of imprecise data. In short, when we identify the requisites of a good scholarly social system for American researchers dealing with past political behavior, we recognize the fairly primitive, present state of our institutions.

By primitive technology, I mean tools, not methodology. If our methodology is primitive, that fact derives from the combined effects of our unsophisticated institutions and technology. With regard to the latter, historians have shown an inability to *command effective use* of computers and other modern data processing and photocopying equipment essential to efficient collection, storage, and analysis of the large masses of diverse data required for systematic substantive research. For certain purposes, pens, typewriters, printing presses, adding machines, and the like do represent advanced tools; they are relatively primitive tools when used to collect, order, and analyze the data actually required by American political historians. Emphasis on data collection does not derive, of course, from the caricature of inductionist method which holds that researchers need do little more than amass mountains of vaguely related "facts" and then, somehow, the mountains themselves will move and reveal the "truth." Quite the contrary. Significant historiographic progress will not be made, I believe, until powerful concepts, theories, and methods are first developed. But we are highly unlikely to get to that advanced stage—even slowly and painfully —unless three conditions are satisfied.

First, basic data, both numerical and non-numerical in original form, must be systematically collected and logically ordered. These materials, indispensable to fruitful research on past and present American political behavior, would include election statistics, demographic data, legislative roll calls, party platforms, standard collective biographies of public officials and party leaders, and so forth. While we have long identified and gathered these items, we have too often been guided by crude methods and theories in doing so. Second, researchers need not individually collect the basic data required for systematic research. Instead, data must be readily available to all professional researchers at no financial cost to individuals, in a form permitting manipulation and analysis in any way researchers believe might prove profitable. Third, historians must effectively command the technology and techniques needed to test their theories.

Have the conditions sketched above been satisfied in the past? The answer obviously is no. Do grounds now exist to believe that they can be satisfied in the future? The answer, I think, is yes—partly because the American Historical Association has created an *ad hoc* Committee to Collect the Basic Quantitative Data of American Political History, a committee whose lengthy title accurately denotes its main function. But the present likelihood that the committee will fulfill its tasks in the future stems largely from its effective collaboration with a recently created, and basically new type of scholarly organization, the Inter-University Consortium for Political Research. Organized in 1962 with eighteen charter members, the Consortium has its executive headquarters at the University of Michigan.[6] It is today perhaps best described as a working confederation of political researchers at more than seventy universities, banded together in a formal organization designed to generate and foster the social relationships postulated by academic ideology and hitherto mocked by academic practice.

Cordially collaborating with the AHA committee, and aided by generous grants from the National Science Foundation and the Social Science Research Council, the Consortium is now developing the cumulative data archives which, in effect, Buckle postulated as necessary to the achievement of "behavioral science." In addition, the Consortium is constructing mechanisms designed to provide individual researchers with ready access to the modern technology and technical services needed to make productive use of central data archives. Moreover, the organizational structure of the Consortium, its sponsorship of coordinated conferences and research seminars, and its rapidly expanding summer training programs aided by a substantial grant from IBM to support historians and staffed by combinations of specialists unavailable at any single university, all enable it to serve as an unprecedentedly effective communications network linking individuals and groups engaged in similar or complementary research. In short, the Consortium, by developing and servicing a computer-oriented central archive for data required by political researchers, and by constructing and utilizing mechanisms for the rapid dissemination and exchange of ideas, skills, and information, has begun to provide the conditions under which political researchers are most likely to engage in fruitful scientific work.

One point cannot be overemphasized. The Consortium is designed to aid researchers who may share widely different approaches to the study of political phenomena, not to centralize research or direct or manipulate individuals into specified types of research for predesigned goals. To revert to my Hobbesian metaphor, the Consortium is best viewed as a prototype of those genuinely *liberal* social inventions which, in the future, will aid scholars both to advance beyond the state of near-natural anarchy lamented by Buckle and simultaneously remain free from the pressures of Leviathan (or his Big Brother). Instead of centralizing power to control individuals, the Consortium centralizes resources, converts them into public goods freely available to all, and thus helps researchers to achieve genuine freedom for creative thought and work. Its organization and rapid growth seem, therefore, to support the claim that the conditions will exist in the not distant future for American political historians to achieve the scientific estate predicted by Buckle, or, more precisely, the claim that such conditions will exist for those individuals able and willing to pay the psychological costs required to break free from old routines. By 1984, I have argued, a significant proportion of American political historians will have proven themselves both able and willing. Henry Buckle will then stand vindicated as a premature prophet rather than a deluded Utopian.

[6] Inquiries about the operations and plans of the Consortium should be addressed to its executive director, Professor Warren Miller, P.O. Box 1248, Ann Arbor, Michigan.

3

ARTHUR SCHLESINGER, JR.

The Humanist Looks at Empirical Social Research

Lee Benson's call for a genuinely scientific history is anathema to many historians who are humanities-oriented. In the following essay, originally presented to the 1962 meeting of the American Sociological Association, Arthur Schlesinger, Jr. speaks for the humanists and registers his caveat against quantitative history. Quantification is not "the central and infallible path" to "social wisdom," says Schlesinger; it is merely one approach, and a weak one at that, since the most important questions are not amenable to quantitative answers. Who, for example, can solve quantitatively the problem of the causes of the Civil War? The quantitative method also rests on false assumptions, according to Schlesinger. Specifically, the author condemns Sir Lewis Namier and B. F. Skinner for asserting that quantitative methods yield "objectivity" and for insisting that man can be programmed.

L E T M E , first, express my great pleasure in being here. An historian among sociologists, I fear, is a case of an inferior Daniel cast into a den of superior lions; but my natural anxiety in facing this assemblage is outweighed tonight by the satisfaction I have in being permitted to join this tribute to your president —a tribute which the humanist claims the right to share along with the

Arthur Schlesinger, Jr., "The Humanist Looks at Empirical Social Research," *American Sociological Review*, XXVII (Dec., 1962), 768–71. Reprinted with permission of the author and the American Sociological Association.

card-holding empirical social researcher. However much one may occasionally differ with Paul Lazarsfeld—and even more, on occasion, with the Lazarsfeldi-ans—one must acknowledge both the brilliance and charm of the man and the notable stimulus the sociologist has provided to all students, humane as well as behavioral, of social processes. I might add that whenever I encounter Paul Lazarsfeld, I recognize the truth of an old adage much cherished by historians: that, inside every sociologist, there is an humanist struggling to get out.

As an historian, I am naturally strongly prejudiced in favor of empirical social research. If I understand this term correctly, it refers, I take it, to two things: first, to gaining the most complete possible factual knowledge about events which have already taken place; and, second, to devising inquiries and experiments which, by enlarging our knowledge about present and future events, may enlarge our understanding of social and human processes in general. No historian can possibly deny the value of empirical social research in both senses: such research is the stuff by which historians live—and by which, I may add, we too often live carelessly and irresponsibly. I am well aware how dismally written history lacks in rigor, how impressionistic the historian's analysis so often is, how imprecise his generation, how loose his language, how literary his whole style of attack. Insofar as empirical social research can drive historians to criticize their assumptions, to expose their premises, to tighten their logic, to pursue and respect their facts, to restrain their rhetoric—in short, insofar as it gives them an acute sense of the extraordinary precariousness of the historical enterprise—it administers a wholly salutary shock to a somewhat uncritical and even complacent discipline.

I would wish everything else I have to say this evening about empirical social research to be construed in the light of this *cri de coeur.* But I know that you have not come tonight to hear how wonderful empirical social research is. Let me therefore conclude this part of my remarks by quickly entering these two points into the record: first, my indebtedness as an historian to the sociologists who have so vastly broadened my own intellectual horizons and refined my own conception of the historical enterprise; and, second, my own intense awareness of the shortcomings, epistemological and methodological, of the enterprise. Let me now pass on to the question whether, granted all this, empirical social research in the sense used by sociologists is *the* key to social knowledge.

This question, it should now be clear, has to do, not with the value of empirical social research *per se,* but with what one must call the *mystique* of empirical social research—the notion that it is, not one of several paths to social wisdom, but the central and infallible path. And this question derives particu-larly from the extent to which empirical social research is taken by its practi-tioners to mean, above all, *quantitative* research—that is, research which deals in quantifiable problems and yields numerical or quasi-numerical conclusions.

Again I do not want to be misunderstood. No historian can deny that quantitative research, complete with IBM cards and computers, can make an important contribution to historical understanding—no historian, that is, who has examined, for example, a recent production by the historical branch of the Lazarsfeld family, *Massachusetts Shipping, 1697–1714,* by the Bailyns. Yet the problem remains: does quantitative research provide the best way of solving significant historical problems?

Your president raised one aspect of this question in a stimulating article in the Winter 1950–1951 issue of the *Public Opinion Quarterly* entitled "The Obligations of the 1950 Pollster to the 1984 Historian." Paul Lazarsfeld proposed here that public opinion data can be of inestimable use to the future historian in defining the 'prevailing values' of a society and in charting the interaction between ideas and social action as well as in analyzing specific events like elections. Similarly, Hadley Cantril in his indispensable survey *Public Opinion, 1935–1946* suggests how useful historians would have found a similar compilation of public opinion polls covering such confused and turbulent epochs of history as the American or French Revolution or the Civil War.

At first, the thought of the availability of such materials is deeply attractive. Yet, on reflection, I wonder whether the existence of public opinion data would, in the end, cause us to write the history of these epochs very differently. What does a public opinion poll report? It reports essentially, I would suppose, what people think they think. It does not report what people really think, because people ordinarily don't know what they really think in advance of a situation which compels them to act on the basis of their thoughts. Public opinion polling, in short, elicits essentially an *irresponsible* expression of opinion—irresponsible because no action is intended to follow the expression. The expression of opinion is not given weight or substance by a sense of accountability for consequences; when that sense of accountability enters, then the expression may very likely be different.

Irresponsible opinion is certainly of interest. It may well tell us a great deal about the general atmosphere of a period. But it is responsible opinion—opinion when the chips are down, opinion which issues directly in decision and action —which is relevant to the historical process and of primary interest to the historian. And public opinion polls do not add greatly to our own knowledge of the evolution and distribution of responsible opinion. The measure of responsible opinion is not answers, but acts. As an experienced student of these matters, Harry S. Truman, once put it, "I think the best poll there is is the count after election."

Polls catch public opinion in a plastic, unfinished, and superficial state, while the historian is concerned with opinion under the stress of decision, opinion as it is crystallized by events and leadership and brought to bear at points of political and intellectual action. The difference between expression without responsibility and expression under responsibility raises problems which go to the root of the whole question of assent. Cardinal Newman's old distinction between "notional assent" and "real assent" represents one salient aspect of the problem involved in the difference between "public opinion" in the polls and "public opinion" in the historical process.

Why does a political leader make a decision? The decision is generally the result of an accommodation between his own views of what is wise and the *felt* pressures on him as to what is possible. The crux of the matter is that the pressures are felt; they are politically kinetic pressures, not inert or latent attitudes. Only a crude politician construes felt pressures in terms of lobbies and pressure groups; a statesman is attuned by his own radar to a whole turmoil of public sentiment; he knows that, by action and by leadership, he can to some degree generate the pressures which will propel him along the course he has already chosen to go. Public opinion data can no doubt provide a kind of measure of his success in marshalling opinion. But his actions and the effective response to them provide a far more reliable measure. Nor do current attempts to evaluate the intensity with which opinions are held really meet the question, since they do not abolish the essential difference between responsible and irresponsible opinion. For this reason, I doubt whether full Gallup, Roper, Michigan, and Harris dossiers on the American or French Revolutions would radically change the historian's view of these historic events. The best poll there is remains the count after election—not what people say they think, but what they do.

Polls represent only one aspect of the attempt to quantify historical data. A number of excellent historians—Sir Lewis Namier and his followers in Great Britain; and certain American scholars under the spell of the behavioral sciences—have mounted more general attacks on classic historical questions in a formidable effort to make them surrender to quantitive solutions. This effort has a pervading complex of assumptions—that the role of human purposes, ideas and ideals in social action is vastly overrated; that history can, in effect, be reduced to a set of social, ethnic, and economic tropisms; and that the quantitive method can transform the historian into a detached and 'scientific' observer. But there seem to me two main troubles with this effort—with an effort, for example, to solve quantitatively the problem of the causes of the Civil War. One is that most of the variables in an historical equation are not susceptible to commensurable quantification; the other is that the observer is too mixed up with the phenomena observed to eliminate the subjective element.

When Sir Lewis Namier condemns the tendency to exaggerate "the importance of the conscious will and purpose in individuals," he holds forth the possibility of a form of historical certitude—but he does so by dismissing a whole range of historical issues which happen not to be susceptible to quantification. This seems to me the essential trick of the quantitative approach. That approach claims a false precision by the simple strategy of confining itself to the historical problems and materials with which quantitative techniques can deal —and ignoring all other questions as trivial. The *mystique* of empirical social research, in short, leads its acolytes to accept as significant only the questions to which the quantitative magic can provide answers. As an humanist, I am bound to reply that almost all important questions are important precisely because they are *not* susceptible to quantitative answers. The humanist, let me repeat, does not deny the value of the quantitative method. What he denies is that it can handle everything which the humanist must take into account; what he condemns is the assumption that things which quantitative methods can't handle don't matter.

I would suggest that these are the things that matter most. Nor can one accept the answer that is all a temporary shortcoming of method—that improvements in technique will soon extend the sway of the quantitative approach until it can subdue all problems. My old friend Professor B. F. Skinner tells us that this is so—and warns us that we must face the consequences. I would not assume that Professor Skinner speaks for all behavioral scientists, but I do feel that he has pursued the logic of the behavioral approach with admirable candor to an ultimate conclusion. His conclusion is briefly that "the application of the methods of science to human affairs" is increasingly and irrevocably "at odds with the traditional democratic conception of man" and "the so-called 'democratic philosophy' of human behavior." The more we understand about human behavior, Professor Skinner tells us, the less we can credit to man himself:

> as such explanations become more and more comprehensive, the contribution which may be claimed by the individual himself appears to approach zero. Man's vaunted creative powers, his original accomplishments in art, science and morals, his capacity to choose and our right to hold him responsible for the consequences of his choice— none of these is conspicuous in this new self-portrait.

Where the democratic view assumes a measure, however limited of free choice and individual responsibility, science, Professor Skinner suggests, refutes such fancies and absorbs everything in a system of comprehensive determinism.

If this is so, then it is so; but the proof does not lie in assertion—or in extrapolation. It can lie only in demonstration—and in a demonstration that has not yet been made. Until it is made, those who accept this view accept it on faith. Science in such terms ceases to be a system of provisional hypothesis and becomes instead a form of poetic myth, almost of religion.

The defenders of behavioral science are sometimes given to the doubtful practice of trying to dispose of its critics by advancing theories about the personal or status insecurities which impel them to criticism. I do not wish to emulate this form of reductionism, and I will refrain, therefore, from speculating about the impulses which divide the world into what William James called the tender-minded and the tough-minded—the impulses which make some people monists and others pluralists. The point is not the psyche of the individuals, but the merit of the arguments.

The key is the demonstration—and one is compelled to doubt whether the necessary demonstration is likely to be made in the near future. For one thing, the vision of comprehensive determinism remains a psychological impossibility in the sense that no human being could conceivably act upon it or live by it. As Sir Isaiah Berlin has put it, "If we begin to take it seriously, then, indeed, the changes in our language, our moral notions, our attitudes toward one another, our views of history, of society and of everything else will be too profound to be even adumbrated." We can no more imagine what the universe of a consistent determinist would be like than we can imagine what it would be like to live in a world without time or one with seventeen-dimensional space. And it is more than a psychological impossibility: it is also a quite illegitimate extension of existing evidence. Until the omnipotence of determinism can be demonstrated by infallibility of prediction and control, one must surely stick with the provable facts and accept the existence of intractable elements in experience which may well, in the future as in the past, continue to defy quantification.

In this belief, I am encouraged by the testimony of Dr. Norbert Wiener, who has done as much as any one to invent the devices which make modern quantitative research possible. Dr. Wiener has noted the contention of behavioral scientists that the main task of the immediate future is "to extend to the fields of anthropology, of sociology, of economics, the methods of the natural sciences, in the hope of achieving a like measure of success in the social fields.

From believing this necessary, they come to believe it possible. In this, I maintain, they show an excessive optimism, and a misunderstanding of the nature of all scientific achievement." Success in exact science, Dr. Wiener points out, has come where there is a high degree of isolation of the phenomenon from the observer—as in astronomy or atomic physics. But the social sciences deal with short statistical runs, and observers are deeply, inextricably and indeterminately involved in what they observe. He concludes:

> Whether our investigations in the social sciences be statistical or dynamic . . . they can never be good to more than a very few decimal places, and, in short, can never furnish us with a quantity of verifiable, significant information which begins to compare with that which we have learned to expect in the natural sciences. . . . There is much which we must leave, whether we like it or not, to the "unscientific," narrative method of the professional historian.

I would qualify Dr. Wiener's conclusion only by expanding it. There is much, I would add, which we must leave, whether we like it or not, not just to historians but to poets, novelists, painters, musicians, philosophers, theologians, even politicians, even saints—in short, to one form or another of humanist. For an indefinite future, I suspect, humanism will continue to yield truths about both individual and social experience which quantitative social research by itself could never reach. Whether these truths are inherently or merely temporarily inaccessible to the quantitative method is a question which only experience can answer.

In the meantime, this humanist is bound to say that, as an aid to the understanding of society and men, quantitative social research is admirable and indispensable. As a guide to the significance of problems, it is misleading when it exudes the assumption that only problems susceptible to quantitative solutions are important. As a means of explaining human or social behavior, it is powerful but profoundly incomplete. As the source of a theory of human nature and of the universe, it is but a new formulation of an ancient romantic myth.

4

ALLAN G. BOGUE

United States: The "New" Political History

In this essay Allan G. Bogue charts the origins, purpose, and goals of political behavioralists and evaluates the contributions of the first generation. Professor Bogue is eminently qualified to introduce the new political history, having served on two key "counters" committees since their inception—the AHA ad hoc committee formed in 1964 to collect the basic quantitative political data for the Inter-University Consortium for Political Research, and the history committee of the Mathematics Social Science Board (MSSB) created in 1964 to update historians in mathematical and statistical techniques.

THOUSANDS OF SCHOLARS study, teach, or write American history. Score upon score of commercial and scholarly presses speed the researches of these scholars to an audience provided by their professional colleagues and the general public. To search for trends or to look for common denominators in this massive outpouring is a task for the brave, the gifted, or the foolish. On occasion, however, accident or incident reveals a purposive current in the relentless tide even to those who lack the ideal qualifications of the historiographer. So was it recently, when a political scientist searched in his midwestern University for a scalogram computer programme and learned that the only deck on campus belonged to a historian. His discovery reflected the growing interest in quantification and social-science theory and method that has been developing among American political historians for some years now.

American historians experimented with quantification in earlier years. Frederick Jackson Turner and some of his Wisconsin students, most notably Orin G.

Allan G. Bogue, "United States: The 'New' Political History," *Journal of Contemporary History*, III (Jan., 1968), 5–27. Reprinted, with slight revisions, with permission of the author and the publisher.

Libby, were industriously mapping election returns and analysing legislative roll calls at the turn of the century. Libby's plea for the systematic study of congressional roll calls appeared in the Annual Report of the American Historical Association in 1896.[1] Turner never lost his enthusiasm for such methods and the imprint of his influence shows in the major publications of a number of scholars. Work in this tradition appeared as late as 1941, but the early interest in quantification and political ecology among historians subsided, perhaps because of the inadequate statistical methods of the pioneers.

At present a small number of historians are trying to apply social-science methods and theory in American political history with varying degrees of rigour. The nine men who were early members of the American Historical Association's ad hoc committee for the collection of the basic quantitative data of American political history, and others who have since become associated with the committee's work in one way or another, are at the centre of the movement. Their seminars are producing recruits for the cause, as are the seminars of some other historians who allow their graduate students to apply methods learned in satisfying the requirements of minor or related fields. During the summer of 1965, thirty-five historians gathered at Ann Arbor for a three-week seminar on voting and legislative behaviour under the auspices of the Inter-University Consortium for Political Research.[2] This group certainly did not include all the professional historians who are interested in such matters and only representative doctoral candidates were invited. Not all those in attendance, however, were deeply dedicated to a quantitative approach. It was an assembly composed in undetermined proportions of prophets, converts, neophytes, seekers, and scoffers. In the argot of the political scientist, slightly corrupted, political historians today number an overwhelming majority of standpatters, a small group of dedicated switchers, and a growing number of their new votaries. Some believe that the members of the last two categories are sufficiently different from the majority of American political historians to justify calling them behavioural historians—understanding behavioural to connote, in this instance, a strong interest in the methods, results, and implications of measurement, combined with some desire to produce research that is respectable by social-science criteria.[3] I realize that the term raises problems, but for our purposes it is a convenient label.

The behavioural historians have not yet produced an impressive body of literature bearing upon American politics. There are in print various voting studies using ecological correlations, most of them quite simple in method; [4] two

[1] Orin Grant Libby, "A Plea for the Study of Votes in Congress," *American Historical Association Report,* 1896, I (Washington, 1897).

[2] This conference is described in a report prepared by Samuel P. Hays and Murray Murphey, "Research Conference on Political Data: Historical Analysis of Quantitative Data—July 26–August 13, 1965, Ann Arbor, Michigan" (mimeographed, 1965).

[3] Robert A. Dahl defines the term in political science in "The Behavioral Approach in Political Science: Epitaph for a Monument to a Successful Protest," *American Political Science Review,* December 1961, p. 767.

[4] George Daniels, "Immigrant Vote in the Election of 1860: The Case of Iowa," *Mid-America,* July 1962; Robert P. Swierenga, "The Ethnic Voter and the First Lincoln Election," *Civil War History,* March 1965; Stanley Parsons, "Who Were the Nebraska Populists?" *Nebraska History,* June 1963; Howard W. Allen, "Studies of Political Loyalties of Two Nationality Groups: Isolationism and German-Americans," *Journal of the Illinois State Historical Society,* Summer 1964; Thomas B. Alexander,

books and a number of articles in which scaling techniques or simpler methods
of roll-call analysis are used; [5] a number of collective biographies of political
elites; [6] a couple of articles dealing with the characteristics of the national
electorate between 1800 and 1840 and another surveying voting trends in
presidential elections; [7] a path-breaking monograph on the importance of the
time dimension in evaluating election returns, as well as a major reassessment of
the political ideology and voting behaviour of the Jacksonian period; [8] and
several contributions concerned with the methods, problems, and promises of
quantitative history.[9] This is the type of work which the behaviouralists have
published so far.

Kit C. Carter, Jack R. Lister, Jerry C. Oldshue, and Winfred G. Sandlin, "Who Were
the Alabama Whigs?" *The Alabama Review,* January 1963; Thomas B. Alexander and
Peggy J. Duckworth, "Alabama Black Belt Whigs During Secession: A New Viewpoint," Ibid., July 1964; Aida DiPace Donald, "The Decline of Whiggery and the
Formation of the Republican Party in Rochester, 1848–56," *Rochester History,* July
1958.

[5] Joel H. Silbey, *The Shrine of Party: Congressional Voting Behaviour, 1841–1852*
(Pittsburgh, 1967); David Donald, *The Politics of Reconstruction 1863–1867* (Baton
Rouge, 1965); John L. Shover, "Populism in the Nineteen-Thirties: The Battle for
the AAA," *Agricultural History,* January 1965; Edward L. Gambill, "Who Were the
Senate Radicals," *Civil War History,* September 1965; Gerald Wolff, "The Slavocracy
and the Homestead Problem of 1854," *Agricultural History,* April 1966; Howard W.
Allen, "Geography and Politics: Voting on Reform Issues in the United States
Senate, 1911–1916," *Journal of Southern History,* May 1961; Glenn M. Linden,
" 'Radicals' and Economic Policies: The Senate, 1861–1873," Ibid., May 1966.

[6] Pioneering work of this type appeared in George Mowry, *The California Progres-
sives* (Berkeley and Los Angeles, 1951), pp. 86–104; Alfred D. Chandler, Jr., "The
Origins of Progressive Leadership," in Elting Morison *et al.* (eds.), *The Letters of
Theodore Roosevelt* (Cambridge, 1951–54), VIII, App. III, pp. 1462–65; David
Donald, "Toward a Reconsideration of Abolitionists," *Lincoln Reconsidered* (New
York, 1961). See also Grady McWhiney, "Were the Whigs a Class Party in
Alabama?" *Journal of Southern History,* November 1957; Ralph A. Wooster, "Notes
on the Georgia Legislature of 1860," *Georgia Historical Quarterly,* March 1961;
"Membership in Early Texas Legislatures, 1850–1860," *Southwestern Historical
Quarterly,* October 1965; Gerald W. McFarland, "The New York Mugwumps of
1884: A Profile," *Political Science Quarterly,* March 1963; William T. Kerr, Jr., "The
Progressives of Washington, 1910–12," *Pacific Northwest Quarterly,* January 1964;
E. Daniel Potts, "The Progressive Profile in Iowa," *Mid-America,* October 1965;
Herbert J. Doherty, Jr., *The Whigs of Florida, 1845–1854, University of Florida
Monographs:* Social Sciences, I, Winter 1959, pp. 63–72. Robert A. Skotheim discusses
some of the methodological problems involved in this type of study in "A Note on
Historical Method: David Donald's 'Toward a Reconsideration of Abolitionists,' "
Journal of Southern History, August 1959.

[7] Richard P. McCormick, "Suffrage Classes and Party Alignments: A Study in
Voter Behavior," *Mississippi Valley Historical Review,* December 1959; "New
Perspectives on Jacksonian Politics," *American Historical Review,* January 1960;
Charles Sellers, "The Equilibrium Cycle in Two-Party Politics," *Public Opinion
Quarterly,* Spring 1965.

[8] Lee Benson, "Research Problems in American Political Historiography," in Mirra
Komarovsky (ed.), *Common Frontiers of the Social Sciences* (Glencoe, 1957); *The
Concept of Jacksonian Democracy: New York as a Test Case* (Princeton, 1961).

[9] Lee Benson, *Turner and Beard: American Historical Writing Reconsidered* (Glen-
coe, 1960); Samuel P. Hays, "History as Human Behavior," *Iowa Journal of History,*
July 1960; "New Possibilities for American Political History: The Social Analysis of
Political Life" (prepared for the American Historical Association meeting, 29
December 1964 and lithoprinted by the Inter-University Consortium for Political
Research); very similar to the latter is "The Social Analysis of American Political
History, 1880–1920," *Political Science Quarterly,* September 1965; "The Politics of
Reform in Municipal Government in the Progressive Era," *Pacific Northwest Quar-
terly,* October 1964.

What kind of findings are emerging from their endeavours? In two important articles Richard P. McCormick has shown that the Jackson elections did not represent the revolution in popular voting behaviour that historians have so confidently assumed for so many years, and that economic class affiliation apparently had little influence in affecting the party choice of voters during the early national period.[10] Lee Benson carried reassessment of Jacksonian democracy still further when he found that content analysis revealed basic ideological differences between Whigs and Democrats, and particularly when he discovered that the multivariate analysis of election returns in indicator precincts in New York showed ethno-cultural conditioning to have been the most important variable associated with party choice in that state.

The writings of McCormick and Benson are perhaps the most impressive exhibits of the new historical persuasion, but a few other studies are representative. Using the Guttman scale as his major analytical tool, Joel Silbey assessed the significance of sectional and party ties in Congress during the 1840s and early 1850s, finding that party ties withstood the impact of the slavery expansion issue much better than some of the conventional literature leads one to expect. George Daniels probed the problem of ethnocultural loyalties and the 1860 election, and his analysis of precinct voting returns in Iowa reinforced Joseph Schafer's rather neglected findings of a generation ago that a majority of German voters in Wisconsin and Illinois remained true to their Democratic party allegiance in the 1860 election.[11] Using multiple correlation techniques, Stanley Parsons destroyed a truism of Populist folklore by showing that populist votes in Nebraska and mortgage interest rates were only slightly correlated, and that in so far as they were associated the correlation was negative rather than positive. In one of the better collective biographies published by a historian to date, William T. Kerr, Jr. has shown that the Progressive leaders of Washington differed in various respects from their conservative counterparts, as well as in the major sources of their support. Thomas B. Alexander and his students have published the initial results of what has since become an elaborate least-squares analysis of social and economic attributes and voting preference in ante-bellum Alabama and which contradicts the old generalization that the "Democrats became the party of poverty and numbers, and the Whigs the party of property and talents."

A number of theses and dissertations dealing with similar or related problems are now complete. Samuel P. Hays drew upon some of these in suggesting that the urban reform movement of the early twentieth century was essentially upper class in origin, and also in proposing an ethno-cultural interpretation of national voting behaviour in the period 1865–1929.[12] Joel Silbey found support in similar materials for his contention that sectionalism was not the only major

[10] Unless otherwise stated, the contributions discussed in the next two paragraphs are those appearing under their authors' names in footnotes 4 through 9.
[11] Joseph Schafer, "Who Elected Lincoln," *American Historical Review,* October 1941. Schafer was a student of Turner and much of his work exemplifies the empirical side of the Turner tradition.
[12] Samuel P. Hays, "The Politics of Reform," and "Political Parties and the Local-Cosmopolitan Continuum, 1865–1929," prepared for the Conference on American Political Party Development, Washington University, 1966, and cited here by permission of Professor Hays and William Nesbit Chambers.

influence shaping American politics during the 1850s.[13] Much other research with a strong quantitative element is under way. These studies include roll-call analyses of Congress in the early national period, during the 1850s, 1860s, and 1870s, and the progressive period, as well as of the Confederate Congress and midwestern state legislatures during the nineteenth century. Historians are preparing studies of the evolution of party structure during the nineteenth century, and others are studying popular voting behaviour in states and regions in the nineteenth and early twentieth centuries. There has also been completed, or is under way, work which has important implications for political history even though its focus is not primarily political—most notably research in historical demography and population mobility, both spatial and social.[14]

Much of the new quantitative history is unsophisticated in social-science terms. A member of the AHA committee on quantitative data estimated recently that there were no more than several dozen members of the history profession at the faculty level who are conversant with statistics through multiple correlation and regression analysis, and if one omits the new breed of economic historian that is, I am sure, true.[15] This state of affairs is changing as history graduates attend statistics courses and social science methodology seminars, but it will be some time before there is a sizable cadre of historians confidently aware of both the promises and the pitfalls inherent in quantification.

Social scientists find the theoretical assumptions of the behavioural historians rather elementary. They are not trying simply to describe "what happened," in the parlance of the old "scientific" historian, but their methods hardly conform to the basic rules of the behavioural approach sketched by David Easton in *A Framework for Political Analysis*.[16] Few behavioural historians are consciously looking for findings with predictive value, or purposefully giving their research a theoretical frame which the results may in part verify, modify, or contradict. Instead, most are still problem or topic-oriented, using social-science techniques or theory to refute or build on the work of past historians or to probe new areas which catch their fancy. Lee Benson is an exception. To a far greater extent than any of the other historical behaviouralists, he tries to make his theoretical commitments explicit and believes that a historian can make a major contribution to the social sciences. He has for instance suggested certain basic propositions which, he argues, illuminate the behaviour of the founding fathers:

> (1) The behavior of men is determined more by the ends they seek
> than by the means they use to achieve those ends; specifically, men

[13] Joel H. Silbey, "The Civil War Synthesis in American Political History," *Civil War History,* June 1964.

[14] Stephan Thernstrom, *Poverty and Progress: Social Mobility in a Nineteenth Century City* (Cambridge, 1964); Samuel B. Warner, *Street-Car Suburbs* (Cambridge, 1962). For those interested in the rural community the work of James C. Malin is still essential; see "The Turnover of Farm Population in Kansas," *Kansas Historical Quarterly,* November 1935, and *The Grassland of North America: Prolegomena to its History* (Lawrence, 1947), pp. 278–315. Several studies bearing on Iowa are summarized with additional data of my own in Chapter I of *From Prairie to Corn Belt: Farming on the Illinois and Iowa Prairies in the Nineteenth Century* (Chicago, 1963).

[15] Samuel P. Hays speaking on "Computers and Historical Research," Purdue Conference on the Use of Computers in the Humanities, 29 October 1965.

[16] David Easton, *A Framework for Political Analysis* (Englewood Cliffs, N.J., 1965), p. 7.

favored the Constitution largely because they favored a Commercial Society, they opposed the Constitution largely because they favored an Agrarian Society. (2) The ends men choose are positively related to the "modes and processes" by which they gain their livelihoods, the social environments in which they live, the social roles they occupy, the groups with whom they identify, and the groups with whom they regard themselves in conflict. (3) In certain historical situations, men who choose certain ends are more likely than their opponents to possess the qualities and resources needed for victory; specifically, in the United States during the 1780s, commercial-minded men like Hamilton possessed the qualities and resources needed to defeat agrarian-minded men like Clinton.[17]

Such behavioural models are rare indeed in the work of historians. Despite his concern for theoretical explication, Professor Benson's work sometimes falls short of the standards that many behavioural scientists consider essential. One searches the first edition of *The Concept of Jacksonian Democracy* in vain for any detailed discussion of the methods by which he selected his indicator precincts, or of the numbers of voters in his sample, or of correlations or significance tests underlying the party preference percentages which he ascribed to the various ethno-cultural groups living in New York during the 1830s and 1840s.[18]

It can indeed be argued that social scientists have written almost as much, if not more, behavioural history than have the political historians. Walter Dean Burnham, William Nesbit Chambers, Robert A. Dahl, Manning J. Dauer, V. O. Key, Theodore J. Lowi, Duncan MacRae, John Schmidhauser, and Ruth C. Silva, have all probed significantly beyond the contemporary scene and produced work that any political historian must use if he wishes to view this nation's political history in fullest perspective.[19]

More significant perhaps than the research achievements of behavioural historians has been their contribution to the building of the historical data archives of the Inter-University Consortium for Political Research, made in co-operation with political scientists. As a number of historians became inter-

---

[17] Lee Benson, *Turner and Beard,* p. 228.

[18] In the introduction to the paperback edition of *The Concept of Jacksonian Democracy* (New York, 1964), Benson includes a specific description of his methodology.

[19] The following list is not intended to be comprehensive: Walter D. Burnham, "The Changing Shape of the American Political Universe," *American Political Science Review,* March 1965; William N. Chambers, *Political Parties in a New Nation: The American Experience, 1776–1809* (New York, 1963); Robert A. Dahl, *Who Governs? Democracy and Power in an American City* (New Haven, 1961); Manning J. Dauer, *The Adams Federalists* (Baltimore, 1953); V. O. Key, Jr., "A Theory of Critical Elections," *Journal of Politics,* February 1955; "Secular Realignment and the Party System," ibid., May 1959; with Milton C. Cummings, Jr., *The Responsible Electorate: Rationality in Presidential Voting, 1936–60* (Cambridge, 1966); Theodore J. Lowi, *At the Pleasure of the Mayor: Patronage and Power in New York City, 1898–1958* (Glencoe, 1964); Duncan MacRae, Jr. and James Meldrum, "Critical Elections in Illinois: 1888–1958," *American Political Science Review,* September 1960; John R. Schmidhauser, "The Justices of the Supreme Court: A Collective Portrait," *Midwest Journal of Political Science,* February 1959; "Judicial Behavior and the Sectional Crisis of 1837–1850," *Journal of Politics,* November 1961; Ruth C. Silva, *Rum, Religion, and Votes: 1928 Re-Examined* (University Park, Pa., 1962).

ested in quantification some years ago, they discovered in discussion that they were wasting their time in searching out and processing quantifiable information which others had already recorded. They agreed that historians needed an inventory of the basic quantitative data of American political history and ultimately, perhaps, a central data archives on which all interested scholars might draw. Following such discussions, Lee Benson, Charles Sellers, Samuel P. Hays, and William Riker (three historians and a political scientist) submitted a memorandum to the Social Science Research Council. In response the Council invited W. Dean Burnham to assess the problems of collecting election statistics in a number of states.

While these developments were taking place, the Inter-University Consortium was also beginning to consider the establishment of a data archives, having as a nucleus the data collected by the Survey Research Center of the University of Michigan. When Professor Burnham's initial investigation was encouraging, the SSRC commissioned him to spend an additional year on the task of inventorying and undertaking an exploratory recovery of data. His labours were so successful that additional organization seemed necessary. Lee Benson organized a committee of historians to assist the Consortium in developing a historical data archives, and the American Historical Association gave it status by designating it an ad hoc committee. In turn the committee organized state committees that undertook to exhume the county election returns from 1824 to the present and other materials. Under the imaginative leadership of its director, Warren Miller, the Consortium obtained funds from the National Science Foundation for the development of the archives and the SSRC continued to be helpful. Dr. Miller appointed a historian, Howard W. Allen, as director of data recovery at the Consortium, and it was hoped that almost all the county election and referenda returns would be available for use by the late fall of 1966. The historians and archivists engaged in this work may be helping to transform one area of history into a cumulative discipline, in which, for the first time, the careful historian need not duplicate every step of the research of predecessors who were interested in the same problem.

While the work of collecting and recording has gone forward at the Consortium, planning conferences have considered the problems of adding legislative materials, primarily roll call votes, to the archives, and various types of economic and ethno-cultural materials which seem necessary for any considered analysis of the basic election data. At the Ann Arbor seminar in 1965, a number of historians expressed interest in essaying the difficult task of retrieving the election returns of the early national period and this work is now under way. The extent to which these collection and service programmes can be maintained and extended will largely depend, of course, on the willingness of granting agencies to subsidize the work and this in turn must depend to a considerable degree on the interest which historians and social scientists show in using the archives.

Its concrete achievements and the ambitiousness of its programme clearly mark the combined Consortium-AHA committee project as the most impressive evidence of the development of a quantifying and behavioural bent in the historical profession. It is not the only organized effort in that direction, however. In 1964 the Mathematics Social Science Board, an offspring of the

Social Science Research Council and the Institute for Advanced Study in the Behavioural Sciences, sponsored the organization of a history committee, headed by Robert Fogel of the University of Chicago.[20] The AHA ad hoc committee is concerned primarily with the development of a data archives and with training programmes geared to its use. The history committee of the MSSB is seeking ways of encouraging the spread of mathematical and statistical expertise within the history profession.

The behavioural movement among American political historians reflects in part a recent tendency among historians to draw more heavily upon the social sciences for method and theory. In his reader, *American History and the Social Sciences,* published in 1964, Edward N. Saveth presents two dozen historians, writing on concepts which are more usually considered to be of primary interest to social scientists. A large number of other scholars could be added to Saveth's list, whose writings in some way reflect the influence of social-science thought or methods. The political behaviouralists, however, are prepared to introduce considerably more quantification and rigour into their work than most such historians.

A few years ago, in a paper paying tribute to a successful revolution—the advent of behaviouralism in political science—Robert Dahl devoted some attention to the causes of this development.[21] He stressed the pioneering work of Professor Merriam at Chicago, the contributions of the European emigré scholars who came to this country during the 1930s, the practical experience of political scientists in government and military service during the Second World War, the empirical promise of survey research techniques, the leadership of the SSRC, and the helping hand of the foundations. No doubt he would agree that the recent tremendous advances in computer technology have helped to confirm the trend.

There are both similarities and differences between the early developments in political science and those now occurring in history. If political science lagged behind sister fields in moving toward behaviouralism, the lag in history has been greater. The commitment of historians to theory was of course typically less than that of political scientists even in the most unsystematic days of political science. There is among the behavioural historians no group analogous to the European emigrés of the 1930s, trained in a different tradition from their American colleagues. Nor can we point to any history department occupying the pre-eminent position of the political science department at the University of Chicago as a disseminating centre of behavioural ideas and methods. For a time in the late 1950s three historians at the University of Iowa were stressing quantification in their seminars and sending their graduates into the methods seminars of their colleagues in political science and sociology. But this group is now dispersed.

There is no pioneer of quantifying techniques in the historical profession comparable in stature to Charles Merriam. But there were a number of historians, active during the 1930s and 1940s, whose writings or seminar offerings anticipated a quantitative approach. During the 1930s James C. Malin

[20] The members of this committee are Robert W. Fogel, Lionel W. McKenzie, Frederick Mosteller, William O. Aydelotte, Oscar Handlin, and Allan G. Bogue.
[21] Robert A. Dahl, *loc. cit.,* note 3.

used manuscript census rolls to prepare demographic studies that modified conventional interpretations of frontier population movements and influenced a considerable number of other scholars either directly or indirectly. This work, plus Malin's emphasis on the intensive study of the local and regional unit, make him one of the progenitors of historical behaviouralism in America, even though in his later work he specifically repudiated the aims and methods of social science.[22]

In reaction against the conventional history fare that he had suffered as a graduate student, Thomas C. Cochran immersed himself during the 1930s in social-science literature, particularly sociology. Exasperated by the traditional views of the craft which several eminent historians expressed at the meeting of the American Historical Association in 1947, he advanced his rebellious ideas in "The 'Presidential Synthesis' in American History" (*American Historical Review,* July 1948). This article was a resounding attack on the traditional method of describing American political history, presidential administration by presidential administration, and a plea for a " 'social science' synthesis of American history." Cochran argued that our political history should be viewed as an outgrowth of fundamental cultural developments, and that it could be attacked most conveniently at the state level. By the 1940s Oscar Handlin at Harvard was emphasizing ethnic group dynamics and their relationship to politics, and a number of students followed his lead, undertaking detailed studies of politics at the local level. At Cornell University, Paul Wallace Gates, although primarily interested in institutional economic history, was asking his graduate students to spend time in other social science departments. No doubt there were others trying to direct the interests of their students into new channels.

If the writings or teachings of Malin, Handlin, Gates, Cochran and others have helped to provide a favourable climate for a more intensive approach to American political history, I must also mention an early research project that had considerable influence upon the profession. During the late 1940s, Merle Curti conceived the idea of studying a frontier county in Wisconsin intensively, and providing a rigorous test of the suggestion that the frontier was a significant factor in shaping American political institutions, the thesis stated so attractively by Frederick Jackson Turner in the 1890s. Professor Curti was a graduate student under Turner at Harvard and was familiar with his interest in systematic political analysis. One of the handful of scholars who established American intellectual history on a firm foundation, he became chairman of the committee on historiography of the SSRC, organized in 1942–43, which prepared the Council's *Bulletin 54,* entitled *Theory and Practice in Historical Study: A Report of the Committee on Historiography,* published in 1946. This report clearly brought out the concern over the problems of objectivity and relativism which had perplexed and disturbed thoughtful American historians during the previous couple of decades. Both the work of his committee and the somewhat acrimonious discussions which its report provoked, turned Professor Curti's mind to the problems of objectively validating historical fact and theory. By this time also he had concluded that study of the frontier hypothesis had reached an

---

[22] James C. Malin, *op. cit.,* note 14. Professor Malin's position on historiographic problems is developed in *Essays on Historiography* (Lawrence, 1946), and in *On the Nature of History: Essays about History and Dissidence* (Lawrence, 1954).

impasse. Margaret Curti, a psychologist with sound training in statistics, had long maintained that historians should concern themselves to a greater extent with quantitative research and with the application of statistics to historical problems. This was the background of a study of Trempealeau county in western Wisconsin, designed to exploit the quantifiable information in the county records and in the manuscript censuses; *The Making of an American Community: A Case Study of Democracy in a Frontier County,* was published in 1959.

Professor Curti's statistical methods were less rigorous than some social scientists demand today and some historians have disputed the study's conclusions, but it is a milestone in American historiography. That a man who had done so much to establish intellectual history should turn his talents to such research gave respectability to quantification, as well as testifying to the versatility and liveliness of Professor Curti's mind.

As in the field of political science, the SSRC has had considerable influence in changing the outlook of historians. It has always aided historians in projects with an inter-disciplinary character. During the last twenty years it has sponsored three monographs concerned with the problems of writing history. *Bulletin 54* looked back to the relativist controversy of the 1930s; in *Bulletin 64, The Social Sciences in Historical Study,* and in the more recent *Generalization in the Writing of History,* we find a real commitment in some of the contributors to both social-science methods and theory.[23] I am not aware that any foundation has been uniquely concerned with promoting behaviouralism among historians, but the action of the Ford Foundation in supporting the Institute for Advanced Study in the Behavioural Sciences has contributed to that end. Since its establishment, the administrators have generously allocated places to historians. Many if not most of the quantifiers among American political historians today have been assisted to some degree either by the SSRC or the Stanford Institute.

There are few more difficult tasks than that of explaining why one man adopts new techniques and another does not. We can point to general conditioning factors and to encouraging elements in the intellectual milieu, and we can discern apparent predispositions in the individuals who innovate, but it is hard to explain in the final analysis why some take the plunge and others do not. If the SSRC has aided many of the behavioural historians it has also assisted dozens of others in the historical profession who have shown no disposition to change their approach. But aid from that agency or from the Stanford Institute must be regarded as one of a number of predisposing or confirming factors.

To some extent the behavioural historians appear to have had a broader training than usual: one was a classics major, another majored in psychology, another had a good training in mathematics and still another a double major. The prodding of graduate directors in the direction of inter-disciplinary work is remembered by members of the group. It is probably no accident that a number of them were initially interested in economic history, which has always had a

[23] Social Science Research Council, *Theory and Practice in Historical Study: A Report of the Committee on Historiography, Bulletin 54* (New York, 1946); *The Social Sciences in Historical Study: A Report of the Committee on Historiography, Bulletin 64* (New York, 1954); Louis Gottschalk, ed., *Generalization in the Writing of History: A Report of the Committee on Historical Analysis of the Social Science Research Council* (Chicago, 1963).

body of theory and statistical method to draw upon, and in which far-reaching developments have occurred during the last fifteen years.

One learns in discussing the origins of their interests with the behaviouralists that they experienced recurrent dissatisfaction with conventional political history and searched for concepts or methods that would give them greater confidence in the results of research or provide a more satisfying framework in which to present them. A number of them were particularly impressed by the work of Lazarsfeld and Key, and probing produces the names of other social scientists who set the thinking of one or more of them on a new track—Rice, Merton, Duverger, Weber, Michels, Lubell, Hannah Arendt, and Riesman. There was some reaction, too, against the practice of borrowing concepts from the social scientists and applying them without rigorous proof. In *The Age of Reform,* for instance, Richard Hofstadter suggested that declining social status was a major motivating factor among both the Populists and the Progressives. Soon status revolution threatened to become a universal historical solvent, applied unfortunately with little resort to the careful quantification that would either corroborate or disprove the hypothesis.

The most influential of the historical behaviouralists specializing in American history is Lee Benson. Having completed a doctoral dissertation on the economic and political background of the Interstate Commerce Act, he went to Harvard to study location theory; there he was greatly impressed by the rigour and precision with which Walter Isard was attacking the problems of location theory, and by the more systematic approach of social scientists in comparison to historians. Moving to Columbia, he met Paul Lazarsfeld and found him appalled both by the flaccidity of historical analysis and by the ignorance of history among social scientists. Professor Lazarsfeld provided funds and encouraged Benson to investigate more precise approaches to American political history. From Benson's work at the Columbia Bureau of Applied Social Research came his long article "Research Problems in American Historiography," which provided concrete illustrations of the way in which simple time series of election results might be used to explode generalizations long cherished by historians. A few historians were already stressing quantification in their seminars, but it is with the publication of this article that the behavioural trend becomes clearly evident in American historical writing. Other research which Lee Benson began in the 1950s matured as papers on the causation of the Civil War and *The Concept of Jacksonian Democracy: New York as a Test Case.* Benson was a committed economic determinist when he began his doctoral work but, particularly in his study of Jacksonian democracy in New York, he discovered that his formula was inadequate. Ethno-cultural conditioning seemed to explain more than did economic interest.

Stimulated by a small group of social scientists at the State University of Iowa during the late 1940s, William O. Aydelotte conceived the idea of a massive study of the Corn Laws Parliament in which biographical data were to be gathered for the 800-odd members of this assembly, and these materials related if possible to party affiliation and voting behaviour. The Rockefeller Foundation launched the project with a grant and Professor Aydelotte has pushed it steadily forward, searching first for basic biographical information both here and abroad, working out satisfactory classifications of the class and business backgrounds of the members of parliament, recording the divisions, subjecting data first to correlation analysis (with rather discouraging results), then moving to scaling techniques, and along the way teaching himself social statistics and learning the technology of data processing and computer research. Given his subject matter, one is tempted to look to Namier for Professor Aydelotte's inspiration, but he maintains that his early work owed much more to Lazarsfeld and to *The People's Choice* than to Namier's studies of the British Parliament. Aydelotte has not yet summarized his research in a book-length monograph, but he has delivered a number of important papers at historical meetings, publishing some of them as articles, and he has discussed the problems and rewards of such research in numerous informal contacts with specialists in both American and European history. Once a historian recognizes that he must explain why men behaved as they did in the past, he must turn if he is a thorough scholar to the disciplines that concentrate on the explanation of human behaviour; the quantification movement in American political history is one aspect of this change of direction; but commitment to quantification is not equally strong among the members of the AHA committee; one of them wrote recently:

> . . . I am not an enthusiast for quantification. Quantifiable data make up only a portion of the evidence available to the historian. Moreover, if quantifiable data are to be used intelligently, one must have a vast knowledge of the historical context of the situation; the data are not self-interpreting. Another grave danger with quantification is that it can lead to an extremely imbalanced emphasis on those factors that can be quantified, to the exclusion of others of equal or greater significance. Quantification, in other words, is merely one tool in the historian's kit; he must not misuse it or throw the other tools away.

In a series of papers and articles, Samuel P. Hays has tried to articulate and to some extent shape the new trend in American political historiography. He has indicted "conventional political history" as "so preoccupied with the outward and formal, the episodic, the unique and the individual, that it has failed to draw attention to some of the most significant developments of our political past." [24] Historians, he urges, must study political structure in detail: the voters, their socio-economic and ethno-cultural groupings, the pressure groups, the leadership cadres and the systems of decision-making that operate at every level of the American political system, as well as the inter-relationships of these elements. By studying these components of American politics in action through time, by pushing beyond the mere description of political institutions and by penetrating the fog of rhetoric and ideology we can, he promises, reach the basic facts of political motivation, influence, and power. In particular Hays emphasizes the need for study of politics at the grass roots in contrast to the national scene, and the benefits to be gained by distinguishing between political rhetoric and political reality. Recently he has settled upon the term, "the social analysis of politics" as the most appropriate description of this approach. He emphasizes that quantitative data are important tools in this analysis and has also stressed the usefulness of drawing upon the social sciences for both method

[24] Hays "New Possibilities," *loc. cit.*

and theory. Even "conventional" historians can argue that much of this pre-scription describes their current operations. The procedures which Professor Hays recommends differ from normal practice in American political history mainly in the relative emphasis that is placed upon local case studies, quantifi-cation, and social science theory. His articles describe what behaviouralists and their students have been doing in varying degree for some time. But if his role so far has been primarily that of publicist and synthesizer, his emphasis on the historian's obligation to set his findings within some sort of conceptual perspec-tive has been salutary. On the other hand, his unfavourable assessment of traditional history seems unnecessary or overdrawn to some behaviouralists.

We can say, quite accurately I believe, that a large proportion of our political historians expend their energies in writing the biographies of individual politi-cians, and that others pursue their research on political bodies, groups, and movements, almost solely in personal manuscripts, newspapers, and legislative debates. Usually American historians have studied elections as unique expres-sions of the popular will rather than as parts of a time series, and limited their consideration of roll calls to final votes, and perhaps those on major amend-ments. We have as historians frequently been more impressed by what our subjects have said than by what they have done. As a group we have been unsystematic in our generalizations and too little interested in comparisons and categorization. We often fail to make our assumptions adequately explicit, and in trying to understand human motivation we often ignore the more sophisti-cated theorizing of the behavioural sciences. The challenge confronting the behavioural historian is to exploit the body of hard quantitative data that exists in election returns, legislative roll calls, court archives, census data (published and unpublished), state, county, and municipal records, and the great accumu-lation of biographical facts available in other types of sources. This involves both learning the methods necessary to master and manipulate these intimidat-ing sources of information, and becoming more sophisticated in the techniques of research design which are necessary to set findings in useful and defensible theoretical frameworks.

Behavioural history does not promise short cuts or easy answers. If historians have over-emphasized some types of source materials, these cannot be ignored by the historian who quantifies. The scales or other devices which reveal legislative voting patterns can be interpreted fully only if we read the preceding debates. Tables, graphs, and correlations do not explain themselves; they are the product of a particular research design and are subject to various interpreta-tions. The politician's oratory may be designed to conceal or obfuscate his behaviour no less than to explain it, and the scholar who uses the *Congressional Globe* is rather like the prospector who examines a salted claim. Manuscript collections, some will say, are more reliable; here the politician lays bare his motives. He may indeed, but again he may not, and it is shocking to discover how little some of the manuscript collections, regularly cited as major sources in historical monographs, actually reveal about the men who accumulated them. In addition, any manuscript collection is at best an accidental historical accre-tion, pointing perhaps to conclusions that are completely different from those we would reach if all the related manuscript collections had been preserved. It is sobering also to remember that whenever a politician evaluates his election chances correctly (few run in anticipation of defeat), there are usually one or more opponents who judge the situation incorrectly. Remembering this, we will treat the explanations of politicians with caution. But the interplay of contemporary observation and explanation with quantitative evidence should allow us to push our understanding further than either type of source can carry us by itself.

In writing of cultural sources and economic change, Thomas C. Cochran points out that no one has yet developed a model in which all the variables can be quantified. "One cannot," he writes, "speak of units or doses of personality or values." [25] We will no doubt become increasingly ingenious in developing ways to measure attitudes or values indirectly; the quantifier may build some dams and breakwaters in what Matthew Arnold unfairly termed "that huge Mississippi of falsehood called history," but there are rapids he will not tame, tributaries he cannot explore, and quicksands he still cannot plumb by quantification. So American political historians are not all going to become quantifiers, and not only for this reason. Much biography and so-called conventional political history is useful and will continue to attract many in the profession. The fact that quantification calls for extra effort rather than a substitution of effort will discourage some from essaying it.

For those who find the fascination of political history in a smooth and colourful narrative, the injection of numbers, tables, and scales may be jarring and unpleasing. The new political history must make its way by appealing to the intellectual curiosity of the reader; its impact must flow from the ideas and the sense of understanding that it imparts rather than from the colourful incident or well-told anecdote. Even so, behavioural historians need not jettison the idea that history is a literary art. There is no reason why political history should not still employ the well-turned phrase or striking illustration, even though based on a foundation of measurement.

For a time in the testing period ahead the behavioural historians may find editors suspicious and cold; their graduate students will encounter difficulties in obtaining proper training in statistics and the use of computers; both faculty and students may find it difficult to obtain financial aid because the National Science Foundation has not officially recognized historians and granting agencies of humanistic temper are not likely to support behavioural history enthusiastically. These problems may in the end be less disturbing than the limitations of the quantitative data of American history and the inadequacies of the techniques now available for analysing them. Since the behavioural historian cannot interview the dead politician of yesteryear, he is forced to place considerable emphasis on the study of aggregate data, particularly in election analysis. Here he encounters the problem of ecological correlations which W. S. Robinson described some fifteen years ago. One cannot, on the basis of correlation analysis, deduce the behaviour of an individual from the behaviour of the aggregate. There is, as Austin Ranney has pointed out, a good deal to be learned from the study of aggregates as aggregates. [26] What is more, it is possible in some instances to produce refined aggregate data. In some states, for

[25] Thomas C. Cochran, *The Inner Revolution: Essays on the Social Sciences in History* (New York, 1964), p. 142.

[26] Austin Ranney, "The Utility and Limitations of Aggregate Data in the Study of Electoral Behavior," in Austin Ranney, ed., *Essays on the Behavioral Study of Politics* (Urbana, 1962), discusses the problems inherent in the use of aggregate data.

instance, poll lists of the nineteenth century and census data can be combined so that we know precisely the voters represented in precinct totals and many of their social characteristics—in contrast to situations in which we know only that voters represent a certain proportion of an electorate that has as a group certain demographic, socio-economic, or ethno-cultural characteristics. Must we stop there, or can we minimize the limits of possible error in moving from aggregate to individual, or work with probabilities rather than correlation analysis? Ferreting out virtually pure ethno-cultural or socio-economic constituencies seems offhand to be a commonsense solution, which election forecasters have used successfully on occasion; but the very purity of such units may impart bias. Assuming that we can use aggregate data in good conscience, we have fewer of them than we would like. One is hard put to it to find historical measures of some of the variables that survey research has found to be important. The emphasis which behavioural historians are placing on the importance of ethno-cultural groups may in part reflect the fact that the ethno-cultural reference group is the easiest to identify in historical data. Moreover, the statistics of social research are unfortunately much more useful in showing the relationships between variables at a particular moment than in demonstrating change over time. Ideally, the behavioural historian requires a statistics of time series, of lag, of transition matrixes, of growth models, and of indirect relationships where the association of two factors is measured by substituting a third for one or the other. Since most social scientists restrict their research to the findings of survey research, there are few outstanding scholars in the behavioural disciplines who are interested in developing or refining the kind of statistical methods that historians would find particularly useful.[27]

Aggregate election data provide evidence of a single act, although to some extent the preparation for this act can be deduced from examination of other variables. The modern panel survey yields information about the period of preparation and sometimes adds retrospective interpretations by the actors as well. Can content analysis of newspapers or other historical documents be refined to the point where it serves in some measure as a substitute for the questionnaire? Its advocates believe that this technique has been greatly improved during the present generation. Contingency and qualitative content analysis in particular seem to promise results that are more interesting to historians than the rather mechanical exercises that were common some years ago. The imaginative and flexible analyst can indeed deduce political values, class structure, influence and power systems, and key election issues from even the highly partisan newspapers of the nineteenth century, provided he remembers that historical evidence may come in all shapes and sizes. But it seems doubtful that content analysis will soon reach the stage where it can be used to detect the exact turning points or the precise importance of the various issues in election campaigns.[28]

---

[27] Gösta Carlsson comments on the "timelessness" of much social theory in "Time and Continuity in Mass Attitude Change: The Case of Voting," *Public Opinion Quarterly*, Spring 1965.

[28] Ithiel De Sola Pool, *Trends in Content Analysis: Papers, Work Conference on Content Analysis* (Urbana, 1959), is a relatively recent survey of the state of the technique.

If the American political historian faces problems in finding adequate quanti-fiable data and in discovering appropriate statistical techniques, he runs other dangers in using political theory in planning and interpreting his research. In effect he may allow such theory or its related concepts to dehumanize his work. When he writes in terms of social role or status revolution, for instance, he may produce a deterministic history in which his central characters are denied the power of choice or the freedom to make rational decisions, but seem instead the captives of forces beyond their control. The predatory railroad tycoon who bribes a legislature may appear as the guardian of his stockholders, and the representative of a peer group of railroad executives rather than as a calculating offender against the ethics or law of the community. The abolitionist or progressive leader becomes a man in unconscious revolt against the societal changes that are depriving him of the position of leadership which his father enjoyed, rather than a public-spirited reformer trying to improve society from rational and philanthropic motives. "If powerful groups are denied access to formal power in legitimate ways," writes Samuel P. Hays, "they seek access through procedures which the community considers illegitimate. Corrupt gov-ernment, therefore, does not reflect the genius of evil men, but rather the lack of acceptable means for those who exercise power in the private community to wield the same influence in governmental affairs." [29] Such explanations may present old material in a new light, but in careless hands they may fit facts to theory rather than using them to test theory; and certainly such analysis gives little hint of the moral indignation that some historians have found in the progressive period. Once such pitfalls are recognized, however, they can be avoided.

Some historians may consider behavioural history to be "consensus" history. In the introduction to *The American Political Tradition,* Richard Hofstadter noted in 1949 that "the common climate of American opinion" had "been much obscured by the tendency to place political conflict in the foreground of history," and showed, in the essays that followed, the very considerable agree-ment that had existed among American political leaders irrespective of section or party. A few years later John Higham detected a growing "cult of 'American consensus'" in both the intellectual and political history of America, and argued that "current scholarship" was "carrying out a massive grading opera-tion to smooth over America's social convulsions." [30] It seems inevitable that the rather precise measurements and the detailed case studies of behavioural history will qualify the bold conclusions reached in some older general studies. The result need not be homogenized history, however. To prove consensus in our political history, the historian must define politics, political ideas, and the American political system narrowly. In reality it is as much a political act to exclude a racial or an economic minority from participation in formal political institutions, or to keep a depressed sector of the population in bondage by failing to provide adequate educational and economic opportunities, as it is to share in the task of choosing a presidential candidate. With this understood, American political life becomes once more the scene of fundamental political

[29] Hays, "Politics of Reform," *loc. cit.,* p. 166.
[30] John Higham, "The Cult of the 'American Consensus': Homogenizing Our History," *Commentary,* February 1959.

conflict. And some of the behaviouralists do bring this broad view to their study of American political history.

Critics of quantification are common in the historical profession. Some of them suspect inter-disciplinary research on general principles. Arguing by aphorism and analogy, one of my colleagues points out that the supreme achievement of hybridization in the animal world is the mule—a creature without pride of ancestry or hope of progeny. Recently Professor Aydelotte discussed quantification in history in a temperate and closely-reasoned article in the *American Historical Review* (April 1966). He divides the arguments of the most vociferous critics of quantification into four categories, questioning specifically: (1) the value of the work that has been done; (2) the feasibility of this approach in view of the admittedly limited materials available to historians; (3) the reliability of the results obtained by these techniques; and (4) the usefulness or significance of the results. There can, in the end, be only one convincing answer to such criticisms: the usefulness and intrinsic interest of the publications of the behavioural historians will determine whether quantification flourishes or withers as a historical technique.

Lee Benson was sanguine about the future of the new political history when he wrote recently, "the prediction does not seem absurd that . . . by 1984, a significant proportion of American historians will have accepted Buckle's two basic propositions: (1) past human behaviour can be studied scientifically; (2) the main business of historians is to participate in the overall scholarly enterprise of discovering and developing general laws of human behaviour." [31] The date is ominous and the future perhaps less assured than Benson believes. But the methods and theory of the social science disciplines seem to promise much. If the behaviouralists retain the broad and critical knowledge of sources found among conventional political historians, their keen awareness of the range of cultural and socio-economic differences at different times, and their willingness to search widely for alternative hypotheses, they may indeed contribute to a richer and more vital political history of the United States.

I am indebted to J. Rogers Hollingsworth and Joel Silbey for critical advice during the preparation of this article. I would also like to thank the many colleagues with whom I have discussed this subject, or who have replied to my enquiries, in particular Thomas B. Alexander, William O. Aydelotte, Lee Benson, Thomas C. Cochran, Merle Curti, Richard P. McCormick, and Rowland L. Mitchell.

[31] Lee Benson, "Quantification, Scientific History, and Scholarly Innovation," *AHA Newsletter,* June 1966, p. 12.

5

MARSHALL SMELSER
AND WILLIAM I. DAVISSON

The Historian and the Computer:
A Simple Introduction to
Complex Computation

Marshall Smelser and William I. Davisson, an historian and an econo-mist respectively, attempt in this essay to overcome the seemingly visceral fear of computers among many historians by explaining that modern man is inescapably surrounded by electronic devices of all kinds. The advantages of computer-aided methods are also clearly illustrated by examples drawn from Davisson's own quantitative studies of colonial estate inventories in Essex County, Massachusetts, and colonial ship registers in the Philadelphia Gazette. *Studying economic history with the aid of digital computers can be called "paleoeconomics," Smelser and Davisson conclude, perhaps with tongue in cheek, since it is as exacting as astronomy and paleontol-ogy. Readers must bear in mind that the authors' admonition against sampling is in the framework of colonial American history where the data are incomplete. For more recent periods in which information is voluminous and nearly complete, such as population census records, sampling is a stark necessity.*

THE HISTORICAL METHOD of learning has recently benefited from several technical developments, such as the rapid methods of copying printed or

Marshall Smelser and William I. Davisson, "The Historian and the Computer: A Simple Introduction to Complex Computation," *Essex Institute Historical Collections,* CIV (Apr., 1968), 109–26. Copyright © 1968 by Essex Institute. Reprinted with permission of the authors and the publisher.

manuscript materials by photography, the portable dictating machine for taking notes or interviewing, and the high-speed electronic data-processor, or computer. Of these new developments the computer has been accepted least readily. Many scholars who have completed their professional training and who have set out to steer their own courses toward new discoveries seem disinclined to use the computer. Computers seem strange, and what is strange is instinctively avoided by many. The computer seems inscrutable because it has been most exploited by people who use numbers better than they use words. The claims they make are cryptic and obscure to the humanist, but the claims, the uses, even the machinery itself, are not really occult. It is the language of the users which is veiled and enigmatic. The use of the computer can be explained in plain English.

The computer is already ubiquitous. A survey of an average middle-class household will probably turn up several computers in daily use to perform menial tasks. Computers measure and thereby can adjust the operation of a machine to its environment. Computers count anything that can be counted.

The most familiar computer is the telephone. One instructs it by dialing the number. The computer then automatically selects the proper number among millions; it searches for unused circuits and switches the call over unused circuits to the proper telephone. Other familiar computers are thermostats. They report temperature to household appliances and tell them to get to work or to knock off work. They command furnaces, air-conditioners, refrigerators and freezers, ovens, toasters, percolators, flatirons, electric skillets, and other gadgets. Few people know exactly how they work, and fewer can heal them when they are ill, but technological ignorance does not prevent people from buying them or having them installed to do the chores. They do *not* think. The effectiveness of their use depends on the intelligence of their owners. Set the electric toaster to burn a piece of bread and it will burn a piece of bread. Dial the telephone incorrectly and it will ring the wrong bell.

The computer is met frequently in daily life by those who use an automatic elevator, in which they trust their lives to the circuits of a computer. The computer in the elevator sleeps until awakened by an electric shock from pressure or from human body-heat applied to a marker inscribed with the number of the floor which is the rider's destination. If there are several riders, the computer learns by successive sensations which floors they wish to go to, sorts out the floors in the order of ascent, makes sure that the car will not stop at a floor no passenger is going to, and is ready to leave. It waits at each floor for a decision by another computer which keeps track of the entrance of passengers (commonly by counting the interruptions in a beam of light across the door). When a sufficient interval indicates that no more are coming aboard it closes the door and tells the elevator to take off. The computer signals the motor and starts counting floors, stopping where stops are wanted, passing unwanted stops, and then returning to ground level when human signaling ceases. The computer, for humanitarian reasons and to avoid law suits, patiently reopens the door when partially closed in the face of a late-comer and also levels the car with the floor to prevent stumbling.

These devices are merely helpers. The computer, like the steam engine, the telephone, the adding machine, the typewriter, is merely a tool for getting things done quickly and inexpensively that could not be done as quickly or as inexpensively before. They will not improve the quality of the workmanship. A typewriter can not confer literary grace, an adding machine will give an incorrect sum if the wrong numbers are punched, no telephone improves the conversation of a bore, and the automated elevator in a library will deliver the student to the floor where rubbish is shelved if rubbish is what he wishes. The people who live with computers have a cant word for it: "GIGO," acronymous for "Garbage in, garbage out."

A scholar may be disinclined to use the computer to learn history, he may even shudder at the thought of trying to master it, but he cannot escape computers if he tries. They are everywhere. Let him conquer his revulsion, look forward to learning something, if only as a spectator, and look at the high-speed computer which serves scholarship. This explanation is not offered as a substitute for the existing body of literature of historical method but as an additional chapter of that useful and perspicacious literature.

For the historian the computer is particularly useful whenever something can be learned by counting. An equally great advantage of the computer is that it may be used for processes other than counting. It may store and retrieve alphabetized data on command. It may find, sort, and arrange variantly-spelled words or information about variant spellings. In short, one of the great advantages of the computer is that it can deal with verbal as well as numerical problems. It is well to illustrate by applications to economic history because that is the kind of history which deals the most with things that can be counted, whether bushels or codfish, ton-miles or insurance premiums, tax dollars or porterage fees, values-added or freight-car loadings. The computer, of course, has value in any kind of history—whether military, political, linguistic, medical, or other—which deals with multitudes of facts in recognizable categories, but we confine ourselves here to economic history.

The obvious advantage of the computer is that it can handle enormous quantities of fact at the rate of a million separate operations per second. A less obvious advantage, but certainly as great, is that it forces the student to ask precise questions. One cannot carry on an unprepared dialogue with a computer. Here the computer itself is no help. It will not refine vague curiosity into sharp and penetrating inquiries. The computer will only give specific answers to specific questions. For thinking original thoughts the computer is a half-wit. Computers can be given responses to chess moves, but, as yet, there is no possibility that a computer will beat a player who is better than the one who composed the responses, or one who, by games theory, randomizes more skillfully. The computer which the humanist or social scientist will use works with the arithmetic of an infant, saying only "yes" or "no," "right" or "wrong." But the computer can combine and recombine yes-no reactions and in minutes produce results that would take a large number of people and many centuries to calculate.

A few generalities will help before getting down to cases. To learn the scientific answer to a question, the question must be sharply defined. The quality of the definition will depend on the quality of the mind which defines. Sharpening the question may be the hardest part of the whole study. Having arrived at a question which will lead to the answer sought, the seeker is still faced with a methodological problem, that is, with finding the right way to get the answer, whether he is using the computer or a pencil and paper. Almost always the inquirer will have to divide his problem into parts and solve each part separately. To put it more conventionally for humanists, he will have to break his problem into elements, collect data about each, construct hypotheses about each of the elements, test these hypotheses, and draw the conclusions into one defensible answer. Certainly the use of the computer or any other system of calculation is here subordinated to the human mind, which must evaluate at every stage, from the formulation of the question to the formulation of an answer derived from mute facts which speak not of themselves but with the voice of their master.

At the risk of repetition, the process can be explained this way: (1) shaping the correct question out of the nebular gases of creative curiosity; (2) developing a method of answering the question defined; (3) applying the method to data which bear directly on the question, which application of method is, first, bibliographical and archival, and, second, mining the sources for their ore; (4) studying or "processing" the facts to put them in an order in which they can be understood; (5) phrasing the answer.

The computer is of use only in the fourth step, but if one wishes to be scientific or definitive about things which can be counted or measured, the computer is indispensable. Without it one is reduced to generalizing from scraps of information. Such generalizations from scraps are often very durable in historical literature. Their durability is probably in direct proportion to their agreement with what logically ought to or could have been the case rather than with what really happened. This is not to adopt the positivist view that if man cannot measure, man cannot know, but to urge the conviction that what can be measured should be measured.

The economic historian has the problem of trying to draw valid answers from questions put to enormous masses of facts, usually expressed in statistics. So large are many of these collections that one student, using pencil and paper, or a small desk calculator, can neither distill nor arrange the total of facts in any way which can be understood, even by him. But the computer is so fast and so accurate that it can produce simple one-page answers to questions which are put to the very largest collections of figures expressing quantities. These brief answers can be produced as tables and graphs, both easily printed by the computer at the command of its user. With the computer *all* of the data can be assimilated. It is no longer necessary to write economic history from scraps and dubious samples.

For example, the inventories of estate in the records of Essex County, Massachusetts, 1640–1682, can be reduced to 26,000 data cards which, together, tell us all that can now be known of the wealth of the county in that forty-two years. To learn the answer to pointedly defined questions about the economy of the county, the manner of holding property, the types of property held, the nature of the wealth of the county and how it grew, the computer, starting at the beginning, can print seven one-page tables and eighteen explanatory graphs in about ten minutes. Such tables and graphs may distill to only a sentence each, but if the author has a good mind each sentence will be the definitive sentence on its subject.

A manual worker would have had to organize and make perhaps 125,000 calculations from the estate records or, more likely, from notes on the estate records, and then draw his graphs and compile his tables. How long would it take? At least five hundred clock hours. Put another way, let it be assumed that two scholars, equally uninformed and of equal ability, approached the study of the seventeenth-century economy of Essex County. The man who used the computer would finish his study of *all* of the data before the manual worker finished a fractional sample. Because of the labor involved, and the sheer impossibility of organizing a huge mass of data by hand or by desk-size mechanical calculators, the constant tendency of writers has been to generalize broadly from narrow spans of data drawn from statutes, from personal memoirs and account books, from such short series of statistics as come readily to hand, and from the tendentious economic writings of contemporaries who were trying to influence public policy. The results can be provocative, even entertaining, but they convey no certitude. One may estimate a man's riches by his manner of life, but one could do more than guess if he could total the figures in the memoranda of his tax accountant.

Computer science—a phrase which need not alarm the historian—is the science of the use of electronic data-processing machines in manipulating data, whether statistical or other kinds. Its practitioners concern themselves with advancing the methods of storing data and recovering or retrieving it in the most useful way. It is a field of learning in itself, in which the degree of Doctor of Philosophy may be earned, but the historian who wishes to use a computer need not become a computer scientist, nor will he usually have the time to learn the science even if he has the kind of mind needed to become a computer scientist. He uses the product and the thinking of the computer scientist just as he uses the product and thinking of the pharmacologist. The principal product of computer science is the computer itself. A computer can be found in almost any university in the United States. If it is not easily found, the historian who wishes to use a computer should look in the yellow pages and telephone for advice from a representative of one of the companies who have applied computer science to the manufacture of the machinery (jargon: "hardware"). Among the best known at present are International Business Machines Corporation, National Cash Register Company, Sperry Rand Corporation, Control Data Corporation, and General Electric Company.

When he finally meets the computer he will also meet its keeper, who may or may not be a professional computer scientist, but who will, in any event, speak an unfamiliar professional slang, which is really an exact vocabulary forming a sub-dialect of engineering. He will bring two or more collections of facts together into one manageable mass. He will create a "universe"—a logically defined and tightly limited field of study. This universe (model), he will say, has a "population"—all of its facts. He will be best acquainted with businessmen and scientists, and he may know very few poets, critics, and historians. If pressed, he will translate his spoken language so that people who do not make their living from computer-tending can understand. He or his employees are the people with whom the historian will work to manage his mountain of quantities and bring them to order so that they can answer questions. The central concern is the computer—a desk calculator plus electric typewriter plus secretary plus file cabinet plus file clerk, all blended and enlarged colossally and working at the speed of electricity, that is to say, at a million separate operations per second. It is not necessary to understand it; it is only necessary to believe it.

Simple faith does not satisfy some humanists and social scientists who have started asking questions of a computer. It is possible to go on and learn more of computer science, that is, the devising of systems by which data may be manipulated correctly within the limitations of the machine and the specific populated universe of data. To learn computer science is to learn how to make curiosity and the machine compatible, and is the first step toward becoming a computer scientist, a most laudable ambition. The least that the humanist or social scientist needs to know is how to instruct the computer, or to instruct his programmer just as he instructs the research assistant or secretary. The average historian will find himself in a foreign land here, and, as in a foreign land, he will decide whether to learn the language or to use an interpreter—the programmer. At the beginning it would be best to rely on an interpreter, who can speak to the computer in its own languages. The interpreter can be one of the computer's keepers, but the researcher will do even better at least at first, with a colleague and research collaborator of the same or a related discipline who is more than a novice in the arts and sciences of research by computer. The interested graduate student, of course, will seek out (or be drafted by) a professor who uses the computer as a tool of his work.

The word-exchange between the historian and the man who has the necessary knowledge of computer technology is not precisely a dialogue. The historian tells the computer scientist about the population of facts which exists in his universe of inquiry, how it has been recorded and what questions he is asking of the data. The programmer, by himself, practices the occult rite known as programming and brings back the answers. There is no qualitative difference in this human contact from the relationship of a historian asking an accounting clerk to extract a tax series from a collection of public finance manuscripts or directing a student research assistant to do any kind of routine manual labor with paper sources or research notes. It must be repeated: the easiest way to get started is to enter a partnership with an accredited scholar of similar interests who has already used the computer in his work. It is a fair bargain. The new partner can provide specialized bibliographical and historiographical knowledge which the experienced quantitative worker would need years to acquire, and the newcomer, as time passes, will begin to ferment with questions to ask the computer. It is useful to know as much statistics and economics as possible, but any university which offers the Ph.D. will be staffed with people willing to instruct the ignorant of any age, and it is not really necessary to be more than a historian.

The special value of the historian is that he knows the field of facts, or universes of data. William O. Aydelotte has pointed out that there have already been many quantitative studies in history. He himself has applied the method to voting patterns in the British House of Commons, and he names nearly a score of such studies which have either upset established generalizations or have provoked intensive re-study by skeptical scholars.[1] These questions could not

[1] William O. Aydelotte, "Quantification in History," *American Historical Review,* LXXI (1965–66), 803–25, an excellent and persuasive study.

have been left to computer scientists; only historians know which superannuated generalizations rest on inadequate statistical support.

The use of high-speed electronic data-processing is not limited to that which can be measured, but may be most useful to the historian of quantities. In the sources, what can be measured is usually, but not always, expressed in statistical tables for the researcher. There are no special problems of the reliability of quantity-sources that differ from those of other sources. A list of quantities can be as false as a list of qualities. The historian will use the same standards of critical scholarship to evaluate quantitative sources as he uses to evaluate any other sources. A bitter old general, writing his memoirs to revenge the blighting of a career, could fake or forget his strength-reports or the strength of the enemy army, just as he could lie about the morals of the civilian directors of strategy, or omit their successes. Actually, the study of quantitative information may offer less critical difficulty than the study of other sources, because it is usually compiled for other than forensic purposes. In economic history it is usually compiled to make money, whether by taxation or profit, and thus it is to the interest of the compiler to take pains to be accurate, in a mood often foreign to the writer of the narrative of a crucial political struggle in which he participated.

Methodologically there are several caveats which must be kept in mind while applying quantitative methods, whether by hand or by machine, to economic history. (1) Although quantities as quantities can be tabulated for very early periods, even from Babylonian records, statistical tables are not numerous and continuous from a time much earlier than the late seventeenth century. The most reliable economic records which predate the last decade of the seventeenth century are estate records, which, incidentally, lend themselves to many interesting inquiries. (2) The names of places, weights and measures, and commodities differ from age to age; these differences pose critical problems which historians are professionally obligated to solve and cannot be accepted as obstacles. (3) Polemic writers, attempting to justify or to change policy, have not been above producing deliberately biased series of quantities for the purposes of persuasion rather than instruction; this problem of tendentiousness is found in all works of advocacy and is no greater in quantitative studies than in other kinds of historical study. (4) In early economic history all of the arithmetic of the Western world seems to have been done manually, even after the abacus and Pascal's wheels were available. Inevitably, clerical errors have crept into records, even the honest records of zealous government departments. Some of these errors of calculation have been quite large. The computer provides a happy remedy. Unlike the manual worker it can recalculate the addition, subtraction, multiplication, and division at a rate which occasions no appreciable loss of time. On the other hand, if the customs' clerk noted down 132 barrels of molasses, when he meant to write 123, the error is unknowable to posterity. And since it was unknowable before the invention of the computer, there is no objection to electronic data-processing.

To use the computer for economic history the historian need not change his habits of thought very much. In individual cases, the principal difference may be that he has been used to formulating a question and then roving in search of data to answer the question. To use the computer correctly the opposite technique is used. First he peoples the relevant universe with all of its data, then he asks the question. Traditionally there have always been two ways of learning history. One student will ask "why did A do B?" and then look for a body of sources which contains the answer. Another will come upon a trove of documents which had not been previously exploited and ask himself "what questions does this collection answer?" The second method *must* be used in studying history by means of the computer. The facts must be assembled to answer every conceivable question which may ever be asked of a given universe. The inquirer never starts with a specific question and proceeds to assemble the data, but starts with the whole body of data and asks questions. After all, what is a collection of historical data but a collection of answers waiting to be questioned? If the questions are unanswerable the answers are unknowable.

It follows that the investigator must have a prior classification scheme and be lavish, profuse, unstinted, even excessive and extravagant in cross-referencing, so that every conceivable future pairing of categories will be possible when the time comes to ask questions. The prior classification scheme is essential, but the data will shape it. In existing statistical tables the original compiler has already suggested the scheme; if one wishes to convert verbal documentary series into tables, he will find that the original clerk will usually have followed a set form, whether for tax assessments, wills, estate inventories, notes of hand, or whatever.

The uniform handwritten note slip, probably corresponding in the researcher's work to a paragraph of information, is replaced by the Hollerith Card (which International Business Machines has persuaded everybody to call an "IBM card"), representing but a single sentence. The hand-worker, studying bankruptcies in Wet Moccasin County, might have listed all of the livestock belonging to a single bankrupt on one three-by-five-inch card. The computer worker will have a card for each animal, with enough other information to tell whose, when, and appraised at how much. As would be said in a computer center, "horse plus modifiers equal IBM card."

Traditionally, historians have perhaps unconsciously felt that a data sample is satisfactory proof. Why not *sample* this data? In the first place, it is unnecessary. The computer can digest it all. In the second place, it is bad methodology. In early economic history there is no easy way to extract *valid* random samples. Historical data is incomplete to begin with. What is left to study is but a sample. Even a private diary entry of the twentieth century is but a sample of the day's data. If there were an adequate series of historical facts, identically complete from start to end, it would be possible to take a pre-set sample which would give very accurate results, as opinion-pollers do at one specific contemporary instant. But there are no such series of past recorded quantities. Each series is a sample. Useful results cannot be obtained in history by sampling samples. The invariable rule must be, get all. The point is illustrated by Table 1.

The table shows graphically every quarter of a year for which complete port information is available. For example, it is arithmetically impossible to find even a ten-year interval with complete data for each tenth year; the closest one can come to it is the series 1724, 1734, 1754, which is anomalous because 1744 is wholly absent. Yet the table is a graph of *all* the data available from which the historian can generalize about the trade of the port of New York from 1715

TABLE 1

COLONIAL NAVAL OFFICE LISTS (C.O. 5)
FOR THE PORT OF NEW YORK
PRO, C.O. 5/1222–1228

Available Naval Office Lists by Years and by Quarters
Quarters change as noted below:

Quarter 1   Dec. 25 to Mar. 25
Quarter 2   Mar. 25 to June 25
Quarter 3   June 25 to Sept. 29
Quarter 4   Sept. 29 to Dec. 25

After 1752, quarters change as follows:

Quarter 1   Jan.   5 to Apr.   5
Quarter 2   Apr.   5 to July   5
Quarter 3   June   5 to Oct. 10
Quarter 4   Oct. 10 to Jan.   5

In the chart below completed squares indicate full years. Missing quarters in partial years are shown by missing sides in the squares, numbered by quarters, as follows:

```
       2
   1 □ 3
       4
```

Year	I	E	Year	I	E	Year	I	E
1715	⌐	⌐	1734	□	□	1753	—	—
1716	□	□	1735	□	□	1754	□	□
1717	□	□	1736	=	⌐	1755	□	⊓
1718	□	□	1737	□	⌐	1756		
1719	⊏	⊏	1738	□	□	1757		
1720	□	□	1739	□	□	1758		
1721	□	□	1740	□	□	1759		
1722	□	□	1741	□	□	1760		
1723	□	□	1742	□	□	1761		
1724	□	□	1743	⌐	⌐	1762		
1725	□	□	1744			1763	□	
1726	□	□	1745			1764	□	□
1727	□	□	1746					
1728	□	□	1747					
1729	□	□	1748	⌐	⌐			
1730	⊓	⊓	1749					
1731	⌐	—	1750					
1732	⌐	□	1751	—	—			
1733	□	□	1752	⌐				

to 1764 inclusive. The impossibility of valid sampling seems plain. Even the making of this graph to determine what is available required analysis and organization of all the data.

As for the apparatus of publication, it may be well to mention that citation of sources is made just as in any other kind of historical writing. Citation is not to the author's computer data-bank but to the source itself. A number of obvious computer-studies have appeared recently which do not mention the computer, nor do they mention the typewriter, the typesetting machine, or the journal-sewing-machine of the bindery. Any study in any art or science (except computer science) which exalts the computer is a rather self-conscious study, more concerned with admiring its own method than with its discipline. To the extent that the computer is mentioned, it should be discussed only as part of the method used to solve the problem. The computer itself is only a piece of hardware that is a means to an end. The set of computer instructions called a *program*—which develops the answers from the computer-stored data-bank—is the most exact of all descriptions of the historian's methodology. And it should be obvious that many users of computers will find occasion to use more traditional manual methods when dealing with small collections of facts. As a rule of thumb, Aydelotte suggests that electronic data-processing be used when dealing with fifty or more cases.[2]

If the reader is still attending to this matter, at about this point he will properly ask, "how do you do it?" He does not need to be able to operate a computer but it helps to have a notion of how it operates. First, the researcher draws a sharp boundary around his finite universe of facts, for example, every fact collected in the census of 1880 in the state of California was collected on a pre-designed form which the researcher cannot improve upon. If he is dealing with less intelligently collected data, he will design a form of his own and will have research assistants transfer the facts from the source to his form. Third, these facts are recorded on Hollerith Cards or on magnetic tape (according to the kind of computer used). This produces a data-bank, before programming, and is called peripheral storage. The people who put the facts on the cards or tape are called key-punchers and work by the hour.

There are two kinds of programming, external and internal. External programming is the familiar operation at the check-out counter of a self-service market. The cashier programs the cash register to produce a paper tape which itemizes the purchases by categories, and adds the total sum due. Every time she punches the cash register, even if only to record no sale, she is programming. A stenographer presses a pair of margin-sets and presses the tabular key several times in preparation for typing a sheet of paper with several columns of figures. She has externally programmed the typewriter to produce a form. When the operator of an adding machine presses the plus or minus button, the machine has been externally programmed. In short, to program is to tell the machine what to do.

Computer programming is internal. All of the instructions are inserted by a programmer before the data-bank of Hollerith Cards or the magnetic tape is drawn upon. It is a good deal more refined than stenography, cashiermanship, or simple bookkeeping. It is a trade which can be learned, but the historian need not learn it. Most universities that offer graduate work have computers, and most institutions that have computers can provide a programmer to write the instructions before the researcher runs his data through the machine. If aid is needed beyond that, the manufacturer of the computer has an interest in seeing that the client gets what he needs and should be kept alert by calls for help. He knows his machine is obsolescent and he will wish to put in a new one within five years; hence he will be friendly to users.

To take a specific case, all of the individual estate inventories of Essex County, Massachusetts, for the years 1640–1682 total 430. In those inventories William I. Davisson found about 26,000 individual items—assets or liabilities,

[2] *Amer. Hist. Rev.* LXXI, 806.

tangible property and intangible property. Each of these individual items could be written as a simple sentence. For example, "in 1666 John Smith had a horse worth six pounds."

Remember, "horse plus modifiers equal sentence." That horse and his modifiers went on one card, punched there by a key-puncher. Thus the known wealth of Essex County for those forty-two years was recorded on 26,000 Hollerith Cards. It so happened that these particular estate inventories had been printed, so the key-punchers worked directly from the bound volumes. They found about 1,500 archaic spellings of words representing over three hundred kinds of personal property. If wanted, these spellings can be accumulated by categories and reduced to standardized spellings by the computer.[3] If they had been in manuscript or microfilm only, the data would have been transferred by hand by clerical workers to a form devised for the purpose, a form simple enough for the key-puncher to follow without being vexed by the necessity for making his own decisions.

The difficult part followed, that of developing instructions for the computer, telling it what to calculate from the 26,000 card data-bank. The historian phrases his questions or directions precisely, for example: (1) did the number of draft animals (horses, oxen) increase from 1640 to 1682? (2) did the number of ships increase from 1640 to 1682? (3) draw one graph showing the increase or decrease of draft animals and ships on the same scale, at five-year intervals (the computer can draw graphs, even maps).[4] The computer, for that matter, could be answering any other conceivable questions simultaneously. How to get the computer to answer to questions and to obey the command is the problem of the programmer. The historian may become a programmer or may engage the services of a programmer. Once the computer understands what is expected, it will do the work in a matter of seconds, reading all of the cards, drawing the graph, and, for good measure, printing a table of the figures it used to arrive at its graph. The answer will be on one sheet of paper.

This illustration from Essex County, Massachusetts, is drawn from the experience of research in progress. In the course of the study, a methodological lesson was driven home painfully. A colleague came upon an essay arguing the literacy of seventeenth-century New England. The computer was commanded to print all of the signatures of the appraisers of the estates of Essex County, from 1640 to 1682, in alphabetical order, with a parallel column of the estates appraised and the dates of their signatures. In only one instance did the phrase "His Mark" occur. This seemed to show a rather high level of literacy. A quick scanning of the source showed that the editors of the published documents had indicated in footnotes whether the signatures were autograph or not. Where the words "His Mark" occurred in the body of the text they had stood, but if absent were not inserted by the editors. Because the nature of the signature did not appear to be an economic fact, the economic historian did not tell the key-

[3] For example, "chair(s)" appeared as: chayre(s), chayrs, chaires, chayer, chares, chaiers, cheares.

[4] The questions above are not fantasies. High-speed computation showed that plough-pulling power and the value of plough-pulling animals declined in Essex County, Massachusetts, as cargo-carrying vessels increased, according to Davisson's study. It would seem impossible to dispute the conclusion that in the years 1640–1682 Salem was changing from a farm village to a commercial center.

punchers to include the footnotes. Hence the degree of literacy of the men appointed appraisers of estates in seventeenth-century Essex County remains a mystery. The methodological moral was clear: get all of the data.

A few unexpected facts, however, justified the computer's few seconds of effort. Two women were thought wise enough to appraise estates. Bearers of honorific titles were rather diffident about signing them in their own hands or else were remarkably few: an "ensigne," a captain, a major, and three misters comprised the peerage. Only two sturdy characters signed themselves with the straightforward title of "Goodman." And poor Giles Corey, the only man in American history to be tortured to death as part of official judicial process (when he refused to plead guilty or not guilty to a charge of witchcraft), was accounted as meritorious enough to appraise an estate in November, 1666.

A good deal of time has been profitably spent on the quantitative study of the wealth of Essex County [5] in the seventeenth century as a microcosm of the colonial economy.

The study of economic history, by studying *all* of the data of its several subdivisions, can lead both to new discoveries and to revisions of old concepts which have been accepted from generation to generation without skepticism. Probably the first task is to re-examine the old generalizations which rest on rather narrow data. One of the most enduring of shibboleths in American historical writing has been the phrase "triangular trade," which has been used to explain the economic growth of the northern colonies which had little to sell directly to Britain. The idea is that in ports from Philadelphia northward merchants loaded their ships with local products, sold them abroad at an apex of the triangle, bought what was normally available at that apex, proceeded to the third apex and sold the second cargo for profit which was used to buy a third cargo. The third cargo was brought home and sold. The cash was then used to buy British manufactures. This explanation has persisted in the conventional wisdom for decade after decade without question. It has been "proved" by descriptions of particular voyages which followed this pattern. The "proof" sufficed to produce a universal truism. Although the above description is a trifle over-simple, triangle after triangle has been described, and often drawn on illustrative maps. The explanation makes a logical sense. That is the way a rational economic system *ought* to work. But where is the evidence?

Choosing a sentence from an excellent university textbook of American economic history one finds, "Best known of the triangles was one that began as a two-way exchange of fish, timber, livestock, and provisions, shipped from the ports of New England, New York and Pennsylvania . . ." [6] That statement categorically puts Philadelphia at the apex of a triangle.

William I. Davisson has accumulated a data-bank from the *Pennsylvania Gazette* (Philadelphia), which lists every ship arrival and departure, every entry and clearance, for the two three-year periods 1733–1735 and 1749–1751. The

---

[5] William I. Davisson, "Essex County Price Trends: Money and Markets in 17th Century Massachusetts," April, 1967 and, "Essex County Wealth Trends: Wealth and Economic Growth in 17th Century Massachusetts," October, 1967, *Essex Institute Historical Collections.*

[6] Ross M. Robertson, *History of the American Economy,* 2d ed. (New York, 1964), p. 81. This use of Robertson is a deliberate choice of one of the most acceptable of books written by one of the most competent authors.

port-of-entry (naval office) revenue records of Philadelphia for those periods have been destroyed by fire. The press is the only surviving comprehensive source for populating this particular universe of data. Davisson, and Lavonne Coffeen of the Sacramento State College Computer Center, queried the Sacramento State College IBM 1620 Computer about the triangle or triangles. The Computer, so to speak, shook its head firmly. On the basis of all the surviving data the Computer provided tables from which Davisson could only deduce the following.[7]

(1) There was no triangular trade which can be associated with Philadelphia in these two three-year periods. (2) Philadelphia shipping ran three shuttle lines, a coastwise North American trade extending to Canada, a trade to and from the Caribbean, and a trade to Europe, usually to British ports. (3) Philadelphia was the *entrepot* for the distribution of goods from Europe and the collection of goods for shipment to Europe. (A corollary finding, for the benefit of maritime buffs, was that practically all of the coastal traffic was the movement of sloops and schooners, while no specific kinds of rig dominated any other aspect of the sea-going trade of Philadelphia.)

Was this a triangle? No. It was more of an "H trade," with the horizontal line representing the trans-Atlantic shuttle.

Admittedly, this one study of two three-year periods was not the funeral of the concept of the "triangular trade," but surely it is unsettling when an age-old generalization fails to survive its first full-scale statistical re-examination. The generalization of the "triangular trade" deserves no more than hypothetical standing until stabilized by a method which can be duplicated. Such a method will require the historian to do more than to present his impression derived from scrutiny of a few ship's logs. To count the number of deep-water sailing ship passages under the Union Jack, from 1741 (when the first comprehensive list begins) until American independence, is beyond the capacity of the unaided human mind. At a guess, they could hardly have been fewer than half a million. When they have been counted, tabulated and analyzed by electronic data-processing, historians of the economy can begin to generalize in a specific sense, instead of searching for what they hope are a few characteristic traits and tendencies which adequately answer the perennial question of history—"what happened?"

In summary, the computer can be used in economic history to manage vast masses of quantitative data, that is, facts about things which can be usefully measured or counted. At a million operations per second it can reduce the reply to any answerable question to a single sheet, either as a table or a graph, or both. Having as many of these answers as he believes he needs, the art of the historian is brought into play to interpret; the merit of the interpretation is his, not the computer's. Computer science, and its technical language, need not directly concern the scholar except insofar as he needs to be able to talk with the operator of a computer, who will serve as interpreter between inquirer and machine.

Economic history, because it can now bring to bear all relevant data, can become a science at least as exact as astronomy or paleontology, both of which

[7] See William I. Davisson, "The Philadelphia Trade" (Abstract), *Western Economic Journal,* III (1965), n.p.

concern themselves with the past, and both of which develop despite the knowledge that there are gaps in their sources which may never be filled. It may sound a bit pretentious but it is tempting to call economic history as studied by high-speed electronic data-processing machines by the precise name "paleo-economics."

6

STEPHAN THERNSTROM

The Historian and the Computer

The application of computers to American urban history is just as filled with possibilities as is research in economic history, according to Stephan Thernstrom. Extensive social data in local tax and school records, city directories, and the like, have never been thoroughly explored—a fact Thernstrom demonstrates in his own research on social mobility in twentieth-century Boston. Thernstrom's claims for quantitative research methods are moderate. He believes that most historical evidence is not amenable to counting and that the computer will not "revolutionize" written history, make traditional historians technologically obsolete, or improve the quality of historical writing, at least in the near future. On the other hand, whenever quantitative data will yield to computerized analysis, the possibility of using larger samples than can be hand-manipulated virtually dictates the use of the electronic machines. But the best argument in favor of quantitative history, Thernstrom avers, "is the simple fact that this approach has already yielded significant new findings."

DOUBTLESS it is true, as historians are fond of telling their freshman classes, that the study of the past enriches the mind and liberalizes the spirit, undermining the instinctive parochial prejudices of those who have been exposed to only one culture, one world-view, one way of life. But it does not follow, I fear, that historians as a breed are conspicuously liberal and open-

Stephan Thernstrom, "The Historian and the Computer," in Edmund A. Bowles, ed., *Computers in Humanistic Research: Readings and Perspectives.* © 1967. Reprinted by permission of Prentice-Hall, Inc., Englewood Cliffs, New Jersey.

minded in their reception of new methodologies and new research technologies. With respect to the subject of this volume, the potential uses of the modern electronic computer, it can only be said that historians have stood not in the vanguard but in the rearguard.

The resistances to computer research have little to do with the machine itself —intimidating beast though it is. They stem rather from hostility toward the concepts and analytical techniques which the computer seems to impose on the user—theoretical constructs, and quantitative techniques borrowed from the other social sciences. The suspicion certain professional historians feel toward such borrowing borders on the pathological, as witness the claim of a very distinguished American historian that "almost all important questions are important precisely because they are not susceptible to quantitative answers." [1] Let me say only that anyone who is not blindly and irrevocably committed to the view that all legitimate history is ideographic rather than nomothetic, an art and not a science, should concede two points: first, that there are a great many historical problems of importance which *demand* the analysis of overtly quantitative data (voting statistics, information on wages and prices, population figures, etc.); and second, that the fabric of even the most conventional historical account is studded with terms which are in some sense *implicitly* quantitative ("representative," "typical," "widespread," "intense," "growing," etc.).[2] It is not always possible to translate these intuitive judgments into explicit claims for which supporting quantitative data can be produced, of course, but it sometimes is, and here is another large area within which the computer and the habit of mind it promotes may yield valuable results. By "substituting an examined generalization for an unexamined one," as W. O. Aydelotte puts it, a quantitative approach checks our natural instinct to remember best the cases which best fit our own prejudices and preconceived hypotheses.[3]

Certainly I would concede that historical evidence which is amenable to quantitative analysis is often scarce or nonexistent. But it has been my experience that such data is far more readily available than is commonly assumed. For instance, in my own field of specialization, American urban history, there are rich veins of untapped material in manuscript census schedules, election returns, local tax and school records, city directories, and similar sources. Often this evidence is of low quality because of the primitive process by which it was gathered and recorded, but this is hardly an objection to quantitative analysis itself. Indeed, the researcher with a sophisticated knowledge of quantitative techniques is much better equipped to use these materials with proper caution than is the conventionally trained historian, who is prone to rely upon his intuitive judgment of what they portend. Another common objection to quantitative historical research is that the availability of data susceptible to quantification exerts an unduly coercive influence upon the scholar, who may forget the

[1] A. M. Schlesinger, Jr., "The Humanist Looks at Empirical Social Research," *American Sociological Review,* XXVII (1962), 770.

[2] L. Benson, "Research Problems in American Political Historiography," in Mirra Komarovsky (ed.), *Common Frontiers of the Social Sciences,* Glencoe, 1957, p. 117.

[3] W. O. Aydelotte, "Quantification in History," *American Historical Review,* LXXI (1966), 803–25. This paper includes keen discussions of several of the issues discussed in the first section of the present paper, and I am heavily indebted to it.

large issues and turn his attention to trivial matters about which statistical data happens to be available. There is some force in this argument, I think, as the painfully trivial character of much contemporary sociological research testifies, but I doubt that scholars sympathetic to quantification are any more exposed to trivializing pressures than those working with other types of evidence—diplomatic notes, let us say. Historians very often let the availability of unanalyzed data rather than the existence of a significant problem determine their choice of subject; thus the cult of manuscript sources, thus the presumption of aspiring biographers that anyone who "hasn't been done" and who has left personal papers behind is worthy of study by virtue of that fact alone.

Perhaps more convincing than any of these general arguments about the value of quantitative historical research, however, is the simple fact that this approach has already yielded significant new findings. Quantitative research in the field of economic history is superabundant, so much so that some of its practitioners have adopted a new disciplinary label, calling themselves *cliometricians*. Their work has already proven of such value that I think we can forgive them that grating neologism.[4] It should be noted in a discussion of the historian and the computer, however, that quantitative research in economic history has tended by and large to be done by men trained by, and holding appointments in, departments of economics rather than history, though recent studies by Bernard and Lotte Bailyn and Theodore Rabb point to a growing interest within history departments as well.[5] The field of political history is humming with activity, and much more can be expected as the resources of the Inter-University Consortium for Political Research become more widely available to scholars. Some of the interesting possibilities here are suggested by Benson's reinterpretation of Jacksonian Democracy on the basis of an investigation into the voting behavior of the New York state electorate, and by Aronson's statistical demolition of the myth of the Jacksonian spoils system. The social characteristics and political activity of elite groups have been illuminated in recently published or forthcoming studies of the French Parliament in the first half of the Nineteenth Century, the English House of Commons in the 1840's, the Reconstruction Congresses, and reformers of the Progressive era. Charles Tilly, who made a major contribution to our understanding of the French Revolution in his investigation of social change and political upheaval in the Vendée, has most recently given us a tantalizing beginning toward a system for classifying and measuring violent political disturbances, and is employing that system in his quantitative study of urbanization and political upheaval in France since 1830.[6]

[4] For an excellent brief survey, see R. W. Fogel, "The Reunification of Economic History with Economic Theory," *Papers and Proceedings of the 77th Annual Meeting of the American Economics Association* (1965), 92–98.

[5] B. and L. Bailyn, *Massachusetts Shipping, 1697–1714: A Statistical Study,* Cambridge, 1961. Rabb's computer study of the Elizabethan trading companies will soon be published.

[6] L. Benson, *The Concept of Jacksonian Democracy: New York as a Test Case,* Princeton, 1961; S. Aronson, *Status and Kinship in the Higher Civil Service,* Cambridge, 1964; W. O. Aydelotte, "Voting Patterns in the British House of Commons in the 1840's," *Comparative Studies in Society and History,* V (1963); C. Tilly, *The Vendée,* Cambridge, 1964; C. Tilly and J. Rule, *Measuring Political Upheaval,* Princeton, 1965. The work of the Higonnets on the French Parliament, David Donald on Reconstruction Congress, and Samuel P. Hays on Progressivism are still in progress or in press.

A specimen the social historian will find of much interest is Merle Curti's computer analysis of social mobility patterns in a Wisconsin frontier community in the 1850–1880 period, though he may remain highly skeptical of Curti's belief that he has provided powerful objective support for Turner's frontier theory—a useful reminder, perhaps, that neither the raw statistical data nor the computer will speak for themselves; that the task of interpreting statistical results is as difficult and fraught with error as other tasks of historical interpretation.[7] Indeed, it is more difficult in one way, for the precision of quantitative data tends to foreclose the common procedure of making sense out of a mass of materials by offering an intuitive generalization which best fits one's own interpretative predilections. Probably this is the reason that quantitative historical studies have more often been effective in dissolving and destroying older categories and hypotheses than in suggesting equally powerful and persuasive new ones. I cannot believe that this is an inescapable problem, and that the scholarly world is destined to remain forever divided between those who offer grand interpretative structures reared on shaky, intuitive foundations and those computer-equipped termites who undermine these grand structures without offering new ones to replace them. Perhaps it will take some academic Lyndon Johnson to smooth over these differences and articulate a new consensus.

That the computer, properly used, can be of enormous utility to the historian dealing with voting records, economic statistics, or the social characteristics of groups of men should be clear. There can be greater argument, however, over the value of computer analyses of materials of a different kind—words, sentences, paragraphs. One ingenious use of the computer to attack a historical problem—Mosteller's count of the frequency distribution of such minor words as *by, from, to,* and *upon* to infer the authorship of the disputed Federalist papers—seems quite persuasive, but authorship problems are a small and special class, and I don't see that the methodology of the study can be easily extended to other issues.[8]

The technique known as content analysis has much wider application. By breaking down the contents of a document into units which are first labeled by a human coder or by the computer itself with the aid of a dictionary programmed into it, and then mechanically tabulating these units, content analysis purports to provide a more objective, systematic, and sensitive rendering of meaning. There are genuine advantages to this procedure, especially when one is asking rather simple questions of otherwise unmanageably large bodies of material, but the results it yields can be no more sensitive than the coding rules or dictionary employed. I would suggest that in such a field as intellectual history there exist ideas and relationships which cannot be reduced to rules which a machine can follow. One thinks, for instance, of Perry Miller responding to a sermon by Jonathan Edwards. Doubtless a computer, at least if its dictionary were prepared by someone who knew as much about Puritanism as Professor Miller, could pick out certain things in a text that a Miller unassisted would miss, even things of consequence in rare instances. But the converse is

    [7] M. Curti *et al., The Making of an American Community: A Case Study of Democracy in a Frontier County,* Stanford, 1959.
    [8] F. Mosteller and D. L. Wallace, "Inference in an Authorship Problem," *Journal of the American Statistical Association,* LVIII (1963), 275–309.

equally true, I suspect. I fail to see how a computer could be given a set of formal rules which would equip it to identify some of the most important and yet most subtle connections in a document of this kind—connections which are often ones of delicate emotional shadings, connections which are poetic rather than prosaic.

This is not to dismiss content analysis as a tool for the historian; Richard Merritt's recent study of symbols of American national awareness in colonial newspapers between 1735 and 1775 is one demonstration of its value in treating a certain class of problems, and there are others.[9] Some of the work currently being done by Professor Pool at MIT and by a Stanford University team on communications and decision-making on the eve of World War I may some day influence historical interpretation of that event.[10] At present, however, this research (being carried out, it should be said, by political scientists rather than historians) has been aimed at testing largely psychological propositions of such simplicity and such universality as to be of little interest to the practicing historian: "People pay more attention to news that deals with them." "The higher the stress in a crisis situation, the greater the tendency to rely upon extraordinary or improvised channels of communication." The problem is not that these propositions are self-evident, common-sense truths and thus unworthy of testing. This common complaint against social science research is usually unfounded, partly because it ignores the fundamental principle that for each and every cliché there tends to be an equal and opposite cliché, partly for reasons too complex to go into here. What bothers me is that generalizations of such cosmic sweep, presumably true (or at least interestingly false) of all times and all places, invariably seem arid and empty. While I urge that historians attempt to translate their intuitive generalizations into explicit generalizations, the generalizations I have in mind are less abstract, less sweeping, and more powerful; they are to some degree relative to the context to which they refer, applying to such entities as "American farmers in the Twentieth Century" or even "middle class residents of large American cities in the period since World War II," and might be considered the counterpart in history to what a leading sociologist calls "theories of the middle range." [11] The social scientist will naturally seek to extend the range of these intermediate generalizations and to test their limits, but long before the initial generalization is converted into a proposition of sufficient abstractness to apply universally, the historian will have lost interest in it and have gone back to his business of dealing with events and processes in a limited context. To the extent, therefore, that content analysis is conducted by scholars dedicated to testing universalist models of human behavior, it is

[9] R. L. Merritt, "Nation Building in America: The Colonial Years," in K. Deutsch and W. Foltz (eds.) *Nation-Building*, New York, 1963, pp. 56–72; Merritt's fuller account of the study has been published under the title *Symbols of American Community, 1735–1775*, New Haven, 1966. Gilbert Shapiro's large-scale study based on content analysis of the *cahiers* of 1789 is mentioned in Chapter 7 above.

[10] I. de Sola Pool and A. Kessler, "The Kaiser, the Tsar, and the Computer: Information Processing in a Crisis," *American Behavioral Scientist,* VIII (1965), 31–38; O. R. Holsti, "The 1914 Case," *American Political Science Review,* LIX (1965), 365–78.

[11] Cf. R. Merton, *Social Theory and Social Structure,* Glencoe, 1949; S. H. Beer, "Causal Explanation and Imaginative Reenactment," *History and Theory,* III (1963), 6–29.

unlikely to influence the mainstream of historical writing.

Let me now turn briefly to a narrower subject on which I can speak with greater expertise, my current research on the social history of modern Boston. This study grew out of my belief that the existing literature in the field of social history dealt inadequately with social structure and basic social processes. Even the best work in the field, I felt, depended excessively on evidence which was removed from the daily lives of individuals. My Newburyport study offered several examples which supported the premise from which I began: that some important historical processes could not be understood without microscopic study of individual human actors.[12]

There are grave limitations, however, to the usual microscopic historical study. Biographers can overlook these limitations by persuading themselves (or deluding themselves) that their subjects are intrinsically important. But the social historian who seeks to treat the lives of common men rather than very uncommon men cannot evade the problem of giving general meaning to his findings. The easiest tactic is to describe one's microscopic examination of an obscure group or neighborhood or community as a "case study," a useful phrase which lends an attractive aura of generality to one's painstaking study of the social origins of Armenian grocers in Boston's North End. But *of what* is this hypothetical investigation a case study? May we generalize from the Armenians to the Greeks, and from them to the Italians and Jews? What does a study set in the North End tell us about the South End, the West End and other neighborhoods of that sprawling complex, Greater Boston? Historians and sociologists alike have been reluctant to consider such questions. Thus William F. Whyte's classic field report on youth in the North End, *Streetcorner Society,* leaves us in the dark as to how much of what the author describes reflects basic patterns of working class life in American cities, and how much is due to the particular ethnic group (Italians), the particular neighborhood (the North End), or the particular historical period (the late 30's) Whyte dealt with. Nor does Herbert Gans' interesting recent work, *The Urban Villagers,* which treats working class Italo-Americans in the West End in the late 50's, go very far beyond *Streetcorner Society* in this respect. Ideally, historical studies of the city should employ microscopic techniques for the depth and richness of detail they alone can provide, but should employ them on a sufficiently spacious canvas—spacious temporally as well as physically—to confront the problems that the label "case study" customarily obscures.

It is here, of course, that the development of the electronic computer affords the social historian a great opportunity, for only through mechanical means can the historian master the vast body of materials that he must consult to do a study of this kind. The sources for a comprehensive grassroots social history of the sort I describe are readily available—manuscript census schedules, city directories, local tax records, school records, etc.—and they have occasionally been utilized by historians. But for the student who must collect and analyze it without the aid of electronic devices, the limits imposed by the sheer bulk of this material (and by the tedium it inspires) are very narrow. My own little study of the social mobility of unskilled laborers in Newburyport, which was

[12] S. Thernstrom, *Poverty and Progress: Social Mobility in a Nineteenth Century City,* Cambridge, 1964.

done without machines, probably involved about as much complexity and drudgery as the ordinary historian can stand, and that study dealt with something less than 10 per cent of the labor force of a city of fewer than 15,000 inhabitants. To trace and analyze the career patterns of several occupational and ethnic groups in a much larger community without mechanical assistance would be an utterly unmanageable task. With the aid of a computer it is possible to draw together, examine, and comprehend the life histories of thousands and thousands of ordinary men and women. The historian's microscope can thus be applied to a large enough population over a broad enough time span to provide a dynamic view of the whole of a complex social organism, including such matters as variations in social mobility opportunities during the course of urban growth and industrial change, ethnic differences in the mobility patterns, the flow of population between districts of the city and into and out of the city itself.

I am now attempting something of this sort, employing a computer to map the demographic and social structure of Boston from 1880 to the present. I am feeding into the computer information about three samples of the population in the community, one drawn from 1880 manuscript schedules of the U.S. Census, one from 1910 marriage license records, and one from 1930 birth certificates. This information deals with a host of social characteristics: occupation, place of residence, age, ethnic and religious affiliations, property holdings, etc. Once the samples were drawn, the subsequent occupations, addresses, and property holdings of these men were recovered from later city directories and tax records, so that for a substantial cross-section of the Boston population I have abbreviated family histories which span several decades. There are several questions I hope to explore with the aid of these data (and the Harvard Computation Center). Are there dramatic signs, as popular belief would lead us to expect, that social mobility opportunities in the community became more constricted during the course of industrialization? Are there dramatic differences between the mobility patterns of different ethnic and religious groups? (Again, there is a flourishing folklore about the characteristics of the Irish, the Italians, the Jews, the Negroes, and others, but remarkably little solid evidence.) What is the relationship between intragenerational and intergenerational mobility (how does a father's mobility influence his son's career prospects?), and how are residential and property mobility connected to occupational mobility? Recent sociological research has focused too narrowly on one simple index of mobility, rates of intergenerational movement between manual and nonmanual occupations. I attempted in my Newburyport study to employ a much broader conception of social mobility, and I hope to test some of the ideas developed there—my discovery, for example, of an inverse relationship between occupational mobility and property mobility for unskilled laborers —with the much larger Boston sample.

A word now about a general problem which faces anyone who attempts a study of this kind—that is, the problem of reducing the chaotic mass of raw data to some categories which make it manageable—of developing, for instance, an occupational classification scheme to reduce the hundreds of specific occupations listed on the census schedules to some general types. Each reduction of this kind, of course, involves a *loss*. To know that a man is a "semiskilled laborer" is less revealing than to know that he is a street-car conductor or an operative in a shoe factory. It is a cruel fact that we give up something every time we use a general social category; obviously we should strive to reduce our raw data to order in a way which gives up as little as possible. The point to stress here is that, contrary to the belief of many (possibly most) historians, in dealing with problems of this kind at least, a computer can tolerate much more complexity than an individual human being, and can thus preserve a degree of concreteness that a historian working without a machine would necessarily sacrifice.

This for two reasons. It is very difficult, as I know from painful experience, for a man to cross-tabulate raw data employing more than a very few categories. If one is computing, for example, differing rates of occupational mobility in seven ethnic groups, it is impossibly tedious to utilize more than a half dozen occupational categories (thus 42 cells), and even more tedious and difficult to consider the influence of other variables at the same time. With the cunning spaciousness of a punched card at one's disposal, however, and a tireless device to sort and count these cards, it is possible to use many more occupational categories and hence to remain much closer to the complex reality that the historian of a handicraft age had to abstract from.

A second reason why the computer permits a more complex and more concrete analysis in investigations of this kind is simply that in any study utilizing sampling techniques, the possibilities for refined analysis are severely restricted by the size of the sample. Even a good-sized sample of the population of a modern city, for example, will contain only a few Italian carpenters, so that to examine differences between literate and illiterate Italian carpenters would be impossible; to test the significance of literacy as an influence on career patterns one would have to lump together all carpenters or all Italians to have enough cases for meaningful analysis. But a machine, of course, can handle many more cases than a man; thus a much larger sample can be gathered, and a more subtle and concrete analysis carried out.

I would end on a note of chastened optimism. I do not believe that the computer will revolutionize historical writing, leaving orthodox historians the victims of technological unemployment. Nor do I believe that the overall quality of historical work with computers in the near future will necessarily be very high. Historians will find it difficult to learn enough about computers to employ them in a sophisticated fashion, and it is not unlikely that some who do succeed in mastering the computer will forget (or never learn in the first place) that technical competence in manipulating statistics cannot make up for ignorance of the social context which produced the statistics. But I remain confident that the remarkable increment the computer provides to our ability to do certain kinds of things to certain kinds of historical material, and the contact it will promote between history and the other social sciences, will prove of net benefit.

PART II

Content Analysis of
Historical Data

WHICH SENSITIVE HISTORIAN has not drawn generalizations from newspaper editorials, legislative journals, or presidential papers without a sense of unease at the largely impressionistic nature of his statements? To handle this type of research, Wood Gray has noted, one needs a "sort of sixth sense that will alert you to tell-tale signs." [1] Content analysis—the systematic examination of style in communications—can sharpen this sixth sense.[2] Content analysis is a supplement to, rather than a substitute for, subjective examination of documents. It allows for greater objectivity, precision, and sensitivity to meaning, and safeguards the historian from selecting examples out of a mass of contradictory data that support his preconceived notions. As any quantitative method, however, content analysis permits no greater precision than what the human coder programs into his data. Perry Miller might have extracted more meat from Jonathan Edwards' sermons with computer-assisted content analysis; but, as Stephan Thernstrom has observed, it is doubtful whether "a computer could be given a set of formal rules which would equip it to identify some of the most important and yet most subtle connections in a document of this kind—connections which are often ones of delicate emotional shadings, connections which are poetic rather than prosaic." [3]

The application of content analysis to historical records dates back to the early decades of this century.[4] The first efforts were crude and unsystematic, yet they laid the foundation for future progress. In 1920, William Bayard Hale undertook a content analysis of the writings of Woodrow Wilson which, unfortunately, was marred by the author's personal aversion to the President.[5] Despite his jaundiced approach, Hale uncovered Wilson's penchant for adjectives, a sign of instability for psychologists of the era. In 1940, David P. Broder traced the adjective-verb quotient in a stratified random sampling of various types of American writing from 1820, specifically in Ralph Waldo Emerson's journals and the letters of William James.[6] A variation on the adjective-verb count was a "value analysis," which John Dollard and O. Hobart Mowrer developed later in the 1940's. This measured tension as expressed in autobiographical and other personal documents by counting words that revealed some

[1] Wood Gray, *Historian's Handbook: A Key to the Study and Writing of History* (Boston, 1959), 36.
[2] Richard L. Merritt defines content analysis in *Symbols of American Community, 1735–1775* (New Haven, 1966), xxi. A more detailed definition is in Ole R. Holsti, "Computer Content Analysis in International Relations Research," in Edmund A. Bowles (ed.), *Computers in Humanistic Research: Readings and Perspectives* (Englewood Cliffs, 1967), 109.
[3] Stephan Thernstrom, "The Historian and the Computer," in Bowles, *Computers in Humanistic Research,* 76.
[4] For an incomplete but perceptive analysis, see John A. Garraty, "The Application of Content Analysis to Biography and History," in Ithiel de Sola Pool (ed.), *Trends in Content Analysis* (Urbana, Ill., 1959), chap. 6.
[5] William B. Hale, *The Story of a Style* (New York, 1920).
[6] David P. Broder, "The Adjective-Verb Quotient; A Contribution to the Psychology of Language," *Psychological Record,* III (Mar., 1940), 310–43.

form of discomfort and relief.[7] More recently, L. Sanders completed a content analysis of John F. Kennedy's first six press conferences,[8] Ithiel de Sola Pool explored the symbols of democracy,[9] Myron Rush examined the Kremlin documents relating to the rise of Khrushchev,[10] Herman Lantz and colleagues looked at the American family patterns revealed in colonial magazines,[11] Ole R. Holsti, Richard A. Brody, and Robert C. North examined the 1962 Cuban missile crisis,[12] Richard L. Merritt studied nascent American nationalism in the Revolutionary era,[13] David Mishkin explored the viticultural schemes of European nations in New World colonization,[14] and J. Zvi Namenwirth and his Yale associates did a content analysis on American newspaper attitudes of the 1950's toward European unification and Red China's prospective intervention in the Korean War.[15] Finally, within the last decade, Philip J. Stone and his colleagues at Harvard University developed the first system for computer content analysis —the "General Inquirer" program—which Ole Holsti subsequently adapted to analyze political and historical documents.[16]

In sharp contrast to the work of these political scientists,[17] historians have barely begun to exploit the possibilities of content analysis, with or without

[7] John Dollard and O. Hobart Mowrer, "A Method of Measuring Tension in Written Documents," *Journal of Abnormal and Social Psychology,* XLII (Jan., 1947), 3–32.
[8] This was Sander's M.A. thesis in radio-television at Ohio State University, 1965. For an abstract see L. Sanders, "A Content Analysis of President Kennedy's First Six Press Conferences," *Journalism Quarterly,* XLII (Winter, 1965), 114–15.
[9] Ithiel de Sola Pool, *Symbols of Democracy* (Stanford, 1952).
[10] Myron Rush, *The Rise of Khrushchev* (Washington, 1958).
[11] Herman Lantz, *et al.,* "Pre-Industrial Patterns in the Colonial Family in America: A Content Analysis of Colonial Magazines," *American Sociological Review,* XXXIII (June, 1968), 413–26.
[12] Ole R. Holsti, Richard A. Brody, Robert C. North, "Measuring Affect and Action in International Reaction Models: Empirical Materials from the 1962 Cuban Crisis," *Journal of Peace Research,* I (1964), 170–90.
[13] Richard L. Merritt, *Symbols of American Community, 1735–1775* (New Haven, 1966).
[14] Mishkin studied some 1200 bibliographic items on American colonization and established the primacy of economic motives behind European overseas expansion, specifically the desire for vineyards. Mishkin's bibliographic index was computer-produced according to a modified Keyword-in-Context (KWIC) data-processing technique. Some 30,000 major information statements were also indexed for computer manipulation. See "The American Colonial Vineyard: An Economic Interpretation," *Journal of Economic History,* XXV (Dec., 1965), 683–85.
[15] For a summary of Namenwirth's work, see Richard L. Merritt, "Political Science and the Computer," in Bowles, *Computers in Humanistic Research,* 94.
[16] See P. J. Stone, *et al., The General Inquirer: A Computer Approach to Content Analysis in the Behavioral Sciences* (Cambridge, 1966), and O. R. Holsti, "An Adaptation of the General Inquirer for the Systematic Analysis of Political Documents," *Behavioral Science,* IX (1964), 382–88.
[17] For a survey of the innovative role of political scientists in content-analysis techniques since the early 1950's, see Harold D. Lasswell, Daniel Lerner, and Ithiel de Sola Pool, *The Comparative Study of Symbols: An Introduction,* Hoover Institute Studies, Series C, No. 1 (Stanford, 1952); Richard L. Merritt, "Political Science and Computer Research," in Bowles, *Computers in Humanistic Research,* 90–107; Philip J. Stone, Dexter C. Dunphy, and Alex Bernstein, "Content Analysis Applications at Simulmatics," *American Behavioral Scientist,* VIII (May, 1965), 16–18; Ole R. Holsti, *Content Analysis for the Social Sciences and Humanities* (Reading, Mass., 1969); George Gerbner, *et al., The Analysis of Communication Content: Development in Scientific Theories and Computer Techniques* (New York, 1969); Robert C. North, *et al., Content Analysis: A Handbook with Applications for the Study of International Crisis* (Evanston, Ill., 1963); and the items cited in footnote 2.

computer aids. Indeed, prime opportunities have been muffed. Thomas Cochran attempted to plumb the attitudes of railroad executives on public questions by scanning some 100,000 letters of the group.[18] But since Cochran's sampling technique was unsystematic, his conclusions are weakened by their impressionistic base. Similarly, Edward Kirkland immersed himself in the voluminous statements of businessmen expressed in books, magazine articles, private correspondence, and statements in newspapers and before Congressional committees. "I have sought through saturation to acquire a sense of the corporate thought of the business community," Kirkland notes in his preface. "When such a consensus eluded me, I have tried to indicate dissents and divergencies. Doubtless those who read this book can provide other exceptions." [19] One can only wonder how often consensus eluded the good professor. As Lee Benson recently declared, "Bluntly stated, we historians need to move beyond that 'brute empiricism' which relies upon 'saturation' in primary sources unguided by canons for generating data and for making inferences from the data generated." Benson demanded "a genuinely scientific study of past public opinion," based on an analytic model or system and aiming at "theory construction and concept and index formation." [20]

   The essay by Richard L. Merritt (7), although not based on an overarching analytic model of public-opinion sampling, is one of the pioneering forays into computerized content analysis in history. Merritt studies the developing symbols of American national consciousness during the mid-eighteenth century as seen in five selected newspaper runs published between 1735 and 1774 in Boston, New York, Philadelphia, Williamsburg, and Charleston. He asked relatively simple questions of his material, but the results are rich indeed. His work is basically a simple counting of English- and American-oriented place names and identification symbols such as "British," "American," "Boston," or implicit identifications such as "here" or "these." With the use of computer routines, Merritt also measured inter-colonial relationships and attitudes, a task too complex for mechanical manipulations. Professor Merritt first reported on his work in 1963. Unfortunately, few historians have taken up his suggestive method of content analysis in order to examine such intriguing problems as the development of Southern nationalism in the antebellum period, the ideology of manifest destiny, the folklore of Populism, the rise of isolationism in the inter-war period of the twentieth century, and a host of other tailor-made questions.[21] Not only is the documentary evidence abundant, but computer programs are available to increase both the complexity and reliability of content analysis and free the researcher from the laborious frequency counts.

---

[18] Thomas C. Cochran, *Railroad Leaders: 1845–1890* (Cambridge, 1953).
   [19] Edward Kirkland, *Dream and Thought in the Business Community, 1860–1900* (Ithaca, 1956), viii.
   [20] Lee Benson, "An Approach to the Scientific Study of Past Public Opinion," *Public Opinion Quarterly,* XXXI (Winter, 1967–1968), 529.
   [21] Several historians have work in progress. Charles M. Dollar and James Henderson of Oklahoma State University are engaged in a preliminary study of revolutionary sentiment between 1763 and 1776, based on a content analysis of public statements issued by provincial and inter-colonial legislative bodies. Melvin Small of Wayne State University is using content analysis in a study of American images of the Soviet Union from 1939 to 1945. Louis Galambos of Rice University is similarly studying the literature of American business firms.

Questions of disputed authorship provide a narrower application of computer content analysis in the field of history than studies of verbal texts. Nonetheless, at least one knotty historical debate has already been silenced and another is nearing solution.[22] The resolved issue is the disputed authorship between Alexander Hamilton and James Madison of a dozen numbers of *The Federalist* papers. Two mathematicians, Frederick Mosteller and David L. Wallace, in their book *Inference and Disputed Authorship: The Federalist* (Reading, Mass., 1964), developed several ingenious statistical methods to measure the probability of Hamilton's or Madison's authorship.[23] The authors conclude that the odds favor Madison by more than 800:1 except for *Federalist* No. 55, for which the odds are only 80:1 for Madison. These findings corroborated historian Douglass Adair's earlier (1944) and more tentative verdict in favor of Madisonian claims, based on a careful scrutiny of the Virginian's papers and the numbers in dispute.[24]

Mosteller and Wallace had been stymied in early attempts to find discriminators—that is, marker words or phrases that were sufficiently sensitive to the stylistic nuances of Hamilton and Madison. But in 1959, Adair unlocked the key to the problem with an intuitive insight. While rereading *The Federalist* papers, the historian discovered that Hamilton used the word "while" whereas Madison in similar situations preferred "whilst." At Adair's urging and with this clue, the statisticians returned to the problem and solved it. With customary parochialism, only one major journal in American history reviewed the mathematicians' book upon its appearance in 1964; the others relegated it to the "book notes" sections or ignored it as non-history.[25]

That the vast statistical processes of the mathematicians should merely confirm Adair's sophisticated hunch may cause historians to gloat; but they need not. As Aydelotte observed in the opening essay on quantification: "Even if research merely confirms in a more conclusive fashion what some people already believe, it is good to have this additional assurance and to establish this belief on a more solid foundation." Mosteller and Wallace have indisputably demonstrated that Madison wrote every *Federalist* number that he claimed. Their "nonintellectual, wholly impersonal, and utterly objective evidence" [26] independently supplements Adair's intellectual, personal, and reasoned judgment based on the best traditional historical methods. And by translating a non-mathematical problem into mathematical terms, the authors provide interested historians with a splendid example of the functional role that statistical techniques can play in their craft.

[22] The problem still under study by Robert E. Kennedy, Jr., and Donald A. Kearns of Merrimack College is that of the disputed authorship of an emigré pamphlet of the French Revolution, *Antidote au Congres de Rastadt* (1798). The authors are using the Mosteller and Wallace approach. See their report in "Computerized Research in the Humanities: A Survey," *ACLS Newsletter, Special Supplement* (June, 1966), 13.

[23] An excellent and readable summary of the book is "Inference in an Authorship Problem," *Journal of the American Statistical Association*, LVIII (1963), 275–309.

[24] See the first item under "References" in Ivor S. Francis' article (8) for the citations of Adair's findings.

[25] The lone exception was the positive review by Linda M. and Stephan S. Webb, *William and Mary Quarterly, Third Series*, XXIII (Apr., 1966), 353–55. Brief mention occurred in *American Historical Review*, LXX (July, 1966), 1233–34; and the *Journal of American History*, LII (June, 1965), 186–87.

[26] Review of *Inference and Disputed Authorship, William and Mary Qaurterly*, 354.

7

RICHARD L. MERRITT *

The Emergence of American Nationalism: A Quantitative Approach

A perennial debate among colonialists revolves around the "timing" of the Americanization process. Did a distinctively American self-consciousness develop gradually or suddenly? If gradually, when did the transition become pronounced? If suddenly, what event precipitated the shift? In the following article, political scientist Richard L. Merritt has attempted a statistical answer to the problem. The method is a content analysis or symbol count of English- and American-oriented words as found in randomly selected issues of five urban newspapers published between 1735 and 1774. Students intrigued by this novel and informative essay should read the author's larger work, Symbols of American Community, 1735–1775 (*New Haven, 1966*). *Two methodological points should be mentioned. Merritt's symbols may be too narrowly political or diplomatic. Should the Great Awakening of the 1740's be considered, for example? And most important, how confident can one be that the urban newspapers in the sample accurately reflect the views of a nation which was 95 per cent rural?*

Richard L. Merritt, "The Emergence of American Nationalism: A Quantitative Approach," *American Quarterly*, XVII (Summer, 1965), 319–335. Copyright © 1965, Trustees of the University of Pennsylvania. Reprinted with permission of the author and *American Quarterly*.

* Without wishing to burden them with responsibility for my remarks, I should like to thank Professors Karl W. Deutsch and Edmund S. Morgan of Yale University, Louis P. Galambos of Johns Hopkins University, and Eugene C. McCreary of Lafayette College for their helpful comments on previous versions of this paper; and the Carnegie Corporation for its generous support of this project.

THE SYMBOLISM of names plays a significant role, not only in the magic of the primitives and the games of children, but in the process of group development and emerging nationalism as well. The designation of a group by a name—a specific name that serves as a symbol under which all would-be members of the group can unite, no less than as a means to differentiate the group from other such groups—is indicative that a group has come of age. In a situation where people are beginning to shift their primary group loyalties, the symbolism of names is particularly important.

Such was the case in the emerging American political community of the eighteenth century. The point at which the colonists stopped considering themselves Englishmen and began more often to think of themselves as Americans was of signal importance in the rise of American nationalism.

If students of the colonial era are fairly unanimous in recognizing the importance of this transitional period, it is not equally true that they agree on when the transition took place. Some writers, such as James Truslow Adams, Michael Kraus, Oscar Handlin and Howard H. Peckham, have suggested that the "Americanization" of the colonists was a gradual and virtually imperceptible process that took place during the whole of the colonial period.[1] A few have associated this transition with specific events. Albert Harkness Jr., for instance, wrote that the use of the terms "Americans" and "Europeans" to differentiate the colonists from their English contemporaries stemmed from the War of Jenkins' Ear, which began in 1739.[2] And Max Savelle found a growing "national" feeling among Americans during the six years between the end of King George's War (1748) and the outbreak of the French and Indian War.[3] It was in the forced association of Americans and Englishmen during the latter war that Carl Lotus Becker found the rise of an American community consciousness.[4] More recently Paul A. Varg wrote that "the development of a nascent nationalism" in the colonies found its first manifestation in the fall of 1759 when, "during the celebrations of the conquest of Quebec, the name 'Americans' became something more than a geographical expression." [5] Other

[1] James Truslow Adams, *The March of Democracy: The Rise of the Union* (New York and London, 1932), p. 54; cf. pp. 74–75; Michael Kraus, *Intercolonial Aspects of American Culture on the Eve of the Revolution, With Special Reference to the Northern Towns* (New York, 1928); Oscar Handlin, *This Was America: True Accounts of People and Places, Manners and Customs, as Recorded by European Travelers to the Western Shore in the Eighteenth, Nineteenth, and Twentieth Centuries* (Cambridge, 1949), p. 7; Howard H. Peckham, *The Colonial Wars, 1689–1762* (Chicago and London, 1964), pp. 219–21.
[2] Albert Harkness Jr., "Americanism and Jenkins' Ear," *Mississippi Valley Historical Review*, XXXVII (1950), 61–90, esp. pp. 89–90.
[3] Max Savelle, *Seeds of Liberty: The Genesis of the American Mind* (New York, 1948), pp. 555, 561.
[4] Carl Lotus Becker, *Beginnings of the American People* (Boston, New York, Chicago, 1915), pp. 191–93. In his brilliant essay, "The Spirit of '76," Becker found that the beginning of the American quarrel with Britain was in 1763, but later noted that, as much as his protagonist, Jeremiah Wynkoop, "admired England as the home of political liberty, he was thoroughly American." Carl Becker, J. M. Clark and William E. Dodd, *The Spirit of '76, and Other Essays* (Washington, D.C., 1927), pp. 10, 14. Cf. also, Lawrence Henry Gipson, "The American Revolution as an Aftermath of the Great War for the Empire, 1754–1763," *Political Science Quarterly*, LXV (1950), 86–104.
[5] Paul A. Varg, "The Advent of Nationalism, 1758–1776," *American Quarterly*, XVI (1964), 169–81; Varg emphasizes that these sentiments did not begin to crystallize until the 1760s.

historians, including such prominent scholars as Allan Nevins, John C. Miller, Carl Bridenbaugh, Edmund S. Morgan and Bernhard Knollenberg, have argued that the sharp increase in the American sense of community came during the critical decade that began with the passage of the Stamp Act and ended with the creation of the first Continental Congress.[6] And Kenneth C. Wheare and others have asserted that no American sense of nationality really existed until long after formal ties bound the colonies into a single federation.[7]

Such a variety of views leaves the student of American nationalism somewhat bewildered. When *did* the transition to Americanism take place? When did the colonists stop referring to themselves as "His Majesty's subjects" or as "British colonists"—perceptions compatible with membership in a British (or possibly Anglo-American) political community—and start more often calling themselves "Americans"? Did this shift occur in all the colonies at approximately the same time? Did the perceptions of colonists with explicit Tory sympathies differ substantially from those of colonial "Sons of Liberty"? Above all, what was the timing of the transition? Did American nationalism blossom in the space of a few weeks or months, in response, perhaps, to some spectacular event or British pronouncement of policy? Or did the colonists "learn" to become Americans over a much longer period of time?

A useful approach to such questions is the method of communication research known as "content analysis." Now, at first blush, the term seems to imply nothing new. Is that not what we do daily when we "analyze" the "content" of a book, letter, speech or other communication? In the modern social sciences the term "content analysis" has come to mean something much more specific. Quantitative content analysis, in the words of Alexander George, "substitutes controlled observation and systematic counting for impressionistic ways of observing frequencies of occurrence" of content variables.[8] Examples of such content variables include words (or symbols), concepts, images, words in context, sentence lengths or structures, and so forth. Thus content analysis is the systematic tabulation of the frequency with which certain predetermined symbols or other variables appear in a given body of data—newspapers, letters, books, speeches or any other form of recorded communication—covering a specific period of time.

This essay uses the type of content analysis that concentrates on words or symbols to explore a key aspect of the emergence of American nationalism: the terms used by the colonists to refer to themselves and to the land they inhabited.

* * *

[6] Allan Nevins, *The American States During and After the Revolution, 1775–1789* (New York, 1924), p. 544; John C. Miller, *Origins of the American Revolution* (Boston, 1949), p. 22; Carl Bridenbaugh, *Cities in Revolt: Urban Life in America, 1743–1776* (New York, 1955), p. 424; Edmund S. Morgan, *The Birth of the Republic, 1763–89* (Chicago, 1956), p. 101; Bernhard Knollenberg, *Origin of the American Revolution, 1759–1766* (rev. ed.; New York, 1961), p. 218.

[7] Kenneth C. Wheare, "Federalism and the Making of Nations," in *Federalism, Mature and Emergent,* ed. Arthur W. Macmahon (Garden City, N.Y., 1955), pp. 33–35; Edward Frank Humphrey, *Nationalism and Religion in America, 1774–1789* (Boston, 1924), pp. 2–4; Esmond Wright, *Fabric of Freedom, 1763–1800* (New York, 1961), pp. 20, 241.

[8] Alexander L. George, "Quantitative and Qualitative Approaches to Content Analysis," in *Trends in Content Analysis,* ed. Ithiel de Sola Pool (Urbana, Ill., 1959), p. 8.

Symbol analysis rests on the assumption that the words a person uses in communicating are indicative of or symbolize his attitude. (This is an assumption to which I shall return in later paragraphs.) To some extent the selection of words by a communicator is a conscious process. Novelists frequently seek to describe characters in their stories in a way that will give their readers a set of vivid images. One thinks of Dickens' Mr. Micawber, always painted in gray tones, or Uriah Heep, who everlastingly sought to impress his " 'umility" upon one and all. Similarly, much as the villain in a nineteenth-century melodrama wore (and was expected to wear) a black hat and a mustache, so villains in modern-day propaganda are clothed in "appropriate" garb. It is not the "United States" that communist newspapers discuss, but rather the "monopolistic" or "imperialistic" United States. And not infrequently do American politicians and writers preface the term "communism" with adjectives bearing a pejorative connotation in American symbol usage, such as "atheistic" or "totalitarian." By the same token, the patriot is the "people's hero," the "friend of peace" or the "red-blooded American."

In contrast to this deliberate use of language, designed to create a particular image for its audience, is what might be termed the "style" of a communication —"the subtle *unconscious* patterning of speech, handwriting, posture, and involuntary movements." [9]

But what is meant by the phrase "unconscious patterning of speech"? In one sense the analysis of such unconscious patterns resembles the psychoanalyst's search for the *lapsus linguae,* the "slip of the tongue" that has become such a prominent aspect of the folklore of psychoanalysis. And yet, quantitative symbol analysis does not place much emphasis upon such speech blunders. The intentional or accidental use of a word, such as "immortality" or "immorality," in a speech or in a diary of such a man as John Adams may mean nothing in itself. It would be, we might say, a random element in an otherwise patterned context, a word that might appear once or perhaps twice in any similar speech or diary.[10]

The symbol analyst most often focuses upon the regularities of speech usage. If a word or phrase is used constantly in some form of communication, it ceases to be a random occurrence, and becomes a stylistic pattern itself. In extreme cases, using the example from above, we would say that the speech or diary was preoccupied with "immortality" or "immorality." The songs that Hitler's Storm-

[9] Harold D. Lasswell, Daniel Lerner and Ithiel de Sola Pool, *The Comparative Study of Symbols: An Introduction* (Series C, No. 1, Hoover Institute Studies [Stanford, Calif., 1952]), p. 21. They continue: "It is a matter of style when we describe the vocabulary, enunciation or gestures of a speaker; or when we describe the grammatical forms, word choice, and sentence length of a writer" (p. 22). Cf. also Mary McCarthy, in an interview by Elizabeth Niebuhr, *The Paris Review,* No. 27 (Spring 1962), p. 79.

[10] More suited to such a task is Alexander George's "qualitative" content analysis, which is interested less in the quantification than in the appearance of key words and phrases, or Philip J. Stone's "General Inquirer" computerized method, which is particularly suitable for the study of psychological variables. See Alexander George, "Quantitative and Qualitative Approaches to Content Analysis," in *Trends in Content Analysis,* ed. Pool, pp. 7–32; and Philip J. Stone, Robert F. Bales, J. Zvi Namenwirth and Daniel Ogilvie, "The General Inquirer: A Computer System for Content Analysis and Retrieval Based on the Sentence as a Unit of Information," *Behavioral Science,* VII (1962), 484–98.

troopers sang as they marched through the streets of Germany during the 1930s, for example, dwelled on death and the dead; similarly, such concepts as "nullification" and "abolition" find an especially prominent place in American writing of the mid-nineteenth century.

The symbol analyst is interested less in whether a particular message represents the communicator's style or his deliberate manipulation of symbols than in the frequency with which certain items occur, in frequency changes over time, in variations in frequency patterns in different communication media or in the same media in different geographic or political areas. He is concerned not with the intention of the message but with its effect, which in turn depends far less upon the subtle psychological motivation of the communicator than upon the qualities of the audience. Taking an example from colonial history, if a Tory newspaper, such as the *Massachusetts Gazette,* devoted an increasing share of its space to American symbols and events as the colonial years passed, or if it increasingly more often identified its readers as "Americans" rather than as "His Majesty's subjects" or even "colonists," we might say that, despite its pro-British point of view, the latent content of its symbol usage encouraged its readers to think of themselves as members of a distinctly American community and to turn their thoughts inward toward that American community.

But let us return to the assumption made earlier: that the words a person uses in communicating are indicative of or symbolize his attitudes. How can we be sure that this is actually the case? In a sense, of course, we can never be completely certain whether or not the communicator is choosing his words carefully to create a particular effect. There are two points to be noted in considering this objection. First of all, certain stylistic elements creep into the person's communication regardless of how hard he may try to exclude them. The passion for anonymity and unity of style that attended the writing of *The Federalist* papers have not been completely successful in disguising their authorship.[11] Similarly, matters of style are very significant in differentiating literary, musical and artistic masterpieces from copies or imitations.

The second point is of a more practical nature. If we do not use words to symbolize attitudes, what else can we use? Sampling the mind of the colonial American through public opinion surveys or through subjective psychological tests is clearly out of the question. Nor is it any more likely, we have learned from psychologists, that a person's actions, while perhaps speaking louder than words, are any more indicative of his true attitudes than the symbols he uses in communicating. In short, we must use available analytical techniques, or devise better ones, to explore the meager data that have come down to us from the colonial era. And, for the most part, these data comprise words—expressions of opinion, musings in a diary, outright propaganda, accounts of events by eyewitnesses, interpretations of these events and of such processes as colonial patterns of behavior or thinking.

The starting place of research using symbol analysis is a grasp of the fundamentals of the analyst's subject of interest: the elaboration of a theoretical

---

[11] Cf. Frederick Mosteller and David L. Wallace, *Inference and Disputed Authorship: The Federalist* (Reading, Mass., Palo Alto, Calif. and London, 1964).

framework; the recognition of problems within that framework that are at once significant and subject to analysis; and the framing of questions as well as the selection of adequate means to answer them. But such tasks are not peculiar to symbol analysis research. They find their place in all types of research in the natural and social sciences.

Symbol analysis is useful only when the researcher has questions of a quantitative nature—how often? how much? how many? with what covariance? —that can be answered by counting the appearance of a limited number of symbols in a given body of data. Whether or not the topic that interests the analyst is subject to such a quantitative analysis rests not upon the nature of this research method alone, but upon the theoretical framework within which he is working. Symbol analysis would not be of much value, for instance, in trying to determine when a particular battle took place, or how much trade passed between colonial New York and Philadelphia. It would be considerably more helpful in trying to establish the nature of the colonists' political allegiances.

Once he has decided that a symbol analysis would be feasible and useful, the analyst must frame his questions (or form his hypotheses) so that quantitative data can answer them clearly, directly and simply. Symbol analysis is not merely a counting process, nor is it what might be termed "brute empiricism" —the amassing of statistics in the hope of finding interesting relationships. Effective symbol analysis is designed to test specific hypotheses by establishing a limited universe of relevant items as well as their alternatives, and by establishing their distribution or changes in the frequency of their appearance. On the basis of the evidence the hypotheses can then be accepted or rejected. An example of such an hypothesis might be: "The colonists' sense of group identification shifted from the British political community to a strictly American political community gradually but steadily from 1735 to 1775." This proposition asserts that the colonists turned away from their British ties in favor of an intercolonial allegiance; and, further, that a trend line showing the growth of an American sense of community would be generally linear, that is, not characteristically marked by sharp shifts in the colonists' community ties.

With his questions or hypotheses in mind, the symbol analyst must outline the technical aspects of his project, determining how to count which symbols in what body of data covering what time period. Objectivity requires that these technical aspects of the symbol analysis be specified in advance, and that throughout the analysis there be strict adherence to the coding procedure. If this requirement is met, an independent research project should be able to verify the findings of a symbol analysis by applying the analyst's coding procedures to the original body of data. If it is impossible or impractical to analyze all the data, the analyst must utilize a sampling technique (about which I shall say more later) designed to produce a representative sample or reproduction in miniature of the entire body or universe of relevant items. A pretest or "dry run" is essential to "indicate whether the prescribed symbol list, coding rules and recording procedures *actually* will produce the statistic wanted." [12] After subjecting a small portion of the sample to analysis, the researcher can often see where he must eliminate and where he must add categories to his symbol list, or

[12] Lasswell, Lerner and Pool, *The Comparative Study of Symbols*, p. 51; italics in the original.

where he must make changes in his hypotheses or coding procedures.

How could we test the hypothesis suggested above—that "The colonists' sense of group identification shifted from the British political community to a strictly American political community gradually but steadily from 1735 to 1775"—using symbol analysis? Since one crucial aspect of group identification is the recognition, both by members of the group and outsiders, of the group's existence apart from other such groups, we can examine the use of self-referent symbols in colonial newspapers.[13] To return to some questions suggested above, when did the colonists (or at least their newspapers) stop referring to themselves as "colonists" or as "His Majesty's subjects," and begin more often viewing themselves as "Americans"? When did they begin identifying the land that they occupied as "America" rather than as "British-America" or the "colonies"? Another aspect of group identification is the amount of attention paid by the members of the group to one another, in contrast to the attention paid to outsiders. When did the colonists begin devoting more space in their newspapers to local events and occurrences in America than they did to European wars and English court gossip? A simple count of symbols in the colonial press referring to place names throughout the world would give us substantial information about the colonists' focus of attention, and about the changes in this focus as they reached the end of the colonial era.

Clearly a certain amount of expertness in the methodology of symbol analysis —whether, when, what and how to count [14]—is important here. Symbol analysis is after all a research tool which, like any other tool or method, has its specific uses, its advantages and its limitations. The analyst must know how to use this research tool, and must be aware of its limitations. This sort of expertness is akin to that of the student of American diplomatic history who, before he can perform competent research, must be familiar with such research aids as bibliographies and dictionaries of biographies; he must be able to evaluate conflicting interpretations of history or of events; he must learn to distinguish between reliable and unreliable sources. The expert symbol analyst, like the expert chemical engineer, strives to clarify his research designs so that even his newest research assistant could carry out at least some of the often tedious testing or counting.

Finally, the analyst must interpret the results of the symbol count in terms of his theoretical framework. That the colonists' use of self-referent symbols changed considerably from 1735 to 1775 is in itself an interesting fact. But where does that fact fit into the development of an American sense of community, the growth of sentiments of separateness from the mother country, the emergence of a desire for independence? It is this relationship—conclusions "formed by means of an inference from observed data to nonobserved continua" [15]—that is the crux of research in the social sciences.

Confronted with the task of analyzing a set of objects or communication media, such as eighteenth-century colonial newspapers, I could follow one of

[13] For a discussion of the value and limitations of newspapers for analyzing colonial attitudes, and of some of the problems encountered in content analyzing them, see Richard L. Merritt, "Public Opinion in Colonial America: Content Analyzing the Colonial Press," *Public Opinion Quarterly*, XXVII (1963), 356–71.

[14] Lasswell, Lerner and Pool, *The Comparative Study of Symbols*, pp. 45–63

[15] *Ibid.*, p. 29.

two different procedures. I could, first of all, examine each item individually; or, alternatively, I could use some sort of sampling method to select a few representative items for close examination. The appropriateness of either procedure rests primarily upon the amount and type of information needed to answer my questions about the class of items, as well as upon what economists call the "opportunity cost" of securing a certain amount of information. If I were interested in newspaper reaction to specific events, the Boston Tea Party, for instance, or the Battle of Golden Hill, I would most likely have to analyze every issue of a given number of newspapers for a certain limited time period. But searching for long-run trends in press attitudes or reporting would pose an entirely different research task.

One means of analyzing long-run trends in the press would be to read through every issue published (or extant) for the years in question. This is the time-honored historical method, and has much to commend it. In this manner the alert and insightful scholar can often spot significant relationships in the data that enable him to formulate interesting research problems and to reach useful conclusions.

That his results are important, however, is no guarantee that they adequately represent the actual content of the newspapers. Three critical types of error might have crept into his findings. We may, first of all, ignore the type of error produced by a writer merely searching for statements fitting his preconceived notions about the content of the press. Charlatanism is possible regardless of the research method used. The occurrence of such instances is nonetheless frequent enough to make us wary. A second and more important type of error occurs when the researcher searches through the newspapers for different points of view. It is sometimes difficult to assess the importance of certain ideas or symbols without some sort of frequency count or other measure of intensity. To ignore this is to run the risk of evaluating widely differing ideas or symbols on a par, assigning equal weights to an argument appearing only occasionally and to one appearing constantly.[16] The third type of error falls into the category of simple human failings. To scrutinize every extant issue of the pre-Revolutionary press would consume an inordinate amount of time. The researcher cannot read every word with equal care. He is generally able to do little more than to scan the newspapers, looking for key words or concepts. Even as Homer nodded, so too the modern writer occasionally slips, momentarily gliding by a few words or even paragraphs as the library grows dimmer, the microfilm copy grows fuzzier or the hour grows later. He may judge certain items to be of only marginal interest when in fact their inclusion would be necessary to give a rounded aspect to his final conclusions. Or, still more likely, the categories of items or concepts he considers of marginal interest may vary from day to day.

The alternative is to utilize some method of sampling. The detailed examination of every *n*th issue of a newspaper, or of a certain number of newspapers selected at random for each year, is as useful in measuring long-run trends in attitude changes as a sampling process is in testing blood or the control of quality on an assembly line. Such a procedure eliminates the necessity of

---

[16] For examples of such an error, see Warren H. Goodman, "The Origins of the War of 1812: A Survey of Changing Interpretations," *Mississippi Valley Historical Review*, XXVIII (1941), 171–86.

scanning large quantities of newsprint as well as errors of the type mentioned in the previous paragraph. The more we can stratify the sample according to some characteristic of the media, according to political sympathies, for instance, or place of publication, or popularity as indicated by circulation, the more refined it will be. But, at the same time, with increasing refinement comes the need for larger sample sizes and hence added expense in terms of the time and money available for research. Ideally, the sample should be small enough to be manageable, and yet large enough to answer the most important questions about the total class of items.

Whether or not a sample is appropriate also rests upon certain empirical tests. One test would be to compare the analysis of the sample with a complete analysis of the larger set from which the sample has been drawn. Since such a procedure would obviate the need of a sample, it would be efficient only if the sampling technique were to be used in analyzing additional bodies of similar data. More frequently it is sufficient to compare the sample with a second sample drawn independently from the same data. If the variation between the two independent samples is not statistically significant, then either could be used within certain limits of probability in analyzing the data. If the variation is significant, then a larger sample, or perhaps one stratified differently, must be used. In my own work on changes in symbol usage in the colonial press, I have found that a random sample of four issues per year of a newspaper is nine-tenths as good as an independently-chosen random sample of twelve issues per year.[17] But, it must be added, although a sample of four issues per year might well measure yearly changes in symbol usage, it would take a more refined sample to analyze changes within any given year.

As a research method symbol analysis is a lengthy process, costly both in time and research money; and, even worse for the person performing the actual counting, an extensive project may become rather tedious. In this sense symbol analysis resembles a large radar network, which is also expensive, time-consuming and tiresome for the person scanning the radar screens. We know that the payoff of the radar net, in terms of national defense, is important. But why bother with symbol analysis? Is the increment in knowledge—about the development of colonial patterns of group identity, for instance—worth the effort involved?

Intrinsically, of course, any increment in man's knowledge that contributes to an understanding of important events and processes is useful. At the very least a symbol analysis of the colonial press would tell us something about the changing perspectives of their editors. To the extent that these perspectives reflected and helped to shape the perspectives of the politically relevant strata of colonial society, they are useful in analyzing attitude changes in eighteenth-century America.

There is another side to the use of information derived from symbol analyses.

---

[17] Independent samples of four and twelve issues per year for ten different years were compared, using the nonparametric "Mann-Whitney U Test." In nine of the ten cases, the tests indicated that no significant differences between the two samples existed. More properly speaking, in nine of ten cases (significant at the .05 level for a two-tailed test) the test did not reject a null hypothesis asserting that there was no significant difference between the sample of four and the independent sample of twelve issues.

In one sense such data are quite different from the standard materials of American history: they are quantitative in nature, based on standard statistical tests of reliability and verification. The information yielded is both impersonal and repeatable, that is, an independent researcher could get similar results by following the same procedures. In another, very important sense, however, this information is not at all dissimilar from any other piece of concrete evidence used in the study of American history. Its usefulness rests upon its interpretation, upon the pattern of events and processes in which the scholar places it. Like custom-house reports on intercolonial shipping patterns, it is evidence that conscientious scholars cannot ignore.

Trend information produced by symbol analysis encourages us to consider history as a continuing process rather than as sets of discrete events in a time series. This fact bears two important implications for research. First of all, trend analyses permit us to fit single pieces of evidence into continuing patterns, giving us a better understanding of the relevance of the single bits of information as well as enriching our understanding of the patterns. In seeking to answer the question, "When did the colonists begin to perceive themselves as Americans rather than as English colonists?" it is often quite tempting to focus upon single documents or single events—occasions upon which the "Americanism" of the colonists was emphasized—and to point to these occasions as the origin of an American sense of nationality. It is an interesting fact, for instance, that documents (letters, battle reports, instructions) written in the Caribbean during the War of Jenkins' Ear frequently used the terms "Americans" and "Europeans" to differentiate colonial from English sailors and marines, but this fact must be considered not in isolation, away from its environment of other relevant information. It is necessary to compare the actual frequency of such usages with the frequency with which common terms were used to refer to colonists and Englishmen alike, and to see how these frequencies changed over time and with the tide of battle. Moreover, the importance of the fact pales if it turns out that the differential usage of nomenclature was restricted to an area of interaction limited in the number of communicators, the time period covered and geographic circumstances. Did the inhabitants of the British Isles or the North American continent adopt such terms? Or were these names like nicknames given one another by children in a summer camp—meaningful at the time, often quite graphic, but soon forgotten when the summer is over? Similarly, how *representative* of more general speech patterns are the statements cited in the writings of others who try to pinpoint in time and place the origin of American nationalism? Did such statements reflect or precede (or even create) a sense of community in the people as a whole? Or were they instances of aberrant or possibly random verbal behavior that found neither basis nor echo in the common language of the day? In sum, an assessment of widely varying points of view about the origins of American nationalism requires adequate information on long-run trends in colonial thinking, the sort of information that symbol analysis can provide.

A second implication for research is that trend data from symbol analyses help us to focus our attention upon years or months of particular importance in the development of American community awareness. If it should turn out that the period during which colonial symbol usage underwent the most radical change was the year 1763 (or, even more specifically, the early summer of that year), then we might do well to commit more of our research resources to an examination of colonial attitudes during that crucial period.

More generally speaking, symbol analysis bears yet another implication for research in the field of colonial history. The training of the top-flight historian, no less so than that of the social psychologist or the political scientist with an interest in communications research, is long and arduous, usually involving a considerable degree of specialization. Can we expect that the historian, having mastered his own trade, will turn to the vast fields of psychology and communications research for further training? There are of course some historians who will do just that. For others, however, the solution may be to encourage interdisciplinary research. The recently developed tools of the social sciences can contribute as much to the study of history as the historian can—by identifying the important and interesting problems in, say, colonial history, as well as the most relevant variables—to contemporary theory in the social sciences.

A systematic analysis of self-referent symbols in the colonial press would tell us much about patterns of nationalism in eighteenth-century America. With this view in mind I examined the news columns of four randomly selected issues per year of newspapers from each of five colonial population centers—Boston, New York, Philadelphia, Williamsburg and Charleston in South Carolina[18]— tabulating each appearance of place-name symbols (such as "Boston," "England," "the colonies," "Americans" or other names of actual places or their inhabitants) during the 41 years from 1735 to 1775. The place-name symbols of particular importance here are self-referent symbols referring collectively to either the colonists or the colonies as a single unit. The tabulation includes both direct symbols (that is, those symbols actually specifying the group or the area, such as "the colonists" or "the colonies") and indirect symbols (those that replace the specific name of the group or area with such terms as "they," "that place" and so forth).

The collective self-referent symbols are categorized in two different ways. One means is by their primary identification content: Do they denote the geographic area that later became the United States, or its population? A second means of categorization is according to the specific label, a so-called secondary symbol, that the self-referent symbols attach when identifying the primary content: Do they associate the land or its population with the British political community or with a distinctly American community? In this respect we can differentiate five groups of such symbols: (1) Symbols of explicit British common identity: "British North America," "the English colonies," "British-America," or "British colonists," "British-Americans," "English provincials"; (2) Symbols of identification with the British Crown: "His Majesty's colonies," "royal colonies" or "crown colonies," "His Majesty's subjects in America," "Royal Americans"; (3) Symbols of implicit British common identity: the

---

[18] The newspapers were: *The Boston News-Letter* (issues from 1735 to 1775) and *The Boston Gazette, and Country Journal* (1762–75); *The New-York Weekly Journal* (1735–51) and *The New-York Mercury* (1752–75); *The Pennsylvania Gazette* (1735–75); the various *Virginia Gazettes* (under William Parks from 1736 to 1750, and under William Hunter and his successors from 1751 to 1775); and *The South-Carolina Gazette* (1735–75).

"colonies" or "provinces," "our colonies in America" (only when used in articles with British datelines), "colonists" or "provincials"; (4) Symbols of implicit American common identity: the "continent" or "country," the "American colonies" or the "colonies in America," the "United Colonies," the "continentals," "American colonists"; and (5) Symbols of explicit American common identity: "America" or "North America," "Americans" or "North Americans." In this paper I shall collapse the first three categories into a single one comprising symbols identifying the colonies and colonists as essentially British, and the last two categories into one of symbols identifying the colonial lands and population as American. Elsewhere I have considered the difference it makes if we categorize self-referent symbols according to whether they appeared in articles with American, British or other foreign datelines; [19] here I shall consider the distribution of symbols only in respect to the total image of the American community presented to the newspapers' readers.

The first point to be noted about the distribution of collective self-referent symbols in the press is that their salience increased dramatically in the years from 1735 to 1775. In the late 1730s, the newspapers as a whole paid little attention indeed to the colonies or colonists as a collective unit. The average issue contained .66 such symbols, that is, in every three issues of a newspaper approximately two self-referent symbols appeared. This figure represented somewhat over 4 per cent of the total number of symbols in the press referring to American place names. The average issue from 1771 to 1775 contained almost 22 collective self-referent symbols, an increase of over 3200 per cent over the 1735–39 period. During the last five colonial years the press devoted about one-quarter of its news space to collective symbols, another quarter to symbols of place names in the colonies publishing the individual journals and about one-half of its space to symbols of place names in other colonies. In sum, a concept that was extremely marginal in the late 1730s was quite salient by the early 1770s.

The process by which the salience of the collective concept for the colonial press increased was cyclical. As may be seen in Table 1, the number of collective self-referent symbols per issue fluctuated considerably during the 41 years from 1735 to 1775. The low points of the cycles occurred in 1736 (or possibly earlier), 1745, 1761 and 1772; the peaks were in 1740, 1756, 1769 and 1775 (or later). Two points are of interest here. First, the peaks of the cycles no less than the troughs were on increasingly higher planes as time passed. Second, in general the cycles were of increasingly shorter duration. Thus, despite fluctuations in the curve, the secular trend in the use of collective self-referent symbols was clearly climbing upward at an ever greater rate.

That the salience of the collective concept in the newspapers rose is of course no indication that the colonists were becoming ever more "nationalistic." It is possible that they could merely have been stressing their allegiance to the British political community more often. As it turns out, however, such was not the case. For the period as a whole about six in ten collective self-referent symbols (58 per cent) identified the colonies or colonists either implicitly or explicitly as American. Again the propensity to use American self-referent symbols rose:

[19] See Richard L. Merritt, *Symbols of American Community, 1735–1775* (New Haven, 1966).

THE FREQUENCY OF COLLECTIVE SELF-REFERENT SYMBOLS IN THE COLONIAL PRESS, 1735-1775

Note: For easier visualization the data are on a semi-logarithmic graph.

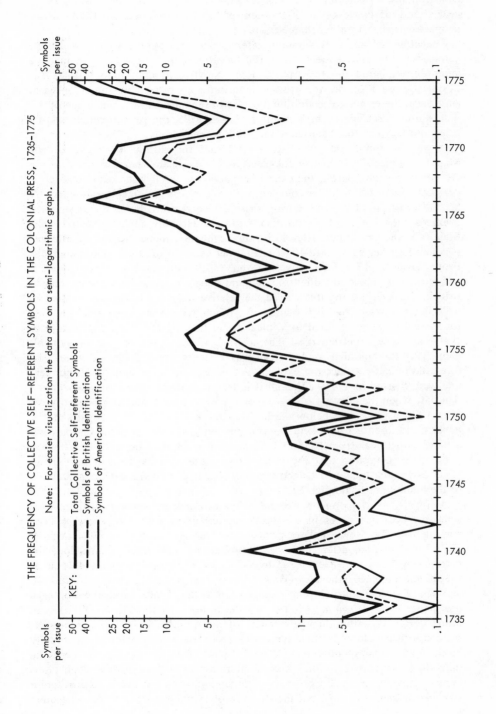

from roughly 43 per cent in 1735–39 to about 63 per cent in 1771–75. In no year after 1755 did less than 50 per cent of these symbols identify the land and people as American rather than British.

Collective self-referent symbols referring to the people appeared in the newspapers far less frequently than did those referring to the land. In fact the latter outnumbered the former by more than five to one. In only one year (1760) before 1765 did the average issue refer collectively to the colonists at least once; the ensuing decade found each newspaper printing an average of 3.7 such symbols, reaching a high point of 10.9 in 1775, the year in which fighting broke out between the Americans and the Redcoats.

It was not until the years after 1764 that the distinction between "His Majesty's subjects" or "British colonists" and "Americans" became a real one in the colonial press. Before then the newspapers were all but unanimous (97.1 per cent) in identifying the colonists with the British political community. By far the most popular terms during these 29 years were those identifying the colonists as subjects of the British Crown—"His Majesty's subjects," "His Majesty's colonists," and, after 1756, the regimental name "Royal Americans" —which together comprised 108 (or 79.4 per cent) of the total of 136 symbols. From 1764 to 1775 almost six in ten (57.0 per cent) of the collective self-referent symbols identified the colonial people as American rather than as British. But even during this period the relative paucity of symbols resulted in wide fluctuations in the distribution of symbols from year to year. If the data for these 12 years are fitted to a linear trend line, however, a clear picture of changing perceptions emerges. The average increase in the use of symbols identifying the colonists as American was 2.3 percentage points per year. The threshold of self-conscious or explicit "Americanism," an imaginary 50 per cent line, was crossed in 1770, although it is true that there were two years before that date when the curve was above the 50 per cent level, and at least two years after 1770 when it was below the halfway mark. (By way of comparison, the linear trend line for symbols identifying the land as American rose 0.8 percentage points per year from 1735 to 1775 and crossed the 50 per cent threshold in 1762, thus suggesting that the perception of the land as being a part of an American rather than a British community clearly preceded a similar perception of the inhabitants of that land.)

As far as newspapers from the individual colonies are concerned, there were some marked differences in their presentation of an image of the American community. The New England prints—the Tory *Massachusetts Gazette* from 1735 to 1764 and, after its level of "Americanism" slipped somewhat, the patriot *Boston Gazette* from 1765 to 1775—led in this respect; the journals of the middle colonies (the *New-York Weekly Journal,* the *New-York Mercury* and the *Pennsylvania Gazette*) lagged until the 1760s; and the southern newspapers (the *Virginia Gazette* and the *South-Carolina Gazette*), after an initial period of rather high awareness of an American political community, seemed to draw closer in their symbol usage to the British political community in the two decades between 1745 and 1764. With the passage of time the individual newspapers not only became more aware of the collective concept, as indicated by the inclusion of an ever larger number of collective self-referent symbols in their columns, but their choice of symbols tended to become quite steady and congruent. Not until the early 1760s, however, did the newspapers of the middle colonies join with the New England prints in a symbol revolution that preceded the outbreak of fighting by more than a decade.

These findings are suggestive of the value of symbol analysis for putting events or specific statements of individuals into a larger time perspective. It becomes clear, for instance, that the "Americanism" that appeared during the War of Jenkins' Ear was not without precedent. Nor did a spirit of American nationalism strike the colonists like a bolt from the blue during the French and Indian War. That spirit was already there. Similarly, the newspapers, which at once reflected and helped to shape the images of the politically relevant strata of colonial society, revealed an upsurge in sentiments of American community during the 1760s. The point, however, is not that such a trend emerged for the first time during the conflicts of that decade. The trend already existed. The crises of the 1760s merely accelerated the pace of that trend toward symbolic separation from the British political community. In short, the changing processes of symbolic identification in the American colonies seem to have been neither revolutionary nor evolutionary in the strictest sense of these terms. Rather, like other learning situations, they were both gradual and fitful, with a few periods of extremely rapid advances (or breakthroughs) interspersed with other periods of more or less mild relapses. Symbol analysis gives us a useful means to examine this process by which the colonists learned to be Americans.

8

IVOR S. FRANCIS *

An Exposition of a Statistical Approach
to the Federalist Dispute

For more than 150 years a controversy has raged over the authorship of 12 papers (out of 77) of The Federalist. *Initially, Hamilton claimed the credit, but after his death Madison insisted on his own authorship. Scholars ever since have taken sides, usually on the basis of political leanings, with Madison's advocates holding a decided edge. Stimulated by Douglass Adair, a noted colonial historian, mathematicians Frederick Mosteller and David L. Wallace brought their statistical expertise to the problem. Ivor S. Francis, an economic and social statistician, served as one of Professor Mosteller's assistants on the* Federalist *project. In the following essay Francis describes the history, methods, and findings of this fascinating investigation. The article is designed for the general reader and has a minimum of technical jargon. Note that the best discriminator words between Hamilton and Madison are not meaningful words like* war, executive, *and* legislature, *but filler words—articles, prepositions, and conjunctions.*

Ivor S. Francis, "An Exposition of a Statistical Approach to the Federalist Dispute," in Jacob Leed (ed.), *The Computer and Literary Style* (Kent, Ohio: Kent State University, 1966), 38–79. Reprinted, with deletion of Sections 10 and 11, with permission of the author.
* The writer acknowledges with thanks the many helpful comments and suggestions of Professor Frederick Mosteller. For work on the manuscripts thanks are due to Miss Marguerite O'Leary, Miss Jacqueline Wollan, and also to Mrs. Marianne

T W O   D A Y S   before his fatal duel with Aaron Burr on July 11, 1804, Alexander Hamilton visited Egbert Benson and ostentatiously concealed in his friend's bookcase a slip of paper. All the *Federalist* papers had been published over the name "Publius," whose identity was a secret. On the slip of paper Hamilton listed by number the authors of the various essays. The three authors were James Madison, John Jay, and himself.

Neither Madison nor Jay chose to challenge the Benson list when it was found. It was not until 1817 that a friend of Madison's challenged the Benson list and claimed for Madison some of the papers that Hamilton had claimed to have written. Then in 1818 Madison formally announced his claim in Jacob Gideon's edition of *The Federalist*. Few of Madison's contemporaries doubted this carefully considered claim and there the matter rested until the Civil War. From 1861 the Virginian's fame as a constitutional statesman declined while Hamilton's reputation grew with the rise of Federalism, so that by 1886, with the publication by Henry Cabot Lodge of a new edition of *The Federalist*, the Benson list was being reconsidered.

Three quarters of a century later the authorship of these disputed papers remained an historical controversy and it was into this arena that two innocent statisticians stumbled. This article describes the attempts made by Frederick Mosteller and David L. Wallace to resolve the controversy, not by the usual methods of historical literary analysis, but by methods of mathematical statistics.

1. Background

The statistical or mathematical approach to the study of language is not new. Whatmough (1957) points out that a Sanskrit grammarian of the Sutra period (500–200 B.C.) gave the number of hymns, verses, words, and even syllables contained in the *Rig-Veda*. More recently, in 1854, George Boole records in *Laws of Thought* how the principle of determinate frequency was applied to the deciphering of Ogam and cuneiform. In 1887 Mendenhall investigated the difference between the literary styles of Dickens and Thackeray insofar as the length of words was concerned. He studied the frequency distribution of the length of words—the proportion of one-letter, two-letter, three-letter words, etc. In a later article (1901) he used word-length frequency distributions in a study of the authorship of Shakespeare's play (see Section 4). Figure I shows the distributions for Bacon (based on a count of 200,000 words from his *Henry VII, The Advancement of Learning,* and many essays) and for Shakespeare (based on a count of 400,000 words including nearly all of his most famous plays).

The frequency distribution of the number of words in a sentence was proposed by Yule (1938) as another element of style that seems to be

Blackwell and Miss Frances Suda. The quotations from the book *Inference and Disputed Authorship: The Federalist,* by Frederick Mosteller and David L. Wallace, are reprinted by permission of the copyright owners, Addison-Wesley Publishing Company, Inc., Reading, Massachusetts. This work was facilitated by a grant from the National Science Foundation (GS-341).

FIGURE I

WORD-LENGTH FREQUENCY DISTRIBUTION FOR BACON AND SHAKESPEARE
REDRAWN FROM MENDENHALL (1901)

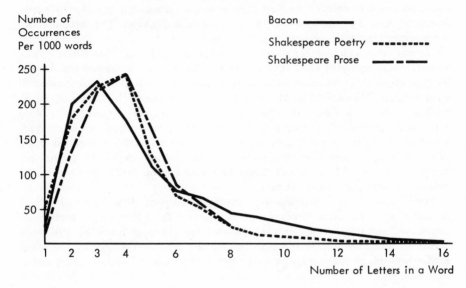

characteristic of an author. He investigated the style of *De imitatione Christi* and compared it, in respect to the distribution of sentence length, to works of Thomas à Kempis and Jean Charlier de Gerson. His results were consonant with the view that à Kempis was, and Gerson was not, the author of the work.

In 1944 Yule published a further attempt to decide the authorship of *De imitatione Christi*. This time he studied a feature of vocabulary, namely the distribution of the number of nouns used once, twice, etc.

In 1941 Frederick Williams introduced Frederick Mosteller to the problem which we shall consider in detail in this paper, namely the problem of the authorship of the disputed *Federalist* papers. Williams and Mosteller, influenced by the work of Yule and of C. B. Williams (1939), studied the undisputed *Federalist* works of Hamilton and Madison but found that sentence length did not discriminate between the two authors. They then computed for each known paper the percentages of nouns, of adjectives, of one- and two-letter words, and of *the*'s. On the basis of these data they constructed a statistic that was intended to separate Hamilton's writings from Madison's. This statistic, however, was not sensitive enough to assign the disputed papers with any degree of confidence, although it pointed to Madison for most of them.

Williams and Mosteller did not resume their joint work and it was only a few years ago that Mosteller's interest was revived. In 1959 Douglass Adair informed Mosteller that he had found a pair of words (later called marker words) that distinguished Hamilton from Madison quite well when the words occurred. Hamilton uses *while* and Madison, in a corresponding situation, uses *whilst*. It was around such words that Mosteller and Wallace built their case described in their book *Inference and Disputed Authorship: The Federalist* and summarized in a paper entitled "Inference in an Authorship Problem" (*J. A. S. A.,* 1963). As mathematical statisticians the authors' major concern was the comparison of a number of statistical methods of discrimination all based on much the same data. But they were also interested in solving the authorship question of the *Federalist* papers and in proposing routine methods for solving other authorship problems. This paper attempts to give readers unfamiliar with mathematical statistics a summary of the problem and the results, besides reporting briefly the authors' advice to those who would undertake similar projects. The writer of this article assisted in several parts of the *Federalist* project and will quote frequently from the book and paper. The tables are taken from the *J. A. S. A.* paper.

For a more detailed account the reader is referred to the book which, though statistically oriented, separates much of the mathematics from the exposition so that a non-mathematical reader should have little difficulty in following the main arguments. A reader who is interested in this study because of its contribution to the literary controversy may feel, after viewing the complexity and power of the main Bayesian study, that nuclear weapons have been used to defoliate a forest when weedkiller would have done the job. He should be reminded that Mosteller and Wallace realized that, though the methods of their earlier work may have been adequate for the immediate purpose of deciding authorship, the problem presented an opportunity for a systematic comparison of two general methods of attack. Thus the study became more involved than a simple resolution of the controversy would have required.

The authors admit in retrospect that the methodological analysis could have been restricted to sets of papers whose authorship is known, but the responsibility of making judgments about authorship in disputed cases added a little hard realism and promoted additional care that might otherwise have been omitted. The book describes four different studies—four different approaches to the dispute. The first, the main study, exhibits the so-called Bayesian approach, and the second, the weight-rate study, follows the so-called classical tradition of statistical inference. These two large-scale studies, parts of which were carried out on a high-speed computer, contrast the two methods of attack. The main study, especially, required considerable use of the computer. Mosteller and Wallace believed that lighter artillery would have done the trick so they carried out two small-scale studies, one Bayesian in character and the other essentially classical. These two studies were less sensitive than the two large-scale studies but required only desk-calculators or slide rules for the calculations. They are described in Chapters 6 and 7 of the book and will not be treated in this paper.

2. The Federalist

The *Federalist* papers were published anonymously over the pseudonym "Publius" in 1787–1788 by Alexander Hamilton, John Jay, and James Madison, to persuade the citizens of the State of New York to ratify the Constitution. Of the 77 essays, 900 to 3500 words in length, that appeared in newspapers, it is generally agreed that Jay wrote five: Nos. 2, 3, 4, 5, and 64. Hamilton and Madison, as well as historians, agree upon the authorship of an additional 57 papers, 43 by Hamilton and 14 by Madison. On the other hand, they dispute the authorship of another 12 papers referred to as the "disputed papers." Finally there are three papers which will be referred to as "joint" papers— Hamilton said they were joint papers, and Madison claimed to have written them using Hamilton's notes. The issue concerning these three papers is the extent of each man's contribution.

Over the past 150 years numerous lists have been published, some claiming the disputed papers for Hamilton and some for Madison. Adair (1944a) has noted that the preference shown for each man's claim has, over the years, swung with the popularity of the man's views. The available historical evidence today is modest enough that a reasonable skeptic can maintain that it is not convincing one way or the other.

This brief summary of the case of Hamilton versus Madison certainly does not do justice to the controversy. The reader is referred to Adair (1944a, 1944b) and Cooke (1961) for more complete historical accounts.

3. Statistics and Style

In Section 1.1 of their book Mosteller and Wallace write: "From the point of view of statistical methods, authorship problems fall into a general area called discrimination or classification problems. In these problems the task is to assign a category to an object or individual whose true category is uncertain. In our authorship problem the objects are essays written by either Hamilton or Madison. We reduce our uncertainty about the authorship of an 'unknown' essay by comparing its properties with information obtained from essays whose authorship is known. Classifying plants in biology, skulls in anthropology, candidates for parole in criminology, and subjects according to personality in psychology are related operations that sometimes employ similar methods, even though the properties that aid the classification vary drastically from one area to another. The methods used to study one problem in discrimination can sometimes be extended to other areas of research." But where does the statistical method stand from the point of view of historical and linguistic methods? How much can we hope to accomplish toward resolving this controversy?

At best we can make statements like "It is very likely that Madison wrote paper No. 57." When we make such a statement about one of the disputed papers, clearly we have no direct evidence that Madison wrote paper 57. We are merely stating that, with respect to certain stylistic attributes, paper 57 is much more like Madison's known writings than Hamilton's. But surely this is nothing new. The difference between the statistical method and the standard methods of historical research is that the stylistic attributes used in the statistical method are formal ones that are treated quantitatively. Mosteller and Wallace treated these attributes merely as fingerprints: fingerprints say nothing about the character of their owner but they do help to identify him. Referring to the selection of vocabulary items for such classification problems, Yule (1944) said: "All these are mere details; details certainly quite useful in relation to the controversy, providing valid evidence . . . *but they give no faintest notion as to what his vocabulary is really like as a whole*. To tell me that there is a small mole on

Miranda's cheek may help me to identify the lady, and may in conceivable circumstances be quite useful information to the police, but it hardly amounts to a description of her alluring features." For the purpose of studying authorship Mosteller and Wallace were not interested in the writers' overall style or in the use of their total vocabulary. They just searched for and found tell-tale fingerprints.

We can take this analogy further. Suppose there are two suspects for a certain burglary. Police are familiar with the techniques of both suspects and are certain that one of the two committed the crime. There were some hairs left at the scene of the crime but, unfortunately for the police, not only do both suspects have the same color hair but the texture is almost identical. Analogously the average sentence length for Hamilton is practically the same as for Madison, and also the variability of sentence length (as measured by the standard deviation) is practically identical for the two authors. So these measures prove to be of no use in detecting authorship for *The Federalist*.

The detectives felt that there were subtle differences between the techniques of the two suspects but had difficulty in putting their fingers on specific things. One thing—there may have been other more subtle clues—that did differentiate the crimes of one suspect from those of the other was the fingerprints. Thus Mosteller and Wallace, as we shall see below, settled on the frequency of occurrence of certain selected words as their clue, these particular words because they had proven successful in differentiating between the known writings of Hamilton and Madison. Note that in this analogy the fingerprints correspond to the particular selected words, *not* to words in general. Words *not* selected correspond to clues such as the hair which did not distinguish between the two suspects, and the admission of inconsequential evidence into a trial will only succeed in clouding the issue and obscuring the important evidence contained in the fingerprints.

The analogy can take us one step further. If only one partly smudged fingerprint could be found, it is doubtful that a jury would be convinced on that evidence alone. Likewise if Mosteller and Wallace based their final classification on only one marker word or pair of marker words, such as "while-whilst" mentioned above, it is doubtful that many people would be convinced. But as another print is found, then another and another, the case tightens, so that with several prints found, smudged though they might be, the evidence points more and more to one of the suspects. Likewise with the *Federalist* problem, each distinctive word by itself is not convincing enough, but the combined evidence of all the selected words presents a case which should convince a very skeptical juror.

4. Sentences, Words and Letters

In most authorship studies the problem of deciding what variables to use as discriminators will be easier than it was in the *Federalist* study. Both Hamilton and Madison had developed a style of writing much admired in their period, rather in imitation of the *Spectator* papers. Douglass Adair (1944a) writes that "like Hamilton and Jay, Madison was a master of that Addisonian prose style which had all but standardized the tone of eighteenth century essays." Also one author might have tried to imitate the other, since they were writing over the same *nom de plume*. So not only were clues that distinguished Hamilton from Madison hard to find, but stylistic attributes which could be easily imitated were not to be trusted.

Sentence length is one attribute that could be easily imitated, and in this respect the two authors are practically identical. In fact any single attribute that can be recognized can be imitated, especially if a writer is given plenty of time. So it would be unwise to attribute authorship to a paper on evidence from one attribute alone.

In this *Federalist* study the researchers went to great lengths in trying to choose variables which were not subject to the whims of the writer. It is unlikely that a writer would be aware of small but consistent changes in the use of high frequency words: for example a change in the use of *an* from 6 times per thousand words to 4½, or a change in the use of *of* from 64½ times per thousand to 58, etc.

Moreover, the attribution of authorship to the disputed *Federalist* papers was based not on a single attribute or variable, but on many variables. Mosteller and Wallace believe that their authorship attributions are not vulnerable to the possibility that one author wrote but the other edited the disputed papers: only a virtual rewriting would provide all the necessary differences (see Section 16, part A). We know that *The Federalist* was written at great speed so the authors were forced to work independently of each other. Adair (1944b) believes that "the very speed with which *The Federalist* had to be written guaranteed that the writing of both men would reveal sharp differences which they had no time to level off into perfect editorial unity."

Another danger with sentence length as a discriminating variable is that the proportion of long and short sentences may differ from one essay to another depending, for example, on context. An essay on law or philosophy may have more long sentences than an essay on farming. In more technical language we would say that the *frequency distribution* or the *probability distribution* of sentence length might depend on context.

The notion of a distribution is important so we shall digress briefly to discuss it. Figure I displays three examples of *frequency distributions*. If we divide the numbers on the vertical axis by 1000, we have three *probability distributions*. For instance, Shakespeare's poetry graph would then give the probabilities attached to each word length for a word drawn at random from Shakespeare's poetry: there is a probability of about .05 (or equivalently, 50 chances in 1000) that this randomly selected word is one letter in length; a probability of .175 that it is two letters long; a probability of .225 that it is three letters long; etc. Since this distribution was obtained from counting the length of several hundred thousand words, it should come very close to his true distribution, his long-run distribution, for poetry. If we took a sample of 500 words from his poetry we would expect the proportions of words of the various lengths to be something like the true or long-run probabilities, but not necessarily very close.

Notice that Shakespeare's poetry distribution is different from his prose distribution. There seems to be a slight but systematic change in his vocabulary when he changes from poetry to prose. It is this kind of change that we were concerned about above when we suggested that the probability distribution of sentence length might depend on context. If it changes significantly when the author changes subject we might be led to believe that it is a different author writing. For this reason Mosteller and Wallace used only those words which were not contextual and which seemed to have consistent rates over a variety of subjects.

The frequency distribution of the length of words might be similarly subject to change in context and therefore suspect as a discriminator. And an author might change his word-length distribution when he imitates another author. Mendenhall (1887, 1901) named the graph of the word-length distribution the *characteristic curve of composition*. In his 1887 paper he pointed out, however, that Mr. Edward Atkinson, in two addresses on the same subject, made greater use of long words in his speech to the alumni of the Andover Theological Seminary than in his speech to a group of working men of Providence. (Some of these items were brought to my attention in an unpublished paper by Patricia Phillips, 1964.)

Again in his 1901 paper Mendenhall studied the characteristic curve, this time for Shakespeare and some of his contemporaries. Shakespeare's curves, differing only slightly between his prose and poetry, were different from the curves of Bacon, Ben Jonson, Beaumont and Fletcher, and others, but were remarkably similar to Marlowe's. But Mendenhall ended by throwing cold water on his conclusions in reporting a count made of a brochure written by Professor Shaler of Harvard University, entitled "Armada Days." Professor Shaler had endeavored to "compose in the spirit and style of the Elizabethan Age. Although too small to produce anything like a 'normal' curve it was counted and plotted, and the diagram indicated that Professor Shaler had not only caught the spirit of the literature of the time, but that he had also unconsciously adopted the mechanism which seems to characterize it. In the excess of the four-letter word and in other respects, the curve was rather decidedly Shakespearean, although it was written before its author knew anything of such an analysis as this" (Mendenhall, 1901, p. 105).

So while there is evidence that an author is consistent in his word lengths in his normal writings—Brinegar (1963) exhibits statistics to indicate that Mark Twain was similarly consistent—there is also evidence that a particular frequency curve can be simulated. One might then question Brinegar's conclusion —that the Quintus Curtius Snodgrass (QCS) letters were not the work of Mark Twain—since it was based on the fact that the frequency curves of Twain and QCS were dissimilar. Twain would seem to have had good reasons for not being identified as QCS; so might he not have affected a different style?

The *Federalist* problem is easier than Brinegar's problem and probably most authorship problems, in that Hamilton and Madison were the only two contenders. Everyone agrees that either Hamilton or Madison wrote the disputed papers; so if we become satisfied that a disputed paper is much more like Hamilton's writing than Madison's, we have resolved the controversy for that paper. But Brinegar had no list of authors which he was certain contained the name of the true author of the QCS letters. So even if he had found Mark Twain's frequency curve (or use of certain words) to be like QCS's, he could not have said that Twain was QCS with the same confidence that we could say that Hamilton wrote the paper in question.

Mosteller and Wallace in their book report briefly on their attempt to use the Mendenhall statistics to discriminate between the known papers. Unfortunately, the variation from paper to paper *within* an author's writings was greater than the difference *between* the two authors.

The reader can probably think of candidates other than sentence length and word length which might be useful discriminators. Section 15 suggests several.

5. Words as Discriminators

Joshua Whatmough (1957) has said that "languages obey laws as stable as any that have been found in human behavior, if not as those of astrophysics (which are not entirely stable)." Kepler's laws provide a mathematical model of the motion of a body, for example, a planet, in the solar system. They describe approximately, in mathematical terms, the path that a planet actually traces in space—approximately because no mathematical model can ever describe a physical process exactly. For instance Kepler's model assumes that a planet is subject only to the attractive force of the sun and neglects the effect of the other planets. So the planet's true path is not quite the ellipse that Kepler's model describes, but for many purposes an ellipse is an adequate description of the path.

A mathematical model enables us to assemble information from different sources to strengthen our inference. "It can be manipulated in the absence of the structure it represents . . . [and] consequences can sometimes be derived from the mathematics that are not obvious from inspection of apparatus or data" (Mosteller and Wallace, 1964, p. 22). The next few paragraphs describe two possible models, one called the Poisson model and the other the negative binomial model, which attempt to describe the process by which an author produces words. We shall see that the negative binomial model, the more complicated of the two, appears to be significantly better than the other in describing the process: that is to say, when the mathematics of the two models is manipulated, the distributions of word occurrences predicted by the negative binomial model are very close to the actual observed distributions.

A simplified model of the use of words by an author could be the following: an author uses each word in his vocabulary at a constant average rate. In addition, the occurrence of a particular word is independent of the previous occurrence of that same word. This is called a Poisson model after S. D. Poisson, a nineteenth century French mathematician.

For example, an author might use the word *on* at the average rate of 5 times per thousand words. This is not to say that *on* will appear 5 times in every block of 1000 words, but he tends to average 5 times per thousand in a very large text.

The independence assumption in the model implies that the occurrence (or non-occurrence) of a particular word gives absolutely no information about its next occurrence—it might come in the same sentence again, or it might not come for another thousand words. The only thing that governs the occurrence of this word is its overall rate.

Notice that this model contrasts with a second, more realistic model in which one occurrence of a certain word would bring two counter-pressures to bear on the next occurrence of that word. A writer's attempt to avoid repetition of a word isolates it and spaces its occurrences, thus making the rate constant. On the other hand, he may repeat a word several times in a brief passage for emphasis, parallelism, or clarity. This tendency to cluster can be built into the more complicated negative binomial model.

If the Poisson model is a reasonable approximation of reality we would expect that the frequency distribution of word occurrences—the proportion of times in passages of fixed length that a word occurs once, twice, etc.—could be

TABLE 1

OBSERVED AND FITTED POISSON AND NEGATIVE BINOMIAL
DISTRIBUTIONS FOR SELECTED WORDS—HAMILTON

| | *Occurrences:* | | | | | | | |
	0	1	2	3	4	5	6	*7 or more*
an								
obs.	77	89	46	21	9	4	1	
Poisson	71.6	88.6	54.9	22.7	7.0	1.7	.4	.1
N.B.	81.0	82.7	49.2	22.0	8.2	2.7	1.0	.2
any								
obs.	125	88	26	7	0	1		
Poisson	126.3	84.6	28.5	6.4	1.1	.2		
N.B.	same as Poisson							
may								
obs.	128	67	32	14	4	1	1	
Poisson	109.9	88.9	36.0	9.7	2.0	.3	.1	
N.B.	128.2	69.4	30.1	12.1	4.6	1.7	.6	.3
upon								
obs.	129	83	20	9	5	1		
Poisson	121.6	86.1	30.6	7.3	1.3	.2		
N.B.	131.1	77.1	27.9	8.2	2.1	.5	.1	
his								
obs.	192	18	17	7	3	2	4	3
Poisson	131.7	82.7	26.2	5.5	.9	.1		
N.B.	192.2	23.8	11.0	6.4	4.0	2.7	1.9	5.0

closely approximated by a Poisson distribution. Consider, for example, the word *any* as used by Hamilton. Mosteller and Wallace broke up a collection of *Federalist* papers into 247 blocks of approximately 200 words, and tabulated the frequency distribution of counts for each of many different words. The distributions for a few words are given for Hamilton in Table 1.

Notice that out of the 247 blocks, 125 had no occurrence of *any*, 88 had exactly 1 occurrence, 26 had exactly 2 occurrences, 7 had 3, no block had 4, 1 block had 5, and no block had more than 5. This gave a total of 166 occurrences in a total of 247 blocks for an average (or mean) number of occurrences in a 200-word block of 166/247, or .672 words per block.

In the specification of the Poisson model above we required two things: independence of one occurrence from the next, and a constant rate. For a particular rate this model gives rise to a particular Poisson distribution, and that distribution is completely specified by that rate. Thus we call the collection of all the Poisson distributions a "one-parameter" family since one number, or parameter (in this case the average rate), specifies which member of the family we are talking about. The Poisson distribution has a mathematical formula, in which this number (parameter) appears, giving the proportions of zero occurrences, one, two, etc., expected under the Poisson model. These proportions will of course depend on the parameter—the average rate. So now we can verify whether Hamilton used "any" as if he followed a Poisson model by comparing the observed frequencies with the frequencies expected from the Poisson distribution which has the same average rate. This process of calculating the observed rate (in our example, .672), then calculating the expected frequencies given by the Poisson distribution having that same rate, is termed "fitting" a Poisson distribution to the data. Recall that the Poisson is a *one*-parameter family: just *one* number specifies a particular Poisson distribution, so that the "fitting" involves the equating of only *one* number (parameter), in this case the mean rate. (Shortly we shall discuss a *two*-parameter family of distributions. The fitting of one of these distributions to some data involves the equating of *two* parameters.)

Returning to the Poisson and our example, we calculate the expected frequencies given by the Poisson distribution having a mean rate .672. The results are in Table 1 under the observed counts for *any*. Out of a total of 247 blocks we would expect 126.3 blocks to have zero occurrences, 84.6 to have one occurrence, etc. It can be seen that the Poisson distribution fits the data very well. (Even if our observed data had come from an artificial process which is truly Poisson, it is quite likely that the observed and expected frequencies would differ by more than they do in this example.) So we can say that in the writings of Hamilton that were studied the word *any* occurs as if it obeyed the Poisson model.

This is gratifying, but a glance at Table 1 will show that not all words are as Poissonian as *any*. The observed frequencies for *may* and *his* differ drastically from those expected from Poisson processes having the same mean rates of occurrence. What we need is another family of distributions which are like the Poisson—because, after all, the Poisson fits *any* very well—but which allows a little more flexibility, or gives us a wider choice of distributions. We say we need a "richer" family. Notice that the tails of the observed distributions (we call the "tail" that part furthest from the mean) are fatter than the tails of the fitted Poisson distributions. This might arise from the word's being repeated for emphasis, and this repetition means that the occurrences of the word are not independent as required by the conditions of the Poisson model.

One way, therefore, in which we would like this new family to be flexible is that it allow for fatter tails. A family which does this is the negative binomial family. The negative binomial model allows the author to vary slightly, from one block of writing to another, his rate of usage of a word. More formally, we suppose that before writing a block the writer chooses a rate for that block and then behaves according to the Poisson theory for that rate and that block. For the next block he chooses another rate and so on. If he chooses his rates randomly in a certain reasonable way, he ends up with a negative binomial model.

But this is no exception to the rule that you never get something for nothing. The negative binomial is a two-parameter family, so we pay for the increased flexibility by having to fit a distribution with two parameters and more generally by having to work with a much more complicated mathematical formula. The first parameter is again the average rate. The second measures how fat the tail of the negative binomial distribution is, compared with the tail of the corresponding Poisson distribution. This parameter is termed the *non-Poissonness parameter*.

Table 1 shows clearly how the negative binomial distributions come very close to the observed data even in the tails.

6. Pools of Words

Initially every word in an author's vocabulary is a candidate for selection as a discriminator. Fortunately many can be rejected immediately. Mosteller and Wallace wanted variables that depended as nearly as possible only on the author and not, for example, on the subject under discussion. For instance the word *war* would likely occur frequently in an essay on the armed forces but seldom in any essay on voting. Such contextual words are probably bad discriminators, and therefore unlikely survivors of a screening test, and they are potentially dangerous if they survive the screening test. That they proved to be bad discriminators and dangerous will be demonstrated later. One source of words, found in an independent study to be largely non-contextual, was a list of "function" words made up by Miller, Newman, and Friedman (1958). Their list gives frequency counts, for 363 words, based on 35,000 words of text taken from the King James Bible, William James, and *The Atlantic* (1957). "Function" words are "filler" words as opposed to "content" words. They would include Russell's "logical" words which are associated with the structure of a sentence so that they may not be changed without changing the structure. It is likely that these words will discriminate, but certain other function words, such as personal pronouns and auxiliary verbs, might be dangerous. The 70 most frequent words of the Miller-Newman-Friedman list became one pool of words along with a random set of 20 from their low-frequency words. The 70 high-frequency function words are listed in Table 2, and the random sample of 20 appear in Table 3.

TABLE 2

FUNCTION WORDS AND THEIR CODE NUMBERS

1 a	11 been	21 had	31 its	41 one	51 that	61 was
2 all	12 but	22 has	32 may	42 only	52 the	62 were
3 also	13 by	23 have	33 more	43 or	53 their	63 what
4 an	14 can	24 her	34 must	44 our	54 then	64 when
5 and	15 do	25 his	35 my	45 shall	55 there	65 which
6 any	16 down	26 if	36 no	46 should	56 thing	66 who
7 are	17 even	27 in	37 not	47 so	57 this	67 will
8 as	18 every	28 into	38 now	48 some	58 to	68 with
9 at	19 for	29 is	39 of	49 such	59 up	69 would
10 be	20 from	30 it	40 on	50 than	60 upon	70 your

TABLE 3

ADDITIONAL WORDS AND THEIR CODE NUMBERS

*71 affect	*83 contribute	*94 innovation	106 still
*72 again	*84 defensive	*95 join	107 those
*73 although	*85 destruction	*96 language	*108 throughout
74 among	86 did	97 most	109 under
75 another	*87 direction	98 nor	*110 vigor
76 because	*88 disgracing	*99 offensive	*111 violate
77 between	89 either	100 often	*112 violence
78 both	*90 enough	*101 pass	*113 voice
*79 city	(and in	102 perhaps	114 where
	sample of 20)		
*80 commonly	*91 fortune	*103 rapid	115 whether
*81 consequently	*92 function	104 same	*116 while
*82 considerable	93 himself	105 second	*117 whilst

A second source of words—chronologically the first—was a screening study. Some known papers of both authors were studied in waves, and words were scored by the number of papers in which they appeared. There were 18 Hamilton and 14 Madison papers. Words like *enough,* which appeared in 14 Hamilton papers and no Madison papers, *commonly* (9, 1), *whilst* (0, 13), and *language* (2, 10), were retained. About 3000 different words started but only 28 survived. The survivors, which by the nature of their selection were low-frequency words, appear in Table 3 with an asterisk beside them.

A number of papers for both authors had been typed on to punched cards, then stored on magnetic tape of a high-speed computer. These papers, 18 by Hamilton and 19 by Madison totalling 70,000 words, provided a concordance of 6700 different words. Those uncontextual words which displayed an uneven split between the two authors were retained. The 48 survivors, which are not listed here, brought the total number of words in the pool to 165.

7. The Main Study: Bayes' Theorem

Statistical inference is the process of drawing conclusions about unknown quantities from propositions which are supposed to be true. For example, knowledge of the characteristics of a sample allows inferences to be made about the population from which the sample was drawn. Or, information about the features of typical Hamilton and Madison essays, together with the corresponding information about a particular disputed essay, allows conclusions to be drawn about the authorship of the disputed essay.

What is the mechanism by which statistical inferences are made? How is evidence combined to change a prior belief into a conclusion or posterior belief? In the main study these questions are answered by Bayes' Theorem. Degrees of belief in propositions such as "Hamilton wrote paper No. 52" are expressed by numerical probabilities, and Bayes' Theorem adjusts the probabilities for the evidence in hand.

Consider the problem of assessing the evidence regarding the authorship of a single disputed paper. With the help of a simple form of Bayes' Theorem we first assess the evidence of a single word, then use the theorem again to combine the evidence from several words.

Suppose that for the word *also* Hamilton's true average rate is known to be .25 words per thousand and Madison's .50, and that both authors follow the Poisson model. Then for a 2000-word paper the probabilities that each author used *also* 0 times through 6 times are given in Table 4. If Hamilton wrote the paper there is a probability of .607 that *also* did not occur at all, a probability of .303 that *also* appeared once, and so on. But if Madison wrote a 2000-word paper there is a probability of only .368 that *also* will not occur at all, and an equal probability that it will occur once, and so on.

Suppose now that *also* appears four times in our disputed paper. Table 4

TABLE 4

POISSON PROBABILITIES FOR A WORD FROM A 2000-
WORD PAPER: HAMILTON'S RATE BEING .25 AND
MADISON'S .50

Frequency	Hamilton	Madison
0	.607	.368
1	.303	.368
2	.0758	.184
3	.0126	.0613
4	.00158	.0153
5	.000158	.00307
6	.0000132	.000511

shows that the probability of *also's* occurring four times in a Hamilton paper is .00158, but in a Madison paper it is .0153, or about ten times as much. A betting man would interpret these numbers as betting odds: if he had only a very vague opinion on the dispute prior to his looking at the evidence from *also*, he now would bet .0153 to .00158, or approximately 10 to 1, that Madison wrote the paper. Thus the data provide evidence in the form of *odds*, or, as the ratio .00158/.0153 is called, in the form of a *likelihood ratio*.

If, however, our betting friend had previously read of this dispute and had formed an opinion on the matter, how should he change his belief in the light of this new, independent information provided by the data? Suppose he could express this prior opinion in the form of odds, say 1 to 3 that Hamilton wrote it. These are his *initial* or *prior* odds. What we want are his *posterior odds* which combine his prior information with that obtained from the data. Appealing to Bayes' Theorem we find that his posterior odds are simply his prior odds multiplied by the likelihood ratio: 1/3 multiplied by 1/10 giving 1/30; that is, his odds now are 1 to 30 that Hamilton wrote the paper.

Notice that a different friend who had prior odds of 2 to 1 in favor of Hamilton now has odds of 1 to 5 in favor of Hamilton, or 5 to 1 in favor of Madison. So the data strengthened the opinion of our first friend, whereas it altered the opinion of our second friend.

8. Combining the Evidence of Several Words

Our first friend now has odds of 1 to 30 that Hamilton wrote the paper in question. Suppose that both authors' use of the word *an* is likewise well

FIGURE II

BLOCK DIAGRAM SHOWING PROGRESSION FROM PRIOR ODDS TO POSTERIOR ODDS

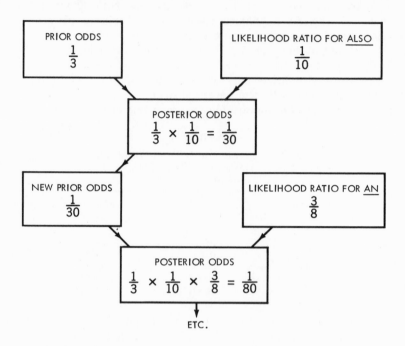

ETC.

represented by independent Poissons, and that for *an* Hamilton is known to have an average rate of 6.00 words per thousand and Madison 4.50. Suppose further that *an* appeared 7 times in the disputed paper in question. From tables of the Poisson distribution we find that the likelihood ratio for this outcome is .0437/.117 or approximately 3/8. Before looking at this new information our friend's *new prior odds* are 1 to 30 (see Figure II). Bayes' Theorem once again tells us how to combine this new evidence and we see that his latest posterior odds are 1/10 times 3/8 or 1/80. So his new odds are 1 to 80 that Hamilton wrote the paper. By repeating this procedure we can combine the evidence of all the words.

Notice that his latest odds, 1/80, factor into the product of the initial odds 1/3 and the combined likelihood ratio of the two words, 3/80. In other words, the assessment of the initial odds can be separated from the statistical analysis needed to determine the likelihood ratio. Because different people have different prior odds, the statistical analysis in this study concentrates on the likelihood ratio term.

9. Criterion for Selecting Final Words

We now have a guide for selecting final words from the three pools described earlier: we select only those whose discriminating power is high, that is, whose likelihood ratio is very different from unity. We saw that the likelihood ratio for 4 occurrences of *also* was approximately 1/10, and for 7 occurrences of *an* it was 3/8. The product of these was 3/80. The addition of a few more good words will build up this combined likelihood ratio to such an extent that it will swamp any reasonable initial odds. In contrast, consider the word *because*. It can never hope to contribute much to the combined likelihood ratio since its individual likelihood ratios for 0, 1, 2, and 3 occurrences are respectively 1.11, 1.00, .90, and .81, so that no matter how many times *because* appears in a disputed paper it will be of very little help in classifying the paper one way or the other. Such words may be discarded since they add significantly to the complexity and cost of the enterprise, yet provide little discriminating power.

What has been described in the last few sections is a simplification of a real-life analysis. Many of the assumptions made are too strong and a real analysis must make allowances for the deviations. For instance, the rates for *also* and *an* were assumed known. If we know the true rates for all words, picking out the best discriminating words does not introduce any bias. But when the rates have to be estimated, the selection and regression effect arises because some of the selected variables are not as good at discriminating as they appear to be. . . .

In the actual problem, of course, the true rates were unknown and had to be estimated from some rather vague prior information and a moderate amount of sample data. The prior information comes from a few existing studies of word rates, and the sample data comes from 94,000 words of Hamilton's text and 114,000 words of Madison's. This is a large amount of text, but for the purpose of estimating rates it is surprisingly little. . . .

Here, for a second time, Bayes' Theorem gets into the act. The prior information about word rates is summarized into a probability distribution—the *prior* distribution of the rates. The information contained in the known works of the two authors concerning the rates of various words is summarized into likelihood ratio terms. Then Bayes' Theorem combines the prior distribution and the likelihood ratio terms into the *posterior* distributions of the rates. Unfortunately these posterior distributions turn out to be very complex and unmanageable even with the help of high-speed computers; so we have to be satisfied with new, improved point estimates derived from the posterior distributions. For example, the rates with which Hamilton and Madison used *also,* as estimated from the known works, are respectively .28 and .71 occurrences per thousand words of text. But the new, improved estimates, which take the prior information into account, are .31 and .67. . . .

Allowances can be made for each of the troubles and the combined allowance will provide an adjustment to the final odds. If the final adjusted odds still favor one author strongly, the conclusions remain strong.

* * *

12. The Selection of Final Words for the Main Study

The 165 words that entered the main study (see Section 6) were reduced to 30 words, classed into 5 groups, before the disputed papers were analyzed. The

30 were selected because they were apparently good at discriminating between the known works of Hamilton and Madison. Since the prior distributions on the parameters had already taken care of the regression effect, the words could be selected for retention by whatever methods were available so long as they were independent of the disputed papers.

The words were grouped according to categories of use and source that were felt to bear on contextuality, so that the performance of different types of words (function words, adjectives and adverbs, etc.) could be evaluated.

Only 45 of the 165 words showed any appreciable discriminating ability as measured by the disparity between the estimated rates for the two authors. A few more of the 45 words were discarded because Madison's rates in *The*

TABLE 6

FINAL WORDS AND WORD GROUPS: ESTIMATED NEGATIVE BI-
NOMIAL PARAMETERS BASED ON UNDERLYING CONSTANTS SET 31

Code No.	Word	μ_H	μ_M
B3A			
60	upon	3.24	.23
B3B			
3	also	.32	.67
4	an	5.95	4.58
13	by	7.32	11.43
39	of	64.51	57.89
40	on	3.38	7.75
55	there	3.20	1.33
57	this	7.77	6.00
58	to	40.79	35.21
B3G			
73	although	.06	.17
78	both	.52	1.04
90	enough	.25	.10
116	while	.21	.07
117	whilst	.08	.42
123	always	.58	.20
160	though	.91	.51
B3E			
80	commonly	.17	.05
81	consequently	.10	.42
82	considerable(ly)	.37	.17
119	according	.17	.54
124	apt	.27	.08
B3Z			
87	direction	.17	.08
94	innovation(s)	.06	.15
96	language	.08	.18
110	vigor(ous)	.18	.08
143	kind	.69	.17
146	matter(s)	.36	.09
151	particularly	.15	.37
153	probability	.27	.09
165	work(s)	.13	.27

Federalist for these words were different from his rates in some of his papers exterior to *The Federalist*. Finally, personal pronouns and auxiliary verbs were eliminated since they were probably contextual. This left 30 words in five groups called B3A, B3B, B3G, B3E and B3Z. Table 6 displays these words, together with their estimated rates for the negative binomial analysis based on set 31 of the underlying constants.

13. Results from the Main Study

It is more convenient to report the results not in odds (for example 150 to 1 in favor of Madison) but in *log odds,* which are simply the natural logarithms of the odds: odds of 150 to 1 for Hamilton become log odds of 5, while odds of 150 to 1 for Madison (or 1 to 150 for Hamilton) become log odds of −5. Table 7 converts odds to log odds.

TABLE 7
Conversion from Log Odds to Odds

Log Odds	Odds
0	1 to 1
2	7 to 1
5	150 to 1
10	22,000 to 1
15	3,300,000 to 1
20	480,000,000 to 1

Most of the following account of the results is taken from Section 6 of Mosteller and Wallace (1963). The account presents only a sprinkling of the results from the 113 papers and the numerous prior distributions. Recall that each prior is characterized by a set of underlying constants.

A. Checking the method

In Table 8 we present the total log odds for 11 papers by each author for three sets of underlying constants. For each author, we give his first 8 papers from *The Federalist,* and 3 papers exterior to *The Federalist*. Papers exterior to *The Federalist* are displayed to give a notion of what happens when the method is applied to a larger variety of writings, and these particular papers are chosen because they contain the one paper most poorly identified by the log odds for each author. Looking first at the negative binomial distribution for set 22 of underlying constants, we see that every Hamilton paper has positive, and every Madison paper negative, log odds. Since these papers contain the worst outcomes, the entire 48 Hamilton and 50 Madison papers have been assigned log odds in the proper direction by this distribution and set of underlying constants.

Looking now at the Poisson model we see that paper No. 134 has log odds pointing mildly in the wrong direction. As a whole, though, the log odds for the three sets of underlying constants point consistently and forcibly in the right direction. Just how strong these odds are can be better appreciated by consult-

TABLE 8

TOTAL NATURAL LOG ODDS FOR PAPERS OF KNOWN AUTHORSHIP, 11 BY
HAMILTON AND 11 BY MADISON; TOTAL FOR 30 FINAL WORDS; 3 SETS OF
UNDERLYING CONSTANTS, 2 DISTRIBUTIONS

Paper number	Paper length (thousands)	Hamilton Negative binomial Set of underlying constants			Poisson Set of underlying constants		
		22	33	21	22	33	21
1	1.6	13.9	11.9	15.7	22.9	20.5	25.7
6	1.9	16.8	15.7	17.7	27.4	25.5	29.2
7	2.2	16.6	14.3	17.5	36.6	33.7	39.0
8	2.0	14.0	13.0	16.5	20.7	18.3	23.8
9	1.6	11.6	10.2	12.6	16.7	15.3	18.0
11	2.5	16.3	15.4	17.2	30.7	28.7	32.2
12	2.1	13.0	11.3	14.1	25.2	23.0	27.3
13	1.0	7.8	7.3	8.0	12.0	11.4	12.4
111	2.9	11.9	12.0	10.9	27.0	26.6	26.5
112	2.5	9.3	7.5	10.0	23.4	21.1	25.3
113*	1.2	3.0	2.2	4.0	2.8	2.0	3.8

Madison

10	3.0	−17.5	−17.2	−18.2	−30.5	−29.5	−31.0
14	2.1	−20.0	−18.5	−22.6	−28.7	−26.5	−31.5
37	2.7	−20.2	−18.9	−23.4	−32.7	−30.4	−35.8
38	3.3	−16.5	−15.3	−19.6	−25.4	−22.9	−29.2
39	2.6	−24.6	−23.6	−26.6	−45.1	−42.5	−47.7
40	2.7	−19.2	−18.5	−20.9	−30.1	−28.6	−31.7
41	3.5	−15.6	−15.1	−17.5	−27.6	−26.5	−28.7
42	2.7	−11.9	−11.1	−13.4	−21.1	−20.0	−22.6
132	2.7	−20.3	−19.3	−22.9	−31.9	−29.3	−35.1
133	2.5	−13.3	−11.7	−15.6	−20.4	−18.7	−22.7
134 *	1.7	−0.8	−0.1	−1.9	0.9	1.4	0.1

* The paper by each author that is most poorly identified.

ing the brief conversion table, Table 7.

Since we know who wrote each of these papers, the log odds in Table 8 offer a check on the method. Essentially, each paper has been treated as if it were a disputed paper, and the log odds computed. And the evidence is that the method works well.

B. *Effects of prior distributions and of data distributions*

Beyond this, we can examine the effect of varying the underlying constants. Visual inspection will assure the reader that the variation in log odds from one set to another is modest compared to the variation from one paper to another. But the change in log odds from the negative binomial distribution to the Poisson is huge.

C. *Who wrote the disputed papers?*

Next, the *piéce de resistance,* Table 9, presents total log odds for the joint and disputed papers. Attending to the 12 disputed papers, we see that every set of underlying constants gives odds for all papers strongly in favor of Madison.

TABLE 9

TOTAL NATURAL LOG ODDS FOR THE PAPERS OF JOINT AND DISPUTED AUTHORSHIP. TOTAL FOR THE 30 FINAL WORDS. 3 SETS OF UNDERLYING CONSTANTS, 2 DISTRIBUTIONS

Paper number	Paper length (thousands)	Negative binomial Set of underlying constants			Poisson Set of underlying constants		
		22	33	21	22	33	21
Joint							
18	2.1	−11.0	−10.8	−11.4	−20.1	−19.5	−20.5
19	2.0	−12.1	−12.0	−12.2	−18.6	−18.4	−18.3
20	1.4	−4.6	−5.0	−3.6	−7.0	−7.6	−6.0
Disputed							
49	1.6	−13.2	−12.2	−14.6	−18.1	−17.1	−19.3
50	1.1	−14.3	−13.7	−15.1	−18.2	−17.5	−18.9
51	1.9	−21.9	−20.9	−24.0	−33.4	−31.3	−35.9
52	1.8	−16.0	−15.7	−16.5	−23.1	−22.5	−23.4
53	2.2	−15.8	−15.0	−17.4	−22.0	−20.7	−23.6
54	2.0	−14.3	−13.6	−15.7	−22.9	−21.7	−24.3
55	2.0	−5.8	−5.5	−6.2	−7.1	−6.6	−7.6
56	1.6	−8.7	−8.2	−9.6	−10.6	−10.0	−11.4
57	2.2	−16.7	−15.7	−18.4	−26.1	−24.2	−28.6
58	2.1	−18.0	−17.1	−19.4	−26.3	−25.1	−27.4
62	2.4	−16.5	−16.0	−17.3	−26.9	−25.6	−28.0
63	3.0	−18.5	−17.7	−19.6	−32.2	−31.2	−32.9

The weakest of these are papers 55 and 56, and the lowest odds for No. 55 are 240 to 1 (log odds of −5.5) in favor of Madison, not absolutely overwhelming, if one had strong initial odds in favor of Hamilton. Essentially, No. 55 does not have its share of marker words, no matter who wrote the paper, and the high-frequency words produced no information.

D. The behavior of word groups

To show how consistently the different word groups behave and to what extent each contributes to the total, we present the log odds by word groups for set 22 in Table 10.

All groups look quite consistent, considering their differing strengths—a weak set must have negative log odds occasionally. This general consistency is a further sign of good discrimination.

The set B3B is stronger than B3A (*upon*), which in turn looks nearly as strong as the other three groups put together. Recall that B3B contains the high-frequency function words: *to, this, there, on, of, by, an, also.* So in the end the high-frequency words outshone all marker words. While this does not prove that cleverness in selecting variables fails to pay, it does show that routine can pay.

E. Summing up

In summary the following points are clear:

1. Madison is the principal author. These data make it possible to say with better foundation than ever before that Madison is the author of the twelve

TABLE 10

Log Odds by Word Groups for Set 22 of Underlying Constants

Paper number	Negative binomial					Poisson				
					Word group					
	B3A	B3B	B3G	B3E	B3Z	B3A	B3B	B3G	B3E	B3Z

Hamilton

1	4.7	2.0	1.9	3.1	2.3	11.6	2.8	2.2	4.0	2.3
6	2.5	9.2	1.7	.3	3.2	5.2	14.3	2.1	.7	5.2
7	6.4	4.6	−.2	2.6	3.3	23.3	6.9	−.3	3.0	3.8
8	1.2	3.0	4.9	2.2	2.8	2.1	5.1	7.4	2.4	3.6
9	2.9	3.5	2.6	1.0	1.6	6.0	5.4	3.0	1.2	1.2

Madison

10	−6.5	−6.8	−.9	−2.1	−1.2	−9.1	−14.1	−1.9	−3.5	−1.8
14	−5.0	−7.9	−1.4	−1.9	−3.8	−6.6	−12.3	−1.5	−2.5	−5.8
37	−3.2	−9.2	−3.1	−1.3	−3.4	−5.5	−16.1	−3.4	−1.2	−6.5
38	.3	−4.6	−6.4	−3.0	−2.9	.8	−8.4	−10.1	−3.4	−4.4
39	−5.8	−11.7	−.8	−2.7	−3.6	−7.9	−21.1	−1.4	−10.0	−4.7

Joint

18	−2.1	−8.1	1.3	−1.0	−1.1	−3.6	−14.4	1.9	−2.7	−1.3
19	−4.8	−7.6	−.9	1.4	−.2	−6.2	−13.0	−.9	1.7	−.2
20	−.9	−7.6	.8	1.0	2.0	−1.6	−9.9	.7	1.1	2.6

Disputed

49	−4.0	−5.5	−.8	−1.3	−1.6	−4.9	−9.4	−.9	−1.1	−1.9
50	−2.9	−9.0	−1.1	.2	−1.5	−3.4	−12.2	−1.2	.3	−1.8
51	−4.6	−9.3	−3.8	−1.9	−2.4	−5.8	−16.4	−5.4	−2.6	−3.3
52	−4.4	−10.2	.2	.2	−1.8	−5.6	−15.9	.1	.4	−2.2
53	−5.1	−6.4	−4.6	1.4	−1.2	−6.6	−10.1	−5.4	1.7	−1.7
54	−.2	−8.6	−1.3	−2.3	−1.9	−.6	−15.2	−1.7	−3.1	−2.3
55	−4.8	−.1	.8	−.7	−1.0	−6.2	1.1	.6	−1.4	−1.3
56	−3.9	−2.4	−3.1	1.0	−.4	−4.8	−3.1	−3.5	1.2	−.4
57	−5.1	−5.9	−2.6	−.9	−2.1	−6.7	−10.9	−5.4	−.8	−2.4
58	−4.9	−8.6	−1.3	−1.3	−2.0	−6.4	−15.1	−1.5	−1.0	−2.4
62	−5.5	−8.1	−.2	−1.5	−1.2	−7.3	−14.1	−.9	−3.2	−1.5
63	−6.6	−8.4	−1.5	.2	−2.3	−9.2	−19.1	−1.6	.6	−2.9

disputed papers. Weakest support is given for No. 55. Support for Nos. 62 and 63, most in doubt by current historians, is tremendous.

2. While the choice of prior distributions matters, it does not matter very much so long as they represent reasonably well the prior information which has come from a fair body of data.

3. The choice of data distribution is important. We notice that in the change from the negative binomial to the Poisson model the log odds are roughly doubled.

4. Routine pays off. We were surprised that in the end, it was the utterly mundane high-frequency function words that did the best job. Though we love

them for their lack of contextuality, their final strength was as unexpected as it was welcome. The result is reminiscent of a hard fact perennially being discovered in the social sciences. For the forecasting of a great many facets of a man's behavior, it is hard to beat the usual tired old socio-economic variables and the standard personal background data.

5. The method performed satisfactorily on both *Federalist* material and on essays exterior to *The Federalist*. Such consistency of the method is encouraging in considering the method for other studies and in assessing the generality of the present inference. The disputed papers could be as contextually disparate as the Pacificus or Helvidius papers for all we know.

6. Two of the joint papers are mainly the work of Madison, the third presents a puzzle. The joint papers Nos. 18 and 19 seem mainly to be the work of Madison. No. 20 presents an interesting new problem: can we sort out the contribution of a possible, unwitting, third party, Sir William Temple, so as to assess properly Hamilton's share?

F. Adjustments to the log odds

The log odds presented depend on many assumptions and approximations. When these are taken into consideration the log odds are decreased by about 25 per cent. Even after this deflation the odds cannot be taken entirely at face value. The possibility of what we call outrageous events, which we regard as outside the framework of the model, must be allowed for. For instance, the possibility of blunders or errors in calculation is always present.

To the statistician who asks how we can get odds of even thousands to one when we have only about 100 papers altogether, the answer is that the distribution theory, which is rather well founded on data, supplies some of this strength, but the major part comes from the independent, fairly modest contributions from many variables.

14. The Weight-Rate Study

The weight-rate study is based on the method of discrimination devised by R. A. Fisher (1936). The Bayesian analysis described in the preceding sections takes its name from the theorem published by the Reverend Thomas Bayes in 1763, but it is only within the last decade that statisticians have begun to think seriously of using Bayesian analysis directly in practical problems. So it is the Fisherian method, and not the Bayesian method, that has been given the title "traditional," or "classical."

One essential difference between a Bayesian analysis and the more traditional method is that the former attempts to assess prior information and then incorporate it into the model, while the latter does not. Critics of the traditional method feel that prior information should be used; "critics of the Bayesian plan usually agree that the inclusion of the information would be an asset, but they regard the proper assessment of this information as a hopeless task" (Mosteller and Wallace, 1964, p. 2). The researchers in this study found it to be, if not a hopeless task, at least a most formidable one. An idea of the relative sizes of a Bayesian and a classical analysis is gained from the fact that in their book describing these studies, Mosteller and Wallace devoted 154 pages to the main Bayesian study but only 15 pages to the classical weight-rate study. This comparison exaggerates the difference a little since much of the mathematics of the latter was omitted while the former was given a full mathematical treatment. The reason for this is twofold: the mathematics of the classical analysis is, for the most part, fairly straightforward while the Bayesian analysis is mathematically complex; secondly, unlike the classical methods, which have been well studied in the literature, Bayesian methods have been applied to actual life-sized problems on very few occasions. This *Federalist* project is one of the first published large-scale statistical studies that involve substantial analyses of data by Bayesian methods.

Nevertheless, a great deal more effort did go into the main study than into the weight-rate study. The Bayesian analysis also included some prior information that was neglected in the classical analysis; so it should not be surprising that the main study produced the more definitive conclusions concerning the authorship of the disputed *Federalist* papers. The researchers might have profitably done a larger job on the weight-rate analysis, but instead they put their extra effort into the Bayesian study.

In the main study the prior distributions on the word rates took account of the selection and regression effect. In the weight-rate study this effect is taken care of by the use of a calibrating set of papers, a procedure which is simple but which is expensive in terms of the amount of data available.

The plan is to construct a linear discriminant function, which is simply a weighted sum of the rates for words. The weights are chosen so that a paper which has typical Madisonian word rates gets a low (actually negative) score, while a Hamiltonian paper produces a high score. Building such a function is just like devising a psychological test to separate high-school students into two groups: one that would make better lawyers and another that would produce better doctors. The first group would probably do better on verbal questions and the second might excel on scientific questions. So if we gave verbal questions a negative weight (negative score) and scientific questions a positive weight, then added the scores on all the questions, prospective doctors would tend to have a positive total score while budding lawyers would tend to have a negative total score. In this way the test separates the students into lawyers (negative) and doctors (positive). Notice that to get a negative total score is not to do poorly in the test. We could just as easily have given the verbal questions a positive weight and scientific questions a negative weight, and then the doctors would score negatively.

The discriminant function to separate Hamilton from Madison is constructed using data from about half of the known papers for each author. These papers are called the *screening set,* and on the basis of the information contained in this set about word rates of the two authors, certain words are selected and weighted for use as discriminators. Once the words are chosen and weighted, the function is tried out on the other half of the material of known authorships, the *calibrating set.* This provides a test of the chosen function and also calibrates the weighted sum on material uncontaminated by the effect of selection, thereby taking account of the regression effect. The calibration gives us an idea how (known) Madison papers and (known) Hamilton papers score on this test function. Now when we apply the function to a disputed paper we can compare the new score with Madison's scores and Hamilton's scores, and decide who wrote the disputed paper.

The conclusions that may be drawn from this study are very similar to those of the main study: paper No. 55 is again the least Madisonian of the twelve. Its score is so close to the midpoint of the average score for the known Hamilton papers and the average score for the known Madison papers that we cannot make a definite classification one way or the other, although it is slightly on the Hamilton side. The rest of the disputed papers, except possibly No. 56, are undoubtedly Madison's.

For a more detailed description of the weight-rate study and of the two small-scale studies the reader is referred to Mosteller and Wallace (1964).

Perhaps it should be pointed out that these results are certainly not independent of the results of the main study; so the fact that this study has agreed with the main study, particularly insofar as it has judged No. 55 to be the least Madisonian of the twelve disputed papers, should not be construed as additional evidence for or against any of the papers. Fifteen of the twenty words used in the weight-rate study were also included in the thirty final words of the main study; so we would have been surprised had the conclusions reached from the two studies been very different.

15. Other Possible Discriminating Variables

The major effort in this attempt to solve the authorship problem went into the study of the differential use of individual words by Hamilton and Madison. The authors realize that the choice of words as the variables of interest can be easily ridiculed as linguistically and stylistically naive and uninteresting, but their defense against this criticism is strong: the use of words was feasible and highly effective for this discrimination problem, whereas other variables that came to mind appeared to have little or no discriminating value. But this is not to say that these other variables might not prove effective discriminators in other studies.

One of the variables that were tried and found to be useless for the *Federalist* study was sentence length. Another was word length. These two were discussed in an earlier section. Other variables that Mosteller and Wallace studied briefly were: (1) pairs of words, e.g., *effect* and *affect;* (2) use of comparative and superlative forms; (3) words with an emotional tone; (4) methods of enumeration; (5) conditional clauses and phrases; (6) the fraction of new material in the paper; (7) the uses of a word; and (8) the length of papers.

The reader can no doubt think of many other aspects of language and style that might be good discriminators. Large areas in the field of literary statistics remain to be explored in an effort to discover new measures of an author's style, measures that are stable within an author's writing but which differ from author to author. Plath (1961) gives a survey of the field of mathematical linguistics up to 1960. As he points out, "Investigations on the syntactive level, including the statistical study of patterns of coordination and subordination and of the types and depths of 'nesting' in sentences, may possibly provide interesting new insights into certain aspects of literary style which have yet to be handled quantitatively." The "depth" of a sentence, a concept due to Yngve (1961), can be measured from the phrase-structure tree of the sentence. Consider, for example, the sentence "The dog chased the cat." In the phrase-structure tree (Figure V) this sentence breaks into two parts, the noun phrase (NP) and the verb phrase (VP). The verb phrase splits into verb (V) and another noun phrase. Then finally both noun phrases split into an article (A) and a noun (N). The depth of each word is calculated as follows: at each node (junction), number the branches 0, 1, etc. from right to left. To compute the depth of a word, add together the numbers written along all branches leading to that word. The depth of the sentence is defined to be the depth of the deepest word. Thus the depth of our sample sentence is 2, since the deepest word is the initial *the* (see Figure III).

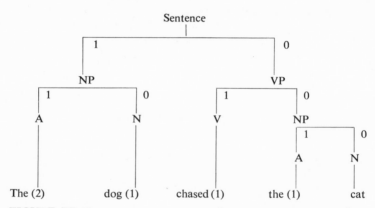

FIGURE III. Phrase structure tree (depths in parentheses).

Depth is one measure of how complex a sentence is, and could well be a variable that has a stable distribution within the writings of one author. In Yngve's model of sentence construction, the depth of the sentence is related to the amount of temporary memory storage that the listener needs in order to comprehend the whole sentence.

In the quotation above, Plath stated that concepts such as depth had not been treated quantitatively, but recently he has indicated (by personal communication) that he now has some data concerning the depth of the writings of some Russian authors. This is a by-product of work that he and others at Harvard have been doing on the machine translation of Russian into English. In the procedure that they use for translation, the amount of temporary computer memory storage (the depth of the predictive pool) required for the translation of a sentence is directly related to Yngve's depth. This amount of temporary storage is recorded for each sentence. Plath has noticed that the late writings of one Russian author were deeper in this technical sense than his early works. So it seems quite possible that the notion of depth could discriminate between two different authors.

Yet we should not be too optimistic about this or any other new variable until we have tried it out. After all, the depth of a sentence will be related to, and perhaps, highly correlated with, the length of the sentence. So measuring depth may be just an expensive way of measuring length, and sentence length did not discriminate between Hamilton and Madison at all. Until we try it out we can only speculate whether sentence depth will do any better.

When it becomes possible to perform syntactic analyses of English sentences on a practical scale—high-speed computers still take several minutes to analyze a complex Russian sentence—linguists will be able to study variables such as depth and use of words much more closely than they can now. But even when these studies become practicable, such simple characteristics of style as the frequency with which certain words are used may turn out to be just as good for use in solving authorship problems as the more complicated characteristics. And a study which uses simpler variables will likely be more economical: the problems of identification and counting will be fewer, and the use of a high-speed computer may be unnecessary.

The mere fact that a study has been carried out on a high-speed computer makes it no better a study than one requiring only desk calculators or even only paper and pencil. The worth of a study depends entirely on the data and ideas that go into it. In the *Federalist* project a computer helped in counting words in some papers, and performed most of the calculations for the main study. About half of the *Federalist* papers were typed on to punched cards, and the machine tabulated the total frequency of every word separately for each paper. Others of the papers were typed on to roll paper and counted by hand. At that time, counting by hand was cheaper than counting by computer, even though time on the computer was paid for at educational rates. However, the output of the computer was much better looking, came in multiple copies, and was easier to read and work with. In addition, the texts and counts of the papers that had been prepared for the machine were stored on magnetic tape; so the data was available for further computations. (A detailed description of the problems experienced in the counting and reconciliation of the counts made by hand and by computer is given in Mosteller and Wallace (1962).) But while the counting could have all been done by hand, the computations for the main study could not have been done in years without the computer.

To the man with an authorship problem Mosteller and Wallace offer some advice on getting started, and give a few suggestions for a small-scale attack which they believe might be widely effective. This is in Section 8.2 of the book. They include a table which should prove useful in picking out good words: the table lists the 165 words used in the study, along with the rates with which they are used by a number of authors. If our man with the authorship problem computes the rates from the known works of his competing authors, and compares them with the rates in the table, he should find a number of words that distinguish between the several authors.

16. Summary

This section quotes or paraphrases some of the conclusions reached by Mosteller and Wallace as reported in their book (1964) and *J.A.S.A.* paper

(1963). It is in two parts: concerning the authorship of the disputed *Federalist* papers, and concerning authorship studies in general.

A. *The authorship of the disputed Federalist papers*

1. Our data independently supplement those of the historian. On the basis of our data alone, Madison is extremely likely, in the sense of degree of belief, to have written the disputed *Federalists,* with the possible exception of No. 55, where our evidence is weak: suitable deflated odds are 80 to 1 for Madison. No. 56, next weakest, is a strong 800 to 1 for Madison. The data are strong for all the rest, including the two papers historians feel weakest about, Nos. 62 and 63.

2. Among the joint papers, Nos. 18 and 19 look as if Madison wrote the lion's share. No. 20 requires a more subtle analysis of its possible contamination by third parties before Hamilton's share can be assessed.

3. We give little credence to the possibility that Hamilton wrote but Madison thoroughly edited the disputed papers, so that they finally looked Madisonian, rather than like a mixture of styles or a parody. The reader must appreciate that such a performance is not so trivial as changing two or three words. Even among the 30 words of the main study, Madison would have to make between 50 and 100 changes in each paper, to say nothing of the further changes these would induce. Since Madison could not know that we planned to use these 30 words, the total revision required, so that an analysis would show clear Madison rates, would have had to be on a scale even more vast.

4. Choice of prior distribution mattered little compared to other sources of variation.

5. Changes in the data distribution had enormous effects on the output, but both Poisson and negative binomial performed better in the disputed papers than the theory of these models forecast.

6. The main study shows stable discrimination for essays on various subjects, the writing spread over a quarter of a century.

7. The weight-rate, the robust Bayes, and the three-category studies give good support for the main study from the point of view of reasonableness of results. (Only the weight-rate and the main studies have been described in this paper.) Paper No. 55 is on Hamilton's side in these studies, although within easy sampling error of the border, and No. 56 is similarly inconclusive, although it is on Madison's side. These studies cannot be taken utterly at face value because of certain technical weaknesses. For this reason, their results do not take precedence over Results 1, derived from the main study.

B. *Authorship problems*

1. The function words of the language are a fertile source of discriminators, and luckily those of high frequency are strong. Our table of rates (discussed in Section 15) should help an investigator form a pattern of rates for a new author and speed him in solving easy authorship problems.

2. Context is a source of risk. We need variables that depend on authors and nothing else. Some function words come close to this ideal, but most other words do not. So many words and other variables depend on topics that their exploration for differences between authors would be a needless waste of funds, and worse, even screening them invites trouble, because some may accidentally

survive. Grouping words or other variables in ways that relate not only to objective properties but also to the investigator's intuitive assessment of their trustworthiness offers a start on screening for context. Those groups which are not discarded out of hand can be studied for their sensitivity to sources of writing. If the investigator has a variety of kinds of writing for each author, he can study variability in rates and have a basis for eliminating or lightly weighting variables or groups that show substantial heterogeneity among the kinds. If the bulk of the members of a group have excessive variability, he should consider guilt by association for the rest. No variable is entirely safe. He should investigate.

3. Hamilton's and Madison's styles are unusually similar; new problems, with two authors as candidates, should be easier than distinguishing between Hamilton and Madison. On the other hand, investigators with problems of selecting one author from many authors or of grouping a collection of essays into clumps by similar authors need all the help they can get.

References

Adair, Douglass (1944a, 1944b). "The Authorship of the Disputed *Federalist* Papers," *The William and Mary Quarterly*, Vol. I, No. 2, pp. 97–122; *ibid.*, Vol. I, No. 3, pp. 235–264.

Brinegar, Claude (1963). "Mark Twain and the Quintus Curtius Snodgrass Letters: A Statistical Test of Authorship," *Journal of the American Statistical Association*, 58:85–96.

Cooke, Jacob E., ed. (1961). *The Federalist*. Cleveland: The World Publishing Company.

Fisher, R. A. (1936). "The Use of Multiple Measurments in Taxonomic Problems," *Annals of Eugenics*, Vol. 7, Pt. 2, pp. 179–188.

Mendenhall, T. C. (1887). "The Characteristic Curves of Composition," *Science*, Vol. 9, No. 214, supplement, pp. 237–249.

———— (1901). "A Mechanical Solution of a Literary Problem," *Popular Science Monthly*, Vol. 60, No. 2, pp. 97–105.

Miller, G. A., E. B. Newman, and E. A. Friedman (1958). "Length Frequency Statistics of Written English," *Information and Control*, 1:370–389.

Mosteller, F., and D. I. Wallace (1962). "Notes on an Authorship Problem," in *Proceedings of a Harvard Symposium on Digital Computers and Their Applications*, pp. 163–197, Cambridge, Mass.: Harvard University Press.

———— (1963). "Inference in an Authorship Problem," *Journal of the American Statistical Association*, 58:275–309.

———— (1964). *Inference and Disputed Authorship: The Federalist*. Reading, Mass.: Addison-Wesley Publishing Company.

Phillips, Patricia (1964). "A Statistical Approach to Some Literary Problems." Unpublished dissertation submitted to the University of Wales towards a Master of Science degree.

Plath, Warren (1961). "Mathematical Linguistics," in Christine Mohrmann, Alf Sommerfelt, and Joshua Whatmough, eds., *Trends in European and American Linguistics, 1930–1960*. Utrecht: Spectrum Publishers.

Whatmough, Joshua (1957). "Mathematical Linguistics," in *Proceedings of the VIIIth International Congress of Linguists*. Oslo University Press.

Williams, C. B. (1939). "A Note on the Statistical Analysis of Sentence-Length as a Criterion of Literary Style," *Biometrika*, 31:356–361.

Yngve, V. (1961). "A Model and an Hypothesis for Language Structure," *Proceedings of the American Philosophical Society*, 104:444–466.

Yule, G. Udny (1938). "On Sentence-Length as a Statistical Characteristic of Style in Prose: With Application to Two Cases of Disputed Authorship," *Biometrika*, 30:363–390.

———— (1944). *The Statistical Study of Literary Vocabulary*. Cambridge University Press.

PART III

Legislative and Judicial Behavior

ROLL-CALL VOTING ANALYSIS is the most common type of statistical research among "new" political historians today. Utilizing techniques of quantitative measurement developed in the past twenty-five years by sociologists, psychologists, and political scientists, the behavioralists are scrutinizing decision-making in the nation's many collegial bodies—national and state legislatures;[1] party and constitutional conventions;[2] the United States Supreme Court and state high courts;[3] and the United Nations General Assembly and Security Council.[4] The objective is to find simplifying variables in the many

[1] Representative works in American history are Duncan MacRae, Jr., *Dimensions of Congressional Voting: A Statistical Study of the House of Representatives in the Eighty-First Congress* (Berkeley, 1958); Leroy Rieselbach, *The Roots of Isolationism: Congressional Voting and Presidential Leadership in Foreign Policy* (Indianapolis, 1966); James S. Young, *The Washington Community, 1800–1828* (New York, 1966), esp. Part 3; Joel H. Silbey, *The Shrine of Party: Congressional Voting Behavior, 1841–1852* (Pittsburgh, 1967); Thomas B. Alexander, *Sectional Stress and Party Strength: A Study of Roll-Call Voting Patterns in the United States House of Representatives, 1836–1860* (Nashville, 1967); Charles H. Gray, "A Scale Analysis of the Voting Records of Senators Kennedy, Johnson and Goldwater, 1957–1960," *American Political Science Review*, LIX (Sept., 1965), 615–21; Gerald Marwell, "Party, Region and the Dimensions of Conflict in the House of Representatives, 1949–1954," *ibid.*, LXI (June, 1967), 380–99; Thomas A. Flinn and Harold L. Wolman, "Constituency and Roll-Call Voting: The Case of Southern Democratic Congressmen," *Midwest Journal of Political Science*, X (May, 1966), 192–99; H. Douglas Price, "Are Southern Democrats Different? An Application of Scale Analysis to Senate Voting Patterns," in Nelson W. Polsby, *et al.* (eds.), *Politics and Social Life: An Introduction to Political Behavior* (Boston, 1963), 740–56; Samuel C. Patterson, "Legislative Leadership and Political Ideology," *Public Opinion Quarterly*, XXVII (Fall, 1963), 399–410. For a state legislative scaling study by a political scientist, see Jack E. Holmes, *Politics in New Mexico* (Albuquerque, 1967), 275–84.

[2] Frank Munger and James Blackhurst, "Factionalism in the National Convention, 1940–1964: An Analysis of Ideological Consistency in State Delegation Voting," *Journal of Politics*, XXVII (May, 1965), 375–94; S. Sidney Ulmer, "Sub-group Formation in the Constitutional Convention," *Midwest Journal of Political Science*, X (Aug., 1966), 288–303.

[3] Major cumulative scaling studies of the U.S. Supreme Court are: Glendon A. Schubert, *The Judicial Mind: The Attitudes and Ideologies of Supreme Court Justices, 1946–1963* (Evanston, Ill., 1965); Schubert, *Quantitative Analysis of Judicial Behavior* (Glencoe, 1959), 269–376; Schubert, *Judicial Behavior: A Reader in Theory and Research* (Chicago, 1964), esp. 548–87; Schubert (ed.), *Judicial Decision-Making* (Glencoe, 1963), esp. 55–108; John R. Schmidhauser, *Constitutional Law in the Political Process* (Chicago, 1963), esp. 486–505; Schmidhauser, "Judicial Behavior and the Sectional Crisis of 1837–1860," *Journal of Politics*, XXIII (Nov., 1961), 615–40; Harold J. Spaeth, "An Analysis of Judicial Attitudes in the Labor Relations Decisions of the Warren Court," *ibid.*, XXV (May, 1963), 290–311; Spaeth, "Judicial Power as a Variable Motivating Supreme Court Behavior," *Midwest Journal of Political Science*, VI (Feb., 1962), 54–82; S. Sidney Ulmer, "Toward a Theory of Sub-Group Formation in the United States Supreme Court," *Journal of Politics*, XXVII (Feb., 1965), 133–52; and the articles by Ulmer cited in footnote 12 below. For a state court study see Ulmer, "The Political Party Variable in the Michigan Supreme Court," *Journal of Public Law*, XI (1962), 352–70.

[4] Hayward R. Alker, Jr., and Bruce M. Russett, *World Politics in the General Assembly* (New Haven, 1965); B. M. Russett, "Discovering Voting Groups in the United Nations," *American Political Science Review*, LX (June, 1966), 327–39. James E. Todd, "An Analysis of Security Council Voting Behavior," *Western Political Quarterly*, XXII (Mar., 1969), 61–78.

votes or decisions, as, for example, the key issues that divide a given body or bloc and factional sub-groups within the body.

The Guttman attitudinal scale has become the standard tool in the mathematical approach to legislative behavior analysis. Developed by social psychologists and refined by political scientists, Guttman scaling measures patterns of individual behavior within a group context on a given issue.[5] Basically, roll-call analysis provides a means to transpose a qualitative set of attitudes—i.e., "liberal"-"conservative"—into a quantitative value and then to test whether such a division of attitudes in fact exists. The underlying assumption is that decision-makers—lawmakers or justices—vote in a generally consistent manner dictated by their ideological posture. When they do not, it is scored as an "error" and too many errors vitiate a scale. Of course, scaling is needless on votes that are unanimous or strictly partisan. Standard computer programs are now available to ease the laborious calculations of scale coefficients.[6]

Scaling is not only computerized but has also reached the predictive stage. In 1968 two political scientists developed the first computer-simulation model of Congressional roll-call voting, based upon twenty-one bills in the 88th Congress dealing with the expansion of the Federal role in government.[7] The model predicted the actual voting pattern with a high degree of accuracy (89 per cent for individuals, 82 and 85 per cent respectively for Republican- and Democrat-sponsored bills).

In the field of jurisprudence, the transition from art to science took shape in the early 1950's among scholars who believed that legal studies should be concerned more with judicial behavior than with legal precedent or the values and personalities of judges.[8] "The long-standing ties that bind the study of law to the philosophical and historical tradition remain," said one advocate in 1963, "but they are being augmented by new bridges across interdisciplinary chasms." [9] The bridge-building reflects a shift not in content but in ethos. The practitioners of *jurimetrics,* as the math-oriented study of law is known, have adopted the experimental method of the laboratory. The goal is that of any

[5] The best methodological sources are Lee F. Anderson, *et al., Legislative Roll-Call Analysis* (Evanston, Ill., 1966); Samuel C. Patterson, *Notes on Legislative Behavior Research* (Iowa City, 1965); George M. Belknap, "A Method for Analyzing Legislative Behavior," *Midwest Journal of Political Science,* II (Nov., 1958), 377–402; Louis Guttman, "The Basis for Scalogram Analysis," in Samuel A. Stouffer, *et al., Measurement and Prediction* (Princeton, 1950); Duncan MacRae, Jr., "A Method for Identifying Issues and Factions from Legislative Votes," *American Political Science Review,* LIX (Dec., 1965), 909–26.

[6] Duncan MacRae, Jr., "IBM 1401 Q-Matrix and Editing Programs for Legislative Votes," *Behavioral Science,* X (July, 1965), 324–25, and "Cluster Analysis of Congressional Votes with the BC TRY System," *Western Political Quarterly,* XIX (Dec., 1966), 631–38.

[7] Michael J. Shapiro, "The House and the Federal Role: A Computer Simulation of Roll-Call Voting," *American Political Science Review,* LXII (June, 1968), 494–517; and Cleo H. Cherryholmes and Michael J. Shapiro, *Representatives and Roll-Calls: A Computer Simulation of Voting in the Eighty-Eighth Congress* (Indianapolis, 1969).

[8] See the items cited in footnote 3 above, especially Glendon A. Schubert, *Judicial Behavior: A Reader in Theory and Research* (Chicago, 1964), and specifically Lee Loevinger, "Jurimetrics," 72–76, and the articles by Samuel Kreslov, Fred Kort, Reed C. Lawler, S. Sidney Ulmer, Stuart S. Nagel, Joseph Tanenhaus, and Glendon Schubert in chap. V.

[9] Schubert, "Prediction from a Psychometric Model," in Schubert (ed.), *Judicial Behavior,* 549.

applied science worth its salt—predictive power. "The ultimate test of our theory and methods lies in our ability correctly to predict judicial decisions," Glendon A. Schubert has insisted. Schubert then laid on the line his methodological beliefs by predicting the outcome of the 1962 Supreme Court term on the basis of a detailed factor analysis of the 1961 Court.[10] But the prediction experiment met with only indifferent success, partly because of the seating of a new justice, Arthur Goldberg, and partly because the Court unexpectedly swung toward a nearly unanimous liberal consensus.[11] S. Sidney Ulmer, another pioneer jurimetrician, enjoyed much greater predictive success by limiting his scope to civil-liberty cases. Using the Guttman scaling method, Ulmer correctly predicted the relative ranking of the justices for seven consecutive Court terms (1955–1961) on the basis of their previous year's voting behavior, a random chance prediction with odds much less than one in a hundred.[12] "The evidence," Ulmer concluded, "is that the Guttman scalogram techniques can be used successfully to predict the relative rank of each justice in terms of attitude toward civil liberty deprivations."[13] The judicial behavioralists, if nothing else, are a confident company of scientists.

Political scientists continue to dominate the behavioral field, but in recent years historians have made major inroads. Since William O. Aydelotte's scalogram analysis of voting patterns in the British House of Commons appeared as an article in 1963, at least two dozen historians have completed scaling studies of the American Congress or state legislatures. Most noteworthy are the full-length accounts of Congressional voting behavior in the nineteenth and early twentieth centuries by Joel H. Silbey, Thomas B. Alexander, Glenn M. Linden, John K. Folmar, George R. Nielson, Jerome M. Clubb, and Charles M. Dollar;[14] and the ambitious state studies of the Illinois legislature in the

[10] *Ibid.*, 548–87.
[11] *Ibid.*, 579–87.
[12] See S. Sidney Ulmer, "Supreme Court Behavior and Civil Rights," *Western Political Quarterly*, XIII (June, 1960), 288–311; "The Analysis of Behavior Patterns in the United States Supreme Court," *Journal of Politics*, XXII (Nov., 1960), 629–53; "Scaling Judicial Cases: A Methodological Note," *American Behavioral Scientist*, IV (Apr., 1961), 31–34; "A Note on Attitudinal Consistency in the United States Supreme Court," *Indian Journal of Political Science*, XXII (Oct.–Dec., 1961), 195–215; "Discriminant Analyses and an Error Criterion," in Schubert, *Judicial Behavior*, 506–17.
[13] Ulmer, "Supreme Court Behavior and Civil Rights," 311. Several jurimetricians, however, have raised serious questions about the utility of the Guttman cumulative scaling model of judicial behavior. See Joseph Tanenhaus, "The Cumulative Scaling of Judicial Decisions," *Harvard Law Review*, LXXIX (June, 1966), 1583–94; and Ira H. Carmen, "One Civil Libertarian Among Many: The Case of Mr. Justice Goldberg," *Michigan Law Review*, LXV (Dec., 1966), 301–36, especially Appendix A, 331–34.
[14] The Silbey and Alexander books are cited in footnote 1 above; Glenn M. Linden, "Congressmen, 'Radicalism' and Economic Issues, 1861 to 1873," (Ph.D. dissertation, University of Washington, 1963) [three published excerpts are in *Journal of Southern History*, XXXII (May, 1966), 189–99; *Civil War History*, XIII (Mar., 1967), 51–65; XIV (Sept., 1968), 240–49]; John K. Folmar, "The Erosion of Republican Support for Congressional Reconstruction in the House of Representatives, 1871–1877; A Roll-Call Analysis" (Ph.D. dissertation, University of Alabama, 1968); George R. Nielson, "The Indispensible Institution: The Congressional Party During the Era of Good Feelings" (Ph.D. dissertation, University of Iowa, 1968); Jerome M. Clubb, "Congressional Opponents of Reform, 1901–1913" (Ph.D. dissertation, University of Washington, 1963); Charles M. Dollar, "The Senate Progressive Movement, 1921–1933" (Ph.D. dissertation, University of Kentucky, 1966).

Jacksonian era by Rodney O. Davis, banking legislation in ante-bellum Iowa by
Erling A. Erickson, and Wisconsin progressivism by Kenneth C. Acrea, Jr.[15]
These are augmented by article-length efforts of John L. Shover on the AAA of
the 1930's, Gerald Wolff on the Homestead Act of 1854, Edward L. Gambill
and Allan G. Bogue on the Civil War Senate, David P. Thelen on the origins of
Progressivism, Jerome Clubb and Howard W. Allen on the Senate in the
Progressive era, and John R. Moore on the southern coalition in the Senate
during the Second World War.[16] At least another two dozen similar scalogram
projects in American history are in progress on such diverse topics as Harry
Truman's Senatorial voting record, Senatorial partisanship in the 77th and 78th
Congresses, the Civil War Congresses, Congressional progressives in the 1920's,
the House of Representatives from 1863 to 1875, tariff legislation in the Senate
from 1909 to 1934, and two massive projects to measure party cohesiveness and
partisan conflict, in the years 1789–1861, and in the twentieth century.[17] With
all the Congressional roll-calls available from the Inter-University Consortium
in machine-readable form, only the premium on computer proficiency stands
between the behavioral researchers and significant results. Perhaps we are closer
than many think to realizing Lee Benson's 1984 prognosis of a truly scientific
historiography in American political history.

[15] Rodney O. Davis, "Illinois Legislators and Jacksonian Democracy, 1834–1841"
(Ph.D. dissertation, University of Iowa, 1966); Erling A. Erickson, "Banks and
Politics Before the Civil War: The Case of Iowa, 1836–1865" (Ph.D. dissertation,
University of Iowa, 1967); Kenneth C. Acrea, Jr., "Wisconsin Progressivism: Legis-
lative Response to Social Change, 1891 to 1909" (Ph.D. dissertation, University of
Wisconsin, 1968).
[16] John L. Shover, "Populism in the Nineteen-Thirties: The Battle for the AAA,"
Agricultural History, XXXIX (Jan., 1965), 17–24; Gerald Wolff, "The Slavocracy
and the Homestead Problem of 1854," *ibid.,* XL (Apr., 1966), 101–11; Edward L.
Gambill, "Who Were the Senate Radicals," *Civil War History,* XI (Sept., 1965),
237–44; Allan G. Bogue, "Bloc and Party in the Civil War Senate, 1861–1863," *ibid.,*
XIII (Sept., 1967), 221–41; David P. Thelen, "Social Tensions and the Origins of
Progressivism," *American Historical Review,* LVI (Sept., 1969), 323–41; Jerome M.
Clubb and Howard W. Allen, "Party Loyalty in the Progressive Years: The Senate,
1909–1915," *Journal of Politics,* XXIX (Aug., 1967), 567–84; Howard W. Allen,
"Geography and Politics: Voting on Reform Issues in the United States Senate,
1911–1916," *Journal of Southern History,* XXVII (May, 1961), 216–28; John R.
Moore, "The Conservative Coalition in the United States Senate, 1942–1945,"
ibid., XXXIII (Aug., 1967), 368–76.
[17] For descriptions of some of the projects in progress, see *Historical Methods
Newsletter,* II (Dec., 1968), 16–20, (June, 1969), 21–26, and (Sept., 1969), 21–25;
Computers and the Humanities, III (Nov., 1968), 114–17 (May, 1969), 317–18.

9

ALLAN G. BOGUE

Bloc and Party in the
United States Senate: 1861–1863

In this essay, a part of his forthcoming full-scale study of the Civil War Congresses, Allan G. Bogue illustrates the use of various statistical techniques—index numbers, cluster bloc, and Guttman scalogram—to measure Senatorial political, factional, and sectional alignments in the first Civil War Congress. Republican Radicals and Moderates are clearly identified on the basis of 368 recorded roll calls and the issues pinpointed on which they divided. "This particular Senate," Bogue concludes, "was hardly a classic illustration of the two party system at work." Factionalism rather than partisanship characterized the dominant Republicans as well as the powerless Democrats, although the Democrats held a slight edge in party cohesion. Even more impressive is the complexity of the issues and variety of responses. The Civil War Senate functioned within a political system in which matters of party, faction, section, and constituency interacted with personal ideals to create a variegated pattern. The application of quantitative techniques may clarify fewer old problems than open up new ones. Why, for example, were New England Moderates more cohesive than Radical Republicans, or Democrats more united than Republicans?

Allan G. Bogue, "Bloc and Party in the United States Senate: 1861–1863," *Civil War History*, XIII (Sept., 1967), 221–241. Reprinted, with slight revision, with permission of the author and publisher.

AS HE FOUGHT FOR ELECTION in 1854, James Harlan explained how he would conduct himself if elected to the Senate of the United States: ". . . in all *Constitutional* questions . . . I would expect to be guided in my action by the decisions of the Supreme Court and the well-settled principles of Constitutional Law—in all questions of *Legislative Expediency,* by the views and wishes of the Legislature and people of Iowa—and in all questions of *Conscience* by the Bible." [1] To understand court, constituency and holy writ was to understand the legislative behavior of Senator Harlan, or so he said. The fact is that it is rather difficult to understand Senator Harlan at times in these terms or by any other simple formula and this is also true of his colleagues in the Senate. Led, some time ago, to the Thirty-seventh or first Civil War Congress by my interest in the great economic legislation of that body, I soon found myself trying to understand the major forces that were reflected in the voting of the congressmen. This paper is an outgrowth of that rather frustrating endeavor—a case study of general voting behavior in the Senate during the second session, the longest and most important of the three legislative sessions of the Thirty-seventh Congress.

The historian who seeks for understanding can, of course, usually find other historians willing to guide him. We are all familiar with the interpretation which pictures a beleagured Lincoln, struggling during the Civil War to maintain his leadership against the determined onslaughts of the Radical faction that dominated his party and the Congress. This organizational theme has been rewarding and, indeed, the authors of some of the historical classics of the Civil War have used it. But recently David Donald has argued that historians have overstressed the difference between Radical and Moderate Republicans and suggested that the importance of party bonds should be emphasized instead.[2] T. Harry Williams, however, continues to believe that the distinction is an important one.[3] If we exclude the executive branch from our discussion and focus on the congressional aspects of the Radical-Moderate controversy it is clear that the problem can be stated more precisely. Did party or did factional groups within the Republican party more significantly influence the voting of Republican senators and representatives during the Civil War years? More recently still, Professor Donald has suggested that the congressional district played a major part in determining the votes of members of the House of Representatives when they were considering reconstruction legislation.[4] Thus in a sense he joined Senator Harlan in emphasizing the importance of constituency in helping to determine congressional voting patterns—a factor which may have accounted for the presence of Moderate and Radical factions among the Republicans, if indeed they did exist.

We remember also that Frederick Jackson Turner had something to say about the relation of constituency to legislative behavior. "A study of votes in the federal House and Senate from the beginning of our national history reveals

[1] Johnson Brigham, *James Harlan* (Iowa City, 1913), p. 87.
[2] David Donald, "Devils Facing Zionwards" in Grady McWhiney (ed.), *Grant, Lee, Lincoln and the Radicals: Essays on Civil War Leadership* (Evanston, 1964), pp. 72–91.
[3] T. Harry Williams, *"Lincoln and the Radicals: An Essay in Civil War History and Historiography,"* ibid., pp. 92–117.
[4] David Donald, *The Politics of Reconstruction: 1863–1867* (Baton Rouge, 1965).

the fact," wrote Turner, "that party voting has more often broken down than maintained itself on fundamental issues; that when these votes are mapped or tabulated . . . a persistent sectional pattern emerges." [5] The Thirty-seventh was of course the first congress of the Civil War and unusual in that most of the representatives of one great section were missing. Although the empty seats render this and the next congress unique in the history of national legislative behavior, Earle Ross and others have maintained that sectionalism, particularly that of East against West, continued to influence the actions of legislators during the Civil War.[6] In the *Congressional Globe* we can easily find proud affirmations of loyalty to constituency, frank declarations of sectional interest, and the appeals of Republican leaders to their colleagues to shun factionalism and cleave to party. But oratorical flourishes can be deceiving; in the end it was the votes of the senators that counted. And what do the votes tell us of geographical bloc, of party faction and of the bonds of party?

When I began this research I selected for analysis all of the substantive votes which were concerned with slavery and confiscation measures, both broadly defined; the tariff and the internal revenue tax bills; legal tenders; the agricultural college bill; the homestead law; the department of agriculture bill; the Pacific railroad act; northern civil liberties and the general conduct of the war, as well as a few important procedural votes that seemed related to such measures. Most of these votes fell into one of three broad categories. Eighty-seven dealt with the confiscation of rebel property or the status of slavery; fifty-one emerged from the debate on the Internal Revenue Act of 1862; and the debates on other major economic legislation of national interest produced thirty-five votes. During the course of the research I broadened the scope of the study to include 368 roll calls of this session, excluding only those that related to appointments.[7] These votes are the major source for the scholar seeking evidence of patterns in the voting of the thirty-one Republicans, eleven Democrats, five Border Unionists and one northern Unionist who sat in the Senate during most of the second session of the Thirty-seventh Congress.[8]

In the following pages I have used a few simple devices that describe legislative behavior in quantitative terms.[9] An index number of cohesion shows

[5] Frederick Jackson Turner, "The Significance of the Section in American History," *Wisconsin Magazine of History,* VIII (1925), 270.

[6] Earle D. Ross, "Northern Sectionalism in the Civil War Era," *Iowa Journal of History and Politics,* XXX (1932), 455–512; Jacque Voegeli, "The Northwest and the Race Issue, 1861–1862," *Mississippi Valley Historical Review,* L (1963), 235–51.

[7] This included votes in the Senate proper, in committee of the whole and in executive session. Tallies used are those recorded in the Senate *Journals,* supplemented occasionally by those in the *Congressional Globe.*

[8] In the Border Unionist category I included five senators of Whig origins from the Border States. I have used the term Northern Unionist to describe Senator Joseph A. Wright of Indiana. A prominent Democrat prior to the Civil War, Wright was selected by Governor Morton to replace Senator Bright and abjured party politics for the duration of the war. See his letter to the Indiana State Union Convention, *National Intelligencer,* June 23, 1862. However, Kenneth Stampp lists him as a War Democrat in *Indiana Politics During the Civil War* (Indianapolis, 1949), p. 237.

[9] These are described in more detail in Lee F. Anderson *et al., Legislative Roll-Call Analysis* (Evanston, 1966) and in Samuel C. Patterson, *Notes on Legislative Behavior Research* (Iowa City, 1965). An index of cohesion may be calculated by subtracting the per cent yea of a party's vote (if the smaller) from the per cent nay (if the larger) or vice versa. When 83 per cent of Republicans voted yea and 17 per cent voted nay on a bill the index number of cohesion is $83 - 17 = 66$. If 75 per cent

the extent to which a political party or group is united in a particular roll call on a scale running from one to one hundred. Similarly, an index number of agreement or likeness measures the degree to which the members of two parties or groups vote alike in a division, and the obverse of such a number can be called an index of disagreement. Thus, if Democrats and Republicans agreed on a particular vote to the amount of 40 per cent of the maximum agreement which would result when all Republicans and all Democrats voted alike, the index of likeness would be forty and the index of disagreement would be sixty.

Other techniques help us to identify groups of legislators that act in concert, or relative differences in attitude among legislators. If we record the number of times that each legislator votes with every other legislator we can find groups of like-minded individuals by fitting the pair-agreement scores into a matrix with the highest agreements in the upper left corner. Legislative groups derived by this process are often called cluster blocs. The Guttman scale deals with association among the senators in a different way. Used originally in psychological testing, Guttman scaling in legislative research is performed in effect by isolating a roll call in which a small group of lawmakers (a) opposed a large majority of the chamber; then searching the votes for another one in which members of that group were again found in agreement but were joined by additional legislators, group (b); then scanning the roll calls for another in which the first two groups (a & b) voted together but were joined by an additional group (c) and so on. Because they could find few who shared their opinion in the original roll call selected, the members of (a) are assumed to have held an extreme or radical position on the matter at issue. The order in which additional legislators were added to the members of group (a) serves the analyst as a ranking of their extremeness (their scale types) on the issues under consideration in the roll calls. The items in a scale matrix of this type are not added in chronological sequence, let it be noted.

The cluster bloc technique may not reveal the shifting patterns of agreement among legislators over time and gives no hint of the relative extremeness in attitude of group members in comparison with the positions taken by the members of other groups. It may require the researcher to make arbitrary decisions concerning the outer limits of the groups or clusters. The scalogram masks but does not completely destroy temporal relationships, does not isolate the members of self-conscious groups, and discards roll calls that will not scale. There also is involved in scaling the assumption that legislators will vote for measures which in their minds represent only half a loaf because half is, after all, better than none. Not all representatives and senators are so logical; some, in frustration, vote against bills because they deem them too weak and there are instances of such behavior in the Thirty-seventh Congress. But in general the principle holds. Indeed, John Sherman stated it neatly on one occasion in this Congress, "It is always better, in a legislative body . . . to do the best you can. It is a principle by which I have always been governed. . . ." [10] Neither the index number approach, the cluster bloc technique, nor the Guttman scale is

of the Democrats and 50 per cent of the Republicans voted yea in a roll call the index of likeness or agreement is $100 - (75 - 50) = 75$.
[10] *Congressional Globe,* 37 Cong., 2 sess., p. 2999.

perfect or all revealing but used together these methods can reveal a great deal about legislative behavior.

We should, of course, avoid imposing unreasonable standards in evaluating the behavior of political groups or individual legislators. To expect voting blocs or factions to maintain the same membership over long periods of time is unrealistic. Wayne Morse, no matter what he would like to think, is hardly a unique creation of this harried age. It is similarly unrealistic to suppose that all legislators will maintain exactly the same ideological position over a period of two or more sessions, or even during one session. It is unreasonable to assume that group feeling must be reflected by agreement across a number of different kinds of issues or that all members of a group should reflect the same intensity of attitude concerning even those issues on which they most strongly agree. The crucial defection or the betrayal of friends provides us with the high drama of political history but such acts must be viewed in the general perspective of voting frequencies and it is with these that we are mainly concerned here.

"We" [of the Northwest], said Senator Grimes, "are the only portion of all the loyal States that feel the effect of this war oppressively. . . . Whilst men who own the railroads in the Northwest are making fortunes out of this war by the transportation of our produce, we are receiving nothing in fact from it." [11] Later in the session, Ten Eyck of New Jersey spoke for the East when he asked: "Now what inducement is there for a Senator from an Atlantic State to vote an appropriation of large sums of money, even in the shape of a loan, to construct a variety of [rail] roads for the advantage of the western States?" [12] These were the oratorical flourishes of eastern and western sectionalism. We can quite easily design a procedure that will reveal the presence of sectional determinants in voting divisions.

In examining the roll calls of the Senate, I assumed that a disagreement index of forty or more represented substantial disagreement between eastern and western Republicans. Western Republican senators included all of those from Ohio or states to the west and eastern Republicans, those members of the party from the states east of Ohio. The states represented by Democrats were few and widely spread; I did not, therefore, use Democratic votes in my search for roll calls that revealed the sectionalism of East and West. By these definitions there was substantial sectional disagreement among eastern and western Republican senators in forty-six of the 368 votes of the second session.[13]

The sectionalism of East and West appeared most frequently in voting on economic measures of national significance.[14] In the original selection of eighty-seven roll calls relating to slavery and confiscation and eighty-six that were linked to major economic legislation only 7 per cent of the slavery and confiscation roll calls showed substantial sectional disagreement between the eastern and western Republicans, in comparison to 25 per cent of the votes on economic policy. Consideration of all 368 roll calls does not change the generalization. In

[11] *Ibid.*, p. 114.
[12] *Ibid.*, p. 2805.
[13] A list of these roll calls is available on request from the author.
[14] Of course, much of the legislation, passed or proposed, concerning the South was "economic" in both its short-run and long-run implications, but for the sake of convenience I will distinguish between legislation on slavery and confiscation (or southern legislation) in contrast to national economic legislation.

voting on slavery and confiscation measures, the Republican senators divided on the basis of East and West in seven substantive votes and in three procedural votes. The same pattern appeared in two roll calls concerning the possibility of expelling Lazarus Powell, senator from Kentucky. Among the votes on economic legislation we find a division between eastern and western Republicans on eight roll calls during the debates on the internal revenue bill; on eight votes in the discussion of the land grant college bill; on three concerning greenback issues; on three during the Pacific railroad debates; and two divisions concerning the tariff. Sectionalism appeared also in three votes relating to the judiciary, three concerning appropriations for the armed forces, and in five roll calls on miscellaneous matters.

Western Republicans ranged themselves against the eastern members of their party most sharply when they voted on the land grant college bill. Eight of the nine roll calls, generated in discussion of this bill, showed substantial disagreement between East and West; the index of disagreement between the sections ranged from seventy-one to eighty-five in the roll calls on the major amendments. In the end both Wisconsin senators and one Republican senator from Iowa, Indiana, and Kansas actually voted against the bill. They were joined by Senator Wright, the northern Unionist from Indiana, whose Republican colleague supported the most severe amendments proposed by the westerners but did not vote on the bill itself. No other economic measure inspired such consistent and strong antagonism between eastern and western Republicans in this session.

Indices of likeness or disagreement do not reveal whether the representatives of a section were more united in their approach to certain categories of legislation than were the legislators of another section. But this was indeed the case among the Republican senators of the Thirty-seventh Congress. The average voting agreement among all possible pairs of western senators was 61 per cent (with absences deleted) in the roll calls on the major national economic legislation and 59 per cent in the votes on the internal revenue bill.[15] In contrast, the eastern Republicans had mean agreements of 76 and 65 per cent. The differences between the two groups of senators would have increased still more had I dropped the senators from the Middle States from the comparison. Six New England senators, Clark (N.H.), Collamer (Vt.), Fessenden (Me.), Foot (Vt.), Foster (Conn.), and Morrill (Me.) were in particularly strong agreement in the votes on economic legislation. Minimal mean agreement among these men was 73 per cent and Clark and Fessenden voted together in 97 per cent of the roll calls on major economic legislation. There was no western group comparable either in numbers or in the strength of agreement among its members.

Among the 368 roll calls of the second session there were ninety-one in which the cohesion indices of eastern and western Republicans differed by as much as forty points. In fifty-nine of these roll calls it was the easterners who showed the greater solidarity. The western Republicans were more cohesive in voting on only thirty-two roll calls of this type. Of the 105 votes in this session which were apparently related to economic measures of national interest,

[15] Absences of individual senators are disregarded in the calculation of these percentages.

thirty-five, or 33 per cent, showed a marked difference in the cohesion of eastern and western Republicans. Of 120 roll calls linked to slavery, confiscation and the general conduct of the war, only eighteen, or 15 per cent, revealed a similar pattern. Thus, economic issues provoked more sectional response between eastern and western Republicans than did legislation concerned with slavery and confiscation, and it is clear also that the eastern Republicans were in greater agreement on the national economic legislation of this Congress than were their western colleagues.

The most striking sectional alignment in Congress during the years before the Civil War had reflected the divergent interests of North and South.[16] During most of the second session of the Thirty-seventh Congress senators represented five slave states. This group, containing both Democrats and former Whigs, guarded the southern heritage insofar as they considered it appropriate and feasible—which was sometimes a good deal further than the Republicans liked. An index of disagreement which compares the voting of the senators from the slave states with that of the senators from the free states shows substantial disagreement on 154 of the 368 Senate roll calls of this session. Sixty-seven of these votes appeared in the original selection of eighty-seven roll calls, related to slavery and confiscation legislation. The slave-state delegation was so small that this bloc's voting was sometimes masked by other voting determinants, but the group could be of major importance when Radical and Moderate Republicans disagreed.

To examine the conflict of Radical and Moderate Republicans is more difficult than it is to examine sectional manifestations in Congress, as we have no ready-made categories to use. But the documentary evidence suggests that the distinction had real meaning among the legislators. In December, 1861, Timothy Howe of Wisconsin predicted factional strife in the party when he wrote:

> Everything about us portends the coming of a rupture in the ranks of the war party and if so, a fierce struggle between the two factions. The organization of a party designing either to rule the administration or to supplant it has I think already commenced. Emancipation—the utter extinction of slavery will be the watchword & the effort of one faction. Where the other faction will plant itself is not so certain.[17]

And if one reads only the debates on the confiscation bills of the next spring one finds the senators describing, explicitly or implicitly, the differences among Republicans. Some opponents of a harsh confiscation bill invoked the Constitution against those who maintained that Congress should exercise war powers and advocated "legislative encroachment upon the prerogatives of the other departments." [18] But men who complained in this fashion, retorted Senator

[16] In "The Civil War Synthesis in American Political History," *Civil War History*, X (1964), 130–40, and in *The Shrine of Party: Congressional Voting Behavior, 1841–1852* (Pittsburgh, 1967), Joel Silbey cautions against over-emphasizing sectionalism in these years.

[17] Timothy O. Howe to Grace Howe, Dec. 13, 1861. Timothy O. Howe Papers, Wisconsin State Historical Society.

[18] *Congressional Globe*, 37 Cong., 2 sess., p. 2919.

Wade, were contending for "the irresponsible power of the Chief Magistrate in time of war," a doctrine which he characterized as "most slavish and un-American." [19] Senator Dixon, who feared that the powers of the states might be diminished, maintained that the rebel states were still within the Union and their residents, therefore, were entitled to the guarantees of the Constitution if they were to be punished. He also implied that the chairman of the Judiciary Committee was an "opponent of this Administration." [20] To this the chairman, Lyman Trumbull, responded by suggesting that Dixon was a "courtier" and a "sycophant" who did "not mean to be in opposition to the Administration let what will happen. . . ." [21] In this exchange we find support of the administration used to distinguish one Republican from another.

Senator Cowan referred to "the ultra school of the Republican party," whose members had decided that the rebellion of "some of the slave States" should be "put down by main force, and by an utter disregard of the will of the whole people of the slave States," and were insisting on measures "utterly obnoxious and distasteful" to every senator from the slave states.[22] More personally still, Wade described himself and his friends as "the earnest, up and down, through thick and thin Republicans of this body," leaving the character of recusant Republicans to the imagination.[23] But on one occasion, Fessenden, in exasperation with Wade and his friends, spoke of "certain gentlemen on this floor," who "seem to think that they are the representatives of all righteousness . . . and that if anybody differs from them he is either a fool or a knave." [24]

Expression of such differences appeared in the correspondence of the senators. Writing to Chandler after the close of the second session and as the election of 1862 neared, Wilkinson worried only about the success of ultra-Radicals like himself.[25] Trumbull, as he reviewed the Illinois election for Chandler's benefit a few weeks later, remarked sarcastically: "Do you think it will be any loss to exchange Browning for a responsible Democrat?" [26] To Browning, after the Thirty-seventh Congress had ended, Harris lamented that the President had "been drawn into the views" unfortunately "of a miserable lot of politicians"; a "lot" of which the New Yorker obviously did not consider himself a member.[27]

Most of the eighty-seven roll calls on slavery and confiscation motions fit into six Guttman scales. Beginning at the end of these scales which, judging by the content of the motions, represented the most extreme position relative to slavery and confiscation, I calculated the mean percentile positions of the senators in each scale and then prepared a weighted average of each senator's various scale positions. The average mean-percentile score of both Wilmot and Wade was nineteen, but the score of Senator Powell, a slave state Democrat at the other end of the political spectrum, was eighty-two. The other senators ranged between these poles, Radical Republicans presumably giving way to Moderate Republicans and War Democrats until finally the most conservative representa-

[19] *Ibid.*, p. 2930.   [20] *Ibid.*, pp. 2924–28, 2973.
[21] *Ibid.*, p. 2973.   [22] *Ibid.*, p. 2993.
[23] *Ibid.*, p. 3002.   [24] *Ibid.*, p. 2203.
[25] Morton Wilkinson to Zachariah Chandler, Oct. 20, 1862. Zachariah Chandler Papers, Library of Congress.
[26] Lyman Trumbull to Zachariah Chandler, Nov. 9, 1862, *ibid.*
[27] Ira Harris to Orville H. Browning, May 30, 1863. Orville H. Browning Papers, Illinois State Historical Society.

TABLE 1

A Voting Pattern on Slavery and Confiscation Measures

Senator	Party	State	Type	N 1	N 2	N 3	Y 4	N 5	N 6	Y 1	Y 2	Y 3	N 4	Y 5	Y 6
Powell	D	Ky.	6	*	*	*	*	*	*						
Kennedy	BU	Md.	6	*	*	*	0	*	0						
Davis	BU	Ky.	6	*	*	*	*	0	*						
Wilson, R.	BU	Mo.	6	*	*	0	*	*	*						
Carlile	BU	Va.	6	*	*	*	0	*	*						
Wright	NU	Ind.	6	*	_	*	*	*	*	x					
Saulsbury	D	Del.	5		*	0	0	*	*	0					
Stark	D	Ore.	5		*	0	0	*	*	0					
Willey	BU	Va.	5		*	*	*	*	*	0					
Henderson	D	Mo.	4			*	*	*	*	*	*				
Cowan	R	Pa.	4			*	*	0	*	*	*				
Browning	R	Ill.	4			*	*	*	*	*	*				
Anthony	R	R.I.	3				*	*	*	*	*	*			
Doolittle	R	Wis.	3				*	*	*	*	*	*			
Collamer	R	Vt.	3				*	*	0	*	0	*			
Sherman	R	Ohio	3				*	*	*	*	*	*			
Foster	R	Conn.	3				*	*	*	*	*	*			
Ten Eyck	R	N.J.	3				*	*	*	*	*	*			
Fessenden	R	Me.	3				*	0	*	*	*	*			
Lane, H. S.	R	Ind.	3				*	*	*	0	*	0			
Simmons	R	R.I.	3				*	*	*	*	*	*			
Howe	R	Wis.	3				*	*	*	*	*	*			
Harris	R	N.Y.	2					*	0	*	*	*	*		
Foot	R	Vt.	2					*	*	*	*	*	*		
Clark	R	N.H.	1						*	*	*	*	*	*	
Hale	R	N.H.	1						*	*	*	*	*	0	0
Wilson, H.	R	Mass.	1						*	*	*	*	*	*	
Sumner	R	Mass.	1						*	*	*	*	*	*	
Morrill	R	Me.	1						*	*	*	*	*	0	
Lane, J. H.	R	Kan.	1						*	*	*	*	*	*	
Harlan	R	Ia.	0							*	*	*	*	0	0
Pomeroy	R	Kan.	0							0	*	0	*	*	*
Grimes	R	Ia.	0							*	0	*	*	*	*
Chandler	R	Mich.	0							*	*	*	*	*	*
Wilkinson	R	Minn.	0							*	*	*	*	*	*
Trumbull	R	Ill.	0							*	0	*	*	*	*
King	R	N.Y.	0							*	*	*	*	*	*
Wade	R	Ohio	0						x	*	*	*	*	_	*
Wilmot	R	Penn.	0							*	0	*	*	*	0

* = pattern vote; –x = deviant vote (error); 0 = absent. Forty-six other roll calls from the original selection fitted into this scale. Missing senators voted in less than half of the divisions shown here. Coefficient of reproducibility = .99.

Voting Key: 1—Final vote on S. 351, supplementary to the act for emancipation in the District of Columbia.

2—Final vote on S. 394, to amend the act calling forth the militia.

3—Sumner's motion to amend S. 351 by inserting, "That in all judicial proceedings . . . there shall be no exclusion of any witness on account of color."

4—Sherman's amendment to S. 394, inserting, "who . . . shall owe service or labor to any person who, . . . levied war or has borne arms against the United States . . ."

5—Sumner's amendment to S. 365, providing for emancipation in the state of West Virginia.

6—King's amendment to the confiscation bill, S. 151, inserting, "persons in the present insurrection levying war against the United States or adhering to their enemies . . ."

tives of the border slave states were reached.[28] Table 1 presents the scale pattern found most frequently in the votes on slavery and confiscation.

A rank-order list of this sort derived from Guttman scaling tells us (if we accept the assumptions of the scaling technique) that one senator was more extreme in his approach to a category of legislation than was another, but it does not divide the legislators into self-conscious groups. Some scholars have tried to solve this problem by dividing scale rankings into thirds or by designating one or more votes within a scale as boundaries. Both systems are arbitrary and I have instead worked out cluster blocs, using the percentages of agreement between every possible pair of senators in the voting on the eighty-seven roll calls on slavery and confiscation in my original selection. Such agreement scores showed considerable harmony among senators like King, Wilmot, Wilkinson, Chandler, and Wade, who stood at the Radical end of the scalogram rank order, and a considerably lower agreement among these men and a group which included Fessenden, Foster and a few other New Englanders who also agreed among themselves very strongly and appeared in the center of the scaling rank order. We can regard these two groups in a sense as the nuclei of the Radical and Moderate Republicans, with other senators forming an outer fringe in both factions. The boundaries of these groups suggested a cutting point in the scale ranking that yielded seventeen Radicals and fourteen Moderates. In this division the marginal Radicals agreed in their voting with the other Radicals substantially more than with the Moderates.[29]

[28] Some students have tried to summarize the voting positions of legislators by summing or averaging their scale type positions in a number of appropriate scales. Unfortunately, such procedure disregards the fact that Guttman scales are ordinal scales and we cannot be sure that the scale types in various scales are equivalent units of measurement. Here, therefore, I have calculated the number of percentiles that the legislators of each scale type occupied and allocated the mean percentile score to each man in the scale type. Such percentile values can, of course, be averaged with those derived from other scales. Actually, the rank ordering of senators derived in this way did not vary greatly from the rank order which resulted when I summed the scale types of the various legislators, although there were some minor differences. But one should not assume that the rank order derived by summing scale types in some published research is inaccurate simply because of the methods used. The results may or may not be correct. I am indebted to Professor Aage Clausen of the Political Science Department of the University of Wisconsin for assistance with this problem.

[29] Some Radical and Moderate Republican Agreement Scores *

	King	Wilmot	Wilkinson	Chandler	Wade	Morrill	Sumner	Collamer	Foster	Anthony	Simmons	Fessenden
King												
Wilmot	97											
Wilkinson	96	98										
Chandler	94	90	91									
Wade	93	93	96	90								
Morrill	89	91	94	88	89							
Sumner	89	86	89	90	81	92						
Collamer	69	63	66	67	74	78	69					
Foster	68	62	68	69	71	81	72	95				
Anthony	68	64	65	69	72	74	71	92	91			
Simmons	55	58	59	55	60	74	61	90	91	93		
Fessenden	68	67	68	67	68	85	74	87	90	86	95	
Cowan	42	36	34	46	39	44	48	69	65	77	71	63

* Per cent agreement in 87 votes on slavery and confiscation; absences are ignored. The cluster-bloc pairing suggests that the Radical who was closest in his voting to the

Having divided the Republicans into Radicals and Moderates by using the scales and cluster blocs found in the original selection of eighty-seven roll calls on slavery and confiscation, I could then compute the index of disagreement of each of the 368 roll calls under study. In all there were fifty-eight roll calls in which the disagreement ranged between forty and one hundred.[30] These fifty-eight roll calls delimit the areas of major conflict between Moderate and Radical Republicans in the Senate during the second session.

Much of the disagreement between Radical and Moderate Republicans was, of course, related to emancipation and to the methods by which this might be achieved. During the discussion of Senate Bill 108, providing for the emancipation of slaves in the District of Columbia, Davis of Kentucky proposed that all individuals who were freed under this act should be colonized and that an appropriation should be made for that purpose. Doolittle moved to amend this, allowing all of the freed men of the District to choose whether or not they wished to emigrate. His amendment specified Haiti or Liberia as the destination of the emigrants or "such other country . . . as the President of the United States" might determine, and limited the expenditures in each individual case to $100. The vote on both the Doolittle amendment and on the amended Davis amendment provoked substantial disagreement between Radicals and Moderates.

In the debate on Senate Bills 384 and 394, to amend the act calling forth the militia, Grimes offered an amendment designed to free the mother, wife and children of those of African descent who served the Union under the amended law, as well as the colored soldier or laborer himself. Moderate colleagues and Border State men opposed this amendment, suggesting that it should apply only to the slaves of traitors, that it should not touch the slaves of loyal slaveowners, or at least that loyal owners in the Border States should be recompensed for losses under it. Eight roll calls on various aspects of this matter produced disagreement of considerable strength. In a more direct blow at the institution of slavery in the Border States, Sumner tried to amend the West Virginia admission act by striking the limited emancipation clause, which provided that all children were to be born free, and substituting the provision that there should be neither slavery nor involuntary servitude in the new state except as criminal punishment. The ringing language of the Northwest Ordinance and of

---

Moderates was Senator Clark, whose average agreement with the men above him in the matrix (the other Radicals) was 83 per cent, and with the Moderates 77 per cent. The scalogram percentile rankings drop Howard below Clark. Howard's mean pairing score with other Radicals was 80 per cent and with the Moderates only 65 per cent. Such variation is attributable to the fact that absences are handled somewhat differently in the cluster bloc and scaling procedures and to the fact that the mean percentile method of ranking is by no means precise since large numbers of tie scores are involved. The only senator to present a real problem in classification was Senator Dixon. Historians usually consider him a Moderate, as he apparently did himself, but both scaling and clustering procedures ranked him among the Radicals. When a cluster-bloc matrix was prepared that counted absences as a third way of agreement between legislators, Dixon's average agreement with the Radicals fell to less than 60 per cent, although it was still somewhat higher than his average agreement with the Moderates. Dixon apparently absented himself on some embarrassing roll calls and I have therefore counted him among the Moderates, although this imparted a slightly conservative bias to the calculation of the index of disagreement between Radicals and Moderates.

[30] A list of these roll calls is available on request from the author.

TABLE 2
REPUBLICAN RADICALS AND MODERATES

Radicals		Moderates	
Chandler (Mich.)	Morrill (Me.)	Anthony (R.I.)	Foster (Conn.)
Clark (N.H.)	Pomeroy (Kan.)	Browning (Ill.)	Harris (N.Y.)
Foot (Vt.)	Sumner (Mass.)	Collamer (Vt.)	Howe (Wis.)
Grimes (Ia.)	Trumbull (Ill.)	Cowan (Penn.)	H. S. Lane (Ind.)
Hale (N.H.)	Wade (O.)	Dixon (Conn.)	Sherman (O.)
Harlan (Ia.)	Wilkinson (Minn.)	Doolittle (Wis.)	Simmons (R.I.)
Howard (Mich.)	Wilmot (Penn.)	Fessenden (Me.)	Ten Eyck (N.J.)
King (N.Y.)	Wilson (Mass.)		
J. H. Lane (Kan.)			

the Wilmot Proviso may have stirred proud nostalgia in many a Republican heart but not one Moderate voted for it.

Various divisive motions related to the disabilities of color, although the implications of the roll calls doubtless ran deeper on occasion. As Senator Clark tried, by amendment, to substitute the select committee version of the confiscation bill in place of the confiscation bill from the House, Sumner attempted to add the words "and in all proceedings under this act there shall be no exclusion of any witness on account of color," to one clause of the senate bill. Almost a full complement of Radicals supported Sumner's amendment and the Moderates massed in opposition to it. When Sumner also tried to attach this amendment both to House Bill 390, "in relation to the competency of witnesses in trials of equity and admiralty," and to a senate bill relating to the judiciary, he encountered strong Moderate opposition in the first instance and less in the second. Radical faced Moderate again when the senators voted on the Border State proposition to amend a naval appropriations bill by barring the use of slaves on the works of the naval service.

The Republican senators disagreed sharply among themselves in the debates on confiscation during the last four months of the session. The discussion focused first on the Trumbull bill, S. 151, which the Illinois senator reported from the judiciary committee. A compromise measure, S. 310, which a select committee under the chairmanship of Senator Clark drafted was considered next and then House Bill 471. Due mainly to the efforts of Moderates, aided by votes from the Border States, the Senate used the amendment process to substitute S. 310 for the bill from the House. Two major questions were involved in the debates: (1) Could Congress reach the property of rebels under powers opened to it by the war crisis or must it be bound by constitutional restrictions on the punishment of treason? (2) What categories of southerners ought to lose their property under the law? The Radicals in general supported the broad application of a law based on the war power; most Moderates fought for judicial processes which they believed were in accord with the treason clause of the constitution and wished to specify limited categories of southerners to whom the law was to apply. Senators introduced various major amendments during the debates and the parliamentary maneuvering was reflected in numerous disagreements between the Radicals and Moderates on procedural matters. In sum, the members of the two groups disagreed substantially in eleven roll calls during the debates on confiscation and the conflict persisted even into the vote on a motion that the Senate withdraw its amendment to the House Bill after the House had asked for a conference committee.

The division between Moderates and Radicals sometimes was revealed in the discussion of matters that at first glance do not relate directly to slavery or confiscation. A bloc of Moderates supported Senator Davis when he tried to amend House Bill 371, "to prescribe an oath of office . . . ," so as to exempt congressmen from its operation. Moderates in some number also supported Henderson's amendment to the same bill, changing the affirmation, ". . . I have never voluntarily borne arms against the United States . . . ," by striking "borne arms" and replacing it by the phrase "levied war." When Sumner tried to amend the internal revenue bill by inserting an additional section that taxed slave holders at the rate of $5.00 for each slave between the ages of ten and sixty, his action inspired a flurry of opposition and counterproposals which generated substantial disagreement between the Republican factions. So, too, did the effort of John Sherman to win reconsideration of a 50 per cent reduction in the cotton tax and Sumner's attempt to strike the tax on book-making materials.

The Radicals and Moderates disagreed in four votes dealing with the seating of Benjamin Stark, the Copperhead senator who replaced Baker of Oregon. A similar division appeared in four roll calls relating to the organization, or emoluments, of the armed forces. It was seen also when Senator Harris attempted to have Senate Bill 200, to establish provisional governments in certain cases, made a special order; on an amendment of Senator Grimes to Senate Bill 89, changing the boundaries of Federal judicial districts; in the case of two votes relating to the water and gas utilities of the District of Columbia; on Trumbull's motion to strike the second section of the extradition treaty with Mexico; and on a motion of Hale concerning the dead letter office. Finally, as the legislators reached mid-June, 1862, the same pattern of Radical in opposition to Moderate appeared in seven votes concerning adjournment and the operation of the Senate rules.

The disagreement indices provide us with some evidence of the duration as well as the intensity of disagreement during the session. Three votes revealed substantial disagreement between Radicals and Moderates during January of 1862 but in June there were nineteen, and in considerably less than a month of debate during July, there were seventeen such confrontations. However, every vote in which the index rose to eighty-five or better occurred in July. Party harmony was obviously in serious jeopardy as the session closed. Although we are tempted to emphasize the confiscation issue and the emancipation of slaves in the District of Columbia in discussing the achievements of Congress during this session, the sharpest disagreement between Radicals and Moderates did not develop in the roll calls on these measures but rather when the senators voted on the emancipation clause of the bills to amend the act calling forth the militia and on Sumner's amendment to provide unlimited emancipation in the new state of West Virginia. The votes on these issues produced disagreement indices that ranged from eighty-five to one hundred.

Although the senators might have explained their differences in terms of constitutional interpretation or conscience, we, as historians, inevitably ask ourselves if the differences between Radical and Moderate Republicans are explainable in terms of the conditioning which these men experienced in the years before the Civil War. Ralph Waldo Emerson was playing this game when he wrote in his journal:

> The Unitarians, born Unitarians, have a pale, shallow religion, but the Calvinist, born and reared under his vigorous, ascetic, scowling creed, and then ripened into a Unitarian, becomes powerful . . . So it is in politics. A man must have had the broad, audacious Democratic party for his nursing-mother, and be ripened into a Free-Soiler, to be efficient. . . .[31]

Emerson's "Law" does have some predictive value when applied to the Republican senators of this session. Of seven former Democrats among the Republicans, six were Radicals, including four of the most Radical complexion, and only Doolittle was a Moderate. Among the senators of Whig antecedents, men who had made some striking commitment to the antislavery cause before 1854 seem in general to have been more extreme than those who made their public commitment in 1854 or thereafter.[32]

In distinguishing between Radicals and Moderates you will remember that I have not arbitrarily selected one or several votes and posited that all who voted one way or another on this limited selection were Radicals or Moderates. Instead I have been concerned with voting frequencies over a rather considerable number of roll calls. This reflects my feeling that it is unreasonable to expect the members of even a closely knit faction to vote together all of the time. And the high disagreement roll calls provide numerous examples of deviation. Sherman, seldom, if ever, considered a Radical, pressed doggedly for the more severe House version of the confiscation bill in preference to the select committee's compromise measure. Of the Radicals, only Wade joined the Moderates in opposition to Sumner's amendment to the West Virginia admission bill although he termed his vote "very harsh and unsavory." [33] The lion could on occasion lie down with the lamb.

Was there any relation between the sectionalism of East and West and the disagreement between Radicals and Moderates in the Republican party? We have already noted that east-west sectionalism was most apparent in the voting on national economic issues, but in a number of votes relating to the South there was some alignment of western Republicans in opposition to eastern Republicans. There are various ways of examining this question. If the Republican Radicals were primarily eastern or western in constituency, roll calls showing a high sectional disagreement between eastern and western men should also have a high index of disagreement between Radicals and Moderates. Ten roll calls are common to the list of forty-six votes in which eastern and western

---

[31] Edward W. Emerson and Waldo E. Forbes, *Journals of Ralph Waldo Emerson, 1820–1876* (Boston, 1913), IX, 407–8. Some of Emerson's illustrations do not actually fit his pattern but the hypothesis is an interesting one.

[32] Basic biographical data were drawn from the *Biographical Directory of the American Congress* (Washington, seriatim); Allen Johnson (ed.), *The Dictionary of American Biography* (New York, 1928+); *The National Cyclopedia of American Biography* (New York, 1892+). When a senator was not listed in the *Dictionary of American Biography,* state and local biographical directories were consulted. Periodical literature and book-length biographies dealing with the senators are uneven in both quantity and quality. There are no published biographies of some of the senators; others are the subjects of a number of studies. Such material has been used wherever possible.

[33] *Congressional Globe,* 37 Cong., 2 sess., p. 3308.

Republicans differed substantially and the group of fifty-eight roll calls that show substantial disagreement between Radicals and Moderates.

We can attack the problem more simply by examining the division of eastern and western Republican senators between the Radical and Moderate factions of the party. Table 3 shows that slightly more than half of the eastern Republicans

TABLE 3*

	Eastern Republican Senators (17)		Western Republican Senators (14)	
Radical Republicans	8	47%	9	64%
Moderate Republicans	9	53%	5	36%

* The contingency coefficient gamma is −.34.

were Moderates and a somewhat larger proportion of western Republicans were Radicals. Antislavery sentiment in the West is sometimes linked to eastern origins and Table 4 presents place of birth as a possible variable.

For what it is worth, the Republican senator most apt to be extreme in his views toward the South and its institutions was a western senator of eastern origins; seven of the nine senators who fitted this description were Radicals (78 per cent). The senator most apt to be a Republican Moderate on the other hand was a western senator of western birth; three out of five, or 60 per cent, in this category were Moderates. But given the relatively small numbers of men

TABLE 4*

	Republican Senators of Eastern Birth (26)		Republican Senators of Western Birth (5)	
Radical Republicans	15	58%	2	40%
Moderate Republicans	11	42%	3	60%

* Gamma is .34

involved, the percentage differences that support a sectional interpretation of the disagreement between Radicals and Moderates are rather small.

The fact that there were proportionately more Radicals in the West has sometimes made it difficult for historians to decide whether the sectionalism of East and West or the division between Radicals and Moderates most influenced a particular vote. The sectional aspect of the voting on the colonization amendment to the bill providing for emancipation of the slaves in the District of Columbia has been emphasized recently but roll call analysis seems to show that we should more appropriately view the issue as an aspect of factionalism between Radical and Moderate Republicans in the Senate.[34]

Historians have toyed with the idea that the Republican Radicals not only agreed strongly among themselves on southern policy but that they were peculiarly the spokesmen of northeastern industrialism.[35] We have in general

[34] See Voegeli, "Northwest and the Race Issue," 235–51. I discuss this matter in more detail in an unpublished paper, "Senators, Sectionalism and the 'Western' Measures of the Republican Party."

[35] See Donald, "Devils Facing Zionwards," pp. 72–3. I find it difficult to interpret T. Harry Williams, *Lincoln and the Radicals* (Madison, 1941), in this light, but it is applied explicitly to the reconstruction years by Howard K. Beale in his article "The Tariff and Reconstruction," *American Historical Review*, XXXV (1930), 276–94, especially 276.

rejected this thesis in recent years and there is little support for it in this research. We can, however, argue that some Republican senators agreed strongly with each other during the second session of the Thirty-seventh Congress both in their voting on slavery and confiscation and on the national economic program of the Republican party. Men like Fessenden, Collamer, Foster, and Anthony tended to agree much of the time, whether the subjects under debate were slavery and confiscation or economic measures of national import. Agreeing strongly with them on economic matters were some of the marginal Radicals from New England, particularly Foot and Clark. If any group of senators can be described as consistently cohesive it was the nucleus of New England Moderates.

Having examined some of the dimensions of geographical bloc and party faction, we can return to the question of whether the historian is justified in emphasizing the internecine conflicts of the Republicans or whether he should stress rather the importance of party and the basic agreement among Republicans. We have seen that eastern and western Republicans differed substantially in forty-six roll calls and that Radical Republican similarly opposed Moderate Republican in fifty-eight votes, with some overlap in the categories. By comparison, the Republican and Democratic parties differed by 40 per cent or more of the total disagreement possible in 161 roll calls. Restating the matter in slightly different terms, a majority of Republicans opposed a majority of Democrats in 180 of the 368 voting divisions. Of the eighty-seven roll calls in my original selection of votes on slavery and confiscation, sixty-five showed a majority of Republicans opposed to a majority of Democrats, and only twenty-one revealed a disagreement index between Moderate and Radical Republicans of substantial size. In these crude terms party was indeed more important than factionalism.

We cannot leave the matter there, however. Howard W. Allen and Jerome M. Clubb calculated the amount of party voting in a total of some twelve hundred votes on the most controversial issues considered in the senates of the Sixty-first, Sixty-second and Sixty-third Congresses, 1909–1915, when the winds of progressivism were blowing strongly. Since Allen and Clubb sifted out some votes on less controversial matters and I considered all roll calls the comparison cannot be exact, but the percentage ranged from 60 to 79 per cent in those congresses, with a mean of 71 per cent.[36] In the second session of the senate of the Thirty-seventh Congress the percentage of party votes in the selection of eighty-seven roll calls on slavery and confiscation issues was seventy-five but this figure drops to 50 per cent when all 368 roll calls are considered. Relatively speaking, party was apparently less significant in the voting of this session than on the more important issues of Progressivism. On the other hand, "party votes," as a percentage of all Senate votes, represented only 45 per cent on the average during the Eighty-fourth through the Eighty-eighth Congresses, 1955–1964.[37]

Yet, if party lines were drawn very sharply on the issues of slavery and

[36] Jerome M. Clubb and Howard W. Allen, "Party Loyalty in the United States Senate in the Taft and Wilson Years." (Mimeographed, Inter-university Consortium for Political Research, Ann Arbor), pp. 1–29. See particularly pp. 7, 8 and fn. 8, p. 28.

[37] *Ibid.*, p. 8, drawn by Clubb and Allen from the *Congressional Quarterly Almanac.*

confiscation during the second session of the Thirty-seventh Congress, one out of every four roll calls on such matters did reveal substantial disagreement between Republican Radicals and Moderates. Traces of this division appeared in many other votes as well. Basically, the differences between Radical and Moderate structured the voting of Republicans in one major category of legislation and also affected a number of other types of legislative action that were only indirectly related to the southern question. Nor should we forget that the division between Radical and Moderate was a more important one than was the distinction between eastern and western legislators.

The relative cohesion of the Democrats and the Republicans has some bearing on the significance of party among the Republicans. In a recent article Leonard Curry has argued that the Democrats were more cohesive during the Thirty-seventh Congress than were the Republicans.[38] My voting analysis of the second session Senate supports his conclusion. The mean Democratic cohesion in my original selection of slavery and confiscation votes was sixty-nine and that of the Republicans was sixty-three. In eighty-six divisions on the major national economic legislation of this session, Democratic cohesion was sixty-six and that of the Republicans was thirty-eight. We have to discount this finding somewhat, however, because the Democratic group was small and absenteeism among its members much more marked than among the Republicans, even after adjustment is made for the illness of several Democratic senators.

To divide the roll calls of this session into those that show sectionalism, those that illustrate the conflict of Radical against Moderate Republican, and those that illustrate party differences is to disregard a considerable number of votes. There were 132 roll calls (again with some overlapping of other categories) in which Republican cohesiveness was sixty or below and in which the likeness indices of East against West and of Radical versus Moderate were quite high. In these divisions, apparently, the idiosyncrasies of the individual constituency or senator were asserted or subregional voting patterns became important. Although it is possible to build some scales from these roll calls, the scalograms include a relatively small number of votes and it is difficult to identify underlying continua of attitude. As I move further into the task of calculating correlations between the various scales I may be able to refine my description of these votes.

In this session of the Civil War Senate, party obviously was an important voting determinant but we cannot disregard the significance of geographical bloc or party faction either, nor the importance of the individual senator and his constituency. And, of course, the decision to vote in sectional grouping or party faction may have come only after much agonizing deliberation. Obviously there is much to be said in support of the interpretations of both David Donald and T. Harry Williams concerning Republican factionalism, but we will profit, I believe, in the future by treating the houses of Congress during the Civil War as political systems in which a variety of determinants of voting behavior were interacting.

This particular senate was hardly a classic illustration of the two-party system at work, with its strong Republican majority, its reeling Democracy, its home-

[38] Leonard P. Curry, "Congressional Democrats: 1861–1863," *Civil War History*, XII (1966), 220–21.

less border Unionists and the unusual pressures of constituency and public opinion that played upon the senators. Comparison with a one-party legislature or a multi-party system may be more revealing than exposition of the conventional two-party model. But party objectives were by no means forgotten; Democrats hoped for a comeback and many Republicans had both the present and the future in mind as they labored during this session. The doctrinaire Hale scoffed that the department of agriculture bill was not the wish of the men who leaned "upon their plow-handles; but . . . the men who want them to take their hands off the plow-handle and vote for them at the ballot-box." [39] The more practical politicians of the new party prevailed against such criticism and the Thirty-seventh Congress bequeathed a formidable legislative legacy to the people of a reunited nation.

[39] *Congressional Globe,* 37 Cong., 2 sess., p. 2014.

RODNEY O. DAVIS

Partisanship in Jacksonian State Politics: Party Divisions in the Illinois Legislature, 1834–1841

Voting patterns in state legislatures provide an unlimited field of study for the statistically inclined scholar. This is true especially for the nineteenth century, when party organization was more vigorous at the state than at the Federal level. Rodney O. Davis is the first historian to undertake a thorough scalogram analysis of a state legislature, in this case the Illinois General Assembly of the Jacksonian era, 1834–1841. By constructing partisan cohesion percentages over time on a series of key issues—banking, corporations, Andrew Jackson, judicial reorganization—Davis attempts to determine whether state-level politicians were as issue-oriented as previous scholars such as Turner and Schlesinger believed. As with much of the behavioral research, Davis' findings support the consensus interpretation of American political history—in this case, specifically, the views of Richard McCormick.

A RECENT REDIRECTION in the historiography of Jacksonian Democracy has been toward de-emphasis of the doctrinal or socio-economic divisions that might have defined American political parties in the second quarter of the

Printed with permission of the author.

nineteenth century. This trend may have come as much from exhaustion as from any devotion to consensus interpretations; the great production of books and articles about Jacksonian Democracy that was first stimulated 25 years ago by Schlesinger's *The Age of Jackson,* if showing no other overall unity, has demonstrated the enormous complexity and variety of party issues and affiliations over both time and space in the Jackson period. Indeed the last two major studies of the era tend to give increased weight to Glyndon Van Deusen's observations that, multiple surface partisan differences notwithstanding, "the political conflicts of the Jacksonian period were fought more often with a view to gaining control of the government than out of any devotion to diametrically opposed political and social ideals." [1]

Much of the work that has led to this new realization of the kaleidoscopic character of Jacksonian politics was the product of the late 1950's and early 1960's. The 1961 publication of Lee Benson's magnificent study of New York politics in the Jackson era was a benchmark in its development. Much of it has been quantitative in methodology and almost all of it has quite reasonably focused on state and local levels of political behavior.[2] For it seems an underemphasized but undoubted fact of political life in early nineteenth-century America that political party organization was strongest at the state, not the national level. The national parties were confederations of state organizations; and the state and local governments which politicians vied to control simply had more impact on Americans than did the Federal government. Before the Civil War the national government probably had a greater effect on more Americans as a mail carrier than it did as tax-collector, land-purveyor, ensuror of domestic tranquility, or arbiter of the nation's financial affairs. It was the states, after all, that most often had direct responsibility for business, banking and credit control, for promoting internal improvements, setting voting requirements, and encouraging public welfare, morals or education.

Unfortunately, much of this recent valuable work is still of somewhat limited perspective because of its emphasis on the acts of "the minority at the top," [3] of vocal politicians whose names and speeches appeared most often in the newspapers or whose letters were saved for posterity.[4] Other studies have tried to

[1] Richard P. McCormick, *The Second American Party System* (Chapel Hill, 1966); Edward Pessen, *Jacksonian America* (Homewood, Illinois, 1969); Glyndon G. Van Deusen, "Some Aspects of Whig Thought and Theory in the Jacksonian Period," *American Historical Review,* 63 (1958), 321–22.

[2] Lee Benson, *The Concept of Jacksonian Democracy: New York as a Test Case* (Princeton, 1961). A few of the other outstanding examples in this voluminous literature include Edwin A. Miles, *Jacksonian Democracy in Mississippi* (Chapel Hill, 1960); Grady McWhiney, "Were the Whigs a Class Party in Alabama?" *Journal of Southern History,* 23 (1957), 510–22; Frank Otto Gatell, "Money and Party in Jacksonian America: A Quantitative Look at New York City's Men of Quality," *Political Science Quarterly,* 82 (1967), 235–52; Thomas B. Alexander, Kit C. Carter, Jack R. Lister, Jerry C. Oldshue, and Winfred G. Sandlin, "Who Were the Alabama Whigs?" *Alabama Review,* 16 (1963), 5–19; Thomas B. Alexander, Peggy Duckworth Elmore, Frank M. Lowery, Mary Jane Pickens Skinner, "The Basis of Alabama's Ante-Bellum Two-Party System, *Ibid.,* 19 (1966), 243–76.

[3] Jesse Lemisch, "The American Revolution from the Bottom Up," in Barton J. Bernstein, ed., *Towards a New Past, Dissenting Essays in American History* (New York, 1968), 4.

[4] See for example William S. Hoffman, *Andrew Jackson and North Carolina Politics* (Chapel Hill, 1958); John Vollmer Mering, *The Whig Party in Missouri* (Columbia, 1967).

surmount this limitation through a deeper-probing empiricism, thus to find the political loyalties of socio-economic, ethnic, or religious groups within state and local societies. In this way these studies have tested the time-honored "Concept of Jacksonian Democracy" whose limits were set most conspicuously by Frederick Jackson Turner and Arthur Schlesinger, Jr.[5] Even this approach, however, tends to freeze the popular electorate and its behavior to perhaps only one voting decision (such as Benson's focus on the presidential election of 1844) or to only one political affirmation (e.g. "I am a Democrat," or "I am a Whig"). What still remains unstudied at the state level for the Jacksonian period, and only recently studied at the national level,[6] is the relatively long-run loyalty of party members to a number of what were or have become identified as party issues. In Edward Pessen's words, "The determination that the Democrats [for example] were the party of this or that group must finally be made not on the basis of statistics or the degree of electoral support the Democracy got from the group in question, but according to an *evaluation* of the party's behavior." [7] Such an evaluation might allow us to correlate the new and the old in Jacksonian historiography; it should show us something about issue-orientation and the strength of doctrinal principles in the Jacksonian period, if less about issues themselves, and perhaps it can reveal the relative priorities of issues and "control of the government."

Evaluating a party's behavior in a state during the nineteenth century can be done very well through studying state legislative activity, an arena in which a wide range of political issues required decisions by party members. Though encompassing a kind of elite group to be sure, state legislatures during the Jacksonian era have, nonetheless, left in their journals the records of roll-call votes taken not only on the passage of certain key bills but also on amendments, second and third readings, and procedural motions. All this material affords a complex and subtle record of many more political transactions than studies of mass electoral voting behavior can reasonably unearth, by many more party members than those in the loquacious minority of public men whose utterances have been preserved. With this record, through systematic legislative roll-call analysis, we can find answers to questions like these: Did issues actually mean much to state-level politicians whom we have been inclined to think of as issue-oriented? What kinds of issues meant the most to them? The least? Was party cohesion greater over some legislative issues than for others? Did the level of cohesion over issues change significantly over time?

A useful analytic tool in this quest is the Guttman scaling technique, a device which assumes a general consistency in voting behavior on the part of the legislators, and which allows the rank-ordering of legislators during a given session according to their positions on sets of related issues as revealed by their

[5] Examples are Benson's *The Concept of Jacksonian Democracy;* Alexandra McCoy, "The Political Affiliations of American Economic Elites: Wayne County, Michigan, 1844–1860, as a Test Case" (Unpublished Doctoral Dissertation, Wayne State University, 1965); and Ronald P. Formisano, "Social Bases of American Voting Behavior, Wayne County, Michigan, 1837–1852, as a Test Case" (Unpublished Doctoral Dissertation, Wayne State University, 1966).
[6] The two studies by historians of nineteenth-century congressional voting behavior are Joel H. Silbey, *The Shrine of Party* (Pittsburgh, 1967); and Thomas B. Alexander, *Sectional Stress and Party Strength* (Nashville, 1967).
[7] Pessen, *Jacksonian America,* 256.

TABLE 1

Corporation Legislation, Illinois Senate, 1840–1841

		Anti-Corporations														Pro-Corporations													
Senator	Score	1	2	3	4	5	6	7	8	9	10	11	12	13	14	1 a	2 a	3 a	4 a	5 a	6 a	7 a	8 a	9 a	10 a	11 a	12 a	13 a	14 a
Markley(D)	0	X	X	X	X	X	X	X	X	X	X			X	X											X	X		
Moore(D)	0	X	X	X	X	X	O	X	X	X	X	X	X	X	X												X	X	
Evans(D)	0	X	X	X	X	X		X		X	X	X	X	X	X						X								
Gaston(D)	0	X	X	X	X	O	X		X	X	X	X	X	X	X				X		X	X							
Harris(D)	0	X	O	O	O	X	X	X	X	X	X	X	X	X	X		X												
Johnston(D)	0	X	X	X	X	X	X	X	X	X	X	O	X	X	X														
Nunnally(D)	0	O	X	O	X	O	O	X	X	X	X	X	O	X	X											X			
Parrish(D)	0	X	X	X	X	O	O	X	X	X	X	X	X	X	X														
Ralston(D)	0	X	X	X	X	X	O	X	X	X	O	X	X	O	O													X	
Wood(D)	0	X	X	X	X	X	O	X	X	X	O	X	X	O	X														
Gatewood(D)	1					X	X	X	X	O	X	X	X	X	X	O					X			X		X			X
James(D)	1	X	X	X	X	X	X	X	X	O	X	X	X	X	X	X	X	X	X	X	X	X	X	X	X	X			
Gibbs(D)	2	X			X	X	X	X	X	O	X	X	X	X	X		X	X	X	X	X		X	X	X				
Pearson(D)	3					X	X	X	X	O	X	X	X	O	X	X	X	X		X	X		X		X	X	X		
Feaman(D)	4	X	X		X			X	X	X	X	X	X	X	X	X	X	X	X	X	X	X	X	X	X	X	X		X
Allen(D)	4		X	X												X	X	X	O	X	X	X	X	O	O	X	X		
Houston(D)	5						X			X						X	X	X	X	X	X	X	X	X	X	X	X	X	X
Hunter(D)	5								X	X	X	X	X	O	X	X	X	X	X	X	X	X	X	X	X	X	X	X	X
Slocumb(D)	5						X			X						X	X	X	O	X	X	X	X	X	X	X	X	X	X
Warren(D)	6			X					X		X	X		X	X	X	X	O	O	X	X	O	O		O	O	O	O	
Witt(D)	6			X				X		X	X					X	X	O	X	O	X	X	X	X	X	X	X	X	X
Fithian(W)	7													X		X	X	O	O	X	X	O	O		O	O	O	O	
Herndon(D)	7															O	O	X	X	O	X	X	X	X	O	X	X	O	X
Baker(W)	7															X	X	X	X	X	X	X	X	X	X	X	X	X	X
Churchill(W)	7															X	X	X	X	X	X	X	X	X	X	X	X	X	X
Cullom(W)	7			X		X				X						X	X	X	X	X	X	X	X	X	X	X	X	O	X
Davidson(W)	7					X				X						X	X	X	O	X	O	O	X	X	X	X	O	X	X
Henry(W)	7					X					X					X	X	X	X	O		X	X	X	X	X	X	X	X

	1	2	3	4	5	6	7	8	9	10	11	12	13	14
Killpatrick(W)						O	X	X	X	X	X	X	X	X
Stapp(W)		X				X	X	X	X	X	X	X	X	X
Harrison(W)			X			X	X	X	X	X	O	X	X	X
Hamlin(W)				X		O	X	X	X	X	X	X	O	X
Sargent(W)				X	X	X	X	X	O	X	X	X	X	X
Stadden(D)					X	X	X	O	X	X	O	X	X	X
Little(W)			X			X	X	X	X	X	X	X	X	X
Ross(W)						X	X	X	X	O	X	X	X	O

Key to Items on Table 1

1. Second reading of a bill to incorporate the Springfield, Jacksonville, and Meredosia Railroad Company. Nay vote is anti.
2. Passage of a bill to authorize the Mt. Carmel and Alton Railroad Company to construct the Southern Cross Railroad. Nay vote is anti.
3. Passage of a bill incorporating the Illinois and Rock River Railroad Company. Nay vote is anti.
4. Tabling of a bill to provide for the completion of the Northern Cross Railroad from Springfield to the Illinois River. Yea vote is anti.
5. Passage of a bill authorizing Samuel Bowen to build a dam across Rock River, amended to allow the governor to sell state stock in the enterprise. Nay vote is anti.
6. Third reading of a bill authorizing Henry Hand to keep a ferry across Rock River. Nay vote is anti.
7. Reconsideration of an amendment to Item 2, allowing the state to repurchase the completed railroad. Yea vote is anti.
8. Amendment to Item 4, allowing the state to repurchase the completed railroad. Yea vote is anti.
9. Third reading of Item 5. Nay vote is anti.
10. Tabling of Item 5, after amendments. Nay vote is anti.
11. Amendment to Item 4, allowing the state an interest in construction of the railroad. Yea vote is anti.
12. Postponement of a bill allowing private construction of the Illinois and Michigan Canal. Yea vote is anti.
13. Amendment to Item 5, shortening the charter's term of years. Yea vote is anti.
14. Amendment to Item 4, requiring that the state receive tolls collected on that portion of the railroad already completed. Yea vote is anti.

Two senators are not included due to absences and ambiguous voting records.
Coefficient of Reproducibility: 90 per cent.

roll-call votes.[8] From a series of roll-call responses related to corporations, for instance, it is possible to classify legislators in terms of their degree of support or non-support for chartered privileges. Corporation-related roll-calls with the fewest favorable votes may be considered as those isolating the most ardent pro-corporation men; those with the most should attract all legislators with any favorable feelings toward corporations whatsoever. Totally unfavorable legislators at the other extreme would be those voting against corporations in every case. Obviously, many possible intervening gradations could exist.

The resultant classifications may be correlated to outside variables, of which party affiliation or sectional origin are the most obvious. It is also often desirable to organize these rank-ordered legislators into such more convenient categories as those encompassing people definitely "pro" or "anti"—the proposition in question, or "moderate" on it. Table 1 is a Guttman scale based on Illinois Senate votes on corporations in 1840–1841 and Table 2 is a somewhat refined abstract of the scale data; together they should make these procedures

TABLE 2

CORPORATION LEGISLATION
Illinois Senate, 1840–1841

	Democrats		Whigs	
	No.	Per Cent	No.	Per Cent
Anti-Corporations	12	52	0	0
Moderate	7	31	0	0
Pro-Corporations	4	17	13	100

clearer. In Table 1 the "anti-corporation" men identified themselves by voting against all or most grants of chartered privileges (Items 1–6), and by favoring amendments that would restrict charters (Items 7–14). Those were considered "moderates" who tended to approve the passage of charter bills (Items 1a–6a) but also approved of limits on corporate privileges (Items 7–14). "Pro-corporation" legislators were those who favored all charters with no strings attached (Items 1a–14a).

Table 2 shows how it is possible to measure political party unity by noting the percentage of a legislative party's membership within each of these categories. The Whigs in this case were obviously totally unified; they were unanimously pro-corporation. Democrats were clearly fragmented. The Whigs' 100 per cent pro-corporation showing may be considered their highest party-unity percentage on corporations in that session; the Jacksonians by contrast could muster a highest-unity percentage of only 52. By constructing time series with these highest-unity percentages, it is possible to determine the changing level of party cohesion on certain sets of especially persistent issues, over several legislative sessions.

The state of Illinois affords a particularly valuable opportunity for the

[8] The clearest discussions of the Guttman technique's use for historians in legislative roll-call analysis are in Silbey, *The Shrine of Party*, 13–16; and in George M. Belknap, "A Method for Analyzing Legislative Behavior," *Midwest Journal of Political Science*, 2 (1958), 377–402.

investigation of party behavior in its legislature during the Jacksonian period. In the 1830's Illinois was geographically pivotal, economically and demographically expansive and, because of her location on both Lake Michigan and the Mississippi, subject to a variety of sectional influences. By 1834 Whigs and Democrats were identifying themselves in the Illinois General Assembly; they represented coalescing political persuasions that were both new and home-grown, for Illinois was too young as a state to harbor any vestiges of the First American Party System.[9]

The public (and sometimes private) images that Illinois Whigs and Democrats cast of themselves and of each other, especially after the Panic of 1837, were not much different from those that historians have derived from the traditional sources. The images were of a Democratic party opposed to such things as corporate charters and reckless paper money issued by an uncontrolled minority because of the danger they posed to liberty and security, and of a Whig party favoring such things, without the same adjectives, because of their advancement of the country's prosperity.[10] In Illinois further emphasis might also be laid on a partisan division (spurious or not) between effete town and hard-working country; a Democratic farmer in Clay County for instance complained in 1838 of the Whiggish "rage to be genteel, extravagant and refined, [which] has raised every upstart in this country, above the decree of his Maker, that man shall gain his bread by the sweat of his brow. . . ."[11] Illinois Democrats accused Whigs of favoring irresponsible banks, moneyed monopolies, and exclusive privilege, and of containing within their ranks "the men who produce nothing, who labor not" and only now and then an honest but deluded working man.[12] They identified themselves as the protectors of the rights of all and the givers of special privileges to none.[13]

Illinois Whigs did not entirely disagree although they were less vocal; it was simply harder to defend banks and corporations enthusiastically in the abstract than it was to assail them. Yet the *Sangamo Journal* usually upheld Illinois' state banks and the sanctity of contract when either seemed in danger,[14] and the Belleville *Register* thought Whigs a group possessed of a "higher state of mental cultivation and a greater share of social refinement," who "embrace a large proportion of the mercantile class—the shifting, bustling, speculative class whose wealth and fortunes enable them to court pleasure and enjoyment of repose. . . ."[15] William Thomas, a Whig lawyer of Jacksonville, wrote early in 1838 that "all our solvent business men in town are opposed to the adm[istration]. We have but two solvent merchants in town as exceptions; they

[9] A convenient recent sketch of Illinois' early party development is in McCormick, *The Second American Party System*, 277–87. The most complete account is Paul David Hebert, "Emergence of the Democratic Party in Illinois" (Unpublished Master's Thesis, University of Illinois, 1963).

[10] See for example Marvin Meyers, *The Jacksonian Persuasion* (New York, 1960), 8–9; Arthur M. Schlesinger, Jr., *The Age of Jackson* (Boston, 1945), 205–7, 334–37; Frederick Jackson Turner, *The United States, 1830–1850* (New York, 1935), 320–27.

[11] *Illinois State Register* (Vandalia), July 27, 1838.

[12] *Ibid.*, November 3, 1837; *Ibid.* (Springfield), May 8, 1840.

[13] *Ibid.* (Springfield), August 31, 1839, December 18, 1839.

[14] *Sangamo Journal* (Springfield), January 21, 1837, July 15, 1837, December 8, 1840.

[15] *Ibid.*, February 16, 1839, citing Belleville *Register*.

are doing small business." [16]

Our problem, then, is to find indications of how strongly such notions of party identity were reflected in Illinois legislative behavior during the Jacksonian period. It was in the legislature, of course, not in the newspapers, that the meaningful political action was taken. If Illinois Jacksonians and Illinois Whigs truly thought of themselves as opposed or devoted, respectively, to special fiscal or corporate privilege, or to the pursuit of commercial success, how vigorously did they act in behalf of these articles of faith? What other matters might have engaged them even more completely as partisan actors?

Illinois legislators had many opportunities to express themselves on the issues of money, banking, and corporations A bankless state before the removal of the Federal deposits from the Bank of the United States in 1834, Illinois found her credit and currency situation particularly urgent since her sole nearby source of reliable bank notes, the St. Louis branch of the national bank, seemed soon to go under. Therefore, although they might disagree about Biddle's bank, both parties collaborated in the Ninth General Assembly's first session (December 1834–March 1835), to erect two new state-chartered fiscal institutions, the State Bank of Illinois and the Bank of Illinois at Shawneetown.[17] Although the State Bank of Illinois failed to be designated a Federal depository—probably because of its violations of its own charter—[18]it remained immune to substantial partisan criticism during the boom period of 1835–1836, and rode out an investigation of its affairs undertaken early in 1837 by a Democratically-dominated legislature.[19] Indeed, so expansive and speculative was the general mood of Illinois legislators in early 1837, that, the investigation notwithstanding, they authorized an increase in the state-chartered banks' capitalization, to most of which increase the state itself was to subscribe.[20] Illinois' economic euphoria subsided, of course, after financial panic broke in April 1837. The state bank was obliged to suspend specie payments, and seemed in danger as its charter required it to resume payments within sixty days or face liquidation. A special session of the Tenth General Assembly in the summer of 1837 gave the bank the reprieve it needed, and also required the bank's severe retrenchment, a cure brought about through the recall of notes, which some thought was as bad as the disease.[21]

Banks came under general Democratic disapprobation after the panic, an ill-favor further encouraged by the Van Buren administration's efforts in behalf

[16] William Thomas to Henry Eddy, January 4, 1838, in Henry Eddy papers (transcripts), Illinois State Historical Library, Springfield.

[17] *Laws of Illinois,* 1834–1835, 7–14; Fuller accounts of the creation of these banks are in George W. Dowrie, "The Development of Banking in Illinois, 1817–1863," in *University of Illinois Studies in the Social Sciences,* 2 (1913), 60–65; and Fred R. Marckhoff, "Currency and Banking in Illinois Before 1865," *Journal of the Illinois State Historical Society,* 52 (1959), 375–82.

[18] See *Illinois Advocate* (Vandalia), March 9, 1836; *Sangamo Journal* (Springfield), March 5, 1836, March 12, 1836.

[19] Illinois *House Journal,* 1836–1837, 195–98; Usher F. Linder, *Reminiscences of the Early Bench and Bar of Illinois* (Chicago, 1879), 260–61.

[20] *Laws of Illinois,* 1836–1837, 18–22; *Illinois State Register* (Vandalia), March 1, 1837; John H. Krenkel, *Illinois Internal Improvements, 1818–1848* (Cedar Rapids, 1957), 127–28.

[21] *Laws of Illinois,* 1837 (Special Session), 6; *Illinois State Register* (Vandalia), June 2, 1837; David Davis to William P. Walker, July 1, 1837, in David Davis papers, Illinois State Historical Library, Springfield.

of an independent treasury. Paper money as well as the agencies that issued it were anathematized during the hard times of the late 1830's in terms that might have seemed irrelevant during the flush years earlier in the decade. The sub-treasury itself would have no significance in Illinois, as Illinois banks had no Federal deposits to surrender, but there seems no doubt that the sub-treasury controversy helped radicalize both pro- and anti-bank feeling in the state. Yet when the Eleventh General Assembly met early in 1839 the Illinois banks were again redeeming in specie. No specific grievance was at issue, but a branch of the State Bank of Illinois at Alton was rumored to have had illegal dealings in goods and wares. On this count, an investigation was unsuccessfully demanded by some Jacksonians. Otherwise, legislators in this session could commit themselves only on such issues as possible future Federal deposits in Illinois banks should the sub-treasury proposal fail.[22]

During the summer of 1839, however, the malodorous details of the Alton branch's speculations came to light.[23] The bank also got entangled in unfortunate litigation regarding its refusal to redeem some burned bank notes; [24] and on October 23 it was forced once again to suspend specie payments. Since the sixty-day limit on suspension was still in force, and the state was now encumbered with an unpayable internal improvements debt, Governor Thomas Carlin called the General Assembly into special session in December to consider the crisis. In that session the bank's charter violations at Alton (and also at Galena and Chicago) received a full airing. Its charter was revived, but against the strong opposition of some Democrats, who did succeed in extracting as a price for reprieve a turnover in the bank's electorate, severe retrenchment once again, and a promise that specie payments would be resumed by the end of the legislature's next session.[25] Some strongly anti-bank Jacksonians undertook to make capital of this last provision in December 1840. By forcing a premature *sine die* adjournment of the Twelfth General Assembly, these Democrats required the state bank to begin redeeming its notes before any other western or southern bank. However, some of the Jacksonians relented enough the next month to allow the bank its third lease on life.[26] In 1841, however, the Illinois State Bank would close its doors as a result of its own mismanagement rather than legislative action.

This extended catalogue of Illinois' banking vicissitudes is background for the data in Table 3. Table 3 is a condensed statement of the General Assembly's actions taken on banks between 1834 and 1841, and reveals that Whig and Jacksonian rhetoric regarding business enterprise was well-reflected in legislative behavior, at least insofar as that enterprise was associated with banks. This fact was much more evident after 1837. Indeed, little overt Jacksonian anti-state

[22] *Illinois State Register* (Vandalia), January 22, 1839.
[23] See Thomas Ford, *A History of Illinois* (Chicago, 1854), 176–78, for an account of these transactions. See also *Illinois State Register* (Vandalia), June 28, 1839, July 5, 1839.
[24] *Illinois State Register* (Vandalia), June 28, 1839; *Ibid.* (Springfield), August 10, 1839; *Sangamo Journal* (Springfield), July 12, 1839, July 26, 1839, October 11, 1839.
[25] The text of the report of the joint committee to investigate the State Bank of Illinois is in Roy P. Basler, ed., *The Collected Works of Abraham Lincoln* (New Brunswick, 1953), I, 185–95. See also *Laws of Illinois, 1839–1840*, 15.
[26] *Sangamo Journal* (Springfield), December 8, 1840, January 8, 1841, January 29, 1841, February 9, 1841; *Laws of Illinois, 1840–1841*, 39–42.

TABLE 3

HIGHEST PARTY UNITY PERCENTAGES, STATE BANKING ISSUES 1834–1841

	Democrats (Anti-bank, unless other- wise noted)		Whigs (Pro-bank, unless other- wise noted)	
	Senate	House	Senate	House
Ninth Gen. Assembly				
1834–1835	50 †	88 *	46	56
Tenth Gen. Assembly				
Reg. Sess., 1836–1837	48	54	55	58
Spec. Sess., 1837	53 *	55	94	48
Eleventh Gen. Assembly				
Reg. Sess., 1838–1839	85	88	80	71
Spec. Sess. 1839–1840	85	64	60	48
Twelfth Gen. Assembly				
1840–1841	84	72	64	86

* pro-bank
† moderate

bank sentiment was abroad in Illinois before the panic. It was still possible to draw a clear distinction between "banks" and "Biddle's bank" when expectant capitalists in towns as well as on farms wanted credit accommodations. Democrats came forth as stronger pro-bank men than Whigs in the Illinois House in 1835; 88 per cent of them were pro-bank men whereas only 56 per cent of the Whigs took that position; and in the Senate 50 per cent of the Democrats were "moderate" instead of radicalized. Even in the summer of 1837 most Democrats in the Senate were pro-bank. But the polarization of legislative attitudes toward banks came dramatically when hard times set in and banks got the blame for them, as sub-treasury propaganda began to make its impact felt, positively or negatively, and as Illinois' fiscal agencies distressingly often confirmed in their own activities what the more radical Jacksonians had to say about all banks.

With corporations and their "monopolistic privileges" however, the case was somewhat different. Both banks and the corporate business formation tended to be regarded by outspoken Democrats and Whigs as either necessary to business prosperity or as irresponsible agencies benefiting only their proprietors and endangering popular sovereignty. But in fact, since Illinois in the 1830's had little revenue, no men of great capital, and was almost totally bereft of substantial public or private administrative or commercial facilities, joint action was often needed to provide these things.[27] It seems probable, therefore, that most corporate charter applications to come before the General Assembly for roll-call votes reflected not monopolistic ambitions on the part of their sponsors, but aspirations to raise capital in excess of the scant resources available to most frontier entrepreneurs.

Indeed a minority of Democratic leaders, most notably Stephen A. Douglas and James Semple, both in the Illinois House in 1837, persistently attacked

[27] See Robert Murray Haig, "A History of the General Property Tax in Illinois," *University of Illinois Studies in the Social Sciences,* 3 (1914), 25–44.

corporate privileges and their sponsors, and held up the charter issue as one which "showed pretty distinctly who were the Democratic as well as the Aristocratic members of the legislature." [28] Efforts were made in the Tenth General Assembly to amend every charter application with a proviso reserving to the legislature the right to alter or repeal the charter.[29] In the Eleventh General Assembly two bills to authorize "limited partnerships" *were* beaten down, but with the collaboration of many Whigs with the Jacksonians.

Table 4 demonstrates that although banks and corporations might be attacked as identically baneful in public prints and pronouncements, Whigs and Democrats never polarized over corporations in the legislature to the extent that they did over banks; both parties tended toward moderation as often as they

TABLE 4

HIGHEST PARTY UNITY PERCENTAGES, CORPORATION ISSUES 1834–1841

| | Democrats (Anti-corp., unless otherwise noted) | | Whigs (Pro-corp. unless otherwise noted) | |
	Senate	House	Senate	House
Ninth Gen. Assembly				
Reg. Sess., 1834–1835		49		50
Spec. Sess., 1835–1836		39 *		64 †
Tenth Gen. Assembly				
1836–1837	41 †	45 †	56	52 †
Eleventh Gen. Assembly				
1838–1839	47 †	55	70 †	38 †
Twelfth Gen. Assembly				
1840–1841	52	50	100	76

* pro-corporation
† moderate

were either pro- or anti-corporation. Democrats never showed as much cohesion on chartered privileges as they had over banking questions; the Jacksonian rank and file simply refused to follow its more radical leadership on this issue. In spite of inflammatory public statements, for instance, Democrats in both chambers of the Tenth General Assembly were most conspicuously "moderate." not "anti-corporation." In terms of actual partisan success, the winning of roll-call votes, Table 4 shows that even the slightly higher Democratic opposition to charter grants after the panic could not match Whig unity in their favor; the overall Democratic split allowed most of the Whig-favored charter-seekers to have their way.

Substantive issues, such as the foregoing ones, might or might not have elicited strong party divisions in the Illinois legislature; but when Illinois' senators and representatives took time to consider the acts and policies of the national administration, they could be quite emphatic in registering their

[28] *Sangamo Journal* (Springfield), January 21, 1837.
[29] Stephen A. Douglas, "Autobiographical Sketch," in Robert W. Johannsen, ed., *The Letters of Stephen A. Douglas* (Urbana, 1961), 68; Illinois *House Journal,* 1836–1837, 438, 454.

collective sentiments. Both houses in January 1835 considered resolutions applauding Andrew Jackson for vetoing the recharter of the Bank of the United States and for removing its Federal funds, and for attacking the Federal Senate for censuring the president and then refusing to register his protest.[30] The following year the Ninth General Assembly's second session considered statements favoring Thomas Hart Benton's resolution expunging the censure from the Federal Senate journal and expressing confidence in the patriotism, integrity, and Democratic Republican principles of Martin Van Buren, Richard M. Johnson, and the convention that nominated them.[31] Late in 1836 the Illinois House prepared a response to the Whiggish Governor, Joseph Duncan, who had intemperately remarked that Andrew Jackson was preparing a despotism potentially "more absolute than that of any civilized government in the world." In the same session the House also considered such matters as the use of its chamber for a local anniversary celebration of the Battle of New Orleans, or the retention of the adjective "entire" in a resolution expressing "entire approbation" of the Old Hero's presidency.[32] Finally the House in the Eleventh General Assembly's first session put itself on record regarding the Independent Treasury and a possible new national bank.[33]

TABLE 5

HIGHEST PARTY UNITY PERCENTAGES, NATIONAL ISSUES 1834–1839

	Democrats (Pro-admin. policies)		Whigs (Anti-admin. policies)	
	Senate	House	Senate	House
Ninth Gen. Assembly				
Reg. Sess., 1834–1835	93	97	64	53
Spec. Sess., 1835–1836	86	91	82	81
Tenth Gen. Assembly				
1836–1837		95		50
Eleventh Gen. Assembly				
1838–1839		83		92

Table 5 indicates much stronger cohesion among Democrats over Andrew Jackson than over banks and corporations; near unanimity was the case in several instances. Although actual partisan bipolarity did not begin to exist until late in the 1830's over the Independent Treasury, it is clear in every case where the majority of Whigs stood. But it is significant that few of these legislative divisions had more than psychological influence in Illinois. Albert J. Beveridge called the battle over the 1835 resolutions "the one notable political contest that took place in the legislature of Illinois during the session of 1834–35," [34] yet we may not exaggerate by saying that this and other notable contests involving national partisan matters were over non-issues in Illinois. Andrew Jackson was

[30] See Illinois *House Journal,* 1834–1835, 216–17; Illinois *Senate Journal,* 1834–1835, 208–9.
[31] Illinois *House Journal,* 1835–1836, 62–63, 211–12; Illinois *Senate Journal,* 1835–1836, 12, 29, 78, 259.
[32] Illinois *House Journal,* 1836–1837, 19–26, 114–18, 121, 217–18, 825–27.
[33] *Ibid.,* 1838–1839, 172–73, 230–31.
[34] Albert J. Beveridge, *Abraham Lincoln, 1809–1858* (Boston and New York, 1928), I, 168–69.

serving out the last of his second term in the White House and would not seek re-election; the Bank of the United States had no Illinois branches; the sub-treasury was of only academic interest since Illinois' state banks had no Federal deposits to hand over to it. Only the convention issue had direct repercussions in Illinois. In short, when grand matters of national policy required local endorsement, Illinois Democrats, and to a lesser extent Whigs, were willing to follow their national leaders; at the very least this would probably help them win votes. But when the further development and welfare of Illinois or localities within Illinois might be concerned, factors other than partisan ones often intervened.

For our final enquiry the evidence is fragmentary, but still provocative. It rises from two cases carried to the Illinois State Supreme Court in 1839. That court had come to have a Whig majority in a Democratic state by the late 1830's, largely as the result of the longevity and shifting political sentiments of its members. This Whiggish court was called upon in July and December 1839 to decide upon the right of an appointive secretary of state who was a Whig to retain his office against the wishes of a Democratic governor and legislature, and on the constitutionality of alien voting in the state.

The Illinois constitution was vague on the officeholding issue and the court was probably correct in guaranteeing the secretary of state's post to the incumbent, A. P. Field,[35] but by so doing the court, and the Whigs by association, became vulnerable to the charge of advocating life tenure for officeholders. The constitution was clearer on immigrant voting; technically, any free, white male of age could vote in Illinois after six months' residence regardless of his nativity or citizenship. Most immigrants voted Democratic, however, much to the chagrin of Whig politicos, who moved to close the franchise to aliens in a lower-court decision in a test case in May 1839.[36] That case was carried to the Supreme Court and delayed there long enough to allow aliens to vote in the 1840 election, but there seemed to be little doubt of the high tribunal's final decision, given its Whig proclivities. A remedy for Democrats against this seeming usurpation was to punish and intimidate the high court by packing it with Jacksonians and to impose a circuit duty on the justices, heretofore unrequired; this remedy was successfully administered by the legislature in February 1841.[37]

In Table 6 we perceive a degree of partisan polarity over the judiciary unseen in previously-investigated issues or set of issues. Only in the resolutions assailing or endorsing Andrew Jackson had the Jacksonians stood more solidly together; and on no previous votes had the Democrats and Whigs shown comparable cohesion simultaneously. The assault on the Illinois judiciary was an act of partisan vindictiveness, meant to punish the Whigs for dominating a branch of government. It must be significant that in a conflict like this, in which ideology was secondary and political power and officeholding were the main considerations, that party division in the Illinois General Assembly was more pronounced than at any other time.

Obviously what this evidence suggests is that on substantive matters such as

[35] Field *v.* People *ex rel.* McClernand, 2 Scammon (3 Illinois), 79–184.
[36] Spragins *v.* Houghton, 2 Scammon (3 Illinois), 211–14, 377–416.
[37] *Sangamo Journal* (Springfield), February 5, 1841; *Illinois State Register* (Springfield), February 5, 1841.

TABLE 6

HIGHEST PARTY UNITY PERCENTAGES, JUDICIAL REORGANIZATION
1841

	Democrats (Pro-reorganization)		Whigs (Anti-reorganization)	
	Senate	House	Senate	House
Twelfth Gen. Assembly	88	90	100	97

banks, Illinois' Jacksonian-era legislators could reveal something like issue-orientation; on others, like corporations, they could not, in spite of the entreaties of their leaders. Relatively safe non-issues which might still have voter impact, like support of a beloved national figure, could draw the Jacksonian party together more profoundly than local issues could; control of the government, it appears, might divide legislators more completely than actual issues. We have not considered other relevant state controversies such as internal improvements, temperance, and depression relief, or non-controversies requiring legislative action such as everyday revenue and appropriation measures. They, obviously, would add further detail to the picture, as would studies of legislative behavior in other states during the age of Jackson.

II

S. SIDNEY ULMER

Supreme Court Behavior and Civil Rights

Judicial decisions reflect behavior patterns as assuredly as do legislative roll calls. In this essay S. Sidney Ulmer examines the voting behavior in civil liberties cases of the United States Supreme Court in the 1956–1957 terms. The author, one of the new breed of jurimetricians who have wedded mathematics and the study of law, utilizes the same statistical method as Bogue and Rodney Davis—the Guttman scalogram. No Supreme Court in American history suffered more carping criticism than the Warren Court. Complaints generally centered on the supposed willingness of the justices to "legislate" on key issues in terms of personal beliefs rather than judicial precedent. The implication is that judicial behavior is irrational and inconsistent. This article, one among a growing body of statistical studies of Supreme Court voting, undercuts the assumption of irrationality by demonstrating the highly consistent position of individual Court justices, at least concerning deprivations of civil liberties. It is a moot question, however, whether Ulmer's predictive scaling method would be equally applicable in the study of appellate and trial courts where the multiplicity of issues have not yet been screened, refined, and specified.

I

THE HIGHLIGHT of the 1956 term of the United States Supreme Court was the expanded protection given civil liberties. Court holdings considerably

S. Sidney Ulmer, "Supreme Court Behavior and Civil Rights," *Western Political Quarterly*, XIII (June, 1960), 288–311. Reprinted with permission of the University of Utah, copyright owners.

weakened the restrictive provisions of the Smith Act,[1] opened FBI files to defendants in certain cases,[2] and established safeguards around the exercise of congressional investigatory powers.[3] The term was also notable for the fact that voting statistics identified the operation of a new libertarian [4] bloc of Douglas, Black, Warren, and Brennan. While the 1957 term continued the same general patterns, analysis reveals several highly suggestive deviations. The purpose of this paper is to explore the patterns of judicial behavior in civil liberties cases decided by the Court in the 1957 term. A focus on this particular area of decision-making is justified by the heavy emphasis in American Public Law on civil liberties problems. Selection of such a focus is buttressed further by the suspicion abroad that attitude on the part of the Court has had too much and the law too little to do with deciding such cases in recent years. One should recognize, of course, that diagnosis of the motives underlying positions taken by Supreme Court justices is fraught with peril. But one cannot ignore phenomena which appear from the record. Nor should one close one's ears to confessions of garrulous judges that it is now popular on the Court "to regard every so-called civil liberties question as constitutionally self-answering." [5]

The identification of civil liberties cases presents some difficulty. But since this discussion is not to explore semantical problems a simple definition is adopted. In this paper a civil liberties case is one involving a claimed right of the type covered by the Bill of Rights and Civil War Amendments to the Constitution. On this definition it makes no difference whether the claim calls for constitutional or statutory interpretation as long as the right involved is primarily a personal rather than a property right.

Within the framework of this definition the Supreme Court decided forty-six civil liberties cases in the 1957 term.[6] This is an increase of twelve over the

---

[1] *Yates* v. U.S., 354 U.S. 298 (1956).

[2] *Jencks* v. *U.S.*, 353 U.S. 657 (1957).

[3] *Watkins* v. *U.S.*, 354 U.S. 178 (1957). On balance the 1956 civil liberties rulings of the Court led to charges that the Court was once again asserting itself as a super-legislature and super-executive. See in this regard Ralph F. Bischoff, "Constitutional Law and Civil Liberties," *Annual Survey of American Law* (1958), pp. 50–81, and the *New York Times*, June 25, 1957, p. 1; July 1, 1957, p. 1.

[4] The terms "libertarian" and "bloc" are defined and discussed at a later point in this paper. "Libertarian" as used here simply means those justices most favorable to civil liberty claims.

[5] Felix Frankfurter, "Mr. Justice Roberts," 104 *U. of Pa. L. Rev.*, 311 (1955).

[6] *Harmon* v. *Brucker*, 355 U.S. 578 (1958); *Kent* v. *Dulles*, 357 U.S. 116 (1958); *Dayton* v. *Dulles*, 357 U.S. 144 (1958); *Perez* v. *Brownell*, 356 U.S. 44 (1958); *Nishikawa* v. *Dulles*, 356 U.S. 129 (1958); *Trop* v. *Dulles*, 356 U.S. 86 (1958); *Lawn* v. *U.S.*, 355 U.S. 339 (1958); *Eubanks* v. *Louisiana*, 356 U.S. 584 (1958); *Benanti* v. *U.S.*, 355 U.S. 96 (1957); *Eskridge* v. *Washington*, 357 U.S. 214 (1958); *Lambert* v. *California*, 355 U.S. 225 (1957); *Staub* v. *City of Baxley*, 355 U.S. 313 (1958); *Ciucci* v. *Illinois*, 356 U.S. 571 (1958); *Hoag* v. *New Jersey*, 356 U.S. 464 (1958); *Thomas* v. *Arizona*, 356 U.S. 390 (1958); *Payne* v. *Arkansas*, 356 U.S. 560 (1958); *Alcorta* v. *Texas*, 355 U.S. 28 (1957); *Moore* v. *Michigan*, 355 U.S. 155 (1957); *Yates* v. *U.S.* (1), 355 U.S. 66 (1957); *Yates* v. *U.S.* (2), 356 U.S. 363 (1958); *Brown* v. *U.S.*, 356 U.S. 148 (1958); *Green* v. *U.S.* (1), 355 U.S. 184 (1957); *Green* v. *U.S.* (2), 356 U.S. 165 (1958); *Rathbun* v. *U.S.*, 355 U.S. 107 (1957); *Conley* v. *Gibson*, 355 U.S. 41 (1957); *Youngdahl* v. *Rainfair*, 355 U.S. 131 (1957); *Sacher* v. *U.S.*, 356 U.S. 576 (1958); *Ashdown* v. *Utah*, 357 U.S. 426 (1958); *Knapp* v. *Schweitzer*, 357 U.S. 371 (1958); *N.A.A.C.P.* v. *Patterson*, 357 U.S. 449 (1958); *Lerner* v. *Casey*, 357 U.S. 468 (1958); *Beilan* v. *Board of Education of the City of Philadelphia*, 357 U.S. 399 (1958); *Abramowitz* v. *Brucker*, 355 U.S. 578 (1958);

previous term. While 71 per cent of the 1956 cases involved claims against the federal government or its officers, only 43 per cent are so classified in the 1957 term. Claims against the state or its officers increased from 29 to 50 per cent. It is unlikely that the number of claims against either state or federal government varied significantly from one year to the next. The figures suggest, therefore, that the Court was less disposed to hear claims against the federal government in the latter term and more disposed to hear claims against the states. One reason for this might be that the Court was less inclined to decide civil liberties claims against the federal government in the 1957 term. On the same basis one should suppose that the Court was more willing to decide against the state. These expectations flow from the fact that the Court has virtually complete control of its docket. Access to this docket, for all practical purposes, is at the discretion of the Court or of four of its justices where the case comes up on certiorari. The first inference is supported by the evidence since only 65 per cent of the cases were decided against the federal government in the 1957 term as against 75 per cent in the preceding term. The inference respecting state cases, however, is not supported by the relevant data. The Court held against the state in 70 per cent of the 1956 cases but in only 52 per cent of those decided in the following term. This points to probable differentiation among blocs of justices on the question of access to the Court. Investigation would likely reveal a higher compositional correlation between blocs bringing up and deciding federal cases than between blocs bringing up and deciding state cases. It is reasonable to surmise that the percentage of state cases gaining access to the Court through permission of minimal four-justice blocs increased from 1956 to 1957. The justices are not likely to bring up cases involving claims against a state for the purpose of affirming the denial of the claim at a lower level. Thus it appears that in a number of instances the four-justice blocs responsible for bringing up the state cases were not able to pick up the fifth vote needed to hold for the claimant. The blocs responsible for bringing up the federal cases do not seem to have had this particular difficulty. A failure of the type indicated should, of course, be reflected in a less favorable disposition of the Court as a whole toward civil liberties claims. Analysis verifies that over-all the Court was more sympathetic to such claims in the 1956 term than in the term following. Thus while 26 per cent of the claims were denied in the 1956 term, the following term featured denials in 41 per cent of the cases. The foregoing data strongly suggests a greater differentiation in the attitudes of Supreme Court justices toward claims against the state than toward claims against the federal government. In short, the present balance of power on the Court seems more permissive toward state activity than toward federal and, overall, more permissive toward governmental activity in general in the civil liberties field.

Wilson v. *Leow's,* 355 U.S. 597 (1958); *First Unitarian Church* v. *Los Angeles,* 357 U.S. 545 (1958); *Valley Unitarian Church* v. *Los Angeles,* 357 U.S. 545 (1958); *Speiser* v. *Randall,* 357 U.S. 513 (1958); *Prince* v. *San Francisco,* 357 U.S. 513 (1958); *Cicenia* v. *La Gay,* 357 U.S. 504 (1958); *Caritativo* v. *California,* 357 U.S. 549 (1958); *Rupp* v. *Dickson,* 357 U.S. 549 (1958); *Jones* v. *U.S.,* 357 U.S. 493 (1958); *Miller* v. *U.S.,* 357 U.S. 301 (1958); *Gore* v. *U.S.,* 357 U.S. 386 (1958); *Crooker* v. *California,* 357 U.S. 433 (1958); *Giordenello* v. *U.S.,* 357 U.S. 480 (1958).

II

The substantive rights most frequently in contention before the Court in the 1957 term were the traditional ones pertaining to speech, counsel, search and seizure, etc. But not quite so traditional was the fact that five of the forty-six civil liberties cases involved claimed rights of citizenship. Table 1 shows that only cases concerning free speech and former jeopardy exceeded in number the citizenship cases.

TABLE 1

CIVIL RIGHTS MOST FREQUENTLY IN CONTENTION IN THE
1957 TERM

Subject Matter	Number of Cases
Former Jeopardy *	6
Free Speech †	6
Rights of Citizenship ‡	5
Search and Seizure §	5 ¶
Jury Trial **	4
Coerced Confessions ††	4
Right to Counsel ‡‡	3

* *Yates* v. *U.S.* (1), *Eubanks* v. *Louisiana, Ciucci* v. *Illinois, Hoag* v. *New Jersey, Gore* v. *U.S., Green* v. *U.S.* (1).

† *Staub* v. *City of Baxley, Youngdahł* v. *Rainfair, First Unitarian Church* v. *Los Angeles, Valley Unitarian Church* v. *Los Angeles, Prince* v. *San Francisco, Speiser* v. *Randall.*

‡ *Trop* v. *Dulles, Perez* v. *Brownell, Nishikawa* v. *Dulles, Kent* v. *Dulles, Dayton* v. *Dulles.*

§ *Benanti* v. *U.S., Rathbun* v. *U.S., Jones* v. *U.S., Miller* v. *U.S., Giordenello* v. *U.S.*

¶ Includes two wiretap cases: *Benanti* v. *U.S.*, 355 U.S. 107 (1957) and *Rathbun* v. *U.S.*, 355 U.S. 96 (1957).

** *Green* v. *U.S.* (2), *Eubanks* v. *Louisiana, Harmon* v. *Brucker, Abramowitz* v. *Brucker.*

†† *Ashdown* v. *Utah, Payne* v. *Arkansas, Thomas* v. *Arizona, Crooker* v. *California.*

‡‡ *Crooker* v. *California, Cicenia* v. *La Gay, Moore* v. *Michigan.*

While constitutional and statutory requirements were certainly important factors in civil liberties decisions in the 1957 term, they were by no means the only factors involved. Indeed in some instances they were perhaps less significant than other so-called nonlegal factors. This seems incontestably clear in several of the citizenship cases. The opinions in *Perez* v. *Brownell* and *Trop* v. *Dulles* show rather vividly that the attitudes of the decision-makers can be of prime importance. One can ignore the importance of the man in the judge only at a serious loss to scholarship. This point has been well stated by Frankfurter, who expresses it this way:

We speak of the Court as though it were an abstraction. To be sure, the Court is an institution, but individuals, with all their diversities of endowment, experience and outlook, determine its actions. The history of the Supreme Court is not the history of an abstraction, but the analysis of individuals acting as a Court who make decisions and lay down doctrines, and of other individuals, their successors, who refine, modify, and sometimes even overrule the decisions of their predecessors, reinterpreting and transmuting their doctrines. In law, also, men make a difference. It would deny all meaning to history to believe that the course of events would have been the same if Thomas Jefferson had had the naming of Spencer Roane to the place to which John Adams called John Marshall, or if Roscoe Conkling rather than Morrison R. Waite had headed the Court before which came the Granger legislation. . . . There is no inevitability in history except as men make it.[7]

Thus we shift here to individual action. Although leading ultimately to comparative evaluation, attitude analysis must concentrate upon the behavior of individual justices. The men who occupy seats on the United States Supreme Court have available to them alternative choices in each specific case situation. The choice configurations sometimes reveal significant relationships which tend to be overlooked in straight legal analysis. For example, we find that in the 1957 term the justices differed appreciably in the extent to which each chose to express himself in written opinions in civil liberties cases. During the term a total of seventy-five opinions were written in such cases. This represented approximately 34 per cent of all opinions written during the term. Justice Clark wrote the largest number, thirteen, followed by Douglas with twelve and Frankfurter with eleven. Clark also had the largest percentage of his total opinions in civil liberties cases. Exactly one half of Clark's opinions are so classified. He was followed in this respect by Brennan and Warren with 40 per cent and by Frankfurter with 34 per cent.[8]

Table 2 gives the opinion record in civil liberties cases of all the justices for the 1957 term. The table also indicates the percentage variance of such opinions from that expected from the fact that these cases constituted approximately 31 per cent of the term total. The variance runs from +19 in the case of Clark to −8.8 in the case of Harlan. This scale might be taken as one indication of the strength of each justice's feeling about civil liberties problems. It would seem from this that Clark had rather intense feelings and perhaps a definite "position" on personal rights issues that came before the Court during the term. Harlan and Whittaker, on the other hand, appear to have been relatively disinterested. Warren and Brennan apparently identified closely with the values represented by the personal claims. It is also possible to interpret the scale as showing the extent to which a particular justice had a unique position. If Justice A can adequately express a point of view it may not be necessary for Justice B

---

[7] Felix Frankfurter, *Mr. Justice Holmes and the Supreme Court* (Cambridge: Harvard University Press, 1938), pp. 8–9.

[8] The percentages for the other justices are: Douglas, 34.2; Black, 31.8; Harlan, 22.2; Whittaker, 23.5; Burton, 33.3.

TABLE 2

WRITTEN OPINIONS OF INDIVIDUAL JUSTICES IN CIVIL LIBERTIES CASES—1957 TERM

Justice	Opinions of Court	Dissenting	Total	Civil Liberties Opinions as % of Total Opinions	Variance from Expectation *
Douglas...............3	9	12	34.2	+3.2
Black................3	4	7	31.8	+ .8
Warren...............4	4	8	40	+9
Brennan..............4	4	8	40	+9
Frankfurter..........4	7	11	34.3	+3.3
Harlan...............6	2	8	22.2	−8.8
Whittaker............3	1	4	23.5	−7.5
Burton..............3	1	4	33.3	+2.3
Clark...............3	10	13	50	+19

* Expected percentage of civil liberties opinions for each justice would be approximately 31 per cent since the civil liberties cases constituted 31 per cent of the opinion cases decided during the term.

to write an opinion. But the more intensely interested one is in a specific problem or problem area, the less likely it is that another's expression will be adequate. Thus the broader interpretation encompasses the more narrow explanation.

The opinion table suggests several additional questions which are directly related to attitude study. For example, one type of power on the Supreme Court is that possessed by the chief justice, or the senior justice in the majority, to assign the writing of the Court's opinion. The choices made in the exercise of this power may reveal something about the attitudinal relationship of one judge to another and about the makeup of dispositional blocs. Analysis of the 1957 term reveals that opinions in all forty-six cases were assigned by Warren or by Frankfurter. This is to say, of course, that Warren and Frankfurter never dissented together. Each time that Warren was in the minority, Frankfurter was in the majority. Moreover, each time Warren was in the dissent he was joined by Black. Otherwise, Black, being senior to Frankfurter, would have assigned the opinions of the Court.

Table 3 shows that Warren assigned twenty-one opinions while Frankfurter assigned twelve. One might generally expect these opinions to be assigned almost automatically in such a way as to equalize work load. While this is plausible in respect to total opinions it is not necessarily reasonable in a selected subject-matter area. Thus one could not easily predict assignment patterns in civil liberties cases. Table 3 reveals the number of times each justice was available for assignment, the number of assignments made and the ratio of the latter to the former.

An assigning justice has a number of alternatives open to him in selecting opinion-writers. He may, for instance, make assignments to members of the Court on the basis of the interagreement rate between himself and each other justice. Tables 3a and b list the names of the justices in order of times available for assignment. If the interagreement rates constitute the basic factor underlying assignment the number of opinions assigned each justice should correlate

TABLE 3a

WARREN OPINION ASSIGNMENTS IN CIVIL LIBERTIES CASES—1957 TERM

Justices	Times Available	Opinions Assigned	Percentage
Warren........................21		4 (1) *	19
Brennan......................20		4	20
Black...........................20		3	15
Douglas......................19		3	15.7
Whittaker...................18		3 (1) *	16.6
Frankfurter................14		0	0
Harlan.........................13		3	23
Burton........................11		1 *	9
Clark............................ 7		0	0

* Decided against the civil liberties claim.

at a high level with the number of opportunities. This turns out to be the case since the coefficient of correlation (r) is .84 for Table 3a and .90 for Table 3b. The coefficient of determination (r^2) is 70 per cent for the Warren assignments and 81 per cent for those by Frankfurter. Thus 70 per cent of the variance in the Warren assignments and 81 per cent of the variance in the Frankfurter assignments can be accounted for by the variance in the number of times the members of the Court were available for opinion assignment.

Delineation of the other factors operating in this choice-making situation must, at this stage, be somewhat speculative. Certain discrepancies in the assignments, however, are noticeable. One of these is that Warren never assigned a civil liberties opinion to Frankfurter even though Frankfurter was available in fourteen instances. This can be explained, of course, in terms of equalizing the work load. Frankfurter and Warren both wrote four opinions of the Court in civil liberties cases in the 1957 term. The tables, in other words, must be read in conjunction. When this is done the equalization-of-work theory seems to explain adequately every case except that of Harlan. It is seen that Harlan wrote six opinions of the Court, two more than any other justice. And his average rate of assignment was approximately 25 per cent in both the

TABLE 3b

FRANKFURTER OPINION ASSIGNMENTS IN CIVIL LIBERTIES CASES—
1957 TERM

Justices	Times Available	Opinions Assigned	Percentage
Frankfurter...............12		4 *	33.3
Harlan.......................12		3 *	25
Burton......................11		2 *	18.1
Clark..........................10		2 *	20
Whittaker.................. 8		1 *	12.5
Brennan...................... 4		0	0
Warren...................... 0		0	0
Black......................... 0		0	0
Douglas..................... 0		0	0

* Decided against the civil liberties claim.

Warren and Frankfurter camps. This is by no means surprising in respect to the Frankfurter assignments. Harlan agreed with Frankfurter in every civil liberties case in which Frankfurter was the senior justice. Moreover, he is so often in agreement with Frankfurter in all types of cases that he is sometimes referred to as one of Frankfurter's "little hot dogs." The over-all rate of agreement between Harlan and Frankfurter in the 1957 term was the highest of each with any justice. These two justices joined in opinion in 95 of the 117 cases in which both participated.[9] Interaction process analysis for the 1957 term indicates that the interaction was predominantly from Harlan to Frankfurter. Thus the opinion data from Table 3b is in line with the normal expectation. The Warren assignments are a little more difficult to explain. Since Harlan wrote three opinions assigned by Frankfurter, it would have been consistent with the equalization-of-work theory for Warren to omit assignments to Harlan as he did to Frankfurter. Other factors appear to be operating in the Harlan case. One possible explanation might be that the figures merely reflect the fact that Harlan occupied a center position on the Court in the civil liberties cases in the 1957 term. This would suggest that his acceptance in both camps merely delineates his role as "swing justice" during the term. The difficulty with this is that Frankfurter and Whittaker occupied essentially the same position. These three were the "swing justices" in civil liberties cases during the term. This is evidenced by the fact that they were in the majority more often than any of the others. But of the three, Whittaker was more often in the majority. Thus, if any one justice is to be characterized as "swing justice" it would have to be Whittaker, not Harlan. We are left with the inference that of the three justices occupying the middle ground in the 1957 term Harlan for some reason was more acceptable to Warren (and probably the libertarian bloc) than Frankfurter or Whittaker. It should be noted that Harlan's role as number one opinion writer for the Court in civil liberties cases is entirely consistent with his indicated disinterested attitude.

III

It has been suggested that the number of opinions that a justice chooses to write in a selected subject-matter area has some significance. It may reveal something about the extent to which he identifies himself with the values encountered in the area. In the civil liberties opinions of the 1957 term we pointed to Clark, Warren, and Brennan as identifying most closely with the allocation of the values in contention. But our opinion evidence did not indicate the *direction* of the identification. This direction can be clearly portrayed through analysis of voting statistics.

In examining the voting statistics in civil liberties cases in the 1957 term one is immediately struck by discrepancies in individual reactions to certain fact-law situations. One cannot, of course, expect a collegial court of nine justices to decide all cases unanimously. Differences in interpretation of Constitution and statute there most assuredly will be. But when the reactions of the justices are markedly different over a long series of cases one is led to suspect that

[9] 72 *Harv. L. Rev.* 103 (Nov. 1958).

individual characteristics are important decision-shaping factors. Analysis reveals that in twenty-two non-unanimous civil liberties cases decided in the 1956 term, Douglas and Black voted *for the civil liberty claim twenty-one times.* Clark, on the other hand voted for the civil liberty claim in one case and *against the claim in twenty-one.* In the 1957 term out of forty-one non-unanimous civil liberties cases Douglas voted *for the claim in forty instances.* Clark, with the same number of opportunities voted *against the claim in thirty-nine cases.*

Certainly discrepancies of this nature are not alone due to mere differences as to the meaning of Constitution or statute. Indeed it is reasonable in this context to suggest that the *attitude* of the judge toward civil liberty claims was the factor shaping the individual decisions. Llewellyn and the legal realists have often noted that the important factor in judicial decision-making is the reaction of the judge to the fact-stimuli of life around him.[10] This observation would seem pertinent in the area of civil liberties decisions if anywhere.

We shall hypothesize, therefore, that the responses of the justices in civil liberties cases are in terms of *one dominant variable: deprivation of a claimed civil liberty.* This hypothesis assumes that the justice will make his decision not by asking "What does the law require?" but by asking himself such questions as: "Shall I allow any deprivation of a claimed civil liberty? Shall I allow deprivation to the extent of X? to the extent of Y? to the extent of Z?" Since the civil liberties cases have been selected in terms of one common factor: *deprivation of a claimed civil liberty,* verification of response to *one dominant variable* will constitute strong support for the hypothesis. Failure to verify *one dominant operative variable* will nullify the hypothesis.

Identification of the operative variable may be attempted through the use of Guttman Scalogram Analysis. This research tool was developed by Louis Guttman in the early 1940's to cope with a basic problem in opinion research. The problem is to determine if questions asked on a single issue have a single meaning for the respondents. Only if such a single meaning is present can respondents be ranked along an attitude continuum in order of favorableness. Scalogram analysis is designed to detect the presence or absence of this single meaning or dominant variable in terms of which responses are made and respondents may be ranked. Such a variable is identified if a "scale" exists. A perfect scale is said to exist if the questions and responses can be arranged in such a way that "persons who answer a given question favorably all have higher ranks than persons who answer the same question unfavorably." [11] From the rank or scale score of the respondent we know exactly which questions he favored and can therefore say that a response to any question defines the respondent's attitude. Perfect scales, however, are not expected in practice. The difference between a perfect scale and a given scale pattern is measured by a coefficient of reproducibility (CR). Guttman has arbitrarily classified any pattern with a CR of less than .90 as non-scale type.

The attitude of a respondent toward a primary operating variable is measured relatively by his rank order. It is denoted numerically by his scale score. Thus,

[10] Karl Llewellyn, *The Bramble Bush* (New York: Oceana Publications, 1951), pp. 45–49, 66–69. Cf. Glendon A. Schubert, *Quantitative Analysis of Judicial Behavior* (Glencoe: Free Press, 1959).

[11] S. A. Stouffer (ed.), *Measurement and Prediction* (Vol. IV of *Studies in Social Psychology in World War II* [Princeton: Princeton University Press, 1950]), p. 5.

the complete behavior of a respondent to a series of questions can be indicated by a numerical score within the margin of error denoted by the CR.

As applied to Supreme Court cases, certain slight modifications in Guttman's techniques are necessary. The cases are conceptualized as posing a series of questions to a population composed of nine Supreme Court justices. The votes in the cases represent responses to the questions. The questions concern the degree of allowable deprivation to which specific civil liberties may be subjected. Each subsequent case in the list is conceptualized as less deprivational than the one preceding it. The non-unanimous civil liberties cases for the 1956 term, when analyzed, form a scale with properties well within the requirements of scale theory. The existence of the scale indicates: (1) a structured attitude continuum along which response is highly consistent, and (2) the presence of one dominant operating variable. The variable hypothesized is the one in terms of which the cases were originally selected: *deprivation of a claimed civil liberty*. Thus, the data for the 1956 term supports the general hypothesis. The scalogram in Figure I ranks the justices in order of favorableness toward civil liberty claims. Douglas and Black turn out to be most favorable toward such claims with Burton and Clark least favorable. Reed's ranking is of little significance due to his large number of nonparticipations. Consistency of the justices in these cases is measured by the coefficient of reproducibility of .957. This indicates that 95.7 per cent of the over-all response can be accounted for by one operating variable.

There were only eight inconsistent votes out of 182 cast. Frankfurter and Harlan had two each for half of the total. Detailed analysis of the data for the 1956 term is omitted here since the material is included for the purpose of comparison with the following term. But before leaving the 1956 scalogram it should be noted that this scale can be used as a predictive device. As long as the same justices sit and the same types of questions are raised, one can predict from the 1956 scale that the relative ranking in terms of favorableness toward civil liberty claims will be maintained. Thus, from the 1956 data, one could have predicted the same relative ranking for the 1957 term.

The analysis of non-unanimous civil liberties cases in the 1957 term produces a scale with a CR of .953 which is very close to that of the preceding term. True to prediction, the relative ranking of the justices is unchanged. Douglas remains most favorable toward civil liberty claims and Clark remains least inclined to support them. Out of 365 responses there were only seventeen inconsistent votes. Frankfurter had the largest number—five, followed by Whittaker with four, and Brennan with three. Warren, Black, and Douglas had a perfectly consistent voting record in the civil liberties cases in the 1957 term. Black also showed perfect consistency in the 1956 term. This suggests that his attitude is perhaps the most rigidly structured in the civil liberties field of any justice on the Court. Frankfurter, on the other hand, would appear to have the least rigid outlook in this area.

Seven of the inconsistent votes were cast by Frankfurter, Harlan, and Brennan in the three cases of *Caritativo* v. *California, Rupp* v. *Dickson* and *Lawn* v. *United States*.[12] Frankfurter and Brennan were both inconsistent in

[12] 357 U.S. 549 (1958); 355 U.S. 339 (1958).

FIGURE 1

SCALOGRAM ANALYSIS: CIVIL LIBERTY CASES—UNITED STATES SUPREME COURT—1956 TERM

	Douglas	Black	Warren	Brennan	Frankfurter	Harlan	Whittaker	Burton	Clark	Reed	Vote
Scale Score	22	22	19	19	14	12	11	5	0	0	
As Percentage of First Rank	100	100	81.7	81.7	63.6	54.5	50	22.7	0	0	
Jencks v. United States	+	+	+	+	+	+	n	+	−	n	7–1
Yates v. United States	+	+	+	n	+	+	n	+	−	n	6–1
Schneiderman v. United States	+	+	+	n	+	+	n	+	−	n	6–1
Richmond v. United States	+	+	+	n	+	+	n	+	−	n	6–1
Boviaro v. United States	+	n	+	+	+	+	n	+	−	n	6–1
Watkins v. United States	+	+	+	+	+	+	n	n	−	n	6–1
Kremen v. United States	+	+	+	+	+	+	n	−	−	n	6–2
Kinsella v. Krueger	+	+	+	+	+	+	n	−	−	n	6–2
Reid v. Covert	+	+	+	+	+	+	n	−	−	n	6–2
Sweezy v. New Hampshire	+	+	+	+	+	+	+	−	−	n	6–2
Chessman v. Teets	−	+	+	+	+	+	n	−	−	−	6–3
Gold v. United States	+	+	+	+	+	+	n	−	−	−	6–3
Fikes v. Alabama	+	+	+	+	+	−	n	−	+	−	6–3
Paoli v. United States	+	+	−	+	+	−	n	−	−	−	4–5
Konigsberg v. State Bar	+	+	+	+	−	−	n	+	−	n	5–3
Petition of Groban	+	+	+	+	−	−	n	−	−	−	4–5
Kingsley Books v. Brown	+	+	+	+	−	−	−	−	−	n	4–5
Nilva v. United States	+	+	+	+	−	−	n	−	−	−	4–5
Pollard v. United States	+	+	+	+	−	−	n	−	−	−	4–5
Breithaupt v. Abrams	+	+	−	−	−	−	−	−	−	n	2–7
Roth v. United States	+	+	−	−	+	+	−	−	−	n	4–5
Alberts v. United States	+	+	−	−	+	+	−	−	−	n	4–5
Number of Participants	22	21	22	19	22	22	5	21	22	6	182
Inconsistencies	1		1		2	2		1	1		8

Legend: + for the civil liberty claim
− against the civil liberty claim
n nonparticipation

Note: Case titles have been shortened in some instances.

Coefficient of Reproducibility = $1 - \dfrac{8}{182} = .957$

FIGURE II

SCALOGRAM ANALYSIS: CIVIL LIBERTY CASES—UNITED STATES SUPREME COURT—1957 TERM

	Douglas	Black	Warren	Brennan	Frankfurter	Harlan	Whittaker	Burton	Clark	Vote
Scale Score	40	36	35	31	16	14	11	8	0	
As Percentage of First Rank	100	90	87.5	77.5	40	35	27.5	20	0	
First Church v. Los Angeles	+	+	+	+	+	+	+	+	−	8–1
Valley Church v. Los Angeles	+	+	+	+	+	+	+	+	−	8–1
Speiser v. Randall	+	+	+	+	+	+	+	+	−	8–1
Prince v. San Francisco	+	+	+	+	+	+	+	+	−	8–1
Nishikawa v. Dulles	+	+	+	+	+	−	+	+	−	7–2
Harmon v. Brucker	+	+	+	+	+	+	+	+	−	8–1
Abramowitz v. Brucker	+	+	+	+	+	+	+	+	−	8–1
Staub v. City of Baxley	+	+	+	+	−	+	+	+	−	7–2
Jones v. United States	+	+	+	+	+	+	+	−	−	7–2
Miller v. United States	+	+	+	+	+	+	+	−	−	7–2
Payne v. Arkansas	+	+	+	+	+	+	+	−	−	7–2
Sacher v. United States	+	+	+	+	+	+	−	n	−	6–2
Giordenello v. United States	+	+	+	+	+	+	−	−	−	6–3
Yates v. United States	+	+	+	+	+	+	−	−	−	6–3
Kent v. Dulles	+	+	+	+	+	−	−	−	−	5–4
Dayton v. Dulles	+	+	+	+	+	−	−	−	−	5–4
Lerner v. Casey	+	+	+	+	−	−	−	−	−	4–5
Beilan v. Board of Education	+	+	+	+	−	−	−	−	−	4–5
Cicenia v. La Gay	+	+	+	n	−	−	−	−	−	3–5
Thomas v. Arizona	+	+	+	+	−	−	−	−	−	4–5
Ciucci v. Illinois	+	+	+	+	−	−	−	−	−	4–5
Hoag v. New Jersey	+	+	+	n	−	−	−	−	−	3–5
Green v. United States (2)	+	+	+	+	−	−	−	−	−	4–5
Brown v. United States	+	+	+	+	−	−	−	−	−	4–5
Trop v. Dulles	+	+	+	+	−	−	+	−	−	5–4
Eskridge v. Washington	+	+	+	+	n	−	−	+	+	6–2

Case										Vote
Green v. United States (1)	+	+	+	+	+	−	−	−	−	5-4
Moore v. Michigan	+	+	+	+	+	−	−	−	−	5-4
Lambert v. California	+	+	+	+	+	−	−	−	+	5-4
Gore v. United States	+	+	+	+	+	−	−	−	−	4-5
Crooker v. California	+	+	+	+	+	−	+	−	−	4-5
Perez v. Brownell	+	+	+	+	+	−	+	−	−	4-5
Knapp v. Schweitzer	+	+	+	+	−	−	−	−	−	3-6
Yates v. United States	+	+	+	+	−	−	−	−	−	3-6
Youngdahl v. Rainfair	+	+	+	+	−	−	−	−	−	3-6
Ashdown v. Utah	+	+	+	−	−	−	−	−	−	2-7
Wilson v. Leow's	+	+	−	−	−	−	−	−	−	1-8
Rathbun v. United States	+	+	−	−	−	+	−	−	−	2-7
Caritativo v. California	+	+	−	−	+	+	−	−	−	3-6
Rupp v. Dickson	+	+	−	−	+	+	−	−	−	3-6
Lawn v. United States	−	−	−	+	+	+	−	+	−	3-6
Number of Participations	41	41	41	39	40	41	41	41	40	365
Inconsistencies				3	5	2	4	1	2	17

Legend: + for the civil liberty claim
− against the civil liberty claim
n nonparticipation

$$\text{Coefficient of Reproducibility} = 1 - \frac{17}{365} = .953$$

Note: Case titles have been shortened in some instances.

Caritativo, Rupp, and *Lawn.* The first two cases were consolidated for judgment which, *per curiam,* held against the civil liberty claim. The cases concerned the treatment of insane criminals who have become insane after conviction. They raised questions of due process rights under the Fourteenth Amendment.

The due process clause of the Fourteenth Amendment requires a fair hearing in the states. But the Court has never held that the clause applies against the states all the procedural requirements of the Bill of Rights. The Court has been selective and has insisted that those procedural rights which are "essential to justice" are protected at the state level. The list of procedural rights "essential to justice" has been greatly expanded since 1923. But this has been done with caution. And the Court has not seen fit to require the federal procedure at the state level, nor the wisest or best conceivable procedure. As a result the requirements of federal due process at the state level are minimal.

Under the California Penal Code, an insane criminal who has become insane after conviction may not be executed. Wardens in the state prisons are obligated to initiate legal proceedings to determine sanity when there appears "good reason" for so doing. Caritativo and Rupp had been sentenced to death upon conviction for first degree murder. They sought suspension of the execution under the statute. *Ex parte,* the warden of San Quentin, refused to initiate the proceedings. His primary reason was that on several occasions psychiatrists had examined the petitioners and advised that they were sane. In the case of Rupp, the warden refused to hear evidence from petitioner and his counsel even though Rupp had a long history of mental illness.

The Supreme Court majority held that the warden's denial did not constitute a violation of due process. The majority reached this conclusion on the authority of *Solesbee* v. *Balkcom,*[13] a case upholding a Georgia statute granting power to determine insanity to the Governor. Frankfurter's dissent (in which Brennan and Douglas joined) in *Caritativo* reiterated in part his dissent in *Solesbee.* The dissent stressed the common-law rule against executing the insane. And it is generally recognized that the Fourteenth Amendment protects against such execution. His complaint, however, was not substantive but procedural. He does not suggest that a person in the place of Caritativo has a right to have his claim tested in a judicial proceeding or in a formal adversary hearing before the warden. He does insist, however, that the warden should be required to hear the claim of the party. What kind of a constitutional right is it, he asks, "the vindication of which rests wholly in the hands of an administrative official whose actions cannot be inquired into, and who need not consider the claims of the person most vitally affected, the person in whom the constitutional right is said to inhere?" The Frankfurter argument is particularly cogent in view of Rupp's long history of mental illness. The inconvenience to penal administration which would result from a change in the procedure is recognized by Frankfurter. But he declares this better than that California "should have on its conscience a single execution that would be barbaric because the victim was . . . mentally unfit to meet his destiny."

In *Lawn* v. *United States,*[14] the Court upheld a conviction for income tax evasion over contentions that tainted evidence had been used to obtain it. This

[13] 339 U.S. 9 (1950).   [14] 355 U.S. 339 (1958).

evidence had been secured by a Grand Jury in 1952. But the indictments voted at the time were later dismissed by the District Court on the ground that the petitioner had not been notified of his constitutional privilege against self-incrimination. The indictment at issue in the instant case was voted in 1953. Lawn contended that conviction on the later indictment was based on evidence obtained in the 1952 investigation thereby violating the Fifth Amendment. The Court found that Lawn's counsel had waived any objection to the introduction of the evidence. Lawn contended that due process of law was denied him by a failure of the District Court to grant him a full hearing to determine the extent to which the 1952 evidence was used in the subsequent proceeding. No merit was found in this contention. Finally, the majority rejected, on the record, petitioner's argument that he was denied an opportunity to examine and cross-examine witnesses at the trial to determine use of the tainted evidence. Harlan, Frankfurter, and Brennan dissented in part.

The three cases here are significant for splitting the libertarian and less-libertarian blocs on the Court. Douglas and Brennan from the libertarian bloc and Frankfurter from the Court's less-libertarian bloc joined in holding for the claim in *Caritativo* and *Rupp.* In *Lawn,* Harlan and Frankfurter from the right and Brennan from the left joined in supporting the claim. The remainder of the Court opposed. The seven inconsistent votes in these three cases can be explained in part by the peculiar nature of the questions raised. All three presented extraordinary problems. In general, the responses indicate the extent to which the justices disagree as to the nature of the "hearing" required by due process of law in criminal proceedings.

The only other case in which there were as many as two inconsistent votes was *Eskridge* v. *Washington,*[15] another case involving a state criminal proceeding. In this, two justices from the right wing of the Court, Burton and Clark, joined the libertarian bloc of Warren, Douglas, Black, and Brennan to hold for the civil liberty claim. *Eskridge* was decided *per curiam* as were *Caritativo* and *Rupp.* The similarities between the three cases do not stop there. All three concerned persons convicted of murder. All three were actions brought by inmates of state penal institutions. In the instant case the petitioner sought and was denied a free transcript of his trial proceedings in order to appeal his murder conviction. Washington law authorized a trial judge to furnish such a stenographic transcript to an indigent defendant at public expense if in the judge's opinion "justice will be done." The judge here opined negatively and the Washington Supreme Court dismissed the appeal.

The majority of the United States Supreme Court found a violation of the Fourteenth Amendment. The opinion pointed out that while the Amendment does not require a state to furnish a transcript in every case involving an indigent defendant, a state denies a constitutional right if it allows all convicted defendants to have appellate review except those who cannot afford to pay for the records of their trial.

This holding was first made in *Griffin* v. *Illinois.*[16] Since *Eskridge* concerned a 1935 conviction Harlan and Whittaker felt that *Griffin* should not control. The point made by Harlan and Whittaker is important since it involved retro-

[15] 357 U.S. 214 (1958).   [16] 351 U.S. 12 (1956).

spective lawmaking. Judge-made law is often distinguished from that of legislatures. It is said that legislative law operates prospectively only while judge-made law has retrospective as well as prospective force. But, the retrospective element is usually considered to be restricted to the case in which the law is made. This appears to be acceptable to Harlan and Whittaker. The burden of their objection seems to be that the retrospective operations of the Court's decisions should be so restricted. Otherwise there would be no objection to applying *Griffin* to a 1935 trial.

The break-point cases in the scalograms identify the points at which the degree of deprivation of the civil liberty involved became acceptable to the respective justices. For Douglas, only the case of *Lawn* v. *U.S.*[17] accomplishes this. Black breaks in *Wilson* v. *Leow's*[18] where he rejected the claim of a "right to work." Petitioner had been blacklisted in the movie industry for invoking the Fifth Amendment before the Congressional Committee on Un-American activities. After granting the writ of certiorari the Supreme Court dismissed the writ as improvident. Douglas dissenting, said he saw no difference between the "right to work" being denied because of race and where, as here, because the witness had exercised a Fifth Amendment right. Both cases, Douglas urged, violated equal protection.

The break-point case for Warren was *Ashdown* v. *Utah*.[19] This case concerned a claim by Milda Ashdown that she had been coerced by Utah authorities into making a murder confession. Miss Ashdown had conversed with the authorities prior to requesting an attorney as well as after making the request. The oral confession was given prior to the first request. The Utah court excluded all testimony of what was said subsequent to the request for counsel but admitted all that was said before the request. The United States Supreme Court on a complete review of the facts found that the confession was admissible and that it had been obtained under constitutional conditions. Douglas dissented, along with Black, on the ground that a request for counsel made by the father and brother of the accused almost immediately after arrest should have been honored.

Ashdown was one of four cases in which the central issue was the claim of a coerced confession. But, it was the only one of the four in which Warren thought the confession admissible.

In *Thomas* v. *Arizona*,[20] the petitioner, a Negro, was convicted of murder and sentenced to death. He asked the Supreme Court to reverse on the ground that his confession, introduced as evidence in the trial, had been coerced by fear of lynching. Such fear was allegedly induced by the fact that when arrested by a sheriff and posse, Thomas had been lassoed around the neck by a local rancher and jerked toward the nearest trees. Writing for the Court, Clark held that the confession, made some twenty hours after the incident, was not induced by fear of lynching. Warren, Black, Douglas, and Brennan in dissent thought otherwise.

In *Payne* v. *Arkansas*,[21] a nineteen-year-old mentally dull Negro was convicted of murder in Jefferson County and sentenced to death by electrocution. The Supreme Court of Arkansas affirmed. The United States Supreme Court

[17] 355 U.S. 339 (1958).   [18] 355 U.S. 597 (1958).
[19] 357 U.S. 426 (1958).   [20] 356 U.S. 390 (1958).
[21] 356 U.S. 560 (1958).

granted certiorari to examine the charge that the petitioner's confession was coerced. Payne alleged that the chief of police had threatened that thirty or forty people were trying to "get him" but that a confession would enable the chief to prevent it.

The chief of police admitted the substance of the statement. Whittaker for the Court found that in addition, the petitioner was (1) arrested without a warrant; (2) denied a hearing before a magistrate at which time he would have been advised of his right to counsel; (3) not advised of his right to remain silent or of his right to counsel; (4) held incommunicado for three days without counsel, advisor, or friend; and (5) denied food for twenty-five hours and then after two sandwiches for fifteen additional hours. The totality of this conduct created such fear, the Court held, as to taint the confession in violation of the Fourteenth Amendment. Burton and Clark in dissent thought that the confession was voluntary.

In *Crooker* v. *California,* the petitioner's claim of coercion was based on a denial of his request to contact counsel. But, in view of the fact that Crooker was educated, intelligent, and informed of his rights, the Court found the confession voluntary.

It is notable that *Thomas* and *Payne* involved Negroes while *Ashdown* did not. Thus, *Ashdown* is distinguishable on that basis. This is not, however, to suggest that such a factor explains Warren's reaction in the three cases. But it is worth noting that two members of the libertarian bloc thought the confessions coerced in all three cases. And of the three members of the Court most favorable to civil liberty claims in the 1957 term only Warren voted against the claim in *Ashdown.*

Perez v. *Brownell*[22] was the first case on the list which found Brennan opposed to the civil liberty claim. *Perez* was one of several important citizenship cases decided during the term. The role of Brennan in two of these deserves some comment. These two, *Perez* and *Trop* v. *Dulles,*[23] concerned expatriation and the rights of the natural-born citizen.

In deciding them, the whole question of the role of the Supreme Court became involved in the differing views of the justices. Remarks from the bench became unusually bitter and waspish, and the philosophic diversity on the Court was clearly revealed. The cases tested the constitutionality of a federal statute depriving native-born Americans of citizenship for certain proscribed acts. In *Perez* v. *Brownell,* petitioner had been deprived of citizenship for voting in a political election in a foreign state in violation of Section 401 of the Nationality Act of 1940.[24] Frankfurter, for the Court, found that Congress was merely exercising its power to regulate foreign affairs. The basic restriction upon this power is that its exercise must be reasonable or have its basis in rationality. It is recognized that voting in foreign elections might well embroil the United States in embarrassing situations to the jeopardy of successful conduct of foreign relations. Frankfurter thought it reasonable, therefore, to discourage the practice. He found nothing unreasonable about the particular means of discouragement chosen by Congress. For, as he put it, "The termination of citizenship

[22] 356 U.S. 44 (1958).   [23] 356 U.S. 86 (1958).
[24] 54 Stat. 1137, 1168–69, as amended 8 U.S.C. at 1481.

terminates the problem." The majority failed to reach the constitutional issue.

In dissent, Chief Justice Warren, joined by Black and Douglas, argued that Congress lacked the power to deprive the native born or the lawfully naturalized citizen of American citizenship. Responding to the Court opinion he asserted that "a government of the people cannot take away their citizenship simply because one branch of that government can be said to have a conceivably rational basis for wanting to do so." The Warren opinion recognized that a citizen may voluntarily relinquish citizenship by renouncing it expressly or by acting in such a manner as to compromise his allegiance. In the latter category he felt that voting in a foreign election might be an act of voluntary relinquishment under appropriate circumstances. But the Nationality statute does not limit the challenged section to "those situations that may rationally be said to constitute an abandonment of citizenship." Pointing out that of eighty-four nations, the United States is the only one specifically to designate foreign voting as an expatriating act, Warren concluded that "the mere act of voting in a foreign election . . . without regard to the circumstances attending the participation, is not sufficient to show a voluntary abandonment of citizenship."

Thus in *Perez*, we find Frankfurter speaking for one view of the Supreme Court's role in its relationship with Congress. The Court, in his view, should defer to Congress on all doubtful questions. The elected branches of the government should have broad power in a democratic system. Congressional statutes should be upheld if Congress has a rational basis for adopting them. This philosophy is anathema to Warren, Black, and Douglas. These justices stand for a more assertive role of the Supreme Court in its relations with Congress. For example, Douglas, in a separate opinion in which he was joined by Black, took sharp issue with the Frankfurter philosophy. He described it as "foreign to our constitutional system . . . this philosophy has no place here." "It gives," he declared, "supremacy to the legislature in a way that is incompatible with the scheme of our written Constitution."

Following Frankfurter's more restrained approach in *Perez* were Clark, Harlan, Burton, and Brennan. The first three of these are often grouped with Frankfurter in such cases. Brennan and Whittaker have said that they subscribe to the philosophy of self-restraint. But in *Perez* and the companion case of *Trop* v. *Dulles* they voted independently and decided the issue in each instance. In *Trop* a native-born American was deprived of citizenship by reason of a court martial conviction for wartime desertion. As in *Perez,* the issue was whether the forfeiture was in violation of the Constitution. The Court, speaking through Warren, decided that the statute providing for loss of citizenship for one dishonorably discharged after conviction for desertion was unconstitutional. Warren attempted to distinguish the instant case from *Perez* on the ground that Section 401 (g) of the 1940 Nationality Act was involved here, while 401 (j) was involved in *Perez*. The Court saw the question posed by 401 (g) as whether or not denationalization may be inflicted as a punishment, even assuming that citizenship may be divested pursuant to some governmental power. (This assumption is specifically rejected by Warren in his *Perez* dissent.) Holding 401 (g) to be a penal statute, the Court found that the Constitution did not permit Congress to take away citizenship as a punishment for a crime. Denationalization as a punishment for crime, Warren declared, is barred by the Eighth

Amendment. For while there may be no physical mistreatment and no primitive torture, "there is instead the total destruction of the individual's status in organized society." This, the Court felt, was cruel and unusual.

The distinction between *Perez* and *Trop* is indeed tenuous at most. The fact is that the vote of eight of the justices reflected the same attitude in both cases. But Brennan switched from the majority position in *Perez* to the majority position in *Trop* constituting the fifth vote in each case. In making this switch Brennan conceded that "It is . . . paradoxical to justify as constitutional the expatriation of the citizen who has committed no crime by voting in a Mexican political election, yet find unconstitutional a statute which provides for the expatriation of a soldier guilty of the very serious crime of desertion in time of war." But, he explained, in *Perez* expatriation was a means reasonably calculated to prevent evils which might obstruct or embarrass our diplomatic interests. In *Trop,* Brennan held, expatriation for desertion in time of war was not a means reasonably calculated to aid in the successful waging of war.

Thus the decision in the case turned upon Brennan's conception of "reasonableness" between ends and means. Clearly, the Trop case overturning a federal statute has at most a tenuous rationale. It is not likely to have much use as precedent. It is precisely the kind of situation in which Frankfurter would say that the legislature should prevail. The Brennan position, which was crucial in the pair of cases, is not easily explainable unless one accepts his comments on "reasonableness" at face value. Refuge in such terminology has too often in the past been taken by judges interested in the manipulation of legal symbols to accomplish desired ends. As a result there is much to be said for the Frankfurter position. Moreover, if "reasonableness" of the relationship between means and ends is to be a vital factor one would expect the Court to consider more than one or two factors in a given situation. It may be reasonable for Congress to ban participation of American citizens in foreign elections where such participation interferes with effective conduct of foreign affairs. But conceivably there are elections where these considerations do not apply. The election of the head of state in the Vatican is a case in point. Certainly, American Cardinals cannot be constitutionally barred from taking part in the selection. Likewise, there may be instances where the foreign state permits voting by resident aliens. Would this interfere with effective conduct of foreign relations? Clearly the nature of the election and the policies of the nation involved are factors that should be considered in determining the "reasonableness" of congressional restrictions.

The break-point case for Justice Frankfurter was *Lerner* v. *Casey*,[25] one of two cases during the term involving the applications of the due process clause of the Fourteenth Amendment to the discharge of public employees. *Lerner* tested the constitutionality of the New York Security Risk Law enacted in 1951. This statute gives the State Civil Service Commission the authority to classify any bureau or agency within the state as a "security agency." The appointing authority of each such agency is then given powers of suspension and dismissal as to any employee whose continued employment would "endanger the security or defense of the nation and the state." Findings may be made upon the

[25] 357 U.S. 468 (1958).

employee's past conduct. Legal rules of evidence do not apply in such cases but the evidence is not to be "limited" to evidence of membership in organizations found by the state Civil Service Commission to be "subversive."

In 1953, the Commission found the New York City Transit Authority to be a "security agency." In March 1954, it found the Communist party to be "subversive." In November, 1954, the appellant was summoned to the office of the Commissioner of Investigations of the city of New York in the course of an investigation being conducted under the Security Risk Law. Being sworn he was asked whether he was then a member of the Communist party. A refusal to answer was based on the Fifth Amendment privilege. The Transit Authority suspended the appellant without pay and advised him that he could appeal within thirty days. Instead of appeal Lerner brought process in the state courts for reinstatement. The state courts refusing relief, the United States Supreme Court reviewed on appeal papers treated as application for Writ of Certiorari. While several claims were advanced the major contention took the line that the administrative finding of reasonable grounds for the belief that the appellant was "of doubtful trust and reliability" and therefore a security risk, offended due process. The finding, Lerner argued, rested on an inference that he was a member of the Communist party. This inference, it was suggested, was drawn from Lerner's invocation of the Fifth Amendment privilege. He asked the Court to recognize that there was no rational connection between the inference and his refusal to answer. This the Court refused to do. Harlan, for the majority, found that Lerner had not been discharged because of any inference about Communist party memberships nor for invoking the Fifth Amendment. The discharge, the Court said, came about because of "doubt created as to his 'reliability' by his refusal to answer a relevant question put by his employer." The discharge rested solely, therefore, on the refusal to respond. The inference as to reliability was based upon lack of frankness in answering relevant questions. Thus, it now appears that federal or state government may ask employees questions relevant to job fitness and fire them for refusing to answer. The fact that the refusal may be accompanied by the assertion of the Fifth Amendment privilege does not taint the constitutionality of the discharge.

Harlan, the man with whom Frankfurter is most often in agreement, split from his mentor in the now famous passport case of *Kent* v. *Dulles* [26] decided June 16, 1958. The Harlan break-point case was one concerning two applications for passports by Rockwell Kent and Walter Briehl, both of which were denied by the Secretary of State. In both instances, the denials were based in general on the failure of the applicants to furnish certain information regarding their alleged participation in Communist activity—specifically the failure to submit an affidavit as to whether the applicants were or had been members of the Communist party. Both applicants defended on the ground that matters unrelated to the question of citizenship were irrelevant to the right of passport. Briehl, in addition, maintained that every American citizen has a right to travel regardless of politics and that the burden was on the Secretary of State to prove illegal activities on the part of the applicant. The District Court upheld the Department of State. The Court of Appeals affirmed *en banc* by a divided vote.

[26] 357 U.S. 116 (1958).

The majority of the United States Supreme Court, per Douglas, noted that for most of our history the passport was not, as presently, a condition of entry and exit. While recognizing that the right to travel is a part of the liberty of which the citizen cannot be deprived without due process, the Court avoided the constitutional issue deciding the case on statutory construction. Congress had not, Douglas declared, delegated to the Secretary of State the authority to deny passports because of beliefs or associations.

Clark wrote a dissenting opinion in which Burton, Harlan, and Whittaker joined. The dissenters thought that Congress had intended that the Secretary should deny passport to those whose travel abroad would be adverse to national security. They would have reached the constitutional issue but declined comment on the constitutional question in view of the majority decision.

Finally, Whittaker and Burton broke respectively in *Sacher* v. *United States* [27] and *Jones* v. *United States.*[28] In *Sacher* the petitioner contested a conviction in the District Court (D.C.) for failure to answer three questions put to him by a sub-committee of the Senate Committee on the Judiciary. The Court of Appeals affirmed. The Supreme Court granted certiorari, and remanded for reconsideration in light of the decision in *Watkins* v. *United States,*[29] decided in the 1956 term. On reargument the Court of Appeals for the District of Columbia sitting *en banc* affirmed by a divided bench. The Supreme Court again granted certiorari. In a *per curiam* opinion the Court held that where the subject matter of inquiry was "recantation of prior testimony by a witness named Matusow" questions concerning "proposed legislation barring Communists from practice at the federal bar" were not pertinent to the authorized subject of investigation. Clark and Whitaker dissenting, objected to the reversal urging upon the Court that "pertinency is clearly established."

In *Jones* v. *United States,*[30] the petitioner was convicted of various violations of federal liquor laws including possession of an illegal still. The District Court entered adverse judgement. The Court of Appeals affirmed. The Supreme Court granted certiorari. Jones made the claim that some of the evidence used against him in the trial should have been suppressed because it was obtained by an unlawful search and seizure. The evidence in question consisted of a boiler, a fuel burner, and fifteen barrels seized in rear rooms and the attic of the house occupied by Jones. Entry into the house had been over the protests of the wife of the accused. Moreover, it had been made at night without a nighttime warrant. The state argued that the question was simply whether the search was reasonable under the circumstances. The officers had reason to suspect that a crime was being committed for they had previously detected mash in a hollow behind the house, the odor of hot mash from the direction of the house, a hose from which mash emerged running in the direction of the house, and the sound of a blower burner from the same direction. It was admitted that the officers had plenty of time in which to obtain a warrant.

The majority noted that it is settled doctrine that probable cause for belief that certain articles subject to seizure are in a dwelling, cannot of itself justify a search without a warrant. The government's answer to this was that entry had been made for the purpose of arrest. While looking for the accused the

[27] 356 U.S. 576 (1958).
[29] 354 U.S. 178 (1957).
[28] 357 U.S. 493 (1958).
[30] 357 U.S. 493 (1958).

government claimed a right to seize all contraband in sight. The Court did not speak to the merits of this theory but merely observed that the record failed to support the argument.

Black concurred without opinion. Clark wrote a dissenting opinion with which Burton concurred. Clark argued that "although there are many ways to kill a cat, drowning remains the most favored. The Court applies that method to this conviction—drowning it by watering down the findings of fact and conclusions of law." Clark would have accepted the judgment of the lower courts and the government that "the officers had authority to enter the house, arrest any persons engaged in the illicit operation, and, not finding petitioner, arrest him upon his return to the scene. . . . Since the entry . . . was lawful," Clark thought the officers had a right to seize the contraband property.

When we look at Clark's position on the scalogram, we find that he has no break point. His voting record reflects a consistent attitude against civil liberty claims. He finds only two of the forty-one non-unanimous cases deprivational enough to justify support for the claim. One of these, *Eskridge* v. *Washington* has already been noted. The other case was *Lambert* v. *California* [31] which raised general considerations of "fairness" under due process requirements.

In *Lambert,* the Court considered the constitutionality of a Los Angeles Felon Registration Ordinance as applied to a person who had no actual knowledge of a duty to register. Douglas, speaking for the majority, held the statute as applied unconstitutional since notice is required in circumstances of this type. The Douglas opinion distinguished the ordinance here from registration laws in general in that violation of the Los Angeles ordinance is unaccompanied by any activity whatever.

In dissenting, Burton declared that no constitutional rights were violated. Frankfurter, joined by Harlan and Whittaker, in a biting dissent charged the majority with (1) drawing a constitutional line between a state's requirement of doing and not doing; (2) quoting Holmes out of context (which Frankfurter remedied by repeating the quotation and including its context); and (3) making a decision that will turn out to be an isolated deviation from the strong current of precedent—"a derelict on the waters of the law."

Justice Clark was one of two justices casting a lone dissent in a non-unanimous civil liberty case during the 1957 term. Douglas cast such a vote in favor of the claim in *Wilson* v. *Leow's,*[32] the "right to work" case. But Clark is the only justice to cast a lone dissent during the term in a case decided for the claim. He does this not once but on six different occasions. There seems little question that his attitude toward civil liberty claims differs in degree from that of the other justices. Indeed, the magnitude of the disparity almost suggests a difference in kind.

If one compares the scales for the two terms of 1956 and 1957, several important facts quickly emerge. First, it is quite clear that the ranking of the justices in the former term is the same as the ranking in the latter. While these two terms constitute too short a period from which to make overly confident predictions, a tentative statement might be made. That is: the ranking of the justices in civil liberties cases during the 1958 term will be identical with that of

[31] 355 U.S. 225 (1957).   [32] 355 U.S. 597 (1958).

the two preceding terms in respect to those justices participating in all three periods.

While the relative ranking of the justices did not change in the two terms the relative positions in the latter period reflect some degree of spatial movement. We may consider the Douglas position in 1956 and 1957 as the "most favorable" toward civil liberty claims. All other ranks may be interpreted in relation to the Douglas pole. The relative positions may then be compared from one term to the next. The data for the 1956 and 1957 terms are suggestive. Obviously, the four justices most favorable to civil liberties claims in the 1956 term may be viewed as a libertarian bloc. The existence of a bloc can be more precisely established by the use of a cohesion index derived by the formula $\dfrac{Ai}{Ai + Aj} \times 100$ where Ai is the number of times Justice A agrees with another and Aj is the number of disagreements between the same two justices. Thus, the index furnishes a percentage rate of agreement between each two justices on a descending scale. We may consider a justice "linked" to a bloc if his percentage rate of agreement with the justice preceding him on the scalogram is 75+. In the 1965 term we identify the existence of two blocs. Douglas and Black link at 95 per cent; Black and Warren at 81 per cent; and Warren and Brennan at 95 per cent. But Brennan and Frankfurter link at the rate of 63 per cent. Thus, Frankfurter is not a member of the first bloc composed of those most favorable to civil liberty claims in the 1956 term. Frankfurter and Harlan form the second bloc since they link at 91. Whittaker and Reed are eliminated from consideration as a result of their large number of non-participations. Since Burton and Harlan link at 57, and Clark and Burton link at 67 we identify only two blocs and two unaffiliated justices.

In the following term we again identify two blocs but these include collectively all nine justices. The four-member bloc of Douglas, Black, Warren, and Brennan occupies the position most favorable to civil liberties claims. The linkage rates within this bloc run from 82 to 98 per cent. Frankfurter's linkage rate with Brennan is again 63 per cent and thus he again constitutes the break-point between blocs. But Frankfurter and the remaining justices on the descending scale all link with scores of 77 per cent and above. Thus we identify two blocs at either end of the Court. We fail to identify a center group although obviously Frankfurter and Harlan and Whittaker are closer to center than other members of the Court. The dispositional status of the two blocs is revealed by the end of the attitude continuum toward which they tend. The justices most favorable to civil liberty claims compose a libertarian bloc which may be called left. Those least favorable to such claims compose a less-libertarian bloc which may be called right.

In terms of relative spatial position, the following may be said. In the libertarian bloc, Black and Brennan are not as closely identified with Douglas as in the 1956 term. Warren, on the other hand, is more closely allied with Douglas than previously. In fact, Warren is the only justice on the Court to move closer to Douglas in civil liberty cases during the 1957 term. Clark is so negative that he has a scale score of zero in both terms. All the justices with scale scores above that level, excepting Warren, are further divorced from the Douglas pole in the 1957 term than in the preceding one. Three possible inferences may be drawn from this. It might be suggested that Douglas stood still spatially with the movement of the remaining justices, excepting Warren, tending toward a less libertarian position. Or it may be thought that the Court stood still, and Douglas and Warren became even more favorable to civil liberty claims. Finally there may have been movement by Douglas and Warren on the one hand and the remainder of the Court on the other, but in opposite directions. The first inference seems to be more consistent with other data.

The break between the blocs is much more conspicuous in the 1957 term. The Court as a whole was less favorable to civil liberty claims in the period. The Douglas position is consistent and equivalent in both terms. Douglas and Black could find not a single non-deserving claim in a non-unanimous civil liberty case in the 1956 term. In the following term Douglas found one such claim but Black found five. The most tenable inference seems to be that the Court cooled toward civil liberty claims with the exception of Douglas and Warren during the most recent term. In addition, the evidence on balance suggests that the 1956 term represents the zenith of favorable Court attitudes toward civil liberty claims as a reaction to the "McCarthy period." The pendulum appears to be tending in the opposite direction; a development consistent with the so-called conservative thinking in the country as a whole in recent times. But it also reflects the impact of the Whittaker appointment to the Court as well as a more conservative outlook on the part of Frankfurter and Harlan.

IV

In conclusion, the analysis of the behavior of the United States Supreme Court in civil liberties cases for the 1957 term produces concrete as well as inferential findings. These may be summarized as follows: (1) The Court was less favorable as a whole toward civil liberty claims in the 1957 term than in the term preceding it. (2) Two distinct cohesion blocs operated on the Court in civil liberty cases in both terms but in the 1957 term these two blocs encompassed collectively all nine justices. (3) The blocs cohered in terms of disposition toward civil liberty claims and can be designated on this basis as libertarian and less libertarian. (4) The relative ranking of the justices in terms of attitude toward civil liberty claims remained the same in both terms. (5) The positions of the justices relative to the Douglas polar position showed movement toward a less libertarian role for all justices except Clark and Warren. (6) In both the 1956 and 1957 terms the Court decided civil liberty claims in terms of one dominant variable: deprivation of a claimed civil liberty. (7) The evidence is that the Guttman scalogram techniques can be used successfully to predict the relative rank of each justice in terms of attitude toward civil liberty deprivations. Thus in the 1958 term,[33] Douglas will be expected to be most favorable toward civil liberty claims with his colleagues ranked [34] behind him in the order of: Black, Warren, Brennan, Frankfurter, Harlan, Whittaker, and Clark.

[33] This paper was written prior to the conclusion of the 1958 term.
[34] Potter Stewart, the 1958 addition to the Court, cannot be ranked until completion of a full term.

PART IV

Popular Voting Behavior

TRADITIONAL POLITICAL HISTORY has come under withering attack in the present generation. This has been true especially since 1948, when Thomas C. Cochran condemned the "presidential synthesis" as futile and sterile and called for the substitution of a "social science synthesis."[1] Subsequently, Lee Benson and Samuel P. Hays have sketched the parameters of the new approach in major methodological papers.[2] Although the social science synthesis has not yet emerged, historians have changed the focus of their work and are much more concerned today than they were in 1948 with the cultural and social dimensions of the American past. Political scientists such as V. O. Key, Jr., Paul F. Lazarsfeld, Angus Campbell, Robert A. Dahl, Warren E. Miller, and Walter Dean Burnham are largely responsible for the change in viewpoint. In the last two decades they have pioneered in popular voting behavior studies based on aggregate election statistics and survey research.[3]

The thrust of the social science approach to political history is the search for structural patterns among the various societal groups—socio-economic, ethno-cultural, local, and cosmopolitan. Since politics involves the clash of interests and values among these groups and the distribution of power which determines the triumph of one goal over another, the social scientist is concerned more with the basic underlying patterns of political life, the sources of conflict, rather than the traditional interest in the formal institutions or leading individuals and events. To understand the "why" of political events, the behavioralists (1) take a long-term perspective by comparing voting results over time, (2) seek to formulate potentially verifiable hypotheses, (3) explore statistical methods of

[1] Thomas C. Cochran, "The Presidential Synthesis in American History," *American Historical Review*, LIII (July, 1948), 748–59.

[2] Lee Benson, "Research Problems in American Political Historiography," in Mirra Komarovsky (ed.), *Common Frontiers in the Social Sciences* (Glencoe, 1957), 113–83, and *The Concept of Jacksonian Democracy: New York as a Test Case* (Princeton, 1961), 270–87. Samuel P. Hays' major "methods" papers are "History as Human Behavior," *Iowa Journal of History*, LVIII (July, 1960), 193–206; "New Possibilities for American Political History: The Social Analysis of Political Life," in Seymour Martin Lipset and Richard Hofstadter, *Sociology and History: Methods* (New York, 1968), 181–227; "The Social Analysis of American Political History, 1880–1920," *Political Science Quarterly*, LXXX (Sept., 1965), 373–94; "Archival Sources for American Political History," *American Archivist*, XXVIII (Jan., 1965), 17–30.

[3] For the major works of Key, Campbell, Miller, Philip E. Converse, Donald E. Stokes, E. E. Schattschneider, and others, see the footnotes in Burnham's article (12). Additional studies are Key, *The Responsible Electorate* (Cambridge, 1965); Campbell, *Elections and the Political Order* (New York, 1966); Robert A. Dahl, *Who Governs? Democracy and Power in an American City* (New Haven, 1961); Paul F. Lazarsfeld, Bernard Berelson, and Hazel Gaudet, *The People's Choice* (New York, 1948); Austin Ranney (ed.), *Essays on the Behavioral Study of Politics* (Urbana, 1962), esp. chap. 2; Duncan MacRae, Jr., and James A. Meldrum, "Critical Elections in Illinois: 1888–1958," *American Political Science Review*, LIV (Sept., 1960), 669–83; Charles Sellers, "The Equilibrium Cycle in Two Party Politics," *Public Opinion Quarterly*, XXIX (Spring, 1965), 16–38; Gerald Pomper, "Classification of Presidential Elections," *Journal of Politics*, XXIX (Aug., 1967), 535–66, and Pomper, *Elections in America* (New York, 1969); Michael P. Rogin, *The Intellectuals and McCarthy: The Radical Specter* (Cambridge, 1967).

inquiry (e.g., correlation coefficients),[4] (4) focus on local history in the knowledge that patterns of political structure develop first at the community level, and (5) freely mine archival source material such as genealogical data, official state manuals, city directories, and manuscript census and election returns.

The following three essays illustrate the major characteristics of the "new" political history. Walter Dean Burnham, in his important article on American voting patterns during the past century, touches each of the five bases—the long sweeping perspective, an hypothesis of political alienation, statistical measurement, detailed study at the local (in this case, state) level, and neglected election and census data. Even more important, Burnham has harmonized the hitherto conflicting perspectives of students of aggregate electoral statistics and survey research. Robert R. Dykstra and Harlan Hahn also adopt the case study method and statistics in their quantitative social analysis of an Iowa state referendum in 1868. State-wide popular referenda on constitutional amendments, initiatives, and other issues of public policy, provide virtually an untapped source for such quantitative studies of electoral behavior.[5] The Inter-University Consortium files now include returns for more than 3000 referenda, and it is estimated that the total universe of such data is at least three times greater.[6] Dykstra and Hahn collaborated to analyze one of these referenda in an attempt to uncover the socio-economic groupings among the Iowa electorate.

Roger E. Wyman's intensive study of the Wisconsin electorate in the 1890 state election is similar to the Dykstra and Hahn essay in statistical method and style, but focuses on the ethno-cultural dimension of electoral behavior in lieu of the social and economic. The American ethnic mosaic has long fascinated historians, but for many years filiopietists dominated the field. Beginning in the 1930's, scholars such as Oscar Handlin turned to sociological constructs (but not the behavioral sciences) in an attempt to discern the tragedy and pathos among the uprooted. Only in the last decade has ethnic history begun to break free of the moralistic, romantic emphasis, largely at the hands of political behavioralists Samuel Lubell and Seymour Martin Lipset, who developed the ethno-cultural approach to political history.[7]

The ethno-cultural view involves the examination of local election returns in the light of the religious and nationality backgrounds of the voters. Lee Benson, in his case study of Jacksonian Democracy in New York, was one of the first historians to follow Lubell's ethno-cultural method. "Ethnic and religious differences," Benson concluded, "have tended to be relatively the most important

[4] For a detailed explanation of correlation techniques, see Hubert M. Blalock, Jr., *Social Statistics* (New York, 1960), chaps. 17–19.

[5] A study similar to Dykstra and Hahn of the ante-bellum suffrage referenda in New York, which also notes the invaluable nature of referenda data, is John L. Stanley, "Majority Tyranny in Tocqueville's America: The Failure of Negro Suffrage in 1846," *Political Science Quarterly*, LXXXIV (Sept., 1969), 412–35.

[6] Inter-University Consortium for Political Research, *Biennial Report, 1966–1968* (Ann Arbor, 1969), 61–62. Regrettably, none of the data is in machine-readable form.

[7] Samuel Lubell, *The Future of American Politics* (New York, 1952), and Seymour Martin Lipset, "Religion and Politics in the American Past and Present," in Robert Lee and Martin E. Marty (eds.), *Religion and Social Conflict* (New York, 1964). See also Gerhard Lenski, *The Religious Factor; A Sociological Study of Religion's Impact on Politics, Economics, and Family Life* (New York, 1961).

sources of political differences." [8] Benson's iconoclastic book has prompted a spate of political studies that focus on such diverse ethnic groups as New York Jewish socialists in 1910–1911, the Rockford Swedish community and German isolationists in Illinois, Dutch and German Democrats in ante-bellum Iowa, Nebraska's Germans in the late nineteenth century, and non-British immigrants in Michigan in the 1830's and 1840's.[9] Wyman's essay is in the mainstream of the Benson tradition. Wyman not only adopted Benson's method of isolating ethnic groups in the various political subdivisions, but also participated in the summer training seminar of the Inter-University Consortium and utilized its computer and data bank of county-level voting and census information.

One aspect of voting behavior into which historians are just beginning to venture is the "historical study of public opinion," especially political opinion. Lee Benson, in a major theoretical essay, recently outlined a general analytic model for such studies, drawing on his own analysis of New York public opinion on the Texas annexation question,[10] and on the earlier pioneering studies of such political scientists as Bernard Berelson, Paul Lazarsfeld, Morris Janowitz, and others.[11] Benson believes that social scientists can study past

[8] Lee Benson, *Concept of Jacksonian Democracy,* 165. This conclusion is buttressed by Michael F. Holt's excellent behavioral analysis of ante-bellum Pittsburgh, *Forging a Majority: The Formation of the Republican Party in Pittsburgh, 1848–1860* (New Haven, 1969).

[9] Arthur Gorenstein, "A Portrait of Ethnic Politics," *Publications of the American Jewish Historical Society,* L (Mar., 1961), 202–38; Dorothy Homer, "The Rockford Swedish Community," *Journal of the Illinois State Historical Society,* LVII (Summer, 1964), 149–55; Howard W. Allen, "Studies of Political Loyalties of Two Nationality Groups: Isolationism and German Americans," *ibid.,* 143–49; George Daniels, "Immigrant Vote in the 1860 Election: The Case of Iowa," *Mid-America,* XLIV (July, 1963), 146–62; Robert P. Swierenga, "The Ethnic Voter and the First Lincoln Election," *Civil War History,* XI (Mar., 1965), 27–43; Frederick C. Luebke, *Immigrants and Politics: The Germans of Nebraska, 1880–1900* (Lincoln, 1969); Ronald P. Formisano, "A Case Study of Party Formation: Michigan, 1835," *Mid-America,* L (Apr., 1968), 83–107; Formisano, "Analyzing American Voting, 1830–1860: Methods," *Historical Methods Newsletter,* II (Mar., 1969), 1–12; and Formisano, "The Social Bases of American Voting Behavior, Wayne County, Michigan, 1837–1852 as a Test Case" (Ph.D. dissertation, Wayne State University, 1966). Other major substantive articles stressing local political issues are: Paul Kleppner, "Lincoln and the Immigrant Vote: A Case of Religious Polarization," *Mid-America,* XLVIII (July, 1966), 176–95; Thomas B. Alexander, *et al.,* "The Basis of Alabama's Ante-Bellum Two-Party System," *Alabama Review,* XIX (Oct., 1966), 243–76; Stanley B. Parsons, "Who Were the Nebraska Populists?" *Nebraska History,* XLIV (June, 1963), 83–99; Richard Jensen, "The Historical Roots of Party Identification," paper delivered to the American Political Science Association, Washington, 1969.

[10] Lee Benson, "An Approach to the Scientific Study of Past Public Opinion," *Public Opinion Quarterly,* XXXI (Winter, 1967–68), 522–67. Benson's substantive contributions include: "Texan Annexation and New York Public Opinion," in *Concept of Jacksonian Democracy,* 254–69; a book in progress with Joel Silbey, tentatively entitled, "New York Public Opinion and American Civil War Causation: An Essay in the Logic and Practice of Historical Explanation;" and a master's essay he directed: Madeleine S. Shapiro, "Michigan Public Opinion, the Mexican War, and the Wilmot Proviso: A Study of Legislative Resolutions as Opinion Indicators" (Wayne State University, 1964).

[11] Bernard Berelson and Morris Janowitz (eds.), *Reader in Public Opinion and Communication,* 2nd ed. (Glencoe, Ill., 1965); Paul F. Lazarsfeld, "Public Opinion and the Classical Tradition," *Public Opinion Quarterly,* XXI (Spring, 1957), 39–53; and Allen H. Barton and Paul F. Lazarsfeld, "Some Functions of Quantitative Analysis in Social Research," *Frankfurter Bertrage Zur Soziology,* I (1955), reprinted as "S-336" in the Bobbs-Merrill Reprint Series in the Social Sciences. On the historical study of public opinion, see Robert T. Brower, "Opinion Research and

public opinion scientifically, despite the lack of relevant opinion polls or surveys and the impossibility of interviewing our deceased forebears. "By selecting documents and, so to speak, 'interrogating' their authors, historical researchers [can] *generate* data designed to answer questions about past public opinion." [12] The interrogation, Benson suggests, should proceed step by step, beginning with the reconstruction of the distribution of opinion on specified issues over time, moving to the reconstruction of the process of opinion formation, and ending with the reconstruction of the impact of opinion on government decisions. What are the opinion indicators? Since voting results directly reflect mass public opinion, they provide the best immediate source of opinion data. Given the ready access to voting data in machine-readable form from the Inter-University Consortium, Benson's sanguine prediction "that major advances will be made in the use of voting behavior as an opinion indicator" is likely to be realized. Other historical documents such as newspaper editorials and personal manuscripts, which may be highly unrepresentative, can serve to supplement the voting indices.

Historical Interpretations of Elections," *Public Opinion Quarterly,* XII (Fall, 1948), 457–58; Herbert H. Hyman, "Toward a Theory of Public Opinion," *ibid.,* XXI (Spring, 1957), 56–57; Hans Spier, "Historical Development of Public Opinion," *American Journal of Sociology,* LV (Jan., 1950), 376–88; Joseph Strayer, "The Historian's Concept of Public Opinion," in Komarovsky, *Common Frontiers of the Social Sciences,* 263–68; Robert A. Kann, "Public Opinion Research: A Contribution to Historical Method," *Political Science Quarterly,* LXXIII (Sept., 1958), 374–96.
[12] Benson, "Scientific Study of Past Public Opinion," 525.

WALTER DEAN BURNHAM

The Changing Shape of
the American Political Universe

Walter Dean Burnham draws on the recent behavioral methods to survey the massive changes in the size and shape of the American electorate since the mid-nineteenth century. In 1962–64 Burnham helped initiate the project of the Inter-University Consortium for Political Research to collect popular election data for presidential elections of the nineteenth century. The present essay utilizes this data as well as census findings to measure voting participation by five criteria: "estimated turnout," "drop-off," "roll-off," "split-tickets," and "partisan swings." The analysis rests largely on the experience of five states, which suggests the possibilities for similar research in other states. Burnham's findings, exploratory as they are, raise disturbing questions about the modern American political system which emerged in the New Deal era. None is more disquieting than the apparent inability to integrate into the system the apolitical half of the American electorate before they are mobilized by a manipulative radicalism of the left or the right.

IN THE INFANCY of a science the use even of fairly crude methods of analysis and description can produce surprisingly large increments of knowledge if new perspectives are brought to bear upon available data. Such perspec-

Walter Dean Burnham, "The Changing Shape of the American Political Universe," *American Political Science Review*, LIX (Mar., 1965), 7–28. Reprinted with permission of the author and the Executive Director of the American Political Science Association.

tives not infrequently require both a combination of methodologies and a critical appraisal of the limitations of each. The emergence of American voting-behavior studies over the last two decades constitutes a good case in point. Studies based on aggregate election statistics have given us invaluable insights into the nature of secular trends in the distribution of the party vote, and have also provided us with useful theory concerning such major phenomena as critical elections.[1] Survey research has made significant contributions to the understanding of motivational forces at work upon the individual voter. As it matures, it is now reaching out to grapple with problems which involve the political system as a whole.[2]

Not at all surprisingly, a good deal of well publicized conflict has arisen between aggregationists and survey researchers. The former attack the latter for their failure to recognize the limitations of an ahistorical and episodic method, and for their failure to focus their attention upon matters of genuine concern to students of politics.[3] The latter insist, on the other hand, that survey research alone can study the primary psychological and motivational building blocks out of which the political system itself is ultimately constructed. Not only are both parties to the controversy partly right, but each now seems to be becoming quite sensitive to the contributions which the other can make. As survey scholars increasingly discover that even such supposedly well established characteristics of the American voter as his notoriously low awareness of issues can be replaced almost instantaneously under the right circumstances by an extremely pronounced sensitivity to an issue, the importance of the time dimension and factors of social context so viewed become manifest.[4] Students of aggregate voting behavior, on the other hand, are turning to the data and methods of survey research to explore the structure and characteristics of contemporary public opinion.[5] A convergence is clearly underway. One further sign of it is the construction of the first national election-data archive, now underway at the Survey Research Center of the University of Michigan.[6] The completion of this

[1] The leading work of this sort thus far has been done by the late V. O. Key, Jr. See, *e.g.,* his "A Theory of Critical Elections," *Journal of Politics,* Vol. 17, pp. 3–18 (1955), and his *American State Politics* (New York, 1956). See also such quantitatively oriented monographs as Perry Howard, *Political Tendencies in Louisiana, 1812–1952* (Baton Rouge: Louisiana State University Press, 1957).

[2] The most notable survey-research effort to date to develop politically relevant theory regarding American voting behavior is Angus Campbell, Philip E. Converse, Warren E. Miller and Donald E. Stokes, *The American Voter* (New York, 1960), especially ch. 20.

[3] V. O. Key, Jr., "The Politically Relevant in Surveys," *Public Opinion Quarterly,* Vol. 24, pp. 54–61 (1960); V. O. Key, Jr., and Frank Munger, "Social Determinism and Electoral Decision: The Case of Indiana," in Eugene Burdick and Arthur J. Brodbeck, eds., *American Voting Behavior* (Glencoe, Ill., 1959), pp. 281–99.

[4] Warren E. Miller and Donald E. Stokes, "Constituency Influence in Congress," this REVIEW, Vol. 57, pp. 45–56 (1963). The authors observe that in the 1958 Hays-Alford congressional race in Arkansas, the normally potential nature of constituency sanctions against representatives was transferred under the overriding pressure of the race issue into an actuality which resulted in Hays' defeat by a write-in vote for his opponent. The normally low issue- and candidate-consciousness among the electorate was abruptly replaced by a most untypically intense awareness of the candidates and their relative positions on this issue.

For an excellent cross-polity study of voting behavior based on comparative survey analysis, see Robert R. Alford, *Party and Society* (Chicago, Rand McNally, 1963).

[5] V. O. Key, Jr., *Public Opinion and American Democracy* (New York, 1961), based largely on survey-research data at the University of Michigan.

[6] This effort, to which the author was enabled to contribute, thanks to a Social Science Research Council grant for 1963–1964, has been supported by the Council

archive and the conversion of its basic data into a form suitable for machine processing should provide the material basis for a massive breakthrough in the behavioral analysis of American political history over the last century and a half.

If controversies over method accompany the development of disciplines, so too does the strong tendency of the research mainstream to bypass significant areas of potential inquiry, thus leaving many "lost worlds" in its wake. One such realm so far left very largely unexplored in the literature of American politics centers around changes and continuities in the gross size and shape of this country's active voting universe over the past century. Key, to be sure, made contributions of the greatest significance to our understanding of the changing patterns of party linkage between voters and government. Moreover, he called attention to the need for quantitative analysis of political data other than the partisan division of the vote for leading offices.[7] E. E. Schattschneider's discussion of the struggle over the scope of political conflict and his functional analysis of the American party system remain a stimulus to further research— not least in the direction of examining the aggregate characteristics of the American electorate over time.[8] Other recent studies, for example, of the turnout of voters in Canada and Indiana, have added to our knowledge of contemporary patterns of mass political involvement.[9] The fact remains, however, that no systematic analysis over lengthy time periods has yet been made of the massive changes of relative size and characteristics in the American voting universe, despite their obvious relevance to an understanding of the evolving political system as a whole.

This article does not purport to be that systematic study. It is, rather, a tentative reconnaissance into the untapped wealth of a whole range of political data, undertaken in the hope of showing concretely some of the potentialities of their study. The primary objective here is the preliminary exploration of the scope of changes since the mid-19th century in turnout and other criteria of voting participation, and the possible substantive implications of such changes.

There is also a second objective. The day is not far distant when a major

---

and by the National Science Foundation. This article is in no sense an integral part of that larger project. But it is proper to acknowledge gratefully here that the S.S.R.C., by making it possible for me to spend a year at the Survey Research Center, has helped to provide conditions favorable to writing it. Thanks are also due to Angus Campbell, Philip E. Converse, Donald E. Stokes and Warren E. Miller for their comments and criticisms. They bear no responsibility for the defects of the final product.

[7] V. O. Key, Jr., *American State Politics, op. cit.,* pp. 71–73, 197–216.

[8] E. E. Schattschneider, *Party Government* (New York, 1942) and *The Semi-Sovereign People* (New York, 1960), pp. 78–96.

[9] Howard A. Scarrow, "Patterns of Voter Turnout in Canada," *Midwest Journal of Political Science,* Vol. 5, pp. 351–64 (1961); James A. Robinson and William Standing, "Some Correlates of Voter Participation: The Case of Indiana," *Journal of Politics,* Vol. 22, pp. 96–111 (1960). Both articles—one involving a political system outside of but adjacent to the United States—indicate patterns of contemporary participation which seem at variance with the conclusions of survey studies regarding the behavior of the American electorate. In Canada rural turnout is higher than urban, and no clear-cut pattern of drop-off between federal and provincial elections exists. Voter participation in Indiana apparently does not increase with the competitiveness of the electoral situation, and does increase with the rurality of the election jurisdiction. With the possible exception of the relationship between competitiveness and turnout, all of these are characteristics associated with 19th-century voting behavior in the United States; see below.

effort will be undertaken to relate the findings of survey research to contemporary aggregate data and then to examine the aggregate data of past generations in the light of these derived relationships. Before such inquiry is undertaken, it will be a matter of some importance to ascertain whether and to what extent the basic findings of survey research about the present American electorate are actually relevant to earlier periods of our political history. Firm conclusions here as elsewhere must await much more comprehensive and detailed study. Even so, enough can be learned from the contours of the grosser data to warrant posting a few warning signs.

I

Several criteria of voting participation have been employed in this analysis: (1) estimated turnout; (2) drop-off; (3) roll-off; (4) split-ticket voting; (5) mean partisan swing. Turnout, the most indispensable of these criteria, is also unfortunately the "softest." A number of errors of estimate can arise from the necessary use of census data. For example, interpolations of estimates for intercensal years can produce significant error when abnormally large increases or decreases in population are bunched together within a few years. Estimates of the alien component in the total adult male population must also necessarily remain quite speculative for the censuses from 1880 through 1900, and are impossible to secure from published census data prior to 1870. No doubt this helps explain why students of voting-behavior research have avoided this area. But we need not reject these admittedly imprecise data altogether, because of their imperfections, when secular changes in turnout levels and variabilities from election to election are of far too great a magnitude to be reasonably discounted on the basis of estimate error.[10]

Moreover, the other criteria employed in this study not only share a very similar directional flow over time, but are directly derived from the voting statistics themselves. Free from the estimate-error problem, they are ordinarily quite consistent with the turnout data.[11] What is called "drop-off" here is the

[10] In computing turnout data, note that until approximately 1920 the criteria for eligibility to vote differed far more widely from state to state than they do now. In a number of states west of the original thirteen—for example, in Michigan until 1894 and in Wisconsin until 1908—aliens who had merely declared their intention to become citizens were permitted to vote. Woman suffrage was also extended piecemeal for several decades prior to the general enfranchisement of 1920. The turnout estimates derived here have been adjusted, so far as the census data permit, to take account of such variations.

[11] If one computes the off-year total vote of the years 1950–1962 as a percentage of the total vote cast in the preceding presidential election, a virtually identical correspondence is reached with estimated off-year turnout as a percentage of turnout in the immediately preceding presidential year:

Year	Total Off-Year Vote as % of Vote in Last Presidential Year	Estimated Off-Year Turnout as % of Turnout in Last Pres. Year
1950	82.9	80.4
1954	69.2	67.5
1958	73.9	72.1
1962	74.4	73.6

familiar pattern of decline in the total vote between presidential and succeeding off-year elections. The drop-off figures usually presented below are reciprocals of the percentage of the presidential-year total vote which is cast in the immediately following off-year election. If the total vote for the two successive elections is the same, drop-off is zero; if the total vote in the off-year election exceeds that cast in the immediately preceding presidential election, drop-off is negative. Secular increases in the amplitude of drop-off could be associated with such factors as a declining relative visibility or salience of off-year elections, or with an increasing component of active voters who are only marginally involved with the voting process as such.

"Roll-off" measures the tendency of the electorate to vote for "prestige" offices but not for lower offices on the same ballot and at the same election. If only 90 per cent of those voting for the top office on the ticket also vote for the lesser statewide office receiving fewest votes at the same election, for example, the roll-off figures stands at 10 per cent. Secular increases in this criterion of voting participation could be associated with such variables as a growing public indifference to elections for administrative offices which might well be made appointive, or with a growing proportion of peripheral voters in the active electorate; or with changes in the form of ballots. Split-ticket voting has been measured rather crudely here as the difference between the highest and lowest percentages of the two-party vote cast for either party among the array of statewide offices in any given election. Zero on this scale would correspond to absolute uniformity in the partisan division of the vote for all offices at the same election. The amplitude of partisan swing is computed in this study without reference to the specific partisan direction of the swing, and is derived from the mean percentage of the two-party vote cast for either party among all statewide races in the same election. Both of these latter criteria are more directly related to changes in the strength of partisan linkage between voters and government than are the others employed in this study.

Two major assumptions underlie the use of these criteria. (1) If a secular decline in turnout occurs, and especially if it is associated with increases in drop-off and roll-off, we may infer that the active voting universe: (a) is shrinking in size relative to the potential voting universe; and (b) is also decomposing as a relative increase in its component of peripherally involved voters occurs. Opposite implications, of course, would be drawn from increases in turnout accompanied by decreases in these rough indices of voter peripherality. (2) If split-ticket voting and the amplitude of partisan swings are also increasing over time, we may infer that a decline in party-oriented voting is taking place among a growing minority of voters. Reductions in these criteria would suggest a resurgence of party-oriented voting.

A recent study by Angus Campbell tends to support the view that the above criteria are actually related to the component of marginal voters and voters with relatively weak partisan attachments in today's active electorate.[12] Campbell argues that surge and decline in voting participation and in partisan distribution of the vote result from two major factors: the entrance into the active electorate

[12] Angus Campbell, "Surge and Decline: A Study of Electoral Change," *Public Opinion Quarterly*, Vol. 24, pp. 397–418 (1960).

of peripherally involved voters who tend to vote disproportionately for such beneficiaries of partisan surges as President Eisenhower, and then abstain from the polls in subsequent low-stimulus elections; and the temporary movement of core voters with relatively low levels of party identification away from their nominal party allegiance, followed by their return to that allegiance in subsequent low-stimulus elections. Campbell's study reveals that split-ticket voting in the 1956 election tended to be heavily concentrated among two groups of voters: those who voted Republican for President in 1956 and did not vote in 1958, and those who voted Republican in 1956 but Democratic in 1958—in other words, among those with peripheral involvement in the political process itself and those with borderline partisan commitments. Moreover, roll-off—the failure to vote a complete ticket in 1956—was heavily concentrated among the non-voters of 1958. It is also suggestive that the level of drop-off in Campbell's panel from 1956 to 1958, 23 per cent, very closely approximates the level of drop-off as measured by the aggregate voting data.[13]

II

Even the crudest form of statistical analysis makes it abundantly clear that the changes which have occurred in the relative size and shape of the active electorate in this country have not only been quantitatively enormous but have followed a directional course which seems to be unique in the contemporary universe of democratic politics. In the United States these transformations over the past century have involved devolution, a dissociation from politics as such among a growing segment of the eligible electorate and an apparent deterioration of the bonds of party linkage between electorate and government. More precisely, these trends were overwhelmingly prominent between about 1900 and 1930, were only very moderately reversed following the political realignment of 1928–1936, and now seem to be increasing once again along several dimensions of analysis. Such a pattern of development is pronouncedly retrograde compared with those which have obtained almost everywhere else in the Western world during the past century.

Probably the best-known aspect of the changing American political universe has been the long-term trend in national voter turnout: a steep decline from 1900 to about 1930, followed by a moderate resurgence since that time.[14] As the figures in Table 1 indicate, nationwide turnout down through 1900 was quite high by contemporary standards—comparing favorably in presidential years with recent levels of participation in Western Europe—and was also marked by very low levels of drop-off. A good deal of the precipitate decline in turnout after 1896 can, of course, be attributed to the disfranchisement of Negroes in the South and the consolidation of its one-party regime. But as Table 2 and Fig. 1 both reveal, non-Southern states not only shared this decline but also have

---

[13] *Ibid.,* p. 413. The percentage of drop-off from 1956 to 1958, as computed from aggregate voting data, was 25.6%.
[14] See, *e.g.,* Robert E. Lane, *Political Life* (Glencoe, Ill., 1959), pp. 18–26.

TABLE 1

DECLINE AND PARTIAL RESURGENCE: MEAN LEVELS OF NATIONAL TURN-
OUT AND DROP-OFF BY PERIODS, 1848–1962 *

Period (Presidential Years)	Mean Estimated Turnout	Period (Off-Years)	Mean Estimated Turnout	Mean Drop-Off
	(%)		(%)	(%)
1848–1872	75.1	1850–1874	65.2	7.0
1876–1896	78.5	1878–1898	62.8	15.2
1900–1916	64.8	1902–1918	47.9	22.4
1920–1928	51.7	1922–1930	35.2	28.7
1932–1944	59.1	1934–1946	41.0	27.8
1948–1960	60.3	1950–1962	44.1	24.9

* Off-year turnout data based on total vote for congressional candidates in off years.

current turnout rates which remain substantially below 19th-century levels.[15]

The persistence of mediocre rates of American voting turnout into the
present political era is scarcely news. It forms so obvious and continuing a
problem of our democracy that a special presidential commission has recently
given it intensive study.[16] Two additional aspects of the problem, however,

TABLE 2

SECTIONALISM AND PARTICIPATION: MEAN TURNOUT IN SOUTH-
ERN AND NON-SOUTHERN STATES IN PRESIDENTIAL ELECTIONS,
1868–1960

Period	Mean Turnout: 11 Southern States	Period	Mean Turnout: Non-Southern States
	(%)		(%)
1868–1880	69.4	1868–1880	82.6
1884–1896	61.1	1884–1896	85.4
1900 (transi-tion)	43.4	1900	84.1
1904–1916	29.8	1904–1916	73.6
1920–1948	24.7	1920–1932	60.6
1952–1960	38.8	1936–1960	68.0

[15] There are, of course, very wide divergences in turnout rates even among
non-Southern states. Some of them, like Idaho, New Hampshire and Utah, have
presidential-year turnouts which compare very favorably with European levels of
participation. A detailed analysis of these differences remains to be made. It should
prove of the utmost importance in casting light upon the relevance of current forms
of political organization and partisan alignments to differing kinds of electorates and
political subsystems in the United States.
[16] *Report of the President's Commission on Registration and Voting Participation*
(Washington, 1963), esp. pp. 5–9. Hereafter cited as *Report*.

emerge from a perusal of the foregoing data. In the first place, it is quite apparent that the political realignment of the 1930s, while it restored two-party competition to many states outside the South, did not stimulate turnout to return in most areas to 19th-century levels. Even if the mere existence of competitiveness precludes such low levels of turnout as are found in the South today, or as once prevailed in the northern industrial states, it falls far short of compelling a substantially full turnout under present-day conditions. Second, drop-off on the national level has shown markedly little tendency to recede in the face of increases in presidential-year turnout over the last thirty years. The component of peripheral voters in the active electorate has apparently under-

FIGURE 1

PATTERNS OF TURNOUT: UNITED STATES, 1860–1964, BY REGION, AND SELECTED WESTERN EUROPEAN NATIONS, 1948–1961.

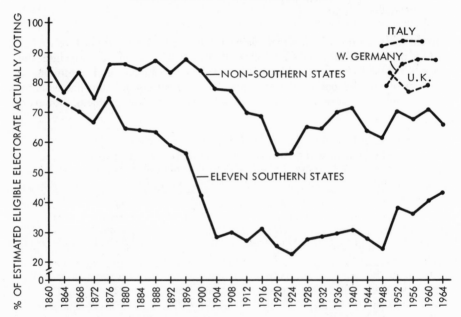

gone a permanent expansion from about one-sixth in the late 19th century to more than one-quarter in recent decades. If, as seems more than likely, the political regime established after 1896 was largely responsible for the marked relative decline in the active voting universe and the marked increase in peripherality among those who still occasionally voted, it is all the more remarkable that the dramatic political realignment of the 1930s has had such little effect in reversing these trends.

At least two major features of our contemporary polity, to be sure, are obviously related to the presently apparent ceiling on turnout. First, the American electoral system creates a major "double hurdle" for prospective voters which does not exist in Western Europe: the requirements associated with residence and registration, usually entailing periodic re-registration at frequent intervals, and the fact that elections are held on a normal working day in this employee society rather than on Sundays or holidays.[17] Second, it is very probably true that 19th-century elections were major sources of entertainment in an age unblessed by modern mass communications, so that it is more difficult for politicians to gain and keep public attention today than it was then.[18] Yet if American voters labor under the most cumbersome sets of procedural requirements in the Western world, this in itself is a datum which tends to support Schattschneider's thesis that the struggle for democracy is still being waged in the United States and that there are profound resistances within the political system itself to the adoption of needed procedural reforms.[19] Moreover, there are certain areas—such as all of Ohio outside the metropolitan counties and cities of at least 15,000 population—where no registration procedures have ever been established, but where no significant deviation from the patterns outlined here appears to exist. Finally, while it may well be true that the partial displacement by TV and other means of entertainment has inhibited expansion of the active voting universe during the past generation, it is equally true that the structure of the American voting universe—*i.e.*, the adult population—as it exists today was substantially formed in the period 1900–1920, *prior* to the development of such major media as the movies, radio and television.

III

As we move below the gross national level, the voting patterns discussed above stand out with far greater clarity and detail. Their divergences suggest something of the individual differences which distinguish each state subsystem from its fellows, as their uniformities indicate the universality of the broader secular trends. Five states have been selected for analysis here. During the latter part of the 19th century two of these, Michigan and Pennsylvania, were originally competitive states which tended to favor the Republican Party. They developed solidly one-party regimes after the realignment of 1896. These regimes were overthrown in their turn and vigorous party competition was restored in the wake of the New Deal realignment. In two other states, Ohio and New York, the 1896 alignment had no such dire consequences for two-party competition on the state level. These states have also shown a somewhat different pattern of development since the 1930s than Michigan and Pennsylvania. Our fifth state is Oklahoma, where a modified one-party system is structured heavily along sectional lines and operates in a socio-economic context unfavorable to the classic New Deal articulation of politics along ethnic-class lines of cleavage.

Michigan politics was marked from 1894 through 1930 by the virtual eclipse of a state Democratic Party which had formerly contested elections on nearly equal terms with the Republicans. The inverse relationships developing between this emergent one-partyism on the one hand, and both the relative size of the

[17] *Ibid.*, pp. 11–14, 31–42.
[18] See, *e.g.*, Stanley Kelley, "Elections and the Mass Media," *Law and Contemporary Problems*, Vol. 27, pp. 307–26 (1962).
[19] E. E. Schattschneider, *The Semi-Sovereign People, op. cit.*, pp. 102–3.

active voting universe and the strength of party linkage on the other, stand out in especially bold relief.

A decisive shift away from the stable and substantially fully mobilized voting patterns of the 19th century occurred in Michigan after the realignment of 1896, with a lag of about a decade between that election and the onset of disruption in those patterns. The first major breakthrough of characteristics associated with 20th-century American electorates occurred in the presidential year 1904, when the mean percentage Democratic for all statewide offices reached an unprecedented low of 35.6 and the rate of split-ticket voting jumped from almost zero to 17.1 per cent. A steady progression of decline in turnout and party competition, accompanied by heavy increases in the other criteria of peripherality, continued down through 1930.

The scope of this transformation was virtually revolutionary. During the civil-war era scarcely 15 per cent of Michigan's potential electorate appears to have been altogether outside the voting universe. About 7 per cent could be classified as peripheral voters by Campbell's definition, and the remainder— more than three-quarters of the total—were core voters. Moreover, as the extremely low 19th-century level of split-ticket voting indicates, these active voters overwhelmingly cast party-line ballots. By the 1920s, less than one-third of the potential electorate were still core voters, while nearly one-quarter were peripheral and nearly one-half remained outside the political system altogether. Drop-off and roll-off increased sixfold during this period, while the amplitude of partisan swing approximately doubled and the split-ticket-voting rate increased by a factor of approximately eight to twelve.

For the most part these trends underwent a sharp reversal as party competition in Michigan was abruptly restored during the 1930s and organized in its contemporary mode in 1948. As the mean Democratic percentage of the two-party vote increased and turnout—especially in off-year elections—showed a marked relative upswing, such characteristics of marginality as drop-off, roll-off, split-ticket voting and partisan swing declined in magnitude. Yet, as the means for the 1948–1962 period demonstrate, a large gap remains to be closed before anything like the *status quo ante* can be restored. Our criteria—except, of course, for the mean percentage Democratic of the two-party vote—have returned only to the levels of the transitional period 1900–1918. As is well known, exceptionally disciplined and issue-oriented party organizations have emerged in Michigan since 1948, and elections have been intensely competitive throughout this period.[20] In view of this, the failure of turnout in recent years to return to something approaching 19th-century levels is all the more impressive, as is the continuing persistence of fairly high levels of drop-off, roll-off and split-ticket voting.[21]

[20] Joseph La Palombara, *Guide to Michigan Politics* (East Lansing, Mich., Michigan State University Press, 1960), pp. 22–35.
[21] This recalls Robinson and Standing's conclusion that voter participation in Indiana does not necessarily increase with increasing party competition. Of the eight Michigan gubernatorial elections from 1948 to 1962 only one was decided by a margin of 55% or more, while three were decided by margins of less than 51.5% of the two-party vote. Despite this intensely competitive situation, turnout—while of course much higher than in the 1920s—remains significantly below normal pre-1920 levels.

TABLE 3

MICHIGAN, 1854–1962: DECAY AND RESURGENCE?

Period	Mean turnout		Mean drop-off	Mean roll-off	Mean split-ticket voting	Mean partisan swing	Mean % D of 2-party vote
	Pres. years	Off-years					
	(%)	(%)	(%)	(%)	(%)	(%)	
1854–1872	84.8	78.1	7.8	0.9	0.8	3.2	43.9
1878–1892	84.9	74.9	10.7	0.8	1.6	2.2	48.0
1894–1908	84.8	68.2	22.3	1.5	5.9	4.7	39.6
1910–1918	71.4	53.0	27.2	3.0	9.8	4.1	40.4 *
1920–1930	55.0	31.5	42.9	6.0	10.0	7.3	29.8
1932–1946	63.6	47.3	25.9	6.7	6.0	7.4	47.9
1948–1962	66.9	53.6	19.1	4.1	5.8	4.9	51.0

* Democratic percentage of three-party vote in 1912 and 1914.

The Michigan data have still more suggestive implications. Campbell's discussion of surge and decline in the modern context points to a cyclical process in which peripheral voters, drawn into the active voting universe only under unusual short-term stimuli, withdraw from it again when the stimuli are removed. It follows that declines in turnout are accompanied by a marked relative increase in the component of core voters in the electorate and by a closer approximation in off years to a "normal" partisan division of the vote.[22] This presumably includes a reduction in the level of split-ticket voting as well. But the precise opposite occurred as a secular process—not only in Michigan but, it would seem, universally—during the 1900–1930 era. Declines in turnout were accompanied by substantial, continuous increases in the indices of party and voter peripherality among those elements of the adult population which remained in the political universe at all. The lower the turnout during this period, the fewer of the voters still remaining who bothered to vote for the entire slate of officers in any given election. The lower the turnout in presidential years, the greater was the drop-off gap between the total vote cast in presidential and succeeding off-year elections. The lower the turnout, the greater were the incidence of split-ticket voting and the amplitude of partisan swing. Under the enormous impact of the forces which produced these declines in turnout and party competitiveness after 1896, the component of highly involved and party-oriented core voters in the active electorate fell off at a rate which more than kept pace with the progressive shrinking of that electorate's relative size. These developments necessarily imply a limitation upon the usefulness of the surge-decline model as it relates to secular movements prior to about 1934. They suggest, moreover, that the effects of the forces at work after 1896 to depress voter participation and to dislocate party linkage between voters and government were even more crushingly severe than a superficial perusal of the data would indicate.

Pennsylvania provides us with variations on the same theme. As in Michigan, the political realignment centering on 1896 eventually converted an industrializing state with a relatively slight but usually decisive Republican bias into a solidly one-party G.O.P. bastion. To a much greater extent than in Michigan, this disintegration of the state Democratic Party was accompanied by periodic outbursts of third-party ventures and plural party nominations of major candidates, down to the First World War. Thereafter, as in Michigan, the real contest between competing candidates and political tendencies passed into the Republican primary, where it usually remained until the advent of the New Deal. In both states relatively extreme declines in the rate of turnout were associated with the disappearance of effective two-party competition, and in both states these declines were closely paralleled by sharp increases in the indices of peripherality.

As Table 4 demonstrates, the parallel behavior of the Michigan and Pennsylvania electorates has also extended into the present; the now-familiar pattern of increasing turnout and party competition accompanied by marked declines in our other indices has been quite visible in the Keystone State since the advent of the New Deal. On the whole, indeed, a better approximation to the *status quo*

[22] Angus Campbell, "Surge and Decline," *op. cit.,* pp. 401–4.

TABLE 4

VOTING PATTERNS IN PENNSYLVANIA, 1876–1962: DECLINE AND RESURGENCE?

Period	Mean turnout		Mean drop-off	Mean roll-off	Mean split-ticket voting	Mean partisan swing	Mean % D of 2-party vote
	Pres. years	Off-years					
	(%)	(%)	(%)	(%)	(%)	(%)	
1876–1892	78.5	69.3	9.4	0.6	0.6	1.4	47.7
1894–1908	75.7	64.7	12.2	5.2	1.3	6.3	38.5
1910–1918	64.0	51.4	20.0	4.3	4.7	5.8	43.6 *
1920–1930	50.4	39.5	28.0	5.2	8.9	7.1	32.8
1932–1948	61.5	51.9	14.9	2.2	1.4	6.1	49.0
1950–1962	67.5	56.3	12.2	1.8	3.1	3.3	49.3

* Combined major anti-Republican vote (Democrat, Keystone, Lincoln, Washington).

ante has been reached in Pennsylvania than in Michigan or perhaps in most other states. But despite the intense competitiveness of its present party system, this restoration remains far from complete.

A more detailed examination of turnout and variability in turnout below the statewide level raises some questions about the direct role of immigration and woman suffrage in depressing voter participation. It also uncovers a significant transposition of relative voter involvement in rural areas and urban centers since about 1930.

It is frequently argued that declines in participation after the turn of the century were largely the product of massive immigration from Europe and of the advent of woman suffrage, both of which added very large and initially poorly socialized elements to the potential electorate.[23] There is no question that these were influential factors. The data in Table 5 indicate, for example, that down until the Great Depression turnout was consistently higher and much less subject to variation in rural counties with relatively insignificant foreign-stock populations than in either the industrial-mining or metropolitan counties.

Yet two other aspects of these data should also be noted. First, the pattern of turnout decline from the 1876–1896 period to the 1900–1916 period was quite uniform among all categories of counties, though the rank order of their turnouts remained largely unchanged. It can be inferred from this that, while immigration probably played a major role in the evolution of Pennsylvania's political system as a whole, it had no visible direct effect upon the secular decline in rural voting participation. Broader systemic factors, including but transcending the factor of immigration, seem clearly to have been at work. Second, a very substantial fraction of the total decline in turnout from the 1870s to the 1920s—in some rural native-stock counties more than half—occurred *before* women were given the vote. Moreover, post-1950 turnout levels in Pennsylvania, and apparently in most other non-Southern states, have been at least as high as in the decade immediately preceding the general enfranchisement of women. If even today a higher percentage of American than European women fail to come to the polls, the same can also be said of such population groups as the poorly educated, farmers, the lower-income classes, Negroes and other deprived elements in the potential electorate.[24] In such a context woman suffrage, as important a variable as it certainly has been in our recent political history, seems to raise more analytical problems than it solves.

Particularly suggestive for our hypothesis of basic changes in the nature of American voting behavior over time is the quite recent transposition of aggre-

---

[23] Herbert Tingsten, *Political Behavior* (Stockholm, Stockholm Economic Studies, No. 7, 1937), pp. 10–36. See also Charles E. Merriam and Harold F. Gosnell, *Non-Voting* (Chicago, University of Chicago Press, 1924), pp. 26, 109–22, for a useful discussion of the effect of woman suffrage on turnout in a metropolitan area immediately following the general enfranchisement of 1920.

[24] Survey-research estimates place current turnout among American women at 10% below male turnout. Angus Campbell *et al., The American Voter, op. cit.,* pp. 484–85. This sex-related difference in participation is apparently universal, but is significantly smaller in European countries which provide election data by sex, despite the far higher European level of participation by both sexes. The postwar differential has been 5.8% in Norway (1945–1957 mean), 3.3% in Sweden (1948–1960 mean), and 1.9% in Finland (1962 general election). While in 1956 only about 55% of American women went to the polls, the mean turnout among women in postwar elections was 76.1% in Norway and 79.4% in Sweden.

TABLE 5

DIFFERENTIALS IN AGGREGATE TURNOUT AND VARIATIONS OF TURNOUT IN SELECTED PENNSYLVANIA COUNTIES: PRESIDENTIAL ELECTIONS, 1876–1960*

County and Type	N	% Foreign stock, 1920 (%)	1876–1896 Mean turnout (%)	1876–1896 Coef. var.	1900–1916 Mean turnout (%)	1900–1916 Coef. var.	1920–1932 Mean turnout (%)	1920–1932 Coef. var.	1936–1960 Mean turnout (%)	1936–1960 Coef. var.
Urban:										
Allegheny	1	56.6	71.8	6.75	56.7	2.45	43.8	10.11	68.9	5.82
Philadelphia	1	54.3	85.2	4.61	72.9	6.42	50.5	12.57	68.8	4.40
Industrial-Mining:	4	49.0	88.1	4.48	72.8	4.41	54.2	11.63	64.7	10.88
Rural:	8	13.5	88.5	3.12	76.4	3.63	56.0	8.09	65.2	13.20

* The coefficient of variability is a standard statistical measure; see V. O. Key, Jr., *A Primer of Statistics for Political Scientists* (New York, 1954), pp. 44–52. Since secular trends, where present, had to be taken into account, this coefficient appears abnormally low in the period 1900–1916. During this period many counties registered a straight-line decline in turnout from one election to the next.

gate turnout and variations in turnout as between our rural sample and the two metropolitan centers. In sharp contrast to the situation prevailing before 1900, turnout in these rural counties has tended during the past generation not only to be slightly lower than in the large cities but also subject to far wider oscillations from election to election. In Bedford County, for example, turnout stood at 82.5 per cent in 1936, but sagged to an all-time low of 41.2 per cent in 1948. The comparable figures in Philadelphia were 74.3 and 64.8 per cent, and in Allegheny County 72.5 per cent (in 1940) and 60.6 per cent.

A major finding revealed by survey research is that the "farm vote" is currently one of the most unstable and poorly articulated elements in the American electorate.[25] It is said that since rural voters lack the solid network of

TABLE 6

URBAN-RURAL DIFFERENCES IN STABILITY OF POLITICAL INVOLVEMENT: 1936–60 MEAN TURNOUT AND VARIABILITY OF TURNOUT AS PERCENTAGES OF 1876–96 MEAN TURNOUT AND VARIABILITY OF TURNOUT, PENNSYLVANIA

County and Type	N	1936–60 Turnout / 1876–96 Turnout	1936–60 Variability / 1876–96 Variability
		(%)	(%)
Urban:			
Allegheny	1	95.9	86.2
Philadelphia	1	80.8	95.4
Industrial-Mining:	4	73.4	249.6
Rural:	8	73.7	447.4

group identifications and easy access to mass-communication media enjoyed by their city cousins, they tend to be both unusually apathetic and exceptionally volatile in their partisan commitments. As rural voting turnout was abnormally low in 1948, its rate of increase from 1948 to 1952 was exceptionally large and —fully consistent with Campbell's surge-decline model—was associated with a one-sided surge toward Eisenhower. A restatement of the data in Table 5 lends strong support to this evaluation of the relative position of the rural vote as a description of the *current* American voting universe.

But the data strongly imply that virtually the opposite of present conditions prevailed during the 19th century. Such variables as education level, communications and non-family-group interaction were probably much more poorly developed in rural areas before 1900 than they are today. Not only did this leave no visible mark on agrarian turnout; it seems extremely likely that the 19th-century farmer was at least as well integrated into the political system of that day as any other element in the American electorate. The awesome rates of turnout which can be found in states like Indiana, Iowa and Kentucky prior to 1900 indicate that this extremely high level of rural political involvement was

[25] *Ibid.*, pp. 402–40.

TABLE 7

PATTERNS OF VOTER PARTICIPATION IN OHIO, 1857–1962: DECLINE WITH-
OUT RESURGENCE?

Period	Mean turnout		Mean drop-off	Mean roll-off	Mean split-ticket voting
	Pres. years	Off-years			
	(%)	(%)			
1857–1879	89.0	78.4	9.7	0.6	0.5
1880–1903	92.2	80.5	11.2	0.8	0.6
1904–1918	80.4	71.2	9.2	2.5	3.3
1920–1930	62.4	45.8	24.1	7.9	9.9
1932–1946	69.9	49.1	27.2	7.6	6.5
1948–1962	66.5	53.3	19.0	8.2	11.1

not limited to Pennsylvania.[26] As a recent study of Indiana politics demonstrates, the primarily rural "traditional vote" in that state was marked prior to
1900 by an overwhelming partisan stability as well.[27]

Perhaps, following the arguments of C. Wright Mills and others, we can
regard this extraordinary change in rural voting behavior as a function of the
conversion of a cracker-barrel society into a subordinate element in a larger
mass society.[28] In any event, this rural movement toward relatively low and
widely fluctuating levels of turnout may well be indicative of an emergent
political alienation in such areas. It is suggestive that these movements have
been accompanied generally in Pennsylvania as in states like West Virginia by a
strongly positive Republican trend in these agrarian bailiwicks during the last
thirty years.[29] The impression arises that the political realignment of the 1930s,
which only imperfectly mobilized and integrated urban populations into the
political system, had not even these limited positive effects in more isolated
communities.

The behavior of the Ohio electorate down to about 1930 closely paralleled
the patterns displayed in its neighbor states, Michigan and Pennsylvania. Since
then a marked divergence has been manifest.

Two-party competition here was far less seriously affected by the sectional

[26] The estimated rates of turnout in presidential elections from 1876 through 1896,
mean turnout in the period 1936–1960 and estimated turnout in 1964 were as follows
in these states:

State	1876	1880	1884	1888	1892	1896	1936–60 (Mean)	1964 (Prelim.)
Indiana	94.6	94.4	92.2	93.3	89.0	95.1	75.0	73.3
Iowa	89.6	91.5	90.0	87.9	88.5	96.2	71.7	72.0
Kentucky	76.1	71.0	68.0	79.1	72.6	88.0	57.6	52.6

[27] V. O. Key, Jr., and Frank Munger, "Social Determinism and Electoral Decision,"
op. cit., pp. 282–88.
[28] C. Wright Mills, *The Power Elite* (New York, Oxford University Press, 1956),
pp. 298–324. See also Arthur J. Vidich and Joseph Bensman, *Small Town in Mass
Society* (New York, 1960), pp. 5–15, 202–27, 297–320.
[29] John H. Fenton, *Politics in the Border States* (New Orleans, Hauser Press,
1957), pp. 117–20.

political alignment of 1896–1932 than in most other northern industrial states. Of the eighteen gubernatorial elections held in Ohio from 1895 to 1930, for example, Democrats won ten. But here as elsewhere are to be found the same patterns of decline in turnout and sharp increases in indices of voter peripherality after 1900. Indeed, while turnout bottomed out during the 1920s at a point considerably higher than in Michigan or Pennsylvania, it had also been considerably higher than in either of them during the 19th century. Here too such variables as woman suffrage seem to have played a smaller role as causal agents —at least so far as they affected the growing tendencies toward peripherality among active voters—than is commonly supposed. Drop-off from presidential to off-year elections began to assume its modern shape in Ohio between 1898 and 1910. As Figure 2 shows, roll-off—an especially prominent feature in contemporary Ohio voting behavior—emerged in modern form in the election of 1914.

Ohio, unlike either Michigan or Pennsylvania, has demonstrated only an extremely limited resurgence since the realignment of the 1930s. Presidential-year voting turnout in the period 1948–1960 actually declined from the mean level of 1932–1944, and was not appreciably higher than it had been in the trough of the 1920s. If mean drop-off has declined somewhat in recent years, it still stands at a level twice as high as in any period before 1920. Moreover, roll-off and the rate of split-ticket voting have actually increased to unprecedented highs since 1948. By 1962 the latter ratio touched an all-time high of

FIGURE 2

INCREASES IN ROLL-OFF: THE CASE OF OHIO, 1872–1962.

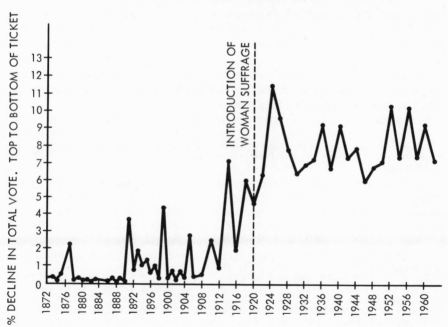

21.3% (except for the three-party election of 1924), suggesting that Ohio politics may be becoming an "every-man-for-himself" affair. This pattern of behavior stands in the sharpest possible contrast to 19th-century norms. In that period turnout had reached substantially full proportions, drop-off was minimal and well over 99 per cent of the voters cast both complete ballots and straight party tickets—an achievement that may have been partly an artifact of the party ballots then in use.[30] The political reintegration which the New Deal realignment brought in its wake elsewhere has scarcely become visible in Ohio.

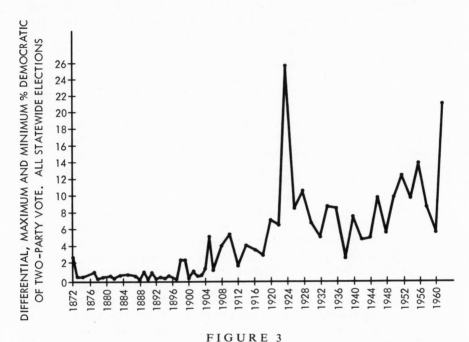

FIGURE 3

INCREASES IN SPLIT-TICKET VOTING: THE CASE OF OHIO, 1872–1962.

Two recent discussions of Ohio politics may shed some light upon these characteristics. Thomas A. Flinn, examining changes over the past century in the partisan alignments of Ohio counties, concludes that until the first decade of the 20th century the state had a set of political alignments based largely on sectionalism within Ohio—a product of the diverse regional backgrounds of its settlers and their descendants. This older political system broke down under the impact of industrialization and a national class-ethnic partisan realignment, but no new political order of similar coherence or partisan stability has yet emerged to take its place.[31] Flinn's findings and the conclusions which Lee Benson has drawn from his study of New York voting behavior in the 1840s are remarka-

[30] However, Ohio's modern pattern of split-ticket voting, formed several decades ago, seems to have been little (if at all) affected by the 1950 change from party-column to office-block ballot forms. See Figure 3.
[31] Thomas A. Flinn, "Continuity and Change in Ohio Politics," *Journal of Politics,* Vol. 24, pp. 521–44 (1962).

bly similar.[32] In this earlier voting universe the durability of partisan commitment and the extremely high levels of turnout appear to have had their roots in
a cohesive and persistent set of positive and negative group referents. These, as
Flinn notes, provided "no clear-cut class basis for statewide party following
from the time of Jackson to that of Wilson." [33]

John H. Fenton, discussing the 1962 gubernatorial campaign, carries the
argument one step further.[34] Basic to Ohio's social structure, he argues, is an
unusually wide diffusion of its working-class population among a large number
of middle-sized cities and even smaller towns. The weakness of the labor unions
and the chaotic disorganization of the state Democratic Party seem to rest upon
this diffusion. Ohio also lacks agencies which report on the activities of
politicians from a working-class point of view, such as have been set up by the
United Automobile Workers in Detroit or the United Mine Workers in Pennsylvania or West Virginia. The result of this is that to a much greater extent than
in other industrial states, potential recruits for a cohesive and reasonably
well-organized Democratic Party in Ohio live in an isolated, atomized social
milieu. Consequently they tend to vote in a heavily personalist, issueless way, as
the middle and upper classes do not. Such a state of affairs may provide clues
not only for the relative failure of voter turnout to increase during the past
generation, but for the persistent and growing indications of voter peripherality
in Ohio's active electorate as well.

The development of the voting universe in New York is more analogous to
the situation in Ohio than in either Michigan or Pennsylvania. In New York, as
in Ohio, two-party competition was not as dislocated by the 1896–1930 alignment as a hasty survey of the presidential-election percentages during that
period might suggest. Democrats remained firmly in control of New York City,
and this control helped them to capture the governorship eight out of eighteen
times from 1896 through 1930. There were other parallels with Ohio as well,
for here too this persistence of party competition did not prevent the normal
post-1896 voting syndrome from appearing in New York. Nor has there been
any pronounced resurgence in turnout levels or convincing declines in the other
variables since the 1930s. Drop-off, roll-off, split-ticket voting and partisan
swing are not only quite high in New York by 19th-century standards, but have
been twice as great as in neighboring Pennsylvania during the past decade. This
relative failure of political reintegration is revealed not only by the data
presented in Table 8 but—in much more dramatic fashion—by the rise and
persistence of labor-oriented third parties which are centered in New York City
and have enjoyed a balance-of-power position between the two major party
establishments. The existence of the American Labor and Liberal Parties, as
well as the continuing vitality of anti-Tammany "reform" factions, are vocal
testimony to the failure of the old-line New York Democratic Party to adapt
itself successfully to the political style and goals of a substantial portion of the
urban electorate.

Curiously enough, examination of the data thus far presented raises some

[32] Lee Benson, *The Concept of Jacksonian Democracy* (Princeton, Princeton University Press, 1961), pp. 123–207, 288–328.
[33] Flinn, *op. cit.*, p. 542.
[34] John H. Fenton, "Ohio's Unpredictable Voters," *Harper's Magazine*, Vol. 225,
pp. 61–65 (1962).

TABLE 8

NEW YORK VOTING PATTERNS, 1834–1962: DECLINE WITHOUT RESURGENCE?

Period	Mean turnout (Pres. years)	Mean drop-off	Mean roll-off	Mean split-ticket voting	Mean partisan swing	Mean % D of 2-party vote
	(%)	(%)	(%)	(%)	(%)	
1834–1858	84.8	3.3	1.6	1.2	1.7	50.9 *
1860–1879	89.3	7.9	0.4	0.6	2.6	50.1
1880–1898	87.9	10.4	1.2	1.6	5.0	50.5
1900–1908	82.5	8.3	1.1	2.2	3.7	47.2
1910–1918	71.9	10.9	5.1	3.3	3.8	46.2
1920–1930	60.4	17.3	5.5	9.5	8.3	49.6
1932–1946	71.3	22.5	4.9	3.4	3.2	53.2 †
1948–1962	67.8	20.6	3.6	6.5	5.8	47.3 †

* Elections from 1854 to 1858 excluded because of major third-party vote.

† The American Labor Party, 1936–46, and the Liberal Party, 1944–62, are included in Democratic vote when their candidates and Democratic candidates were the same.

doubt that the direct primary has contributed quite as much to the erosion of party linkages as has been often supposed.[35] There seems to be little doubt that it has indeed been a major eroding element in some of the states where it has taken root—especially in states with partially or fully one-party systems where the primary has sapped the minority party's monopoly of opposition. But comparison of New York with our other states suggests the need of further concentrated work on this problem. After a brief flirtation with the direct primary between 1912 and 1921, New York resumed its place as one of the very few states relying on party conventions to select nominees for statewide offices, as it does to this day. Despite this fact, the post-1896 pattern of shrinkage in turnout and increases in our other indices of political dissociation was virtually the same in New York as elsewhere. To take a more recent example, New York's split-ticket-voting ratio was 16.1 per cent in 1962, compared with 21.3 in Ohio, 7.1 in Michigan and 6.8 per cent in Pennsylvania. The overall pattern of the data suggests that since 1932 the latter two states may have developed a more cohesive party politics and a more integrated voting universe with the direct primary than New York has without it.

If the data thus far indicate some link between the relative magnitude of voter non-participation and marginality with the cohesiveness of the local party system, even greater secular trends of the same sort should occur where one of the parties has continued to enjoy a perennially dominant position in state politics. Oklahoma, a border state with a modified one-party regime, tends to support such an assumption.[36] The relatively recent admission of this state to the union naturally precludes analysis of its pre-1896 voting behavior. Even so,

[35] This would seem to suggest a limitation on Key's findings, *American State Politics, op. cit.,* pp. 169–96.

[36] This designation is given the state's political system in Oliver Benson, Harry Holloway, George Mauer, Joseph Pray and Wayne Young, *Oklahoma Votes: 1907–1962* (Norman, Okla., Bureau of Government Research, University of Oklahoma, 1964), pp. 44–52. For an extensive discussion of the sectional basis of Oklahoma politics, see *ibid.,* pp. 32–43, and V. O. Key, Jr., *American State Politics, op. cit.,* pp. 220–22.

TABLE 9

VOTER PERIPHERALITY AND PARTY DECAY? OKLAHOMA, 1907–1962

Period	Mean turnout (Off-years)	Mean drop-off	Mean roll-off *	Mean split-ticket voting *	% of State and Congressional elections uncontested by Republicans	
					Per cent	Mean N †
	(%)	(%)	(%)	(%)		
1907–1918	52.9	12.1	6.1	3.6	2.1	32
1922–1930	40.1	13.0	13.9	9.7	2.1	31
1934–1946	37.1	32.2	16.4	8.1	14.8	32
1950–1962	44.5	26.3	14.0	10.5	41.3	29

* Roll-off and split-ticket voting are computed for contested elections only.
† Mean number of state and congressional races in each off-year election.

it is quite clear that the further back one goes toward the date of admission, the closer one comes to an approximation to a 19th-century voting universe. In Oklahoma, curiously enough, the secular decline in turnout and increases in the other indices continued into the New Deal era itself, measured by the off-year elections when—as in a growing number of states [37]—a full slate of statewide officers is elected. Since 1946 very little solid evidence of a substantial resurgence in turnout or of major declines in drop-off, roll-off or split-ticket voting has appeared, but there is some evidence that the minority Republican Party is atrophying.

The magnitude of drop-off and roll-off has become relatively enormous in Oklahoma since the 1920s, with a very slight reduction in both during the 1950–1962 period. While turnout has correspondingly increased somewhat since its trough in the 1934–1946 period, at no time since 1914 have as many as one-half of the state's potential voters come to the polls in these locally decisive off-year elections. Still more impressive is the almost vertical increase in the proportion of uncontested elections since the end of World War II. The 1958 and 1962 elections, moreover, indicate that the trend toward decomposition in the Republican party organization and its linkage with its mass base is continuing. In 1958 the party virtually collapsed, its gubernatorial candidate winning only 21.3 per cent of the two-party vote. Four years later the Republican candidate won 55.5 per cent of the two-party vote. The resultant partisan swings of 34.2 per cent for this office and 22.0 for all contested statewide offices was the largest in the state's history and one of the largest on record anywhere. But while 1962 marked the first Republican gubernatorial victory in the state's history, it was also the first election in which the Republican Party yielded more than half of the statewide and congressional offices to its opposition without any contest at all. Even among contested offices, the Oklahoma electorate

[37] In 1936, 34 states (71%) elected governors for either two- or four-year terms in presidential years, and the three-year term in New Jersey caused major state elections to coincide with every fourth presidential election. By 1964, only 25 of 50 states (50%) still held some of their gubernatorial elections in presidential years. Two of these, Florida and Michigan, are scheduled to begin off-year gubernatorial elections for four-year terms in 1966.

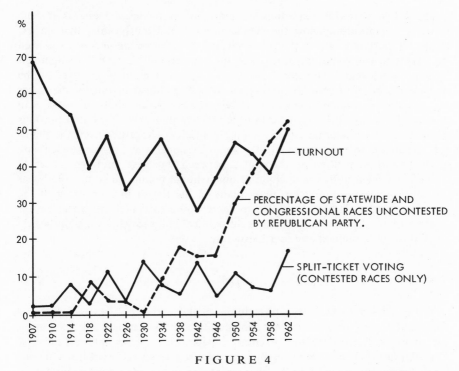

FIGURE 4

PATTERNS OF POLITICAL EVOLUTION: THE CASE OF OKLAHOMA, 1907–1962.

followed a national trend in 1962 by splitting its tickets at the unprecedented rate of 17.3 per cent.

As Key has suggested, the direct primary has almost certainly had cumulatively destructive effects on the cohesion of both parties in such modified one-party states as Oklahoma.[38] The rapidly spreading device of "insulating" state politics from national trends by holding the major state elections in off years has also probably played a significant role. Yet it seems more than likely that these are variables which ultimately depend for their effectiveness upon the nature of the local political culture and the socio-economic forces which underlie it. Pennsylvania, for example, also has a direct-primary. Since 1875, it has also insulated state from national politics by holding its major state elections in off years. Yet since the realignment of the 1930s, both parties have contested every statewide office in Pennsylvania as a matter of course. Indeed, only very infrequently have elections for seats in the state legislature gone by default to one of the parties, even in bailiwicks which it utterly dominates.[39]

[38] *American State Politics, op. cit.*, pp. 169–96.
[39] In the period 1956–1962 there have been 840 general-election contests for the Pennsylvania House of Representatives. Of these all but six, or 0.7%, have been contested by both major political parties. No Pennsylvania state Senate seat has been uncontested during this period. Despite the 1962 Republican upsurge in Oklahoma, however, there were no contests between the parties in 11 of 22 Senate seats (50.0%) and in 73 of 120 House seats (60.9%). All the uncontested Senate seats and all but two of the uncontested House seats were won by Democrats.

These five statewide variations on our general theme suggest, as do the tentative explorations below the statewide level in Pennslyvania, that an extremely important factor in the recent evolution of the voting universe has been the extent to which the imperatives of the class-ethnic New Deal realignment have been relevant to the local social structure and political culture. In the absence of an effectively integrating set of state political organizations, issues and candidates around which a relatively intense polarization of voters can develop, politics is likely to have so little salience that very substantial portions of the potential electorate either exclude themselves altogether from the political system or enter it in an erratic and occasional way. As organized and articulated in political terms, the contest between "business" and "government" which has tended to be the linchpin of our national politics since the 1930s has obviously made no impression upon many in the lowest income strata of the urban population. It has also failed to demonstrate sustained organizing power in areas of rural poverty or among local political cultures which remain largely pre-industrial in outlook and social structure.

IV

The conclusions which arise directly out of this survey of aggregate data and indices of participation seem clear enough. On both the national and state levels they point to the existence and eventual collapse of an earlier political universe in the United States—a universe in many ways so sharply different from the one we all take for granted today that many of our contemporary frames of analytical reference seem irrelevant or misleading in studying it. The late 19th-century voting universe was marked by a more complete and intensely party-oriented voting participation among the American electorate than ever before or since. Approximately two-thirds of the potential national electorate were then "core" voters, one-tenth fell into the peripheral category, and about one-quarter remained outside. In the four northern states examined in this survey the component of core elements in the potential electorate was even larger: about three-quarters core voters, one-tenth peripherals and about 15 per cent non-voters.

In other ways too this 19th-century system differed markedly from its successors. Class antagonisms as such appear to have had extremely low salience by comparison with today's voting behavior. Perhaps differentials in the level of formal education among various groups in the population contributed to differentials in 19th-century turnout as they clearly do now. But the unquestionably far lower *general* level of formal education in America during the last century did not preclude a much more intense and uniform mass political participation than any which has prevailed in recent decades. Though the evidence is still scanty, it strongly implies that the influence of rurality upon the intensity and uniformity of voting participation appears to have been precisely the opposite of what survey-research findings hold it to be today. This was essentially a pre-industrial democratic system, resting heavily upon a rural and small-town base. Apparently, it was quite adequate, both in partisan organization and dissemination of political information, to the task of mobilizing voters on a scale which compares favorably with recent European levels of participation.

There is little doubt that the model of surge and decline discussed above casts significant light upon the behavior of today's American electorate as it responds to the stimuli of successive elections. But the model depends for its validity upon the demonstrated existence of very large numbers both of peripheral voters and of core voters whose attachment to party is relatively feeble. Since these were not pronounced characteristics of the 19th-century voting universe, it might be expected that abnormal increases in the percentage of the vote won by either party would be associated with very different kinds of movements in the electorate, and that such increases would be relatively unusual by present-day standards.

Even a cursory inspection of the partisan dimensions of voting behavior in the 19th century tends to confirm this expectation. Not only did the amplitude of partisan swing generally tend to be much smaller then than now,[40] but nationwide landslides of the 20th-century type were almost non-existent.[41] Moreover, when one party did win an unusually heavy majority, this increase was usually associated with a pronounced and one-sided *decline* in turnout. Comparison of the 1848 and 1852 elections in Georgia and of the October gubernatorial and November presidential elections of 1872 in Pennsylvania, for example, makes it clear that the "landslides" won by one of the presidential contenders in 1852 and 1872 were the direct consequence of mass abstentions by voters who normally supported the other party.[42] Under 19th-century conditions, marked as they were by substantially full mobilization of the eligible electorate, the only play in the system which could provide extraordinary majorities had to come from a reversal of the modern pattern of surge and decline—a depression in turnout which was overwhelmingly confined to adherents of one of the parties.[43]

[40] Mean national partisan swings in presidential elections since 1872 have been as follows: 1872–1892, 2.3%; 1896–1916, 5.0%; 1920–1932, 10.3%; 1936–1964, 5.4%.

[41] If a presidential landslide is arbitrarily defined as a contest in which the winning candidate received 55% or more of the two-party vote, only the election of 1872 would qualify among the 16 presidential elections held from 1836 to 1896. Of 17 presidential elections held from 1900 through 1964, at least eight were landslide elections by this definition, and a ninth—the 1924 election, in which the Republican candidate received 54.3% and the Democratic candidate 29.0% of a three-party total—could plausibly be included.

[42] The total vote in Georgia declined from 92,203 in 1848 to 62,333 in 1852. Estimated turnout declined from about 88% to about 55% of the eligible electorate, while the Democratic share of the two-party vote increased from 48.5% in 1848 to 64.8% in 1852. The pattern of participation in the Pennsylvania gubernatorial and presidential elections of 1872 is also revealing:

Raw Vote	Governor, Oct. 1872	President, Nov. 1872	Absolute Decline
Total	671,147	562,276	− 108,871
Democratic	317,760	213,027	− 104,733
Republican	353,387	349,249	− 4,138

Estimated turnout in October was 82.0%, in November 68.6%. The Democratic percentage of the two-party vote was 47.3% in October and 37.9% in November.

[43] The only apparent exception to this generalization in the 19th century was the election of 1840. But this was the first election in which substantially full mobilization of the eligible electorate occurred. The rate of increase in the total vote from 1836 to

This earlier political order, as we have seen, was eroded away very rapidly after 1900. Turnout fell precipitately from 19th-century levels even before the advent of woman suffrage, and even in areas where immigrant elements in the electorates were almost nonexistent. As turnout declined, a larger and larger component of the still-active electorate moved from a core to a peripheral position, and the hold of the parties over their mass base appreciably deteriorated. This revolutionary contraction in the size and diffusion in the shape of the voting universe was almost certainly the fruit of the heavily sectional party realignment which was inaugurated in 1896. This "system of 1896," as Schattschneider calls it,[44] led to the destruction of party competition throughout much of the United States, and thus paved the way for the rise of the direct primary. It also gave immense impetus to the strains of anti-partisan and anti-majoritarian theory and practice which have always been significant elements in the American political tradition. By the decade of the 1920s this new regime and business control over public policy in this country were consolidated. During that decade hardly more than one-third of the eligible adults were still core voters. Another one-sixth were peripheral voters and fully one-half remained outside the active voting universe altogether. It is difficult to avoid the impression that while all the forms of political democracy were more or less scrupulously preserved, the functional result of the "system of 1896" was the conversion of a fairly democratic regime into a rather broadly based oligarchy.

The present shape and size of the American voting universe are, of course, largely the product of the 1928–1936 political realignment. Survey-research findings most closely approximate political reality as they relate to this next broad phase of American political evolution. But the characteristics of the present voting universe suggest rather forcefully that the New Deal realignment has been both incomplete and transitional. At present, about 44 per cent of the national electorate are core voters, another 16 or so are peripheral, and about 40 per cent are still outside the political system altogether. By 19th-century standards, indices of voter peripherality stand at very high levels. Party organizations remain at best only indifferently successful at mobilizing a stable, predictable mass base of support.

The data which have been presented here, though they constitute only a small fraction of the materials which must eventually be examined, tend by and large to support Schattschneider's functional thesis of American party politics.[45] We still need to know a great deal more than we do about the specific linkages between party and voter in the 19th century. Systematic research remains also to be done on the causes and effects of the great post-1896 transition in American political behavior. Even so, it seems useful to propose an hypothesis of transition in extension of Schattschneider's argument.

1860 was 60.0%, the largest in American history. Estimated turnout increased from about 58% in 1836 to about 80% in 1840. This election, with its relatively one-sided mobilization of hitherto apolitical elements in the potential electorate, not unnaturally bears some resemblance to the elections of the 1950s. But the increase in the Whig share of the two-party vote from 49.2% in 1836 to only 53.0% in 1840 suggests that that surge was considerably smaller than those of the 1950s.

[44] *The Semi-Sovereign People, op. cit.,* p. 81.

[45] *Ibid.,* esp. pp. 78–113. See also his "United States: The Functional Approach to Party Government," in Sigmund Neumann, ed., *Modern Political Parties* (Chicago, University of Chicago Press, 1956), pp. 194–215.

The 19th-century American political system, for its day, was incomparably the most thoroughly democratized of any in the world. The development of vigorous party competition extended from individual localities to the nation itself. It involved the invention of the first organizational machinery—the caucus, the convention and the widely disseminated party press—which was designed to deal with large numbers of citizens rather than with semi-aristocratic parliamentary cliques. Sooner than the British, and at a time when Prussia protected its elites through its three-class electoral system, when each new change of regime in France brought with it a change in the size of the electorate and the nature of *le pays légal,* and when the basis of representation in Sweden was still the estate, Americans had elaborated not only the machinery and media of mass politics but a franchise which remarkably closely approached universal suffrage. Like the larger political culture of which it was an integral part, this system rested upon both broad consensual acceptance of middle-class social norms as ground rules and majoritarian settlement (in "critical" elections from time to time), once and for all, of deeply divisive substantive issues on which neither consensus nor further postponement of a showdown was possible. Within the limits so imposed it was apparently capable of coherent and decisive action. It especially permitted the explicit formulation of sectional issues and—though admittedly at the price of civil war—arrived at a clear-cut decision as to which of two incompatible sectional modes of social and economic organization was henceforth to prevail.

But after several decades of intensive industrialization a new dilemma of power, in many respects as grave as that which had eventuated in civil war, moved toward the stage of overt crisis. Prior to the closing years of the century the middle-class character of the political culture and the party system, coupled with the afterglow of the civil-war trauma, had permitted the penetration and control of the cadres of both major parties by the heavily concentrated power of our industrializing elites. But this control was inherently unstable, for if and when the social dislocations produced by the industrial revolution should in turn produce a grass-roots counterrevolution, the party whose clienteles were more vulnerable to the appeals of the counterrevolutionaries might be captured by them.

The take-off phase of industrialization has been a brutal and exploitative process everywhere, whether managed by capitalists or commissars.[46] A vital functional political need during this phase is to provide adequate insulation of the industrializing elites from mass pressures, and to prevent their displacement by a coalition of those who are damaged by the processes of capital accumulation. This problem was effectively resolved in the Soviet Union under Lenin and Stalin by vesting a totalitarian monopoly of political power in the hands of Communist industrializing elites. In recent years developing nations have tended to rely upon less coercive devices such as non-totalitarian single-party systems or personalist dictatorship to meet that need, among others. The 19th-century European elites were provided a good deal of insulation by the persistence of

[46] Clark Kerr, John T. Dunlop, Frederick S. Harbison and Charles A. Myers, *Industrialism and Industrial Man* (Cambridge, Harvard University Press, 1960), pp. 47–76, 98–126, 193, 233. Walt W. Rostow, *The Stages of Economic Growth* (Cambridge, Cambridge University Press, 1960), pp. 17–58.

feudal patterns of social deference and especially by the restriction of the right to vote to the middle and upper classes.

But in the United States the institutions of mass democratic politics and universal suffrage uniquely came into being *before* the onset of full-scale industrialization. The struggle for democracy in Europe was explicitly linked from the outset with the struggle for universal suffrage. The eventual success of this movement permitted the development in relatively sequential fashion of the forms of party organization which Duverger has described in detail.[47] In the United States—ostensibly at least—the struggle for democracy had already been won, and remarkably painlessly, by the mid-19th century. In consequence, the American industrializing elites were, and felt themselves to be, uniquely vulnerable to an anti-industrialist assault which could be carried out peacefully and in the absence of effective legal or customary sanctions by a citizenry possessing at least two generations' experience with political democracy.

This crisis of vulnerability reached its peak in the 1890s. Two major elements in the population bore the brunt of the exceptionally severe deprivations felt during this depression decade: the smaller cash-crop farmers of the Southern and Western "colonial" regions and the ethnically fragmented urban working class. The cash-crop farmers, typically overextended and undercapitalized, had undergone a thirty-years' decline in the prices for their commodities in the face of intense international competition. With the onset of depression in 1893, what had been acute discomfort for them became disaster. The workers, already cruelly exploited in many instances during this "take-off" phase of large-scale industrialization, were also devastated by the worst depression the country had thus far known. Characteristically, the farmers resorted to political organization while the workers sporadically resorted to often bloody strikes. The industrializers and their intellectual and legal spokesmen were acutely conscious that these two profoundly alienated groups might coalesce. Their alarm was apparently given quite tangible form when the agrarian insurgents captured control of the Democratic Party in 1896.

But the results of that great referendum revealed that the conservatives' fears and the anti-industrialists' hopes of putting together a winning coalition on a Jacksonian base were alike groundless. Not only did urban labor *not* flock to William Jennings Bryan, it repudiated the Democratic Party on an unprecedented scale throughout the industrialized Northeast. The intensity and permanence of this urban realignment was paralleled by the Democrats' failure to make significant inroads into Republican strength in the more diversified and depression-resistant farm areas east of the Missouri River, and by their nearly total collapse in rural New England. The Democratic-Populist effort to create a coalition of the dispossessed created instead the most enduringly sectional political alignment in American history—an alignment which eventually separated the Southern and Western agrarians and transformed the most industrially advanced region of the country into a bulwark of industrialist Republicanism.

This realignment brought victory beyond expectation to those who had sought to find some way of insulating American elites from mass pressures without formally disrupting the pre-existing democratic-pluralist political struc-

[47] Maurice Duverger, *Political Parties* (New York, 2d. ed., 1959), pp. 1–60.

ture, without violence and without conspiracy. Of the factors involved in this victory three stand out as of particular importance. (1) The depression of 1893 began and deepened during a Democratic administration. Of course there is no way of ascertaining directly what part of the decisive minority which shifted its allegiance to the Republican Party reacted viscerally to the then incumbent party and failed to perceive that Cleveland and Bryan were diametrically opposed on the central policy issues of the day. But contemporary survey findings would tend to suggest that such a component in a realigning electorate might not be small. In this context it is especially worth noting that the process of profound break with traditional voting patterns began in the fall of 1893, not in 1896. In a number of major states like Ohio and Pennsylvania the voting pattern of 1896 bears far more resemblance to those of 1893–1895 than the latter did to pre-1893 voting patterns. Assuming that such visceral responses to the Democrats as the "party of depression" did play a major role in the realignment, it would follow that the strong economic upswing after 1897 would tend to strengthen this identification and its cognate, the identification of the Republicans as the "party of prosperity."

(2) The Democratic platform and campaign were heavily weighted toward the interests and needs of an essentially rural and semi-colonial clientele. Considerably narrowed in its programmatic base from the farmer-labor Populist platform of 1892, the Democratic Party focussed most of its campaign upon monetary inflation as a means of redressing the economic balance. Bryan's viewpoint was essentially that of the smallholder who wished to give the term "businessman" a broader definition than the Easterners meant by it, and of an agrarian whose remarks about the relative importance of farms and cities bespoke his profound misunderstanding of the revolution of his time. Silver mine owners and depressed cash-crop farmers could greet the prospect of inflation with enthusiasm, but it meant much less to adequately capitalized and diversified farmers in the Northeast, and less than nothing to the depression-ridden wage earners in that region's shops, mines and factories. Bryan's appeal at base was essentially Jacksonian—a call for a return to the simpler and more virtuous economic and political arrangements which he identified with that by-gone era. Such nostalgia could evoke a positive response among the native-stock rural elements whose political style and economic expectations had been shaped in the far-away past. But it could hardly seem a realistic political choice for the ethnically pluralist urban populations, large numbers of whom found such nostalgia meaningless since it related to nothing in their past or current experience. Programmatically, at least, these urbanites were presented with a two-way choice only one part of which seemed at all functionally related to the realities of an emergent industrial society. With the Democrats actually cast in the role of reactionaries despite the apparent radicalism of their platform and leader, and with no socialist alternative even thinkable in the context of the American political culture of the 1890s, the Republican Party alone retained some relevance to the urban setting. In this context, its massive triumph there was a foregone conclusion.

(3) An extremely important aspect of any political realignment is the unusually intense mobilization of negative-reference-group sentiments during the course of the campaign. 1896 was typical in this respect. Profound antago-

nisms in culture and political style between the cosmopolitan, immigrant, wet, largely non-Protestant components of American urban populations and the parochial, dry, Anglo-Saxon Protestant inhabitants of rural areas can be traced back at least to the 1840s. Bryan was virtually the archetype of the latter culture, and it would have been surprising had he not been the target of intense ethnocultural hostility from those who identified with the former. He could hardly have appeared as other than an alien to those who heard him in New York in 1896, or to those who booed him off the stage at the Democratic Convention—also in New York—in 1924. Moreover, his remarks about the Northeast as "the enemy's country"—anticipating Senator Goldwater's views about that region in 1964—could only intensify a broadly sectional hostility to his candidacy and deepen the impression that he was attacking not only the Northeast's industrializing elites but the Northeast itself. Both in 1896 and 1964 this region gave every visible evidence of replying in kind.

As Schattschneider has perceptively observed, the "system of 1896" was admirably suited to its primary function. One of its major working parts was a judiciary which proceeded first to manufacture the needed constitutional restraints on democratic political action—a development presaged by such decisions as the Minnesota railroad rate case of 1890 [48] and the income tax cases of 1894–1895 [49]—and then to apply these restraints against certain sensitive categories of national and state economic legislation.[50] Another of the new system's basic components was the control which the sectional alignment itself gave to the Republican Party, and through it the corporate business community, over the scope and direction of national public policy. Democracy was not only placed in judicial leading-strings, it was effectively placed out of commission— at least so far as two-party competition was concerned—in more than half of the states. Yet it was one of the greatest, if unacknowledged, contributions of the "system of 1896" that democratic forms, procedures and traditions continued to survive.[51] Confronted with a narrowed scope of effective democratic options, an increasingly large proportion of the eligible adult population either left, failed to enter or—as was the case with Southern Negroes after the completion of the 1890–1904 disfranchisement movement in the Old Confederacy—was systematically excluded from the American voting universe. The results of this on the exercise of the franchise have already been examined here in some detail. It was during this 1896–1932 era that the basic characteristics associated with today's mass electorate were formed.

These characteristics, as we have seen, have already far outlived the 1896 alignment itself. There seems to be no convincing evidence that they are being progressively liquidated at the present time. If the re-emergence of a competitive party politics and its at least partial orientation toward the broader needs of

[48] Chicago, Milwaukee & St. Paul Railway Co. v. Minnesota, 134 U.S. 418 (1890).
[49] Pollock v. Farmers' Loan & Trust Co., 157 U.S. 429 (1895); (rehearing) 158 U.S. 601 (1895).
[50] The literature on this process of judicial concept-formulation from its roots in the 1870s through its formal penetration into the structure of constitutional law in the 1890s is extremely voluminous. Two especially enlightening accounts are: Benjamin Twiss, *Lawyers and the Constitution* (Princeton, Princeton University Press, 1942), and Arnold M. Paul, *Conservative Crises and the Rule of Law* (Ithaca, Cornell University Press, 1960).
[51] Paul, *ibid.,* pp. 131–58.

an urban, industrialized society were welcome fruits of the New Deal revolution, that revolution has apparently exhausted most of its potential for stimulating turnout or party-oriented voting in America. The present state of affairs,
to be sure, is not without its defenders. The civics-minded have tended to argue
that the visible drift away from party-oriented voting among a growing minority
of voters is a sign of increasing maturity in the electorate.[52] Others have argued
that mediocre rates of turnout in the United States, paralleled by the normally
low salience of issues in our political campaigns, are indicative of a "politics of
happiness." [53] It is further contended that any sudden injection of large numbers
of poorly socialized adults into the active voting universe could constitute a
danger to the Republic.[54]

But there is another side to this coin. The ultimate democratic purpose of
issue-formulation in a campaign is to give the people at large the power to
choose their and their agents' options. Moreover, so far as is known, the blunt
alternative to party government is the concentration of political power, locally
or nationally, in the hands of those who already possess concentrated economic
power.[55] If no adequate substitute for party as a means for mobilizing non-elite
influence on the governing process has yet been discovered, the obvious growth
of "image" and "personality" voting in recent decades should be a matter of
some concern to those who would like to see a more complete restoration of the
democratic process in the United States.

Moreover, recent studies—such as Murray Levin's examinations of the
attitudes of the Boston and Massachusetts electorate—reveal that such phenomena as widespread ticket splitting may be associated quite readily with
pervasive and remarkably intense feelings of political alienation.[56] Convinced
that both party organizations are hopelessly corrupt and out of reach of popular
control, a minority which is large enough to hold the balance of power between
Republicans and Democrats tends rather consistently to vote for the lesser, or
lesser-known, of two evils. It takes a mordant variety of humor to find a kind of
emergent voter maturity in this alienation. For Levin's data are difficult to
square with the facile optimism underlying the civics approach to independent
voting. So, for that matter, are the conclusions of survey research about the
behavior of many so-called "independent" voters.[57]

Findings such as these seem little more comforting to the proponents of the
"politics of happiness" thesis. Granted the proposition that most people who
have been immersed from birth in a given political system are apt to be
unaware of alternatives whose explicit formulation that system inhibits, it is of

---

[52] See, among many other examples, *Congressional Quarterly Weekly Report,* Vol.
22 (May 1, 1964), p. 801.
[53] Heinz Eulau, "The Politics of Happiness," *Antioch Review,* Vol. 16, pp. 259–64
(1956); Seymour M. Lipset, *Political Man* (New York, 1960), pp. 179–219.
[54] *Ibid.,* pp. 216–19; Herbert Tingsten, *Political Behavior, op. cit.,* pp. 225–26.
[55] V. O. Key, Jr., *Southern Politics* (New York, 1949), pp. 526–28; E. E.
Schattschneider, *The Semi-Sovereign People, op. cit.,* pp. 114–28.
[56] Murray B. Levin, *The Alienated Voter* (New York, 1960), pp. 58–75, and his
The Compleat Politician (Indianapolis, 1962), esp. pp. 133–78. While one may hope
that Boston and Massachusetts are extreme case studies in the pathology of
democratic politics in the United States, it appears improbable that the pattern of
conflict between the individual's expectations and reality is entirely unique to the Bay
State.
[57] Angus Campbell *et al., The American Voter, op. cit.,* pp. 143–45.

course difficult to ascertain whether their issueless and apathetic political style is an outward sign of "real" happiness. We can surmise, however, that the kind of political alienation which Levin describes is incompatible with political happiness, whether real or fancied. A great many American voters, it would seem, are quite intelligent enough to perceive the deep contradiction which exists between the ideals of rhetorical democracy as preached in school and on the stump, and the actual day-to-day reality as that reality intrudes on his own *milieu*. Alienation arises from perception of that contradiction, and from the consequent feelings of individual political futility arising when the voter confronts an organization of politics which seems unable to produce minimally gratifying results. The concentration of socially deprived characteristics among the more than forty million adult Americans who today are altogether outside the voting universe suggests active alienation—or its passive equivalent, political apathy—on a scale quite unknown anywhere else in the Western world. Unless it is assumed as a kind of universal law that problems of existence which can be organized in political terms must fade out below a certain socio-economic level, this state of affairs is not inevitable. And if it is not inevitable, one may infer that the political system itself is responsible for its continued existence.

Yet such an assumption of fade-out is clearly untenable in view of what is known about patterns of voting participation in other democratic systems. Nor need it be assumed that substantial and rapid increases in American voting participation would necessarily, or even probably, involve the emergence of totalitarian mass movements. The possibility of such movements is a constant danger, to be sure, in any polity containing so high a proportion of apolitical elements in its potential electorate. But it would be unwise to respond to this possibility by merely expressing the comfortable hope that the apoliticals will remain apolitical, and by doing nothing to engage them in the system in a timely and orderly way. It is much more to the point to seek a way, if one can be found, to integrate the apolitical half of the American electorate into the political system before crisis arises.[58] Such integration need not be out of the question. The United States, after all, enjoyed intense mass political involvement without totalitarian movements during the last part of the 19th century, as do other Western democracies today.

No integration of the apoliticals can be carried out without a price to be paid. Underlying the failure of political organizations more advanced than the 19th-century middle-class cadre party to develop in this country has been the

---

[58] The line of reasoning developed in this article—especially that part of it which deals with the possible development of political alienation in the United States— seems not entirely consistent with the findings of Gabriel A. Almond and Sidney Verba, *The Civic Culture* (Princeton, Princeton University Press, 1963), pp. 402–69, 472–505. Of course there is no question that relatively high levels of individual satisfaction with political institutions and acceptance of democratic norms may exist in a political system with abnormally low rates of actual voting participation, just as extremely high turnout may—as in Italy—be associated with intense and activist modes of political alienation. At the same time, the gap between American norms and the actual political activity of American individuals does exist, as Almond and Verba point out on pp. 479–87. This may represent the afterglow of a Lockean value consensus in an inappropriate socio-economic setting, but in a polity quite lacking in the disruptive discontinuities of historical development which have occurred during this century in Germany, Italy and Mexico. Or it may represent something much more positive.

deeper failure of any except middle-class social and political values to achieve full legitimacy in the American political culture. It may not now be possible for our polity to make so great a leap as to admit non-middle-class values to political legitimacy and thus provide the preconditions for a more coherent and responsible mode of party organization. But such a leap may have to be made if full mobilization of the apolitical elements is to be achieved without the simultaneous emergence of manipulative radicalism of the left or the right. The heart of our contemporary political dilemma appears to lie in the conflict between this emergent need and the ideological individualism which continues so deeply to pervade our political culture. Yet the present situation perpetuates a standing danger that the half of the American electorate which is now more or less entirely outside the universe of active politics may someday be mobilized in substantial degree by totalitarian or quasi-totalitarian appeals. As the late President Kennedy seemed to intimate in his executive order establishing the Commission on Registration and Voting Participation, it also raises some questions about the legitimacy of the regime itself.[59]

[59] "Whereas less than sixty-five percent of the United States population of voting age cast ballots for Presidential electors in 1960; and
"Whereas popular participation in Government through elections is essential to a democratic form of Government; and
"Whereas the causes of nonvoting are not fully understood and more effective corrective action will be possible on the basis of a better understanding of the causes of the failure of many citizens to register and vote . . ." (emphasis supplied) The full text of the executive order is in *Report,* pp. 63–64. Compare with Schattschneider's comment in *The Semi-Sovereign People, op. cit.,* p. 112: "A greatly expanded popular base of political participation is the essential condition for public support of the government. This is the modern problem of democratic government. The price of support is participation. The choice is between participation and propaganda, between democratic and dictatorial ways of *changing consent into support, because consent is no longer enough.*" (Author's emphasis)

13

ROBERT R. DYKSTRA AND HARLAN HAHN

Northern Voters and Negro Suffrage: The Case of Iowa, 1868

Referenda on Negro rights were held in almost every Northern state in the Reconstruction era, not infrequently on a repeated basis. The questions of black enfranchisement became a volatile social and political issue which polarized political parties, ethno-cultural groups, and economic interests. Iowa and Minnesota were the only states in 1868 to adopt impartial suffrage by referendum majorities, and these victories, according to James M. McPherson, gave a major boost to the movement for a Fifteenth Amendment.

In their investigation of election returns in the Iowa referendum of 1868, Robert R. Dykstra and Harlan Hahn attempt to isolate several major political, ethno-cultural, and economic factors that may help explain the vote. By measuring the association of variables through the statistical technique of correlation coefficients, the authors demonstrate the highly partisan nature of the suffrage vote, the surprising support from small towns and economically prosperous rural areas, and the opposition from German and Irish immigrant groups, large cities, and economically backward areas. How typical the Iowa experience was is a question that can be answered only by similar analyses of referenda data in other Northern states between the years 1865 and 1870.

Robert R. Dykstra and Harlan Hahn, "Northern Voters and Negro Suffrage: The Case of Iowa, 1868," *Public Opinion Quarterly*, XXXII (Summer, 1968), 202–215. Reprinted, with slight revision, with permission of the authors and the editor of *Public Opinion Quarterly*.

A L T H O U G H American race prejudice is usually viewed as a Southern-born phenomenon that came North only with urbanization, Northern prejudice itself has a long history. Formal discrimination against the Negro in the North was probably most severe in the decades before the Civil War.[1] But the wartime triumph over slavery did not automatically bring an end to Northern discrimination. The result in many ways was a widespread crisis of conscience: having fought a war to preserve the Union that had developed into a crusade against slavery, would northerners yield to the moral implications of their victory and grant full civil rights—everywhere—to the Negro?

Between Appomattox and the promulgation of the Fifteenth Amendment in 1870, proposals that would allow Negroes to vote became burning political issues in several Northern states. The confrontation of views on the suffrage question during this period has been too long neglected by scholars interested in the relationship of race prejudice to the history of Negro civil rights.[2] While attitudes on Negro suffrage may not have been *precisely* related to race prejudice, it seems a proper if unverifiable assumption that those opposed to suffrage extension were opponents of racial equality. An examination of the Negro suffrage question of the 1860's, therefore, should lend insights into an important area of social relations in a historical era as well as perhaps help clarify more recent social and political behavior.

On the eve of the Civil War, only five New England states permitted Negroes to vote. New York had a limited provision for Negro suffrage. Four other states had altered their constitutions to exclude Negroes from the franchise, and in eight Northern states Negroes had always been legally deprived of the right to vote.[3] Opposition proved so strong prior to the Civil War that, in the estimation of one student, "the problem of Negro suffrage eclipsed the problem of the foreigner." [4] The question, however, was not resolved by the war. Between 1865 and 1870 proposals for Negro suffrage were defeated in at least 14 Northern states.[5] In addition, Colorado Territory jeopardized its admission to the Union in 1865 by a favorable referendum vote on a constitution restricting the franchise to "every white male citizen of the age of twenty-one and upward." [6] In New Jersey, the question of Negro suffrage was never submitted to a referendum, although the state's legislators rejected it decisively by a vote in

---

[1] See Leon F. Litwack, *North of Slavery: The Negro in the Free States, 1790–1860*, Chicago, University of Chicago Press, 1961. For the intellectual bases of race prejudice in the United States in the nineteenth century, see especially William Stanton, *The Leopard's Spots: Scientific Attitudes Toward Race in America, 1815–1859*, Chicago, University of Chicago Press, 1960; Thomas F. Gossett, *Race: The History of an Idea in America*, Dallas, Southern Methodist University Press, 1963, Chaps. 4–13.

[2] For a brief overview, see Leslie H. Fishel, Jr., "Northern Prejudice and Negro Suffrage, 1865–1870," *The Journal of Negro History*, Vol. 39, 1954, pp. 8–26. See also James M. McPherson, *The Struggle for Equality: Abolitionists and the Negro in the Civil War and Reconstruction*, Princeton, Princeton University Press, 1964, pp. 236–37, 333–34, 377, 382–83, 419 ff.

[3] Litwack, *op. cit.*, pp. 74–93; Kirk H. Porter, *A History of Suffrage in the United States*, Chicago, University of Chicago Press, 1918, pp. 89–92; Stephen B. Weeks, "The History of Negro Suffrage in the South," *Political Science Quarterly*, Vol. 9, 1894, p. 677.

[4] Porter, *op. cit.*, p. 62.

[5] James Albert Hamilton, *Negro Suffrage and Congressional Representation*, New York, Winthrop Press, 1910, pp. 21–23.

[6] *The American Annual Cyclopaedia and Register of Important Events of the Year 1865*, New York, D. Appleton and Co., 1866, p. 178.

1867 [7] and by a subsequent resolution denouncing Negro enfranchisement.[8]

Rejection of Negro suffrage by Northern states in the Reconstruction era placed the Republican "radicals" in Congress in a serious dilemma. At the same time that most of them demanded the right to vote for Southern Negroes, some on the grounds of principle, others to establish a Republican foothold in the South, their constituents blocked similar plans in the North.[9] The political advantages of the situation were not lost on President Andrew Johnson, who taunted Northern Congressmen for the inconsistencies in their position.[10] One of the relatively few prominent radicals who urged that Negroes universally be permitted to vote was Senator Charles Sumner of Massachusetts. Many other Congressmen, however, championed Negro suffrage in the South without risking the political consequences of advocating a similar program for the North. In these circumstances the Fifteenth Amendment, by prohibiting racial qualifications for voting in any state, provided a means to resolve the embarrassing issue without the need for various state constitutional referenda, although the battle still had to be waged in the state legislatures.[11]

Meanwhile, expressions of public opinion on Negro suffrage gave the radicals little encouragement. Since politicians generally were reluctant to decide the issue themselves, franchise extension became a frequent subject of referendum voting in the late 1860's. The per cent of the vote in opposition to Negro suffrage in ten Northern state referenda is contained in Table 1. There was no decided trend in favor of extending the franchise to Negroes. Although border states evidenced somewhat more resistance to Negro suffrage than states farther north, the years in which the referenda were held seemed to have little effect on the outcome. In general, there were few differences in the outcome of referenda held in 1868 and those held earlier.

While most Northern states confronted the issue directly, proponents of Negro suffrage in a few states attempted relatively circuitous methods of gaining approval for the measure. In Michigan, for example, voters were presented with a totally new constitution that quietly omitted the word "white" from the qualifications for voting.[12] In Illinois, a Negro suffrage amendment

[7] *Annual Cyclopaedia* (1867), p. 539.
[8] *Annual Cyclopaedia* (1868), pp. 541–42.
[9] Eric L. McKitrick, *Andrew Johnson and Reconstruction,* Chicago, University of Chicago Press, 1960, pp. 55–58.
[10] Charles H. Coleman, *The Election of 1868: The Democratic Effort to Regain Control,* New York, Columbia University Press, 1933, p. 19. For the most important recent scholarship on the party conflict over a Reconstruction policy for the defeated South, see LaWanda Cox and John H. Cox, *Politics, Principle, and Prejudice, 1865–1866: Dilemma of Reconstruction America,* New York, Free Press, 1963; W. R. Brock, *An American Crisis: Congress and Reconstruction, 1865–1867,* New York, St. Martin's, 1963; Kenneth M. Stampp, *The Era of Reconstruction, 1865–1877,* New York, Knopf, 1965; David Donald, *The Politics of Reconstruction, 1863–1867,* Baton Rouge, Louisiana State University Press, 1965.
[11] For the most recent book-length study of the Fifteenth Amendment issue, see William Gillette, *The Right to Vote: Politics and the Passage of the Fifteenth Amendment,* Baltimore, Johns Hopkins University Press, 1965. For a recent article taking issue with the prevailing view that most national Republican figures were cynically political in their approach to the Negro suffrage question see LaWanda and John H. Cox, "Negro Suffrage and Republican Politics: The Problem of Motivation in Reconstruction Historiography," *Journal of Southern History,* Vol. 33, 1967, pp. 303–30.
[12] Fishel, *op. cit.,* pp. 20–21.

TABLE 1

PER CENT OF THE VOTE IN OPPOSITION TO NEGRO SUF-
FRAGE IN NINE STATE REFERENDA, 1865–1868

State	Per Cent against Negro Suffrage
District of Columbia (1865)	99.5
Connecticut (1865)	55.2
Wisconsin (1865)	54.4
Kansas (1867)	65.1
Ohio (1867)	55.2
Minnesota (1867)	51.2
Michigan (1868)	53.1
Missouri (1868)	57.3
Iowa (1868)	33.5

SOURCE: *Annual Cyclopaedia*, 1865–1870.

had been overwhelmingly defeated in 1862. Six years later, Illinois voters endorsed a plan for a constitutional convention by a scant majority of 704 out of 444,860 ballots cast.[13] The convention delegates struck the word "white" from the suffrage requirements of the new constitution but refused to refer the issue to the voters as a separate amendment, thus forestalling its rejection.[14]

The presidential election of 1868 represented a peak time for voting on Negro suffrage. In that year voters approved franchise extension in Iowa and Minnesota, but rejected it in Michigan and Missouri.[15] In Minnesota, Negro enfranchisement was adopted, after two previous defeats in referenda, only when the question was submitted to voters as "an amendment of section 1, article 7, of the constitution"—without any direct reference to impartial suffrage.[16] Negro suffrage also won in Wisconsin that year, but through a decision of the State Supreme Court rather than a popular vote.[17] Thus the only straightforward victory for Negro suffrage in 1868 occurred in Iowa; and as the only state that adopted franchise extension by means of a single, uncomplicated referendum, Iowa appears to offer productive opportunities for investigating postwar popular attitudes toward Negro rights in the North.

The analysis of voting returns is a particularly appropriate method of studying historical public opinion.[18] Even though previous research suggests that aggregate election data may not correlate precisely with individual opinions,[19]

[13] *Annual Cyclopaedia* (1868), p. 351.
[14] *Annual Cyclopaedia* (1870), p. 392.
[15] Coleman, *op. cit.*, p. 18.
[16] *Annual Cyclopaedia* (1868), p. 505.
[17] *Annual Cyclopaedia* (1865), p. 823.
[18] For a comprehensive discussion of the application of such methods to historical problems, see Samuel P. Hays, "New Possibilities for American Political History: The Social Analysis of Political Life," unpublished paper presented at the meeting of the American Historical Association, Washington, D.C., December 29, 1964; see also William O. Aydelotte, "Quantification in History," *American Historical Review,* Vol. 71, 1966, pp. 803–25.
[19] W. S. Robinson, "Ecological Correlations and the Behavior of Individuals," *American Sociological Review,* Vol. 15, 1950, pp. 351–57; Herbert Menzel, "Com-

voting statistics remain the only quantitative measure of "grass roots" attitudes before the twentieth century. Clearly, the alternative to using election statistics is to ignore them entirely and continue to place exclusive emphasis on random estimates of public opinion—usually highly subjective—hazarded by contemporary politicians and journalists. While one may, of course, lament the nonexistence of such ideal aids as opinion surveys, much more historical election data can be recovered than is sometimes imagined, and much can be accomplished with it through the use of modern analytical techniques.

The principal sources of data for this study were the election returns from 97 counties and 437 townships for Iowa's 1868 referendum on the Negro suffrage question. Surprisingly, the location of voting statistics proved a much less severe problem than anticipated. County election returns were recovered from the state archives and the township reports were obtained from an exhaustive review of extant local newspapers. The statistics were then internally verified to ensure their accuracy.

Census material comprised a second important source of data for this study, especially the published state censuses of 1867 and 1869 and the federal manuscript census of 1870. Unfortunately, the unusual mobility of the Iowa population in the late 1860's required the exercise of considerable caution at some points, especially in positing relationships between the 1868 voting and 1870 demographic characteristics. Yet, the over-all richness of the census data greatly facilitated the research. When the analysis of voting and demographic patterns was supplemented by information from newspapers and other historical records, a relatively comprehensive picture emerged.

The issue of Negro suffrage was first presented to Iowans in 1857. After the 1854 election of a Whig as governor had dislodged Democrats from control of public offices in the state, considerable agitation developed for a new constitution that would remove the prohibition on banks and effect other changes. An ensuing constitutional convention produced a number of important alterations in the basic framework of Iowa government, but disagreement over a Negro suffrage proposal proved sufficiently intense to inspire the delegates to refer it to the voters as the only separate amendment to the new constitution.[20] Although Iowans approved the new constitution by a slight majority, they turned down the proposal to strike the word "white" from its suffrage provisions by an overwhelming margin of 85.4 per cent. But at the same time, more than one-fourth of the people who cast ballots on the new constitution failed to vote on the suffrage amendment.

An examination of the 1857 voting returns by area permits some interesting insights. Only two counties in the state recorded a majority for the amendment. In Mitchell County, which contained a large Scandinavian settlement, the proposal received a plurality of less than one per cent; but a unanimous vote of 284 to 0 was delivered for it in Cedar County, at that time populated almost exclusively by Quakers. By arbitrarily dividing the state along geographic lines, the location of centers of support and opposition becomes apparent. Counties in

————
ment on Robinson's 'Ecological Correlations and the Behavior of Individuals,' " *ibid.*, p. 674.
    [20] Carl H. Erbe, "Constitutional Provisions for the Suffrage in Iowa," *The Iowa Journal of History and Politics*, Vol. 22, 1924, pp. 185–207.

the northern half of the state, for example, provided nearly 10 per cent fewer votes in opposition to franchise extension than southern counties, in which settlers from below the Mason-Dixon Line predominated. The largest vote against Negro suffrage was recorded in southeastern Iowa, which contained the state's earliest and most Southern settlements.[21]

Resistance to Negro rights was manifested in several areas of Iowa during the Civil War, although the attitudes of many residents undoubtedly underwent profound changes during the war years. Iowa, for example, contributed more men per capita to the Union army than any other state. As an area subjected to the agitations and dislocations of the war during a formative period of its history, perhaps Iowa was particularly affected by doctrines and arguments promulgated in support of the Union position.

The results of the second referendum in 1868 suggested that a major shift in opinion had occurred. The vote for Negro enfranchisement increased from 14.6 per cent in 1857 to 66.5 per cent in 1868. Furthermore, the total vote cast on Negro suffrage was within five per cent of the total vote in the 1868 presidential contest, which was on the ballot at the same time.

The 1868 referendum presented voters with five different amendments to strike the word "white" from the Iowa constitution. The first amendment removed the qualification of race from voting requirements; the second, third, and fourth amendments eliminated similar restrictions from census and apportionment regulations; and the fifth amendment voided racial limitations on the composition of the state militia. A sixth discriminatory clause in the state constitution, confining membership in the legislature to free whites, was overlooked in the haste to prepare amendments, but voters repealed this provision in 1880 by a margin of 63.4 per cent.[22] The 1868 vote on the five amendments varied by only 202 out of more than 186,000 cast. Consequently, the vote on the first amendment has been employed as the principal measure of attitudes in this analysis.

Since the vote for Negro suffrage varied by five per cent or less between different sections of the state in 1868, more precise statistics were examined. The associations between the vote for franchise extension and several major political, social, and economic variables by county have been recorded in Table 2. Perhaps the most striking feature of the table is the high association between party preferences and voting on Negro enfranchisement. The township voting statistics also revealed the strength of this association. In 367 out of the 437 townships, there was a difference of only 10 per cent or less between the vote on suffrage and the presidential returns. At the township level, the coefficient of correlation between the percentage of the vote for U. S. Grant, the Republican candidate for President, and the percentage of the vote in favor of Negro suffrage was +.91. This correlation probably reflects the success of Republican leaders who sought to identify their party with the cause of extending additional liberties to Negroes in the postwar era.

As early as 1866, Iowa was the only state in which the Republican party had

---

[21] Alice Lucile Hahn, "Exercise of the Electoral Franchise in Iowa in Constitutional Referenda, 1836–1933," Des Moines, Drake University, unpublished master's thesis, 1933, pp. 63–66.

[22] *Ibid.,* pp. 74–76.

TABLE 2

CORRELATION BETWEEN VOTE FOR NEGRO SUFFRAGE IN 1868 AND POLITICAL, SOCIAL, AND ECONOMIC CHARACTERISTICS, BY COUNTY

Political, Social, and Economic Characteristics	*Correlation with Vote for Negro Suffrage*	*p*
Per cent of vote for Republican candidate for Secretary of State (1867)	+.92	.001
Per cent of vote for Republican candidate for Governor (1867)	+.84	.001
Per cent of vote for Republican candidate for President (1868)	+.86	.001
Per cent of eligible voters in incorporated towns (1867)	−.32	.01
Per cent of population Negro (1867)	−.23	.05
Per capita value of manufactures (1868)	−.26	.05
Value of farm produce sold per unit of production (1868)	+.31	.01
Average value of land per acre (1868)	−.30	.01

strongly endorsed Negro suffrage.[23] The particular zealousness of Iowa Republicans on the suffrage question also probably reflected the bitter factional dispute between James Harlan, Secretary of the Interior in Lincoln's Cabinet, and wartime Governor Samuel J. Kirkwood, who, along with General Grenville M. Dodge, led the radical reconstructionists of Iowa. Agitation for the radical cause in the party became so intense that Congressman John A. Kasson, Lincoln's First Assistant Postmaster General, was purged by Dodge at least in part for his failure to espouse Negro suffrage.[24] The power of the radical faction in the Iowa Republican party of 1868 was implicitly echoed by one Republican editor, who proclaimed, "A vote for Grant and Colfax in Iowa, is *not a true, honest, Republican, vote,* unless it contain[s] the clause striking the word 'White' from the Constitution." [25] The high association between the vote for Republican candidates and for suffrage extension indicates that a large number of Iowa Republicans heeded such exhortations.

Party regularity, however, does not provide the only explanation for the remarkable discipline the parties apparently exerted on the referendum vote. The balloting on Negro suffrage also was somewhat related to settlement patterns. Several measures of population characteristics suggest that the greatest support for Negro enfranchisement was concentrated in rural or farming regions and that its principal opponents were located in the relatively urbanized or densely settled areas of the state. Both the proportion of eligible voters living in incorporated towns and the per capita value of manufacturing were negatively related to the vote for Negro suffrage. On the other hand, a positive association was found between support for franchise extension and such rural indices as the percentage of enclosed areas devoted to the cultivation of wheat (+.41) and the proportion of rural voters in the county population (+.34).

A somewhat clearer picture of the differences between urban communities and farming areas emerged from an examination of the vote in the 437

[23] Fishel, *op. cit.,* p. 17.
[24] Edward Younger, *John A. Kasson,* Iowa City, State Historical Society of Iowa, 1955, pp. 182–206.
[25] Davenport *Western Soldier's Friend,* Oct. 24, 1868.

townships by type of population unit. Small towns (2,500 population or less) gave slightly more support to the Republican party and to Negro suffrage, and they had higher levels of voter participation in both the election and the referendum, than either farm areas or large towns (more than 2,500 population).[26] Although the amazingly large percentages of eligible voters who everywhere cast ballots on both questions are consistent with the findings of prior research on voter turnout in the late nineteenth century, the data did not support the conclusion that rural or farm settlers voted in greater proportions than the residents of urban communities generally.[27]

The tendency of small towns to support both the Republican candidate for President and Negro suffrage in 1868 is consistent with previous research indicating that the residents of small towns are less likely to depart from traditional party orthodoxy than other segments of the voting population.[28] A number of special factors probably influenced the vote in both rural townships and relatively large communities, where the pro-suffrage total was 10 per cent below the state plurality for Negro suffrage. Large towns normally contained large concentrations of Democratic voters, who, as Democrats, had little sympathy for Republican-sponsored proposals to secure Negro rights. On the other hand, the relative lack of enthusiasm for Negro suffrage displayed in farm townships perhaps was affected by the special status of the Negro in a rural environment. By the end of the Civil War, the few Negroes in Iowa, who constituted only one half of one per cent of the population of the state, had begun to filter thinly into the Iowa countryside. Many of them, perhaps lacking the skills and training qualifying them for work in populous areas, were probably compelled to perform marginal work without steady employment. There did not seem to be a role for the Negro in a rural economy. In these circumstances, the farmer whose status was subject to the fluctuations of an unpredictable market perhaps had little difficulty in conjuring a vision of colored immigrants flooding the rural landscape from outside the state, attracted by guarantees of equal rights.

Support for the idea that rural areas facing the specter of economic insecurity were the most susceptible to fears of displacement through Negro immigration was discovered in documents from that era. The 1868 campaign rhetoric reflected both intense partisan disagreements and a possible explanation for the strong correlation between party preferences and positions on the suffrage question. While Republicans enlisted the "bloody shirt" and appeals to conscience in their efforts to enfranchise the Negro, Democrats often sought to arouse fears concerning economic status as a means of stimulating opposition to the measure. Some Democratic spokesmen attempted to expose Negro suffrage

[26] In small towns, 98 per cent of the population voted in the 1868 presidential election and 95 per cent on the Negro suffrage question; 65 per cent of the vote went to Grant and 61 per cent for Negro suffrage. In rural townships, 89 per cent voted in the presidential election and 87 per cent in the suffrage referendum; 62 per cent voted for Grant and 56 per cent for Negro suffrage. In large towns, 84 per cent voted in the presidential election and 80 per cent in the suffrage referendum; the vote for Grant and for Negro suffrage was, respectively, 61 and 56 per cent.
[27] Walter Dean Burnham, "The Changing Shape of the American Political Universe," *American Political Science Review*, Vol. 59, 1965, pp. 16–17.
[28] Harlan Hahn, "One-partyism and State Politics: The Structure of Political Power in Iowa," unpublished doctoral dissertation, Cambridge, Harvard University, 1964.

as a device for attracting cheap labor with which white voters would be forced
to compete. For example, a stump-speaking innkeeper from Clayton County,
the seat of a large concentration of foreign-born voters with Republican
proclivities, admonished his fellow citizens to vote for "a free white Democratic
ticket." His argument was a cunning amalgamation of "populist" economic
rhetoric and appeals to race prejudice:

> You voted for "Abraham Lincoln;" this made you "loyal;" you freed
> the negro; you put down that awful curse *"negro* slavery" and
> fastened eternal white slavery upon yourselves and children by lower-
> ing and knuckling to the most absolute, despotic and exacting, intrud-
> ing slave driver, that ever marked the poor man's path—the Giant
> God of Moloch—the monied mon[o]polies of the country. Good bye
> laboring man! The bondocracy of New England have fixed your
> status.[29]

This was a somewhat circumlocutory appeal to white status panic with respect
to the Negro; and, in fact, few such Democratic exhortations were issued
straightforwardly and openly. But Republican spokesmen acknowledged them
to be a potent factor affecting the decisions of white voters. *"That man is a
Coward who fears negro suffrage,"* argued the Republican editor quoted previously. ". . . It is not the color of the skin you fear, it is the fear you have,
that the negro will outstrip you in the race of life." [30] Another Republican
editor addressed the question at some length. "A Democratic friend in Eden-
ville," he wrote,

> . . . contends that he wants laws passed which shall give him a better
> chance in life than is given the colored man. He thinks it should be
> made by law easier for him to get his living—that in the race and
> struggle of life he should have advantages, while the black, already
> borne down by the prejudice of color, should be made to labor under
> positive disabilities. . . . Either our Edenville friend is very uncharita-
> ble at heart, or he is afraid that "the nigger" will get the start on him
> in the race of life and in the struggle for preferment. . . . How
> narrow, contemptible, illiberal, unjust and mean, is the prejudice,
> which would hamper the colored man in the pursuit of an industrious
> livelihood. . . .[31]

Since the economic consequences of extending Negro rights were debated
primarily by party spokesmen, the effectiveness of appeals to white anxieties
over the threat of economic displacement is difficult to assess. By removing the
influence of partisan considerations, however, some indications can be gained
about the independent impact of the argument. Table 3 contains the partial
correlations between the vote for Negro suffrage and several social and economic variables by county, controlling on the percentage of the vote for the

[29] McGregor *North Iowa Times,* Sept. 30, 1868. For the speaker's personal
characteristics, see *History of Clayton County, Iowa,* Chicago, Inter-State Publishing
Co., 1882, pp. 819–20. A summary of the economic issues in the 1868 campaign is
given by Coleman, *op. cit.,* pp. 24–44.
[30] Davenport *Western Soldier's Friend,* Oct. 24, 1868.
[31] Marshalltown *Times,* Sept. 26, 1868.

TABLE 3

PARTIAL CORRELATIONS BETWEEN VOTE FOR NEGRO SUFFRAGE IN 1868
AND SOCIAL AND ECONOMIC CHARACTERISTICS, BY COUNTY

Social and Economic Characteristics	*Partial Correlation with Vote for Negro Suffrage* [a]	*p*
Per cent of eligible voters in incorporated towns (1867)	+.15	n.s.
Per cent of population Negro (1867)	−.01	n.s.
Per capita value of manufacturers (1868)	−.16	n.s.
Value of farm produce sold per unit of production (1868)	+.49	.001
Average value of land per acre (1868)	+.23	.05

[a] Controlling on the per cent of the vote for the Republican candidate for Secretary of State in 1867.

Republican candidate for Secretary of State in 1867. Table 3 reveals that, with the effect of the Republican vote eliminated, the associations between variables measuring agricultural prosperity and positions on Negro suffrage are altered considerably. The correlations with the indicators of urbanization and the percentage of Negroes are substantially reduced. But the relation between farm prosperity as measured by the relative value of farm produce and the suffrage vote is strengthened. Perhaps even more striking is the coefficient of correlation between the average value of land per acre and the vote in favor of Negro enfranchisement, which changes from a negative to a positive direction when the Republican vote is introduced as a control. Apparently, support for Negro suffrage was related to economic success in rural areas, independent of the effects of partisan allegiances. Since rural workers in relatively prosperous areas had less to fear from economic displacement than those in poor farming areas, they seemed to be more resistant to the imagined threat of Negro immigration.

In addition, the township data were used to measure the association between the difference in the vote on Negro suffrage and the Republican presidential vote, and the percentage of the population that was Negro. In farm townships, but in neither small nor large towns, the Negro proportion of the population correlates positively and significantly with the size of this difference. Only in rural areas was it found that the greater the relative number of Negroes, the greater was the difference between the percentage of the vote for Grant and the percentage for Negro suffrage. Although the relation between the fear of economic competition and race prejudice among the residents of large towns and cities has been popularly accepted, patterns in the 1868 Iowa vote indicate that similar conclusions may be equally and perhaps particularly applicable to rural areas.

The results of the 1868 referendum and the partisan elections of the 1860's also indicate that immigrant townships, which were perhaps most vulnerable to anxieties about Negro economic competition, were more consistently opposed to both Republican candidates and Negro suffrage than native American areas. The mean percentage of the vote in selected townships of Iowa for three elections is contained in Table 4. Fortunately, information on the predominant

TABLE 4

VOTE IN TOWNSHIPS, BY NATIVE ORIGINS OF VOTERS, IN
THREE ELECTIONS IN IOWA, 1860–1868

Townships [a]	Number of Townships	Per Cent for Grant (1868)	Per Cent for Negro Suffrage (1868)	Per Cent for Lincoln (1860)
Upper Ohio Valley (voted Republican by 75% or more in 1860)	8	81	77	82
Upper Ohio Valley (voted Democratic by 60% or more in 1860)	7	42	37	31
German (voted Democratic by 60% or more in 1860)	5	22	18	23
Irish (voted Democratic by 60% or more in 1860)	4	16	12	12

[a] As identified by George H. Daniels, "Immigrant Vote in the 1860 Election: The Case of Iowa," *Mid-America*, Vol. 44, July 1962, pp. 159–162.

ethnic composition of Iowa townships is contained in a prior study, which discovered that townships dominated by Irish and German voters provided overwhelming support for Democratic candidates before the Civil War.[32] By comparing the vote in various townships, it is possible to determine areas of support and opposition to Negro suffrage and changes in voting patterns that may have occurred over time.

German and Irish townships not only expressed the greatest opposition to Negro suffrage, but they also were least inclined to 'depart from Democratic allegiances. Townships dominated by natives of the Upper Ohio Valley that had voted overwhelmingly for Lincoln in 1860 gave the most support to Grant and Negro suffrage in 1868. But while the Republican vote in *Democratic* townships dominated by voters from the Upper Ohio Valley increased markedly between 1860 and 1868, the presidential vote and the vote on Negro suffrage in Irish and German townships remained relatively stable. Thus townships with a high proportion of foreign-born voters yielded more opposition both to Republican candidates and to Negro suffrage than even traditionally Democratic townships settled by native Americans from the Upper Ohio Valley.

Another measure of the opposition of immigrant groups to Negro enfranchisement was provided by isolating the several townships casting the heaviest vote against the referendum proposal. So far as is known, all of the townships that voted less than 10 per cent for Negro suffrage also were among the most Democratic townships in the state in both the 1860 and the 1868 elections. Even more striking, however, the electorates of all were over 48 per cent foreign-born in 1870. Voters of Irish birth dominated five, Germans one, and Irish and Norwegians shared dominance in another.[33]

[32] George H. Daniels, "Immigrant Vote in the 1860 Election: The Case of Iowa," *Mid-America,* Vol. 44, 1962, pp. 159–62.
[33] The townships were: Washington Twp., Clinton County; Iowa Twp., Liberty Twp., Prairie Creek Twp., Washington Twp., all in Dubuque County; Butler Twp., Jackson County; and Washington Twp., Jones County. The mean percentage of the

Although partisan loyalties and ethnic group identifications overlapped to a great extent in Iowa during this period, it was possible to identify three traditionally Republican townships in which foreign-born voters predominated over residents of native birth. Two of the townships were dominated by Germans, and the other by Norwegians. In all three, the discrepancy between the Republican vote in 1868 and the vote in support of Negro suffrage exceeded, though slightly, the state average.[34] Despite the limited amount of evidence, therefore, the data did suggest a cautious finding that even Republican immigrant voters gave somewhat less support to franchise extension than native Americans.

The explanation of these phenomena is not difficult to discern. A ranking of ethnic backgrounds reveals that the three largest foreign-born groups in Iowa in 1870 were the Germans, the Irish, and the Scandinavians. They constituted 9 per cent, 6 per cent, and 3 per cent, respectively, of the total labor force in the state. In many of the jobs requiring few skills, however, they congregated in larger numbers than their relative proportions of the working population. More than 37 per cent of the common laborers in Iowa at this time were German, Irish, and Scandinavian. Nearly 25 per cent of all railroad employees were Irish, and 13 per cent were Scandinavian.[35] Consequently, immigrants were less immune to fears of economic displacement should Negroes be attracted to Iowa by the extension of suffrage than were native Americans who held occupations providing greater security and status.

Referenda on Negro rights in the years after the Civil War created major problems and conflicts for many groups of voters. Perhaps the group that experienced the greatest difficulty with the Negro suffrage question in that period was the Republican party. While Congressmen who endorsed radical Reconstruction programs demanded Negro suffrage in the South, they experienced serious resistance to the imposition of Negro suffrage on their own Northern constituencies. In Iowa the suffrage vote was closely related to partisan loyalties. Republican discipline may have been less effective in some other Northern states. Yet, significantly, opinions on Negro suffrage everywhere were clearly divided along party lines during this period. Republicans generally endorsed the extension of Negro rights, and Democrats frequently were obliged to defend themselves against charges of anti-Negro prejudice.[36] The Democratic strategy of opposing Negro suffrage as a potential invitation to the influx of cheap labor was directed particularly at immigrant groups, which most feared economic competition.[37] Probably appeals contrived to portray Negro rights as a social and economic threat contributed to Democratic strength in the predominantly Republican era of the 1860's.

---

vote for Negro suffrage in the seven townships was 5.0, the mean percentage of the vote for Grant was 7.1, and the mean percentage of foreign-born voters in 1870 was 71.9.

[34] These townships were: Garnavillo Twp., Volga Twp., and Marion Twp., all in Clayton County.

[35] Calculated from *United States Census* (1870), Vol. 1, p. 733.

[36] Horace Samuel Merrill, *Bourbon Democracy of the Middle West, 1865–1896,* Baton Rouge, Louisiana State University Press, 1953, pp. 13–17.

[37] Frank L. Klement, *The Copperheads in the Middle West,* Chicago, University of Chicago Press, 1960, pp. 13–14, 105.

The results of Iowa's referendum voting indicate that Democrats generally were successful in arousing antipathy to Negro suffrage among immigrants. The vote on Negro suffrage also was closely related to social and economic characteristics. Although small towns cast somewhat larger majorities in favor of Negro suffrage than rural townships or urban areas, the only positive association between the presence of Negroes in the population and the Republican presidential vote minus the vote for Negro suffrage was found in farming areas. The white farmer in Iowa apparently experienced a reaction to potential Negro competition similar to the response of other groups enjoying few economic privileges.

Whether the case of Iowa in 1868 was or was not typical for the North in the 1860's is a question that can be answered only by similar research for other states. The historical bases of race prejudice, despite the complexities involved in attempting to assess them, are certainly worthy of continued investigation. The analysis of popular referenda on Negro suffrage held prior to the Fifteenth Amendment would appear to be one fruitful approach.

14

ROGER E. WYMAN *

Wisconsin Ethnic Groups and the Election of 1890

This article, awarded the William B. Hesseltine Award for 1967–1968, applies the statistical technique of correlation coefficients to assess the strength of the association between voting behavior and ethnic, religious, and nationality variables. The study centers primarily on two laws, one state and one national, which stirred more than ordinary community reactions—the Bennett Law of 1889 prescribing English-language instruction in Wisconsin schools (at least for certain subjects), and the McKinley Tariff of 1890. Professor Wyman concludes that the Bennett Law with its suspected nativist bias caused mass defections of German and Scandinavian Protestants from Republican ranks, especially in the eastern part of the state. This, coupled with Republican losses in western Wisconsin due to the tariff issue, gave the Democrats a landslide victory in 1890 and shaped the political fortunes of the state for the remainder of the decade. Wyman's conclusions on western Republican defections need further statistical analysis of voting trends; but if his eastern Wisconsin findings are valid, as they seem to be, it appears that local issues and personalities overshadowed national questions such as the tariff in determining voting patterns.

Roger E. Wyman, "Wisconsin Ethnic Groups and the Election of 1890," *Wisconsin Magazine of History,* LI (Summer, 1968), 269–93. Reprinted with permission of the publisher.
* The author is grateful to the Inter-University Consortium for Political Research at the University of Michigan for making it financially possible to attend its summer

THE BENNETT LAW controversy of 1889–1890 was one of the most exciting chapters in Wisconsin's colorful political history. The furor over this law, a seemingly innocuous child labor and compulsory education act which also stipulated that certain subjects had to be taught in the English language, created a brief but major upheaval in Wisconsin politics, and the debris left in its wake cast a shadow over the political life of the state for a decade.

The ethnic and religious antagonisms that the Bennett Law aroused were the bitterest ever experienced in Wisconsin. Defenders of the law asserted that it was necessary for the preservation of the public school system, but Germans saw it as an attempt by Americanizing Yankees to extinguish the German language in the United States; Catholics and Lutherans viewed it as a direct threat to their system of parochial education. As a result, in the election of 1890, a unified German and Catholic vote handed the Wisconsin Republican party its worst defeat until 1932; and in 1892 the lingering emotions among the law's opponents enabled a Democratic presidential candidate to carry the state for the first time since 1852.

Wisconsin has long been known for its large foreign population, particularly its sizable German contingent in Milwaukee and surrounding areas. Throughout the last half of the nineteenth century, the state consistently had the largest percentage of foreign-born population east of the Mississippi River. In 1890 people of foreign parentage—those of foreign birth plus native-born of foreign parents—composed 73.7 per cent of Wisconsin's 1,686,880 inhabitants.[1] The Germans were by far the most numerous of the various ethnic groups represented in the state. In 1890 they made up 37.1 per cent of the total population. Scandinavians were the second largest ethnic group: Norwegians, Swedes, and Danes composed 10.9 per cent of the total population. Immigrants from Ireland, Great Britain, Poland, Canada, Bohemia, Holland, Belgium, and Switzerland also made up important segments of the population in various areas.[2]

The injection of religious and ethnic conflict into Wisconsin politics was not peculiar to 1890; indeed, ethnic and religious tensions between native Americans and foreigners and between the different ethnic groups were reflected in state politics as early as the 1840's. The suffrage provisions of the state constitution of 1848 made the immigrant a force to be reckoned with in Wisconsin politics, for the right to vote was given to all adult males who had lived in the state for one year and who had declared their intention to become an American citizen.

The pattern of ethnic political allegiances that the Bennett Law campaign of 1890 disrupted was formed prior to the Civil War. By the late 1850's a protracted struggle over prohibition, and then the slavery question, had pro-

training seminar in 1966 and for providing computer time and much of the county-level data used in this study. The author also thanks Professor Allan G. Bogue, Professor E. David Cronon, and Mr. Stanley Mallach for their critical readings of the manuscript. Responsibility for any errors remains solely with the author.

[1] *United States Census, 1890,* Part I, pp. lxxiii, cxxxix, clxvi–clxvii, 606–9, 667–68.

[2] Germans made up more than 50 per cent of the state's population who were of foreign parentage. There were almost 260,000 German-born residents alone, totaling 15.4 per cent of the state's population. Norwegians were the most numerous Scandinavian nationality, composing more than 65 per cent of Scandinavian immigrants. *Ibid.*

duced relatively permanent attachments between the various ethnic groups and the Republican and Democratic parties. There never was a "foreign vote" as such; the immigrant groups divided their loyalties between the two parties. The Irish, Bohemians, Polish, and Dutch and German Catholics provided the bulk of immigrant support for the Democrats. The Republicans, in addition to commanding the loyalty of a majority of native-born American Protestants, received the votes of the English, Welsh, and Scotch; the Scandinavians; the Dutch Protestants; and an increasingly larger share of the German Protestants. Strong support from the Scandinavians and German Protestants was a major factor in Republican ascendancy in Wisconsin during the last half of the nineteenth century. The Republican party was deposed only twice between its formation and 1900. In both cases, in 1873 over the Republican-sponsored Graham liquor law, and in 1890 over the Bennett Law, the German vote defected *en masse* to the opposition party.[3]

Overt ethnic and religious antagonisms periodically crept into Wisconsin election campaigns. Any type of liquor legislation immediately drew protests from the German population and often evoked cries of nativism and "Know-Nothingism." Antiforeign sentiment, nationality antagonisms, and anti-Catholicism were all exploited regularly by politicians of both parties. The gradual shift of German Protestants to the Republican party in the 1870's and 1880's was largely the result of subtle exploitation of the inherent religious antagonisms between Catholic and Protestant Germans by Republican party leaders.

In light of the furor it created, it is ironic that the Bennett Law passed virtually unnoticed through the 1889 legislature. Republican Governor William D. Hoard had advocated a compulsory education law in his inaugural address, and the subsequent bill, introduced by young Iowa County assemblyman Michael J. Bennett, passed through the legislature without debate. The law was enacted on April 17, at the end of the session, and signed by Governor Hoard the following day.[4] It required compulsory attendance for each child of school age in "some public or private day school in the city, town or district in which he resides" for at least twelve weeks. The heart of the law, in the eyes of its opponents, was section five:

> No school shall be regarded as a school, under this act, unless there
> shall be taught therein, as part of the elementary education of chil-

[3] For the crucial role of the Germans in Wisconsin politics, see Herman J. Deutsch, "Yankee-Teuton Rivalry in Wisconsin Politics of the Seventies," in the *Wisconsin Magazine of History*, 14:262–82, 403–18 (March, June, 1931); Wilhelm Hense-Jensen and Ernest Bruncken, *Wisconsin's Deutsch-Amerikaner, bis zum schluss des neuenzehnter jahrhunderts* (2 vols., originally published in Milwaukee, 1900–1902. Translated into English by Joseph C. Schafer, typewritten manuscript in the Joseph C. Schafer Papers, State Historical Society of Wisconsin), chaps. 10–13.

[4] The Bennett Law was not Wisconsin's first compulsory education law; a law requiring school attendance had been passed in 1879. Another 1889 bill which required private schools to make annual reports to the Superintendent of Public Instruction had aroused protests from both clergymen and laymen and elicited 40,000 signatures on petitions opposing it. The bill was allowed to die. The only notice the Bennett bill received was one small petition supporting it. There is no evidence to support the contention current at the time that it came from a secret "bill factory" maintained by anti-Catholic groups in the East. See William F. Whyte, "The Bennett Law Campaign in Wisconsin," in the *Wisconsin Magazine of History*, 10:377 (June, 1927): Janet C. Wegner, "The Bennett Law Controversy in Wisconsin, 1889–1891" (unpublished Master's thesis, Brown University, 1966), 6–9.

dren, reading, writing, arithmetic and United States history, in the English language.[5]

The last four words—"in the English language"—ignited the political explosion which followed.

Concerted opposition to the Bennett Law did not develop for several months. In June, 1889, three German Protestant bodies denounced the law as an attack upon German churches, schools, and language, but the undercurrent of opposition remained below the surface until early in 1890.[6] The Republican *Milwaukee Sentinel* was largely responsible for fomenting much of the bitterness of the ensuing battle. It undertook an aggressive and belligerent campaign to defend the law as necessary for the preservation of the common school system and the speedier assimilation of all immigrants. It wrapped the law in a mantle of Americanism and patriotism, belittling the opponents of the law as enemies of the public schools, narrow-minded clerics, or self-seeking politicians. Day after day the *Sentinel* filled its editorial pages with defenses of the law, strongly worded attacks on its opponents, and exposés of American-born adults who could not speak, read, or write English.[7]

The *Sentinel's* intransigence made it impossible to keep the issue out of the spring municipal elections. In Milwaukee, anti-Bennett Law clubs were formed in several wards; individual German Lutheran parishes established their own political organizations. Three weeks before the April 1 election the state's three German-born Catholic bishops, who had been content to let the Lutherans lead the assault, entered the fray. They issued a Bishops' Manifesto which contended that the real object of the law was to bring parochial schools under state regulation and ultimately to destroy the parochial school system altogether. They denounced the law as unnecessary, offensive, and unjust, and advocated the support of candidates who favored its repeal.[8]

[5] *Laws of Wisconsin, 1889,* 729–33. The law's progressive child labor provisions were ignored in the protest. They prohibited employment of children under 13, unless exempted by a judge for specific purposes, and provided strict penalties for violations. *Ibid.*

[6] The three groups, whose conferences all met in June, were the Wisconsin Conference of the Evangelical Association and two predominantly German Lutheran bodies—the Missouri Synod and the Wisconsin Synod. Wegner, "Bennett Law Controversy," 42; Otto Hattstaedt, *History of the Southern District of the Evangelical Synod of Missouri, Ohio and Other States* (translated from the German. Works Progress Administration. Wisconsin Historical Records Survey, 1941), 76.

[7] Whyte, "Bennett Law," 377–78. Not a day passed in February and March, 1890, without an editorial or several letters to the editor regarding the Bennett Law appearing on the editorial page of the *Sentinel.* The *Evening Wisconsin,* another Milwaukee Republican daily, pursued a similar course, although in a more moderate fashion. See, for example, the issue of March 13, 1890.

[8] The bishops were Archbishop Michael Heiss, who died a few days before the election; Frederick X. Katzer of Green Bay, who later succeeded Heiss as Archbishop; and Kilian C. Flasch of La Crosse. *Catholic Citizen* (Milwaukee), March 15, 1890; *Milwaukee Sentinel,* March 1, 2, 6, 30, 1890; Whyte, "Bennett Law," 381–82.

The *Catholic Citizen* represented the Irish-American viewpoint, but to maintain its semiofficial status in the German-dominated diocese, it avoided the nationality conflict which rent the Wisconsin Catholic Church at this time. It had ignored the Bennett Law controversy until the Bishops' Manifesto appeared. Thereafter, it criticized the law on the basis of state interference with parochial education and quietly ignored the language issue which had so aroused the German element. See the issues of March 22, 29, 1890.

In an atmosphere of such agitation, neither party could avoid the issue. Despite the efforts of state Republican chairman Henry C. Payne to effect a compromise, the Republican platform upheld the law. The influential Protestant German weekly, *Die Germania*, usually staunchly Republican, then deserted to the Democrats, who had denounced the law unequivocally in their platform.[9]

The Bennett Law was the only issue of consequence in the ensuing campaign. The Democrats assailed the law but denied they opposed public schools. Their main target was the consequences of the law; the Democratic mayoralty candidate, humorist George Peck, the author of *Peck's Bad Boy*, went so far as to call it a forerunner of prohibition.[10] The *Sentinel*, still outwardly confident and aggressive, finally realized the gravity of the situation when German Lutheran clergy and lay leaders applied religious fervor to political activity. As the campaign closed, the *Sentinel* attempted to hold Lutherans in the Republican fold by arousing anti-Catholic feelings. It warned Lutherans of the evil consequences of an alliance with their Catholic enemies and denounced the political activity of both Catholic and Lutheran clergymen. It also exaggerated support for the law among Irish, Polish, Bohemian, and American Catholics.[11]

The election results shattered the *Sentinel's* illusions of support for the Bennett Law. Peck and the entire Democratic ticket won in a landslide, carrying all but three of the city's eighteen wards. An unusually large turnout gave Peck an absolute majority of votes cast in a three-way contest. The amazing gains which Peck made in normally Republican German wards surprised both parties. In three of the four heaviest German wards—all of which usually turned in solid Republican majorities—Peck more than doubled the vote of his Republican opponent, incumbent mayor Thomas H. Brown. German Lutheran votes also enabled Peck to carry other normally Republican wards. The Bennett Law was an issue in other Wisconsin cities as well, and Democratic mayoralty candidates scored victories in several normally Republican cities, including Eau Claire, Chippewa Falls, Wausau, Cedarburg, Ripon, Waupun, and Fort Atkinson.[12] The *Sentinel*, undaunted by its stunning defeat, regarded the result as only a "Bull Run" in the larger war to follow, confidently stating that voters outside heavily German Milwaukee would uphold the law. Other Republican papers denounced clergymen for preaching politics from the pulpit. It was obvious that the Bennett Law would become a prime issue in the autumn gubernatorial campaign.[13]

[9] *Catholic Citizen,* March 6, 1890; Whyte, "Bennett Law," 381; *Milwaukee Sentinel,* March 25, 26, 1890.

[10] *Milwaukee Sentinel, Milwaukee Journal,* March 25, 1890; *Milwaukee Sentinel,* March 30, 1890.

[11] The *Sentinel's* exaggeration of support for the Bennett Law and the Republican ticket often approached absurdity, such as the contention that nine out of ten Germans supported the law. See issues of March 15, 16, 17, 30, 1890. See also *Evening Wisconsin,* April 1, 1890; for a refutation of the *Sentinel's* assertions, see *Catholic Citizen,* March 22, 1890.

[12] Peck received 16,216 votes to 9,501 for Brown and 5,316 for the Citizen's ticket (labor) candidate. *Milwaukee Sentinel, Milwaukee Journal, Evening Wisconsin,* April 2, 1890. Previous voting returns were from *Milwaukee Sentinel,* April 4, 1886, April 4, 1888.

[13] *Milwaukee Sentinel, Evening Wisconsin,* April 2–5, 1890; *Wisconsin State Journal* (Madison) denounced the comments of the German sectarian press, which had rejoiced in the outcome, as "anti-American and unpatriotic to the last degree." April 5, 1890.

The April victories spurred the anti-Bennett Law forces to greater political agitation. Once again the German Protestants led the opposition and called a huge Anti-Bennett Law Convention for June. Largely a German Protestant affair, the convention laid the groundwork for a statewide network of anti-Bennett Law organizations with the formation of the Anti-Bennett Law State Central Committee. The uncompromising tone of the speeches and the enthusiastic response served notice that the German community was solidly behind opposition to the law.[14]

The speeches of the convention confirmed what many of the law's proponents had averred all along: that by and large the Germans were more opposed to the English language provision than they were to the principle of state interference with private education. But they also feared that state interference in parochial education threatened more than just the Lutheran parochial schools. They were afraid that it might lead to the forced disintegration of the German-American way of life. Both Catholic and Protestant Germans saw the Bennett Law as the first assault on "Germanism" (*Deutschtum*). Throughout much of eastern Wisconsin, the German immigrants jealously guarded what they regarded as their right to preserve many of the customs they brought with them from Europe. The dream some had had of creating a German state in America had long passed, but many still insisted on preserving *Deutschtum* within an American context.[15]

At the heart of *Deutschtum* was the German language. Although most German parents recognized the necessity and desirability of their children learning English, they realized that a thorough knowledge of the mother tongue was essential if German theater, literature, music, and even the Lutheran religion were to survive on American soil. The German parochial schools provided the means by which the mother tongue was taught to the young and were thus essential to the persistence of *Deutschtum*. Again and again, regardless of the official protests against the Bennett Law on the basis of state paternalism, the central concern of Germans involved the language provision. Some of the more zealous Lutherans even contended that if the German language were given up, it would spell the end of Lutheranism.[16] "Strike the two words 'in English' from the law," one newspaper commented, "and not a churchman in the State could be found to raise his voice against it."[17]

[14] For accounts of the convention, see Hense-Jensen and Bruncken, *Wisconsin's Deutsch-Amerikaner* (Schafer translation), chap. 13, pp. 15–19; Wegner, "Bennett Law Controversy," 74–75.

[15] For other explanations of *Deutschtum* and the extent of Germanism in some Wisconsin areas, see Robert J. Ulrich, "The Bennett Law of 1889: Education and Politics in Wisconsin" (unpublished Ph.D. thesis, University of Wisconsin, 1965), chap. 1; Louise Kellogg, "The Bennett Law in Wisconsin," in the *Wisconsin Magazine of History*, 2:8–12 (September, 1918); Whyte, "Bennett Law," 372–73.

[16] The thought of worshipping in the English language was astounding to many Germans. As one pioneer in using English later reminisced: "It had been a well-settled tradition . . . that when mother tongue was given up mother Church must be sacrificed." He recalled that when one young pastor once dared to speak to an audience in English, he was shouted down with the cry *"Unser Herr Gott ist ein deutscher Gott!"* ("Our God is a German God!"). G. H. Gerberding, "Reminiscent Pioneering and Moralizing," in *Historical and Reminiscent Sketches, English Evangelical Lutheran Synod of the Northwest* (n. p., 1916), 5–9.

[17] *Manitowoc County Chronicle*, quoted in Wegner, "Bennett Law Controversy," 18. Wegner stresses the point that the language provision was the central basis of

Perhaps no better indication that Germanism and not state paternalism motivated the almost unanimous German protest was the fact that both Lutheran and Catholic Germans stood united and even co-operated in their efforts. The *Germania* came close to admitting the true source of opposition to the Bennett Law when it labeled the April victory in Milwaukee as "a wonderful victory of Germandom over narrow-hearted nativism." It continued:

> And that Germandom went into this fight tolerably well united, may be partly ascribed to the attacks made for several months past by the English press of our city against it. These attacks brought into line the large majority of Germans, rank and file. The Germans recognized that with the German parochial schools one of the firmest bulwarks of Germandom was becoming endangered and, with the fullest determination, stepped forward to protect this very bulwark.[18]

Since the 1850's Germans had generally divided their political allegiances along religious lines, the Catholics supporting the Democrats and the Protestants and free-thinkers the Republicans. But unlike some other ethnic groups, Germans did not form rigid attachments to either party. However, on occasion particular issues, such as prohibition and hard money, transcended religious antipathies and temporarily unified German political sentiment. Thus the Bennett Law crisis witnessed not only unceasing activity among the normally politically passive Germans but also extraordinary co-operation between German Catholics and Protestants. The Lutheran-dominated state central committee published volumes of pamphlets, and many of the state's most prominent Lutheran clergymen and laymen took the stump or headed various committees.[19] The Catholics, although fearful that the Republicans might placate the Lutherans at the last moment, remained somewhat aloof from the struggle, content to let the Lutherans wage the battle. Catholics participated in the work of the Anti-Bennett Law State Central Committee, but much of the work was done by priests among their own flocks, most of which were already favorable to the Democrats. The Bishops' Manifesto and continued pleas by local priests were helpful in keeping non-German Catholics in the anti-Bennett Law ranks.[20]

The Republicans, stunned by their Milwaukee defeat, were bitterly divided over the course to pursue regarding the Bennett Law. For Governor Hoard and his associates, vindication by standing firm on the issue was the answer. Hoard had stated earlier that he would stand or fall on the school issue if necessary, and he refused to adopt a more conciliatory position. The day after the

---

opposition to the law. *Ibid.*, 30, 33–34, 74–75, 98. Bruncken also recognizes the multi-faceted nature of German opposition. *Wisconsin's Deutsch-Amerikaner* (Schafer translation), chap. 13, *passim*.

[18] *Die Germania*, quoted in *Milwaukee Sentinel*, April 3, 1890.

[19] The pamphlets published by the Anti-Bennett Law State Committee and the synodical school committees strongly disavowed opposition to the English language (although firmly asserting that German was not a foreign language) and based opposition to the law on state paternalism. They carefully cited pages of statistics of German schools using English. Christian Koerner, *The Bennett Law and the German Protestant Parochial Schools of Wisconsin* (Anti-Bennett Law State Central Committee, 1890).

[20] *Catholic Citizen*, June 14, 1890; Wegner, "Bennett Law Controversy," 104.

Milwaukee election Hoard delivered a speech to a teachers' group in which he stoutly defended the law and denounced its enemies.[21]

Hoard and many other supporters of the Bennett Law firmly and sincerely believed that it was necessary for the preservation of the common school system. To the governor, still a political neophyte, it was a matter of firm conviction and principle—one which could not be compromised. Norwegian-American Congressman Nils P. Haugen believed that it was "the old fight of the Church on the Common School" and that it was "absolutely essential to the future welfare of the state that Hoard and the Common School be endorsed by the people" in November.[22] In addition, Hoard, Haugen, the *Sentinel,* and many other Republican leaders believed that sentiment outside of Milwaukee was solidly in favor of the law, and they were confident of carrying the state on the issue. Haugen, Wisconsin's most prominent Scandinavian politician, was blinded by the strong Scandinavian support of compulsory education and by a lack of understanding of the mentality of the Germans in the eastern part of the state. Admitting that things looked bad for the Republicans in 1890, he wrote that "if anything saves the state it will be the Bennett law." Haugen also denounced "the truckling, whimpering attitude" of Payne and other Milwaukee Republican leaders toward the law.[23]

Republican leaders with more experience in statewide politics—Payne, Senator John C. Spooner (whose seat was at stake in the election), and Secretary of Agriculture and former governor Jeremiah Rusk—saw things differently. Not only did they understand the German attitude but they also realized the size of the German Lutheran vote, which they estimated at about 40,000. Payne and other leaders had opposed Hoard's nomination in 1888 and viewed his Bennett Law crusade as folly, leading only to defeat.[24] The tradition of renomination of a governor for a second term was a strong one: a fight to dump Hoard might prove disastrous.[25] Forced to accept Hoard, party leaders hoped to allay German fears by adopting a moderate platform statement on the law to salvage what they could of the Lutheran vote. Payne and Spooner undertook a feverish but futile campaign to retain the Lutherans and the *Germania.*

The attitudes of Haugen and Hoard dominated the Republican convention, which stood firmly for the law. The entire Republican campaign effort centered on the Bennett Law as necessary for the preservation of the common school system. The slogan became "The Little School House—Stand By It." A picture of a school, with an American flag flying above it and the slogan written on its

[21] *Evening Wisconsin,* March 13, April 2, 1890.

[22] Wegner, "Bennett Law Controversy," 84–85; Nils P. Haugen to W. D. Parker, April 4, 1890, Haugen letterbooks, in the Nils P. Haugen Papers, State Historical Society of Wisconsin. See also Haugen to Parker, April 13, 1890. Haugen's views were colored by a strong anti-Catholicism, typical of many Scandinavians.

[23] Haugen to Parker, April 13, 1890; to Ernest Timme, April 12, 1890; to Charles Smith, June 7, 1890, in the Haugen letterbooks.

[24] Dorothy Ganfield Fowler, *John Coit Spooner, Defender of Presidents* (New York, 1961), 146–50; Wegner, "Bennett Law Controversy," 80–81. The estimate of about 40,000 German Lutheran votes corresponded closely to Democratic estimates. See Ellis B. Usher to Calvin Brice, August 15, 1890, Usher letterbooks, in the Ellis B. Usher Papers, State Historical Society of Wisconsin.

[25] Nevertheless, in an editorial entitled "A Modern Jonah," the *Evening Wisconsin* suggested that Hoard be dumped overboard to save the endangered Republican ship. March 14, 1890.

roof, decorated the editorial pages of Republican newspapers and the stationery of campaign committees. In letters and speeches full of Biblical rhetoric and imagery, Hoard insisted that the public schools were in danger and defended the necessity that "the poor little German boy" learn English if he were to become a useful American citizen.[26]

As early as the autumn of 1889 Democratic party leaders realized that they might profit by the dissatisfaction of German Lutherans with the law but were afraid to inject such an emotion-laden issue into the campaign. Even after the landslide for Peck in April, party leaders were still divided as to whether or not the issue should be exploited.[27]

The younger and bolder party managers, particularly former state chairman Ellis B. Usher and new chairman Edward C. Wall, denounced such indecision. They saw a golden opportunity to capture the predominantly Republican German Protestant vote by a strong stand against the law. Usher wrote that "Hoard and the *Sentinel* and the Republicans . . . have fully aroused the opposition in the Lutheran and Catholic churches. Neither side can or will quit. The course therefore is clear to me. We must meet it whether we will or not." [28] Wall agreed and attacked the timidity of Democrats who favored silence on the issue. "The idea that a subject that fills the papers daily, that the Governor of the state speaks on every time he addresses the people, that a large portion of the voters of the state protest against, not being *an issue*," Wall thought, was utterly foolish and weak. *"It is an issue. A great big one. It must be met."* [29]

Wall and Usher decided to press the issue immediately by opposing the law as paternalistic and undemocratic. This would put the Republicans on the defensive, forcing them to "defend their child." A firm stand would force the Republicans either to desert Hoard or else to defend the law. In either case, Wall felt, the Republicans would lose the Lutheran vote.[30] Once the decision to oppose the law unequivocally was made, Wall moved to bring dissident leaders and newspapers into line. By cajolery and persuasiveness he convinced former Secretary of the Interior William F. Vilas and other lukewarm Democrats of the merits of his course of action. With the same persuasiveness plus a little arm-twisting, Wall got the state's Democratic press to fall into step by June, and

[26] Wegner, "Bennett Law Controversy," 84–85; Whyte, "Bennett Law," 385. "The Little School House" became the focus of the campaign in much of the state. The Milwaukee Young Men's Republican Club solemnly resolved: "We stand by the little school house. In its defense we invite the co-operation of all patriotic people." The *Evening Wisconsin* reported that "prominent men in all sections of the state are coming out bravely in favor of Gov. Hoard and the little red school house. . . ." Quoted in *The Little School House,* a pamphlet included in *Bound Bennett Law Pamphlets,* State Historical Society of Wisconsin.
Even the Democratic press got into the act. It ran the identical cut of the school, including the 'Stand By It,' but added under it: "Peck and All the Schools."
[27] Usher to Rush Winslow, November 4, 1889, in the Usher letterbooks; *Milwaukee Journal,* April 4, 1890; Horace S. Merrill, *William Freeman Vilas, Doctrinaire Democrat* (Madison, 1954), 162.
[28] Usher to Edward C. Wall, April 6, 1890, in the Usher letterbooks.
[29] Wall to Usher, April 27, 1890, in the Usher Papers. To Wall, timid Democrats were "cowards, so many weak men that could run after Greenbackers, labor voters and all kinds of 'unclean girls' " in the past but now held back on the Bennett Law for "conscience sake." *Ibid.*
[30] *Ibid.;* Wall to Usher, May 1, 1890, Usher Papers; Usher to Wall, May 26, 1890, Usher letterbooks; Wall to William F. Vilas, May 16, June 25, 1890, in the William F. Vilas Papers, State Historical Society of Wisconsin.

then supplied papers throughout the state with editorial matter prepared by the state committee.[31]

The next step for Wall was co-operation with the anti-Bennett Law religious groups. He established smooth relations with the Catholic hierarchy and may have had a hand in formulating their policy of quiet opposition. In the fall the Church became more active and played an important role in keeping most Catholic voters in the Democratic column. Most of Wall's indefatigable energy and organizational talent was devoted to securing the German Lutheran vote. After the June convention Wall continued to work closely with Lutheran leaders, providing them with campaign material, consulting them on the formulation of party policy, and winning their confidence.[32] The anti-Bennett Law plank of the Democratic party was scrutinized carefully by religious leaders. After the Catholics approved it, Wall showed it to the Lutherans who made a few changes but called the platform a masterpiece. Considerable effort was also made in keeping the influential *Germania* from backsliding to the Republican party.[33] As early as June, Wall was so confident of success among the Lutherans [34] that he suggested the party press devote a month's time to stress other issues. The Bennett Law would "take care of itself; the Catholics and Lutherans will do the fighting," he wrote.[35]

National issues also worked to the benefit of the Democrats. The Republicans worried about the effect of the tariff issue in the farming areas. An agricultural depression had plagued much of the west since the mid-1880's, and in 1890 Farmers' Alliances and other agricultural political organizations grew rapidly. Wisconsin was not troubled by these divisive political organizations, although discontent erupted in isolated areas in the northwestern part of the state. The new McKinley tariff of 1890 was viewed with more uncertainty than damnation or praise; still, Democratic promises of tariff reform appealed to discontented farmers and urban consumers.[36]

The Bennett Law dominated the campaign. The Democrats nominated Milwaukee's "happy mayor," George W. Peck, for governor and demanded the

[31] Wall sent an aide on a tour of the state to get the Democratic press to act in concert. He recognized that Vilas' support was instrumental and worked hard to secure it. Wall to Usher, May 5, 1890, in the Usher Papers; Wall to Vilas, May 9, 13, 16, 28, 1890, in the Vilas Papers.

[32] Wall worked early with prominent Lutherans. He arranged to have the *Milwaukee Journal* sent to every Lutheran clergyman in the state, and in mid-May he met quietly with the Lutheran anti-Bennett leaders. He assured Vilas that although a few desired reconciliation with the Republicans, the more influential leaders and the mass of the clergy opposed it. The firm resolutions of the convention made it easier for Wall to establish close relationships with the Lutheran leadership. Wall to Vilas, May 16, June 25, 1890, in the Vilas Papers.

[33] Wall to Vilas, June 25, August 22, September 10, 1890, in the Vilas Papers (additions).

[34] A Milwaukee Lutheran clergyman told Wall that "he had some 400 male communicants, who prior to this spring always voted the republican ticket, and not one of them a democrat and that now not one of them was a republican for, he said, it is a party of cranks." Wall to Vilas, June 25, 1890, in the Vilas Papers.

[35] Wall to Usher, June 11, 1890, in the Usher Papers.

[36] Harold U. Faulkner, *Politics, Reform and Expansion, 1890–1900* (New York, 1959), chap. 3, pp. 105–17; Merrill, *Vilas,* 160–68; Griff Jones to Haugen, June 4, 1890, in the Haugen Papers. For Democratic hopes of winning votes on the tariff issue, see Clarence Clark to Vilas, July 29, 1890; C. W. Graves to Vilas, October 16, 1890, in the Vilas Papers.

law's repeal. Both parties, plus the Lutheran and Catholic organizations, kept up an incessant torrent of charges and countercharges concerning the law. In the last weeks of the campaign, Vilas, who had stressed national issues in most of his speeches, delighted Wisconsin German audiences with his comment that it did not matter whether a person said "two plus two make four" or *"zwei und zwei machen vier."* [37]

The 1890 election campaign witnessed the most blatant ethnic and religious appeals in the state's history. The Germans called on their brethren to defend the mother tongue and Germanism; pro-Bennett Law advocates charged the Germans with reverse know-nothingism. Much of the pro-Bennett Law literature and press had a distinct antiforeign and anti-Catholic tone. The *Sentinel* and other Republican papers attacked the Lutheran clergy almost as vociferously as the Catholic hierarchy. Latent nationality and religious prejudices were aroused on both sides.

Ethnic campaigning rose to a peak in both parties. By fall the Republicans were resigned to losing most of the German vote, but they hoped to offset it by gains among native and Irish-American Democrats who supported the law. The Irish, engaged in an often bitter running battle with German Catholics over the use of English or German in individual parishes and for control of the state Catholic hierarchy,[38] were strong supporters of the public schools. Most Irishmen educated their children there, and many served as teachers and administrators. John Nagle, superintendent of Manitowoc County schools and editor of the Manitowoc *Pilot,* was a leader of the largely Irish-American Democratic Bennett Law League. The League received a big play in the Republican press but was numerically weak. Despite Republican overtures, most Irish-Americans, loyal Catholics, and their clergy opposed the law because of the possibility of its use against parochial schools.[39]

More important to Republican success was the usually solid Scandinavian vote. The Scandinavian Lutheran churches which operated parochial schools usually did so in the summer months, when public schools were not in session. Only in rare instances did they compete with public schools.[40] Scandinavian opposition to the law centered on the district clause and the implications of the law for all parochial schools. Scandinavians generally approved of the law's Americanizing features, but rumors of breaks in their support for the Republicans persisted. The Republicans made a concerted effort to keep them in line, and leaders such as Haugen were kept scurrying around the state mending fences among the dissidents.[41]

[37] Merrill, *Vilas,* 167–68; Whyte, "Bennett Law," 386.
[38] For ethnic conflict within the Wisconsin Catholic church, see Colman J. Barry, *The Catholic Church and German Americans* (Milwaukee, 1953), chaps. 2–3; Sister Justille McDonald, *History of the Irish in Wisconsin in the Nineteenth Century* (Washington, 1954), 172–76.
[39] McDonald, *History of the Irish in Wisconsin,* 172–76; Wall to Vilas, September 15, 1890, in the Vilas Papers (additions).
[40] George M. Stephenson, *The Religious Aspects of Swedish Immigration: A Study of Immigrant Churches* (Minneapolis, 1932), 409–10; Ruth G. Sanding, "The Norwegian Element in the Early History of Wisconsin" (unpublished Master's thesis, University of Wisconsin, 1937), 137, 169–70.
[41] Wegner, "Bennett Law Controversy," 31, 100; R. H. Gile to Haugen, October 21, 1890; O. M. Kalheim to Haugen, October 8, 1890; Walter L. Houser to Haugen, October 21, 1890, in the Haugen Papers.

The Democrats' main efforts were aimed at securing the German Protestant vote and at keeping their usual support from German, Irish, Polish, and Bohemian Catholics. Wall also set up a special Scandinavian bureau to proselytize among the Norwegians. Expecting considerable defection from Scandinavians over both the Bennett Law and the tariff, the Democrats sent speakers and literature into Norwegian areas at an unprecedented rate. Wall relied heavily on the Catholic hierarchy to keep the Polish and Irish vote solidly Democratic, but extra efforts were made in Irish wards and townships. In addition to the earlier Bishops' Manifesto, the three bishops spoke against the law, and circulars opposing it were read from Catholic pulpits. In an Oshkosh speech, Bishop Frederick X. Katzer even intimated that those Catholics who failed to vote against the law were traitors to the church.[42]

The earliest returns left no doubt about the outcome: it was a Democratic landslide. Although Governor Hoard ran 6,000 votes ahead of the Republican ticket, he was inundated. Hoard's 1888 plurality of 20,273 was transformed into a 28,320 vote margin for Peck, and the entire Democratic state ticket was swept into office. The cruelest blow to the Republicans came in the congressional and legislative races. Nils P. Haugen, secure in his heavily Scandinavian district, was the only one of seven Republican incumbents to survive. The Democrats also captured a solid majority in both houses of the legislature, thus assuring that a Democrat would replace John C. Spooner in the United States Senate.[43]

The Democrats registered large gains in all parts of the state. In 1888 they had won only fifteen of sixty-eight counties, most of which were concentrated in the traditionally Democratic eastern and lakeshore counties. In 1890 Peck captured forty-one counties; in the entire eastern half of Wisconsin, only six counties remained loyal to the Grand Old Party. The Republican percentage of the total vote declined in every single county in the state.[44] Except for four heavily Anglo-American counties along the southern border, the great majority of Republican counties in 1890 were in the western and northwestern part of the state, in areas populated largely by Scandinavians and native Americans.

It was obvious that the Bennett Law was at the root of the upheaval in the state's political composition. In the heavily German areas, rejoicing over the results was unparalleled.[45] The Democrats, hoping to make their control of the state permanent, were almost as jubilant. Chairman Wall agreed that the Bennett Law had given them their victory: "It *was* our position on the law that

[42] Wall to Rasmus B. Anderson, May 26, 1890, in the Rasmus B. Anderson Papers, State Historical Society of Wisconsin; Wall to Vilas, September 15, 1890, in the Vilas Papers; *Milwaukee Sentinel,* November 1, 1890.
[43] Only holdover Republican senators prevented the election from becoming a complete rout. Democrats won 15 of the 17 seats up for re-election, but the Republicans held a 12 to 4 edge on the holdover seats. Democrats gained a 19 to 14 edge in the senate and a 66 to 33 margin in the assembly. All election returns, unless noted otherwise, are from the *Wisconsin Blue Book* of the year following the election.
[44] Democratic percentages, however, declined in six counties at the same time the Republicans lost ground; this is largely the result of an upswing in Prohibition party vote. Some dissatisfied Republicans may have voted Prohibition rather than aid the Democrats.
[45] A German-American historian who was active in the campaign wrote many years later that "unless one lived through this period, one cannot appreciate the jubilations in our congregations" over the outcome. Hattstaedt, *History of the Southern Wisconsin District,* 77.

made it complete," he wrote Vilas. "By declaring for democratic principles we drew the Germans to us and made a victory we can be proud of." Vilas, in private, held that the party could have won the state on either the tariff or the school law.[46]

Republicans were equally convinced as to the cause of their defeat. It was inevitable, Spooner wrote. "The school law did it—a silly, sentimental and damned useless abstraction, foisted upon us by a self-righteous demagogue." An ex-Congressman expressed similar sentiments: "Hoard with his school question drove all the Lutherans away from our party, the German Lutherans especially, and the Norwegians stayed away from the polls." Although many Republican politicians looked upon the party's stand with dismay, the Bennett Law's ardent defenders voiced little regret. Horace Rublee, editor of the *Sentinel,* recognized the political error for which he had to take much of the blame, but offered no apologies. He felt that no American-born citizen could have foreseen "the wild and unreasonable opposition" to the law.[47] The rhetoric of defeat was similar to that of April: It was only the "Bull Run" of a much larger struggle for the vindication of the common school. The more rabid Bennett Law proponents blamed the results on the evil influences of clergymen in politics. Perhaps the best assessment by a prominent Republican came two years later, when the Bennett Law still haunted state politics. An aging "Boss" Elisha W. Keyes stated that either the tariff or the Bennett Law could have cost the Republicans the state in 1890. "If the school question had been out of the canvass, the heavy weight of the McKinley bill would have beaten the state ticket; but we should probably have saved the legislature. The school bill was the cause that lost us the legislature." [48]

Republican party leaders also blamed voter apathy for their defeat, lamenting that the total vote cast fell far below that of 1888. While Peck received almost 5,000 votes more than the Democratic candidate in 1888, Hoard's vote fell by more than 40,000. Historians who have studied the Bennett Law also noted this "stay at home" Republican vote.[49] But such a blanket comparison of the total vote figures for 1888 and 1890 on the statewide level leads to considerable distortion. In the first place, it is misleading to compare the total vote of a presidential year (1888) with a nonpresidential election; a sharp drop in the total vote cast should be expected in 1890. A more reasonable comparison would be to examine how the drop in total vote between 1888 and 1890 compared with the drop-off between the presidential election of 1884 and 1886.

[46] Wall to Vilas, November 10, 1890, in the Vilas Papers; Vilas to Wendall Anderson, December 10, 1890, in the Wendall Anderson Papers, State Historical Society of Wisconsin.

[47] Spooner to H. M. Ketchin, November 18, 1890, quoted in Merrill, *Vilas,* 169; George Hazelton to John Hazelton, December 4, 1890, quoted in Fowler, *Spooner,* 153; Horace Rublee to Jeremiah Rusk, December 2, 1890, quoted in Richard N. Current, *Pine Logs and Politics: A Life of Philetus Sawyer, 1816–1900* (Madison, 1950), 254.

[48] *Milwaukee Sentinel,* April 2–5, 1890; Wegner, "Bennett Law Controversy," 121; William F. Vilas, "The 'Bennett Law' in Wisconsin," *Forum,* 12:197 (1891); Elisha W. Keyes to Rusk, July 6, 1892, quoted in Current, *Pine Logs and Politics,* 254. Joseph C. Schafer also agreed with Keyes. See "Editorial Comment," in the *Wisconsin Magazine of History,* 10:458–59 (June, 1927).

[49] Ulrich, "Bennett Law of 1889," 469; Wegner "Bennett Law Controversy," 123–26.

The total vote for the state as a whole fell 10.8 per cent in 1886 and 12.8 per cent in 1890. At first glance, then, the drop-off in 1890 seems just slightly higher than usual. The individual county totals, however, give a different picture. In 1890 many counties suffered a decline in total vote of at least 20 per cent, some in excess of 30 per cent. The statewide total of 12.8 per cent is strongly influenced by the more populous counties, particularly Milwaukee, which had four times as many voters as any other and whose total vote actually increased. If each county is taken as a unit, the average drop-off would be closer to 20 per cent.

Looking at the individual county totals points out a second distortion which can arise when only the statewide totals are used—the geographic distribution of the vote decline. There was a distinct geographical pattern to the spectacular drops in the vote; every county in which the total vote decreased by more than 25 per cent was in the western or northern section of the state. Conversely, with one exception, counties which had a low drop-off or whose total vote increased were in the eastern or north central part of the state. This geographic pattern followed distinct ethnic lines as well. Most of those counties with a small drop-off had large German populations, and none had many Scandinavians. On the other hand, many of those countries suffering large drops in total vote were among the heaviest Scandinavian counties, and none had a large German contingent.[50] Certainly, in the eastern part of Wisconsin—the most heavily German—there was little voter apathy in 1890, as the Bennett Law agitation kept the total vote almost at the level for a presidential election. In the western part of the state, the drop-off was much larger than usual but, as will be shown later, was due not to apathy but dissatisfaction with Republican national policies on the part of particular segments of the population.

The Democratic landslide of 1890 was more than a response of Germans and Catholics to the Bennett Law. Republicans suffered heavy losses in all sections of the country, particularly in the Middle West and the Plains States. Many normally rock-ribbed Republican states, unplagued by issues such as the Bennett Law, elected Democratic governors and sent Democratic delegations to Congress. With Republican defeats occurring throughout the Middle West, the 1890 election in Wisconsin cannot be considered an isolated phenomenon resulting solely from distaste for an obnoxious school law. Boss Keyes' observation that either the Bennett Law or the tariff could have led to a Democratic victory is essentially correct. But it was the simultaneous convergence of both of these powerful issues that produced the ignominious Republican defeat. Not only did dissatisfaction over the tariff cost the Republicans the votes of many who might have supported them on the Bennett Law, but the two issues may have *interacted* to lose them more votes. In other words, many voters might not have disliked the Bennett Law or the tariff alone enough to vote Democratic, but the cumulative negative effect of both of the unpopular measures might have led to a decision to vote a straight Democratic ticket.

None of the previous studies of the Bennett Law analyze the election of 1890 in any systematic manner, although a few demonstrate a general relationship between the German population in some counties and the rise in the Democratic vote in 1890. None attempt to separate the effect of the Bennett Law and

[50] The ethnic composition of Wisconsin counties was determined from the 1890 federal census.

the tariff on the outcome.[51] A careful analysis of Wisconsin election returns between 1884 and 1890, combined with an equally careful comparison of this data with ethnic, religious, and other census material, conducted on both the county and township level, leads to very definite conclusions about the relative impact of the Bennett Law and the tariff upon the voting behavior of some of Wisconsin's major ethnic and religious groups. These conclusions are supported and enhanced by the application of statistical analysis to the election and census data.[52]

Careful scrutiny of the election returns on both the county and precinct level reveals the all-encompassing effect of the Bennett Law. Both the normal ethnic and religious basis of party division in Wisconsin, and the extent to which it was increased by the emotional campaign of 1890, can be shown by applying the standard statistical technique of correlation to county-level data.[53] Table 1 correlates the Republican and Democratic percentages of total vote for governor in 1888 and 1890 with ethnic and religious categories obtained from federal censuses.[54]

TABLE 1

CORRELATION COEFFICIENTS: REPUBLICAN AND DEMOCRATIC GUBERNATORIAL VOTE, 1888 AND 1890, WITH ETHNIC AND RELIGIOUS CENSUS DATA

Variable	Republican Governor 1888	Republican Governor 1890	Democratic Governor 1888	Democratic Governor 1890
Native-Native	.595	.656	−.544	−.551
Anglo-American	.585	.665	−.536	−.550
Scandinavian	.510	.501	−.554	−.688
German	−.593	−.706	.628	.799
Catholic	−.646	−.583	.681	.609
Yankee Protestant	.344	.526	−.425	−.466
Republican Ethnic Groups	.789	.847	−:838	−.915
Democratic Ethnic Groups	−.612	−.682	.672	.811

[51] Ulrich, "Bennett Law of 1889," 502–3, 521–28; Wegner, "Bennett Law Controversy," 126–32. Wegner deals only with raw vote totals and county level population statistics. Ulrich looks at some German and Scandinavian townships but uses no systematic criteria for selection. Neither presents much convincing evidence for their conclusions. Joseph C. Schafer had a more sophisticated understanding of German voting in 1890 but never wrote on it at length. He discusses the election somewhat in *Four Wisconsin Counties, Prairie and Forest* (Madison, 1927), *passim,* as well as in his "Editorial Comment" on Whyte's 1927 article.

[52] Preliminary computer analysis of the county-level data was done at the University of Michigan, utilizing the facilities of the Inter-University Consortium for Political Research. Most of the analysis utilized the STATJOB system of the University of Wisconsin Computing Center.

[53] The statistical technique used is the standard Pearsonian product-moment correlation coefficient. This coefficient is a measure of association between two variables, measuring the extent to which they vary in respect to each other. The coefficient has an upper limit of 1.0 and a lower limit of −1.0. A value of 1.0 indicates a perfect positive association, −1.0 a perfect negative one. A value of zero suggests no linear relationship between the two variables. For a more comprehensive explanation, see Hubert M. Blalock, *Social Statistics* (New York, 1960), chap. 17; V. O. Key, Jr., *A Primer of Statistics for Political Scientists* (New York, 1954), chap. 4.

[54] County-level election data was provided on IBM cards by the Inter-University Consortium for Political Research; this information was verified and corrected by the

The polarization between Yankee and Teuton and between Protestant and Catholic in 1890 is clear from the table. The Republican percentage of the vote correlates strongly with the percentage of native born of native parents in 1888 (.595) and increases in 1890 (.656). If we add together the percentage of Methodists, Presbyterians, and Congregationalists for each county to form a category of "Yankee Protestant," the result is similar. The considerable increase in the correlation coefficient between Yankee Protestant and Republican vote (from .344 in 1888 to .526 in 1890) is evidence of the ardent support Hoard and the Bennett Law received from native American Protestants. On the other hand, a solidly negative relationship exists between Republican vote and Catholic percentage. The relationships between the religious variables and the party vote hold up when we take the analysis one step farther and introduce partial correlations to control for the effects of ethnicity.[55]

The German shift to the Democratic party is obvious from the table. There is a sharp rise in the correlation between per cent German and Democratic vote in 1890; the value of .799 establishes a firm relationship between the two variables. An equally sharp increase in the negative correlation between per cent German and the Republican vote also demonstrates the severity of the German reaction to the Bennett Law. Wisconsin's Scandinavians continued to support the Republicans strongly in both 1888 and 1890. The negative relationship between Scandinavians and Democratic vote was even stronger in 1890 (−.688, compared to −.554 in 1888), but the correlation between Scandinavian and Republican vote dipped slightly as a result of the stay-at-home tendency of many Wisconsin Scandinavian voters in 1890.

Further evidence of intensified ethnic divisions in 1890 can be obtained by adding together percentages of voters for several ethnic groups known to tend to vote either Democratic or Republican and by correlating those values with the party vote. The Republican ethnic variable was composed of the percentages of native born of native parents, Scandinavians, and British; the Democratic variable, of Germans, Irish, Polish, and Bohemians. The result obtained in this manner provide solid evidence in support of the contention that ethnicity was a primary determinant of voting behavior in the late nineteenth century as well as pointing out the sharp increase in ethnic-oriented voting in 1890. In table 1 the correlation between these Republican-tending ethnic groups and the Republican

author. The Consortium also provided most of the census data used in tables 1 and 2, which were calculated from the 1890 federal census. The percentages used in the calculations are estimates (according to a formula developed by the Consortium) of the total number of voters (i.e., adult males) for each group; the percentages used in the variables native-native and Anglo-American were computed by the author from the 1900 federal census. After scattergram analysis, an extreme case was eliminated in a few of the variables before computer analysis.

[55] Partial correlation is a more sophisticated statistical technique which permits the effect of one or more variables to be held constant. For a detailed explanation, see Blalock, *Social Statistics,* chaps. 18–19.

The relationship between Catholic and party vote is even strengthened by holding German constant. The partial correlations between Catholic and Democratic vote, controlling for German, are: for 1888, .717; for 1890, .727; between Catholic and Republican vote, −.663 and −.622, respectively. The correlation between Yankee Protestant and party vote is considerably reduced, however, when we control for native-born of native parents. The partial correlations between Yankee Protestant and Democratic vote are −.202 for 1888 and −.249 for 1890; between Yankee Protestant and Republican vote, .054 and .287.

vote for governor in 1888 is a very strong .789, rising in 1890 to .847. The values of the coefficients of this same variable with the Democratic vote are even more extraordinary, changing from −.838 in 1888 to an amazing −.915 in 1890. A strong relationship between the Democratic ethnic groups and the Democratic vote also emerges; the correlation between these two variables also increases sharply, from .672 in 1888 to .811 in 1890.[56]

An even better indication of ethnic and religious polarization in 1890 can be obtained by correlating the changes in Republican and Democratic percentages of the total vote between 1888 and 1890 with the same census categories.[57] If a group supported either party with about the same strength in both 1888 and 1890, the values of the correlation coefficients should be near zero. If a group shifted toward the Democratic party in 1890, a positive value would result; similarly, if it supported the Republican party more strongly in 1890 than in 1888, a negative value should be obtained.

Table 2 underscores the significant gains that the Democrats made among Germans in 1890; the correlation between per cent German and Democratic

TABLE 2

CORRELATION COEFFICIENTS: REPUBLICAN LOSS
AND DEMOCRATIC GAIN IN GUBERNATORIAL
VOTE BETWEEN 1888 AND 1890 WITH ETHNIC
AND RELIGIOUS CENSUS DATA

Variable	Republican Loss 1888–1890	Democratic Gain 1888–1890
Native-Native	−.170	−.186
Anglo-American	−.223	−.212
Scandinavian	.075	−.451
German	.252	.627
Catholic	−.133	.000
Yankee Protestant	−.481	−.289

gain is a strong .627. The negative correlations of Republican loss with native born of native parents and with Anglo-American stock show that these groups supported the Republican cause with greater fervor in 1890 than in 1888, despite the over-all Republican losses around the state. The same is true for the Protestant categories, composed largely of native Americans. The discrepancy in the correlation coefficients involving Scandinavians again reflects the Scandinavian stay-at-home vote as well as their continued support for the Republican party.

[56] Such extremely high values, either negative or positive, are rare in much of the literature of the social sciences. Given a large enough number of cases (the number used here, 68, is quite sufficient), values of plus or minus .5 are usually considered high enough to establish a firm relationship. The extremely high values revealed by this analysis can be considered conclusive.

[57] To obtain the Republican loss, the Republican percentage for 1890 was subtracted from the Republican percentage for 1888 for all counties; to get Democratic gain, the Democratic percentage for 1888 was subtracted from that for 1890.

The role of the Germans in the landslide of 1890 can easily be shown by analysis of the election returns. The Democratic party made its largest gains in heavily German areas. The predominantly German counties were usually among the banner Democratic counties; they remained so in 1890, and each boosted its Democratic percentage. Ozaukee County, which had the highest proportion of Germans in the state, gave 83.5 per cent of its vote to Peck. Of the ten counties with the largest Democratic gains, nine were among the fifteen most German counties. In 1888, three of the ten most German counties—Milwaukee, Green Lake, and Taylor—posted Republican pluralities; in 1890 they all had Democratic majorities of at least 55 per cent of the total vote.

The pervasiveness of the German defection from the Republican party is more clearly revealed at the township and ward level. Many townships around the state had a preponderant majority of voters who were either German-born or born of German parents. Table 3 shows the total vote and the Republican

TABLE 3

VOTE ANALYSIS: TEN TOWNS WITH THE HIGHEST PERCENTAGE OF GERMAN FAMILY HEADS. TOTAL VOTE, 1884–1890, AND REPUBLICAN PERCENTAGE OF TOTAL VOTE, 1884–1890

Town and County	Total Vote Cast				Republican Percentage of Total Vote			
	1884	1886	1888	1890	1884	1886	1888	1890
Hamburg (Marathon)	101	100	123	100	33	32	32	22
Seneca (Shawano)	44	47	63	61	34	43	49	20
Berlin (Marathon)	196	195	205	190	25	22	24	3
Herman (Sheboygan)	432	370	388	368	40	47	41	20
Schleswig (Manitowoc)	374	291	388	326	25	39	25	21
Wolf River (Winnebago)	145	140	171	175	31	29	29	14
Mosel (Sheboygan)	179	155	171	132	49	53	44	33
Polk (Washington)	301	285	325	250	44	44	45	32
Hartford (Shawano)	241	212	226	207	44	56	47	23
Belgium (Ozaukee)	302	264	282	293	2	2	5	10

percentage of total vote for the ten most German townships in the state for 1884 through 1890.[58] Each township was more than 90 per cent German.[59] By and large, these townships were Democratic in all four elections (two voted Republican in 1886); there was also very little difference in the Republican percentage of the vote between 1884 and 1888. In 1890, however, the Republican percentage fell off precipitously in nine of the ten; in four cases the drop exceeded 20 per cent, and although four towns had given Hoard more than 40

[58] All township ethnic percentages cited herein are from the 1905 state census; the ethnic composition of Wisconsin townships, particularly in the eastern part of the state, changed little between 1890 and 1905. The percentages are based upon the total number of family heads (a good estimation of voters) in the given town, village, or ward in 1905. They are taken from a retabulation of the 1905 census directed by George W. Hill of the University of Wisconsin Rural Sociology Department in 1940. See "Cultural-Ethnic Backgrounds in Wisconsin, 1905" (11 vols., 1940, typewritten manuscript in the possession of the Rural Sociology Department of the University of Wisconsin).

[59] In each of these ten towns in 1905 more than 95 per cent of the family heads were of German stock. Although the actual percentage may have been different in 1890, each of them was as thoroughly German in 1890.

per cent in 1888, only two gave him more than 30 per cent in 1890. The average Republican percentage for the ten towns fell from 34.1 in 1888 to 19.4 in 1890. In Berlin township in Marathon County, the Republican share of the vote fell to a meager three per cent! The overriding concern of Germans over the Bennett Law can be seen in the total vote figures. The normal drop-off in a non-presidential year failed to occur: in two towns the total vote actually exceeded that for 1888, providing a striking contrast with the state as a whole.

Democratic gains in many other German areas, particularly in German Lutheran settlements, were even more spectacular. Losses in the Republican share of the vote exceeded 30 per cent in several townships. In six predominantly German townships, the Republican percentage of the vote fell by more than 40 per cent. (See table 4.)

TABLE 4

GERMAN TOWNSHIPS WITH REPUBLICAN LOSSES GREATER THAN 40 PER CENT, 1890

Town and County	% Republican 1888	% Republican 1890	Loss 1888–1890
Bloomfield (Waushara)	75	24	49
Crystal Lake (Marquette)	62	13	49
Jackson (Washington)	60	18	42
Elba (Dodge)	60	19	41
Fountain Prairie (Columbia)	86	46	40
Newton (Marquette)	48	8	40

Large-scale defections from Republican ranks were not limited to closely-knit German "islands" in rural areas, but also occurred among German residents in both large and small cities. They were the most important in Milwaukee, where the Republicans lost more than 1,000 votes. In four heavily German wards the Republican percentage of the vote fell between 11 and 22 per cent from its 1888 level; the Democratic percentage in the same wards increased between 19 and 35 per cent. In one precinct of the eleventh ward, the Democratic percentage increased from 22 per cent in 1888 to 75 per cent in 1890. In each of these four wards—the ninth, tenth, eleventh, and thirteenth—the total vote surpassed that for 1888 by more than 200 votes. Milwaukee was no exception: German-dominated wards in cities in all parts of Wisconsin were also more Democratic. Republican percentages fell in Portage's fourth ward by 25 per cent and in Eau Claire's eighth ward and Wausau's seventh ward by 17 per cent.

Nor was desertion from the Republican party confined to the areas of concentrated German settlement. It appeared wherever German voters were scattered around the state. In predominantly Scandinavian Vernon County, the only two normally Republican townships to vote Democratic in 1890 were Hamburg, which had the highest percentage of German voters in the county, and Hillsborough, whose population was composed mostly of Germans, Bohemians, and Irish. In Adams County, the most native American of all the sixty-eight Wisconsin counties, the only township to change its allegiance to the Democracy was Quincy, which had the largest percentage of Germans.

Throughout the state, virtually every area witnessing heavy Democratic gains had a large proportion of German voters.

It is significant that those German areas which recorded the heaviest Republican losses were predominantly Protestant. In most of them Lutherans dominated, but in some there were substantial numbers of Reformed, Evangelical Association, Evangelical United Brethren, or other Protestant denominations. All of the six towns shown in table 4 were heavily Protestant, and the pattern was true for German areas in all parts of the state. In Ozaukee County, for example, the greatest drop in Republican percentage occurred in the two largely Protestant towns, Cedarburg and Mequon. This certainly does not mean that in 1890 Protestant Germans were more Democratic than their Catholic brethren. It serves only to point out that prior to 1890 more Catholic than Protestant Germans supported the Democratic party; consequently, in 1890 the Republican losses were higher in German Protestant areas.[60]

The reaction of Wisconsin's other ethnic groups to the Bennett Law was not so violent as that of the Germans. Their response varied considerably. Scandinavians were the second largest ethnic group in Wisconsin. Their voting behavior in 1890 differed from that of previous years, although by no means did it approach the severity of the German reaction. The drop in sentiment for the Republican party among Scandinavians, as described later, reflected their dissatisfaction with Republican national policy rather than with the Republican position on the Bennett Law. During the campaign there was great uncertainty among both Republican and Democratic politicians regarding the Scandinavian vote; their performance in the election satisfied neither party, although it contributed to the Democratic victory.

Scandinavians had ambivalent attitudes toward the Bennett Law. In general they approved of its Americanizing tendency. Most Scandinavians were quick to learn English or at least make sure that their children did; they resented the Germans' opposition to the English language requirement. The attitudes of many Scandinavians were also conditioned by their inherent anti-Catholicism; like Congressman Haugen, some regarded the Bennett Law fight as one of the Catholic Church against the public schools. On the other hand, Scandinavians feared any law interfering with parochial education.[61]

Dissatisfaction with the Republicans among Scandinavians was more serious regarding the McKinley tariff. Scandinavian farmers in western Wisconsin felt the prolonged agricultural depression acutely and had grave doubts about the wisdom of the new tariff. A small number of Scandinavians had supported the

---

[60] Religious statistics at the township level are difficult to find and are often unreliable. The relative strength of Catholic and Protestant among the German towns was ascertained from several sources. Instrumental were Harry J. Heming, *The Catholic Church in Wisconsin* (Milwaukee, 1895–1898); the manuscript census report for the Archdiocese of Milwaukee, 1902, Milwaukee Archdiocese Archives, Chancery office (copy in the possession of the Research Division, State Historical Society of Wisconsin); county histories; and examination of several plat maps for the relevant counties, in the collections of the State Historical Society of Wisconsin. For Ozaukee County, see Schafer, "Editorial Comment," 459–60.

[61] On Scandinavian anti-Catholicism, see Kendrick C. Babcock, *The Scandinavian Element in the United States* (Urbana, 1914), 114; Stephenson, *Religious Aspects of Swedish Immigration,* 1; Sanding, "Norwegian Element," 167; O. F. Ander, "The Swedish-American Press and the American Protective Association," in *Church History,* 6:168 (June, 1937).

Democrats in 1888 on the tariff issue, and larger defections were expected in 1890.[62]

The voting decision of Scandinavians in 1890 was torn by cross-pressures. Their traditional anti-Catholicism and their distaste for German opposition to Americanization reinforced their usually staunch Republicanism. On the other hand, they disliked many features of the Bennett Law and distrusted the McKinley tariff. Recent studies of voting behavior by social scientists indicate that people faced with such cross-pressures very often take the path of least resistance and stay away from the polls.[63] This evidently was the case among Wisconsin Scandinavians in 1890. Obviously dissatisfied with the Republicans, most Norwegians and Swedes who opposed the Bennett Law or the tariff did not vote Democratic; many of them just refused to vote.

Consequently, heavily Scandinavian areas did not go Democratic in 1890. They remained Republican, but because of the lower total vote, the plurality was sharply reduced. In many Scandinavian areas the Democratic vote remained about what it was in 1888, while the Republican vote fell off sharply. This Scandinavian stay-at-home vote was an important factor in the Democratic victory; it deprived the Republican party of thousands of desperately needed votes. It was previously noted that those counties registering the greatest Democratic gains all had large German populations. The same is not true, however, of those counties which witnessed the greatest Republican losses: three of the ten counties registering the greatest Republican losses had German populations of less than 5 per cent. These three counties—Bayfield, Douglas, and Jackson, all of which remained Republican—ranked third, fourth, and eighth, respectively, in percentage of Scandinavian voters. In addition, the drop in total vote in Bayfield (37.2 per cent of the 1888 vote) and Jackson (23.0 per cent) was well above the state average of 12.8 per cent.

An examination of the townships having the greatest concentration of Scandinavians demonstrates the patterns described above. (See table 5.) The 1890 total vote in some of the heavily Norwegian and Swedish towns fell almost as much as 50 per cent. Comparing the vote totals for 1884 and 1886 with those for 1888 and 1890, it becomes obvious that this sharp drop-off was not the result of the normal lessening of political interest in a nonpresidential election; the drop-off in 1886 was much smaller. The fact that many of the heavily Scandinavian towns were in rapidly growing areas makes the low turnout in 1890 more spectacular; in only two of the nine most Norwegian towns did the 1890 vote exceed that of 1886, and in no cases was it greater than in 1888 or 1884. The Republican percentage of total vote was steady between 1884 and 1888, but fell off noticeably in 1890 as a result of the lower total vote.

The two most Norwegian towns in the state, Coon and Christiana in Vernon County, and the most Swedish town, Trade Lake in Burnett County, serve as good examples. In Coon, the 1890 vote was about one-half of the 1888 total, and was smaller than the vote for 1884 or 1886 as well. The Democratic vote

---

[62] Usher to Calvin Brice, August 15, 1890, in the Usher letterbooks; Clarence Clark to Vilas, July 29, 1890, in the Vilas Papers; Merrill, *Vilas,* 160–62.

[63] Paul F. Lazarsfeld, Bernard Berelson, and Hazel Gaudet, *The People's Choice* (New York, 1944), 45–49, 53–64; Berelson, Lazarsfeld, and William McPhee, *Voting* (Chicago, 1954), 27, 130–31; Seymour Martin Lipset, *Political Man: The Social Bases of Politics* (Garden City, 1963), 211–13, 223–26.

TABLE 5

VOTE ANALYSIS: WISCONSIN TOWNS WITH THE HIGHEST PERCENTAGE OF NORWEGIAN AND
SWEDISH FAMILY HEADS. TOTAL VOTE, 1884–1890, AND REPUBLICAN PERCENTAGE OF TOTAL
VOTE, 1884–1890

	Total Vote Cast				Republican Percentage of Total Vote			
Town and County	*1884*	*1886*	*1888*	*1890*	*1884*	*1886*	*1888*	*1890*
Norwegian:								
Coon (Vernon)	220	215	251	129	85	80	83	73
Christiana (Vernon)	287	334	335	227	97	90	85	64
Scandinavia (Waupaca)	245	218	284	220	92	89	94	85
Pleasant Springs (Dane)	340	353	369	271	81	77	79	68
Preston (Trempealeau)	348	325	395	249	83	74	72	71
Franklin (Jackson)	105	87	119	98	77	82	79	68
Iola (Waupaca)	244	230	271	159	87	92	93	83
Christiana (Dane)	549	539	574	424	67	67	61	60
Northfield (Jackson)	142	133	153	116	79	83	70	51
Swedish:								
Trade Lake (Burnett)	—	130	205	111	—	61	60	55
Stockholm (Pepin)	181	135	158	85	92	73	92	68
Wood River (Burnett)	94	91	105	56	99	86	56	50

declined by four votes, but the Republican decline of 110 votes caused a drop
of 10 per cent in the Republican percentage. In Christiana, the Democrats
gained only thirteen votes, but increased their share of the total vote by 11 per
cent. In Trade Lake, the total vote was almost cut in half, but the Prohibition
party, which received 41 per cent of the vote, benefited more than the Democrats. In none of these towns did the Democrats win a plurality. Scandinavian
voters maintained their strong tie with the Republican party and posted substantial Republican majorities, but their countrymen who stayed away from the
polls cost the Republicans several thousand votes.

The rest of Wisconsin's ethnic groups were less influential, numerically at
least, in shaping the outcome in 1890. The Bennett Law had a marked effect on
the usual voting patterns of a few of these groups, however, particularly the
Bohemians, Belgians, and Swiss. By the late 1880's the majority of the state's
Bohemians supported the Democratic party; in 1890 they did so with increased
fervor. As in the German areas, the total vote was nearly equal to the 1888
level. In four heavily Bohemian towns [64] the Republican vote dropped sharply
in two and slightly in the other two. In Richland and Vernon counties,
townships with large numbers of Bohemians were among those which suffered
the largest Republican losses.

Wisconsin's Belgians, who were concentrated in the Green Bay area and who
were the only Catholic ethnic group in the state to vote Republican regularly,
also leaned towards the Democrats in 1890. In the almost wholly Belgian
township of Red River in Kewaunee County, the vote was cut in half, and the
Republican percentage fell from 79 to 66 per cent. In four other Belgian towns,

[64] Franklin, Montpelier (Kewaunee County); Milladore (Wood); and Castle Rock
(Grant).

the total vote decreased slightly, but the Republican share of the vote fell between 18 and 34 per cent in each.[65]

The fact that Wisconsin's Swiss population was largely German may account for their defection from the Republicans. New Glarus in Green County, normally about 40 per cent Republican, gave Hoard only 28 per cent of its vote in 1890. In Buffalo County, towns with large Swiss populations (which also had large German populations) witnessed large Democratic gains.

The normal voting behavior pattern of the state's remaining ethnic groups did not change in 1890. Evidently neither the Bennett Law, the tariff, nor any other issue affected their usual patterns of support for one party or the other. The most important instance was the Irish. The expected defection of Irish-Americans to the Republican party in support of the Bennett Law never occurred. Irish areas were as strongly Democratic in 1890 as they had been in 1888. The only change in normal voting patterns of the most Irish townships occurred in Mitchell in Sheboygan County; its unusually large turnout and large Democratic gain can be attributed to the large number of Germans also residing there. Evidently their traditionally fierce Democratic partisanship and the opposition of the Catholic clergy to the law kept the Irish vote in line. English and Welsh areas remained about as Republican as they had in 1888. Two English towns gave Hoard a slightly higher percentage in 1890 than in 1888, suggesting that the Bennett Law may have gained some votes for the Republicans among British immigrants.[66]

The remaining groups voted precisely as they had in 1888. Wisconsin's rapidly growing Polish population remained as solidly Democratic as usual (in only one of the six most Polish areas did Hoard get more than 10 per cent of the vote).[67] Dutch Catholics continued to be strongly Democratic; Dutch Protestants did not deviate in their support of the Republicans. Except for a somewhat higher turnout in Polish areas, thus boosting the Democratic vote, none of these groups contributed to the realignment of voters which produced the Democratic landslide.

The patterns of ethnic voting behavior in 1890 that have been described above may better be illustrated by examining a few cities or counties as a unit, rather than townships inhabited by any one particular group. One of the best examples of ethnocentric voting in 1890 is the small city of Hartford, in heavily German Washington County. The city was divided into two wards, one predominantly German and the other mostly Yankee.[68] In 1888, the Yankee ward gave Hoard 61 per cent of its vote, the German ward 50 per cent. As in most of Washington County, the total vote increased in 1890; the Yankee ward again voted 61 per cent for Hoard, but the Republican percentage in the German

[65] The other Belgian towns were Green Bay, Humboldt (Brown County); Union, and Brussels (Door).

[66] The two English towns which boosted their Republican percentage were White Oak Springs and New Diggings in Lafayette County. A third predominantly English town, Linden in Iowa County, registered 62 per cent Republican in both elections.

[67] The Polish areas were the towns of Hull, Sharon (Portage County), Pike Lake (Marathon), and Dodge (Trempealeau); and wards 14 and 18 in Milwaukee.

[68] Examination of a plat map of Hartford makes the division of the city more evident. In addition to the differences in the surnames of land owners, the first ward's churches were Congregational and Methodist. The second ward had three churches: a German Catholic, a Lutheran, and Zion Evangelical.

ward fell to 29 per cent. Milwaukee's ethnic ward patterns are much more complex, but looking at the city as a whole, it is obvious that the .total vote increased sharply in only those wards heavily populated by Germans or Poles. The Poles voted even more solidly Democratic than usual; the shifts in the German wards have already been discussed. Changes in the other Milwaukee wards were minor; for the most part, the turnout declined by a few hundred votes, which was normal for an off-year election, and the Republican percentages paralleled those of 1888.

Waupaca County, which had large German and Scandinavian populations, provides a handy microcosmic view of the behavior of both of these groups. Waupaca remained Republican in 1890, but its plurality fell from 1,616 to 450 votes, and the Republican percentage dropped 10.5 per cent. The difference between the German and Scandinavian towns within the county is striking. The 10 per cent drop in the county's total vote was below the state average, but was not evenly distributed: the total vote fell greatly in the Scandinavian towns (41.3 in Iola), but actually increased in three of the heavily German towns. (The total vote and Republican percentages for 1884–1890 for the six most German, the four most Scandinavian, and the one heavily native town are summarized in table 6.) The German townships all experienced a marked shift to the Democratic party in 1890. Seven voting units in the county—four townships and three cities—shifted from the Republican to the Democratic column; all but one had a majority of voters of German stock. The six towns and one city which posted heavy Republican majorities in both 1888 and 1890 offer a sharp contrast. None had German populations greater than 20 per cent, and most were smaller than 10 per cent. Six of the seven had significant percentages of Norwegian, Swedish, or Danish residents; the seventh, Dayton, had the largest

TABLE 6

VOTE ANALYSIS, 1884–1890, OF THE MOST GERMAN AND MOST SCANDINAVIAN TOWNS, WAUPACA COUNTY

Town	Total Vote Cast				Republican Percentage of Total Vote			
	1884	1886	1888	1890	1884	1886	1888	1890
Heavily German:								
Caledonia	150	120	149	185	10	56	23	9
Larabee	235	170	226	253	64	74	66	34
Dupont	270	233	278	259	69	61	59	44
Fremont	154	140	147	150	42	51	40	27
Union	170	141	173	162	31	44	47	40
Bear Creek	180	139	173	160	39	53	39	28
Heavily Scandinavian:								
Scandinavia	245	218	284	220	92	89	94	85
Iola	244	230	271	159	87	92	93	83
Farmington	218	212	253	220	88	94	89	81
St. Lawrence	192	196	230	196	86	88	89	86
Heavily Native and Scandinavian:								
Dayton	179	189	210	168	73	74	82	79

proportion of native-born Americans in the county, and Scandinavians made up most of its foreign-born voters.

The pattern described above was by no means peculiar to Waupaca County. Buffalo County, populated by Germans and Swiss along the Mississippi River and by Scandinavians in the inland towns, was almost identical in its behavior, and other counties which had concentrations of both German and Scandinavians voted similarly.

The role of national issues, especially that of the McKinley tariff, in the election of 1890 has to some extent been obscured and underestimated by historians, to whom the excitement of the Bennett Law has been particularly appealing.[69] Democrats made striking gains around the nation. In terms of congressional losses, many states paralleled Wisconsin's loss of six of its seven Republican members: Iowa lost six of ten, Michigan five of nine, Minnesota four of five. Republican losses in the agriculturally depressed Plains States were even more spectacular.[70]

Clearly the agricultural decline which had plagued the midwestern farmer since the 1870's, and which had become more acute since the mid-1880's, was beginning to be felt in politics. The pinch of lower commodity prices and rising consumer prices was felt most severely by staple crop farmers; by 1890 corn-hog areas also were struck, and hog prices reportedly hit new lows in 1890. In the wheat-growing areas, the Farmers' Alliances multiplied with amazing rapidity, and many of the congressional losses in Minnesota and the Plains States in 1890 were to Farmers' Alliance candidates or Democratic candidates having Alliance support. In state after state in 1890, the McKinley tariff was blamed for rising consumer prices and consequently for the Republican defeats which followed. In a few states, ethnic-oriented issues such as prohibition in Iowa and a school law similar to the Bennett Law in Illinois also assisted the Democratic party.[71]

Wisconsin's agriculture was undergoing a transition during the late 1880's and managed to escape much of the general decline. The predominantly dairy economy in the eastern and southern parts of the state was not struck by the depression which haunted commodity producing regions. The western, northwestern, and some central areas of the state were in the last phase of a transition from an economy based on wheat and other staples to a more balanced one of dairy farming and livestock production.[72] In some respects these regions were like parts of Minnesota and Iowa which felt the decline sharply and which were prone to support splinter agrarian parties. The rise in consumer prices in 1890 affected this part of the state more than the dairy regions.

There is no doubt that in eastern Wisconsin the dominant issue was the

[69] Schafer was the only student of the controversy to stress the importance of the tariff issue in addition to the Bennett Law. See "Editorial Comment," 458–59. Another reason for the neglect of the tariff issue may be the reliance of other scholars upon Milwaukee and other eastern Wisconsin newspapers; the Bennett Law did not receive such full attention in the western part of the state.

[70] *Ibid.;* Faulkner, *Politics, Reform and Expansion,* 112–18.

[71] Faulkner, *Politics, Reform and Expansion,* chaps. 3, 5; Merrill, *Vilas,* 160–63.

[72] Eric E. Lampard, *The Rise of the Dairy Industry in Wisconsin: A Study in Agricultural Change, 1820–1920* (Madison, 1963), 115. See also Joseph C. Schafer, *A History of Agriculture in Wisconsin* (Madison, 1922), chaps. 6, 8.

Bennett Law. The eastern and northeastern counties contained the bulk of Wisconsin's German population as well as the majority of the state's Catholics; it was the center of the conflict over the public and parochial school issue. Although some of the western counties, particularly those along the Mississippi, had large German concentrations, the area as a whole was dominated by the native American and Scandinavian elements. It was in this half of the state that the tariff issue proved decisive. Dissatisfaction with the McKinley tariff evidently persuaded many farmers and workers to vote Democratic, particularly in the congressional contests. Many other Republicans, although equally dissatisfied with the tariff but loath to vote Democratic, stayed away from the polls. Both responses were detrimental to the Republicans.

In 1888, not a single county in the western and northwestern regions voted Democratic; in 1890, nine shifted to the Democracy, a much lower percentage than in the eastern half. Although most western counties remained Republican, many of them suffered some of the largest declines in Republican percentage of the total vote. In many cases these losses were sustained in heavily Scandinavian counties as well as in German areas. Dissatisfaction with Republican national policies rather than with the Bennett Law was primarily responsible for the downturn in Republican fortunes in western Wisconsin.

Wisconsin Republicans had taken note of the situation early. One of Haugen's correspondents blamed the defection on "bad conditions with farmers, poor crops, low prices and all that—believed by them to be worse than they really are. . . ." Profit-seeking retail merchants raised prices and placed the blame on often nonexistent increased duties in the new law.[73]

An important indication of the importance of the tariff in the minds of voters was that in western Wisconsin the Bennett Law took a decided second place to the tariff in the local press of both parties, a direct reversal of the situation in the eastern counties.[74] When a group in central Wisconsin invited Vilas to address them on "the issues of the day, especially the tariff," they added parenthetically, "the Bennett Law cuts no figure here."[75]

The importance of the tariff in the western part of Wisconsin can be shown by a comparison of the vote for governor and that for Congress. With the exception of Haugen, Wisconsin's Republican Congressmen tried hard to keep the Bennett Law out of their campaigns, claiming it was a state issue only. They were fully aware, however, that the law might lose them normally Republican votes. Haugen's largely Scandinavian district was staunchly Republican enough to sustain both him and Hoard. Haugen ran slightly behind Hoard, a normal occurrence, but the Democratic congressional candidate ran 857 votes ahead of Peck.

The two remaining western districts, the third and seventh, show the role of

[73] Griff O. Jones to Haugen, June 4, 1890, Haugen Papers. Haugen recalled a local merchant who told him he would have to raise the price of sugar because of the new tariff; in reality, the McKinley law put sugar on the free list. *Pioneer and Political Reminiscences* (Madison, 1929), 94–95.
[74] For example, the columns of the Eau Claire *News* (Democratic) and *Leader* (Republican) were filled with attacks and defenses, respectively, of the new tariff. Even with Eau Claire's sizable German element, the Bennett Law controversy took second place in both papers.
[75] H. M. Ayer (Lodi) to Vilas, October 18, 1890, in the Vilas Papers.

the tariff more clearly. In the third district, three-term incumbent Robert M. La Follette was at first overconfident and spent valuable time campaigning in other districts. La Follette had also made a few political blunders in the distribution of his patronage in 1889 which had created animosity towards him among some local leaders in Grant and Iowa counties who refused to work for his re-election.[76] These local squabbles, however, could have cost La Follette no more than a few hundred votes. The Bennett Law did have some effect in the district, particularly among the heavily Catholic population in parts of Grant County,[77] but the tariff was primarily responsible for La Follette's defeat by more than 1,000 votes.

It was the major issue in the campaign. "You hear little else than tariff on the street," one of La Follette's correspondents reported; he also wrote that twenty Platteville tobacco workers were going Democratic because of the tariff. A Dane County worker warned of defections among lifelong Republicans who believed that the McKinley tariff hurt the laboring class.[78] In the vote tally, Hoard polled fifty-nine votes more than La Follette in the five-county district.[79] The Democratic congressional candidate, however, ran more than 600 votes ahead of Peck to post his sizable plurality over La Follette.

In the seventh district, north of La Follette's along the Mississippi, Hoard carried the seven counties by a slim 282 votes; Republican Congressman Ormsby Thomas lost by 2,002 votes.

The difference in support for governor and Congressman reflects the dissatisfaction over the tariff. Hoard's only connection with the tariff was his Republican party label, whereas the Republican Congressmen had helped frame and pass the tariff law. Evidently in the western part of the state a large number of Republicans supported Hoard and the Bennett Law but scratched the party's congressional candidate in opposition to the McKinley tariff. Comparison with the eastern part of the state bears this out. The congressional districts in the east, where the tariff took a back seat to the Bennett Law, provide a decided contrast. The vote for Congress followed the normal pattern relative to the gubernatorial vote; the vote for Congressman of both parties ran slightly behind that for the governor and other state officers.

This detailed, statistical analysis of the Republican defeat in 1890 has revealed that: (1) the Republicans lost thousands of votes on both the Bennett Law and McKinley tariff issues; (2) either issue, by itself, might have cost the

[76] "Phil" to Sam Harper, October 24, 1890; Charles Harper to Sam Harper, October 27, 1890, in the Robert M. La Follette Papers, State Historical Society of Wisconsin.

[77] La Follette's managers worried about the German vote in Grant County, but hoped that some who cut Hoard would still vote for La Follette. They worked quietly among German Lutheran ministers to secure their support for La Follette. They feared desertion by Catholics, however, as reports were received of Catholic priests instructing congregations to vote straight Democratic tickets. See Charles Harper to Sam Harper, August 1, October 27, 1890; W. A. Johnson to Sam Harper, October 23, 1890, in the La Follette Papers.

[78] Charles Harper to Sam Harper, October 22, 27, 1890; James F. Taylor to Sam Harper, October 23, 1890, in the La Follette Papers.

[79] La Follette's assertion in his *Autobiography* that he ran 700 votes ahead of his ticket is erroneous. His claim that "the machine leaders" worked secretly against him in his district while he was away is also not supported by evidence. See Robert M. La Follette, *A Personal Narrative of Political Experiences* (Madison, 1913), 133–34.

Republicans the loss of the state, but the landslide which occurred was not possible without both issues acting together; (3) in general, each of the two issues operated within its own geographical and ethnic sphere: the Bennett Law dominated in the eastern part of the state, which contained most of the ethnic groups who reacted the most violently to the law; the tariff dominated in the western part of the state, where there were fewer Germans and where economic conditions made it easier to look upon the tariff issue as crucial.

In the final analysis, it is clear that of the two issues, the Bennett Law was the more important, not only in determining the outcome in 1890, but also in shaping the state's politics for the next several years. The Bennett Law was responsible for swinging the most votes into the Democratic column; the nature of those votes was also crucial. The shift of thousands of German Protestant votes demonstrated both to the political parties and to the Germans themselves the key position of the German-American vote in Wisconsin. As in 1873, the German vote, particularly the German Protestant vote, had proved to hold the balance of power. The bitterness and depth of the emotions incited in 1890 plagued the conduct of Wisconsin politics for almost a decade, as each party continued to exploit for its own purposes the ethnic and religious antagonisms aroused during the campaign. These antagonisms dominated the voting decisions of thousands of Wisconsin voters until the free silver crusade of the mid-1890's and the new issues of the emerging progressive movement once again pushed ethnic and religious considerations into the background.

For both parties in 1890, however, the debate over the relative causes of the election results had little relevance. What concerned the Republicans was how they could regain their usual ascendancy in the state; the Democrats were equally concerned about how they could consolidate their gains. Many leaders in both parties hoped that the impending repeal of the Bennett Law would remove it permanently from the state's politics. The prejudices and emotions which the controversy had aroused or intensified, however, were not so easily suppressed or forgotten.[80]

[80] The Bennett Law was repealed by the 1891 legislature.

PART V

The "New" Economic History

I N T H E *American Economic Review* (March 1963), Douglass C. North reported that "a revolution is taking place in economic history in the United States." According to Professor North, the revolution has been "initiated by a new generation of economic historians who are skeptical of traditional interpretations of U.S. economic history and convinced that a new economic history must be firmly grounded in sound statistical data." [1] The new generation, led by North, Alfred H. Conrad, Lance E. Davis, Robert W. Fogel, Robert E. Gallman, Jonathan R. T. Hughes, William N. Parker, and their younger counterparts Stanley L. Engerman, Albert Fishlow, Peter D. McClelland, Robert P. Thomas, and Peter Temin (to name only a few), share a common positivistic *Weltanschauung* which stresses the importance of data that can be counted and the relevance of economic theory.[2] Essentially, the "new" economic history, also known as econometrics or "cliometrics," seeks to apply to history the methods and theory developed in economics. The goal is to wed economic theory to statistical reconstruction and the indirect measurement of historical data. Explicit theory is the crucial element. As Fogel states: "Regardless of whether the central task of a particular study is the reconstruction of missing data, the construction of new measurements or the indirect measurement of a process, theory plays an integral part in the quantitative work of the new economic history." [3]

Econometric history has had a rapid rise to its present eminence since 1957. In that year Alfred H. Conrad and John P. Meyer challenged the profession to adopt the analytic tools of scientific inference in economic historiography and then demonstrated the rich rewards to be gained by a statistical study of the question of slavery profitability.[4] Also in 1957 three economic historians at

[1] Douglass C. North, "Quantitative Research in American Economic History," *American Economic Review*, LIII (Mar., 1963), 128. See also North, "Economic History: Its Contribution to Economic Education, Research, and Policy, The State of Economic History," *ibid.*, LV (May, 1965), 86–91; and North's essay "Economic History" in David L. Sills (ed.), *International Encyclopedia of the Social Sciences*, 6 vols. (New York, 1968), VI, 468–74.

[2] This point is argued persuasively by Fritz Redlich in " 'New' and Traditional Approaches to Economic History and Their Interdependence," *Journal of Economic History*, XXV (Dec., 1965), 480–95, and "Potentialities and Pitfalls in Economic History," *Explorations in Entrepreneurial History, Second Series*, VI (Fall, 1968), 93–108. The case for theory is made clearly in George G. S. Murphy, "The 'New' History," *ibid.*, II (Winter, 1965), 132–46.

[3] Robert W. Fogel, "Reappraisals in American Economic History—Discussion," *American Economic Review*, LIV (May, 1964), 380. Other relevant works by Fogel are: *Railroads and American Economic Growth: Essays in Econometric History* (Baltimore, 1964), esp. chap. 6; "The Reunification of Economic History with Economic Theory," *American Economic Review*, LV (May, 1965), 92–98; "The New Economic History, Its Findings and Methods," *Economic History Review, Second Series*, XIX (Dec., 1966), 642–63; "The Specification Problem in Economic History," *Journal of Economic History*, XXVII (Sept., 1967), 283–308.

[4] John R. Meyer and Alfred H. Conrad, "Economic Theory, Statistical Inference and Economic History," *Journal of Economic History*, XVII (Dec., 1957), 524–44; and Alfred H. Conrad and John R. Meyer, "The Economics of Slavery in the Ante-Bellum South," *Journal of Political Economy*, LXVI (Apr., 1958), 95–123.

Purdue University launched extensive data-processing studies that eventually dwarfed the impact on the profession of Conrad and Meyer's work. Lance Davis explored the sources of American industrial capital in the nineteenth century, especially in textiles, while his colleagues Jonathan R. T. Hughes and Stanley Reiter produced the first *tour de force* of econometric history, a quantitative and computerized analysis of the British steam merchant fleet in the first half of the nineteenth century.[5] The Purdue cliometricians took their next major step in December 1960 by instituting the Purdue Seminar on Quantitative Methods in Economic History.[6] The Seminar, an annual event until its demise in 1969, brought together in working conferences scholars interested in quantification. For the initial meeting, the organizers had difficulty finding thirty interested individuals; in recent years the problem has been to select several dozen participants from among the many applicants. The more than sixty papers exposed at these conferences have done much to stimulate research in the application of econometrics to the study of history. In addition to launching the "Cliometric Society" meetings, Davis and Hughes, with Duncan McDougall, published in 1961 the first textbook which concretely applied quantitative methods and economic theory to the study of American economic growth.[7] Since then, Douglass North's *Economic Growth of the United States, 1790–1860* (1961) and *Growth and Welfare in the American Past: A New Economic History* (1966) have hastened the reorientation.

In a lucid essay in the *Times Literary Supplement* a few years ago, Peter Temin suggested that "the easiest way to distinguish between a 'new' and an 'old' economic historian" is to ask him whether his degree is in economics or in history. "The answer will be misleading from time to time," Temin added, "but no other single question will serve to discriminate as well."[8] Temin's observation is correct, although one of the authors in this section took his degree in history and yet has been identified at least tenuously with the new economic historians. Two factors perhaps which might account for this identification are the author's application of the computer to a mass of quantitative data and his

---

Both essays are reprinted in Alfred H. Conrad and John R. Meyer, *The Economics of Slavery and Other Essays in Econometric History* (Chicago, 1964).

[5] Lance E. Davis, Jonathan R. T. Hughes, and Stanley Reiter, "Aspects of Quantitative Research in Economic History," *Journal of Economic History,* XX (Dec., 1960), 539–47; Lance E. Davis, "Sources of Industrial Finance: The American Textile Industry, A Case Study," *Explorations in Entrepreneurial History,* IX (Apr., 1957), 789–803; Lance E. Davis, "Stock Ownership in the Early New England Textile Industry," *Business History Review,* XXXII (Summer, 1958), 204–22; Lance E. Davis, "The New England Textile Mills and the Capital Markets: A Study of Industrial Borrowing, 1840–1860," *Journal of Economic History,* XX (Mar., 1960), 1–30; Jonathan R. T. Hughes and Stanley Reiter, "The First 1,945 British Steamships," *American Statistical Journal,* III (June, 1958), 360–81. These essays and many which appeared subsequently are reprinted in the *Purdue Faculty Papers in Economic History, 1956–1966,* Herman C. Krannert Graduate School of Industrial Administration, Purdue University Monograph Series, Vol. 4 (Homewood, Ill., 1967).

[6] For a list of the papers read at each conference from 1960 through 1966, see *Purdue Faculty Papers,* vii–viii.

[7] Lance E. Davis, Jonathan R. T. Hughes, Duncan M. McDougall, *American Economic History, The Development of a National Economy* (Homewood, Ill., 1961). This work is the first to use the phrase "new economic history," vii.

[8] Peter Temin, "In Pursuit of the Exact," *Times Literary Supplement* (July 28, 1966), 652.

attempt to define his problem explicitly and in an operational manner (17).[9]
Since neither indirect measurements nor models are employed, however, he can
at best make only a partial claim.

Research in the new economic history can be divided roughly into three
methodological categories.[10] The simplest form involves classification and processing of quantitative data by rigorous methods and computer aids, as exempli-
fied in Swierenga's essay (17). A more sophisticated level is the reconstruction
of missing data or the construction of new measurements to analyze existing
data through the application of economic and statistical theory. The most
complex type is the use of the counterfactual conditional argument—that is,
measuring the significance of events that happened by quantifying "what might
have happened." The work of Robert W. Fogel is usually characterized by the
second and third types—the use of synthetic statistics and the hypothetical
alternative.[11] This is readily evident in Fogel's article (16), which questions one
of the major tenets of American history—that railroads were indispensable to
the growth of the American economy. To test this thesis, Fogel reconstructs
statistics on the inter-regional distribution of foodstuffs and then builds a model
of a non-rail economy in 1890 (the hypothetical alternative being canals and
wagon roads). The model permits him to estimate the difference between actual
gross national product in 1890 (based on a rail economy) and what GNP
would have been without the fabled iron horse. This difference is the "social
saving" attributable to the railroad in the inter-regional shipment of major
agricultural commodities, a saving which the author finds is almost negligible.
Subsequent research may indicate that Fogel's estimate is understated.[12] But

[9] E. H. Hunt, "The New Economic History: Professor Fogel's Study of American
Railways," *History*, LIII (Feb., 1968), 5; Lance E. Davis, "Monopolies, Speculators,
Causal Models, Quantitative Evidence, and American Economic Growth," paper read
to the Organization of American Historians, Chicago, April, 1967, 4–5, 9–10, 13. For
a juxtaposition of the traditional and quantitative approaches in American economic
history, see Peter D. McClelland's review essay of Malcolm J. Rohrbough, *The Land
Office Business* (New York, 1968), and Robert P. Swierenga, *Pioneers and Profits:
Land Speculation on the Iowa Frontier* (Ames, Iowa, 1968), entitled "New Perspec-
tives on the Disposal of Western Lands in Nineteenth-Century America," *Business
History Review,* XLIII (Spring, 1969), 77–83.
[10] E. H. Hunt, "The New Economic History," 4–7.
[11] See Robert W. Fogel, *The Union Pacific Railroad: A Case in Premature
Enterprise* (Baltimore, 1960); *Railroads and American Economic Growth;* Fogel and
Stanley L. Engerman, *The Economics of Slavery*, Report No. 3803, Center for
Mathematical Studies in Business and Economics, University of Chicago, Dec., 1967;
Fogel and Engerman, "A Model for the Explanation of Industrial Expansion during
the Nineteenth Century: With an Application to the American Iron Industry,"
Journal of Political Economy, LXXI (June, 1969), 306–28; Fogel and Jack Rutner,
"The Efficiency Effects of Federal Land Policy in the Nineteenth Century," paper
read to the Conference on Applications of Quantitative Methods to Political, Social,
and Economic History, University of Chicago, June 6, 1969; Fogel and Engerman
(eds.), *The Reinterpretation of American Economic History* (New York, 1970). A
sympathetic evaluation of Fogel's work is Lance E. Davis, "Professor Fogel and the
New Economic History," *Economic History Review, Second Series,* XIX (Dec.,
1966), 652–63.
[12] Critics have argued that Fogel's social saving estimate is too low. The best
analyses are Peter D. McClelland, "Railroads, American Growth, and the New
Economic History: A Critique," *Journal of Economic History*, XXVIII (Mar., 1968),
102–23; Louis M. Hacker, "The New Revolution in Economic History: A Review
Article based on *Railroads and Economic Growth: Essays in Econometric History,* by
Robert W. Fogel," *Explorations in Entrepreneurial History, Second Series,* III
(Spring-Summer, 1966), 160–75; E. H. Hunt, "The New Economic History," 10–18;

such a finding would be anticlimactic. As a demonstration of the fascinating possibilities of econometric history, Fogel's work is a *fait accompli*. In evaluating the role of railroads, he has built an economic model (the counterfactual condition), quantified a number of variables not quantified before (by linear programming), and constructed new measurements (social saving).

As can be expected, some scholars have criticized the new economic history, especially the use of the counterfactual or hypothetical alternative. They have dubbed it "quasi-economic history," "cliomagic," "analogous to science fiction." [13] Admittedly, counterfactual excursions spanning many decades became increasingly abstract and unrealistic because situations change. Nonetheless, every explanatory statement implies a reasonable alternative. The statement "The railroad was indispensable for American economic growth" implies the opposite, "Income in the United States would have been significantly less had there been no railroad." [14] Other evaluations of econometric history stress the obvious limitations of the attempt to apply operative models to economic data. "Statistical model-builders have to go where the numbers are," says Thomas C. Cochran, "not where the worries and concerns of the present age call them." [15] And the number of measurable variables is really quite small. In addition, Cochran insists, theoretical models are always unrealistic, at least in part, because models pre-suppose rationality and consistency when in fact entrepreneurs are fallible humans who frequently function in an imperfect market. Ignoring institutional processes in favor of quantitative measurement may also lead to scholarly myopia. One cannot understand the patterns of frontier land speculation, for example, without weighing carefully the institutional decisions of federal and state governments. Both the quantity of public land offered for sale and the statutory minimum price were set with little regard for the market situation. The peculiar type of land credit that developed on the midwestern frontier, the "time-entry system," can likewise be understood only in light of federal land bounties to veterans and state usury laws, both institutional arrangements.[16]

Despite limitations of the model-building approach, the new economic historians have sparked a renewed interest in the major processes of economic development—foreign trade, productivity gains, growth cycles, capital formation, income distribution, technological innovation, and demographic changes. They have explored movements in national income; the social return on investments in railroads, western lands, education, and hybrid seed-corn re-

---

Albert Fishlow, *American Railroads and the Transformation of the Ante-Bellum Economy* (Cambridge, 1965), 57–62, 145–49; Marc Nerlove, "Railroads and American Economic Growth," *Journal of Economic History,* XXVI (Mar., 1966), 107–15; Stanley Lebergott, "United States Transport Advances and Externalities," *ibid.,* XXVI (Dec., 1966), 437–61; and Harry N. Scheiber, "On the New Economic History—and Its Limitations: A Review Essay," *Agricultural History,* XLI (Oct., 1967), 387–90.
    [13] Fritz Redlich, " 'New' and Traditional Approaches," 486; Charlotte J. Erickson, book review of Fogel's *Railroads and American Economic Growth* in *Economica, New Series,* XXXIII (Feb., 1966), 107; Hacker, "The New Revolution in Economic History: A Review Article," 175; Scheiber, "On the New Economic History," 383.
    [14] Douglass C. North, *Growth and Welfare in the American Past: A New Economic History* (Englewood Cliffs, 1966), 12–14.
    [15] Thomas C. Cochran, "Economic History, Old and New," *American Historical Review,* LVI (June, 1969), 1561–72.
    [16] This is evident in Swierenga, *Pioneers and Profits,* chap. 6.

search; the profitability of slavery; the effects of the Civil War on economic growth; the financial cost to the colonies of British mercantilism; and the contribution of labor to economic growth. Most of the findings have appeared in article form, especially in the *Journal of Economic History* and *Explorations in Economic* (formerly *Entrepreneurial*) *History,* in anthologies such as the *Purdue Faculty Papers in Economic History* and Ralph Andreano's *New Views on American Economic Development,* and in the excellent interpretive surveys of Douglass North and Stuart Bruchey.[17] Less than two dozen monographs representing the fruit of econometric methods are in print, but more are in preparation, primarily by graduate scholars fresh from new economic history seminars that have sprouted at the major universities. The cliometricians have not yet formulated a large, grand-scale generalization in the style of Charles A. Beard to explain American economic growth (perhaps there is none), but they have constructed new statistical series on the basis of valid, testable, and explicit hypothetical models and have placed the study of economic history squarely on the road of scientific methodology. In the words of Lance Davis, "It may not be literature; it's certainly not without problems; but the new history has made a substantial contribution to both history and theory."

[17] North, *Growth and Welfare,* and Stuart Bruchey, *Roots of American Economic Growth, 1607–1861* (New York, 1965).

LANCE E. DAVIS

"And It Will Never Be Literature"—
The New Economic History: A Critique

Louis M. Hacker has warned econometricians that "the hunt for invariant law in history—to explain the past, manipulate the present, and predict the course of the future—has all the dangers of a fall into a deep and possibly bottomless pit." Lance E. Davis, one of those poised at the edge of the pit, attempts to answer Hacker and other critics in the following article, which was originally read at the American Historical Association meeting, August 29, 1967. In a tone both moderate and conciliatory (somewhat of a rarity for a new economic historian), Professor Davis shows (1) that econometric history is relevant to the traditional study of an important historical event such as the Tennessee Valley Authority project; (2) that the explicit use of the hypothetical alternative does not differentiate new and traditional approaches; and (3) that some of the models of the new historians, although impeccable logically, have failed to conform to historical reality.

I. Introduction

THE TERM "new economic history" was coined by my ex-colleague, J. R. T. Hughes, and in the words of the typical British female detective story-

Lance E. Davis, " 'And It Will Never Be Literature'—The New Economic History: A Critique," *Explorations in Entrepreneurial History, Second Series,* VI (Fall, 1968), 75–92. Copyright © Graduate Program in Economic History, University of Wisconsin, 1968. Reprinted with permission of the author and the publisher.

writer, "if he had known then what he knows now," I am sure he would not have done it. Any discipline (and that includes economic history) progresses only if substantive work is done, and the controversy over the "new" history has certainly diverted resources away from that end. The young (or perhaps not so young) Turks have latched onto the term and proclaimed that their work is "new"; and their elder (or, perhaps, "traditional" might be a better word) counterparts have been equally definite in asserting that the work is not new and/or not history. Claims of these sorts act on any profession like a young boy standing on a corner in a slum area yelling, "Fight, fight." Economic historians, both new and traditional, have dropped whatever they were doing and "come a running." As a result, the past few years have seen a transfer of energies from serious work to methodology; and I, for one, cannot think of a better way to kill any profession. Although I personally believe that the "new" history is both new (if you will accept as a definition of new—outside the mainstream rather than without antecedents) and history (if you will include as history anything that contributes to our understanding of the past), I think the argument is quite sterile, and I would much prefer to see the "new" discipline judged on its substantive contributions.

Given these reservations, I would like to narrow my comments on this twentieth-century *Methodenstreit* to three questions. How does the "new" economic history relate to the field of economic history as a whole? Does the dependence of the new history on the hypothetical alternative differentiate it from the more traditional? And finally, have some of the models chosen by the "new" historians clouded rather than cleared our view of the past?

II. The Scope of the "New" History

If the "new" discipline is defined as that portion of history that relies on the use of explicit models, it can never encompass more than the theories that underlie those models. If one argues that the models can be drawn from any of the social sciences, then the "new" history would encompass all the areas about which we can make scientific statements. Even that, however, is a relatively narrow area (although one that is likely to expand as social and political theories become more operational). If, on the other hand, the term is narrowed to those questions amenable to economic analysis (and this definition would cover almost all of the work in the new history to date), the area is quite small indeed.

Although the distinction is somewhat artificial, consider four classes of historical questions: (1) those that can be dealt with within the framework of existing economic theory, (2) those that are amenable to analysis, but by some other than economic theory, (3) those that cannot be answered within the framework of existing theory but might in the future be amenable to analysis by theory drawn from one of the social sciences, and (4) those that involve several disciplines and depend therefore on the existence of some "unified field theory" in the social sciences. Questions of types (1) and (2) can be treated in a scientific manner by the "new" history. Questions of types (3) and (4) are outside the "new" methodology. The latter can be examined by historians, events can be described, certain assertions of a non-scientific nature can be made, and these descriptions and assertions may be useful in themselves and/or they may suggest modifications in existing theory or new theories that will help explain similar constellations of events in the future.

To understand better the limits of the "new" discipline, let us look at the history of the Tennessee Valley Authority.[1] Because it presents a mix of social, economic, political, and welfare questions, as well as problems of both a static and dynamic nature, the definitive history of that organization has yet to be written. This paper will not attempt to write such a history, but it will attempt to use the experience of the Authority as a case study in the limits and potentialities of the "new" history. The TVA is a natural subject for historical inquiry, and the complexes of that socio-politico-economic organism make its development a natural setting within which to examine what the "new" history can and cannot do.

The outlines of the history of the TVA are well known: the early attempts at the improvement of navigation on the river, the first dams begun by the Corps of Engineers during World War I, the nitrate plants of the same period, the debates over the sale of the facilities to the private sector that occupied the twenties, the decision to expand the operation under public control during the early 1930's, the legal assaults on federal power by the private utilities during the 1940's, and finally, the completed complex of flood control devices, navigational aids, recreational facilities, and electric power generation stations.[2] Here our interest in the TVA is limited to some examples of questions to which the techniques of the new history might be applied and some that the current state of theory puts outside the "new" history.

Much of the best of the "new" economic history has been concerned with questions of the rate of return or the social savings engendered by particular investment policies. Similar techniques could be brought to bear on the question of the contribution of the TVA. Professor Robert Fogel explicitly introduced the concept of social savings to economic history in his attempt to assess the contribution of the Union Pacific Railroad to the American economy.[3] He noted that all profits do not accrue to the decision-making unit and wanted to measure the total (private plus social) return of the government's decision to underwrite the construction of the UP. Although his measure of total returns was at best a partial one, his conclusion (that the rates were very high) appears to be well-substantiated. More recently, Fogel, Albert Fishlow, and Stanley Lebergott have all employed a concept of social savings in their attempts to assess the total contribution of the railroads to economic growth. The controversy among the three points up the real strengths of the "new" economic history. Fogel attempts to contrast the actual cost of shipping agricultural products in 1890 with the hypothetical cost in a world without railroads, and he

[1] The focus on the TVA was suggested by Professor H. Scheiber at the recent OAH meeting. See H. Scheiber, "Lance Davis and the 'New Economic History.'"
[2] The historical evidence on the TVA has been taken from W. Droze, *High Dams and Slack Water* (Baton Rouge, La., 1958), D. Lilienthal, *TVA: Democracy on the March* (New York, 1953), and P. Habbard, *Origins of the TVA* (Nashville, Tenn., 1961).
[3] R. Fogel, *The Union Pacific Railroad: A Case of Premature Enterprise* (Baltimore, Md., 1960).

concludes that the social savings of the railroads, while not insignificant, were not as high as others had implied.[4] Fishlow's model is similar but he concludes that while the social savings were fairly small in 1859, at a later date (1890, for example) they must have been quite high—as high, perhaps, as earlier writers had suggested.[5] Finally, Lebergott has argued that these attempts to measure total savings are doomed by the lack of adequate theory on which to base a counterfactual measurement, and he instead attempts to estimate the potential profitability of railroads as seen by an ante-bellum investor.[6] His conclusion (based on a model of investment choice) is that the railroads would have appeared very profitable when compared with a technology based on canals and wagons. Similar techniques could be applied to the TVA.

The casual reader may be a bit disturbed by the claim that this debate over the contribution of the railroads represents the best of the "new" history, or that, if it does, the "new" history is worth discussing. How useful can any discipline be if three authors using very similar operational concepts can conclude (1) that railroads were not indispensable in 1890, (2) that they were not indispensable in 1859 but were in 1890, and (3) that they were indispensable even before 1859? The answer lies in the nature of the models selected and in each author's view of the relevant alternative. Thus, while Fishlow and Fogel compare "actual" trade with hypothetical trade, Lebergott compares capacity trade with railroads (*i.e.,* he assumes full capacity utilization) with capacity no rail trade. Again, while Fogel is willing to build new canals, Fishlow is not; and Lebergott does not want to assume any secondary and tertiary changes. Disagreement, certainly, but in each case the reader is made aware of what has been done and what has been assumed. It is this explicit unveiling of hypotheses that is the strength of the new economic history. If the "new" historians were to turn their attention to the TVA, the effort might well yield several quite different estimates of the social returns; however, each would be accompanied by an explicit statement of the assumptions on which it rests. Progress can come not only from discovering new "truths," but also from providing a basis for meaningful dialogue. Such work is not figmentary history.

In a similar vein, Zvi Griliches has produced an excellent study on the social returns on the investment in research and development in hybrid corn during the early twentieth century.[7] Griliches combines his data with an explicit model of the rate of return and with some educated guesses about the relevant elasticities and discovers that the social rate of return from this investment was an incredibly high 700 per cent. A similar model could certainly be built to examine the expenditures on the TVA, and, in fact, Griliches explicitly shows the relationship between his rate of return and the cost-benefit ratio frequently employed by the Corps of Engineers in their economic feasibility studies. Once

[4] R. Fogel, *Railroads and Economic Growth: Essays in Econometric History* (Baltimore, Md., 1964).

[5] A. Fishlow, *American Railroads and the Transformation of the Ante-Bellum Economy* (Cambridge, Mass., 1965). Fishlow's product coverage is greater than Fogel's, he permits less adjustment in his counterfactual world, and he is more concerned with actual trade flows.

[6] S. Lebergott, "United States Transport Advance and Externalities," *Journal of Economic History,* December, 1966.

[7] Zvi Griliches, "Research Costs and Social Returns: Hybrid Corn and Related Innovations," *Journal of Political Economy,* 1961.

again, however, it is clear that other models based on other assumptions could yield quite different conclusions.[8] It is equally clear that even if all of these studies indicated a rate of return in excess of that which could have been earned elsewhere, that conclusion is not equivalent to the argument that general welfare has been increased (or vice versa) by the TVA.

A good deal of the controversy surrounding the TVA turns on the relative efficiency of the government power generation facilities versus those owned by private industry. This question again ought to be amenable to analysis by the techniques of the "new" economic history. Economists utilize a number of logical constructs, and among these the production function is one of the most common. Moreover, a great deal of empirical work in agricultural economics and engineering economy involves estimation of the parameters of particular production functions under certain specific assumptions. Given a number of plants and a set of theoretical assumptions, it is possible to construct a function relating inputs to outputs for a "typical" firm. If some firms use fewer units of input per unit of output, it can be argued that these firms are relatively more efficient. Robert Fogel has adopted a similar technique in his study of the quality of public land alienated under the Homestead Act. Utilizing a sample of the farms drawn from the manuscript census, he constructs a production function for an "average" farm. He then tests to determine if the form of land alienation contributes to the "efficiency" of an individual farm (that is, he looks to see if the inclusion of a variable representing the form of alienation contributes significantly to the "explanation" of the observed data). Fogel is, of course, assuming that all farms are employing the same technology, that the quality of management is uniformly distributed across farms, and that differences in productivities reflect differences in the qualities of the soil. In the case of the TVA, one would assume that the technologies are identical, that there are no private-public locational differentials, and that productivity differences reflect managerial skill. Although both Fogel's work and the proposed TVA study can yield suggestive results, they cannot ever produce *certain* results. The conclusions will always depend on the assumptions of the particular model employed, and it will never be possible to compare the generation facilities of Wheeler Dam operating under public and under private management with nothing else having changed.

Since the depression of the thirties and the anti-depression policy of the Federal Government are a subject of concern to historians, one might be interested in the impact of TVA spending on the short-run level of income both in the region served by the Authority and in the rest of the country. E. Cary Brown in his classic study of fiscal policy in the thirties has shown the power of a relatively simple Keynesian model in analyzing government policy in a historical situation.[9] Brown has shown that (contrary to the well-established view) one can hardly talk about a conscious economic policy aimed at achieving full employment (in fact, the size of the government sector relative to the total economy changes hardly at all over the period). Moreover, his work

[8] For example, even in Griliches' work an inclusion of the early (*i.e.*, 1876–1902) expenditures on research drastically reduces the social return. See D. Beebe, "The Rate of Return in Hybrid Corn Research 1876–1965," unpublished manuscript.
[9] E. Cary Brown, "Fiscal Policy in the '30's, a Reappraisal," *American Economic Review*, 1956.

indicates that, whatever actual economic effects federal legislation did have, they tended to be the unconscious (and at times unwanted) results of laws passed not for economic but for social and political reasons. With little modification, one could use Brown's model to examine the impact of the TVA on the aggregate level of activity, and with some change a similar model could yield estimates of the impact on the region's economy. Once again, however, since the TVA did exist, it is not possible to "know" for certain what an economy without the TVA would be like.

From the short-run impact on the region to the role of the TVA in the region's growth is a logical step; and regional development is another subject to which the new economic history has made substantial contributions. The more we learn about the American economy in the nineteenth century, the more we realize that there was no *American* economy. Instead, there appears to have been a number of regional economic units only gradually linked together by expanding transport and communication systems. The work of Douglass North on the ante-bellum economy makes this point quite clear.[10] However, North's own model is not well-specified and, as a result, it is at times difficult to follow his argument.[11] Despite the lack of adequate specification, the type of regional analysis that he suggests appears particularly appropriate for examining the impact of a particular disturbance (in this case the TVA) on the economy of the upper South. To accomplish this end, however, a more formal model than North's would almost certainly be required; and some form of a regional input-output model appears appropriate. The new history has produced two successful applications of the Leontief technique to historical situations. John Meyer has employed an input-output model in his examination of the effect of a retardation in the rate of growth of the foreign sector on the British economy in the late nineteenth century.[12] The model allows him to measure both the direct and indirect effects of the decline in the rate of growth, and he shows that the total effects of that fall are sufficient to account for the lag in aggregate British growth. Again, William Whitney has used a similar model to examine the impact of changes in the tariff level on the growth of American manufacturers in the same period.[13] The work on regional models has been less rewarding, but the theory has been worked out. Moreover, the attempt by Davis, Quirk, and Saposnik to simulate the Northean world (while extremely naive and yielding hardly earthshaking results) suggests that it is possible to apply these regional techniques to historical situations.[14] Moreover, the work of Walter Isard on

[10] But we should bear in mind that much of traditional history is also written within the framework of regional development. Perhaps, then, North's real contribution was to convince the "new" historians that more complicated models are necessary.

[11] Douglass North, *The Economic Growth of the United States 1790–1860* (New York, 1961).

[12] J. Meyer, "An Input-Output Approach to Evaluating British Industrial Production in the 19th Century," in J. Meyer and A. Conrad, *The Economics of Slavery* (Chicago, 1964).

[13] W. Whitney, "The Structure of the American Economy in the Late 19th Century, An Exercise in Historical Input-Output Analysis," a paper presented at the Fifth Purdue Conference on the Application of Economic Theory and Quantitative Techniques to Economic History, 1965.

[14] L. Davis, J. Quirk, and R. Saposnik, "A Simulation Model of the Northean World," a paper given at the Second Purdue Conference on the A of ET and QT to EH, 1962.

Philadelphia indicates that for the recent past at least the data problem is not insuperable.[15] Once again, however, the results would be a comparison of the Tennessee Valley in the period 1930–1960 with and without the TVA.

Not all questions, however, need be strictly in the area of economic history. It is impossible to talk about the decision to launch the TVA without reference to politics, and every assessment of the value of the Authority involves not only economic variables but political and social ones as well. Throughout much of the thirties, for example, there was continual discussion between the Authority and Congress about the size and timing of expenditures. To analyze these developments, economic analysis is not always relevant and almost always not sufficient. However, some of the work done by Otto Davis and others on non-market decision-making might provide the necessary theoretical models.[16] Again, a historian could well be interested in the sources of legislative support for the Authority, and recent work in political science has made it possible to build empirical models of the voting behavior of political parties (or other coalitions).[17] Techniques of this sort have already made substantial contributions to our understanding of party structure in both U.S. and English history.[18] Moreover, since there appears to have been a substantial change in Congressional attitude over the decades preceding the depression, it might be interesting to examine the history of bloc and party in their response to TVA related legislation as far back as World War I. Finally, although operational theory in sociology is even more primitive than the theories of political and administrative sciences, that field too yields certain theoretical propositions that appear to be of value in writing the history of the TVA. No evaluation of the Authority could be complete without some discussion of the social changes that have been produced, and in that area some of the work utilizing models like ecological correlation might make it possible to understand changes in social structure and mobility.[19]

It would be "a nice thing" to be able to assert that today's theory is adequate to deal with all the problems that historians must face. Unfortunately, not only are political and social theory inadequate, but even economic theory cannot be brought to bear on some of the most pressing problems. How, for example, can one discuss the history of the Authority during the 1930's without reference to

[15] W. Isard, "An Interregional Interindustry Model for the Philadelphia Metropolis," paper presented to the First World Econometric Conference, Rome, 1965.

[16] O. Davis, M. Dempster, and A. Wiloavsky, "A Theory of the Budgeting Process," *American Political Science Review,* 1966, and Davis, Dempster and Wiloavsky, "On the Process of Budgeting: An Empirical Study of Congressional Appropriation" in G. Tullock (ed.), *Papers on Non-Market Decision Making* (Charlottesville, Va., 1966).

[17] L. Guttman, "The Basis for Scalogram Analysis," in Stauffer (ed.), *Measurement and Prediction,* Volume 4 in *Studies in Social Psychology During World War II* (Princeton, N.J., 1949).

[18] See, for example, A. Bogue, "Bloc, Party, and the Senators of the First Civil War Congress," paper delivered to the OAH 1967 and W. Aydelotte, "The Conservative and Radical Interpretations of Early Victorian Social Legislation," paper presented at the Seventh Purdue Conference on the A of ET and QT to EH, 1967.

[19] For example, it might be interesting to see if the Valley becomes "dissimilar" from the surrounding area in terms of certain social factors after the completion of the Authority's major programs. For a discussion of ecological correlation, see L. Goodman, "Some Alternatives to Ecological Correlation," *American Journal of Sociology,* 1959.

the famous feud between Chairman Arthur Morgan and board members David Lilienthal and Harcourt Morgan? Clearly the "civil war" seriously disrupted the organization and had important overtones for the future direction of the Authority; however, the dispute at least was partly the result of personality conflicts. Although economic theory can be usefully brought to bear on many situations, it does not help explain the particular actions of particular individuals. Nor can theory provide much help in answering the question, "Is the nation better off with the TVA?" hardly an unimportant question.

The "new" history may provide estimates of the increases (if any) in personal income that have come from the project, and, perhaps, even some suggestions as to how these income changes were distributed. Assuming for the moment that the changes were positive and large and the redistribution in the direction of greater equality, these findings still do not imply an increase in general welfare. Work in economic theory has shown that statements involving interpersonal comparisons can be made only under very restrictive sets of assumptions. While such results may well warn the economic historian to be careful in making welfare judgments, they do not help the historian who would like to be able to assess the total contribution of the Authority. Similarly, much of economic theory is static, but history by its very nature is dynamic, and our dynamic theory is woefully inadequate. Moreover, not only is the theory inadequate, but what we do have suggests that ofttimes static theory (the best set of tools in the economic workshop) may provide misleading dynamic results.[20] Recent work, for example, has shown that it is possible for short-run optimization procedures to lead the economy off the long-run optimum growth path. As a result, the "new" history can contribute considerably less than one might hope to our understanding of the relationship between the TVA and the growth of the American economy. It has provided the basis for a few halting steps toward a dynamic theory, but it has not produced a usable theory, and it is the historian who must suffer.[21] Finally, almost all the theory that we do have is

[20] This point was made long ago by Schumpeter who argued that while monopolies might distort the allocation of resources in the short run, they might also underwrite a more rapid rate of growth than that engendered by competitive firms. See J. Schumpeter, *Capitalism, Socialism, and Democracy* (New York, 1950).

[21] For example, Richard Easterlin has reached into the American past to provide a model of "long swings" where demographic changes provide the exogenous stimuli to the economic model. Dorothy Brady has turned traditional price studies inside out by systematically investigating changes in the cross-section of prices as a first step toward an understanding of the relationship between technological change, demand, and economies and diseconomies of scale. In a similar vein, several studies have examined the relationship between changes in economic institutions (institutions usually assumed fixed in economic theory) and economic growth. Douglass North has shown that it was not technological change in ship design but institutional adaptations in policing methods and market organization that underwrote the decline in shipping rates in the eighteenth and nineteenth centuries. Lance Davis and J. R. T. Hughes have argued that it is misleading to assume that the "gold standard" operated in the classic manner before the last quarter of the nineteenth century, and that in earlier years that institution was undergoing continual change. Davis has shown that in both the United States and England the development of a national capital market depended on the innovation of new, and the adaptation of old, financial institutions to meet the demands of new industries and new regions.
R. A. Easterlin, "Economic-Demographic Interactions and Long Swings in Economic Growth," *American Economic Review*, December, 1966. Dorothy Brady, "Relative Prices in the Nineteenth Century," *Journal of Economic History*, June, 1964. D. C. North, "Determinants of Productivity in Ocean Shipping," paper given to

highly compartmentalized: we have economic theory, social theory, and political theory, but we don't have a "unified field theory" for the social sciences. As a result, while the application of theory to history has yielded significant (but narrow) results, it has not been able to push into the border areas relating one discipline to another, and it is in this area that many important problems lie. As Professor Redlich has pointed out, economics has (perhaps unfortunately) not become more social (to say nothing of more philosophical). This failure is apparent from any reading of the literature in economic development, and it is at least equally vexing to the economic historian.

In summary then, as dismal as it may be, if a "new" historian were writing about the TVA, he would be unable to explain particular actions of individuals, he would be unable to demonstrate that the TVA has been a "good" thing, he would be unable to prove that the Authority's policies have resulted in more rapid economic growth, and he would be unable to explore the interrelationships between the economic activities of the TVA and the social and political behavior that underlay and were produced by them. While the new history might well provide substantial insights into certain aspects of the Authority, clearly there is still considerable room for the gifted insights and interpretations of the traditional historian.

III. The Counterfactual

The foregoing discussion of the "new" history should have indicated how sensitive its findings are to the nature of the hypothetical alternatives drawn. No aspect of the methodology of the "new" economic history has generated more fire (but perhaps less light) than its practitioners' insistence on the explicit use of the counterfactual (or contrapositive or hypothetical alternative). To many "traditional" historians, counterfactual history is anti-history or non-history, but these same historians continually employ implicit counterfactual arguments. The difference between the old and the new is in the *explicit* use of the contrapositive, not in the innovation of the counterfactual argument.

In a recent article my co-speaker, Professor Redlich, has divided all of the new history into three parts: Class I, those "new" historians who are really old historians and write real history (he includes me in this category); Class II, the "theoretical" new historians who are primarily concerned with hypothesis testing and write near history (in this group he puts, for example, Douglass North); and Class III, the "counterfactual" historians who depend on "figments" and who do not write history at all (and here he places Fogel and Meyer and Conrad).[22] The difficulty with this triparte division lies not alone in its artificiality (the counterfactual is used in some form by all three groups) but, more important, in its suggestion that the best of the "new" historians are

the International Historical Society, Vienna, 1965. L. Davis, "Capital Immobilities, Institutional Adaptation, and Financial Development: The United States and England, an International Comparison," paper given to the International Econometric Conference, Rome, 1965, and "The Investment Market 1870–1914: The Evolution of a National Market," *Journal of Economic History,* September, 1965.

[22] F. Redlich, "New and Traditional Approaches to Economic History and Their Interdependence," *Journal of Economic History,* 1965.

those who do not make explicit use of the counterfactual and that the worst are those who do. In fact, most "new" historians would argue that the reverse is true.

It is certainly possible to describe objects or events without reference to any counterfactual world. Historians can talk about American immigrants in terms of their age and sex composition, about frontier banks in terms of their capital and loans, or about ante-bellum plantations in terms of their work force, acreage, and output. To this extent, therefore, it is possible to write "non-figmentary" history. Few historians (new or traditional) would, I think, be willing to limit themselves to pure description. Instead, most would argue that the unique contribution of the historian lies in his ability to understand sequences of events (*i.e.*, to interpret causal relationships). Any step in this direction, however, leads necessarily to the use (implicit or explicit) of a counterfactual argument. Take, for example, the work of Professor Harry Scheiber, one of the young critics of the "new" history. In a recent article he has described settlement in the northwestern corner of Ohio.[23] To the extent that his work is limited to that description, he has no need for a contrapositive argument. But to the extent that his work is so limited, so is his contribution. In fact, the importance of Scheiber's work (since others had already described settlement in similar terms) lies in his analysis of the causes of the particular pattern of settlement. Scheiber argues that settlement was much slower than one would have expected and that the explanation for the delay lay not, as others have implied, in the physical characteristics of the area, but in the particular land policy that led to large purchases by "speculators." [24] Scheiber's arguments are compelling, and I, for one, am convinced; but his argument by its very nature is a contrapositive one. Scheiber implicitly (by using terms like "slower") compares a situation that was (the actual distribution of the land) with one that never was (a land distribution policy designed to get the land quickly into the hands of the farmer). Moreover, he goes on to assert something about the character of that "never, never land" (*i.e.*, he argues that the experience of five nearby counties in Indiana can be used as a proxy for Ohio with a different land policy), and finally he concludes that in some sense the economy was made "worse off" by the particular system of land distribution that was employed. This explanation is not meant as a criticism of Scheiber's work (his article is a very good one) but to show that he has written counterfactual history. There is, in fact, no way that cause and effect can be discussed without comparing the observed with the hypothetical.

Granted then that counterfactual arguments are a part of all but purely descriptive history, can we ever be certain about the nature of the contrapositive world that we postulate? Its character will always depend on the implications of the model that we choose. Although Robert Fogel's name is anathema to some historians, the social savings controversy, as we have seen, nicely illustrates the question of the relevant counterfactual. What the controversy indicates is that there is no "correct" counterfactual. The one you choose depends on the model

[23] H. Scheiber, "State Policy and the Public Domain: The Ohio Canal Lands," *Journal of Economic History,* 1965.
[24] Scheiber never defines the term "speculator," but it appears that he means sales to persons who themselves did not farm the land.

you select. What Fogel, Fishlow, and Lebergott have done is to make their models explicit, and this is the strength of the new discipline. There is a basis for a dialogue with both point and focus. Differences certainly, but no question about the nature of these differences. Fogel, Fishlow, and Lebergott all know where they stand and so, more importantly, do their readers.

But what of the other two categories of the "new" history to which Professor Redlich alludes? Redlich places the work of Douglass North on the regional growth of the ante-bellum economy in Class II (near history). Does North not employ the technique of figmentary history? North uses a theoretical model that relates shifts in the foreign demand for cotton to both secular and cyclical changes in income in the United States. From this model he concludes that the dependence of the South on cotton caused income growth in that area to lag and that the growth of income in the West can be attributed to the secondary effects of the foreign demand for cotton coupled with that region's ability to isolate itself from world markets. Certainly, his argument contains an implicit counterfactual world without cotton and interregional trade, with higher tariffs, with a different distribution of income, and, perhaps, with a host of other characteristics as well. In fact, the most serious criticism of North's work turns on his failure to specify his model and the resulting inability to formulate adequately the nature of the relevant counterfactual. Without that counterfactual it is not possible to test his model in any meaningful fashion.[25]

Finally, in Class I (real history) Redlich cites with approval the work of certain of the new economic historians whose method, he argues, depends on neither theory nor counterfactuals. Take as example of Class I history my work on the evolution of the capital markets in the U.S.[26] Far from denying models and counterfactuals, the work depends on them, and serious criticism can be raised over my failure to specify them adequately. The model assumes that initially markets were essentially local, and there was no mechanism capable of sustaining arbitrage. As a result, there was no force producing capital transfers and no move to equilibrate interest rates between the markets. It further assumes that, over time, certain institutional innovations made regional arbitrage possible, caused capital to flow from low to high interest areas, and eliminated (or at least reduced) the interest differentials. Implicit in this theory is a counterfactual world without such financial innovations. Clearly a myriad of other theories (not based on a lagged supply model) could be called on to explain this constellation of events, and, in fact, Professor Stigler has suggested a single market model that he feels is more relevant.[27] Ultimately certain tests can be brought to bear on the issues and some of the questions between Stigler and myself can perhaps be resolved, but certainly the discussion of the evolution of the capital market is theoretical history, and the nature of the counterfactual is relevant.

[25] At the simplest level, although North himself talks of a world with only some five or six commodities, a minimum of thirty-six are implicit, and since there are at least three regions, the minimum number of commodities that must be treated are one hundred eight (3 x 36).
[26] L. Davis, "Capital Immobilities and Finance Capitalism," *Explorations of Entrepreneurial History*, 2nd series, 1963; "The Investment Market, 1870–1914: The Evolution of a National Market," *Journal of Economic History*, 1965; "The Capital Markets and Industrial Concentration: The U.S. and U.K., a Comparative Study," *Economic History Review*, 1966.
[27] G. Stigler, "Imperfections in the Capital Market," unpublished manuscript.

Professor Redlich is correct in arguing that Class I is the nearest to traditional history and Class III the furthest removed. He is, however, incorrect in inferring that it is the existence or absence of the counterfactual that provides the basis for this comparison. All three classes contain counterfactual arguments. The differences lie in the degree to which the theories have been specified. The weakness of traditional history (and of Class I and, to a lesser extent, Class II "new" history) lies in the lack of explicit models from which explicit counterfactuals can be deduced. The strength of the type of work typified by Fogel, Fishlow, and Lebergott lies in the complete specification of the model. Each of the three has suggested a different standard against which to measure the contributions of the railroads. Another example of the power of the "new" history is produced by Conrad and Meyer's work on the profitability of slavery. Not everyone agrees with their conclusions, but their model is specified, their counterfactual is explicitly drawn, and their critics know what assumptions they have made and how their evidence relates to their conclusions. Criticism has, therefore, been directed towards building models based on alternative sets of assumptions and on examining their evidence at the crucial points.[28] Agreement and certainty are, like motherhood, a "good thing," but an explicit statement of the basis for disagreement also represents progress. On the TV show "To Tell the Truth" resolution occurs when the Master of Ceremonies says, "Will the real Ignantz Jastro please stand up?" The "real" counterfactual will never be so easily identified (after all, it does not exist), but meaningful discussions leading to better understanding can come when the basis for the choice of counterfactual and the characteristics of that contrapositive are known. The five Indiana counties may or may not provide an adequate proxy for Scheiber's northwest Ohio sans speculation, but unless the reader is aware of the theoretical model used, he has no basis for deciding if the proxy is relevant.

IV. Theory, the Siren Lure

While the "new" economic history has been frequently criticized for what it has done right, it has been far less frequently criticized for what it has done wrong. No impartial survey of the discipline could fail to turn up examples of scholarship that would not be tolerated in any undergraduate history department in the country, nor could it fail to indicate the subject bias that appears to reflect the ease of access of sources far more than the importance of subjects themselves. The most pernicious failure, however, lies in the formulation and application of irrelevant models to history. As long as one is interested solely in the mathematics of an argument, its elegance and cleverness are important, but its applicability is not. If, however, one wants to employ a model to explain

[28] A. H. Conrad and J. R. Meyer, "The Economics of Slavery in the Ante-Bellum South," *Journal of Political Economy,* 1958. For an example of alternative models see Y. Yasuba, "The Profitability and Viability of Plantation Slavery in the United States," *Economics Studies Quarterly,* 1961, or R. Sutch, "The Profitability of Ante-Bellum Slavery—Revisited," *Southern Economic Journal,* 1965. For the questions of evidence see E. Genovese, "Food Costs of Slaves and the Profitability of Slavery in the Ante-Bellum South," paper given at the 3rd Purdue meeting on the A of ET and QM to EH, 1963, or E. Sarayder, "A Note on the Profitability of Ante-Bellum Slavery," *Southern Economic Journal,* 1964.

some aspect of reality, the latter quality assumes prime importance. Some of the "new" historians have failed to understand this point, or if they do understand they have chosen to ignore it. It is, however, in this area that the traditional historian, although undoubtedly aggrieved by what he must realize is a twisting of the past into unrecognizable shapes, is least capable of formulating a relevant objection. Theory *can* be useful in understanding history; it does not, however, follow that all theory is useful. A particular theory (no more logically valid than any of an infinite number of other theories) can aid the understanding of the past only if it has some relevance to the conditions it is attempting to explain. While this proposition may seem eminently sensible and so obvious that it is not worth discussing, it has been ignored by some of the "new" economic historians. Here, then, is real "figmentary history."

Paul David, in his extremely facile analysis of the innovation of the reaper, develops the concept of a threshold farm size (*i.e.,* a minimum size below which the farmer would find it more profitable to harvest by hand than by machine).[29] He produces a model that allows him to estimate the threshold, notes that many farms moved above that level during the 1850's, argues that the increase in wheat prices caused that increase in farm size, and concludes that it was in this manner that the increase in demand for wheat speeded the process of reaper innovation. Here we have a theoretical argument about an historical process. The model is logically valid, but the question remains: Does the model help us to understand the process of innovation? David's model applies to a world where the services of a reaper are indivisible; and the conclusions would not necessarily hold if such services were not indivisible. It is obvious that the reaper is mechanically indivisible (at least within the limits of an 1850 technology). The argument, however, does not rest on the indivisibility of the machine, but on the indivisibility of the services of that machine. The evidence on that point is less clear. Today, for example, such divisibility of services is achieved both through the cooperative purchases of reapers and through the growth of firms specializing in reaping. Did similar institutions exist in the 1850's? The evidence suggests that they did. In the words of Allan Bogue: "I gave this problem to a graduate student one morning at eight o'clock and he was back in my office by ten with a long list of cooperative purchases." [30] While David's model is extremely clever, it is doubtful that it can be directly applied to the American economy in the 1850's (*i.e.,* it has little historical reality). If David wishes to use the model as an explanation of the process of innovation, he must show either that Bogue's evidence is wrong, or that in some regions there were legal or other institutional barriers to cooperative ventures or the growth of reaping firms. In the absence of this additional evidence, it can scarcely be argued that the model has made a substantial contribution to our understanding of the process of innovation.

Similarly, Peter Temin has employed a *very* formal model in an attempt to resolve the questions raised by Rothbart, Habbakkuk, and others about the nature of technology in Great Britain and the United States in the nineteenth

[29] P. David, "The Mechanization of Reaping in the Ante-Bellum Midwest" in H. Rosovsky (ed.), *Industrialization in Two Systems* (New York, 1966).
[30] Bogue notes that no other graduate student could have found the evidence so quickly; this one was particularly well acquainted with the McCormick papers.

century.[31] His model is logically impeccable, and he derives some very strong (not to say, very strange) conclusions about the nature of innovation in the United States and about the nature of the U.S. economy itself. For example, he argues that innovations tended not to be labor-saving and capital-using, but capital-saving and labor-using and that real wages in the U.S. were lower than real wages in the U.K. Since these conclusions are at odds with most of the received doctrine about American development, the work (if it is correct) represents a major revision of economic history. The evidence, however, appears to belie these conclusions, and even Temin is obliged to try to explain this variance. He argues, for example, that while the U.S. appears to have utilized a great deal of capital, it was not very good capital. The problem, however, may not lie in the evidence but in the model which Temin has chosen. While his conclusions are strong, so are his assumptions; and not only are they very strong, but they postulate a world which is quite unlike any that we have ever known. While simplified models are the stock in trade of every economist, oversimplification can lead to lack of explanation. Occam's razor, after all, can help us choose between models only if both predict equally well. In Temin's case, although his general model postulates the traditional three factors of production, only two (labor and capital) are used in manufacturing and only two (land and labor) are used in agriculture. Every historian recognizes that agriculture does use capital and, if one is willing to broaden the definition of land to include raw materials, that manufacturing uses land. If Temin's model is reformulated with these additions, it is possible to conclude that innovations would be labor saving and that real wages would be higher in the U.S.[32] Theory is important—the explicit use of theory is the contribution of the new economic history—but *no* economic historian (be he old or new) should allow himself to be so completely seduced by the logic of theory that he forgets the facts. Theory can help us order and understand facts, but the facts can also suggest that certain theories are inappropriate as explanatory devices.

V. Summary

What then is the current state of the "new" economic history? It has produced some substantial results, but it is certainly not free from criticism. Its critics have, however, frequently misunderstood its methodology; and, as a result, many of their barbs have been aimed at its strengths rather than at its weaknesses. A decade of work within the new framework has produced some substantial revisions of our understanding of historical relations. Some aspects of theory have been modified to make them more useful, and a great deal of meaningful debate has been conducted on issues which are still unresolved. It may not be literature; it's certainly not without problems; but the new history has made a substantial contribution to both history and theory.

[31] P. Temin, "Labor Scarcity and the Problems of American Industrial Efficiency in the 1850's," *Journal of Economic History,* September, 1966.
[32] Temin's work has been criticized along these lines by E. Ames and N. Rosenberg, "The Enfield Arsenal in Theory and History," *Krannert Institute Paper No. 153,* and R. Fogel, "The Specification Problem in Economic History" (revised), *Journal of Economic History* (forthcoming).

16

ROBERT W. FOGEL *

A Quantitative Approach to the Study of Railroads in American Economic Growth: A Report of Some Preliminary Findings

Robert W. Fogel is the most brilliant practitioner of cliometrics to-day. In the last decade he has imaginatively applied the tools of econometrics, synthetic statistics, and the hypothetical alternative to several major problems of the nineteenth century—the effect of railroads on American economic growth, Federal land distribution policy, American agriculture, and the slave system. He is also developing an explanatory model of American industrial expansion and is reconstructing statistics on the growth of the iron industry in the nineteenth century. In the following article, read at the first Purdue cliometrics conference as a trial balloon for his full-length study Railroads and American Economic Growth *(1964), Fogel makes a frontal assault on a major thesis in economic history—that railroads were vital to the American industrial "take-off."*

The article examines only one aspect of railroad economics, the

Robert W. Fogel, "A Quantitative Approach to the Study of Railroads in American Economic Growth: A Report of Some Preliminary Findings," *Journal of Economic History,* XXII (June, 1962), 163–97. Reprinted with permission of the author and the Economic History Association.

* This paper was originally presented in December 1960 at the Purdue Conference on Quantitative Methods in Economic History and at the St. Louis meeting of the Econometric Society. It is a progress report on one aspect of a larger study entitled *Railroads and American Economic Growth: Essays in Econometric History.* The study is being conducted under the supervision of Simon Kuznets and G. Heberton Evans, Jr. They, of course, are not responsible for any errors which appear below. All computations presented in the paper are preliminary and subject to revision. I am grateful to the Social Science Research Council, which generously supported portions of the research on which this paper is based.

"social saving" resulting from the inter-regional rail transport of major foodstuffs. This social saving, Fogel found, is small—less than 1 per cent of GNP, a figure which the author subsequently revised downward to .06 per cent. Also, in the larger work Fogel calculated the social saving of intra-regional agricultural shipments (1 per cent), the transport of all non-agricultural products (4.7 per cent), and the direct and indirect impact of railroads on suppliers and consumers (zero savings). The crude total of social saving, then, is 6.3 per cent of GNP in 1890. Whether this is significant depends on one's perspective. Six per cent of GNP today is more than $50 billion, hardly an infinitesimal sum, even by Defense Department standards. However one interprets the results, Fogel's work is a landmark in the application of econometric and statistical techniques to the problems of economic history.

> Is it legitimate for the historian to consider alternative possibilities to events which have happened? . . . To say that a thing happened the way it did is not at all illuminating. We can understand the significance of what did happen only if we contrast it with what might have happened.
>
> MORRIS RAPHAEL COHEN

I

LELAND JENKS'S article describing the pervasive impact of the railroad on the American economy first as an idea, then as a construction enterprise, and finally as a purveyor of cheap transportation, has become a classic of economic history.[1] The particular contribution of the Jenks article was not the novelty of its viewpoint, but the neat way in which it summarized the conclusions both of those who lived during the "railroad revolution" and those who later analyzed it through the lens of elapsed time. Out of this summary the railroad emerges as the most important innovation of the last two thirds of the nineteenth century. It appears as the *sine qua non* of American economic growth, the prime force behind the westward movement of agriculture, the rise of the corporation, the rapid growth of modern manufacturing industry, the regional location of industry, the pattern of urbanization, and the structure of interregional trade.

Research since the Jenks article has further buttressed the idea that the railroad was an imperative of economic growth. Christopher Savage, in his recent *Economic History of Transport*, states that the influence of the railroad in American development "can hardly be overemphasized" since "agricultural and industrial development and the settlement of the West would scarcely have

[1] Leland H. Jenks, "Railroads as an Economic Force in American Development," THE JOURNAL OF ECONOMIC HISTORY, IV, No. 1 (May 1944), 1–20; reprinted in F. C. Lane and J. C. Riemersma, *Enterprise and Secular Change* (Homewood, Ill.: Richard D. Irwin, 1953), pp. 161–80; and in J. T. Lambie and R. V. Clemence, *Economic Change in America* (Harrisburg, Pa.: Stackpole Co., 1954), pp. 52–68.

been possible" without it.[2] W. W. Rostow has administered an even stronger fillip to this viewpoint. In the projection of his concept of a "take-off into self-sustained growth," Rostow assigns railroads a crucial role. The railroad, he argues, was "historically the most powerful single initiator of take-offs." It "performed the Smithian function of widening the market," it was a "prerequisite in many cases to the development of a major new and rapidly expanding export sector," and most important, it "led on to the development of modern coal, iron and engineering industries." Rostow lists the United States first among the countries in which the influence of the railroad was "decisive." [3]

The idea of a crucial nexus between the railroad and the forward surge of the American economy following 1840 appears to be supported by an avalanche of factual evidence. There is, first of all, the impact of the railroad on the growth of cities. Atlanta was transformed from a spot in the wilderness to a thriving metropolis as a result of the construction of the Western and Atlantic. Chicago eclipsed St. Louis as the commercial emporium of the West by virtue of its superior railroad connections. And Louisville throttled the growth of Cincinnati by its ability to deny the "Porkopolis" rail connection with the South.[4] Further, the decisive victory of the railroads over canals and rivers in the contest for the nation's freight is beyond dispute. One waterway after another was abandoned as a result of its inability to compete with the locomotive. The Pennsylvania Main Line Canal was driven out by the Pennsylvania Railroad, the Blackstone by the Providence and Worcester Railroad, and the Middlesex by the Boston and Lowell line.[5] The Mississippi, which in the early decades of the nineteenth century was the main traffic highway of the center of the continent, had fallen into relative disuse by the end of the century. In 1851–1852 boats carried six times as much freight as railroads; in 1889 the railroads carried five times as much freight as boats.[6]

Finally, there is the high correlation between new railroad construction and both population growth and commercial activity. Illinois, Michigan, and Ohio, for example, experienced a marked increase in population, construction, and manufacturing following the completion of rail lines within and across their borders. For the country as a whole, the undulations in indexes of total output seem to follow closely the cycles in railroad construction.[7] Of particular note is

[2] Christopher I. Savage, *An Economic History of Transport* (London: Hutchinson & Co., 1959), p. 184.

[3] W. W. Rostow, *The Stages of Economic Growth* (Cambridge: The University Press, 1960), p. 55.

[4] See, for example, Wyatt W. Belcher, *The Economic Rivalry Between St. Louis and Chicago, 1850–1880* (New York: Columbia Univ. Press, 1947), and "Cincinnati Southern Railway: Struggle Between Two Rival Cities for Metropolitan Dominance," in N. S. B. Gras and Henrietta M. Larson, *Casebook in Business History* (New York: F. S. Crofts, 1939).

[5] A table of the canals abandoned during the nineteenth century is given in U.S. Congress, Senate, *Preliminary Report of the Inland Waterways Commission,* Doc. No. 325, 60th Congress, 1st Sess. (1908), pp. 205–9.

[6] There was double counting in the data on which these ratios are based. U.S. Congress, Senate, *Andrews Report,* Executive Doc. No. 112, 32nd Cong., 1st Sess. (1853), pp. 903–6; U.S. Census Bureau, *Eleventh Census of the United States: 1890, Report on the Transportation Business in the United States,* Part I, pp. 452, 548, 640; Part II, pp. 9, 10, 163, 308, 384, 436, 479.

[7] Walter Isard, "Transport Development and Building Cycles," *Quarterly Journal of Economics,* LVII, No. 1 (Nov. 1942), 90–112; Jenks, "Railroads as an Economic Force," pp. 4–5.

the apparent upsurge in manufacturing output which paralleled the boom in railroad construction. Between 1839 and 1859 railroad mileage in the United States increased by 26,000 miles.[8] The construction of such an immense transportation network required a large volume of manufactured goods, especially iron, lumber, and transportation equipment. Between 1841 and 1850, for example, when railroad mileage increased by 160 per cent, lumber production rose by 150 per cent and pig iron by 100 per cent.[9]

The evidence is impressive. But it demonstrates only an association between the growth of the rail network and the growth of the economy. It fails to establish a causal relationship between the railroad and the regional reorganization of trade, the change in the structure of output, the rise in per capita income, or the various other strategic changes that characterized the American economy of the last century. It does not establish even *prima facie* that the railroad was a necessary condition for these developments. Such a conclusion depends not merely on the traditional evidence, but also on implicit assumptions in its interpretation.

One cannot, for example, leap from data that demonstrate the victory of railroads over waterways in the competition for freight to the conclusion that the development of the railroad network (particularly the trunk lines) was a prerequisite for the rapid, continuous growth of the internal market. The only inference that one can safely draw is that railroads were producing the same (or a similar) service at a lower cost to the buyer. For if rail transportation was a perfect, or nearly perfect, substitute for the canal, all that was required for a large shift from canal to railroad was a small price differential in favor of the latter. Whether the shift produced a significant increase in the size of the internal market depends not on the volume of goods transferred from one medium to the other, but on the magnitude of the associated reduction in transportation costs. If the reduction in cost achieved by the railroads was small, and if canals and rivers could have supplied all or most of the service that railroads were providing without increasing unit charges, then the presence of the railroads did not substantially widen the market, and their absence would not have kept it substantially narrower. The conclusion that the railroad was a necessary condition for the widening of the internal market flows not from a body of observed data, but from the assumption that the cost per unit of transportation service was significantly less by rail than by water.

Other propositions regarding the role of the railroad involve even stronger assumptions than the one just cited. The view that the quantity of manufactured goods used in the construction and maintenance of the railroad was of decisive importance in the upward surge of manufacturing industry during the two decades preceding the Civil War involves a minimum of three assumptions. It not only assumes that the volume of the goods purchased by the railroad was large relative to the total output of the supply industries, but also that railroad purchases were directed toward domestic rather than foreign markets. It assumes further that if there had been no railroad, the demand for manufactured goods by the other forms of transportation would have been significantly less or

[8] U.S. Census Bureau, *Historical Statistics of the United States, Colonial Times to 1957* (Washington: Govt. Printing Office, 1960), p. 427.
[9] U.S. Agriculture Dept., *Yearbook of Agriculture, 1933,* p. 748; Frank W. Taussig, "The Tariff, 1830–1860," *Quarterly Journal of Economics,* II (1888), 379.

its impact strategically different from the demand associated with railroads.[10]

The preceding argument is aimed not at refuting the view that the railroad played a decisive role in American development during the nineteenth century, but rather at demonstrating that the empirical base on which this view rests is not nearly so substantial as is usually presumed. The fact that the traditional interpretation involves a number of basic assumptions is not in itself a cause for rejecting it. In the absence of data, the economic historian has no alternative but to make the best possible guess. Without such guesses or assumptions, no analysis is possible. The only question is, "How good are the guesses?" Is there any way of testing them?

It is always easier to point out the need to test a given set of assumptions than to propose a feasible method for testing them. The remainder of this paper deals with the problems involved in evaluating one of the most common presumptions regarding the influence of the railroad on American economic development. The question to be considered is: did the interregional distribution of agricultural products—a striking feature of the American economy of the nineteenth century—depend on the existence of the long-haul railroad? To answer the question, I define a concept of "social saving" in interregional transportation attributable to the existence of the railroad, and propose a method of measuring it. The discussion that follows turns largely on the consistency between the size of this "social saving" and the hypothesis that railroads were a necessary condition for interregional agricultural trade. However, the analytical approach described below transcends the particular hypothesis to which it is applied. The same method is being used to obtain information on such additional questions as the effect of the railroad on the determinants of urbanization, the developmental consequences of various trade rivalries, and the extent to which railroads increased the utilization of land and other resources. The basic issue posed by this paper is the feasibility of applying the analytical techniques of contemporary economics to the re-evaluation of one of the major questions in American history—the influence of railroads on economic growth.

II

The massive change in the geographical pattern of agricultural output during the nineteenth century has been a leading theme of American historiography. The meager data at the start of the century strongly suggest that the main sections of the nation were agriculturally self-sufficient.[11] By 1890 the North

[10] The relationship between the railroads and the growth of manufacturing industries is the subject of one of the other essays in *Railroads and American Economic Growth: Essays in Econometric History*.

[11] New England is the only notable departure from this pattern of complete, or virtually complete, agricultural self-sufficiency. Even here the deficiency in grain appears to have been relatively small. Thomas Jefferson, writing in 1808, estimated that "90,000 persons in Massachusetts subsisted on imported flour." This implies that, although deficient, the state's output of wheat was large enough to meet the needs of 80 per cent of the population. And the Massachusetts deficit was offset, at least in part, by the surpluses of Vermont and New Hampshire. Percy W. Bidwell and John I. Falconer, *History of Agriculture in the Northern United States, 1620–1860* (Washington: Carnegie Institution of Washington, 1925), p. 236; U.S. Census Bureau, *Historical Statistics*, p. 13.

Atlantic, South Atlantic, and South Central divisions, containing twenty-five states and 60 per cent of the nation's population, had become a deficit area in various agricultural commodities, particularly foodstuffs.[12] The greatest deficits appear in the North Atlantic region, that is, New England, New York, New Jersey, and Pennsylvania. In 1890 this division produced only 36 per cent of its estimated wheat consumption, 45 per cent of the corn requirement, 33 per cent of the beef requirement, and 27 per cent of the pork requirement.[13] The South produced a bigger share of its local needs, but it too had to look outside its borders for a significant part of its food supply. The local supply of foodstuffs in the deficit regions appears even more inadequate when the product needed for the export market is added to domestic consumption. In the North Atlantic division, for example, local production of wheat supplied only 24 per cent of the combined local and export requirement.[14]

In contrast to the decline in regional self-sufficiency in foodstuffs in the East and South, the North Central division of the country had become a great agricultural surplus area. Virgin territory at the start of the century, these twelve states were producing 71 per cent of the country's cereal grains by 1890 and were also the national center of cattle and swine production.[15] The magnitude of their surpluses is well illustrated by wheat. In the crop year 1890–1891, the twelve states produced 440,000,000 bushels. At five bushels per capita this was enough to feed 88,000,000 people—four times the region's population.[16] Approximately two thirds of the grain surplus of the North Central states was consumed in the East and South, and one third was exported to Europe and South America.

The process by which the agricultural surpluses of the Midwest were distributed can be divided into three stages. In the case of grain, the first stage was the concentration of the surplus in the great primary markets of the Midwest: Chicago, Minneapolis, Duluth, Milwaukee, Peoria, Kansas City, St. Louis, Cincinnati, Toledo, and Detroit. Over 80 per cent of the grain that entered into interregional trade was shipped from the farms to these cities.[17] The second stage involved the shipment of the grain from the primary markets to some ninety secondary markets in the East and South.[18] Among the most important

[12] U.S. Census Bureau, *Eleventh Census of the United States, Compendium,* Part I, p. 2.

[13] Estimated local requirements and supplies for the North Atlantic region (in thousands of tons) are:

	Wheat	Corn	Dressed Pork	Dressed Beef
Local requirement	2,507	4,956	297	381
Local supply	895	2,219	79	127
Deficit	1,612	2,737	218	254

The procedure followed in the construction of these estimates is discussed below, Section IV.

[14] Wheat exports from ports in the North Atlantic region were approximately 1,260,000 tons. St. Louis Merchants' Exchange, *Annual Report, 1890,* p. 168.

[15] U.S. Congress, House, *Report of the Industrial Commission on the Distribution of Farm Products,* Doc. No. 494, 56th Cong., 2nd Sess. (1901), p. 37.

[16] U.S. Statistics Bureau, *Wheat Crops of the United States, 1886–1906,* Bulletin No. 57 (1907), p. 18.

[17] See below, Section IV.

[18] *Ibid.,* Section IV.

secondary markets were New York City, Baltimore, Boston, Philadelphia, New Orleans, Albany (N.Y.), Portland (Me.), Pittsburgh, Birmingham, and Savannah. The third stage was the distribution of the grain within the territory immediately surrounding the secondary markets, and exportation abroad. The distributional pattern of meat products roughly paralleled that of grain. Perhaps the most important difference was that the first stage of the distribution process —concentration of livestock in the primary markets—was dominated by only four cities: Chicago, St. Louis, Kansas City, and Omaha.

With this background it is possible to give more definite meaning to the term "interregional distribution." For the purposes of this paper, "interregional distribution" is defined as the shipments of commodities from the primary markets of the Midwest to the secondary markets of the East and South. For all other shipments—from farms to primary markets and from secondary markets to the points immediately surrounding them—the term "intraregional distribution" is used. Similarly, the term "interregional railroad" is reserved for lines between primary and secondary markets, and the term "intraregional railroad" is used for all other lines. These terms are useful in distinguishing between the railroad in its role as a long-distance mover of agricultural products and its other functions.[19] It also helps to clarify the hypothesis to be examined in this paper, which can now be stated as follows:

> Rail connections between the primary and secondary markets of the nation were a necessary condition for the system of agricultural production and distribution that characterized the American economy of the last half of the nineteenth century. Moreover, the absence of such rail connections would have forced a regional pattern of agricultural production that would have significantly restricted the development of the American economy.

III

In the year 1890, a certain bundle of agricultural commodities was shipped from the primary markets to the secondary markets. The shipment occurred in a certain pattern, that is, with certain tonnages moving from each primary market city to each secondary market city. This pattern of shipments was carried out by some combination of rail, wagon, and water haulage at some definite cost. With enough data, one could determine both this cost and the alternative cost of shipping exactly the same bundle of goods from the primary to the secondary markets in exactly the same pattern without the railroad. The difference between these two amounts I call the social saving attributable to the railroad in the interregional distribution of agricultural products—or simply "the social saving." This difference is in fact larger than what the true social

---

[19] A progress report on the essay dealing with the impact of the railroad on the intraregional distribution of agricultural commodities ("The Social Saving Attributable to American Railroads in the Intraregional Distribution of Agricultural Products in 1890") was presented at the New York meeting of the Regional Science Association in December 1961.

saving would have been.[20] Forcing the pattern of shipments in the nonrail situation to conform to the pattern that actually existed is equivalent to the imposition of a restraint on society's freedom to adjust to a new technological situation. If society had had to ship interregionally by water and wagon without the railroad, it could have shifted agricultural production from the Midwest to the East and South, and shifted some productive factors out of agriculture altogether. Further, the cities entering our set of secondary markets and the tonnages handled by each were surely influenced by conditions peculiar to rail transportation; in the absence of the railroad some different cities would have entered this set, and the relative importance of those remaining would have changed. Adjustments of this sort would have reduced the loss in national income occasioned by the absence of the railroad, but estimates of their effects lie beyond the limits of tools and data. I propose, therefore, to use the social saving, as defined, as the objective standard for testing the hypothesis stated above.

With such a test, one cannot make definite statements about the relationship between the social saving and the geographic structure of agricultural production except for extreme values of the social saving as measured. If the calculation shows the saving to be zero, then obviously the absence of the interregional railroad would not have altered the existing productive pattern. On the other hand, if the social saving turns out to be very large, say on the order of magnitude of national income, it would be equally obvious that in the absence of the interregional railroad all production of surpluses in the Midwest would have ceased. For small differences in the cost differential, there is very little that can be said about the change in the geographic structure of output. It is theoretically conceivable that even a social saving as small as one fourth of 1 per cent of national income would have ended all or most surplus production in the North Central states. But this limitation in the proposed index is not quite so serious as it might seem. For the central concern here is with the influence of the railroad on the course of American economic development. The crucial question is not whether the absence of the railroad would have left agricultural production in a different regional pattern, but whether such a pattern would have significantly restricted economic growth. Sharp regional shifts in production associated with very small values of the social saving would be immaterial from this point of view. They would have served to demonstrate that many geographic patterns of production were consistent with a given rate of economic

[20] The definition of social saving used in this paper is the difference between the actual level of national income in 1890 and the level of national income that would have prevailed if the economy had made the most efficient possible transport adjustment to the absence of the interregional railroad. As noted in the text, this figure is larger than the more ideal social saving figure, which would take into account the production adjustments that would obtain with a different system of transportation.

In treating the differential in transportation costs as a differential in levels of national income, I am assuming that there would have been no obstacles to an adjustment to a nonrail situation. In other words, I am abstracting from market problems by assuming that national income would have dropped only because it took more productive resources to provide a given amount of transportation, and that all other productive resources would have remained fully employed. The relationship between the railroad and the demand for output is the subject of one of the other essays in my study (cf. note 10).

development, and the geographic pattern of agricultural production could be dismissed as a significant element in the growth of the American economy.

The social saving is calculated in my estimates for only one year, 1890. Yet the hypothesis to be tested refers to a period covering almost half a century. How sound an inference about the significance of the railroad's role with respect to agricultural development over such a period can be made on the basis of only one year's data? The answer depends on the relative efficiency of the railroad in 1890 as compared to earlier periods. If the railroad was relatively more efficient in 1890 than in any previous year, the social saving per unit of transportation in 1890 would have exceeded the saving per unit in all previous years. The available evidence suggests that this was indeed the case.[21] The four decades between 1850 and 1890 were ones of continuous advance in efficiency. The size, speed, and pulling capacity of the locomotive were steadily increased, as was the weight of the load a freight car could carry. At the same time, the scattered rail lines were integrated into a network, thus eliminating or reducing transshipment costs. Terminal facilities were expanded, and such important loading devices as the grain elevator were brought into general operation. Perhaps the most significant indication of the increase in the railroad's relative efficiency is the very considerable shift of heavy, low-value items away from water carriers. In 1852 boats and barges dominated the interregional transportation of these items, while in 1890 they were carried mainly by the railroad. Since the volume of agricultural commodities transported between regions had also increased over the period in question, it seems apparent that the social saving in 1890 exceeded in absolute amount the saving of previous years. While it is true that national income rose over the period, the amount of agricultural goods shipped interregionally appears to have risen just as rapidly. In the case of wheat, population and production figures suggest that local requirements in the deficit states were at least 1.1 million tons less in 1870 than they were in 1890. Export requirements were 1.8 million tons less. These figures indicate that the quantity shipped interregionally increased by 145 per cent over two decades —showing approximately the same rate of growth as real national income.[22] Thus, if it is shown that the social saving of 1890 was quite small relative to national income, the relationship would hold with equal force for the half-century preceding 1890.

The problem posed here would be trivial if the wagon were the only alternative to the railroad in interregional transportation. By 1890 the average cost of railroad transportation was less than a cent per ton-mile. On the other hand, the cost of wagon transportation was in the neighborhood of twenty-five cents per ton-mile.[23] According to estimates made here, approximately 7.7

[21] See, for example, J. L. Ringwalt, *Development of Transportation Systems in the United States* (Philadelphia: the author, 1888); Walter A. Lucas, ed., *100 Years of Steam Locomotives* (New York: Simmons-Boardman, 1958); Thomas C. Clarke, *et al., The American Railway: Its Construction, Development, Management and Appliances* (New York: Scribner & Sons, 1892); Baldwin Locomotive Works, *History of the Baldwin Locomotive Works, 1831 to 1907* (Philadelphia: Edgell Co., 1907).

[22] U.S. Statistics Bureau, *Wheat Crops of the U. S.*, p. 7; U.S. Census Bureau, *Historical Statistics*, pp. 12, 13, 139; U.S. Statistics Bureau, *Exports of Farm Products from the United States, 1851–1908*, Bulletin No. 75 (1910), pp. 44, 46.

[23] U.S. Statistics Bureau, *Changes in the Rates of Charge of Railway and Other Transportation Services*, Bulletin No. 15, rev. (1901), p. 14; U.S. Congress, House,

million tons of corn and 5.0 million tons of wheat entered into interregional transportation.[24] Taking the differential between rail and wagon transportation at twenty-five cents per ton-mile, the social saving involved in moving these 12.7 million tons one mile would have been $3,180,000. Assuming that on the average the corn and wheat shipped interregionally traveled nine hundred miles, the total social saving would have been $2,860,000,000. Even this figure is low, since wagon rates did not reflect the cost involved in road construction and maintenance. If account were taken of these and other omitted charges, and if a similar calculation were performed for livestock, the figure for the social saving would probably increase by 50 per cent, to four billion dollars, or more than one third of gross national product in 1890.[25] This magnitude exceeds Gallman's 1889 estimate of gross income originating in agriculture by 43 per cent.[26] Such a loss would have pushed the economy back two decades and probably cut 'the rate of investment by a third.[27] The calculation is very crude, of course, but there seems little doubt that the order of magnitude is correct.

The problem is not trivial, because water transportation was a practical alternative to the railroad in interregional transportation. A glance at a map will show that all of the primary market cities were on navigable waterways. Duluth, Milwaukee, Chicago, Toledo, and Detroit were on the Great Lakes; Omaha and Kansas City were on the Missouri; Minneapolis and St. Louis were on the Mississippi; Cincinnati was on the Ohio; and Peoria was on the Illinois River, midway between the Mississippi and Lake Michigan. The lakes, inland rivers, canals, and coastal waters directly linked the primary market cities to most of the secondary market cities. Of the forty-three most important secondary markets, thirty-two were located on navigable waters still in use in 1890. Seven were on waterways that had been forced into inactivity as a result of railroad competition, but which could have been used in the absence of the railroad. Only four cities were without direct water connection to the Midwest, and each of these was within a relatively short wagon haul of a major water artery.

The importance of a water-route alternative lies in the fact that on a per ton-mile basis, water rates were not only less than wagon rates but also less than railroad rates. The all-rail rate on wheat from Chicago to New York, for example, was about 0.52 cents per ton-mile, or nearly four times as much as the ton-mile rate by water.[28] This fact does not, of course, imply that the social cost or even the private cost on a given tonnage was less when shipped by water. Water routes were much more circuitous than rail routes, and the time in transit was considerably greater. Loss of cargo was more frequent. Terminal charges were higher. These and other problems raised the cost of water transportation to a point where shipments between most primary and most secondary markets

---

Report of the Industrial Commission on Agriculture and Agricultural Labor, Doc. 179, 57th Cong., 1st Sess. (1901), X, 690–91.

[24] See below, Section IV, and Table 6.

[25] U.S. Census Bureau, *Historical Statistics,* p. 139.

[26] Robert E. Gallman, "Commodity Output in the United States," *Trends in the American Economy in the Nineteenth Century.* Studies in Income and Wealth of the National Bureau of Economic Research, Vol. 24 (Princeton: Princeton Univ. Press, 1960), p. 47.

[27] This statement is based on the assumption of the relative constancy of the saving and capital-output ratios over the range of national income being considered here.

[28] U.S. Congress, House, *Distribution of Farm Products,* p. 142.

were cheaper by rail than by boat. What makes the problem interesting is that
the amount by which water costs exceeded railroad costs is far from obvious.
As has already been suggested, the massive switch from rail to water transportation by no means implies that the cost differential was large. Consider the
hypothetical case of a Chicago wheat shipper who made a profit of 10 per cent
on the Chicago price of wheat or nine cents per bushel on a price of ninety
cents. If the cost of shipment, all factors considered, was the same by both
water and rail, the shipper would be indifferent as to which form he used.
Suppose now that technological advances made it possible for the shipper to get
his bushel to market for two cents less than before. How strong an inducement
to switch from water to rail transportation would such a differential generate?
By reducing his cost two cents per bushel, the shipper could increase his profit
by 22 per cent. Clearly, the implication of this example is that a differential of
two cents per bushel would have created a very strong pressure to shift all
wheat that had been transported by water to railroads. Yet the social saving
involved in such a shift would have been just $3,300,000—much too small an
amount to prove the indispensability of the interregional railroad to American
economic growth.[29]

Until now, the discussion has been carried on as if all the agricultural
commodities that entered into interregional trade were to be included in the
estimate. In fact, the estimate will be based on only four commodities: wheat,
corn, beef, and pork. These four accounted for 42 per cent of income originating in agriculture in 1889.[30] Neglect of the other products is not so serious as it
first seems. What is important is not the share of wheat, corn, beef, and pork in
total output, but their share in that part of output which entered interregional
trade. Obviously, if none of the neglected 58 per cent of output moved
interregionally, the restriction is of no real consequence. The most important of
the omitted items is cotton, which represented 11 per cent of output.[31] But
relatively little cotton entered interregional transportation as here defined, and a
large part of the crop shipped interregionally was carried by water.[32] This is
illustrated by the distribution of the 1898–1899 crop. Of the output of that
season, 79 per cent was shipped from southern farms to southern seaport cities,
and carried from there by boat to Europe or to northern ports in the United
States. Another 13 per cent was consumed in the South. Hence, at most only 8
per cent or 225,000 tons of cotton (that is, 900,000 bales) could have entered
into interregional rail transportation.[33] But 225,000 tons is only 1.8 per cent of
the combined wheat-corn tonnage. The case of dairy products, which accounted
for 12 per cent of total product, is similar.[34] There are three main dairy
products: milk, butter, and cheese. Of these, milk was entirely an intraregional
product. Census data on butter and cheese production in the Midwest indicate
that the amount entering interregional trade was about 166,000 tons or 1.3 per

[29] The average wholesale price in Chicago of a bushel of wheat during 1890 was
eighty-seven cents. U.S. Census Bureau, *Historical Statistics*, p. 123.
[30] Gallman, "Commodity Output," pp. 46–48.
[31] *Ibid.*
[32] U.S. Congress, House, *Monthly Summary of Commerce and Finance*, Doc. 15,
Part 7, 56th Cong., 1st Sess. (1900), pp. 2545–2636.
[33] U.S. Congress, House, *Distribution of Farm Products*, p. 174.
[34] Gallman, "Commodity Output," pp. 46–48.

cent of the wheat-corn tonnage.[35] Again, while virtually all wool was transported from west to east, it was less than 1 per cent (closer to one half of 1 per
cent) of the wheat-corn tonnage. In short, neglected items probably do not
account for more than 10 per cent of the goods entering into interregional
trade, and would not justify the effort required to include them.

The most direct method of determining the social saving is to find the 1890
pattern of the shipments of the four commodities, and then estimate both the
actual cost of the pattern and the cost that would have obtained if the pattern
had been executed with only boats and wagons. This method requires the
following data: the amount of each commodity shipped from each primary
market, the amounts received by each secondary market, the routes over which
they were shipped, and the transportation costs by each medium. But not all of
these data are available. The total volume of shipments from each of the
primary markets can be determined, but not their destination and routes.
Receipts of the secondary markets can be estimated, but not the markets from
which these goods came. The impasse is, of course, only apparent. The gap in
the statistics can be bridged by linear programming techniques which yield the
solution at a cheaper cost in terms of data requirements. It seems likely,
incidentally, that in this case and in others as well mathematical techniques of
analysis can reduce the amount of information required to evaluate a given
hypothesis.[36] The linear programming problem is not solved in this paper, but a
short discussion will indicate its possibilities.

The actual method of analysis is simple. It involves a pair of linear programming models for each commodity. The procedure can be illustrated by considering the case of wheat. In 1890, a certain amount of wheat was shipped from the
Midwest to the secondary markets. The first linear programming model will find
the least cost of carrying the wheat from the primary to the secondary markets
without imposing any restraint on the means of transportation that can be used
—that is, allowing the shipments to be made in the cheapest manner, regardless
of the transportation medium. The second model imposes the restriction that
railroads cannot be used, and then finds the least cost of shipping the same
quantity of wheat from the primary to the secondary markets. Presumably these
two least-cost figures will differ; but this difference will reflect only the absence
of the railroad, since the quantities shipped from each of the primary markets
and the requirements of each of the secondary markets will be the same in both
models. The difference between the two least-cost figures is the estimate of social saving due to the use of the railroad in the interregional transportation of
wheat. The cost differential obtained from such a pair of linear programming
models will exceed the true social saving for the reasons specified in Section III,
above.

The water rates to be used in the second model must (with some exceptions)

---

[35] This estimate is based on data for 1899. U.S. Census Bureau, *Twelfth Census of
the United States, Agriculture,* Part I, pp. clxxxii–clxxxiii.

It should be remembered that the East did not run the heavy deficits on dairy
products that it did on grains and meats. New York and Pennsylvania were two of
the three largest producers of dairy products. U.S. Congress, House, *Distribution of
Farm Products,* pp. 268–69.

[36] Cf. Robert W. Fogel, *The Union Pacific Railroad: A Case in Premature
Enterprise* (Baltimore: The Johns Hopkins Press, 1960), especially pp. 81–85.

be those that actually prevailed in 1890. Even if water rates in 1890 equaled marginal costs, their use in the second model would introduce a bias, since these rates applied to a tonnage which is less than the amount specified in the model. To use them is equivalent to assuming that the marginal cost of water transportation was constant over the relevant range. This assumption probably accentuates the upward bias of the estimate. If all costs except the construction of canals and channels are considered variable, then it seems quite reasonable to assume that marginal costs were constant or declining. The basic operating unit in water transportation was the boat, and boat building may have been subject to economies of scale. In any case, most water routes were greatly under-utilized in 1890 and would have been under-utilized even if they had carried some considerable share of the additional interregional tonnage. Maintenance and other operating costs (for example, dredging, repairing locks, supplying water) would have increased only slightly with additional tonnage. To the extent that these tendencies were operative, the 1890 water rates impart an upward bias to the estimate of social saving.[37] Finally, it is important to note that the published 1890 rates did not reflect all of the costs involved in water transportation. In order to avoid introducing a downward bias into the calculations, it will be necessary to take account of such factors as spoilage, transit time and the unavailability of water routes for five months out of the year. The manner in which these factors will be dealt with is discussed in the final section of this paper.[38]

[37] Preliminary calculations suggest that the Erie Canal was the only waterway on which a bottleneck might have arisen. In 1890 the Erie carried 3,200,000 tons. Capacity at the time was 10,000,000 tons. It is possible that without the railroad, the agricultural products shifted to the canal would have exceeded 7,000,000 tons, thus taxing the capacity of the Erie. On the other hand, it appears that the most the additional tonnage could have been was 10,000,000 tons. However, 13,000,000 tons was well below the capacity of the New York State Barge Canal. If the linear programming solution leads to shipments which exceed the capacity of the Erie, I will apply the cost figures of the Barge Canal, adequately adjusted for differences in the price level, etc., and find a new solution. The use of Barge Canal rates would further buttress the assumption of constant or declining marginal costs in water transportation.

[38] As already noted, the estimate of the social saving in the interregional transportation of wheat, corn, pork, and beef requires a pair of linear programming models for each commodity. It might be thought that more than one pair of programs is required for each commodity. Wheat, for example, was carried east both as wheat and as flour. Pork was transported in an even wider variety of forms, including live swine, dressed pork, canned pork, mess pork, ham, bacon, etc. To the extent that each form of pork or wheat is considered a different product, one might be inclined to argue that a separate pair of models is required for each form. This costly complication can be avoided if (in the case, say, of wheat) the ratio of wheat to flour demanded in each secondary market was roughly the same, and with information on the quantities of wheat and flour shipped from each primary market. For then, knowing the wheat equivalent of a given quantity of flour as well as the cost of shipping each form, there is obviously some transportation cost at which X ton-miles of flour can be converted into Y ton-miles of wheat. The assumption of a constancy in the ratio of wheat to flour shipments tends to introduce an upward bias in the estimate of social saving. If the relative transportation costs of flour and wheat were the same by both forms of transportation, no bias would be introduced. However, the cost of shipping flour relative to the cost of shipping wheat was greater by water than by rail. Hence, in the absence of the railroad more wheat and less flour would have been shipped. However, the conversion of flour into a grain equivalent is based on the proportions of each that were actually shipped in 1890.

IV

Use of linear programming would reduce, but does not eliminate, the data problem. An enormous amount of information, some of which cannot be obtained directly, is needed. This section seeks to demonstrate how the necessary estimates can be derived from existing, but largely neglected, bodies of data. What is involved is the application of the estimating techniques usually reserved for the construction of national income accounts to a specific historical problem. It should be emphasized that the results presented below are tentative; many obvious adjustments have not yet been made. Nevertheless, the figures on tonnages entering interregional trade are sufficiently close to the truth for the use to which they are put in the final section of this paper. The problems encountered in translating a theoretically conceived estimate into an actual one can best be discussed by grouping them under four headings: shipments, requirements, railroad rates, and water rates.

Much has been written on the internal agricultural trade of the United States during the nineteenth century. In addition to Schmidt's series of articles in the *Iowa Journal of History and Politics* (1920–1922), there are the studies in the *Census of Agriculture* for 1860 and 1880, the biennial reports on internal commerce issued by the Treasury Department between 1876 and 1891, the volume on the distribution of agricultural products compiled by the Industrial Commission of 1900, and a series of articles which appeared in the *Monthly Summary of Commerce and Finance* in 1900.[39] All of these studies examined the system of primary markets, and they provide a considerable amount of data on the relative importance of the various cities. Surprisingly enough, however, these sources—whether considered separately or together—fail to yield enough data to compile a complete schedule of the shipments of grains and provisions for any year during the nineteenth century. Schmidt comes the closest, giving a schedule of the receipts of grains by primary markets for the year 1890. While there is a relationship between receipts and shipments, Schmidt does not indicate how to convert one into the other. An even more difficult problem is the absence of a complete series on shipments of provisions.

Fortunately, the desired data were relatively easy to obtain. Figures on the shipments of each of the various commodities were taken from the reports of the produce exchanges, the boards of trade or chambers of commerce of each of the primary market cities. These documents contain much highly reliable information, but except in the cases of Chicago, St. Louis, and New York, they have been badly neglected. Table 1 gives the preliminary figures on the shipments of corn and wheat from the primary markets.[40] The compilation of data on meat shipments is still in process.

The estimation of requirements of the secondary markets is much more

[39] The pattern of trade is summarized in Emory R. Johnson, *et al., History of Foreign and Domestic Commerce of the United States* (Washington: Carnegie Institution of Washington, 1915), Parts I and II.
[40] Table 1 includes only grain which was unloaded in the primary markets. Additional amounts were shipped through the primary markets without unloading. Obviously, these neglected amounts will eventually have to be included.

difficult than the shipments from the primary markets. The problem here is not merely the absence of a convenient series on the requirements of the various secondary markets; with the exception of such obvious places as New York, Baltimore, and New Orleans, there was no way of knowing which of the various cities of the East and South comprised the relevant set of secondary markets.

The first task, then, was to find some basis for dividing the deficit regions into marketing areas and for determining the cities which served as distributing centers of the area. The basic reference for making this division was a study of wholesale grocery territories carried out by the Department of Commerce in the

TABLE 1
SHIPMENTS OF CORN AND WHEAT FROM PRIMARY MARKETS, 1890
(thousands of tons)

Primary Market	Wheat [a]	Corn [b]
Chicago	950	2,536
Minneapolis	1,322	53
Duluth-Superior	793	41
Milwaukee	516	7
Peoria	35	211
Kansas City	181	505
St. Louis	522	1,218
Cincinnati	181	70
Toledo	309	463
Detroit	125	32
Total	4,934	5,136

[a] Includes flour converted into wheat at the rate: one barrel of flour equals 0.1430 tons of wheat.
[b] Includes corn meal converted into corn at the rate: one barrel of corn meal equals 0.1262 tons of corn.
Sources: See discussion in text, pp. 293, 301–02.

1920's.[41] This study divided the country into 183 trading areas. Each of the areas was composed of a group of counties served by a single city. The Boston trading area, for example, was determined by a survey of the wholesale firms situated in Boston, and comprised the six counties immediately surrounding the city.

Since grain and provisions were wholesale grocery products, the Department of Commerce survey provided an appropriate framework for the estimates. That the territories it defined pertained to the economy of the 1920's is not a crucial consideration. The basic rail network, especially in the East, was well established by 1890 and remained stable over the ensuing three decades. In the 1920's, trucks had not yet altered existing geographical patterns of trade. They

[41] U.S. Foreign and Domestic Commerce Bureau, *Atlas of Wholesale Grocery Territories,* Domestic Commerce Series, No. 7 (1927).

appear to have affected the size of the inventories carried by outlying retailers rather than the boundaries of the marketing areas. The impression that motor vehicles conformed to, rather than altered, pre-existing patterns is buttressed by a study of wholesale territories made in the late 1930's. The trading areas described by this survey were virtually identical with the earlier set.[42]

This demarcation of trading territories made it possible to devise a procedure for estimating the requirements of each territory by commodity. The area requirement for a given commodity was the difference between the area's total demand for the commodity (including exports) and the amount of the commodity supplied from within the area. Thus, to determine the requirements, estimates of both total demand and local supply were needed. The procedure for arriving at these estimates can be illustrated by the case of wheat.

The total demand for wheat in a given area consisted of two parts: the local demand and the export demand. The export demand was determined directly from export statistics provided by the Treasury Department; the local demand had to be estimated indirectly. The local demand for wheat was almost entirely for human consumption. For the country as a whole, about 10 per cent of the annual wheat crop was set aside for seed and about 2 per cent for animal feed.[43] However, the share of wheat demanded for seed in the deficit regions was considerably less than the national share, since wheat production was quite small. This was especially true in New England, where wheat used as seed was only one half of 1 per cent of the quantity consumed by humans. Similarly, the practice of feeding wheat to animals appears to have been practiced primarily in the areas of surplus production. Hence, the estimate of local demand was largely a matter of determining human consumption.

Total human consumption in a trading area was equal to per capita consumption multiplied by the population of the area. Statistics on area population were obtained from the 1890 census. The tentative estimate of average consumption by regions was calculated from a 1909 survey of urban workers conducted by the British Board of Trade.[44] Based on these data, the estimated per capita consumption of wheat is 4.80 bushels per year in the North and 4.70 bushels per year in the South. These figures do not include an adjustment for urban-rural differences in wheat consumption. However, it does not seem likely that the adjustment, when it is made, will significantly alter the results. A 1913–1914 survey indicates an average per capita wheat consumption of 5.08 bushels

[42] U.S. Foreign and Domestic Commerce Bureau, *Atlas of Wholesale Grocery Trading Areas,* Market Research Series, No. 19 (1938).

[43] U.S. Agriculture Dept., *Yearbook of Agriculture, 1923,* p. 1140; U.S. Statistics Bureau, *Wheat Crops of the U.S.,* p. 18.

[44] Great Britain, Board of Trade, *Cost of Living in American Towns* (London: H. M. Stationery Office, 1911); reprinted in U.S. Congress, Senate, Doc. 22, 62nd Cong., 1st Sess. [ser. no. 6082].

The data needed to convert statistics on bread, cake, and macaroni consumption into a wheat equivalent were obtained from U.S. Experiment Stations Office, *Bulletin,* Nos. 35 (1896) and 156 (1905); cf. U.S. Agriculture Dept., *Farmers Bulletin,* Nos. 23, 1450; William G. Panschar and Charles C. Slater, *Baking in America* (2 vols.; Evanston: Northwestern University Press, 1956).

A convenient review of various budget and diet studies is contained in Faith M. Williams and Carle C. Zimmerman, *Studies of Family Living in the United States and Other Countries,* U.S. Agriculture Dept., Miscellaneous Publications No. 223 (1935).

among 421 farm families in five North Atlantic states, and an average per capita consumption of 5.13 bushels among 149 families in three southern states.[45]

The local supply of wheat in a trading area was the sum of the annual local production of wheat and the supply (positive or negative) out of local inventories. The Department of Agriculture has published estimates of the production of wheat in 1890 by states but not by counties. However, county data were needed to determine local production in a trading area. The 1889 census production data by counties were multiplied by the 1890:1889 ratio of output for the state in which the particular county was located. Inventories of wheat were held by two main groups: wholesalers in the central cities of the trading areas, and farmers. It was not possible to obtain data on changes in the inventories of wholesalers. However, reports on the inventories in the hands of farmers on March 1, 1890 and March 1, 1891 were published by the Department of Agriculture.[46] It was therefore possible to estimate the change in farmers' inventories which, as a factor in supply, was probably more significant than the change in wholesalers' inventories.

The estimate of total wheat requirements of all the secondary markets in the deficit regions is given in Table 2. It is broken down into a local consumption deficit (obtained by subtracting local production and changes in farm inventories from my estimate of the local demand in each area) and foreign exports. The latter figure is based on the *Commerce and Navigation Reports* of the Treasury Department.

It is possible to test the procedure for estimating local requirements of wheat.

[45] W. C. Funk, *Value to Farm Families of Food, Fuel, and Use of House*, U.S. Agriculture Dept., Bulletin No. 410 (1916), pp. 5, 18. Funk's figures were in consumption per equivalent adult, with children twelve and under counted as one half of an adult. Funk's data were converted to a per capita basis on the assumption that the average proportion of persons twelve and under in all the families in his sample residing in a particular state was the same as that state's proportion of persons twelve and under in the rural population in 1910.

The finding that average wheat consumption in the South was about as large as in the North requires some explanation. The letters, journals, and diaries of noted travellers usually stressed the importance of corn in the southern diet. There is no necessary contradiction between the data culled from the budget studies and the commentaries of distinguished observers. Corn *was* the dominant breadstuff in the southern diet. During the period in question, southerners probably consumed an annual average of about six bushels per capita; the rest of the nation used about a bushel per person. One can easily see why travellers would stress the unique element of the southern diet, while passing over the fact that wheat was also consumed in sizeable quantities. Historians have inferred that since the quantity of corn used was unusually large, the consumption of wheat must have been quite small. The budget studies suggest another interpretation: while some corn was substituted for wheat, even larger quantities were substituted for other commodities, especially dairy products. Average caloric intake in the South also appears to have been greater than in the North [Edith Hawley, *Economics of Food Consumption* (New York: McGraw-Hill Book Co., 1932), p. 75].

A high rate of wheat consumption may have been characteristic of the South for the whole last half of the nineteenth century. Schmidt, in his series of studies on the grain trade, noted that the South imported an average of 10,000,000 bushels of wheat per year during the decade leading up to the Civil War. He estimated consumption of wheat for the year 1860 at 4.5 bushels per capita in the South, and placed the national at 5.5 bushels [Louis B. Schmidt, "The Internal Grain Trade of the United States, 1850–1860." *Iowa Journal of History and Politics*, XVIII, No. 1 (Jan. 1920), 101, 106].

[46] Baltimore Corn and Flour Exchange, *Annual Report, 1889, 1890*.

TABLE 2

ESTIMATED REQUIREMENTS OF SECONDARY MARKETS
(thousands of tons)

	1	*2*	*3*
	Local Consumption Deficits	*Exports*	*Total Requirements (Col. 1 plus Col. 2)*
Wheat [a]	3,099	1,916	5,015
Corn [b]	5,415	2,320	7,735
Dressed Pork	729	347	1,076
Dressed Beef	701	304	1,005

[a] Includes flour converted into wheat at the rate: one barrel of flour equals 0.1430 tons of wheat.
[b] Includes corn meal converted into corn at the rate: one barrel of corn meal equals 0.1262 tons of corn.
Sources: See discussion in text, Section IV.

Data are available in reports of local boards of trade on the receipts and foreign exports of the five largest secondary markets. Abstracting from inventory fluctuations, the receipts minus foreign exports will be equal to the local consumption requirement, providing that no wheat is grown locally. This method of estimation cannot be used for three of these largest marketing areas (New York, Philadelphia, and Baltimore) since they grew considerable quantities of wheat, an undetermined amount of which was processed at merchant mills for local consumption, and failed to enter into board of trade statistics. However, only 441 bushels of wheat were grown in the Boston trading area and 120 bushels in the New Orleans trading area, so virtually all the wheat demanded by these markets originated outside the trading areas and was recorded in commercial statistics. To eliminate inventory fluctuations, a nine-year average (centered on 1890) of receipts minus exports was taken. As shown in Table 3, local requirements estimated in this way tend to support the basic estimating procedure. The figure on the New Orleans marketing region (with 64 per cent of the

TABLE 3

A COMPARISON OF THE ESTIMATES OF THE LOCAL CONSUMPTION
DEFICITS OF WHEAT FOR TWO TRADING AREAS
(thousands of bushels)

	1	*2*	*3*
	Method One (local demand minus local supply)	*Method Two (nine-year average of receipts minus exports)*	*Column One as a per cent of Column Two*
Boston	6,996	7,215	97
New Orleans	3,504	3,070	114

population living in rural areas) lends support to the finding that wheat consumption in the South was considerably higher than has been generally realized.[47]

The procedure followed in estimating corn requirements was similar to that used in the case of wheat. The most important difference was that human consumption represented only 8 per cent of the total demand for corn. Estimates of average animal consumption per head were obtained for each of the main categories of animals.[48] But these averages were only available on a national basis. To the extent that there were regional differences in animal consumption of corn, the estimates tend to overstate requirements of some areas and understate those of others.

In estimating the local demand for beef and pork, national per capita disappearance figures were first obtained, following the method of the Department of Agriculture. The national figures were transformed into regional per capita estimates by using weights taken from a 1901 budget study conducted by the Bureau of Labor. Supply was determined in the manner described by Strauss and Bean.[49] Table 2 presents tentative estimates of the requirements of meat in the deficit areas. These figures will also have to be adjusted for urban-rural differences in consumption, but the adjustment will not significantly alter the aggregate meat requirement of the deficit areas. Funk's 1913–1914 study indicates that average consumption of beef and pork together in 570 northern and southern farm families was 157 pounds per equivalent adult. Department of Agriculture data indicate that for the population as a whole the corresponding 1913 figure was about 160 pounds per equivalent adult. However, since farm families ate considerably more pork than beef, the urban-rural adjustment will reduce the estimated amount of the aggregate beef deficit and increase the amount of the aggregate pork deficit in about the same proportions.[50]

Standard sources such as the *Annual Reports* of the Interstate Commerce Commission, the Treasury Department *Reports on Internal Commerce,* and the

[47] Baltimore Corn and Flour Exchange, *Annual Report, 1890–1894;* U.S. Census Bureau, *Eleventh Census of the United States, Population in the United States,* Part I, Tables 8 and 89; cf. note 45, above.

[48] These estimates are based on data for the years 1910–1914. The relevant figures are: horses, 27.811 bushels; hogs, 16.568; dairy cattle, 5.112; other cattle, 2.460; sheep, 0.413; poultry, 0.671. U.S. Agricultural Research Service, *Consumption of Feed by Livestock, 1909–1956,* Production Research Report No. 21 (Nov. 1958), pp. 28–31, 80.

[49] U.S. Agriculture Dept., *Consumption of Food in the United States, 1909–1952,* Agricultural Handbook No. 52 (1953); U.S. Labor Bureau, *Eighteenth Annual Report of the Commissioner of Labor, Cost of Living and Retail Food Prices* (1904). Frederick Strauss and Louis H. Bean, *Gross Farm Income and Indices of Farm Production and Prices in the United States, 1869–1937,* U.S. Agriculture Dept., Technical Bulletin No. 703 (1940).

[50] Funk, *Value to Farm Families of Food,* pp. 5, 20; U.S. Agriculture Dept., *Livestock and Meat Statistics,* Statistical Bulletin No. 230 (July 1958), pp. 283, 284; U.S. Agriculture Dept., *Consumption of Food in the U.S.,* p. 197. Two adjustments were made to the Agriculture Department data to make them comparable to Funk's: the per capita estimates were transformed to equivalent adult estimates on the assumption that the proportion of persons twelve years old and under was the same in 1913 as in 1914 (cf. note 45); edible offals were added to the Agriculture Department figures on beef and pork, since farm families generally consumed all parts of the animals they slaughtered [Carle C. Zimmerman, *Consumption and Standards of Living* (New York: D. Van Nostrand, 1936), pp. 81–82].

report of the Aldrich Committee provide information on less than 10 per cent of the relevant interregional routes. Fortunately, the tariffs filed with the Interstate Commerce Commission under the Interstate Commerce Act of 1887 are available. These files contain the published rates on all of the desired routes.

To the extent that rebating took place, published rates exceeded actual rates. State and Federal investigations produced voluminous reports and documents on the rebating problem. These contain data that can be used to adjust some of the published rates. Continuing research in archives may yield additional information. However, some procedure will have to be devised by which one can both check the reliability of the evidence in the public record and estimate rebates for which no direct evidence exists. One possible approach involves the use of published rates for a year like 1910, when rebating was rather generally eliminated. Abstracting from changes in the price level, the fall in average published rates between 1890 and 1910 is attributable to two factors: the elimination of rebating and the decline in actual rates.[51] Therefore, the differences between average published rates in 1890 and in 1910 (adjusted for changes in the price level) are the most that the average rebate could have been. Thus, by multiplying appropriate ratios of average 1910 rates to 1890 rates by the actual 1890 rates, one obtains an estimate of the least that average actual rates could have been in 1890.

Water transportation was dominated by three main routes: the Great Lakes and Erie Canal route, the Mississippi route and the intracoastal route. Every movement from a primary to a secondary market can be divided into a movement along one or more of these lines, plus an additional short movement along some other body of water. Rates on the main water highways are available in board of trade reports, tariffs filed with the Interstate Commerce Commission, and other documents. Thus only a small part of the charge to a shipper will have to be estimated. Moreover, possible deviations between published and actual water rates are less troublesome. To the extent that such deviations existed, the upward bias of the estimated social saving will be further accentuated.

V

There is no reliable way to predict the outcome of the linear programming problems. In computations of this sort, surprises are common. Even if all the required data were compiled, it would be difficult to anticipate such results as the efficient patterns of trade in the rail and nonrail situations or the breakdown of the social saving by products, routes, and regions. However, a crude estimate

[51] That actual rates declined between 1890 and 1910 is suggested by the fact that average freight revenue per ton-mile (adjusted for changes in the price level) declined by over a third (U.S. Census Bureau, *Historical Statistics*, p. 43). Of course, the decline in average revenue could have taken place even though actual rates were rising if there had been major changes in the composition of freight traffic. However, the available data suggest that the composition and pattern of traffic remained relatively stable during this period. Cf. data in U.S. Census Bureau, *Eleventh Census of the United States: 1890, Transportation*, Part I, and Interstate Commerce Commission, *Twenty-Fourth Annual Report on the Statistics of Railways in the United States for the Year Ending June 30, 1911* (Washington: Govt. Printing Office, 1913).

of the *aggregate* social saving is possible. The calculation that follows involves guesses about average transit distances and average freight rates by both water and rail—averages that cannot reliably be calculated until the linear programming problems are solved. Despite its crudity, the calculation is useful for two reasons. First, it provides a convenient format for demonstrating the ways in which a number of costs—costs that have been considered unquantifiable—can be quantified. Second, it provides a rough idea of the magnitude of the aggregate social saving that one can expect to obtain from the models.

The starting point of the calculation is the difference between the average ton-mile transportation rate by water and by rail. Various experts on transportation have pointed out that water rates were generally less than railroad rates.[52] Thus, over the route from Chicago to New York, the average all-rail rate on wheat in 1890 was 0.523 cents per ton-mile while the average all-water rate was 0.139 cents per ton-mile.[53] Casual examination of the available data suggests that these figures are approximately the same as those applying to all grains on this and other routes.[54] Hence, for the purposes of calculation it will be arbitrarily assumed that the New York to Chicago all-water rate per ton-mile on wheat equaled the average all-water rate (per ton-mile) on all grains over all the relevant routes. The assumption to be made on the all-rail rate is symmetric.

For the crude calculation of the social saving, the average national rate at which grain was actually transported in 1890 is needed. This actual rate must have been less than the all-rail rate. Not all grains shipped interregionally were carried exclusively by rail. Considerable quantities were shipped by a combination of rail and water or completely by water. In contrast to the 0.523 cents all-rail rate per ton-mile on wheat transported from Chicago to New York, the lake-and-rail charge was 0.229 cents, and the lake-and-canal charge was 0.186 cents.[55] The average of these three rates, weighted by the quantities of grain shipped under each one, is 0.434 cents (see Table 4). This last figure will be taken as the "actual" national average rate on grains per ton-mile in 1890. In passing, it may be noted that the adjustment produced a figure which is less than a mill below the all-rail rate.

In the case of meat and livestock products, the calculation is based on the St. Louis to New Orleans rates on pork. The all-rail rate was 1.07 cents per ton-mile and the all-water rate was 0.45 cents.[56] Again, these rates are comparable to those that prevailed on other meat products shipped on this and other

[52] See, for example, Jenks, "Railroads as an Economic Force," pp. 12–13; and Harold G. Moulton, *Waterways versus Railways* (Boston: Houghton Mifflin, 1912), pp. 12–13, 33–38.

[53] U.S. Congress, House, *Distribution of Farm Products*, p. 142.

[54] See, for example, data in U.S. Statistics Bureau, *Changes in Rates;* U.S. Congress, Senate, *Preliminary Report of the Inland Waterways Commission;* and Louisville and Nashville Railroad, *Southwestern Freight Tariff*, No. 9 (Nov. 16, 1890).

[55] The lake-and-canal rate differs from the all-water rate cited in the previous paragraph by 0.047 cents because the former includes transshipment and insurance charges. The lake-and-rail rate includes insurance but not transshipment costs, since the ex-lake rail rates included transshipping charges. Cf. notes to Table 4.

[56] The water rate is the highest that prevailed during the 1890 season of navigation. U.S. Congress, Senate, *Preliminary Report of the Inland Waterways Commission*, p. 343. The rail rate is taken from Louisville and Nashville Railroad, *Southwestern Freight Tariff*, No. 10.

TABLE 4

ESTIMATE OF THE AVERAGE ACTUAL RATE

	1	*2*	*3*
Type of Transportation	*Rate per Ton-Mile (cents)*	*Wheat and Corn (millions of tons)*	*Col. 1 × Col. 2 (cents)*
1. All-water	0.186	1.254	0.2332
2. Water and rail	0.229	2.423	0.5549
3. All-rail	0.523	9.073	4.7452
4. Sum of columns		12.750	5.5333
5. Average actual rate in cents per ton-mile (sum of Col. 3 ÷ sum of Col. 2)			0.434

Sources and Notes:

Column 1. The three rates were determined by taking the Chicago-to-New York charges on wheat (including transshipment and insurance costs) and dividing each charge by the appropriate distance. U.S. Congress, House, *Distribution of Farm Products*, VI, 142; George G. Tunell, "The Diversion of the Flour and Grain Traffic from the Great Lakes to the Railroad," *Journal of Political Economy*, V, No. 3 (June 1897), 345; U.S. Congress, Senate, Select Committee on Transportation—Routes to the Seaboard, *Report No. 307*, Part 1, 43rd Cong., 1st Sess., p. 17; below, Table 6.

Column 2, Line 1. This is the total amount of wheat (including the grain equivalent of flour) and corn shipped by canal from the lake ports of Buffalo, Oswego and Tonawanda plus the quantity of the same commodities shipped by river from St. Louis. The amount of flour shipped from St. Louis by boat was obtained by multiplying the proportion of flour shipped by river in 1898 by the total 1890 shipments of flour. *Line 2* is the amount of wheat (including the grain equivalent of flour) and corn received at the lake ports of Erie, Buffalo, Oswego and Ogdensburg minus the grain shipped from lake ports by canal. *Line 3* is the total quantity of wheat and corn shipped interregionally minus lines 1 and 2. Buffalo Merchants' Exchange, *Annual Report, 1891*, pp. 71, 106, 108, 109, 112; U.S. Congress, House, *Report on the Internal Commerce of the United States for the Year 1891*, Executive Doc. No. 6, Part 2, 52nd Cong., 1st Sess., XXVI; U.S. Statistics Bureau, *Monthly Summary of Commerce and Finance*, 7 (Jan. 1900), pp. 2006–7, 2009; U.S. Congress, Senate, *Wholesale Prices, Wages, and Transportation (Aldrich Report)*, Report No. 1394, Part 1, 52nd Cong., 2nd Sess., p. 558; Table 6, below.

routes. Furthermore, since the quantity of meat shipped by water was a small part of the total interregional tonnage, no further adjustment need be made; that is, the all-rail rate on pork will be assumed to equal the actual average rate on all meat products.

The quantity of corn, wheat, pork, and beef shipped interregionally in 1890 was approximately equal to the net local deficit of the trading areas plus net exports.[57] Assuming that half of the meat products was shipped as livestock and half as dressed, the amount transported interregionally was 15,700,000 tons.[58]

Estimates of average distances are based on a sample of thirty routes (pairs

[57] See above, Table 2.
[58] A breakdown of this figure is given in Table 6.

of cities). The sample was randomly drawn from a population of 875 routes. The average rail distance in the sample was 926 miles, and the average water distance was 1,574 miles.[59] Since only small amounts of meat were transported by water, 926 miles will be assumed to be the average distance over which meats were actually shipped in 1890. In the case of grains, an adjustment should be made for the tonnage that was carried partly or wholly by water. The adjusted figure, 1,044 miles, represents the estimate of the average distance over which grains were actually shipped in 1890.[60]

If rates and ton-miles were the only elements entering into the cost of transportation, it would have been cheaper to have shipped interregionally by water than by rail. As shown in Table 5, the social saving calculated on the basis of these elements is negative by about $38,000,000. This odd result is not difficult to explain. While the estimated actual cost of transportation includes virtually all relevant items, the estimated cost of water transportation does not. In calculating the cost of shipping without the railroad, one must account for six neglected items of cost not reflected in the first approximation: cargo losses in transit, transshipment costs, wagon haulage from water points to secondary markets not on water routes, the cost resulting from the time lost when using a slow medium of transportation, the cost of being unable to use water routes for five months out of the year, and finally, capital costs not reflected in water rates.

When account is taken of the six neglected costs, the loss attributable to the railroad will be transformed into a saving. How big must the neglected costs be to produce a positive saving of 1 per cent of national income? In 1890 gross national product was about $12,000,000,000, and 1 per cent of this amount is $120,000,000. Without the neglected costs, interregional shipment of the four commodities would have been $38,000,000 cheaper by water than by rail. Consequently, in order to reach a social saving of 1 per cent of gross national product, the neglected costs will have to be approximately $158,000,000.

The literature on the interregional transportation of agricultural products indicates that cargo losses were greater on water shipments than on rail shipments. Insurance rates can be used to estimate the cost of these water transit losses. Since the average value of a loss on a given shipment was approximately equal to the insurance charge on the shipment, the total value of cargo losses in the absence of the railroad would have been approximately equal

[59] The averages are simple arithmetic means.
Water distances between the points in the sample are an average of 70 per cent longer than rail distances. This suggests a somewhat greater degree of circuity in water transportation than was indicated by the study of the Bureau of Railway Economics, *An Economic Survey of Inland Waterway Transportation in the United States,* Special Series, No. 57 (Washington: Bureau of Railway Economics, 1930).
[60] The adjustment was made in the following manner:

	1	2	3
Method	Distance (miles)	Tons of Grain (millions)	Millions of Ton-Miles (Col. 1 × Col. 2)
1. All-rail	926	9.073	8,402
2. Water-and-rail	1,302	2.423	3,155
3. All-water	1,398	1.254	1,753
4. Totals		12.750	13,310
5. Average distance (sum of Col. 3 ÷ sum of Col. 2)			1,044 miles

TABLE 5

First Approximation of the Social Saving

Commodity	1 Quantity Shipped (millions of tons)	2 Millions of Ton-Miles of Water Transportation (Col. 1 × 1,574 miles)	3 Water Rate per Ton-Mile (dollars)	4 Cost of Water Transportation in Millions of Dollars (Col. 2 × Col. 3)	5 Average Actual Distance (miles)	6 Millions of Ton-Miles of Actual Transportation (Col. 1 × Col. 5)	7 Actual Rate per Ton-Mile (dollars)	8 Cost of Actual Transportation in Millions of Dollars (Col. 6 × Col. 7)	9 Social Saving in Millions of Dollars (Col. 4 − Col. 8)
Meats	3.000	4,722	.00451	21.296	926	2,778	.01071	29.752	−8.456
Grains	12.750	20,069	.00139	27.896	1,044	13,311	.00434	57.770	−29.874
Totals	15.750	24,791		49.192		16,089		87.522	−38.330

Sources: See notes to Tables 4, 6 and text, Section V.

TABLE 6

ESTIMATED COST OF INSURANCE

	1	2	3	4	5
	Tons Shipped Interregionally	Price per Ton	Value (Col. 1 × Col. 2)	Insurance Rate as a Proportion of Value	Cost of Insurance (Col. 3 × Col. 4)
1. Cattle	949,000	$ 97	$ 92,100,000	.01	$ 921,000
2. Dressed beef	503,000	138	69,400,000	.01	694,000
3. Hogs	1,008,000	79	79,600,000	.01	796,000
4. Dressed pork	538,000	110	59,200,000	.01	592,000
5. Corn	7,735,000	13	100,600,000	.01	1,006,000
6. Wheat	5,015,000	30	150,500,000	.01	1,505,000
7. Totals	15,748,000		551,400,000		5,514,000

Sources and Notes:

Column 1. Estimates of tons shipped interregionally are based on the local net deficits of the secondary markets plus exports. In the case of meats, it was assumed that half the deficit was shipped as dressed meats and half as livestock. Dressed pork was converted into a live weight equivalent at the rate of one pound of dressed pork equal to 1.874 pounds of live weight; for beef the conversion factor was one pound of dressed beef equal to 1.887 pounds of live weight. See above, Section IV.

Column 2. The figures cited are the average Chicago wholesale prices except for dressed meats, which are New York quotations. In the case of wheat and corn, the prices represent unweighted averages of the twelve average monthly prices, with averages of missing months determined by linear interpolation. George K. Holmes, *Meat Situation in the United States*, U.S. Agriculture Dept., Departmental Report No. 109, Part I, pp. 289–98; U.S. Congress, Senate, *Aldrich Report*, Part 2, p. 10; U.S. Census Bureau, *Historical Statistics of the United States, Colonial Times to 1957* (Washington: Govt. Printing Office, 1960), p. 123.

Column 4. Insurance rates varied with the distance of a shipment and the route. In 1850, average insurance rates on the Mississippi and Ohio were about 1 per cent of the value of the cargo per thousand miles. In 1870, the rate on the Great Lakes was about the same. However, scattered data suggest that in subsequent years marine insurance rates fell sharply. By the 1890's, insurance on the Lakes was 0.3 per cent per thousand miles. A decade later the rate on cargo from Pittsburgh to New Orleans was about 0.7 cents per thousand miles, while the intracoastal rate was about 0.1 cents. In the absence of the railroad perhaps half of the tonnage would have been carried over the Lakes on intracoastal routes. In view of the foregoing, it seems reasonable to assume that in the absence of the railroad, the average insurance rate probably would not have exceeded the later Mississippi rate, that is, 0.7 cents per thousand miles or approximately 1 per cent for 1,574 miles. Louis C. Hunter, *Steamboats in Western Rivers* (Cambridge: Harvard Univ. Press, 1949), pp. 368–69; U.S. Congress, Senate, Select Committee on Transportation—Routes to the Seaboard, *Report No. 307*, Part 1, p. 17; George J. Tunell, "The Diversion of Flour and Grain Traffic," p. 345; U.S. Congress, Senate, *Preliminary Report of the Inland Waterways Commission*, pp. 332–33.

to the average insurance charge on a water shipment multiplied by the total value of the goods transported interregionally. Moreover, since railroad rates included insurance, this figure would also represent the neglected cost of cargo losses. The calculation is shown in Table 6. The cost of insurance (cost of cargo losses) in the absence of the railroad would have been approximately $6,000,000. Subtracting this figure from $158,000,000, there is left $152,000,000 to cover the remaining costs.

Transshipping costs were incurred whenever it became necessary to switch a cargo from one type of vessel to another. Grain shipped from Chicago to New York, for example, was transferred at Buffalo from lake steamers to canal barges. In the absence of the railroad there would probably have been an average of two transshipments on each ton carried from a primary to a secondary market. At a cost of fifty cents per ton per transshipment, transshipping charges on the grain and meat products in question would have been $16,000,000.[61] Subtracting this amount from $152,000,000, there is left $136,000,000 to cover the remaining costs.

The two indirect costs of water transportation most frequently cited are the cost of time lost in shipping by water and the cost of being unable to use water routes for about five months out of each year. Arguments based on the time factor and the limited season of navigation have been decisive in ruling out the possibility that water transportation could have been a good substitute for the railroad. Once invoked, these arguments are invincible, since the costs involved seem to be limited only by the intuition of the disputants. Without a means of quantifying the cost of time and the cost of the limited season of navigation, the hypothesis posed in this paper cannot be tested.

The key to quantifying the cost of the time that would have been lost in water transportation is the nexus between time and inventories. If entrepreneurs could replace goods the instant they were sold, they would, *ceteris paribus,* carry zero inventories. Inventories are necessary to bridge the gap of time required to deliver a commodity from its supply source to a given point. If, on the average, interregional shipments of agricultural commodities required a month more by water than by rail, it would have been possible to compensate for the time lost through an inventory increase in the secondary markets equal to one twelfth of annual shipments. Hence the cost of the time lost in using water transportation was the 1890 cost of carrying such an additional inventory.[62]

[61] The cost of transshipping meat products appears to have been included in the water rate. U.S. Corporations Bureau, *Report of the Commissioner of Corporations on Transportation by Water in the United States.* Part III, *Water Terminals* (Washington: Govt. Printing Office, 1910), pp. 329–34.

[62] The assumption that boats took an average of a month longer than trains to provide the same transportation service introduces an upward bias into the estimate of the cost of time. The minimum time required by *express* freight trains on the run from New York to Chicago in 1896 was seventy-five hours, indicating an average speed of twelve miles per hour (Joint Traffic Association, *Proceedings of the Board of Managers, 1896,* p. 627). About the same time, boats on the Great Lakes made the round trip from Duluth to Buffalo in nine days, indicating an average speed of over nine miles per hour [Joseph E. Ransdell, "Legislative Program Congress Should Adopt for Improvement of American Waterways," *Annals* of the American Academy of Political and Social Science, XXXI, No. 1 (Jan. 1908), 38]. In 1912 the average speed of freight boats on rivers was about seven miles per hour. (U.S. Agriculture Dept., *Bulletin No. 74,* p. 36.) These facts suggest that the average time advantage of railroads in the interregional transportation of agricultural products was less than a

The problems inherent in the limited season of water transportation could also have been met by an increase in inventory. Since water routes were closed for five twelfths of the year, I will assume that the absence of railroads would have increased the inventories of agricultural commodities held in secondary markets by five twelfths of the annual interregional shipment. It should be noted that this assumption overstates the additional inventory requirement. Abstracting from risk considerations, the limited season of navigation would— at least with respect to grains—have had no effect on the inventory requirements of the nation. A crop once harvested was placed in inventory and drawn down throughout the year. A shorter transportation season would only have affected the way in which a fixed total inventory was divided between the Midwest and the secondary markets. Exclusive reliance on water routes would have increased the inventory total only if risk factors were operative. Under conditions of risk, the availability of a central depository reduces the size of the stock that must be held by a given set of cities. Nevertheless, the five-twelfths assumption will be adopted to simplify the computation.

The cost of time lost in water transportation and the limited season of navigation would thus not have exceeded the cost incurred in carrying an inventory equal to one half of the annual amount of agricultural products that were transported interregionally. As shown in Table 6, the Chicago wholesale value of the corn, wheat, beef, and pork shipped interregionally was about $550,000,000. Another $43,000,000 should be added to approximate wholesale value at seaboard.[63] Hence, in the absence of the railroad, the limited season of navigation would have required an increase in the value of inventories of about $297,000,000. The cost of carrying such an additional inventory would have included the forgone opportunity of investing the same amount elsewhere. If it is assumed that on the average capital earned 6 per cent in 1890, the alternative cost of the investment in additional inventory would have been about $18,000,000 per year. To this, one must add about $30,000,000 for storage charges.[64] Subtracting $48,000,000 from $136,000,000 leaves $88,000,000 to account for the two remaining costs.

Cities receiving approximately 10 per cent of the interregional shipments were not on water routes. If these cities were an average of fifty miles from the

---

week. Some observers argued that in the transportation of bulk items boats actually provided quicker service than trains (Ransdell, "Improvement of American Waterways," p. 38).

[63] To the Chicago values shown in Table 6, $2.83 per ton was added for wheat, $2.59 for corn, $4.00 for cattle and $5.00 for hogs. Dressed meats in Table 6 are quoted at the New York prices, so no further adjustment was necessary. U.S. Congress, Senate, *Aldrich Report,* I, 518–19, 526.

[64] The cost of elevating and storing grain in Buffalo from November 10 to the opening of navigation (about five months) was two cents per bushel or .4 cents per bushel per month (Buffalo Merchants' Exchange, *Annual Report, 1890,* pp. 88–89). At this rate, storage charges on the six months of additional inventory of wheat and corn would have amounted to $5,300,000. In 1910 cold storage rates were $4.96 per ton per month on beef and $4.70 on pork (U.S. Agriculture Dept., *Statistical Bulletin No. 493,* p. 44). At these rates, the additional storage charges on beef and pork would have been $31,000,000 in dollars of 1910 or $25,000,000 in dollars of 1890. However, cold storage would have been the most costly way of maintaining the additional inventory of meat. It would have been cheaper to store meat in the East by sending live animals to eastern feeders. In this case, the cost of storage would have been essentially the cost of shipping more feed but smaller animals.

nearest water point, the cost of wagon haulage (at twenty-five cents per ton-mile) would have been $20,000,000. Subtracting this amount from $88,000,000 leaves $68,000,000 to account for the last item—neglected capital charges.

Water rates failed to reflect capital costs to the extent that rivers and canals were improved or built by the government and financed out of taxes rather than tolls. If a complete statement of these uncompensated expenditures were available, one could easily estimate the neglected capital costs. Data exist on capital expenditures for water transportation, but much work remains to be done to develop a consistent and complete statement of uncompensated investment. Federal expenditures on river improvement over the years between 1802 and 1890 appear to have amounted to $111,000,000. Canals still in operation in 1890 were built at a cost of $155,000,000. In addition, there were abandoned canals which would have been in use in the absence of the interregional railroad. These were built at a cost of $27,000,000.[65] The total of the three items, $293,000,000, may either overstate or understate the uncompensated capital involved in water transportation. Assuming that the various upward and downward biases, the omitted items and the double counting, cancel each other out, at an interest rate of 6 per cent the neglected capital costs would have been about $18,000,000—$50,000,000 short of the amount required to bring the social saving to 1 per cent of gross national product.[66]

Thus casual examination of the available data suggests that the social saving attributable to the railroad in the interregional transportation of agricultural products was about 1 per cent of national income.[67] The calculation is, of course, subject to considerable error; but there are grounds for having confidence in the result. Four of the estimates—those dealing with transshipment,

[65] U.S. Congress, Senate, *Preliminary Report of the Inland Waterways Commission,* pp. 180–81, 193–97, 202–3, 205–9; cf. U.S. Census Bureau, *Transportation by Water,* pp. 44–46.

[66] The preceding calculation may be summarized as follows:

First approximation of social saving	$ −38,000,000
Neglected cargo losses	6,000,000
Transshipping costs	16,000,000
Additional inventory costs	48,000,000
Supplementary wagon haulage	20,000,000
Neglected capital costs	18,000,000
Total	$ 70,000,000

[67] How significant is a social saving of 1 per cent of national income? This question cannot be answered without making further assumptions as to how the economy would have adjusted to the absence of the railroad. One consequence of the absence of the railroad would have been a rise in the seaboard prices of agricultural commodities. This could have had a significant effect on the U.S. balance of trade. Similarly, a shift from railroad to water and wagon transportation may have been a shift from a more to a less capital-intensive activity. Such a change might have aggravated market problems in the capital goods sector. On the other hand, it might have increased the demand for labor.

If one abstracts from these essentially Keynesian issues of insufficient demand and focuses on the economy's production possibilities, it is possible to interpret the social saving in a fairly simple way. Assuming that the marginal aggregate savings and capital-output ratios would have been what in fact they were when national income was 99 per cent of the 1890 level, the absence of the interregional railroad would have retarded the development of the economy by about three months.

wagon haulage, time lost, and the limited season of navigation—probably overstate the actual cost of water transportation. While the estimates of some of the other items may be too low, it does not seem likely that the errors are large enough to alter substantially the magnitude of the indicated social saving. Suppose, for example, that railroad rates on a ton-mile basis were not above water rates, as has generally been assumed. If the initial water-rail rate differential had actually been zero on all commodities, the elimination of this error would increase the estimated social saving by only $56,000,000. Indeed, if railroad rates are assumed to have been zero, the social saving would rise to only $158,000,000, or about 1.3 per cent of gross national product.

This paper has focused on one aspect of the influence of the railroad on American economic development. A small aggregate social saving in the interregional transportion of agricultural products would not prove that the railroad was unimportant in American development. Conclusions regarding the over-all impact of the railroad require, as Simon Kuznets has suggested, a thorough examination of all the avenues through which the most celebrated innovation of the nineteenth century may have exercised a strategic influence on economic growth. In this connection it is important to re-emphasize that the linear programming models referred to earlier will do more than refine the crude estimate of the aggregate social saving. They will provide information on efficient patterns of agricultural distribution both in the rail and nonrail situations, as well as breakdowns of the interregional social saving by regions and commodities. This type of information, supplemented by similar data on intraregional transportation, will facilitate a re-evaluation of such questions as the developmental significance of various commercial rivalries (for example, the triumph of Chicago over St. Louis and Cincinnati), the determinants of the geographic pattern of urbanization, and the extent to which the railroad promoted a more efficient utilization of certain productive resources.

17

ROBERT P. SWIERENGA *

Land Speculator "Profits" Reconsidered: Central Iowa as a Test Case

Allan G. Bogue and Margaret B. Bogue in 1957 first developed a formal analytic model to examine the profitability of land specula- tion. The results were exceptionally rich and justly so, considering that the authors laboriously hand-tabulated all their data. Because of the technical handicaps and limited data, the Bogues recognized the provisional nature of their findings and called for "careful studies of returns from frontier land speculation on an area basis." This sug- gestion and the availability of central Iowa land records did much to shape the following study, although the project would not have been feasible without the electronic computer. The study shows that large- scale investments in government land in central Iowa proved to be immensely profitable, upwards of 50 per cent annually in the ante- bellum decade.

Since Iowa land is not typical, perhaps the fortunes of the large land investors in the Hawkeye State were not typical either. The state contains one fourth of the richest agricultural land in the nation, yet the government's policy of flooding the land market virtually ensured

Robert P. Swierenga, "Land Speculator 'Profits' Reconsidered: Central Iowa as a Test Case," *Journal of Economic History*, XXVI (March, 1966), 1–28. Reprinted with permission of the Economic History Association.

* Research funds for this study were provided by counsel for the present Sac and Fox and Iowa Indian tribes, for which the author gives grateful acknowledgment. He is also indebted to Allan G. Bogue of the University of Wisconsin for assistance in formulating the theoretical framework and for a critical reading of the draft. Robert R. Dykstra of the University of Iowa also provided valuable editorial assistance. Gerard P. Weeg, director of the University of Iowa computer center, kindly formu- lated the polynomial equation to compute rates of return, which industrial engineer- ing graduate student James Thoreson transposed into Fortran IV computer language for the University IBM 7044 digital computer.

*that the auction price would not climb much above the statutory
minimum of $1.25 per acre. This was far below actual market value
at the time and guaranteed a high profit rate on a short-term speculation. Whether Iowa investors benefited from the largess of the government more than speculators in government lands elsewhere in the
nineteenth century can only be determined by other area-wide studies
of original land entry records.*

"S H O W   U S a non-resident who has made money speculating in western
land," wrote a frontier newspaper editor in 1850, "and we will show you a rare
bird, more rare by far than a successful gold hunter." [1] Despite this warning and
dozens like it, thousands of investors ventured surplus or borrowed funds on
frontier land throughout the nineteenth century. Many, in fact, jumped from
one frontier to the next on the heels of government surveyors and land officers.
Either these businessmen were gluttons for punishment, or speculating in
government land was far more rewarding than some contemporaries were
willing to admit.

A growing number of twentieth-century students of American economic
development have turned their attention to this question of " 'Profits' and the
Frontier Land Speculator," to use the title of the pathbreaking article by Allan
G. Bogue and Margaret B. Bogue, published in this journal in 1957.[2] In their
perusal of the literature the Bogues found that most researchers neither used
adequate mathematical techniques to measure returns nor gave sufficient weight
to the costs involved in land ownership. Few, indeed, even explained their
methods of computation. Of those that did, most ignored such fixed costs as
agents' commissions for buying and selling, land office fees, and taxes. More
important, none attempted to calculate an annual rate of return per dollar
invested. Nearly all of the analysts, the authors also reported, agreed that
speculation in frontier lands was generally a losing proposition mitigated only
by the occasional bonanza.[3]

After outlining the inadequacies of previous studies, the Bogues demonstrated
their new concept—the annual rate of return per dollar invested—in an analysis
of 77,500 acres of agricultural land in east-central Illinois and eastern Nebraska. Although their data suggested that profits may have been greater than
previous students have allowed, they warned against any generalized conclusions on such scattered evidence as they and earlier scholars had amassed.
Rather, they challenged the profession to make careful studies of returns from
frontier land investments on an area basis.[4]

[1] Madison (Wisc.) *Argus,* cited in Benjamin H. Hibbard, *A History of the Public
Land Policies* (New York: Macmillan, 1924), p. 221.
[2] *Journal of Economic History,* XVII, No. 1 (Mar. 1957), 1–24. The reader is
referred to this article for a resumé of much of the literature on the subject.
[3] *Ibid.,* 2–7.
[4] *Ibid.,* 24.

Prior to the age of the electrical computer, scholars understandably shunned the herculean task of undertaking area studies with sufficiently large samples and the requisite theoretical and mathematical precision.[5] With the increasing availability of data computation facilities, however, economic historians are now in a better position to attack this significant question. This paper presents a theoretical framework for analyzing land speculation, a workable mathematical formula to calculate rates of return readily adaptable to computer use, and a summary of the results obtained when these techniques were applied to speculative activity in a twelve-million-acre area of central Iowa.[6] The study, it should be noted, deals with the large speculators as a whole in a given delimited area rather than with certain individuals or land companies.

I

Initial problems concerned definition of terms and data collection. Some historians have followed Horace Greeley in considering a speculator to be anyone, nonresident or settler, who entered more land than he could develop.[7] While accurate enough, this is a difficult yardstick to use since there is no way of knowing exactly how many acres any one person or family might utilize. Few would argue, however, that anyone needed as much as a thousand acres.[8]

[5] As Hibbard observed, "It would be an endless task to trace the land sales for any considerable area with a view to determine the extent of speculation" (p. 224). Two University of Mississippi graduate students each devoted his master's thesis to the measurement of speculation in only one county. See Mattie Russell, "Land Speculation in Tippah County 1836–1861" (unpublished M.A. thesis, 1940); Edwin W. Chapman, "Land Speculation in Tate County 1836–1861" (unpublished M.A. thesis, 1942). Three University of Nebraska graduate students likewise devoted their theses to land disposal in single counties. See John A. Caylor, "The Disposition of the Public Domain in Pierce County Nebraska" (unpublished Ph.D. dissertation, 1951); Evan E. Evans, "An Analytical Study of Land Transfer to Private Ownership in Johnson County Nebraska" (unpublished M.A. thesis, 1950); James A. Stone, "Disposition of the Public Domain in Wayne County, Nebraska, 1868–1893" (unpublished M.A. thesis, 1952).

[6] Central Iowa is the focus of this study because alphabetical tabulations of Federal land entry records, recently prepared by counsel for the Sac and Fox and Iowa Indian tribes for an Indian claims case, were made available to me. I am indebted to several Iowa abstracting firms for granting free access to their tract books, which facilitated the tracing of resales in the county deed registers. Erling A. Erickson and Michael D. Green assisted in abstracting resale data.

[7] Duncan, Charles T. (ed.), *An Overland Journey from New York to San Francisco in the Summer of 1859 by Horace Greeley* (New York: Alfred A. Knopf, 1964), pp. 52–56. For historians who have adopted this position see Paul W. Gates, "The Role of the Land Speculator in Western Development," *Pennsylvania Magazine of History*, LXVI, No. 3 (July 1942), 316; Ray Allen Billington, "The Origin of the Land Speculator as a Frontier Type," *Agricultural History*, XIX, No. 4 (Oct. 1945), 206; Thomas Le Duc, "History and Appraisal of U.S. Land Policy to 1862," in Howard W. Ottoson (ed.), *Land Use Policy and Problems in the United States* (Lincoln: University of Nebraska Press, 1963), pp. 9–15.

[8] Other researchers have arbitrarily selected other acreage figures as the minimum. Russell, p. iv, and Chapman, p. ii, set the minimum at two thousand acres, but this appears too large by Iowa land-use standards. The same figure was used by Mary E. Young, *Redskins, Ruffleshirts, and Rednecks: Indian Allotments in Alabama and Mississippi, 1830–1860* (Norman: University of Oklahoma Press, 1961), p. 99. Paul G. Minneman, "Large Land Holdings and Their Operation in Twelve Ohio Counties" (unpublished Ph.D. dissertation, Ohio State University, 1929), used five hundred acres, as did Harry N. Scheiber, "State Policy and the Public Domain: The Ohio

For convenience, therefore, in this analysis speculators are defined as individuals who entered one thousand acres or more of "Congress land." On this assumption lists of large buyers were compiled from the books of original entry of thirty-three counties of central Iowa, lying mainly within the confines of Royce Cession 262, as indicated by the shaded area of the map (Figure 1).[9] The result was an enumeration of nearly one thousand investors whose total entries topped three million acres.

Having identified the largest speculators and the specific tracts that they entered, the initial resale information was abstracted from county deed registers. The mass of data required concentration on resales in the earliest years—from 1846 through 1860—in only nine counties (indicated on Figure 1 by cross-hatching), chosen carefully in terms of geography and soil type as representative of the entire cession area.[10] For the ten largest entrants in each of

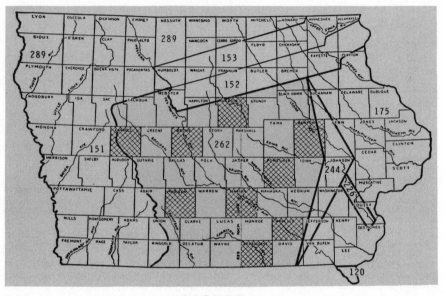

FIGURE 1

ROYCE CESSION 262, SHOWING THE NINE COUNTIES OF CENTRAL IOWA IN WHICH
LAND SALES WERE ANALYZED.

Canal Lands," *Journal of Economic History,* XXV, No. 1 (Mar. 1965), Table 3, p. 95. Midwestern students have used both one thousand acres and 640 acres. See Caylor, pp. 34–35, and Stone, pp. 44–47.

[9] The map was adapted from Map Plate CXXXI in U.S. Congress, House, *Indian Land Cessions of the United States,* by Charles C. Royce (Bureau of American Ethnology, "18th Annual Report, 1896–1897"), 56th Cong., 1st Sess., 1899, H. R. 736. Cession 262 actually contains the major portion of thirty-four counties, but a courthouse fire destroyed the Decatur County book of original entries.

[10] The nine counties were Appanoose, Benton, Boone, Carroll, Hardin, Madison, Marion, Poweshiek, and Wapello. When abstracting, all types of deeds (warranty, quitclaim, and indenture) were used except the following: those that clearly pertained to town lots, those containing metes and bounds descriptions or lot or block numbers that could not easily be translated into sectional descriptions, those reciting nominal considerations (twenty cents per acre or less), those that are illegible, those with obviously defective dates or descriptions, and those with sale dates prior to the date of original entry (such were usually quitclaims deeding only a color of title). When

the nine counties, however, the deed registers were searched for the initial resale of *all* original-entry tracts—the final sale occurring in 1889.[11] Thus limited in geographic area and somewhat in time, the resale acreage to be analyzed amounted to 460,119 acres—about 4 per cent of Royce Cession 262.[12]

The method of calculating returns on the investments of the speculators was a refinement of the technique outlined in the Bogues' seminal article. For each parcel of land sold, a data card was punched recording among other things the acreage, entry and sale price, month and year of entry and sale, the standard fee charged by real estate agents and land officers for locating and entering, and the realtor's commission for selling.[13] A tax series for each county based on the

---

the deed contained two or more descriptions the total consideration was apportioned on the basis of the acreage for each description. When buyers defaulted and tracts were resold, the latter deed was used. Of the 984 entrants with a thousand acres or more in the thirty-three-county area, 299, or about one third, purchased land in the nine selected counties.

[11] Breaks in title due to the failure to record deeds, common especially in the early years, made it impossible to chart about 3 per cent of the initial resales. An additional 10 per cent were dropped because the deeds cited nominal considerations of less than twenty cents per acre.

[12] This smaller sample, it was expected, would be representative of the larger group, but a comparison of resales of the two groups in the period 1845–1860 showed that the ten largest entrants were not quite as successful in their speculations as the other large-scale buyers. In the period after 1860, therefore, when the data rest on the activity of the smaller group only, the rates are probably somewhat lower than if all resales of the large buyers had been included.

[13] All fractional acres were rounded to the nearest whole acre. The entry and sale prices (recorded in dollars and cents) were those given in the books of original entry and deed registers, respectively. The entry price was set at $1.25 per acre if not given in the tract book. All dates were rounded to the nearest whole month. Also included on the data card was a tract identification number corresponding to a tract in the book of original entry, a county and buyer identification number, and a consecutive-data card number. The ten largest original entrants were distinguished from the other large entrymen. Warrant entries were distinguished from cash entries, and tracts sold above $1.25 per acre were differentiated from those sold from twenty cents to $1.25 per acre.

Speculators often entered land for other buyers under a "time entry" agreement (see following). In such cases, borrowers paid land office fees and taxes; agent fees were deducted when loans were repaid. To distinguish credit entries from cash entries (when investors entered land on their own account and paid all fees and taxes themselves), the following rule of thumb was used: credit entries were classified as those in which the land was sold within two years after entry for less than $3.00 per acre or within one year for less than $2.00 per acre. Cash entries were all those in which land was sold twenty-five months or more after entry, or was sold within two years at a greater per acre price than $3.00 or within one year at a greater per acre price than $2.00. Two and three dollars were chosen as safe limits because, at the standard interest rate of 40 per cent on credit sales, approximately 50 cents per year was added to the usual land office price of $1.25 per acre.

Fees and commissions were quite standard for the period. On land warrant entries, agent fees were $5.00 for locating and entering forty-acre tracts, $7.00 for eighties, $8.00 for 120's, and $10.00 for 160's. On cash entries, the fee was reduced by $1.00 for each forty acres since the land office fee was abrogated. Beginning in 1856 when the flood of warrants issued under the liberal bounty act of 1855 (U.S. *Statutes at Large*, X, 701–2) hit the market, standard agent fees were reduced for warrant entries to $2.50 for forty acres, $5.00 for eighties, $7.50 for 120's, and $10.00 for 160's with the corresponding reduction for cash entries. See advertisements in Iowa City *Iowa Capital Reporter,* Jan. 11, 1854; Iowa City *Daily Evening Reporter,* May 28, 1856; Fairfield *Iowa Sentinel,* Jan. 8, 1857; Fairfield *Ledger,* Apr. 30, 1857. See also LeGrand Byington, "Circular No. 4, Iowa General Land Agency, Iowa City," Iowa State Department of History and Archives, Des Moines. Selling commissions varied between 2.5 and 5 per cent of the sale price, but the larger percentage seemed to be more common and was used in this study.

average yearly per acre tax on unimproved land for the period 1845 to 1889 was also transferred to data cards.[14] Other possible cost items necessarily had to be ignored—such as the owner's management time and expense and discounts on drafts and exchange—as well as any possible revenue prior to sale from rents and abortive sales.[15] For each tract of land the rate of interest was computed which, when compounded [16] annually against the original investment

[14] The average yearly tax was based on a "visual mean average" of the annual tax assessments on unimproved lands recorded in the county tax registers. Tax records in three counties had been destroyed; in these cases, the rates of the nearest sample county for which the data were available were substituted—Madison for Appanoose County, Hardin for Boone County, and Marion for Wapello County. Average yearly tax rates rose steadily from one cent per acre in the early years to approximately twenty cents per acre by the 1880's. For a tax series on one section of improved farm land in eastern Iowa, see Allan G. Bogue, *From Prairie to Corn Belt: Farming on the Illinois and Iowa Prairies in the Nineteenth Century* (Chicago: University of Chicago Press, 1963), p. 189.

[15] Additional costs might be postage, fees for notarizing deeds and paying taxes, revenue stamps on deeds (required after 1863), title abstract investigations, blank deeds and record books, redemption of tax-deeded land, defalcations of funds by agents, court litigation costs, and faulty assignments of warrants. The cost of investment capital might also be considered as a possible cost item, although scholars disagree sharply on this point. Offsetting factors were that much of the land was entered with warrants purchased at a discount and that some counties allowed payment of the county portion of the taxes with depreciated "county orders."

Rental income, a much overemphasized aspect of speculation in Congress land in the Midwest, was not a factor in this study. Available evidence indicates that, at least in frontier Iowa, the large speculators primarily engaged in the "time entry," not the rental, business. For example, over 85 per cent of the 328,508 acres of Congress land in Iowa entered by James S. Easley of Halifax, Virginia—the largest nonresident investor in the Hawkeye State—were secured for second parties under credit arrangements (see Robert P. Swierenga, "Pioneers and Profits: Land Speculation on the Iowa Frontier" [unpublished Ph.D. dissertation, University of Iowa, 1965], ch. vii, tables 1 and 2). Moreover, during the twenty-seven years (1852–1879) of his career in the Iowa land business, the Virginian rented not a single acre of the 47,546 acres which he entered "for future speculation." As late as the 1870's he insisted that his raw land remain unencumbered with any rental agreements. Even the seemingly innocuous request in 1875 by an Iowa farmer to fence one of Easley's long-vacant tracts in exchange for its use as a pasture met with a sharp rejection (James S. Easey to B. F. Yelter, Mar. 20, 1875, Easley Letter Books, XIV, 47, James S. Easley Papers, Alderman Library, University of Virginia, Charlottesville). Easley's non-rental policy apparently was not unique. The extant correspondence of John A. Roebling of Trenton, N.J., Nathaniel Gordon of Exeter, N.H., and Andrew J. Sterrett of Erie, Pa.—all large investors in frontier Iowa in the pre-Civil War decades—similarly makes no reference to rental of agricultural lands. Neither do any of the countless newspaper advertisements of Hawkeye land agents. This is not to assert, however, that all large investors discouraged tenancy. Some may have rented part of their holdings, especially in the postwar period. For example, Paul W. Gates, who several decades ago used the now-unavailable account books and business correspondence of Miles and Elias A. White of Baltimore—second only to Easley, among non-Iowans, in the volume of their Iowa land entries—reported that the Whites "liked to keep tenants on their land" ("The Homestead Act in Iowa," *Agricultural History*, XXXVIII, No. 2 [Apr. 1964], 68).

[16] Compound rather than simple interest was used because all contemporary evidence indicates that this was the customary practice. Computing with simple interest, of course, is the standard procedure in many present-day financial arrangements. This method, however, would result in a considerably *higher* rate of return than the rates here presented because interest is not computed on the accrued interest of previous years. For example, $80 invested for 5 years at 5 per cent simple interest would yield $100, whereas $80 invested for the same period at 4½ per cent compounded annually would likewise yield $100.

Use of constant dollars, often desired by purists in economic studies, was not considered necessary in this study. Unsophisticated mid-nineteenth century investors seemingly were not aware of the subtleties of price comparisons over time. Alternative investments, moreover, offered no escape, since price changes affected all forms

plus selecting, locating, and entering fees and subsequent costs, gave a total investment at the date of sale equal to the sale price minus the sale commission.[17] This interest was called the net rate of return on invested capital. This rate, of course, is not the equivalent of profit. To obtain a figure which can be called profit, one must allocate an interest rate to the invested capital and subtract this from the rate of return. If the researcher hopes to be still more precise and to specify net profit, he must subtract an allowance for the time spent by the investor in managing his real estate.[18]

Following the calculation of the annual rate of return for each tract, a new data card was automatically punched containing the original plus the newly computed data. With the use of a card-sorting machine and simple computer programs, the various rates of return per tract were then combined into weighted means.[19] These show the average rate of return per dollar invested for

---

of investment, not only capital sunk in land. Converting to constant dollars, in any case, would not have altered significantly the overall average rates of return. In the first place, adding annual taxes and realtor sale commissions to the initial investment provides a built-in hedge against the effect of price changes. During an inflationary period, for example, converting taxes and sale commissions into constant dollars would result in smaller dollar amounts, thus increasing returns; at the same time, converting revenue from land sales into constant dollars would, of course, reduce rates of return. Secondly, general price indexes during the period of this study (1846–1889) fluctuate over time and, therefore, inflationary losses of one period might well be canceled out by gains from subsequent deflationary periods or vice versa. In the pre-Civil War period (1846–1860), the Snyder-Tucker general price index (Base: 1913 = 100) shows a general inflationary trend—from a low of 66.5 in 1846 to a high of 79.6 in 1857—while in the postwar years there is a marked deflation—from a high of 129 in 1864 to a low of 76 in 1886 (see U.S. Bureau of the Census, *Historical Statistics of the United States, 1789–1945: A Supplement to the Statistical Abstract of the United States* [Washingon: U.S. Government Printing Office, 1949], Series L1, pp. 231–32).

[17] See Appendix I for a more complete explanation of the computation procedure. The polynomial equation used to determine interest rate r was $\text{Poly} = PV \, (1 + r)^{nyear} \, (1 + r \times \text{mons}/12) + (1 + r \times \text{mons}/12) \, \Sigma T(I) \, (1 + r)^{ntyr-1...n} - SV = O$ when PV is the land office price (plus selecting and entering fees), *nyear* is the number of whole years between the entry and sale date, *mons* is the fractional months remaining, $T(I)$ is the annual tax, *ntyr* is the number of whole tax years, and SV is the sale price (less the sale commission). The first factor in the equation compounds interest annually on the initial investment, while the second factor compounds interest annually on taxes. When converting to annual rates of return, all investment periods of less than one full year were computed as being equivalent to one year. This was necessary to avoid gross distortion, although it reduced the rate of return considerably. For example, if an investment of one month's duration yielded a return of 20 per cent, this, rather than 240 per cent (20 × 12), was called the annual rate.

Taxes, computed only on noncredit entries, were determined by multiplying the tract acreage by the tax rate per acre for the respective years. Interest on these yearly tax investments was compounded annually (for a decreasing number of periods) from the date of the first tax payment, due under Iowa law on the second January after entry (see State of Iowa, *Revised Code*, 1860, pp. 110, 117), until the last January before the sale date. Interest on this final tax payment was computed at simple interest for the period from January 1 of the year of sale until the sale date. The prorated tax amount levied against the property during the calendar year of sale was simply subtracted from the sale price, although speculators frequently passed this cost to the buyer. For a column-by-column explanation of the information recorded on the eighty-column data cards and a complete listing of the PROFIT program in FORTRAN IV language for use on an IBM 7040–7044 digital computer, see Swierenga, "Pioneers and Profits," appendices XV and XVI.

[18] Bogue and Bogue, JOURNAL OF ECONOMIC HISTORY, XVII (1957), 22.

[19] These means were obtained by multiplying the entry price of each tract by the rate of return which it earned and dividing the sum of the products by the sum of the entry prices. In addition to listing all of the input data, the computer "print-out" contained the following output data for each tract: the per acre sale price, the

all tracts in the sample, or for those bought or sold in the same year or in the
same county, or by any of several other measures.

II

The Iowa lands on which resale data were collected were confined to nine
counties in the central and south-central portion of the state, as indicated on
Figure 1. Three of the counties—Wapello, Marion, and Boone—straddle the
Des Moines River and represent the fertile river-valley area. Appanoose County
to the south adjoins the Missouri border, while Madison and especially Carroll
represent the interior west-central area where prairie predominated. Hardin
County on the Iowa River typifies the north-central mixed prairie-timber area.
Benton and Poweshiek in the east-central region compare favorably with much
of eastern Iowa and its combination of timber, prairie, and water resources.

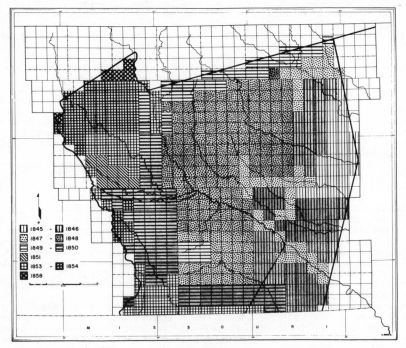

FIGURE 2

YEARS WHEN TOWNSHIPS OF ROYCE CESSION 262 WERE OFFERED FOR SALE.

absolute percentage increase or decrease between the net entry and net sale price, the
gross and net rates of return, and the total time held (in months). For any aggregate
group of tracts (either all tracts within one county or all bought or sold in the same
year, for example) totals were also printed, listing the total acres in the series, the
total entry price, total fees, total sale price, total commissions, weighted average sale
price per acre, weighted average gross and net rates of return, weighted average
absolute percentage increase or decrease between the net entry and net sale prices,
and the weighted average months per acre that all the tracts in the group were held
between the entry and sale dates.

Speculative activity was an important ingredient in the alienation of the public domain in all nine counties, but the amount of investment varied somewhat, depending apparently on the general business condition of the nation when the particular areas were first offered for sale. Wapello County on the Des Moines River in the southeastern sector was directly in the path of settlement when Cession 262 was first thrown open in 1843. Consequently, settlers quickly preempted much of it, and in 1846 and 1847 when the Government first offered the area at public auction (see Figure 2) [20] the large speculators had to be content with only 14.7 per cent of the original entry acreage in the county, as Table 1 indicates. Competition from settlers was less intense in the other

TABLE 1

ORIGINAL ENTRY ACREAGE OF LARGE ENTRYMEN (ONE THOUSAND ACRES OR MORE) IN NINE SAMPLE COUNTIES OF CENTRAL IOWA, 1845–1864

County	Original Entry Acreage in County	Acreage Entered by Large Entrymen	Percentage
Appanoose	264,712	64,108	24.2
Benton	411,933	108,712	26.4
Boone	228,938	87,598	38.3
Carroll	192,958	87,956	45.6
Hardin	299,550	100,617	33.6
Madison	324,917	106,485	32.8
Marion	257,588	75,763	39.4
Poweshiek	341,389	135,337	39.6
Wapello	178,043	26,220	14.7
Totals	2,500,028	792,796	
Weighted average			31.7

counties, however, and the large entrymen were able to absorb between one fourth and one half of all Congress land. On a percentage basis, the northwestern county of Carroll witnessed the greatest speculative activity, with the large investors acquiring 45.6 per cent of the original-entry acreage. In terms of total acreage, on the other hand, the large entrymen together engrossed over 100,000 acres in each of four counties—Benton, Hardin, Madison, and Poweshiek— mainly in the years 1853 to 1856 as the business cycle climbed to its peak. Except for three townships in Boone and Carroll counties, buyers took up over 90 per cent of the original-entry acreage in the nine counties within ten years (see Figure 3). The average purchase price on all but land warrant entries was the Congress minimum of $1.25 per acre.

Occupationally, the nearly one thousand large speculators on which this analysis is based were engaged in the typical western pursuits—real estate and banking, merchandizing, farming and stock-raising, law, medicine, government service, and many of the trades. About one third were from out of state while

[20] For figures 2 and 3 I am indebted to Raleigh Barlowe of Michigan State University.

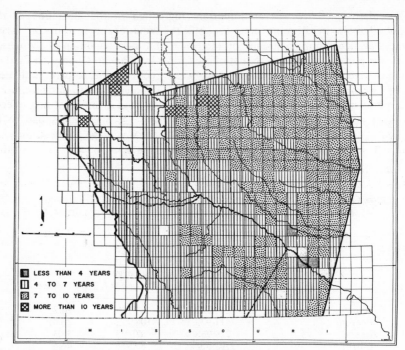

FIGURE 3

NUMBER OF YEARS FROM OPENING OF TOWNSHIP LAND SALES IN ROYCE CESSION 262 UNTIL
90 PER CENT OF THE ORIGINAL ENTRY ACREAGE WAS TAKEN.

the remainder were Iowans. The Iowans were often not residents in the counties
of their major speculative activities, so were as much nonresidents as the
non-Iowans, at least from the standpoint of local residents.[21]

Despite their diversity of background, the investors tended to fall into two
broad categories—those looking for long-term investments which required little
day-to-day supervision and the professionals who devoted all or nearly all of
their attention to the business. The members of the first group typically invested
their surplus capital through frontier real estate brokers, although they frequently commenced their ventures with a personal excursion to the West to
familiarize themselves with local conditions and to strike up connections with

[21] Specifically, of the 984 large buyers, deed records reveal that 648 (65.9 per cent)
lived in Iowa while 310 (31.5 per cent) resided in twenty-four other states and
territories plus the District of Columbia. The residence of 26 buyers (2.6 per cent)
could not be determined. Only nine states were not represented, seven of these being
in the deep South. Biographical data uncovered for 263 Iowans in county histories
and manuscript Federal population census rolls indicated that 106, or 40 per cent,
were primarily engaged as realtors and bankers during the period of their land
entries. Many of these, of course, doubled as lawyers, government officials, merchants, farmers, and even clergymen. The 70 local farmers who comprised the second
largest occupational group speculated on a comparatively smaller scale—all but nine
entered less than 2,000 acres. Most of the remaining investors were principally
employed as merchants, lawyers, physicians, and county officials, with a scattering of
land office personnel, manufacturers, carpenters, clergymen, grocers, clerks, and
newspaper editors. Information obtained on 81 non-Iowans showed that 25, or almost
one third were realtors and bankers, while another 25 were merchants. The others
were mostly farmers and stock-raisers, lawyers, physicians, and government officials.

prospective agents. The latter group—the realtors, bankers, moneylenders, and land capitalists—often began with borrowed capital and operated on a margin, buying and selling land and extending credit at rather fixed interest rates to obtain a quick return and rapid turnover of their funds. Many of these professionals engaged in the widespread frontier practice of entering land "on time" for settlers or speculators who lacked the necessary cash—the so-called "time entry" or "bond for a deed" system. Under this credit arrangement, the prospective buyer designated a desired tract, whereupon the moneylender entered the land in his own name (to protect the loan) but under bond to transfer the title when the loan was paid, usually in one or two years. The standard interest rate on such transactions was 40 per cent per annum, which in part explains the high rates of return described below.

Land historian Benjamin Hibbard compiled statistics on the extent of large-scale speculation by two hundred of the largest investors in early Iowa but did not find it feasible to follow the records of sales "minutely enough to determine what became of these big purchases or how well the purchasers fared." He suggested, however, that most speculators sold their land within a few years at about the same amount as the purchase price. Real estate values could not rise much, he believed, because of the abundance of Congress land offered at the minimum price and of free land available from 1862 until well into the seventies in the northwestern part of the state. "The result was that the big speculators . . . sold out long before land reached twenty or even ten dollars per acre"; thus few, Hibbard concluded, reaped "immense fortunes." [22]

It is true that most Iowa speculators unloaded the bulk of their lands within a few years: for the acreage analyzed in this paper, the average investment period per acre was only 31.6 months or slightly more than 2.5 years. (See Table 2, following.) It is also true that most speculators sold before land prices had increased tenfold: the average sale price of the land included in this study was only $3.10 per acre. Yet, to conclude from this that investments in frontier real estate were therefore unprofitable is erroneous. If land purchased for $1.25 per acre (or less if military bounty land warrants were used) was sold within a year for twice that amount and the money immediately reinvested to the same advantage, it is clear that such dealings could be "immensely profitable." Certainly one investor was satisfied with such returns. Norman Densmore of Emerald Grove, Wisconsin, entered Congress land in Iowa in 1854 at the minimum price and sold it a year later for $2.50 per acre. "If I can succeed in locating land where it will double the entrance money in one year I shall feel well satisfied," he concluded as he made plans for reinvesting. [23]

If Densmore doubled his money in a year, were other investors as successful? At least one member of Congress thought so. "Are there not gentlemen within the sound of my voice," asked Representative Francis Johnson of Maryland, "who have purchased land of the Government, within the last twelve months, and have realized more than a hundred per cent upon it?" [24] That the lawmaker

---

[22] Hibbard (cited in n. 1), pp. 224–25. Cf. p. 221.
[23] Norman Densmore to Benjamin Densmore, Oct. 25, 1855 (Benjamin Densmore Letters, Wisconsin State Historical Society, Madison).
[24] U.S. Congress, *Congressional Globe*, 25th Cong., 2d Sess., 1838, Appendix, p. 547.

knew the facts is evident from Table 2, which presents resale and rate-of-return data on 460,119 acres of unimproved central-Iowa real estate entered by large speculators in the immediate pre-Civil War decades. The table is based on the land office price of each tract; or if entered with land warrants or scrip or the price is not recorded in the land book, the minimum price of $1.25 per acre was substituted.

While the average net rates of return varied widely between counties, from a low of 14.3 per cent per year in Wapello County to a high of 115.2 per cent in Poweshiek, the weighted average returns on the total investments of the large speculators was a stunning 53.4 per cent compounded annually.[25] Appanoose and Marion counties shared low rates with Wapello—averaging 16.8 and 17.7 per cent respectively—while Carroll County speculators (at 95.9 per cent) made out nearly as well as those in Poweshiek. Returns in Benton, Boone, and

TABLE 2

AVERAGE SALE PRICES AND ANNUAL NET RATES OF RETURN
EARNED BY CENTRAL-IOWA LARGE ENTRYMEN IN NINE
SELECTED COUNTIES, 1845–1889
(WITH LAND WARRANT ENTRIES VALUED AT $1.25 PER ACRE)

County	Acres Sold	Range in Price per Acre	Average Price per Acre	Average Net Rate of Return	Average Investment Period per Acre (Months)
Appanoose	40,424	$.29–45.00	$2.82	16.8	30.5
Benton	59,739	.27–30.00	3.09	31.8	37.3
Boone	51,904	.80–12.50	2.70	35.8	45.1
Carroll	50,346	.78–16.25	3.18	95.9	21.2
Hardin	60,056	.50–16.67	2.65	51.7	26.7
Madison	56,781	.55–37.50	2.59	39.3	23.5
Marion	44,029	.20–18.17	2.51	17.7	29.3
Poweshiek	77,315	25–20.00	4.17	115.2	26.9
Wapello	19,525	.20–25.00	4.55	14.3	69.1
Total	460,119				
Weighted averages			$3.10	53.4	31.6

[25] Although not discussed here, the gross rate of return was also calculated for each tract by ignoring taxes, fees, and commissions. This raised returns by an average of approximately 10 per cent. Readers familiar with the Bogues' study and the generally lower rates of return earned on frontier land investments which they presented will recall the major differences between that study and this, which make comparison difficult. Their data reflected the experience of six specific investor groups, of which the three largest—accounting altogether for over 90 per cent of the acreage in the sample—were largely real estate developers who put tenants on their land. The entries of these investors, moreover, varied widely in time—three acquired their land in the 1830's, two in the 1840's and 1850's, and one in the 1870's. In addition, these investors purchased almost 75 per cent of their sample acreage in the post-Civil War period, 30 per cent of it from land-grant railroads and state governments at prices from two to five times greater than the Congress minimum of $1.25 per acre. Finally, the Bogues lacked precise information on the market price quotations of land warrants.

Madison counties fell in the 30 per cent range, while Hardin County averaged 51.7.

III

It is difficult to explain the reasons for the wide variance in annual rates of return between counties. Specific factors that must be considered, however, are the date of entry, the time span of the investment, peculiarities in the action of individual speculators, general estimates of agricultural potential, and proximity to projected internal improvements and railroads. Speculators, for example, first reached Carroll County in 1854 and 1855, just as the business expansion of the fifties was nearing its peak. Under the speculative boom, eager investors snapped up all of the Congress land in a matter of months, with nonresidents acquiring over 95 per cent of it. In the face of such tremendous demand, prices rose sharply and the original large entrymen unloaded quickly to other speculators. Only twenty-one months on an average separated the dates of entry and of sale—the shortest average time among the counties studied. Consequently, yearly rates of return were nearly 100 per cent in Carroll County.

The experience in Wapello County, on the other hand, illustrated the time element in an adverse way. Although speculators there realized a higher average sale price ($4.55 per acre) than in any other county in the study, they yet earned the lowest average returns because they carried their land investments, on an average, more than twice as long as speculators in the other counties. This not only added to the tax burden but sharply reduced annual returns.

Circumstances surrounding the activities of several large buyers in Marion County illustrate how composite analyses such as this must be used with care. Speculators in that county seemingly earned an average net return of only 17.7 per cent compounded annually. However, nearly one thousand Dutch immigrants chose Marion as their home in 1847 under the guidance of a leader who entered nearly eighteen thousand acres in his own name and that of a friend.[26] Much of this acreage, located largely with land warrants, was in turn deeded to the colonists at Government price ($1.25 per acre) or only a slight advance above it. Some might argue, with good reason, that such entries were not speculative in intent and should not have been included in the sample; in any case, this acreage lowered the average rates in Marion by a considerable margin.

Poweshiek County is the best example of the influence of location, strategically situated as it was on the proposed line of the Rock Island and Pacific Railroad and midway between the temporary state capital at Iowa City and the proposed new site at Des Moines. Nonresident investors found themselves attracted as by a magnet. Altogether, the large entrymen entered 135,337 acres, or 39.6 per cent of all the public land in the county. On the 77,315 acres for which resale data were collected, average net returns were 115.2 per cent compounded annually.

Actual returns earned by the average speculators were even higher than the

[26] Jacob Van Der Zee, *The Hollanders of Iowa* (Iowa City: State Historical Society of Iowa, 1912), p. 71.

figures thus far presented. In nearly 60 per cent of their entries the large investors used land warrants, available in the middle 1850's at discounts of 5 to 15 per cent below the land office price.[27] In addition, 87,376 acres, or 20 per cent of the total acreage in the study, were sold at prices between twenty cents and $1.25 per acre—in other words, apparently at no profit. But it is very doubtful if many of these recorded prices were bona fide. Some involved partial financing in which the buyer provided part of the purchase price but the speculator entered the land in his own name to protect the loan. When such loans were repaid and the title transferred, the recorded consideration on the deed could range well below $1.25 per acre.[28] Similarly, when no down payment was involved, the credit arrangement might call for repayment of the original loan at the land office price plus an annual premium of fifty cents per acre. In such cases the actual sale price would be fully 40 per cent higher than the price of $1.25 per acre shown on the deed.

Other sales at prices below the land office minimum covered transfer of land between members of the same family or, as in the case of the Marion County Dutch, from the immigrant leader to his individual colonists. Some deeds were only quitclaims involving tax-clouded or contested land to which the seller had merely a color of title. Sheriff's sales for taxes or other liens and quitclaim deeds to replace earlier unrecorded deeds that had been lost or destroyed also accounted for a few sales below the Government minimum price. At least some sales below $1.25 per acre were bona fide, however, especially in the early years from 1847 to 1852 when land warrants sold at discounts of 50 to 60 per cent. Speculators interested in short-run gains not infrequently entered land with them, resold quickly at prices equal to or slightly below the Government minimum, and immediately reinvested. Such activity could be very rewarding even though sale prices were far below the actual value of the land.

That speculators would sell one fifth of their land at a loss also seems illogical and does not conform to the assertion of one of the largest Iowa investors. In 1867 an Iowan charged that a Virginia speculator, James S. Easley, had in the 1850's agreed through one of his western agents to sell an eighty-acre tract in the Hawkeye State for $100 but had since refused to convey title. Easley replied in indignation that it was preposterous to think that he would have paid a commission to an agent to sell land at $1.25 per acre when it had cost him that amount; he continued,

> We think this would have been rather an unprofitable [sale] & . . . it is the only case of the kind we ever heard of & at the time this land was entered for us, it was considered by all land dealers that lands at that time were as soon as they were entered worth from $2.50 to $3.00 pr acre. . . . This is the first [instance] in buying & selling

[27] In six counties in the sample area, 173,064 acres out of 291,378 were entered with warrants. Boone, Hardin, and Madison county tracts were deleted from this part of the analysis because the records do not differentiate between cash and land-warrant entries. In the state as a whole, warrants were used in lieu of cash in 52 per cent of all entries of Congress land.

[28] For example, if a settler provided three fifths of the land office price but borrowed the remainder, the average consideration recorded at the time of sale might range below $1.00 per acre, even if the interest cost was included.

several hundred thousand Acres through agents that we have ever known them to buy at $1.25 & sell at $1.25.[29]

In order to ascertain more realistic rates of return, the data were recalculated after deleting all tracts selling at the land office minimum or less. The result, as indicated in Table 3, was to raise the average rates more than 15 per cent—from 53.4 (see Table 2) to 67.8 per cent. However, in Appanoose, Marion, and Wapello—counties where investors seemingly earned the lowest returns—the

TABLE 3

AVERAGE SALE PRICES AND ANNUAL NET RATES OF RETURN EARNED
BY CENTRAL-IOWA LARGE ENTRYMEN IN NINE SELECTED COUNTIES,
1845–1889
(WITH LAND WARRANT ENTRIES VALUED AT $1.25 PER ACRE AND ALL
SALES AT $1.25 PER ACRE OR LESS DELETED)

County	Acres Sold	Average Price per Acre	Average Net Rate of Return	Average Investment Period per Acre (Months)
Appanoose	26,570	$3.72	33.7	38.9
Benton	48,324	3.58	44.6	42.2
Boone	42,855	3.06	45.5	40.4
Carroll	43,516	3.52	112.5	18.3
Hardin	55,477	2.77	56.9	27.2
Madison	47,284	2.87	49.1	23.4
Marion	27,608	3.29	34.3	42.6
Poweshiek	68,804	4.55	131.3	27.3
Wapello	13,305	6.17	27.1	86.7
Total	373,743			
Weighted averages		$3.56	67.8	33.2

average rates were doubled by the new calculation, illustrating that a greater than normal number of non-bona fide sales had been recorded in the deed registers of these counties.

IV

Not only must the diligent researcher weigh the factor of non-bona fide sales, he must also consider the effect of the use of land warrants on profits—an element never measured very precisely by previous scholars. In the six counties in the study where land records distinguished between cash and land warrant entries, the average per acre selling price of warrants on eastern markets during the month of entry (plus five cents per acre to approximate western rates) was substituted for the land office price on all warrant entries and the rate of return

[29] Easley and Willingham to Head and Russell, Aug. 23, 1867 (Easley Letter Books, VII, 146–47).

was recalculated.[30] Again, the upward trend was marked, as Table 4 shows, with the overall average climbing from 53.4 to 72.2 per cent. Limited only to sales above $1.25 per acre, as in Table 5, the average rate reached 82.2 per cent. Average annual returns in Poweshiek and Carroll counties jumped to 130.5 and 144.0 per cent respectively.

Reckoned with estimated warrant prices, the results in Wapello County also become more realistic, since the large investors used warrants for 90 per cent of their entries in that county. The average net rate of return increased from 14.3 to 34.6 per cent when based on current warrant prices in the West, and increased again to 39.3 per cent when the acreage was restricted to sales above $1.25 per acre. Taking warrant entries and seemingly non-bona fide sales into

TABLE 4

AVERAGE SALE PRICES AND ANNUAL NET RATES OF RETURN EARNED
BY CENTRAL-IOWA LARGE ENTRYMEN IN SIX SELECTED COUNTIES,
1845–1884
(WITH LAND WARRANT ENTRIES VALUED AT CURRENT MARKET RATES) *

County	Acres Sold	Average Price per Acre	Average Net Rate of Return	Average Investment Period per Acre (Months)[a]
Appanoose	40,424	$2.82	25.8	30
Benton	59,739	3.09	38.3	37
Carroll	50,346	3.18	135.1	21
Marion	44,029	2.51	30.9	29
Poweshiek	77,315	4.17	120.0	27
Wapello	19,525	4.55	34.6	69
Total	291,378			
Weighted averages		$3.37	72.2	32

* Boone, Hardin, and Madison county books of original entry do not distinguish between cash and land warrant entries.
[a] Rounded to whole months.

[30] For the purposes of this study, the midpoint between the monthly high and low retail price quotations, based on 160-acre warrants on the New York and Washington markets, was designated as the "average per acre selling price" for each month. The table of monthly warrant-selling prices in New York and Washington is in my "Pioneers and Profits," p. 211. The data for the table were kindly supplied by Miss Natalie Disbrow, St. Petersburg, Florida, who is researching the land-warrant market for her doctoral thesis at Cornell University, Ithaca, New York. The title of her study is "Mexican War Bounty Land Warrants." See U.S. Department of the Interior, Bureau of Land Management, *Public Lands Bibliography* (Washington: U.S. Government Printing Office, 1962), p. 95. Adding five cents per acre to approximate western rates was arbitrary. The spread between eastern and western retail prices varied somewhat over time, depending on factors of supply and demand. In late 1852, one Iowa agent (Byington, "Circular No. 4") offered a premium of 15 per cent (ten to twelve cents per acre) above current New York warrant price quotations; in 1855 another local land agent noted that warrants were worth from four to eight cents per acre more in Iowa than in New York ("Letters of J. W. Denison," *Iowa Journal of History and Politics*, XXXI, No. 1 [Jan. 1933], 94).

TABLE 5

AVERAGE SALE PRICES AND ANNUAL NET RATES OF RETURN EARNED
BY CENTRAL-IOWA LARGE ENTRYMEN IN SIX SELECTED COUNTIES,
1845–1884
(WITH LAND WARRANT ENTRIES VALUED AT CURRENT MARKET RATES AND ALL
SALES AT $1.25 PER ACRE OR LESS DELETED) *

County	Acres Sold	Average Price per Acre	Average Net Rate of Return	Average Investment Period per Acre (Months) [a]
Appanoose	32,161	$3.27	37.3	34
Benton	52,964	3.37	45.7	40
Carroll	47,230	3.34	144.0	17
Marion	39,673	2.66	35.9	31
Poweshiek	71,795	4.42	130.5	27
Wapello	18,467	4.78	39.3	69
Total	262,290			
Weighted averages		$3.63	82.2	32

* Boone, Hardin, and Madison county books of original entry do not distinguish between cash and land warrant entries.
[a] Rounded to whole months.

account, in short, radically transforms the image of Wapello as a relatively poor place to invest.

V

Returns from land investments, it is generally recognized, varied over time as well as between different areas. The dates of purchase and of sale in relation to the business cycle and the rapidity of settlement in the vicinity of one's landholdings were factors that could affect the profitability of investments. To test the time variable, all of the tracts in the study were arranged first by year of sale, then by both the year of entry and the year of sale. The figures for tracts sold in the same year are presented in Table 6.

The volume of sales and the average returns fluctuated widely. In the first years, 1846–1848, the number of acres traded was not sufficient to enable one to reach valid conclusions; in addition, they mainly involved the immigrant land distribution in Marion County. From 1849 through 1860, however, sales were frequent as speculators unloaded the great bulk of their holdings. Indeed, in the brief period from 1854 through 1856, the large investors sold almost one half of all the acreage in the sample. Rates of return were as encouraging to speculators as the volume of sales, ranging as high as 156.6 per cent in 1854, and averaging 78.1 per cent for the period 1846–1860.[31]

Until 1865 returns remained extremely high, with annual averages topping 100 per cent in both 1859 and 1863 as they had in 1854. Apart from 1861,

[31] This is based on actual land warrant costs. If limited only to tracts sold above $1.25 per acre, the rate was 202.0 per cent.

TABLE 6

AVERAGE RETURNS ON IOWA LAND STUDIED, BY YEAR OF SALE, 1845–1884
(WITH LAND WARRANT ENTRIES VALUED AT CURRENT MARKET RATES)

Year	Acres Sold	Range in Price per Acre	Average Price per Acre	Average Net Rate of Return	Average Investment Period per Acre (Months) [a]
1846	160	$ 2.50–	$ 2.50	70.2	13
1847	8,520	1.25– 2.50	1.26	16.3	1
1848	232	1.25–	1.25	2.7	3
1849	6,298	.25–10.00	2.01	52.9	13
1850	5,896	.30– 6.50	1.75	58.2	10
1851	8,899	.27–10.00	1.33	19.1	13
1852	16,390	.97–10.00	1.67	27.1	14
1853	22,426	.53–12.50	1.67	21.2	13
1854	46,904	.62–17.50	3.54	156.6	9
1855	45,904	.57–15.00	2.86	60.1	15
1856	29,720	.69–25.00	2.90	72.5	19
1857	17,949	1.22–30.00	4.73	66.3	31
1858	14,051	1.00–25.55	4.73	73.2	36
1859	23,153	1.17–18.53	3.65	155.9	17
1860	13,319	.56–17.50	3.77	45.0	53
1861	2,206	1.25– 5.00	2.84	6.9	78
1862	3,195	1.34–19.40	3.81	32.2	92
1863	2,948	1.67–18.17	3.95	107.1	72
1864	3,214	.82–10.00	3.94	31.4	97
1865	2,998	1.25–15.56	6.13	10.8	151
1866	5,805	.78–14.00	3.55	4.1	120
1867	1,551	.62–12.50	6.81	9.8	155
1868	4,143	3.00–45.00	8.60	12.1	163
1869	546	3.75–31.25	12.87	12.3	186
1870	490	1.51–15.33	7.90	8.3	185
1871	40	3.75–	3.75	4.5	191
1872	125	4.00–13.33	7.36	6.3	214
1873	285	1.45–12.66	7.42	5.7	243
1874	760	5.62–25.00	20.38	10.1	292
1875	560	5.62–25.00	21.16	10.8	282
1876	502	.25–25.00	8.36	−4.5	289
1877	349	5.62–10.00	8.60	5.9	308
1878					
1879	240	6.25–10.00	7.50	6.4	256
1880	560	3.00–25.00	14.95	6.5	319
1881	480	7.00–25.00	16.48	6.9	336
1882	240	3.09– 7.50	3.83	− .7	317
1883					
1884	320	15.62–	15.62	6.2	358

[a] Rounded to whole months.

when the unsettled conditions of the nation reduced returns to 6.9 per cent, the average annual rates of return remained above 30 per cent until 1865. In that year a decided break is noticeable as the average ownership time increased suddenly from six to a dozen or more years. Correspondingly, returns declined sharply to an average of approximately 8.5 per cent for the period from 1866 until 1871, when, with another slight break, they tended to level off at an average of about 5 per cent until the final sales in 1884. During the entire time span of the study, average returns dipped into the net-loss column only twice, in 1876 and 1882—years when a mere 742 acres were involved. Of course, during every year some losses occurred, or at least so it appears from the considerations recorded in the deed registers.[32]

One can conclude from the data in Table 6 that land sold in the booming fifties, as nine tenths of it was, brought extremely high short-term profits. On the other hand, if the buyer retained title to his land until the postwar years, he could expect rather stable earnings averaging about 8 or 9 per cent per annum (compounded annually) until the early seventies, and about 5 per cent thereafter. This steady earning rate, despite rising tax costs and the compounding of interest on interest, resulted because land prices in Iowa advanced steadily as the state gradually neared the stage of full agricultural development.

TABLE 7

Most Profitable Combinations of Buying and Selling Years in Iowa
(with Land Warrant Entries Valued at Current Market Rates)

Year of Entry	Year of Sale	Acres Sold	Average Net Rate of Return	Year of Entry	Year of Sale	Acres Sold	Average Net Rate of Return
1848	1849	552	196.2	1856	1857	20,717	80.7
1848	1850	1,325	60.3	1858	1858	4,767	262.2
1849	1849	2,634	66.1	1858	1859	3,128	188.0
1853	1855	6,842	98.7	1858	1860	1,520	56.7
1854	1854	35,774	188.4	1859	1859	14,776	200.6
1854	1855	46,145	54.4	1859	1860	3,000	162.6
1854	1856	14,736	53.9	1862	1862	160	481.2
1854	1857	7,368	50.0	1862	1863	440	116.2
1855	1856	46,172	57.4	1863	1863	920	316.2
1855	1857	8,467	64.7	1864	1864	640	151.5
1856	1856	13,247	110.6				

To determine the combinations of years which proved most profitable for buying and selling Iowa land, averages were calculated on all tracts entered in the same calendar year and sold in the same calendar year. For example, tracts purchased in 1848 and sold the same year were averaged separately from those entered in 1848 and sold in 1849 or bought in 1848 and alienated in 1850. Table 7 lists only those combinations of years when average returns were above 50 per cent per annum. In the 1840's the highest returns came to those who bought in 1848 and sold the next year. In the next decade the most profitable earnings came in 1854, 1858, and 1859 on land bought and sold the same year. The Civil War years, 1862–1864, were also extremely profitable for investors but relatively few acres were sold.

[32] In the six counties in which original entry books distinguish land warrant from cash entries, investors suffered net losses on 34,937 acres, or 11.8 per cent of their acreage. However, on sales above $1.25 per acre only, the net loss figure dips to 5,094 acres, or 1.6 per cent—a remarkably small amount.

These years of highest earnings conform, in general, to the business cycle of the period. The peak years were in the late 1840's and mid 1850's, with the troughs occurring in the early and late fifties. The high earnings on sales during 1858 and 1859—normally considered depression years—are therefore difficult to explain. Yet as the figures in Table 6 also indicated, average rates of return seemingly were not affected by the recession, although the volume of sales steadily declined after 1857.

A somewhat similar picture is presented when the speculative tracts are grouped according to year of entry as in Table 8. The large buyers completed

TABLE 8

AVERAGE NET RATES OF RETURN BY YEAR OF ENTRY, 1845–1864
(WITH LAND WARRANT ENTRIES VALUED AT CURRENT MARKET RATES)

Year of Entry	Acres Enterea	Average Net Rate of Return	Average Investment Period per Acre (Months) [a]
1845	160	70.2	13
1846	560	7.2	113
1847	13,114	17.8	20
1848	6,269	47.5	70
1849	13,200	32.0	43
1850	27,306	20.0	48
1851	20,179	19.8	26
1852	22,649	23.6	19
1853	40,690	44.2	21
1854	136,078	79.9	34
1855	98,487	41.1	35
1856	45,960	73.8	23
1857	240	40.0	7
1858	12,295	152.4	45
1859	20,652	180.7	18
1860	40	−3.0	3
1861	80	−5.0	2
1862	600	128.3	8
1863	920	316.2	3
1864	640	151.5	1

[a] Rounded to whole months.

the bulk of their entries in the period from 1850 through 1856. Since the depression of 1857 did not strike until autumn, the dearth of entries in that year can be explained only by the Government's closing of most of the land offices in 1856. They were not reopened until 1858, when investors had a final opportunity to buy the small amount of the public domain in central Iowa that remained unsold. That this was a profitable opportunity is evident by the high earnings on entries of 1858 and 1859. Actually, however, annual average rates of return were encouraging during the entire twenty-year period, except for 1846, 1860, and 1861; and in those years investors wisely bought virtually no land.

VI

Frontier land was only one of many avenues of investment in the nineteenth century. The researcher is impelled, therefore, to compare earnings returned on frontier land speculation in Iowa with average rates of interest and market yields of possible alternate investments. Prime market yields of long-term, high-grade bonds of the United States Government, municipalities and states, and railroads provide valid indexes for comparison, as do common-stock yields and savings bank deposit rates. Since many frontier real estate investments were short term in nature, interest rates on good commercial paper and call money —both ideal for short-term investments—can also be used in comparison.

In Table 9, ten-year averages of annual compound net rates of return on frontier land investments in Iowa for the period 1840–1890 are listed beside ten-year average yield rates of Federal Government bonds, New England municipals, high-grade railroad bonds, common stocks, commercial paper and call money, and rates on savings deposits. Compared to these alternative investments, it is readily apparent, as pictured in Figure 4, that returns per dollar invested in frontier Iowa land, while fluctuating a great deal more from year to year, far outstripped the very best average bond and stock yields as well as the more speculative commercial-paper and call-money rates. This was particularly true in the decade 1850–1859, when speculators sold 83.9 per cent of all the land here analyzed.

That many eastern capitalists realized the bonus that could be earned on frontier land investments is evident from the high proportion of easterners among the large entrymen in Iowa. As noted previously, a third of the nearly one thousand large speculators in central Iowa were not residing in Iowa at the time they invested. The correspondence of the largest eastern investor in Iowa, James S. Easley of Halifax, Virginia, also provides insights into the thinking of capitalists faced with the need to choose between various forms of investment. Easley noted on several occasions that he could earn at least 10 to 12 per cent interest on his money at home by discounting good commercial paper, buying railroad bonds, or simply lending his funds.[33] Promoters also bombarded him with prospectuses offering stock in various manufacturing companies and public utilities. Easley, however, largely spurned these alternatives and continued to invest in raw land or tax titles in the West until his death in 1879. "We have never been able to make anything by trading [western land] for Stocks," Easley wrote to his Chicago agent in 1869 in reply to a proposal to swap one thousand acres of his tax-ridden Wisconsin lands for Illinois Gas Company stock.[34]

[33] Easley to J. D. Blair, Feb. 22, 1872 (Easley Letter Books, XI, 201); Easley to E. S. Hedges, Apr. 17, 1872 (*ibid.*, 288); Easley to J. P. Casady, July 21, 1874 (*ibid.*, XIII, 220); Easley to G. W. Grance, May 18, 1875 (*ibid.*, XIV, 165).
[34] Easley and Willingham to Josiah Bond, Jan. 12, 1869 (*ibid.*, VIII, 365). This was the only such stock offer that Easley accepted, mainly because he could unload some of his unprofitable Wisconsin lands. See letters of Jan. 28 and Feb. 16, 1869 (*ibid.*, 389, 438). In the sixties Easley invested $10,000 in Danville & Richmond Railroad bonds at 10 per cent and $1,300 in United States bonds. Earlier he had put $2,000 in Virginia coupon bonds. See *ibid.*, VIII, 194; IX, 402, 419, 486; XI, 201.

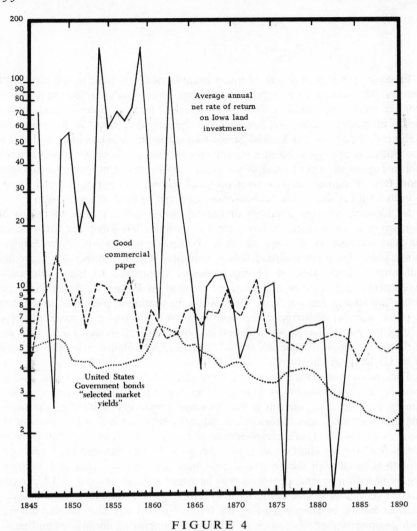

FIGURE 4

Average Annual Net Rate of Return on Frontier Iowa Land Investments as Compared with Long-Term United States Government Bonds "Selected Market Yields," and Short-Term Good Commercial Paper Interest Rates, 1845–1890.

In conclusion, this study has indicated by a careful quantification of data in Government land records that per dollar earnings on frontier land investments in central Iowa in the mid-nineteenth century were superior to many other contemporary investment outlets. Eastern as well as western capitalists realized this fact and were quick to profit from it. Since many of these entrepreneurs operated on successive frontiers throughout the Middle West, one would suspect that statistical analyses of investments in other regions would be equally sanguine. In any case, it is regrettable that most previous scholars have, after only cursory examination of the early land records, created such a dismal and probably erroneous picture of frontier land investments. If the speculator who

TABLE 9

AVERAGE TEN-YEAR RATES OF RETURN ON FRONTIER LAND INVESTMENTS IN IOWA AS COMPARED WITH AMERICAN INTEREST RATES, SHORT AND LONG TERM, 1840–1889 *

Years	Frontier Land Investments in Iowa [a]	Percentage of Land Sold	United States Government Bonds "Selected Market Yields"	New England Municipal Bond Yields	High-Grade Railroad Bond Yields	Common Stock Yields	Commercial Paper Rates	Call Money Rates	Savings Bank Rate: Regular Deposits
1840–49	9.94 (4-yr. av.)	5.2	5.41 (8-yr. av.)	5.02			7.99		5.00
1850–59	71.66	83.9	4.33	5.06	6.50 (3-yr. av.)		8.49	6.30 (3-yr. av.)	5.00
1860–69	30.96	9.1	5.34	5.10	5.90		7.07	6.50	5.00
1870–79	5.97	1.3	3.75	4.98	5.67	5.94 (9-yr. av.)	6.46	5.73	6.00
1880–89	3.88 (5-yr. av.)	.5	2.71	3.60	4.00	4.80	5.14	3.98	4.00

* Common stock yields adapted from Series Ya indexes, p. 372 ff., in Alfred Cowles, 3d, *et al.*, *Common Stock Indexes, 1871–1937* (Bloomington, Ill.: Principia Press, Inc., 1938). Cowles' Series Y-1, p. 270 ff., gives slightly lower yield rates. All other data are in Sidney Homer, *History of Interest Rates* (New Brunswick, N.J.: Rutgers University Press, 1963), pp. 287–88, 318–20, a work which neatly summarizes data from Frederick R. Macaulay, *Some Theoretical Problems Suggested by the Movement of Interest Rates, Bond Yields, and Stock Prices in the United States since 1856* (New York: NBER Publications, No. 33; NBER, 1938).

[a] Based on data in Table 6. Total land sales by decades were: 1846–1849—15,210 acres; 1850–1859—244,611 acres; 1860–1869—26,606 acres; 1870–1879—3,897 acres; 1880–1884—1,600 acres.

made money in frontier land was in truth a "rare bird," as the western editor quoted at the outset of this paper asserted, then the American menagerie must have been well stocked with odd specimens. More likely, however, the investor who failed to show a profit was truly the rare bird.

APPENDIX 1

Computation Procedure (in Brief) of the PROFIT Program

1. The total time period of the investment (in months) was determined by subtracting the year of entry from the year of sale, multiplying by twelve, and adding the sum of the month of sale (expressed in arabic numerals) minus the month of entry. When the total investment period was zero (i.e., fifteen days or less), .5 or one half of a month was substituted. The rationale is that in rounding the days of entry and of sale to the nearest whole month, one half month is the midpoint random average investment period. If zero time is not converted, calculations are impossible as the answer lies in infinity. When the total time period was less than twelve months, it was set equal to twelve months (see n. 17 above).

2. The total compounding period (*nyear*) was determined by dividing the total time in months that the tract was held by twelve. For any fractional part of a year remaining (*mons*), the rate of return was prorated $[(1 + r \times mons/12)]$. This is the standard procedure of banks when dealing with investments covering only a fractional part of a year. The rate of return can also be compounded annually to the full number of whole years plus the fractional part of the year remaining, if any, by the use of fractional exponents $[(1 + r)^{mons/12}]$. For example, an investment held 1½ years would be compounded as $(1 + r)^{1.5}$. Using the fractional exponent method of calculation on the 460,119 acres studied, it was found that the overall average rate of return was not even 1 per cent less per dollar invested than when simple interest was prorated for the remaining fractional part of a year.

3. The total number of tax years (*ntyr*) was determined by subtracting the month of entry (expressed in arabic numerals) from twenty-five, subtracting this total from the total time in months, and dividing the result by twelve. (If January was the month of entry, taxes were due and payable on the first January after purchase, in which case the month of entry was subtracted from thirteen instead of twenty-five.)

4. To solve the polynomial equation (see n. 17 above) it was first necessary to test whether the sign was positive or negative by subtracting the entry price and all subsequent costs from the sale price. If positive, the computer was instructed to iterate by the interval-halving technique between the limits of zero and 6,100 per cent. (The upper limit was set deliberately large to obtain a safe margin.) If negative, the standard logarithm routine was used. The log routine is necessary because, in the interval-halving technique, any number of negative roots may solve the equation and there is no easy way to determine which is correct. There is only one positive root, however.

5. Upon the completion of the calculations for each individual tract, weighted averages and totals were calculated for groups of tracts. Weighted averages for the gross and net rates of return per dollar invested and the percentage difference between the net entry and net sale prices were obtained by multiplying the entry price of each tract by the gross and net rates of return and the percentage change which it returned and dividing the sum of the products by the sum of the entry prices. The weighted average time in months per acre was obtained by multiplying the acreage of each tract by the number of months it was held and dividing the sum of the products by the sum of the acreage.

PART VI

The "New" Social History

SOCIAL HISTORIANS have lagged behind their counterparts in political and economic history in the application of quantitative techniques and theoretical constructs to social data, but they are rapidly closing the gap. Several dozen promising studies are currently under way in diverse areas of research, especially social mobility, political leadership elites, ethnic group structures, collective biographies, school reform movements, and urban ecological patterns. Only a few of these projects, however, have reached the publication stage, a fact testifying to the recent redirection in social history.[1]

Social history traditionally has had no governing method. Diversity is its principal attribute. "Ideally considered," according to a recent account, social history is the "study of the structure and process of human action and interaction as they have occurred in sociocultural contexts in the recorded past." [2] In practice, however, few social historians demanded such rigor; most have been content to follow Herodotus and Tacitus and merely describe societal folkways and institutions. Of late, this "pots and pans" approach is less common, and much of the research in progress is statistical and computerized, strongly analytical, and explicitly theoretical or "sociologized." [3] Sheldon Hackney's research on patterns of violent behavior in America (18) clearly illus-

[1] In addition to the essays in this book there are several other important studies. Most impressive is P.M.G. Harris "The Social Origins of American Leaders: The Demographic Foundations," *Perspectives in American History,* III (1969), 159–343, based on 15,000 sketches in the *Dictionary of American Biography* and 2500 biographies of Harvard and Yale graduates in the colonial era. Michael B. Katz, *The Irony of Early School Reform: Educational Innovation in Mid-Nineteenth Century Massachusetts* (Cambridge, 1968), utilizes a judicious combination of local history, political sociology, social psychology, and statistical analysis. Stephan Thernstrom and Richard Sennett (eds.), *Nineteenth-Century Cities: Essays in the New Urban History* (New Haven, 1969), contains several major quantitative studies. Other pioneering studies in social history are Sam B. Warner, Jr., *Streetcar Suburbs: The Process of Growth in Boston, 1870–1900* (Cambridge, 1962), and *The Private City: Philadelphia in Three Periods of Growth* (Philadelphia, 1968); and Richard Sennett's community study of Chicago's Union Park, *Families Against the City* (Cambridge, 1970). Work in progress is described periodically in the *Historical Methods Newsletter* and *Computers and the Humanities.*

[2] J. Jean Hecht, "Social History," in David L. Sills (ed.), *International Encyclopedia of the Social Sciences,* 6 vols. (New York, 1968), VI, 455.

[3] Seymour Martin Lipset and Richard Hofstadter, *Sociology and History: Methods* (New York, 1968), 14–15. The new *Journal of Social History* (Fall, 1967–   ) has encouraged the redirection. See, for example, Mario S. DePillis, "Trends in American Social History and the Possibilities of Behavioral Approaches," I (Fall, 1967), 38–60. Some of the best examples of quantitative research are in American family history. See the review essay of Philip J. Greven, Jr., "Historical Demography and Colonial America," *William and Mary Quarterly,* XXIV (July, 1967), 438–54, and the substantive article of Greven, "Family Structure in Seventeenth-Century Andover, Massachusetts," *ibid.,* XXIII (Apr., 1966), 234–56; John Demos, "Families in Colonial Bristol, Rhode Island: An Exercise in Historical Demography," *ibid.,* XXV (Jan., 1968), 40–57; and Kenneth A. Lockridge, "The Population of Dedham, Massachusetts, 1636–1736," *Economic History Review, Second Series,* XIX (Aug., 1966), 329–39. Edward Saveth discusses the limits of quantitative family analysis in "The Problem of American Family History," *American Quarterly,* XXI (Summer, 1969), 323–29.

trates the present trend and points up the utility of social statistics and sociological theories as aids in understanding historical phenomena. The appearance of several inter-disciplinary anthologies on history and sociology—by Edward N. Saveth, Werner J. Cahnman and Alvin Boskoff, Seymour Martin Lipset and Richard Hofstadter, and Stephan Thernstrom and Richard Sennett —have also fostered a closer relation between history and sociology and helped to mute some of the long-festering antipathy.[4]

The archival source materials being ferreted out by the new social historians are as varied as the areas of research. Many are virtually untapped. Materials range from census and tax data, which the "Vanderbilt School" of Frank L. Owsley and his students first exploited in the 1930's,[5] to city directories, militia rolls, building permits, probate court estate records, school board minutes, government agency reports, vital statistics, genealogical and biographical data, and even obituaries.[6] Most current research projects use a judicious combination of several of these materials. Nineteenth-century census returns, for example, are especially rich in personal information, but usually must be augmented with tax records, contemporary biographical sketches and city directories, newspapers, and memoirs. Agricultural historians James C. Malin, Mildred Throne, and Allan G. Bogue pioneered in the demographic analysis of census data.[7] But Stephan Thernstrom was the first urban historian to mine these rich social sources in a systematic manner, beginning his research in the early 1960's. Thernstrom's statistical analysis of occupational mobility of unskilled laborers in Newburyport, Massachusetts, published in 1964 (19), and his more ambitious computerized study of Boston's social structure since 1880 have fostered a spate of similar urban projects.[8] Most noteworthy are the mobility

---

[4] Edward N. Saveth (ed.), *American History and the Social Sciences* (Glencoe, 1964); Werner J. Cahnman and Alvin Boskoff (eds.), *Sociology and History: Theory and Research* (Glencoe, 1964); Lipset and Hofstadter, *Sociology and History: Methods;* and Thernstrom and Sennett, *Nineteenth-Century Cities.*

[5] Frank L. Owsley, *Plain Folk of the Old South* (Baton Rouge, 1949).

[6] Guido A. Dobbert used the computer to analyze migration patterns and social and economic mobility trends among the German immigrant elite of Cincinnati, Ohio, based on obituaries of the German pioneer society. See *Computers and the Humanities,* III (May, 1969), 313, and an unpublished paper, "The Obituary in the Analysis of Social Structure: Promises and Pitfalls," read at Yale University, October, 1968.

[7] James C. Malin, "The Turnover of Farm Population in Kansas," *Kansas Historical Quarterly,* IV (Nov., 1935), 339–72: Mildred Throne, "A Population Study of an Iowa County in 1850," *Iowa Journal of History,* LVII (Oct., 1959), 305–30; Allan G. Bogue, *From Prairie to Corn Belt: Farming on the Illinois and Iowa Prairies in the Nineteenth Century* (Chicago, 1963), chap. 1.

[8] Stephan Thernstrom describes his Newburyport study in *Poverty and Progress: Social Mobility in a Nineteenth-Century City* (Cambridge, 1964). Partial findings on the more sophisticated Boston study, nearing completion, are reported in: "Urbanization, Migration, and Social Mobility in Late Nineteenth-Century America," in Barton Bernstein (ed.), *Towards a New Past: Dissenting Essays in American History* (New York, 1967), 158–75; "Notes on the Historical Study of Social Mobility," *Comparative Studies in History and Theory,* X (Jan., 1968), 162–72; "Computers for Social History: A Study of Social Mobility in Boston," *Computers and the Humanities,* I (Nov., 1966), 84–90; "Immigrants and WASPS: Ethnic Differences in Occupational Mobility in Boston, 1890–1940," in Thernstrom and Sennett, *Nineteenth-Century Cities,* 125–61; "Poverty in Historical Perspective," in Daniel P. Moynihan (ed.), *On Understanding Poverty: Perspectives from the Social Sciences* (New York, 1969); "Quantitative Methods in History: Some Notes," in Lipset and Hofstadter, *Sociology and History,* 59–78; and "Religion and Occupational Mobility in Boston, 1880–1963,"

studies by Stuart Blumin and Peter R. Knights of Philadelphia, Kingston (New York), and Boston in the ante-bellum decades;[9] and of Poughkeepsie (New York), South Bend, Cincinnati, and Springfield (Mass.), for the years 1850 to 1880, by Clyde Griffen, Dean R. Esslinger, Zane Miller, and Michael H. Frisch, respectively.[10] These nineteenth-century surveys are vitally necessary to overcome the "parochialism of presentism" inherent in most of the sociological literature on mobility. Apart from C. Wright Mills and his followers, sociologists have restricted their research largely to the post World War II era. But one cannot hope to understand modern mobility trends and the class structure without reliable data from yesteryear. As Thernstrom declared recently: "A sense of the past, an ability to see his subject in historical depth, is not a luxury but a necessity for the student of social mobility."[11]

Since society is composed of groups, social historians have also been compelled to explore the difficult subject of group structure and especially leadership groups or "elites." Charles A. Beard in 1913 first devised a method for analyzing a large elite group, the Founding Fathers.[12] Beard's technique, known today as career-line analysis or collective biography, was to gather personal background data on each member of the Philadelphia Convention and then correlate the findings and generalize from it. Following the Second World War, many distinguished scholars found Beard's career-line analysis extremely useful. Examples are studies of the backgrounds of business leaders by C. Wright Mills, William Miller, Frances W. Gregory and Irene D. Neu, Reinhard Bendix and Frank Howton, and Thomas C. Cochran;[13] of the Philadelphia gentlemen by E.

paper presented to the Conference on Applications of Quantitative Methods to Political, Social and Economic History (Chicago, June, 1969).

[9] Stuart Blumin, "Mobility and Change in Ante-Bellum Philadelphia," in Thernstrom and Sennett, *Nineteenth-Century Cities,* 165–208, and "The Restless Citizen: Social Mobility, Migration, and Community Participation in Nineteenth-Century America [Kingston, N.Y.]," paper read to the Brockport, N.Y., conference on "The Historian and the Social Sciences," October, 1969; Peter R. Knights, "Population Turnover, Persistence, and Residential Mobility in Boston, 1830–1860," in Thernstrom and Sennett, *Nineteenth-Century Cities;* 258–74. Both authors have also published "methods" articles. See Blumin, "The Historical Study of Vertical Mobility," *Historical Methods Newsletter,* I (Sept., 1968), 1–13, and Knights, "City Directories as Aids to Ante-Bellum Urban Studies: A Research Note," *ibid.,* II (Sept., 1969), 1–10.

[10] Clyde Griffen, "Workers Divided: The Effect of Craft and Ethnic Differences in Poughkeepsie, New York, 1850–1880," and Michael H. Frisch, "The Community Elite and the Emergence of Urban Politics: Springfield, Massachusetts, 1840–1880," in Thernstrom and Sennett, *Nineteenth-Century Cities,* 49–97, 277–96. The studies by Dean R. Esslinger and Zane Miller (the latter assisted by Guido A. Dobbert) are still in progress.

[11] Thernstrom, "Historical Study of Social Mobility," 162. An excellent brief study which includes a survey of the literature is Otis D. Duncan, "The Trend of Occupational Mobility in the United States," *American Sociological Review,* XXX (Aug., 1965), 491–98.

[12] Beard, *An Economic Interpretation of the Constitution of the United States* (New York, 1913), esp. chap. 5.

[13] C. Wright Mills, "The American Business Elite: A Collective Portrait," *Journal of Economic History,* V (Supplemental issue, 1945), 20–44, reprinted in Irving Horowitz (ed.), *Power, Politics and People: The Collected Essays of C. Wright Mills* (New York, 1962), 110–39; Reinhard Bendix and Frank W. Howton, "Social Mobility and American Business Elite," in Reinhard Bendix and Seymour Martin Lipset (eds.), *Social Mobility in Industrial Society* (Berkeley, 1959), 114–43; William Miller, "American Historians and the Business Elite," *Journal of Economic History,* IX (June, 1949), 184–208, reprinted in William Miller (ed.), *Men in Business: Essays*

Digby Baltzell;[14] of reform groups by David Donald, George Mowry, Alfred D. Chandler, Jr., Geoffrey Blodgett, and Ari Hoogenboom;[15] and of colonial political elites by Jack P. Greene.[16] These collective biographical analyses were sometimes weak in method and logically flawed. Especially serious was the failure to compare the elite group under study with other groups to determine its degree of uniqueness. If, for example, Republican radicals had career patterns no different from Republican moderates or conservatives in the Reconstruction era, then, as Samuel P. Hays has warned, "one can no longer explain the peculiar background of reformers in terms of a background not peculiar to them."[17] In the 1960's, younger scholars added further statistical refinements to collective biography studies and avoided some of the earlier pitfalls by capitalizing on the mistakes of their predecessors.[18] But only in the last few years with

on the Historical Role of the Entrepreneur (New York, 1962), 309–28; Frances W. Gregory and Irene D. Neu, "The American Industrial Elite in the 1870's: Their Social Origins," in Miller, *Men in Business,* 193–211; Thomas C. Cochran, *Railroad Leaders, 1845–1890* (Cambridge, 1953).

[14] E. Digby Baltzell, *Philadelphia Gentlemen* (Glencoe, 1958), and *The Protestant Establishment: Aristocracy and Caste in America* (New York, 1964).

[15] David Donald, "Toward a Reconsideration of Abolitionists," in Donald (ed.), *Lincoln Reconsidered: Essays on the Civil War Era,* 2nd ed. (New York, 1961), chap. 2; George Mowry, *The California Progressives* (Berkeley and Los Angeles, 1951); Alfred D. Chandler, Jr., "The Origins of Progressive Leadership," in Elting Morison, *et al.* (eds.), *The Letters of Theodore Roosevelt,* 8 vols. (Cambridge, 1951–1954), VIII, 1462–64; Geoffrey Blodgett, *The Gentle Reformers: Massachusetts Democrats in the Cleveland Era* (Cambridge, 1966); Ari Hoogenboom, "An Analysis of Civil Service Reformers," *The Historian,* XXIII (Nov., 1960), 54–78, *Outlawing the Spoils: A History of the Civil Service Reform Movement, 1865–1883* (Urbana, 1961), and "Industrialism and Political Leadership," in Frederick C. Jaher (ed.), *Age of Industrialism in America* (New York, 1967), 49–78.

[16] Jack P. Greene, "Foundations of Political Power in the Virginia Houses of Burgesses, 1720–1776," *William and Mary Quarterly, Third Series,* XVI (Oct., 1959), 485–506.

[17] Samuel P. Hays, "The Social Analysis of American Political History, 1880–1920," *Political Science Quarterly,* LXXX (Sept., 1965), 378. Other perceptive critiques are Robert A. Skotheim, "A Note on Historical Method: David Donald's 'Toward a Reconsideration of Abolitionists,'" *Journal of Southern History,* XXV (Aug., 1959), 356–65; H. J. Bass, review of Hoogenboom's *Outlawing the Spoils* in *Mississippi Valley Historical Review,* XLVIII (Mar., 1962), 714–16; Bonnie R. Fox, "The Philadelphia Progressives: A Test of the Hofstadter-Hays Thesis," *Pennsylvania History,* XXXIV (Oct., 1967), 372–94.

[18] Noteworthy elite studies are Ralph A. Wooster, *The People in Power: Courthouse and Statehouse in the Lower South, 1850–1860* (Knoxville, 1969); Jackson T. Main, *The Upper House in Revolutionary America 1763–1788* (Madison, 1967); Otis L. Graham, Jr., *An Encore for Reform: The Old Progressives and the New Deal* (New York, 1967); Samuel P. Hays, "The Politics of Reform in Municipal Government in the Progressive Era," *Pacific Northwest Quarterly,* LV (Oct., 1965), 157–69; William T. Kerr, Jr., "The Progressives of Washington, 1910–1912," *ibid.,* LV (Jan., 1964), 16–27; Richard E. Beringer, "A Profile of Members of the Confederate Congress," *Journal of Southern History,* XXXIII (Nov., 1967), 518–41; Gerald W. McFarland, "The New York Mugwumps of 1884: A Profile," *Political Science Quarterly,* LXXVIII (Mar., 1963), 40–58; Frank Otto Gattell, "Money and Party in Jacksonian America: A Quantitative Look at New York City's Men of Quality," *ibid.,* LXXXII (June, 1967), 235–52; Richard B. Sherman, "The Status Revolution and Massachusetts Progressive Leadership," *ibid.,* LXXVIII (Mar., 1963), 59–65; E. Daniel Potts, "The Progressive Profile in Iowa," *Mid-America,* XLVII (Oct., 1965), 257–68; Frederick C. Luebke, "German Immigrants and Churches in Nebraska, 1889–1915," *ibid.,* L (Apr., 1968), 116–30; Sandra A. McCoy, "The Political Affiliations of American Business Elites: Wayne County, Michigan, 1844, 1860, as a Test Case" (Ph.D. dissertation, Wayne State University, 1965); David N. Young, "The Mississippi Whigs," (Ph.D. dissertation, University of Alabama, 1968).

the research of the Higonnet brothers, P.M.G. Harris, and Richard Jensen and his students has a truly quantitative methodology emerged in elite studies.[19]

Sampling, computerized data-manipulation, and statistical measurements are the hallmarks of the new social history. Where research in quantitative social history will lead is still not entirely clear. It is certain, however, that with the new sources and techniques, our knowledge of the social structures and group dynamics of the past will increase in geometric proportions. The discovery of a "culture of poverty" in nineteenth-century America—the land of opportunity —is only the first of many startling findings that can be expected from quantitative social history.

[19] Patrick L. R. Higonnet and Trevor B. Higonnet, "Class, Corruption, and Politics in the French Chamber of Deputies, 1846–1848," *French Historical Studies,* V (Fall, 1967), 204–24; P.M.G. Harris, "Social Origins of American Leaders." Except for the essay in this book (20), the research of Richard Jensen and his students has not yet appeared in print. Unpublished results are Jensen, "The Historical Roots of Party Identification," paper delivered to the American Political Science Association meeting, Washington, D.C., Sept., 1969; Thomas Kerwin, "The Chicago Elite of 1910: A Statistical Study in Collective Biography" (seminar paper, Washington University, 1969). George R. Shockey, Jr., and Barry Parker have completed similar studies for the cities of St. Louis and Wichita respectively. Other group studies are Melwyn Hammarberg's analysis of the leaders in Hendricks County, Indiana; James H. Soltow's comparative study of American businessmen in the late nineteenth century in Michigan, Pennsylvania, and Oregon; Catherine Silverman's comparison of the Redeemers in Virginia and North Carolina in the Reconstruction era; and Dale E. Benson's quantitative analysis of revolutionary leaders in Virginia. For references to the work in progress, see *Historical Methods Newsletter,* I (Dec., 1968), 18; II (June, 1969), 21, and (Sept., 1969), 22–23.

18

SHELDON HACKNEY

Southern Violence

Sheldon Hackney's statistical study of Southern violence is an excellent example of the new social history. Professor Hackney used multiple regression analysis to compare the crime and suicide rates in 1940 and the level of modernization as evidenced by data on urbanization, education, income, unemployment, wealth, and age. "South" is added as a "dummy" variable to determine if sectionalism is an explanatory factor in violence. The resulting coefficients demonstrate that Southernness is most positively related to the high incidence of violent crime among Southern whites. Violence, apparently, is the result of cultural patterning. Because every significant change in Southern life has been initiated by external forces, a paranoiac "siege mentality" grips the South, a persecution complex that rests on the un-American experiences of guilt, defeat, poverty, and an overwhelming sense of grievance. To test this intriguing hypothesis is the task of future scholarship. Professor Hackney outlines the techniques and suggests the relevant areas to be explored by quantitative methods —immigration patterns, demographic changes, religious characteristics, and international comparative studies.

A TENDENCY toward violence has been one of the character traits most frequently attributed to southerners.[1] In various guises, the image of the violent

Sheldon Hackney, "Southern Violence," *American Historical Review*, LXXIV (Feb., 1969), 906–25. Reprinted with permission of the author.
    [1] See, e.g., Charles O. Lerche, Jr., *The Uncertain South: Its Changing Patterns of Politics in Foreign Policy* (Chicago, 1964), 48–49. Representative comments can be found in John Richard Alden, *The South in the Revolution, 1763–1789* (Baton

South confronts the historian at every turn: dueling gentlemen and masters whipping slaves, flatboatmen indulging in rough-and-tumble fights, lynching mobs, country folk at a bearbaiting or a gander pulling, romantic adventurers on Caribbean filibusters, brutal police, panic-stricken communities harshly suppressing real and imagined slave revolts, robed night riders engaged in systematic terrorism, unknown assassins, church burners, and other less physical expressions of a South whose mode of action is frequently extreme.[2] The image is so pervasive that it compels the attention of anyone interested in understanding the South.

H. C. Brearley was among the first to assemble the quantitative data to support the description of the South as "that part of the United States lying below the Smith and Wesson line."[3] He pointed out, for example, that during the five years from 1920 to 1924 the rate of homicide per 100,000 population for the southern states was a little more than two and a half times greater than for the remainder of the country. Using data from the *Uniform Crime Reports* concerning the 1930's, Stuart Lottier confirmed and elaborated Brearley's findings in 1938. For this period also he found that homicide was concentrated in the southeastern states. Of the eleven former Confederate states, Louisiana showed the lowest homicide rate, but it was 74 per cent greater than the national average, and no nonsouthern state had a higher rate. It is interesting that while murder and assault were oriented to the southeastern states, robbery rates were highest in the central and western states.[4] These findings were replicated in 1954 using data on crime for the years 1946–1952.[5] The pattern of high rates of serious crimes against persons and relatively lower rates of crimes against property for the South is consequently quite stable.

At the time that Brearley was setting forth the evidence for southern leadership in physical aggression against people, another statistical study primarily of American suicide rates revealed that the South was the area in which people had the least propensity to destroy themselves.[6] Austin Porterfield, in 1949, using mortality tables from *Vital Statistics of the United States,* brought the murder and the suicide indexes together and showed that there was a general inverse relationship between the two rates among the states and that the

---

Rouge, La., 1957), 34–35, 41; Clement Eaton, *A History of the Old South* (2d ed., New York, 1966), 260, 395, 404, 407, 415; John Hope Franklin, *The Militant South, 1800–1861* (Cambridge, Mass, 1956); David Bertelson, *The Lazy South* (New York, 1967), 101–13, 241; H. V. Redfield, *Homicide, North and South: Being a Comparative View of Crime against the Person in Several Parts of the United States* (Philadelphia, 1880).

[2] A stimulating essay on this theme is Frank Vandiver, "The Southerner as Extremist," in *The Idea of the South,* ed. id. (Chicago, 1964), 43–56. A lighter treatment of the same subject is Erskine Caldwell, "The Deep South's Other Venerable Tradition," New York *Times Magazine,* July 11, 1965, 10–18.

[3] H. C. Brearley, "The Pattern of Violence," in *id., Culture in the South,* ed. W. T. Couch (Chapel Hill, N.C., 1934), 678–92; and H. C. Brearley, *Homicide in the United States* (Chapel Hill, N.C., 1932).

[4] Stuart Lottier, "Distribution of Criminal Offenses in Sectional Regions," *Journal of Criminal Law and Criminology,* XXIX (Sept.–Oct., 1938), 329–44.

[5] Lyle Shannon, "The Spatial Distribution of Criminal Offenses by States," *ibid.,* XLV (Sept.–Oct. 1954), 264–73.

[6] Louis I. Dublin and Bessie Bunzel, *To Be or Not to Be: A Study of Suicide* (New York, 1933), 80, 413.

South ranked highest in homicide and lowest in suicide.[7] In 1940 the national average rate of suicide per 100,000 population was 14.4 and of homicide was 6.2, but the old and cosmopolitan city of New Orleans had a suicide rate of 11.1 and a homicide rate of 15.5. Even though some southern cities exceed some nonsouthern cities in suicide rates, the New Orleans pattern of more homicides than suicides is typical of the South but not of the nation. Porterfield comments that "suicide in every non-Southern city exceeds homicide by ratios ranging from 1.19 to 18.60, while suicide rates exceed homicide rates in only 8 of the 43 Southern and Southwestern cities, 5 of these being in the Southwest."[8]

Violence in the South has three dimensions. In relation to the North, there are high rates of homicide and assault, moderate rates of crime against property, and low rates of suicide. The relationship between homicide and suicide rates in a given group is best expressed by a suicide-homicide ratio (SHR = 100 [Suicides/Suicides + Homicides]). The European pattern, shared by white northerners but not by Negroes or white southerners, is for suicides to far outnumber homicides so that the SHR is in excess of 80. The ratios in Table 1,

TABLE 1

SUICIDE-HOMICIDE RATIOS FOR FOUR CATEGORIES OF AMERICANS, 1920–1964[9]

Year	United States White SHR	Southern White SHR	United States Negro SHR	Southern Negro SHR
1920	69.3	43.4 *	11.2	05.6 *
1925	70.9	53.5 *	09.2	05.0 *
1930	75.0	61.1 *	11.9	06.0 *
1935	76.2	59.9	11.4	06.3
1940	83.3	68.5	09.6	06.5
1945	80.3	66.4	11.1	06.8
1950	82.4	69.8	12.4	09.3
1955	88.3	73.1	15.6	09.7
1960	82.0	74.4	17.0	12.2
1964	81.1	73.2	16.7	11.1

displayed graphically in Figure 1, measure the difference between southerners and other Americans with regard to violence. Because the statistics for "the United States" include the statistics for the southern states, the differences between southern and nonsouthern suicide-murder ratios are understated. Even so, the differences are significant. In the North and the South, but more so in

[7] Austin L. Porterfield, "Indices of Suicide and Homicide by States and Cities: Some Southern-Non-Southern Contrasts with Implications for Research," *American Sociological Review,* XIV (Aug. 1949), 481–90.
[8] *Ibid.,* 485.
[9] Suicide-Homicide Ratio = 100 (Suicides/Suicides +Homicides). As the ratio approaches 100, it registers the increasing preference for suicide rather than murder among the members of a given group. The ratios were computed from figures taken from Forrest E. Linder and Robert D. Grove, *Vital Statistics Rates in the United States, 1900–1940* (Washington, D.C., 1943); and US, Department of Health, Education, and Welfare, *Vital Statistics of the United States,* for the appropriate years. The asterisks in the table indicate that: in 1920 all of the former Confederate states were included in the figures except Alabama, Arkansas, Georgia, and Texas; Arkansas, Georgia, and Texas were still not reporting in 1925, but by 1930 only Texas was excluded; since 1935 all southern states are included.

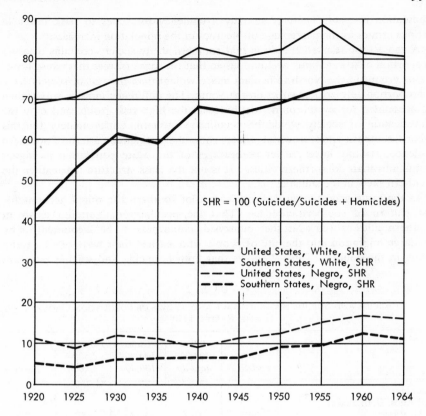

SHR = 100 (Suicides/Suicides + Homicides)

———— United States, White, SHR
———— Southern States, White, SHR
– – – United States, Negro, SHR
▬ ▬ ▬ Southern States, Negro, SHR

the South, Negroes commit murder much more often than they commit suicide. Among white Americans, southerners show a relatively greater preference than do nonsoutherners for murder rather than suicide.

High murder and low suicide rates constitute a distinctly southern pattern of violence, one that must rank with the caste system and ahead of mint juleps in importance as a key to the meaning of being southern. Why this should be so is a question that has puzzled investigators for a long time, and their answers have been various. When one loyal southerner was asked by a probing Yankee why the murder rate in the South was so high, he replied that he reckoned there were just more folks in the South who needed killing.

Few apologies surpass this one in purity, but there is a more popular one that tries to explain the high homicide rates in the southern states by the extremely high rates of violence among Negroes who constitute a large part of the population. As Table 1 indicates, however, southern whites considered by themselves vary from the national norm in the same direction as Negroes, though to a much lesser extent. In addition, Porterfield points out that for the twelve southern states with the heaviest Negro population, the coefficient of correlation between serious crimes and the percentage of Negroes in the population is —.44. There is actually a tendency for states to rank lower in serious crimes as the percentage of Negroes in the population increases.[10]

A more sophisticated theory is that southern white society contains a larger proportion of lower status occupations so that the same factors that cause lower status groups in the North to become more violent than the rest of society have a proportionately greater effect on the South. The difference in rates would then be accounted for by the numerical bulge in the high risk group, and only the stratification of society would be peculiarly southern. Unfortunately for this theory, southern cities, in which whites show the distinctive pattern of southern violence, actually have greater percentages of the white population in higher status jobs than do northern cities.[11] It is not the class structure that causes the southern skew in the statistics.

In the same way, the agricultural nature of southern life might account for the pattern of southern violence. That the peculiar configuration exists in southern cities as well as in the countryside could possibly be accounted for by the large migration into the city of people who learned their ways of living and dying in the country. Table 2 shows that both homicide and suicide rates are

TABLE 2
HOMICIDE AND SUICIDE RATES BY RACE AND BY SIZE OF POPULATION GROUP, UNITED STATES, 1940[12]

	US	Cities 100,000 and up	Cities 10,000– 100,000	Cities 2,500– 10,000	Rural
Suicide (All Ages, Both Sexes)					
All Races	14.4	16.8	15.6	15.1	12.0
White	15.5	17.8	16.4	16.0	13.3
Nonwhite	4.6	7.2	5.8	4.5	3.0
Homicide (All Ages, Both Sexes)					
All Races	6.2	7.1	5.7	7.3	5.7
White	3.1	3.2	2.5	3.7	3.3
Nonwhite	33.3	43.4	43.0	51.9	23.1

lower for rural districts than for urban areas. This results in an SHR for the white population of rural districts considered by themselves of 80.1, as compared with an SHR of 83.7 for the white population of the nation as a whole. The SHR of 68.8 in 1940 for southern whites, both urban and rural, is significantly lower than the national ratios and indicates that southern whites

[10] Austin L. Porterfield, "A Decade of Serious Crimes in the United States," *American Sociological Review*, XIII (Feb. 1948), 44–54; see also James E. McKeown, "Poverty, Race, and Crime," *Journal of Criminal Law and Criminology*, XXXIX (Nov.–Dec. 1948), 480–83.

[11] Norval D. Glenn, "Occupational Benefits to Whites from the Subordination of Negroes," *American Sociological Review*, XXVIII (June 1963), 443–48, esp. Table 1.

[12] The source for this table is Linder and Grove, *Vital Statistics Rates in the United States, 1900–1940*, Table 24.

tended more to act out their aggressions than the white population of either the cities or the countryside in the rest of the nation.

Another way of testing the notion that the rurality of the South may be the root of its strange configuration of violence is summarized in Table 3, a comparison of the SHR's of the eleven former Confederate states with those of the eleven most rural nonsouthern states. The nonsouthern states, mostly western, are closer in time to frontier days and are currently much more subject

TABLE 3

SUICIDE AND HOMICIDE RATES AND SUICIDE-HOMICIDE RATIOS FOR SOUTHERN STATES AND ELEVEN MOST RURAL NONSOUTH-ERN STATES, 1940 [13]

Population Group	Suicide-Homicide Ratio
Southern Nonwhite	6.7
National Nonwhite	12.2
Southern White	68.8
Nonsouthern, White Rural (11 states)	79.0
National White Rural	80.1
National White	83.7

	White				White	
Southern States	Suicide Rate	Homicide Rate	Rural Non-southern States	Suicide Rate	Homicide Rate
Alabama	11.7	6.9	Arizona	15.2	7.5
Arkansas	8.0	5.1	Idaho	17.7	3.3
Florida	19.8	7.5	Iowa	15.2	1.3
Georgia	12.1	5.6	Kansas	13.0	1.1
Louisiana	12.4	5.5	Montana	21.1	4.8
Mississippi	10.1	5.7	Nebraska	16.8	.7
North Carolina	10.4	4.0	New Mexico	14.2	5.7
South Carolina	9.7	5.0	North Dakota	9.7	1.4
Tennessee	10.0	7.1	South Dakota	10.5	1.8
Texas	13.6	5.3	Vermont	16.7	.8
Virginia	18.4	5.0	Wyoming	23.5	4.5
Averages	12.4	5.6	Averages	15.8	4.2

to instability caused by in-migration than are the southern states, but otherwise the two sets of states are similar enough for purposes of comparison. In 1940 the percentage of population living in the urban areas of the southern states ranged from 13.4 per cent to 36.7 per cent, with the mean falling at 26.1 per cent, while in the eleven nonsouthern states the degree of urbanization ranged from 13.6 per cent to 36.7 per cent, with the mean at 31.2 per cent. In order not to distort the picture more than necessary, Nevada, with an extraordinary suicide rate of 41.3 per 100,000 population, is omitted from the comparison. At the same time, Virginia and Florida, with nonsouthern SHR's, are retained in

[13] The source for Table 3 is *ibid.*, Table 20. All rates are per 100,000 population.

the southern sample. The results still show a significant difference between the suicide-murder ratio of the southern states and that of the most rural nonsouthern states. The strange bent of southern violence cannot be accounted for by the rural nature of southern society.

Poverty is also a logical factor to suspect as the underlying cause of the South's pattern of violence. Howard Odum computed that in 1930 the Southeast had 20.9 per cent of the nation's population but only 11.9 per cent of its wealth.[14] Whether or not the region was poor before it was violent is undetermined. Even more to the point, poverty alone cannot explain high homicide rates. The decline of homicides during business depressions in the United States underlines this argument, as does the fact that crime rates among second-generation immigrants are much higher than among first-generation immigrants despite increased material welfare of the former.[15] One study has found no significant correlation between crime rates and the proportion of the population on relief by county in Minnesota, whereas there was a strong correlation between crime rates and the degree of urbanization. Like the rural poor in Minnesota, the Japanese of Seattle were poor but honest and nonviolent.[16]

Though the data are extremely questionable, there is, nevertheless, a significant positive correlation between the SHR for the fifty-six world polities for which information is readily available and almost every measure of modernization that can be quantified.[17] It is difficult to determine whether it is underdevelopment or the process of change that accounts for this, for scholars have noted that the process of modernization generates various sorts of conflict and violence.[18] For both developing and industrialized nations, education is the most powerful predictor of a country's SHR, but indexes of industrial and urban activity, along with reflections of the society's general welfare, are also significantly correlated with the SHR. This is true for the fifty-six world polities considered together as well as for the European nations as a group and for the non-European countries taken together. That southerners over the past half century have been growing more similar to nonsouthern Americans in their tastes in violence as the gap between the nation and the South in economic development has slowly narrowed also argues that there may be no increment of violence in the South that is not "explained" by the relative slowness of the region's development.

[14] Howard Odum, *Southern Regions of the United States* (Chapel Hill, N.C., 1936), 208.
[15] Edwin H. Sutherland and Donald R. Cressey, *Principles of Criminology* (6th ed., New York, 1960), 92, 146–49.
[16] Van B. Shaw, "The Relationship between Crime Rates and Certain Population Characteristics in Minnesota Counties," *Journal of Criminal Law and Criminology*, XL (May–June 1949), 43–49.
[17] Simple intercorrelations were run between the indexes of homicide and suicide and measures of social and economic activity using data from *World Handbook of Political and Social Indicators*, ed. Bruce M. Russett *et al.* (New Haven, Conn., 1964); and Statistical Office of the United Nations Department of Economic and Social Affairs, *Demographic Yearbook, 1963* (New York, 1964), Table 25.
[18] Richard S. Weinert, "Violence in Pre-Modern Societies: Rural Colombia," *American Political Science Review*, LX (June 1966), 340–47; *Internal War, Problems and Approaches*, ed. Harry Eckstein (New York, 1964); E. J. Hobsbawm, *Primitive Rebels: Studies in Archaic Forms of Social Movement in the 19th and 20th Centuries* (New York, 1959). An important synthesis and statement of theory is Ted Gurr, "Psychological Factors in Civil Violence," *World Politics*, XX (Jan. 1968), 245–78.

Multiple regression analysis offers a technique for testing the possibility that variations in the key indexes of modernization operating in an additive fashion might account for the South's particularity in rates of violence. Six independent variables measuring the four factors of wealth, education, urbanization, and age are included in this analysis. Except where indicated below, their values are taken from the *United States Census* for 1940. Urbanization is stated as the percentage of the population living within towns of 2,500 or more; education is measured by the median number of school years completed by persons twenty-five years old and older; "income" is the state's per capita personal income in dollars for 1940; unemployment is expressed as the percentage of the working force out of work; "wealth" is the state's per capita income in dollars in 1950; and age is the median age of the population. The values of each variable except "income" are recorded by race. "South" is a dummy variable included in the analysis in order to see if any of the unexplained residue of the dependent variable is associated with the fact of its occurring either inside or outside the South. All of the former Confederate states were assigned the value of one, while all nonsouthern states were recorded as zero. The dependent variables that require "explaining" are the suicide rate, the homicide rate, the sum of the suicide rate and homicide rate, and the suicide-homicide ratio. Even though these rates are taken from the most reliable source, *Vital Statistics of the United States*, there may be large errors between the published rates and the true rates. Some violent deaths are never recorded, and many are improperly classified, but there is no reason to suspect that there has been a long-term, systematic bias in the collection and recording of the statistics for the southern states. For the purpose of the crude comparison between South and non-South, the *Vital Statistics* are acceptable.

The results of the analysis are summarized in Table 4. The coefficient of correlation between each of the independent variables and the dependent variable is found in the column labeled "Simple." The percentage of the variation in the dependent variable that is associated with, and thus "explained" by, the variation in the independent variable is found by squaring the coefficient of correlation. Education, for example, is the best single predictor of the white suicide rate. The simple coefficient of correlation of .62 between education and suicide in Table 4 indicates that approximately 38 per cent of the variation in the white suicide rate among the forty-eight states in 1940 is associated with variations in the educational level of the populations. The positive correlation means that the suicide rate tends to rise from one state to the next as the educational level rises. The negative coefficients of correlation between each of the independent variables, except South, and the white homicide rate indicate, conversely, that the homicide rate tends to decline as the indexes of development rise.

The effect on the dependent variable of all of the independent variables considered together is measured by the coefficient of multiple correlation, "R." Thus 72 per cent of the white suicide rate and 52 per cent of the white homicide rate are explained by the seven independent variables operating in an additive fashion. The coefficient of partial correlation expresses the relationship of each independent variable with the unexplained portion of the dependent variable after the independent variables acting collectively have done all the explaining possible. The coefficient of partial correlation for the dummy variable (South)

TABLE 4

Multiple Regression Analysis
Violence, Development, and Sectionalism in the United States, 1940 [19]

Dependent Variables by State	R² Variation Explained	Urbanization		Education		Income		Unemployment		Wealth		Age		South	
		Simple	Partial	Simple	Partial	Simple	Partial	Simple	Partial	Simple	Partial	Simple	Partial	Simple	Partial
White Suicide Rate	.72 *	.25	−.64 *	.62 *	.52	.56 *	.14	.22	.33	.53 *	.35	.55 *	.59 *	−.31	.42 *
White Homicide Rate	.52 *	−.45 *	−.24	−.17	.09	−.42	.23	−.13	.26	−.42	−.12	−.58 *	.24	.54 *	.49 *
White Homicide plus Suicide Rate	.57 *	.07	−.59 *	.52	.44 *	.36	.20	.15	.35	−.34	.22	−.30	.41 *	−.09	.50 *
White Suicide-Homicide Ratio	.72 *	.53 *	−.02	.40 *	.11	.63 *	−.24	.25	−.18	.62 *	.29	.76 *	.49 *	−.68 *	−.53 *
Nonwhite Suicide Rate	.30	.08	−.13	.30	.25	.47 *	.26	.15	−.09	.34	−.00	.13	−.04	−.34	.08
Nonwhite Homicide Rate	.25	−.07	−.28	−.19	−.25	−.11	.18	−.17	.21	−.09	−.04	.04	.40 *	.28	.37 *
Nonwhite Homicide plus Suicide Rate	.22	−.02	−.30	−.03	−.12	.13	.27	−.08	.15	.09	−.04	.10	.35	.09	.37 *
Nonwhite Suicide-Homicide Ratio	.35	.27	.32	.36	.31	.43 *	.18	.30	−.11	.36	−.10	.12	−.40	−.36	−.09

[19] The asterisks in the table denote that the chance that a random ordering of the data would produce a relationship this strong is less than one in one hundred.

is the most important yield of the multiple regression analysis.

Even though the seven independent variables acting together explain 72 per cent of the variation of the white SHR among the forty-eight states in 1940, 28 per cent ($r = -.53$) of the remaining portion of the variation of the white SHR is associated with the South. This means that the white SHR is lower in the South than can be accounted for by the lower indexes of urbanization, education, wealth, and age. There is, similarly, a significant portion of the variation from state to state in the white homicide rate, and in the white suicide rate, that is not explained by variations in measures of development, but that is explained by southernness.

If the deviation of the South from the national norms for violence cannot be attributed to backwardness, or at least not to the static measures of underdevelopment, there are other possible explanations that should be considered. The concept of anomie, developed by Émile Durkheim in his study, *Suicide,* in 1898, is frequently mentioned as an explanation of both homicide and suicide. Anomie has meant slightly varying but not contradictory things to different investigators. It is most generally understood to be a social condition in which there is a deterioration of belief in the existing set of rules of behavior, or in which accepted rules are mutually contradictory, or when prescribed goals are not accessible through legitimate means, or when cognition and socialization have been obstructed by personality traits that cluster about low ego-strength.[20] As it is manifested in the individual, in the form of anomy, it is a feeling of normlessness and estrangement from other people. An anomic person feels lost, drifting without clearly defined rules and expectations, isolated, powerless, and frustrated. In this state, there is a strong strain toward deviant behavior in various forms. The problem is that both homicide and suicide are thought to be related to it, and the theory does not predict what sorts of people or what groups will favor one form of behavior rather than another.

To look at southern violence as the product of anomie in any case would involve a great paradox. The most popular explanation of the high rates of violence in America as compared to Europe places the blame on the rapid urbanization, secularization, and industrialization of the United States and on the social characteristics associated with this remarkable growth: geographic and status mobility, an emphasis upon contractual relationships and upon social norms rather than upon personal relationships, competitive striving, and a cultural pluralism that involves a high level of dissonance among the values that everyone tries to put into practice.[21] The South has traditionally served as the counterpoint to the American way of life because it seemed to differ from the North in these very aspects.[22] Southerners have a greater sense of history than northerners, a greater attachment to place, and more deferential social customs.

[20] Herbert McClosky and John H. Schaar, "Psychological Dimensions of Anomy," *American Sociological Review,* XXX (Feb. 1965), 14–40.
[21] David Abrahamsen, *The Psychology of Crime* (New York, 1960), 18–21, 177–83. These relationships are greatly illuminated by the discussion in David Potter, *People of Plenty: Economic Abundance and the American Character* (Chicago, 1954).
[22] William H. Taylor, *Cavalier and Yankee: The Old South and American National Character* (Garden City, N.Y., 1963); C. Vann Woodward, *The Burden of Southern History* (Baton Rouge, La., 1960), 109–40.

By all reports, southerners place more emphasis on personal relations and on ascribed statuses than do northerners. Not only do southerners prize political and social cohesion, but by most measures the South is much more homogeneous than the non-South.[23] Yet, though the South differs from the North on so many of the factors that supposedly contribute to anomie and thus to violence, the South is the nation's most violent region.

One body of theory seems to predict higher rates of violence precisely because of the South's homogeneity. Reformulating the observations of George Simmel and Bronislaw Malinowski, Lewis Coser writes that "we may say that a conflict is more passionate and more radical when it arises out of close relationships." "The closer the relationship," so the reasoning goes, "the greater the affective investment, the greater also the tendency to suppress rather than express hostile feelings. . . . In such cases feelings of hostility tend to accumulate and hence intensify." Such a theory fits the empirical observation that individuals who express hostility retain fewer and less violent feelings of antagonism toward the source of their irritation.[24] But Coser himself states that, though conflicts within close relationships are likely to be intense when they occur, "this does not necessarily point to the likelihood of more *frequent* conflict in closer relationships than in less close ones." There are situations in which accumulated hostilities do not eventuate in conflict and may even serve to solidify the relationship.[25]

The frustration-aggression hypothesis involves similar perplexities.[26] One of the alternative ways of adapting to frustration is, for example, to turn the frustration inward upon the self. In extreme cases this can result in suicide.[27] A psychoanalyst has concluded after an extensive study that a major portion of Sweden's high suicide rate is caused by the frustrations arising from a highly competitive, success-oriented society.[28] The general rise in suicide rates in the United States during economic downturns argues that the same mechanism is at work among some segments of the population. Consequently, nothing in the frustration-aggression hypothesis predicts the direction the aggression will take.

There are currently two theories that attempt to explain the generally inverse relationship between homicide and suicide as reactions to frustration. The first, developed by Andrew F. Henry and James F. Short, Jr.,[29] is based on the assumption that both homicide and suicide are the result of frustration-aggression and builds upon Porterfield's initial suggestion that the strength of the

[23] Jack P. Gibbs and Walter T. Martin, *Status Integration and Suicide: A Sociological Study* (Eugene, Ore., 1964), esp. Table 6.
[24] Lewis A. Coser, *The Functions of Social Conflict* (New York, 1956), 57, 62, 71; Albert Pepitone and George Reichling, "Group Cohesiveness and Expression of Hostility," in *Personality and Social Systems*, ed. Neil J. Smelser and William T. Smelser (New York, 1963), 117–24.
[25] Coser, *Functions of Social Conflict*, 72.
[26] John Dollard *et al., Frustration and Aggression* (New Haven, Conn., 1939); Leonard Berkowitz, *Aggression: A Social Psychological Analysis* (New York, 1962); Aubrey J. Yates, *Frustration and Conflict* (New York, 1962).
[27] Karl Menninger, *Man against Himself* (New York, 1938), 23. The assumption that homicide and suicide are simply aggressions manifested in different directions is the basis of the concept of the suicide-homicide ratio.
[28] Herbert Hendin, *Suicide and Scandinavia: A Psychoanalytic Study of Culture and Character* (Garden City, N.Y., 1965), Chap. v.
[29] Andrew F. Henry and James F. Short, Jr., *Suicide and Homicide: Some Economic, Sociological, and Psychological Aspects of Aggression* (Glencoe, Ill., 1954).

relational system might have something to do with an individual's choice of either homicide or suicide.[30] Henry and Short adduce data on the relationship of homicide and suicide rates to the business cycle and to certain statistically distinct groups. They reason that overt aggression against others "varies directly with the strength of external restraint over the behavior of the adult—external restraint which is a function of strength of the relational system and position in the status hierarchy." [31] According to this theory, overt aggression increases as the strength of the relational system increases and as a person's position in the status hierarchy decreases.

Martin Gold has pointed out, however, that contrary to the hypothesis of Henry and Short, upper status people are likely to be more restrained by the expectations of others than are lower status people. Even more damaging is Gold's demonstration that the Henry and Short hypothesis does not correctly predict the greater preference of women for suicide rather than homicide; [32] nor does it correctly predict that suicide rates are lower among the middle classes than at either extreme of the social scale.

The second theory, fashioned by Gold, attempts to relate differences in child-rearing practices to preferences for hostility or guilt as an accommodation to frustration. Gold shows, specifically, that there is a positive correlation between the incidence of physical punishment commonly used in the child-rearing practices of certain groups and the rate of homicide for that group. His conclusion is that physical disciplining of children leads to aggression against others rather than against the self.[33] To confound the theory, restrictive child-rearing practices in Europe evidently do not lead to the physical violence that such practices among the lower classes in America are supposed to produce. It is also doubtful that there is a significant class differential in the degree of physical punishment used to discipline children.[34] William and Joan McCord found in their study of juveniles that there was no strong relationship between disciplining methods and criminality except when a child is rejected by his parents or when his parents provide him with a deviant role model; harsh discipline does less damage than neglect.[35] Despite such complexities, it is reasonable to suppose that there is some causal relationship between the socialization of aggression and a group's SHR, but before such a relationship can be a useful ingredient of an explanation of southern violence, anthropologists and historians need to know much more about regional differences in child-rearing techniques.

[30] Porterfield, "Indices of Suicide and Homicide," 488.

[31] Henry and Short, *Suicide and Homicide,* 119.

[32] Martin Gold, "Suicide, Homicide, and the Socialization of Aggression," *American Journal of Sociology,* LXIII (May 1958), 651–61. Gold originated the SHR, which he called the "suicide-murder ratio."

[33] *Ibid.*

[34] Melvin L. Kohn, "Social Class and the Exercise of Parental Authority," in *Personality and Social Systems,* ed. Smelser and Smelser, 297–314; Martha Sturm White, "Social Class, Child Rearing Practices, and Child Behavior," *ibid.,* 286–96; Bernard C. Rosen and Roy D'Andrade, "The Psychosocial Origins of Achievement Motivation," *Sociometry,* XXII (Sept. 1959), 185–215, cited in *Anomie and Deviant Behavior: A Discussion and Critique,* ed. Marshall B. Clinard (New York, 1964), 260–61; Bernard Berelson and Gary A. Steiner, *Human Behavior: An Inventory of Scientific Findings* (New York, 1964), 479–81.

[35] William McCord and Joan McCord. *Origins of Crime: A New Evaluation of the Cambridge-Somerville Youth Study* (New York, 1959), 172, 198.

Whether or not the cause can be located in child-rearing practices, several bodies of evidence point to the conclusion that southern violence is a cultural pattern that exists separate from current influences. For instance, several commentators have suggested that the habit of carrying guns in the South made murder a much more frequent outcome of altercations among southerners than among northerners. This argument is buttressed by a 1968 survey, reported in Table 5, which showed that 52 per cent of southern white families owned guns, as opposed to only 27 per cent of their nonsouthern white counterparts. It may be, however, that this differential in ownership of guns is the result of a violent turn of mind rather than the cause of violence. This is the implication of the fact that when the House of Representatives in 1968 passed a weak gun control bill to restrict the mail-order sale of rifles, shotguns, and ammunition by the

TABLE 5

PER CENT OF FAMILIES OWNING FIREARMS [36]

	Yes	No	Not Sure
Total White	34	65	1
South	52	45	3
Non-South	27	72	1
Total Nonwhite	24	70	6
South	34	61	5
Non-South	15	78	7

overwhelming vote of 304 to 118, representatives of the eleven former Confederate states nonetheless voted 73 to 19 against the bill.[37] It should be noted, too, that while some southern states have relatively strict firearms laws, these laws do not dramatically affect their homicide rates.[38] Furthermore, the assault rate is extremely high in the South, indicating that southerners react with physical hostility even without guns.

A glance at Table 4 reveals that for Negroes either the data are grossly skewed or there is little relationship between violence and the selected indexes of social welfare. The barest hint exists that, controlling for the selected factors, there is some explanatory value in sectionalism, a conclusion that has independent verification. Thomas F. Pettigrew and Rosalind Barclay Spier found that the major correlate of the Negro homicide rate in the North was the proportion of Negroes in a given area who had been born and raised in the South and that this was in addition to the effect of migration itself. It had long been known that homicide was much less frequent among northern than among southern Negroes; this finding suggests that violence in the South is a style of life that is handed down from father to son along with the old hunting rifle and the family Bible.[39]

[36] The source of Table 5 is a survey of national statistical sample by Opinion Research, Inc., for a Columbia Broadcasting System program, September 2, 1968.
[37] New York *Times,* July 25, 1968.
[38] Carl Bakal, *The Right to Bear Arms* (New York, 1966), 346–53.
[39] Thomas F. Pettigrew and Rosalind Barclay Spier, "The Ecological Structure of Negro Homicide," *American Journal of Sociology,* LXVII (May 1962), 621–29.

The great contribution to the discussion of southern violence made by Wilbur J. Cash in his book *The Mind of the South* was precisely that southern violence is part of a style of life that can only be explained historically.[40] According to Cash's own poetic and impressionistic rendering, violence grew up on the southern frontier as naturally as it grows up on any frontier. Violence was an integral part of the romantic, hedonistic, hell-of-a-fellow personality created by the absence of external restraint that is characteristic of a frontier. The cult of honor, with its insistence on the private settlement of disputes, was one manifestation of the radical individualism of the South, but there were other influences at work. The plantation, the most highly organized institution on the southern frontier, reinforced the tendency toward violence that had been initiated by the absence of organization. This was so, Cash argues, for two reasons: whites on the plantation exercised unrestrained dominance over blacks; and whites were generally raised by blacks and consequently were deeply influenced by the romantic and hedonistic Negro personality. Cash does not explicitly say what forces produced this Negro personality, but the implication is that it is fixed by the laws of genetics. But if the more likely position is taken that Negro and white personalities are shaped by environment and experience, then the reader is left with yet another Cashian paradox: violence in the white personality stems at the same time from the effect of being unrestrained and from imitating the Negro personality which was formed out of a situation of dependency and subordination.

The mediating variable that brings together the various inconsistencies in Cash's explanation of how violence came to be established in the late ante bellum period as part of the southern personality may be the absence of law. Not disorganization nor individualism, not dominance nor submission, not lack of restraint—none of these forces played as important a role as the absence of institutions of law enforcement in compelling southerners to resort to the private settlement of disputes. Cash makes this explicit in his treatment of Reconstruction, the second frontier.

During Reconstruction, according to Cash, southern whites resorted to individual and collective violence because the courts were dominated by carpetbaggers and scalawags. Though this is logical, it is not consistent with Cash's earlier argument that the growth of law had been inhibited on the ante bellum frontier by the desire of southerners to provide their own justice. Apparently the direction of causation in the relationship between law and violence changes in accordance with the needs of Cash's interpretation.

Just as the first and second southern frontiers simultaneously promoted social solidarity and individualism, the third southern frontier, progress, changed the South in the direction of the American norm of Babbittry while at the same time accommodating continuity in the basic traits of the southern mind. A further paradox is involved in the impact of progress on the pattern of violence. Because violence originally arose from individualism, Cash says, the growth of towns should have brought a decrease in rates of violence. This decrease did not materialize because progress also brought poverty, and poverty destroys individualism. Cash argues in effect that individualism produced violence in the ante

[40] Wilbur J. Cash, *The Mind of the South* (New York, 1940; Vintage ed., 1960), 32–34, 44–52, 76, 115–23, 161, 220, 424.

bellum period and the loss of individualism produced violence in the twentieth century.

Though Cash failed to formulate a coherent theory of southern violence, he did focus on two factors that are obvious possibilities as the chief motive forces of southern violence: the frontier experience and the presence of the Negro. The American frontier did spawn violence, but it seems improbable that the frontier could have much to do with the fact that in the twentieth century southern states on the eastern seaboard have much higher rates of violence than the nation at large. There is also considerable difficulty with the notion that the presence of large numbers of Negroes accounts for the great propensity of whites for violence. There is, in fact, little interracial homicide,[41] and there is no reason to question John Dollard's hypothesis that Negroes murder and assault each other with such appalling frequency because of their daily frustrations in dealing with white men. Because aggressions against whites would call forth extreme negative sanctions, frustrated Negroes transfer their aggressive feelings to other Negroes.[42] If this is the case, it is difficult to see how high rates of violence among the dominant white group would also be attributed to the white-Negro relationship, especially when the presence of Negroes in the North is not accompanied by a proportionate rate of violence among the whites. It is also interesting that whites in South Africa who also experienced frontier conditions and a subordinate nonwhite population have a homicide-suicide ratio almost identical to the ratio for the American North but quite different from that of the South.

Subservience, rather than dominance, may be the condition that underlies a pattern of low SHR's. In his extremely popular book *The Wretched of the Earth,* Franz Fanon suggests that the oppressed status of a colonial people produces a pattern of aggressiveness directed against fellow colonials and a need to achieve manhood through violence. The task of revolutionaries is to mobilize the aggressive drives, provide them a sustaining ideology, and direct them against the oppressors.[43] Defeat in the Civil War and the South's resulting position as an economic dependency of the industrial Northeast qualify it for consideration as a violent colonial region. In addition to the difficulty of separating the effects of subservience from the effects of sheer underdevelopment, the problem with this line of reasoning is that the heroic myths created about the Lost Cause and the relatively early return of home rule after the Civil War may have mitigated the trauma of defeat and social dislocation. It would be difficult to maintain that the South's historical experience as a region is the equivalent of the sort of cultural conflict that leads to the loss of self-esteem, disrupts the processes of socialization, and initiates the cycle of self-crippling behavior within the subordinate group.[44] Furthermore, American Indians have responded to their experience of defeat and repression with higher rates of suicide and other intrapunitive behavior rather than with aggression against

[41] Marvin E. Wolfgang, *Patterns in Criminal Homicide* (Philadelphia, 1958), 222–36.

[42] John Dollard, *Caste and Class in a Southern Town* (3d ed., Garden City, N.Y., 1949), Chap. xiii.

[43] Franz Fanon, *The Wretched of the Earth* (New York, 1963).

[44] Thomas Stone et al., "Poverty and the Individual," in *Poverty and Affluence,* ed. Leo Fishman (New Haven, Conn., 1966), 72–96.

others. Similarly, while industrialization was transforming and disrupting its established folk culture, Harlan County, Kentucky, had the highest homicide rates in the country, but a study of community growth in New England finds suicide and depressive disorders highly correlated with the disruptive impact of geographic mobility.[45]

Though the social sciences offer no clearly authenticated hypothesis that predicts the relationship in different populations between homicide and suicide rates,[46] there are some potentially illuminating investigations currently in progress. Assuming that depressed mental patients are people who have turned anger inward through introjection and guilt when under chronic stress, while paranoid patients are those who have turned anger outward through denial and projection, one study has found an interesting association between the pattern of intrafamily communication and the direction taken by mental pathology when it occurred. Depressed patients in this study came from families in which as children they were forced to try by themselves to attain the desired forms of behavior through positive, "ought" channels. Paranoid patients came from families in which they were forced into acceptable modes of behavior by negative "ought not" procedures.

> In families of *depressed* patients the child comes to view his environment as non-threatening to him physically. It is something to be manipulated by him in order to bring about the desired effects that will win approval. There is directionality here, and it is *from* the child *toward* his environment. On the other hand, in families of paranoid patients the child comes to view his environment as having potentially harmful properties that he cannot control and that must be avoided in some way. Here the directionality is *from* the environment *toward* the child.[47]

The hypothesis is that a manipulative attitude toward the environment will be associated with intrapunitive behavior and that a passive attitude toward the environment, with the absence of the internalization of a feeling of responsibility for the self, will be correlated with a greater use of projection in ego-defense.

There are firm indications that cultural patterning as well as child-rearing techniques will affect the perception of the environment and the orientation of the personality on the paranoia-depression continuum. In Burma, a hierarchical society in which a person's prestige and authority increase as he gets older, the social and physical environment is typically perceived as potentially harmful, and Burma has one of the highest homicide rates in the world.[48] There is also the possibility of a connection between the high rates of violence among

[45] Paul Frederick Cressey, "Social Disorganization and Reorganization in Harlan County, Kentucky," *American Sociological Review*, XIV (June 1949), 389–94; Henry Wechsler, "Community Growth, Depressive Disorders, and Suicide," *American Journal of Sociology*, LXVII (July 1961), 9–16.
[46] Jack O. Douglas, *The Social Meanings of Suicide* (Princeton, N.J., 1967), 3–160.
[47] Hazel M. Hitson and Daniel H. Funkenstein, "Family Patterns and Paranoidal Personality Structure in Boston and Burma," *International Journal of Social Psychiatry*, V (Winter 1959).
[48] *Ibid.*

Afro-Americans and the recent diagnosis that the Negro psyche has been rendered paranoiac by the hostile American environment.[49]

Testing the hypothesis that a paranoid perception of the environment is the root cause of the pattern of violence in the white South is a problem for future scholarship. The most immediately useful technique would be a survey of attitudes toward violence, perceptions of the environment, feelings of personal efficacy, and other measures of alienation. There may be regional differentials in these categories as well as class, age, and sexual differentials. A rigorous comparison of rates of violence in perhaps a Kentucky county and an Ohio county at comparable stages of settlement is also a promising approach. The records of the county court, the reports of the state attorney general, and newspaper surveys might produce useful data on both individual and collective violence. Some effort must be made to determine when the South became violent; timing may reveal much about the relationship of slavery to violence. The possible effects of Scotch-Irish immigration, population density, temperature, and religious fundamentalism should be investigated with quantitative methods. Even though the SHR's of Australia and Canada fit the European mold, some insight may derive from pursuing such comparative cases in a detailed manner. Much can be done.

Meanwhile, in the search for a valid explanation of southern violence the most fruitful avenue will probably be one that seeks to identify and trace the development of a southern world view that defines the social, political, and physical environment as hostile and casts the white southerner in the role of the passive victim of malevolent forces. When scholars locate the values that make up this world view and the process by which it was created and is transmitted, the history of the South will undoubtedly prove to have played a major role. The un-American experiences of guilt, defeat, and poverty will be major constituents of the relevant version of that history,[50] but perhaps they will not loom so large as the sense of grievance that is at the heart of the southern identity.

Southern self-consciousness was created by the need to protect a peculiar institution from threats originating outside the region. Consequently, the southern identity has been linked from the first to a siege mentality. Though southerners have many other identities, they are likely to be most conscious of being southerners when they are defending their region against attack from outside forces: abolitionists, the Union Army, carpetbaggers, Wall Street and Pittsburgh, civil rights agitators, the federal government, feminism, socialism, trade-unionism, Darwinism, Communism, atheism, daylight-saving time, and other by-products of modernity. This has produced an extreme sensitivity to criticism from outsiders and a tendency to excuse local faults as the products of forces beyond human or local control. If the South was poor, it was because the Yankees stole all the family silver and devastated the region in other ways after the Civil War. If industrialization seemed inordinately slow in the South, it was because of a conspiracy of northern capitalists to maintain the region as an economic colony. Added to this experience with perceived threats has been the fact that almost every significant change in the life of the South has been

[49] William H. Grier and Price M. Cobbs, *Black Rage* (New York, 1968).
[50] Woodward, *Burden of Southern History,* 3–26.

initiated by external powers. This is even true of industrialization. Though there was a fervent native movement to sponsor industrialization, absentee ownership has been characteristic. Furthermore, the real qualitative change in the southern pattern of low-wage industry came as a result of World War II and the activities of the federal government.

Being southern, then, inevitably involves a feeling of persecution at times and a sense of being a passive, insignificant object of alien or impersonal forces. Such a historical experience has fostered a world view that supports the denial of responsibility and locates threats to the region outside the region and threats to the person outside the self. From the southern past arise the symbiosis of profuse hospitality and intense hostility toward strangers and the paradox that the southern heritage is at the same time one of grace and violence.

19

STEPHAN THERNSTROM

The Dimensions of Occupational Mobility

The notion of America as the "promised land" rests largely on the supposed equal opportunity to climb to the top. The self-made man of the Horatio Alger image personifies the American dream. But did equal opportunity exist in fact? Apart from studies of the "agricultural ladder" for tenant farmers by James C. Malin and his students, mobility patterns in the nineteenth century remain terra incognita. *Sociologists have been interested in social mobility, but have focused their efforts on trends of the last generation, as, for example, W. Lloyd Warner's* Yankee City *(Newburyport) series and Robert and Helen Lynd's* Middletown *(Muncie) surveys. Both works seem to indicate a low rate of upward mobility, and the authors express concern about this apparent vitiation of the American dream. Perhaps, however, it was as difficult for an unskilled urban worker to climb the social ladder in 1860 as it is today. Only in the light of mobility trends of a century ago can we assess the present data.*

Stephan Thernstrom is the first to attempt a statistical analysis of occupational mobility among unskilled urban labor in the nineteenth century. The testing ground is Newburyport, Massachusetts, where the unskilled comprised about one tenth of the labor force. The decennial manuscript Federal population censuses of 1850 through 1880 provided the basic resource, which the author supplemented with local censuses, city directories, tax lists, and savings bank accounts. Thernstrom's Newburyport study is not statistically sophisticated or computerized, as is his subsequent Boston study from 1880 to the present. It is, however, a lucid demonstration of how simple relationships, refined by control variables, can increase our knowledge of social phenomena. Although Professor Thernstrom uncovered no degraded or fixed proletarian class in Newburyport, there was little inter-generational mobility in occupations either. Sons of common laborers themselves filled the ranks of the unskilled day workers. The high geographical mobility of 60 per cent may have skewed the results somewhat, especially if resettling led to a better job and improved economic status.

JOHN R. FOWLE was an ordinary workman of Newburyport, nothing more. Born in New Hampshire in 1802, Fowle was listed variously as "laborer," "gardener," and "porter" in the census schedules and local city directories of the 1850–1880 period. Nor did he display any great talent for saving money; the census and the tax assessor's records show him without any property holdings during these years. Fowle had five daughters and four sons; none of them received much education. Two of the sons left Newburyport while still youths. A third started work as a common laborer, but after a few years of unskilled labor, and a few more as an operative in a shoe factory, he was able to open a small grocery; the shop was rented, and his inventory was valued at $300.

John Fowle's youngest son, Stephen, had a more striking career. Where he obtained the capital for his first venture into business is unknown. In 1856, a lad of twenty-two, he paid only a poll tax. Two years later tax records show him the owner of a house and lot valued at $1100, and the city directory lists him as a "newsdealer." His news agency prospered, and Stephen was willing to take risks. He sold the house for $1250 in 1862, and looked for new possibilities. Not long after, with the aid of $4500 borrowed from the Institution for Savings, he entered into a series of transactions which gained him a home just off the best residential street (High) and a shop on the main business thoroughfare (State). His real estate holdings reached $8000 by the time of the Census of 1870; his inventories of periodicals, fruit, and sundries approached $2000. The Fowle store is still doing well on the same site after ninety years, though the family itself has disappeared from the city.

Michael Lowry, born in Ireland in 1815, came to the New World in the great exodus following the famine. Lowry settled in Newburyport in the late forties, and worked there as a day laborer the rest of his life. His eight sons were put to work as soon as they were able, but the family remained propertyless, living in rented quarters along the waterfront. One son, James, had a minor success; he saved $450 out of his wages as a mariner to purchase a house. None of the other children appear to have advanced in the slightest; all were unskilled laborers or seamen in 1880, lacking property holdings or savings accounts. Thomas Lowry did embark on certain ventures which might have produced a considerable income, but his brief career as a housebreaker ended with five years behind bars.

Pat Moylan was one of the few laborers in Newburyport who owned his own home in 1850. Moylan too was Irish, but he had immigrated to America well before the Great Famine, and had married a native-born girl. His successes over this thirty-year period were moderate, but they were sufficient to allow his children greater career opportunities than was common at this social level. Sometime in the 1850's Moylan found the job he was to hold until his death—night watchman at a textile mill. If his daily wages were not much higher than they had been as a common laborer, he was now sure of steady employment. His Olive Street home, valued at $700, made it unnecessary to pay out a large portion of his income in rent; he reported an additional $300 in personal proverty on the Census of 1870. Moylan's children were freer than most of their companions from compelling pressure to enter the labor market at the earliest possible age. Two of his five daughters graduated from the Female High School, a rare achievement for a working class girl at this time. Moylan's eldest son became a factory operative at sixteen, but during the Civil War decade acquired the skills of a blacksmith. Albert and James entered more promising situations; one was employed as a clerk in a cotton mill in 1880, while the other was still studying at Brown High School.

William Hardy, like John Fowle, was a native-born day laborer; like Fowle, Hardy never succeeded in accumulating any property. Hardy's two eldest sons did little better; one became a seaman, the other a factory operative. His two younger boys, however, were able to move into a skilled manual calling. Neither James, a machinist, nor Frank, a molder, could claim any property holdings in 1880, but each had entered occupations with earning opportunities well above those for unskilled labor.

The families of Michael and Jeremiah Haley achieved impressive property mobility without any occupational mobility at all. Michael and Jeremiah were recorded as common laborers in the Eighth, Ninth, and Tenth United States Censuses. In 1860 Michael owned property on Monroe Street worth $700; Jeremiah had none. In 1864 Jeremiah, who had three young children working to supplement his income, bought a half share in the Monroe Street house for $400; Michael used this sum to purchase another lot. Michael added steadily to his holdings; by 1880 he paid taxes on $1700 in real estate. In 1870 Jeremiah sold his half share back to Michael, and invested in a larger place on Dove Street, valued at $900 in 1880. The two brothers between them had five sons, none of whom entered any skilled or nonmanual occupation. One of Jeremiah's sons, Pat, did save enough money to build a small house next door to his father's, but he too remained but an ordinary unskilled manual laborer.[1]

These few sketches make one thing quite clear. The situation of the hundreds of Newburyport residents ranked common laborers on the United States Census of 1850, 1860, and 1870 had seemed bleak: these men and their families shared a common plight as members of the lowest social stratum in the community. As these cases reveal, however, not all of these families remained at the very

[1] Information for these cases was drawn from the following sources: manuscript schedules of the Seventh, Eighth, Ninth and Tenth U.S. Censuses; Newburyport Assessor's Valuation Lists, 1850–1880; local city directories; newspapers; a series of manuscript volumes of registrations for the Putnam, Brown, and Female high schools for this period (scattered years). The school registration records are stored in the office of the Superintendent of Schools at the Newburyport High School.

bottom of the Newburyport social ladder. Some, like the Lowrys, were trapped in poverty and illiteracy; others were socially mobile in a variety of ways. This much can be established by examining the life histories of a few families. But a handful of instances cannot reveal what *proportion* of the laboring population of Newburyport reaped the benefits of social mobility, nor can it indicate what *avenues* of social advance were of particular significance to the working class. Perhaps the Lowry family was typical, and the Fowles a curious exception; perhaps the embittered editor of the Boston *Pilot* was right that 95 out of 100 workmen in America were fated to "live and die in the condition in which they were born." [2] Or was Stephen Fowle a representative man, an example of the opportunities open to a wide segment of the working class? To answer the question requires a statistical analysis of social mobility.

Social mobility refers to the process by which individuals alter their social position. But to say this, unhappily, is to say nothing until social position has been defined. The terms social status and social class raise perilously complex and disputed problems of definition. A brief comment at this point will clarify the approach taken here; the subject will be considered further in a later chapter. One major sociological school—represented by W. Lloyd Warner and his followers—emphasizes the prestige dimension of class; the study of social mobility becomes the study of the subtle "climbing" tactics by which the ambitious manipulate others in an effort to improve their prestige rank. Status is measured by polling the community social elite; great emphasis is placed on the intricacies of etiquette. Whatever the merits of this subjective approach to social class and social mobility, it is of little value to the historian, for historical records rarely yield the information necessary to apply prestige categories systematically to societies of the past. [3]

The historical study of social mobility requires the use of objective criteria of social status. The most convenient of these is occupation. Occupation may be only one variable in a comprehensive theory of class, but it is the variable which includes more, which sets more limits on the other variables than any other criterion of status. [4] An analysis of the occupational mobility of unskilled laborers and their sons in Newburyport, therefore, is an appropriate starting point. [5] But such an analysis must take into consideration the changing composition of the Newburyport laboring class.

[2] *Pilot,* Jan. 6, 1855.

[3] Chap. 8 and the appendix [of *Poverty and Progress*] present a detailed critical analysis of Warner's stratification theory.

[4] Gösta Carlsson, *Social Mobility and Class Structure* (Lund, Sweden, 1958), pp. 44–45. Virtually every significant theorist of class sees occupation as a central determinant. Cf. Leonard Reissman, *Class in American Society* (Glencoe, Ill., 1959), p. 158.

[5] The primary source of data for this analysis was the manuscript schedules of the U.S. Census for 1850, 1860, 1870, and 1880. The sample consisted of all Newburyport residents who listed their occupation as "laborer" on the Census of 1850, 1860, or 1870, and all male children of these men. Errors undoubtedly were made in tracing the careers of these hundreds of individuals. For a variety of reasons such errors are most likely to have led to some overestimation of the extent of migration out of the community and perhaps some underestimation of the frequency of upward occupational mobility. However a cross check against the Newburyport Assessor's lists revealed few mistakes and suggests that the margin of error in gathering data was relatively small. One obvious source of possible error is that some of these individuals may have changed their names during the period of the study, a common

Men on the Move: The Problem of Geographical Mobility

Observers of cities have too often treated the modern community as a self-contained entity with a stable population core. A city like Newburyport, whose total population has varied little in the past century, is particularly conducive to such illusions. It is hardly surprising that Lloyd Warner's volumes on Newburyport social life miss the significance of migration in and out of the community and view social mobility exclusively as a reshuffling of its inhabitants into different social classes.

A careful scrutiny of the composition of the Newburyport laboring class in the 1850–1880 period suggests how misleading the myth of stability can be. The most common, if most easily overlooked, form of mobility experienced by the ordinary laborers of nineteenth century Newburyport was mobility out of the city. Slightly less than 40 percent of all the unskilled laborers and their children living in the community at mid-century were still listed there in the Census of 1860; of the 454 men in this class in 1860, but 35 percent were to be found in the city a decade later; the comparable figure for 1870–1880 was 47 percent. (Local health records indicate that deaths accounted for few of these departures.) The first generalization to make about the "typical" Newburyport laborer of this period, it appears, is that he did not live in Newburyport very long! Contemporary observers were correct in characterizing the new working class as floating. For a majority of these permanent transients, Newburyport provided no soil in which to sink roots. It was only one more place in which to carry on the struggle for existence for a few years, until driven onward again.

Even before the effects of occupational and property mobility are taken into account, therefore, it is evident that Newburyport did not develop a degraded proletarian class with fixed membership in the 1850–1880 period. The founders of Lowell had thought of the factory labor force as being made up of "a succession of learners"; to a striking extent this was true of the lowest stratum in Newburyport. A large and steady stream of working class men poured out of the community during these years. Their places were taken by masses of newcomers. Ireland was a continuing source of fresh unskilled labor throughout this period; a smaller but still important group came from the stagnant farms of Vermont, New Hampshire, and Maine. These streams of migration in and out of the community resulted in a turnover of more than half of the local unskilled labor force each decade.

Two of the chief social trends of nineteenth century America—the mass influx of immigrants from the Old World, and the drift of population from country to city—thus appear on our small stage. This volatile society made a

---

tactic of socially ambitious ethnics. I doubt that this was a factor of much significance for this group, though. None of my laborers are recorded on the *List of Persons Whose Names Have Been Changed in Massachusetts, 1780–1883* put out by the Secretary of the Commonwealth (Boston, 1885). Some may have changed their names without legal formalities, of course. But the device itself made most sense for the geographically mobile individuals; a new name was most useful in a new place (or a different neighborhood in a great metropolis), where people did not know the old one. This subject, unhappily, cannot be explored within the confines of a community study like the present one.

hero of the man on the road, heading for the Great West or the Great City.[6]
And American folklore equated movement with success—the hero was on the
make as well as on the move. A few shreds of evidence from recent sociological
inquiries support this old belief that geographical mobility and upward social
mobility are positively related, but whether the myth had any foundation in fact
in nineteenth century America is unknown.[7]

This whets our curiosity about the subsequent career patterns of the hundreds
of laborers who worked in Newboryport for a short time in the 1850–1880
period and then moved on. It is quite impossible, let it be said immediately, to
trace these individuals and thereby to provide a certain answer as to how many
of them later won fame and fortune. Without a magical electronic device
capable of sifting through tens of millions of names and locating a few hundred,
there is no way of picking out former residents of Newburyport on later
national censuses. We do know something, however, about the experiences of
these men in Newburyport, about the circumstances in which they departed
from the community, and about the New England labor market at this time. On
the basis of this information we may venture certain inferences about their
future with a degree of confidence.

In only a handful of all these cases was the laborer migrating from Newburyport in a particularly strategic position to take advantage of new opportunities
in another community. For instance, if the son of a laborer, unencumbered as
yet with family responsibilities, was fortunate enough to possess a substantial
savings account and perhaps a high school education or some experience in a
skilled or nonmanual occupation, his employment prospects after migration
were obviously excellent. Such cases, however, were rare. The great majority of

[6] The volatility of the population in nineteenth century America has not received
the scholarly attention it deserves. A few recent studies report exceptionally high
rates of population turnover in various kinds of communities. Curti found that less
than 50 percent of each occupational group remained resident in Trempealeau
County, Wisconsin, for as long as a decade in the 1850–1880 period (*The Making of
an American Community*, pp. 65–77). The population of Rochester, New York,
appears to have been even less stable at this time: only 47 percent of a sample of 500
names drawn from the 1849 city directory could be located in the 1855 edition, and
the figure fell to 20 percent in 1859 (Blake McKelvey, *Rochester, the Flower City,
1855–1890*, Cambridge, Mass., 1949, p. 3). For statistical data on the rapid turnover
of workers in the textile mills of Holyoke, Massachusetts, in the 1850's, see Ray
Ginger, "Labor in a Massachusetts Cotton Mill, 1853–1860," *The Business History
Review*, 28 (1954): 67–91. The whole question requires systematic study by social
and economic historians. For some valuable methodological suggestions see Eric E.
Lampard, "Urbanization and Social Change: on Broadening the Scope and Relevance
of Urban History," in Oscar Handlin and John Burchard, ed., *The Historian and the
City* (Cambridge, Mass., 1963), pp. 225–47. Cf. Rowland T. Berthoff, "The American Social Order: A Conservative Hypothesis," *American Historical Review*, 65
(1960): 495–514.

[7] Richard Scudder and C. Arnold Anderson, "Migration and Vertical Occupational
Mobility," *American Sociological Review*, 19 (1954): 329–34; Ronald Freeman and
Amos Hawley, "Migration and Occupational Mobility during the Depression," *American Journal of Sociology*, 55 (1950): 171–77; Lipset and Bendix, *Social Mobility in
Industrial Society*, pp. 206–18. A close study of population mobility in Norristown,
Pennsylvania, however, shows that a majority of migrants to the community experienced no change in occupational status as an accompaniment of the migration
process. And among those who did shift occupational level, a higher proportion
were mobile in a downward direction! See Sidney Goldstein, *Patterns of Mobility,
1910–1950: The Norristown Study; A Method of Measuring Migration and Occupational Mobility in the Community* (Philadelphia, 1958), p. 53.

laborers who left Newburyport departed under less auspicious circumstances. Without financial resources, occupational skill, or education, frequently with heavy family responsibilities, the range of alternatives open to these men in their new destination was slender. Laborers like these were not lured to leave Newburyport by the prospect of investing their savings and skills more profitably elsewhere; they left the city when the depressed state of the local labor market made it impossible for them to subsist where they were. As a result of the collapse of 1857, for example, Newburyport suffered a population decline estimated by the *Herald* at "more than one thousand." Most of these departures, it was thought, were cases of workers moving to "locations where work is more abundant." [8]

That the geographical mobility of such laborers dramatically improved their opportunities for upward social mobility seems highly unlikely. The telling objection which has been advanced against the famous "safety valve" theory of the frontier applies here.[9] Migrant laborers from the city rarely had the capital or the knowledge necessary to reap the benefits of the supply of "free land" at the frontier. It seems to have been largely artisans, schoolteachers, farmers, and unsuccessful businessmen who sought their fortunes in Illinois wheat or California gold. The Newburyport newspapers of the 1850–1880 period reported but a single instance of a local laborer who successfully settled in the West, and his was not a case of which Horace Greeley could be proud. The *Herald* of June 22, 1878, carried news of a letter from one Michael Welch, then in Nevada. Welch, the son of a local laborer, had been the treasurer of one of Newburyport's volunteer fire companies; when he left for the frontier he took the treasury with him! Welch advised his parents that he was doing very well in Nevada, and would soon repay the stolen funds. Few workmen in the city, needless to say, found capital to finance a trip west so readily available.[10]

Neither were laborers migrating from Newburyport likely to discover acres of diamonds on the urban frontier. The community fell within the orbit of Boston, which became a great industrial center in the middle decades of the century partly because of the vast reservoir of cheap labor provided by immigration. The unskilled labor market which was centered in Boston included Lowell, Lawrence, Lynn, and smaller cities like Newburyport and Chicopee.

[8] *Herald*, May 28, 1858.

[9] Carter Goodrich and Sol Davison, "The Wage Earner in the Westward Movement," *Political Science Quarterly*, 50 (1935): 161–85 and 51 (1936): 61–110; Fred A. Shannon, "A Post Mortem on the Labor Safety Valve Theory," *Agricultural History*, 19 (1945): 31–37; Clarence H. Danhof, "Farm-Making Costs and the 'Safety Valve'; 1850–1860" *Journal of Political Economy*, 49 (1941): 317–59.

[10] *Herald*, June 22, 1878. Cf. Cole, *Immigrant City*, pp. 132–33. Cole believes that the frontier was somehow a source of hope for the ordinary workman of Lawrence in this period: "For those whose future seemed completely hopeless there was the possibility of moving west." He does not, however, produce any evidence demonstrating that significant numbers of manual laborers from the community actually moved west. It is impressive that sample surveys conducted in Saskatchewan and Alberta in 1930–1931 revealed that a significant number of the farm operators of the prairie provinces had some previous experience in unskilled or semiskilled employment; see C. A. Dawson and Eva R. Younge, *Pioneering in the Prairie Provinces: The Social Side of the Settlement Process* (Toronto, 1940), pp. 120–23, 318. But many of these men had been born and raised on farms, and it is probable that relatively few of them had ever worked as laborers in cities hundreds of miles from the frontier. For other negative evidence on this point, see Handlin, *Boston's Immigrants*, p. 159, and the literature cited there.

There was a high rate of labor mobility from city to city within this market, the flow varying with local fluctuations in the demand for unskilled workers.[11] In these circumstances, differences not only in wages and working conditions but in promotion opportunities as well probably were marginal. Certainly it is doubtful that a workman without capital or skills would have found it markedly easier to advance himself in Boston than in Newburyport. The great metropolis offered alluring opportunities at the top to those with the proper requisites, but to the common laborer who drifted there from Newburyport it probably meant only more of the same. Indeed, occupational opportunities for the unskilled may have been somewhat less in a great city like Boston, where many of the most helpless and destitute members of the working class tended to cluster.

The social mobility study described below necessarily gives disproportionate attention to the settled minority of workmen who remained within the community for a decade or more and whose careers could therefore be traced. It is highly improbable, however, that our lack of precise knowledge of the later careers of migrants from Newburyport has led to an underestimation of the upward mobility eventually achieved by laborers in the sample. The circumstances in which they departed and the character of the unskilled labor market in New England make it unlikely that large numbers of these workmen were more successful in their new places of residence than were their counterparts who remained in Newburyport.

An inquiry of this kind, in fact, is biased to some degree in the opposite direction. To analyze the social adjustment of workmen who settled in a particular city long enough to be recorded on two or more censuses is to concentrate on laborers who were most resistant to pressures to migrate, and these tended to be men who had already attained a modicum of economic security in the community. Thus four fifths of the local unskilled laborers who owned real property in 1850 were still living in Newburyport in 1860, a persistence rate of 80 percent; the comparable figure for propertyless laborers in this decade was 31 percent. Migration was, in this sense, a selective process. Masses of unskilled newcomers—from rural areas and from abroad—streamed into the nineteenth century city. Large numbers of these men were unable to establish a secure place for themselves in the community. Unemployment was always a possibility, and all too often a grim reality. When jobs were too few to go around, the rumor of work in Lawrence, or Lynn, or Holyoke was enough to draw these men on. Workmen who remained in Newburyport for any length of time were therefore a somewhat select group, because to find sufficiently stable employment to maintain a settled residence in a community was itself success of a kind to the laborer. In tracing the changing social position of groups of Newburyport workmen we must keep this relationship between geographical mobility and social mobility clearly in mind. The process of internal migration within the unskilled labor market removed many of the least successful laborers from the community; the following analysis of occupational and property mobility in Newburyport applies primarily to a settled minority from the total

[11] Cf. Handlin, *Boston's Immigrants*, chap. iii, esp. pp. 70–71; Percy Wells Bidwell, "Rural Economy in New England at the Beginning of the Nineteenth Century," *Transactions of the Connecticut Academy of Arts and Sciences*, 20 (1916): 383–91; Shlakman, *Economic History of a Factory Town*, chaps. iii, v. and vi.

unskilled laboring population which passed through the community between 1850 and 1880.

The Nature of the Occupational Hierarchy

To speak of occupational mobility presupposes the social gradation of occupations, a gradation implied in such phrases as the social ladder and the occupational pyramid. The question we should now turn to is, in effect, how to justify the use of these metaphors in a specific historical context. The sociologist is able to go about this task more directly than the historian; by various polling devices he may ask the members of the society he studies how they rank various occupations.[12] While the historian may extrapolate certain of these findings back into the past, he must rely chiefly on indirect evidence to support his judgments as to the nature of the occupational hierarchy.

The occupational classification scheme used in this study is simple, designed to make possible some immediate generalizations from the census data. Occupational mobility is defined as a move from one to another of the four broad categories: unskilled manual occupations, semiskilled manual occupations, skilled manual occupations, and nonmanual occupations. Moves within these categories, involving more subtle changes in status, will be ignored for the present; they will receive some attention at a later point.

The superior ranking of nonmanual occupations seems incontestable. Status differences between manual and nonmanual callings have narrowed somewhat in recent years, with some overlapping between highly skilled manual jobs and certain routine nonmanual occupations. In the nineteenth century, however, the gulf between the two was wide. The annual income of the ordinary white collar worker was at least twice that of the typical laborer.[13] Newburyport papers of the period spoke of "the general belief" that manual work was undesirable; it was often complained that far too many young men were irrationally eager to become clerks and professionals, that not enough were willing to learn a secure manual trade.[14]

Within the broad category of manual labor, three levels of occupational status must be distinguished. If the social distance between these three was less than that between manual and nonmanual occupations as a group, status distinctions within the working class occupational world were nonetheless important. At the top of the manual laboring group stood the skilled craftsmen, artisans, and mechanics—carpenters, caulkers, sailmakers, master mariners, tailors, butchers, and so forth. (Some Newburyport artisans in this period were self-employed and owned significant amounts of capital; these were considered small businessmen and placed in the nonmanual category.) Certain of these trades were prospering during these years, while others were declining from changes in technology and market structure. Even the stagnating trades, how-

[12] For a useful guide to the abundant sociological literature on this matter, see Albert J. Reiss, Jr., *Occupations and Social Status* (Glencoe, Ill., 1961).
[13] Robert K. Burn estimates that in 1890 the average white collar wage was twice the wage for manual labor; see "The Comparative Economic Position of Manual and White Collar Employees," *Journal of Business*, 27 (1954): 257–67.
[14] *Union*, Oct. 30, 1849; *Herald*, April 15, 1856, Sept. 16, 1857, Oct. 29, 1870. Cf. Bureau of Labor, *Fourth Annual Report*, pp. 393–94.

ever, remained markedly superior to other sources of manual employment. The artisan possessed a special skill; he had a "vocation," a "calling," rather than a mere "job." His earnings, as Tables 1 and 2 clearly show, were much higher than those of the semiskilled or unskilled workman; his wife and children were under much less pressure to enter the labor market themselves to supplement the family income.

Status differences between unskilled and semiskilled occupations were less dramatic, but they did exist. The situation of the ordinary unskilled manual laborer of Newburyport at mid-century was analyzed at length in Chapter Two.

TABLE 1

OCCUPATIONAL DIFFERENCES IN EMPLOYMENT AND ANNUAL EARN-
INGS, ESSEX COUNTY, MASSACHUSETTS, 1875 [a]

	Number in sample	Days worked [b]	Mean annual earnings
Skilled occupations			
machinist	135	272.4	$601.94
blacksmith	68	260.0	567.60
carpenter	359	218.0	534.40
mason	101	177.6	524.02
cotton spinner (male)	14	280.5	523.75
shoecutter (male)	254	243.1	521.05
painter	108	207.8	474.79
Semiskilled occupations			
shoecutter, undesignated	883	234.3	418.68
factory operative, undesignated (male)	191	249.6	379.62
Unskilled occupations			
common laborer	412	230.6	358.68

[a] Compiled from the Massachusetts Bureau of Statistics of Labor, *Seventh Annual Report*, pp. 122–199.

[b] On the basis of a six-day week, without considering holidays, the number of possible work days in a year is 312.

The common laborer was, to an extreme degree, at the mercy of the harsh uncertainties of the casual labor market. Without a specific economic function to perform regularly for a predictable reward, he was forced to take his chances daily in the competition for temporary employment. His wages were invariably below those of his fellow workmen in other occupations, and his children were the first to be forced to seek work to keep the family going.

By the criteria of earnings, skill required, and definiteness of function, semiskilled jobs were a cut above this. The ordinary operative in a shoe factory or textile mill, the gardener, or the night watchman did not perform as complex a task as the spinner, shoecutter, or mason, and his wages were correspondingly lower.[15] But it would be a mistake to suppose that such jobs required no "skill"

[15] It should be noted that the shoemakers of the community—a very large group—were ranked as semiskilled rather than skilled workmen. The old-fashioned master of the bench has often been portrayed as the archetypal skilled craftsman, but by 1850 the traditional artisan had largely disappeared from the Newburyport shoe

TABLE 2

OCCUPATIONAL DIFFERENCES IN ANNUAL WAGES AND PROPOR-
TION OF FAMILY INCOME EARNED BY FAMILY HEAD, MASSACHU-
SETTS, 1874 [a]

	Number in sample	Mean annual wage of family head	Percent of total family income
Skilled occupations			
machinist	41	$746.54	89.5
carpenter	44	716.57	86.6
teamster	6	646.67	86.2
Semiskilled occupations			
mill hand	13	594.31	71.9
shoemaker	22	527.41	68.4
Unskilled occupations			
laborer	43	414.42	56.8

[a] Compiled from the Massachusetts Bureau of Statistics of
Labor, *Sixth Annual Report*, pp. 221–354. The wage levels here,
it will be noted, are consistently higher than those reported for
Essex County a year later (Table 1). This is largely because the
1874 sample was gathered in a way which biased the findings
toward the more prosperous representatives of each occupation.
We are interested in relative differentials here, so the bias is unimportant.

at all, and that they were in no way superior to common laboring positions. The
semiskilled workmen of Newburyport had a somewhat more secure and re-
spected position than the general laborers. Their function was more clearly
defined, their wages were a bit higher and a bit more regular, and they were
better able to support their families on their own income.[16]

industry. A few independent masters still made entire shoes in their shops at
mid-century, but the bulk of production was carried on through a putting-out system.
The mobile laborers who became "shoemakers" in the fifties, sixties, and seventies
seem not to have served any apprenticeship at all. Their task was to perform simple,
semiskilled operations on leather farmed out to them by Lynn entrepreneurs. The
status of these men, judging from their wages, working conditions, and training, must
have been essentially the same as operatives in the textile mills and comb factory,
rather than carpenters, masons, and similar artisans. By the 1870's, the local shoe
industry had moved into the factory, and most "shoemakers" were simply operatives,
except for a skilled minority who did specialized tasks—shoecutting, for example.
Such specialized workmen have been ranked in the skilled class, of course. For the
shoe industry in Newburyport, see J. D. Parsons, *Newburyport: Its Industries*
(Newburyport, 1887), pp. 20–21; *Union*, Jan. 12, Jan. 14, 1853. On the evolution of
American shoe manufacture, see Blanche Hazard, *The Organization of the Boot and
Shoe Industry in Massachusetts before 1875* (Cambridge, Mass., 1921); John R.
Commons, "American Shoemakers, 1648–1895," *Quarterly Journal of Economics*, 24
(1909): 39–84. Warner and Low, *The Social System of the Modern Factory* is a
fanciful account of the changing status of the Newburyport shoemaker.
[16] Tables 1 and 2 indicate these differences clearly. For comparative evidence
supporting this line of argument, see Wilbert E. Moore, *Industrialization and Labor:
Social Aspects of Economic Development* (Ithaca, 1951), esp. chap. iv; Charles
Booth, *Life and Labour of the People in London* (9 vol. ed., London, 1892–1897),
vol. VIII; R. Dahrendorf, "Unskilled Labor in British Industry" (unpubl. diss.,
London School of Economics, 1956). The only occupational prestige poll which has
included a broad range of manual laboring jobs ranked casual laborers, farm

One further question about the Newburyport occupational hierarchy must be considered. The shape of a community's occupational structure is obviously a prime determinant of the range of occupational mobility opportunities there. Consider an extreme case—a city in which 95 percent of the labor force holds unskilled jobs, with only 5 percent in the higher occupational categories. Even if the occupants of these few high status positions were continually recruited from the bottom class, the majority of men in this community would remain laborers all their lives. The opposite polar type would be a city with only a small fraction of its residents in lowly occupations; here a much slower turnover of personnel in high status jobs would mean relatively greater mobility opportunities for lower class persons. The significance of data about occupational mobility in a given community cannot be grasped without some sense of the range of mobility which could be "expected" within that community.[17]

The Newburyport occupational structure at mid-century resembled the second polar type more closely than the first. Only about 8 percent of the labor force held unskilled jobs; three times as many occupied nonmanual positions of some kind. Approximately one quarter of the employed males of the city were semiskilled workers, while almost 40 percent were skilled laborers. The diversity of skilled trades was striking—thirty-nine varieties of artisan could be counted on the local census schedules for 1850. It is misleading to classify mid-century Newburyport a "mill town"; its occupational structure was not heavily weighted toward unskilled and semiskilled callings. The community had a highly diversified craft economy, with almost two thirds of its labor force in the top two occupational categories and less than a tenth at the very bottom.

Between 1850 and 1880 the main outlines of the Newburyport occupational structure did not change drastically. A distinct shrinking of employment in the skilled trades did occur, matched by a moderate expansion of both semiskilled and nonmanual callings. But the local economy, which had reached a plateau after the rapid growth of the 1840's, did not undergo large-scale technological changes which fundamentally altered the opportunity structure. The declining proportion of skilled positions in the city, and the expansion of semiskilled and white collar occupations reflect national trends of the period, but in Newburyport these tendencies manifested themselves more slowly than in other more dynamic nineteenth century cities.[18] The local occupational structure offered a

laborers, and laundry workers well below ordinary factory operatives; Raymond B. Cattell, "The Concept of Social Status," *Journal of Social Psychology,* 15 (1942): 293–308. See also Michael Young and Peter Willmott, "Social Grading by Manual Laborers," *British Journal of Sociology,* 7 (1956): 337–45.
[17] Sociologists have developed elaborate statistical techniques for distinguishing "pure mobility" from mobility caused by overall changes in the occupational structure. Typical applications of contingency analysis to this problem are found in Natalie Rogoff, *Recent Trends in Occupational Mobility* (Glencoe, Ill., 1953); David V. Glass, ed., *Social Mobility in Britain* (London, 1954); Joseph A. Kahl, *The American Class Structure* (New York, 1957). It was not appropriate to utilize these techniques in the present study, both because of the smallness of the sample and because there were no major changes in the Newburyport occupational structure between 1850 and 1880.
[18] These observations about the Newburyport occupational structure are based on my tabulation of the occupations of all Newburyport males listed in the manuscript schedules of the U.S. Census of 1850, and a summary of the occupations of Newburyport citizens in 1875; see the Commonwealth of Massachusetts, *The Census of Massachusetts, 1875: Population and Social Statistics* (Boston, 1875), I, 502.

relative abundance of high status positions in 1850; its general shape seemed equally favorable to upward occupational mobility in 1880.

Intra-generational Occupational Mobility, 1850–1880

The career patterns of hundreds of unskilled laborers of nineteenth century Newburyport are summed up in Table 3. A simple generalization immediately suggests itself: less than half of the unskilled laborers listed in the city on the Census of 1850, 1860, or 1870 remained there for as much as a decade, and

TABLE 3

OCCUPATIONAL AND GEOGRAPHICAL MOBILITY OF THREE GROUPS OF LABORERS, 1850–1880

Year	Occupational status attained				Rate of persist- ence [a]	Number in sample
	Unskilled	Semiskilled	Skilled	Nonmanual		
1850 Census group						
1860	64%	16%	15%	5%	32%	55
1870	36	39	9	15	64	35
1880	57	21	7	14	40	14
1860 Census group						
1870	74	12	8	5	33	74
1880	69	19	6	6	65	48
1870 Census group						
1880	79	6	10	5	41	102

[a] This column provides a measure of the geographical mobility of workmen in the sample. The rate of persistence of a group for a particular decade is defined as that proportion of the group recorded on the census at the start of the decade that is still present in the community at the end of the decade. Thus 32 percent of the unskilled laborers of 1850 still lived in Newburyport in 1860; 64 percent of the men in this group as of 1860 still lived in Newburyport in 1870, and so forth.

only a minority of those who did attained a higher status occupation.* The experiences of these obscure workmen, however, were sufficiently varied and complex to merit closer scrutiny.[19]

Of the 171 common laborers employed in Newburyport in 1850, fully two thirds had disappeared from the city by 1860. A few of these had died; most had moved away. Of those who remained, almost two thirds were still ordinary

* A word of warning is in order here. The discussion which follows is based on a series of tables which display in percentages the changing occupational distribution of several groups of men and boys. Scrutiny of the absolute numbers from which these percentages were calculated will reveal that, in some instances, occupational shifts by relatively few men appear as a rather dramatic percentage change. These changes in the occupational adjustment of even a small group of individuals are suggestive, but the reader must recall that this is an interpretative essay based on fragmentary data, not a large-scale, definitive statistical study.

[19] The career patterns of three groups of laborers are traced here. The first of these groups consists of Newburyport residents listed as unskilled laborers on the manuscript schedules of the U.S. Census of 1850. The second consists of men first listed as laborers in Newburyport on the Census of 1860, and the third of unskilled workmen new to the community in 1870.

unskilled laborers after a decade. Only 5 percent had risen into a nonmanual calling. Upward mobility was restricted almost entirely to the skilled and semiskilled occupations; a sixth of these men acquired semiskilled positions by 1860, a slightly smaller proportion found skilled employment.

During the Civil War decade, however, this group fared better. Its members were older, and more securely settled in the community; the persistence rate of the group for 1860–1870 was twice that for 1850–1860. Their occupational adjustment improved markedly in one respect. While two thirds of them had made no occupational gains at all between 1850 and 1860, by 1870 only one third of the group still held completely unskilled laboring jobs.

Almost all of the upward mobility attained by these men in the Civil War decade involved one small step up the occupational ladder. The dramatic shift out of the unskilled occupations was accompanied by only a small expansion of the nonmanual category and by an actual decrease in the skilled category. By far the most widespread form of upward mobility was into positions of only slightly higher status than unskilled labor—semiskilled jobs of various kinds.

Occupational opportunities for the immigrants from rural New England and abroad who arrived in Newburyport *after* 1850 were somewhat less favorable. The laborers first listed in Newburyport in the Census of 1860 remained more heavily concentrated in unskilled jobs ten and twenty years later than the men of the 1850 group. Three quarters of them attained no occupational mobility after a decade in the community, and nearly 70 percent were still common laborers after two decades. One laborer in twenty from those who stayed throughout the Civil War decade obtained a nonmanual position of some kind by 1870; no further gains of significance were made in this category during the seventies. The prospects of moving into a skilled manual job were also remote: only 8 percent held skilled positions after a decade in the city, and the proportion fell to 6 percent by 1880. The most marked difference between the attainments of the 1850 and 1860 groups, however, was in the semiskilled occupations. The unskilled laborer who came to Newburyport after 1850 had fewer prospects of attaining the very modest advance in status involved in becoming a fisherman, a factory operative, a gardener, a night watchman.

The shrinkage of semiskilled opportunities is even more evident from the experiences of the laborers first listed in the Census of 1870. Some two thirds of the men in the 1850 group remained trapped in the unskilled category after a decade; the comparable figure for the 1860 group was three fourths; in the case of the 1870 group, four out of five men remained laborers for at least a decade. This unfavorable trend, however, did not mean the appearance of new barriers against movement into the skilled and nonmanual occupations. The prospects of becoming a grocer or a mason were quite similar for members of all three groups. The chief advantage of the more successful group was that they enjoyed superior access to jobs of a semiskilled character.

It is tempting to conclude flatly that a change somewhat unfavorable to common laborers occurred in the Newburyport occupational structure during these years. But a different explanation of the pattern of declining opportunities can be conceived. We know that the industrial transformation of the Newburyport economy coincided with the arrival of masses of impoverished Irish peasants, and that the proportion of foreign-born men in the local working class rose steadily through the 1850–1880 period. It is possible that foreign laborers had fewer opportunities than their native counterparts throughout this period and that the two later groups had a larger proportion of immigrants than the 1850 group.

Did Yankee workmen climb into higher status occupations more easily than immigrant laborers in these years, as many observers believed, or were ethnic differences in mobility opportunities actually negligible? The relationship between occupational mobility and ethnicity is displayed in Table 4; while the absolute numbers from which these distributions were calculated were tiny in some instances, the uniformity of the pattern which emerges is impressive. The immigrant workman in Newburyport was markedly less successful than his native counterpart in climbing out of the ranks of the unskilled in the 1850–1880 period. In each of the three groups at each census disproportionately high numbers of the foreign-born remained concentrated at the bottom of the occupational scale. The disadvantages of the newcomers were reflected, to some extent, in their underrepresentation in the skilled and nonmanual callings. But the sharpest difference in mobility opportunities was not in the two highest occupational categories but in the semiskilled field. The distribution of the 1850 group in 1870—with 77 percent of its native-born members and 14 percent of its immigrants holding semiskilled jobs—is only the most dramatic illustration of a tendency evident throughout Table 4. Evidently many local employers shared Francis Bowen's belief that "the rude labor" to which the newcomers had become accustomed had "so incapacitated them for higher tasks" that a factory could not be profitably run if more than a third of its labor force was made up of immigrants. "Foreigners generally, and the Irish in particular," wrote Bowen, "cannot be employed at all" in the factory, "except in that small proportion to the total number of hands which will make it possible to restrict them to the lower or less difficult tasks." [20] In the Newburyport factories of this period the proportion of immigrant workmen on the payroll was kept well below that supposedly dangerous level.

The shrinking of opportunities in the semiskilled occupations, therefore, was intimately connected with the changing ethnic composition of the Newburyport laboring class. The proportion of foreign-born men in the community labor force was steadily rising, and in these years the immigrants had particularly restricted access to employment in the occupations most open to the ambitious common laborer. It is noteworthy, however, that the special handicaps of immigrant laborers do not fully account for the inferior showing of the 1860 and 1870 groups. When the occupational experiences of native and foreign laborers are tabulated separately—as in Table 4—the pattern of declining mobility shows up in the figures for both groups.

A few general conclusions about the mobility patterns of common laborers in Newburyport in the 1850–1880 period can now be suggested. The composition of the community's unskilled laboring force was extremely fluid: a majority of the men registered as laborers on a United States Census in these years left the city before a second census was taken. These high rates of migration from the community significantly affected occupational adjustment; the improved occu-

[20] Bowen, *Principles of Political Economy,* pp. 86–87.

TABLE 4

ETHNIC DIFFERENCES IN INTRA-GENERATIONAL OCCUPATIONAL MOBILITY

| | Occupational status attained | | | | | | | | Number in sample | |
| | Unskilled | | Semiskilled | | Skilled | | Nonmanual | | | |
Year	Native	Foreign	Native	Foreign	Native	Foreign	Native	Foreign	Native	Foreign
					1850 Census group					
1860	47%	72%	32%	8%	15%	14%	5%	6%	19	36
1870	15	55	77	14	0	14	8	18	13	22
1880	25	70	25	20	25	0	25	10	4	10
					1860 Census group					
1870	50	83	30	5	5	10	15	2	20	54
1880	50	74	30	15	10	5	10	5	10	38
					1870 Census group					
1880	60	84	15	4	15	9	10	4	20	82

pational distribution of the three groups was partly due to the simple fact that unsuccessful laborers were quicker to leave Newburyport than successful ones.

Surprisingly, however, variations in the flow of migrants from the city were not closely related to variations in occupational opportunities there. The persistence rates of the 1850 and 1860 groups (Table 3) were almost identical—32 and 33 percent respectively the first decade, 64 and 65 percent respectively in the second decade—even though the occupational gains of the two were not. The 1870 group departed somewhat from the pattern; 41 percent of its members remained in Newburyport for at least a decade. This instance hints at a mild negative relationship between group persistence and occupational mobility, since the most stable of the three groups was also the least mobile occupationally. Ethnic differences in migration seem to have followed no consistent pattern. Foreign-born laborers were less successful occupationally than their native competitors throughout these three decades; the persistence rates of the newcomers, however, were lower in 1860 and 1870 and much higher in 1880. The rate of emigration, therefore, was an independent variable which strongly influenced the occupational adjustment of unskilled laborers; it did not vary in response to changes in occupational mobility opportunities in the community.

The common workman who remained in Newburyport in these years had only a slight chance of rising into a middle class occupation, even if "middle class" is generously defined to include the ownership of a subsistence farm. Only one laborer in twenty succeeded in making this advance during his first decade in the city. In the case of the 1850 group this proportion increased to three in twenty after two decades, but the two-decade figure for the 1860 group remained one in twenty. Moreover, neither politics nor religion, often assumed to have been important channels of upward mobility for immigrant groups, provided any opportunities for these men. Not one instance of ascent of this kind was recorded in the 1850–1880 period. The climb into a nonmanual occupation was not impossible for the unskilled workman, but it was achieved by only a tiny minority.

It is perhaps not very surprising that men without capital, education, or special training of any sort should have had limited access to nonmanual occupations. More noteworthy is the fact that these laborers found so little opportunity to enter skilled manual occupations. Approximately a third of the total Newburyport labor force in this period was made up of artisans and craftsmen of various sorts, but few laborers found openings here.

In none of the groups of laborers did as much as a quarter of the men succeed in obtaining either skilled or nonmanual positions in the period studied. From 75 to 85 percent of them remained near the bottom of the social ladder in the low-skill, low-pay occupational universe. The great majority continued to work as day laborers; most of those who did change occupations became semiskilled workmen, performing simple manual tasks at slightly higher wages and with somewhat more regular employment than they had previously enjoyed.

The opportunity to take this very modest step upward into the semiskilled category varied in two significant ways—according to the laborer's nativity and to his time of arrival in the community. Compared to the Yankee, the foreign-born workman was generally underrepresented at all occupational levels above unskilled labor, but his chief disadvantage was not at the top of the occupational ladder but at the second rung. Similarly, the growing tendency of laborers who arrived in Newburyport after 1850 to remain fixed in unskilled occupations involved a relatively small reduction in mobility into skilled and nonmanual positions; most of the change was due to the restriction of employment opportunities in the semiskilled category.

Inter-generational Occupational Mobility, 1850–1880

If nineteenth century Americans were optimistic about the laborer's chances of "pulling himself up by his own bootstraps," they were more optimistic still about his children's prospects for success. The following analysis of career patterns of sons of Newburyport laborers will help to determine to what extent such optimism was justified.

Intra-generational mobility is computed by comparing men's occupations at two or more points in their career, but the task of estimating inter-generational mobility is rather more complicated. A comparison of the status of two different individuals—father and son—is sought. At what point in the careers of the two is it appropriate to make the comparison? Half of this problem has been solved here by arranging the data on sons' occupations by age group, so that the occupational status of sons at varying stages of their careers is displayed (Table 5). Control for age is particularly important in this case because most boys entered the labor market in their early teens, and there is good reason to doubt that the jobs they held at that tender age provide a reasonable measure of inter-generational mobility. It is obviously important to determine how closely the adult occupations of these sons corresponded to the occupations they held while in their teens. One recent study revealed that well over half of a sample of white collar and professional workers in Oakland, California, had worked in a manual laboring position at some point in their early career, persuasive evidence of the dangers of ignoring intra-generational mobility in a study of inter-generational mobility.[21] By utilizing age groups in analyzing the career patterns of laborers' sons this danger can be avoided.

There remains the difficulty that not all of the fathers of these men continued to be unskilled laborers through the entire period of the study. Some, we have seen, moved up the occupational ladder themselves. How did a father's mobility or lack of mobility influence his son's prospects for occupational advance? This question will be considered at a later point. For the present it will simplify matters to ignore occupational advances made by the father and to consider all fathers laborers. Most of them did in fact remain laborers, and, as we shall see later, those who did climb a notch or two upwards had little success in passing on their advantage to their offspring.

Perhaps the most important question to ask about the hundreds of laborers' sons whose careers are recorded in Table 5 is whether or not they customarily inherited the occupation of their fathers and themselves became unskilled day

[21] Lipset and Bendix, *Social Mobility*, p. 168.

TABLE 5

OCCUPATIONAL AND GEOGRAPHICAL MOBILITY OF SONS OF LABORERS, 1850–1880 [a]

Year	Occupational status attained				Rate of persistence	Number in sample
	Unskilled	Semiskilled	Skilled	Nonmanual		
Youths born 1830–1839						
1850	39%	56%	6%	0%	—	18
1860	10	76	7	7	29%	41
1870	11	48	30	11	56	27
1880	11	42	37	11	63	19
Youths born 1840–1849						
1860	11	84	2	4	54	57
1870	28	45	17	10	32	58
1880	21	46	17	17	33	24
Youths born 1850–1859						
1870	23	59	11	7	54	95
1880	33	40	20	8	44	76
Youths born 1860–1869						
1880	25	60	7	8	56	73

[a] The reader may be surprised to see the number of youths in a group increasing from decade to decade in some instances, at the same time that the persistence rate figure indicates that half to two thirds of the group members left Newburyport each decade. The explanation is that large numbers of youths were coming *into* the city during these years as well, and that these have been included in the analysis.

laborers. The answer is apparent in a glance. In none of the age groups at any of the four censuses between 1850 and 1880 did a majority of sons hold unskilled jobs. The most frequently chosen occupation in every instance was in the semiskilled manual category. More often than not, it has been shown, the unskilled Newburyport workman remained an unskilled laborer throughout this period; more often than not the son of such a man became a semiskilled worker.

The really dramatic opening up of semiskilled employment opportunities to laborers' sons occurred in the 1850's. Even in 1850 a slight majority of the handful of sons old enough to be employed held semiskilled positions, but the extent of direct occupational inheritance was still quite high for this group—close to 40 percent. A decade later the situation was strikingly different: almost 85 percent of the boys in the teen-age group held semiskilled jobs, and 75 percent of the youths aged 20–29; only a tenth of the members of either group were mere common laborers! Very few, on the other hand, had climbed more than one rung up the status ladder. Barely 5 percent of the teen-agers working in 1860 had entered skilled or nonmanual callings. The comparable figure for youths in their twenties was higher, but even this meant no more than one in thirteen held a skilled job and one in thirteen a nonmanual job. By far the most common form of inter-generational mobility evident by 1860 was into semi-skilled occupations.

After 1860 there continued to be a heavy concentration of laborers' sons in semiskilled callings, but a significant tightening up occurred. Eighty-five percent of the teen-agers in 1860 held semiskilled jobs, less than 60 percent of the teen-agers in 1870. For the group aged 20–29 in 1860 the drop was from 76 percent to 45 percent. A great wave of working class children entered the labor market during the Civil War decade, and the local employers hiring semiskilled labor did not expand their activity sufficiently to absorb all of them. Indeed, one major source of semiskilled employment began to dry up during this decade. Almost half of the laborers' sons who held semiskilled jobs at the time of the Census of 1860 listed themselves as "fisherman" or "seaman." Both the fishing industry and the coasting trade carried on out of Newburyport experienced a sharp decline during the sixties; by 1870 the maritime industries accounted for only a quarter of the semiskilled jobs held by these youths and by 1880, less than 15 percent. Semiskilled employment was coming increasingly to mean factory employment.

What happened to the boys for whom the cotton mills and shoe factories of Newburyport had no room? The narrowing of semiskilled opportunities in the sixties forced increasing numbers of the fathers of these youths to remain common laborers. This happened to some extent to the sons as well; the 1870 Census showed a rise in the concentration of sons in unskilled positions. It is striking, however, that this decade also saw a corresponding increase in mobility into the two higher occupational classes. In the case of the two younger groups in 1870, the increase in direct occupational inheritance was approximately equal to the increase in the skilled and nonmanual category. For men in the 30–39 age bracket in 1870 the constriction of semiskilled opportunities during the Civil War decade resulted in a substantial rise in the proportion holding high status jobs, but virtually no increase at all in the unskilled category.

A certain number of laborers' sons gained a foothold in the white collar world after 1860—ten members of the group became clerks between 1860 and 1870, for example. But the skilled crafts were a more important source of upward mobility. The 1870 and 1880 figures show that it was uncommon for more than one in ten to cross the barrier dividing manual from nonmanual occupations, while two to three times as many youths characteristically found skilled employment. No single craft or group of crafts appears to have been unusually open to penetration from below; there was a broad scattering of upwardly mobile sons throughout the trades. The 1870 group, for example, included four blacksmiths, two carpenters, two machinists, two painters, two iron molders, a tailor, a baker, and a mason.

Two other aspects of the process of inter-generational mobility require comment—the role of ethnic differences and the influence of geographical mobility. It has already been demonstrated that the immigrant workman was markedly less successful than his native counterpart in climbing up the occupational ladder. Did the children of immigrant laborers face similar handicaps, or did ethnic barriers to mobility affect only the first generation immigrant? A comparison of the occupational distribution of native and foreign sons in 1850, 1860, 1870, and 1880 is presented in Table 6. The conclusion to be drawn from it is obvious: sons of Yankee laborers obtained high status employment in Newburyport much more easily than sons of foreign-born workmen in these years. The proportion of native youths in skilled and nonmanual positions was consistently higher than the proportion of foreign sons; the latter clustered heavily near the bottom of the occupational scale. But, unlike their fathers,

TABLE 6

Occupational Distribution of Sons of Native and Foreign-born Laborers, 1850–1880

Occupational category	1850		1860		1870		1880	
	Native	Foreign	Native	Foreign	Native	Foreign	Native	Foreign
Number in sample	19	14	34	76	37	148	37	158
Unskilled	26%	71%	12%	8%	8%	27%	19%	27%
Semiskilled	53	21	53	88	38	55	38	50
Skilled	21	7	18	3	27	14	24	15
Nonmanual	0	0	18	1	27	5	19	8

immigrant children were not thought "incapacitated" for factory employment. The upper levels of the factory hierarchy were completely closed to them, but a high proportion found semiskilled positions in local factories.[22]

These ethnic differences in mobility opportunities narrowed somewhat in the post-Civil War years. The censuses of 1870 and 1880 showed gains for foreign sons in both the skilled and nonmanual categories. The popular belief that second-generation Americans labored under no special handicaps in the race for occupational status was excessively optimistic, but the evidence of Table 6 hints at the beginning of a trend toward some equalization of opportunities. It is interesting to note, however, that by 1880 none of these youths had advanced through the mobility channels so often stressed in impressionistic accounts of immigrant life—politics and religion. To become a priest required education; to become a ward boss required some education too, and a well-organized, politically conscious constituency. The Irish of Newburyport, and later immigrant groups as well, eventually attained these requisites, but only after long years of struggle.

Like their fathers, these youths tended to be transient members of the community, and migration seems to have influenced their occupational adjustment in much the same way. A certain number of working class youths who had already attained some occupational mobility in the community left Newburyport during these years, but the net effect of emigration was to improve the occupational distribution of the group as a whole by removing a disproportionately large number of the least successful. The persistence of these laborers' sons (Table 5) varied roughly by age: very young children and men above thirty tended to be relatively stable members of the community; boys in their teens and twenties were most likely to move on. The persistence rates of sons of native-born laborers were generally, but not uniformly, higher than those of immigrant children. None of these variations can be clearly attributed to changes in the occupational structure.

Fathers and Sons

This survey of the career patterns of Newburyport laborers and their sons in the 1850–1880 period suggests the following conclusions.*

1) Unskilled manual laborers characteristically remained common laborers;

[22] Cf. the assertion of Warner and Srole that in these years "openings created by the general expansion of the economic system, particularly the establishment of large factories, were filled almost entirely by natives. . . . Only unskilled occupations were available to the Irish as farm laborers, stevedores, carters, hod carriers, and domestics" (*The Social Systems of American Ethnic Groups*, p. 31). This is a mistaken judgment for the Irish immigrants of Newburyport, and a grossly mistaken one for the children of such immigrants. Warner's error may in part be attributed to the fact that he based his opinion on an analysis of data drawn from local city directories, and these provide no information on the occupations of young men still living with their parents. For further critical discussion of Warner's analysis of social mobility in Newburyport, see Chap. 8 and the appendix [of *Poverty and Progress*].

* It must be remembered, of course, that these conclusions refer not to the entire working class population of the community but to *unskilled* laborers and their sons. Recent mobility research suggests the likelihood that an investigation of the career patterns of *skilled* families would have revealed substantially greater movement into nonmanual occupations. Presumably it would also have disclosed evidence of downward occupational mobility, since skilled workmen (unlike common laborers) have status to lose.

the odds that an unskilled laborer living in Newburyport would hold the same lowly position ten years later were at least two to one throughout this period. The sons of these laborers, by contrast, typically became semiskilled workmen; no more than one in four inherited the exact occupation of his father and remained in it.

2) Relatively few of the adult laborers studied worked their way up into a position in a skilled craft—approximately one in ten. The sons of these men were considerably more successful in penetrating the skilled trades, at least after 1860; the 1870 and 1880 figures for sons in their twenties or older holding skilled jobs range from 17 to 37 percent.

3) The contrast between generations was less sharp at the top of the occupational scale. Entry into a nonmanual occupation was almost as difficult for the son of a common laborer as for his father. Since working class families frequently found education for their children a luxury, this is not surprising. The possibility of purchasing a farm or opening a small business existed for both generations; approximately one laborer in ten was able to do this in the three decades studied.

4) The composition of the Newburyport working class was highly unstable. Large numbers of unskilled workmen drifted into the community, but only a minority remained for long. Migration was an important mechanism of occupational adjustment in that it was selective; the successful were less likely to leave than the unsuccessful.

5) Foreign-born workmen and their sons were handicapped in the occupational competition. The sons, however, experienced fewer obstacles to occupational mobility than their fathers; ethnic differences in inter-generational occupational mobility were narrowing somewhat by 1880.

6) Adult laborers employed in Newburyport in 1850 had somewhat greater prospects for occupational advance than those who arrived after 1850. In the case of the sons of these men, however, the trend was in the opposite direction. Some four fifths of the laborers' sons who entered the labor market during the 1850's found semiskilled positions; while the shrinking of semiskilled opportunities after 1860 forced some of these youths back into unskilled jobs, an equally large group rose into skilled and nonmanual callings.

Thus we can conclude that while these laborers and their sons experienced a good deal of occupational mobility, only in rare cases was it mobility very far up the social ladder. The occupational structure was fluid to some degree, but the barriers against moving more than one notch upward were fairly high. Success of the kind achieved by Stephen Fowle was attainable, but only the few were able to grasp it.

20

RICHARD JENSEN *

Quantitative Collective Biography: An Application to Metropolitan Elites

Historians have long studied individual American leaders through their personal manuscripts and published biographical portraits, but only in the last two decades with the work of Miller, Cochran, Chandler, Mowry and others, have scholars sought to analyze groups of leaders. Thus far, the focus has been on national and state-level elites. However, a great wealth of information is also available on hundreds of thousands of local leaders. The available number of city directories, social registers, Who's Whos, biographical dictionaries, gazetteers, and yearbooks is staggering. City directories through 1860 alone number more than 1600 volumes, according to Dorothy N. Spear's bibliography, and almost all are now available on microfiche. Biographical dictionaries at the county and city level probably number more than 3000, judging from Clarence Peterson's bibliography.

The following original essay by Richard Jensen is an inter-city comparative analysis of Chicago and Wichita leaders in the early twentieth century, based on a statistical profile sample drawn from one major biographical directory in each city.

Despite editorial bias in the selection of biographees for inclusion in the directories, a fact of which Professor Jensen is acutely aware, these biographical sources provide the only systematic information on the numerous "prominent" citizens ranking below the top level. Carefully coded and subjected to multivariate analysis by computer, the data yields rich results in Jensen's skilled hands on the socio-political characteristics of midwestern urban leaders.

Printed with permission of the author.
 * The author is indebted to Thomas Kerwin, Barry Parker, and Ann Safier for coding and analyzing parts of the data.

NO SATISFACTORY HISTORY of urban America is possible without knowledge of the business and professional leaders of the cities. The few studies of businessmen by historians and sociologists have concentrated on the upward mobility of only the most important financiers and corporate officials, and provide very little information on the leadership community in any one city. This study, by focusing on Chicago in 1911 and comparing the patterns there with several other Midwestern cities, penetrates well below the level of millionaire bankers, railroad executives, and corporation presidents to encompass a broad cross section of active and influential men. Multivariate statistical techniques, made possible by the use of computers, permit detailed analysis of the characteristics of different occupational groups and age cohorts in the cities as well as the opportunity to test hypotheses suggested by non-quantitative investigations.

The definition of a city's "elite" is necessarily arbitrary. A strict definition limited to outstanding leaders with recognizable power and national reputations would concentrate so heavily on New York and a few other major cities that no conclusions could be drawn about the characteristics of lesser men or smaller cities. Historians have typically adopted restrictive definitions of the elite, not because of lack of interest in middle-level business and professional leaders, but because of the severe difficulties of gathering information about forgotten men and of analyzing the data without computers.[1]

The definition of elite used here is very broad and somewhat arbitrary since it depends upon the criteria used by contemporary observers instead of the criteria that could be established by historical hindsight. The men studied here were those considered influential enough at the time to be included in several city directories edited by John Leonard and Albert Nelson Marquis, the first and second editors of *Who's Who in America*. The compilers apparently sent standardized questionnaires to lists of prominent citizens nominated by a variety of business, professional, and civic sources. The autobiographical responses were then edited to a uniform format, identical to that of *Who's Who in America,* and published in a single volume to be sold to the biographees.

No two investigators are likely to agree on a single list of prominent men in a community, so the directories can hardly be termed definitive. Nevertheless, the editors were experts at their work and built strong reputations on the basis of the fairness, accuracy, and comprehensiveness of their product. The first edition of Marquis' Chicago directory appeared in 1905. The second edition of 1911, in which numerous oversights were corrected, formed the basis of this study, together with the fourth Chicago edition (1926), Marquis' second Saint Louis (1912) and Detroit (1914) editions, and his only edition for the state of Minnesota (1907). Also used were the first edition of Leonard's *Who's Who in Finance* (1911) and the only edition of a directory for Wichita, Kansas (1929), which, while not compiled by Marquis or Leonard, met comparably high editorial standards, and provided a comparison with a smaller city.[2]

[1] For the best studies see especially Stephen S. Visher, *Geography of American Notables* (Bloomington, 1928), which concentrates on scientists from the Midwest; Mabel Newcomer, *The Big Business Executive: The Factors that Made Him, 1900–1950* (New York, 1955); and Eleanor S. Bruchey, *The Business Elite in Baltimore, 1880–1914* (Unpublished Ph.D. Dissertation, Johns Hopkins University, 1967).
[2] The directories were: *The Book of Chicagoans* (Chicago, 1911, 1926), *The Book of St. Louisans* (St. Louis, 1912), *The Book of Minnesotans* (Chicago, 1907), and

Although from 2000 to 10,000 names appeared in each of the various directories, some very prominent men were missing, and doubtless many secondary figures were left out. A few eminences refused to cooperate despite repeated appeals; others were never invited. The omissions will not distort the overall results unless there was a systematic bias against certain classes of prominent men. A cross check against various lists of civic leaders in Chicago indicates that the great majority of the city's upper crust found a place in the directory. Marquis did discriminate, however, against "disreputable" types, such as hack politicians and underworld characters.[3] Leaders of labor and ethnic communities were absent, unless they were also prominent in government or religion, or like Demetrius Jannopoulo, the Greek leader in Saint Louis, they were "president of the Missouri Tent and Awning Co.," or some other species of successful businessmen. Before the Nineteenth Amendment was passed, no women, not even Jane Addams or Mrs. Potter Palmer, received separate entries.[4] Keeping in mind these omissions, and the fact that men in their twenties and thirties rarely had acquired solid business or professional reputations, it is difficult to discern any other systematic biases that would make the patterns revealed by the directories significantly different from the patterns that would be displayed by some ideally "perfect" list. The strongest criticism would be the editors' choice of what proportions of men from each particular occupational or professional group would be included. This criticism can be met by analyzing the data chiefly in terms of occupational categories.[5]

The shortcomings, real or imagined, of the directories should not be allowed to obscure their immense advantages for the urban historian. They cover thousands of merchants, railroad managers, manufacturers, real estate operators, editors, corporate officials, educators, investors, philanthropists, consultants, civic leaders, physicians, traders, judges, lawyers, engineers, wholesalers, dentists, politicians, artists, social workers, brokers, bankers, and clergymen who ran the affairs of a great city, but who otherwise would be totally unknown or obscure today. For the vast majority of these men, the directories provide information that historians could otherwise obtain only by fantastically difficult searches through obituaries, clipping files, tax records, manuscript censuses, marriage licenses, and family bibles.

No historian can digest 6000 autobiographies, however brief, just by reading through them. A systematic research strategy, relying primarily upon quantifi-

---

The Book of Detroiters (Chicago, 1914), all published by Marquis and edited by Marquis or Leonard; John William Leonard, ed., *Who's Who in Finance* (New York, 1911); and Sara Mullin Baldwin, ed., *Who's Who in Wichita: 1929* (Wichita, 1929).

[3] In 1912 the 74,000 men arrested by the Chicago police included 102 lawyers, 318 physicians, 7 stock dealers, 109 brokers, and 10 clergymen. *The Daily News Almanac and Year-Book for 1914* (Chicago, 1913), 529; this yearbook also provided numerous lists of civic leaders.

[4] However, see John William Leonard, ed., *Women's Who's Who in America* (New York, 1914).

[5] The directory listed half the bankers counted by the census of 1910 (350 out of 706), one-third of the lawyers (1300 out of 3866), one-seventh of the physicians (600 out of 4032), one-eighth of the manufacturers (1400 out of 11,166), and only one-ninth of the clergymen (200 out of 1693). Obviously if these proportions had been changed, the aggregate elite would have a somewhat different profile, but the lawyers, physicians, etc., would have about the same profile. Bureau of the Census, *Thirteenth Census . . . 1910*, v. 4, "Population: Occupational Statistics" (Washington, 1914), 157, 161, 163, 165.

cation, is necessary to deal adequately with this large and important body of men. The easiest decision is to punch all the data on IBM cards and let a computer do all the work. But computer programs are purely mechanical devices that perforce have no historical imagination or sense of the past built into them. The challenge is to code the autobiographies so that numerical values stand for characteristics expressed in words, and to use computers to perform routine statistical manipulations. The historian—not the programmer or statistician—must then search the printout for meaningful patterns. If the historian wants to discuss urban elites on the basis of more than a handful of remarkable cases he will have to adopt a quantitative research strategy equal to the exigencies of dealing with great masses of data.

These exigencies demand the use of very simple codes. The computers that guide men to the moon can, it is true, store any information a historian can find, but any coding scheme elaborate enough to retain one-tenth of the richness of the information in the stylized little autobiographies would be a hundred times too complicated to use in statistical analysis. The state of the art of statistics, not computers, is the limiting factor. Furthermore, if all the information were to be stored on cards, it would take months to write programs that could, say, extract a man's age at marriage! Of course, historians oversimplify complex attributes all the time; they have to call a man who raises mules, sells corn, and speculates in real estate a farmer if they expect to understand agriculture.

Coding schemes have to be simple, but they do not have to be naïve. The questions one asks determine the codes one uses. If migration patterns are of concern, it makes sense to set up a series of categories—place of birth, distance and direction from destination, size of birthplace, location of college, number of places lived in, year of arrival in destination, and so on. Such information may not be given explicitly in the source, but can be extracted with the help of gazetteers. If the historian specifies his basic questions, he can approach the directories like a detective looking for implicit clues that can be made explicit by careful searching and ingenious codes.

The codes, also, must be prepared with an eye to the limitations of IBM cards and statistical routines. Each person receives one (or more) cards, with each bit of information recorded in one or more columns. To simplify rechecking, each Chicagoan received an identification code consisting of his abbreviated name and his page number. The first variable for analysis was the last two digits of his year of birth; the second indicated place of birth, both by region and state or foreign country; and the third was a one-column code for size of birthplace at the time the subject was born.[6] In like manner 65 of the 80 columns of a single IBM card were filled with codes for 48 different variables. To keep the printout manageable, facilitate the use of library computer programs, and avoid complicating the statistics, only the digits 0 through 9 were used in any one column after the name. (It is undesirable to use symbols like + and −.) The fewer the categories for any one variable the easier the statistical analysis becomes.

[6] The code was 0 = unknown, 1 = farm, 2 = rural non-farm; 3 = town under 2500 at time of birth; 4 = small city 2500 to 20,000; 5 = city 20,000 to 200,000, 6 = metropolis over 200,000.

Hence, frequent use was made of two-valued or dichotomous codes and of geometric-progression codes.[7]

It was unnecessary to code every name in every directory since a random sample provides virtually the same results with much less effort. For Chicago one name in ten was selected at random (or approximately one name per page), and for Wichita one name in five. The designated autobiographies were then coded and the data transferred to punch-cards. The other directories were not coded and computerized. Instead, whenever a particular question arose, an ad-hoc random sample was chosen and the desired information tabulated by hand. The manual tabulations provided both comparative perspective between cities and deeper explorations of particular groups, but could not generate new patterns the way the computer did. Random samples produce patterns that closely resemble, but are not identical with, the patterns that would result from using every name in the directories. The larger the sample, the smaller the error, and for a sample size (or N) of 746 for Chicago, the average sampling error is reasonably small, of the order of a few per cent. (Quadrupling the sampling size would quadruple coding time, but would only reduce the already small sampling error by half.) [8]

The chief reward for computerizing a collective biography is the ease in cross-tabulating variables, an extremely laborious process otherwise. Not only did the computer count the number of men in each category for each variable, but it automatically counted the number of men in every possible combination of categories for two variables, and it generated thousands of special tables incorporating three variables. Thus the printout not only indicated how many men were in each age cohort, but it also told how many financiers, lawyers, manufacturers, etc., were in each cohort. Furthermore, it reduced the tabulations to percentages, computed chi-square (a measure of strength of relationship), and calculated an "expected" number of men in each cell in the table.[9] (The "expected" number of lawyers born in the 1850's equals the percentage of all men who are lawyers, times the total number of men born in the 1850's.) The total number of tables in such cross-tabulations equals the square of the number of variables used—20 variables produce 400 tables (of which 210 are superfluous), 50 variables produce 2500 tables, and 100 variables produce 10,000! When the ancillary tables are added, the number of tables increases by 300 per cent. Statistical methods of pattern searching, therefore, are essential to indicate whether the pattern displayed in each table is random or not.

Quite simply, a random pattern occurs when each column of the table (in percentage form) is roughly identical. That is, the distribution of Republicans by age is parallel to the distributions of Democrats and nonpartisans by age. (See the part of Table 11 headed "Finance and Manufacturing" for an

[7] For example, 1 = Mason and 0 = not a Mason, was a dichotomous code; 1 = lived one year or less in city, 2 = 2 or 3 years, 3 = 4 to 7 years, 4 = 8 to 15 years, 5 = 16 to 31 years, 6 = 32 or more years, 0 = no information, was a geometric code.

[8] An elementary introduction to sampling theory appears in Hubert M. Blalock, *Social Statistics* (New York, 1960), Chap. 22.

[9] The most useful cross-tabulation program in wide circulation is NUCROSS, as described in Kenneth Janda, *Data Processing: Applications to Political Research* (Evanston, 1965). Most computer centers have a library of "canned" programs such as this for historians unfamiliar with FORTRAN.

example). In this case, age does not differentiate partisan attributes; age and partisanship are unrelated for the sample, and hence for the entire elite. The historian, unless he is perplexed by this result, should pass over to the next table. If it is non-random, the columns differ sharply when put in percentage form. For example, the foreign-born might be old, the easterners middle-aged, and the Chicago-born young. That is worth looking into. For a series of tables dealing with the same number (N) of men, the chi-square statistic will order the tables from low to high according to randomness.[10]

However, when it is necessary to compare tables with different N's, the chi-square values are misleading. A variety of measures of association exist to bridge this gap, of which Pearson's contingency coefficient C seems to be the most useful.[11] The behavior of C somewhat resembles the well known correlation coefficient r, which cannot be used with categorical data. The value of C ranges from 0 (randomness) to nearly +1.0 (very strong pattern). Table 1 for which C = .85, illustrates a strong pattern for the Chicago elite—a man's first occupation was, except for financiers, usually his current occupation. A high value of C does not mean that a particular table is important—there may be elementary reasons for the high value, but these can quickly be observed upon inspecting the table. The recommended strategy for a first scanning of the printout is to investigate the tables with values of C greater than .3 or .4. This reduces the double dangers of overlooking important patterns and wasting time on uninteresting tables. The C values can also be used to compare the strength of patterns in entirely different tables, even in different samples. Of course, there is no substitute for common historical sense in interpreting patterns, so long as one has a precise pattern to interpret.

The most important result of the study was that the exact physiognomy of the elite emerged from the shadows of myth and guesswork. The elite, as expected, differed sharply from the general population. In 1910, 62 per cent of all Chicagoans aged between 45 and 64 had been born abroad, in contrast to only 14 per cent of the elite. Fully 60 per cent of the men had attended college, a privilege denied to all but a handful of other Chicagoans of the same age. In a predominantly Catholic city, only 4 per cent of the elite acknowledged a Catholic affiliation (only 3 per cent were Jewish), while 35 per cent belonged to Protestant bodies. The remainder did not mention a religious affiliation, but were clearly of Protestant background. The largest Protestant denominations—Methodist, Lutheran and Baptist—were represented by only 69 men, in contrast to 164 members of the much smaller Congregational, Episcopalian, and Presbyterian bodies. One unexpected statistic (see Table 2) was the relationship between religion and education, the Catholics being the best educated and the Jews the least. This pattern also held for Saint Louis, and was due to the prominence of Catholic lawyers and Jewish merchants and manufacturers.

The birthplace information proved to be among the most valuable. It showed that the older men came from farther away (Europe and the Northeast), while

---

[10] On chi-square, see Blalock, *Social Statistics,* 212–20; for measures of association, see *ibid.,* 225–31, and Richard Jensen and Charles Dollar, *Quantitative Historical Research* (New York, 1970), Chap. 3.

[11] The value of C equals $\sqrt{X^2/(X^2 + N)}$ where X^2 is chi-square for the table, and N is the number of men included in that table.

TABLE 1
First Occupation by Current Occupation, Chicago, 1911

First Occupation	Current Occupation						All
	Finance	Trade & Transportation	Manufacturing	Law	Medicine	Other Professional	
Finance	44.6%	2.6%	2.1%	0.8%	0.0%	0.0%	7.9%
Trade & Transportation	23.2	65.6	15.5	2.3	3.1	8.7	25.9
Manufacturing	1.8	3.1	59.2	2.3	0.0	0.0	12.9
Law	7.1	5.1	1.4	80.6	0.0	1.1	16.8
Medicine	1.8	0.5	0.7	0.8	84.4	1.1	8.0
Other Professional	6.3	6.7	4.9	7.0	9.4	81.5	15.8
Manual	2.7	4.6	5.6	3.9	1.6	1.1	3.8
Other & Unknown	12.6	11.8	10.5	2.3	1.6	6.5	9.0
Totals	100.0	100.0	100.0	100.0	100.0	100.0	100.0
N	112	195	142	129	64	92	746

chi-square = χ^2 = 2027
contingency coefficient = C = .85

TABLE 2
EDUCATION BY RELIGION, CHICAGO, 1911

Education	Religious Affiliation None Mentioned	Protestant	Catholic	Jewish
Some college	54.8%	67.3%	80.0%	20.0%
High school or less	35.8	31.9	16.7	80.0
Not given	9.4	0.8	3.3	0.0
Total	100.0	100.0	100.0	100.0
N	436	260	30	20

(Chi–square = 84, and C = .32 for entire table, of which this is a condensation.)

younger men came from Chicago and the Midwest (see Table 3). A similar pattern occurred in the smaller boom city of Wichita in 1929 (see Table 4).

Three different hypotheses may explain the observed phenomenon: (1) long-distance geographical mobility among the elite was declining in the late nineteenth and early twentieth century; (2) migration rates remained the same, but older men typically have had more opportunities to move in their lifetime, and so tended to be farther from their birthplaces in 1911; (3) Chicago-born sons of the older members of the elite had an easier time entering the directory lists than young men from outside who lacked local connections. There is no way to choose among the three alternatives on the basis of the cross section of the elite in 1911. It is necessary to compare a cross section taken at a later or earlier date, and the 1926 edition of the directory provides this opportunity. Hypothesis (1) predicts additional shifts toward both Chicago and Midwestern birthplaces for each age category in 1926. Hypothesis (2) predicts a pattern in 1926 virtually identical to that of 1911. Hypothesis (3) predicts that Chicago-born will increase faster than any other category, and that paternal relationships should be observable. Table 5 shows the birthplace of the 1926 elite by age, and Table 6 shows the percentage differences between each entry in Table 5 and the corresponding entries in Table 4, that is, the change in rates.

TABLE 3
PLACE OF BIRTH BY AGE, CHICAGO, 1911

Birthplace	28–40	41–50	51–60	60+	All Ages
Chicago	26.2%	18.9%	10.2%	2.4%	15.1%
Other Midwest	45.3	36.8	39.0	16.0	35.2
Other U.S.	15.4	28.9	32.2	52.0	31.7
Foreign	13.1	15.5	18.7	29.6	18.0
Total	100.0	100.0	100.0	100.0	100.0
N	137	264	177	125	723

(Chi-square = 132 and C = .39 for original table; 23 men omitted for lack of birthplace data.)

TABLE 4

NEARNESS OF BIRTHPLACE, BY AGE,
WICHITA, 1929

	Born within 500 miles	*Born beyond 500 miles*
Age		
45 and over	36.9%	65.1%
44 and under	63.1	34.9
Total	100.0	100.0
N	313	146

(Chi-square = 37 and C = .28 for this table; for the original table, chi-square = 62 and C = .34.)

TABLE 5

PLACE OF BIRTH BY AGE, CHICAGO, 1926

Birthplace	Age 28–40	41–50	51–60	60+	All Ages
Chicago	36.9%	28.5%	23.9%	13.3%	23.0%
Other Midwest	34.9	40.0	37.2	36.0	37.9
Other U.S.	22.8	20.0	27.5	32.0	25.9
Foreign	5.4	11.5	11.5	18.7	13.1
Total	100.0	100.0	100.0	100.0	100.0
N	149	270	113	75	282*

*Pooling of two random samples; does not add horizontally.

TABLE 6

CHANGE IN PLACE OF BIRTH, BY AGE, CHICAGO, 1926 VERSUS 1911

Birthplace	Age 28–40	41–50	51–60	60+	All Ages
Chicago	+10.7	+9.6	+13.7	+10.9	+7.9
Other Midwest	−10.4	+3.2	−1.8	+20.0	+2.7
Other U.S.	+7.4	−8.9	−4.7	−20.0	−5.8
Foreign	−7.7	−4.0	−7.2	−10.9	−4.9

The 1926 patterns of birthplaces show a marked movement toward Chicago in all age groups, and a lesser movement toward the Midwest for all age groups over 40. The other American states and Europe supplied a decreasing proportion of the Chicago elite. Obviously hypothesis (2) must be rejected—the geographical mobility patterns did change in the short span of 15 years. Hypothesis (1), in predicting the contraction of geographical mobility, is justified for each age group except the youngest. There, the proportion of

Chicagoans did go up 10.7 points, but the proportion of Midwesterners fell 10.4 points and the proportion of men from other states increased 7.4 points, which was the opposite of the prediction. Only hypothesis (3) seems to be consistent with all the patterns in Table 6. Further checking indicates that 31 per cent of the Chicago-born elite of 1911 had a relative (father, brother, father-in-law, or son) in the same directory, in contrast to only 16 per cent of the 1911 elite born outside Chicago. For 1926, fully 33 per cent (77) of a sample of 232 men born in the city after 1880 were sons of men listed in at least one edition of the directory (1905, 1911, 1917, or 1926); doubtless, many others were nephews or in-laws of elite members. Thus hypothesis (3) is consistent with all the findings, but there is some doubt whether it can alone account for the magnitudes of the shifts. It seems likely that two effects were operating simultaneously, that is, that both hypotheses (1) and (3) are correct.

Chicago was the only large city that was the birthplace of more than 3 per cent of the 1911 elite. Of the 467 native born (excepting the Chicago-born and those for whom birthplace data is missing), only 7 per cent (32 men) were born in a city of more than 200,000 population, and 11 per cent (50) came

TABLE 7

PARTISANSHIP BY CITY AND OCCUPATIONAL GROUP,
MIDWESTERN BUSINESS AND PROFESSIONAL ELITES, 1907–1929

	Per cent Republican	*Per cent Democrat*	*Per cent None, NA & other*	*N*
Chicago (1911)				
All *	47.7%	9.2%	43.1%	698
Finance	58.9	5.6	35.5	107
Manufacturing	50.4	10.2	39.4	137
Trade & Transportation	46.3	7.3	46.3	179
Medicine	35.5	0.0	64.5	62
Law	60.3	22.6	16.1	124
Other Profession	22.5	3.4	74.1	89
Wichita (1929)				
All *	56.3	14.1	29.6	480
Business	57.8	14.8	27.4	303
Clergy	58.8	0.0	41.2	17
Education	38.3	14.9	46.8	47
Medicine	47.4	18.4	34.3	38
Law	71.9	18.7	9.4	32
Detroit (1914)				
All Business	53.2	10.4	36.3	77
Automobiles	47.5	7.5	45.0	80
Railroad	47.7	9.5	42.8	42
Heavy Mfg. (ex. auto)	53.4	6.3	40.3	189
Construction	47.0	13.0	40.0	15
Real Estate	66.1	7.1	26.8	56
Law	51.8	22.8	25.3	162
Medicine	41.5	6.2	52.3	65

* In Chicago and Wichita, all names were drawn from one systematic random sample, so the marginal totals can be added; in the other cities, separate samples were drawn for each occupation.

TABLE 7 *(Continued)*

	Per cent Republican	Per cent Democrat	Per cent None, NA & other	N
St. Louis (1912)				
All Business	36.2%	19.1%	44.7%	544
Shoes	31.6	34.2	34.2	38
Beer	36.7	13.3	50.0	30
Real Estate	37.4	33.3	29.3	75
Construction	50.0	14.3	35.7	28
Railroad	19.2	23.3	57.5	73
Law	37.6	42.7	17.7	170
Medicine	25.2	23.2	51.6	147
Twin Cities (1907)				
All Business	41.1	6.8	52.1	73
Banking	43.9	9.9	46.2	41
Lumber	46.7	0.0	53.3	30
Newspapers	42.5	2.5	55.0	40
Law	55.0	10.0	35.0	60
Middle-Sized Minnesota Cities (8000 to 75,000 pop) (1907)				
All Business	43.0	22.0	36.0	14
Banking	60.0	7.0	33.0	15
Lumber	50.0	7.0	43.0	16
Newspapers	55.0	35.0	10.0	20
Law	50.0	27.5	22.5	40
Minnesota: Small Cities and Towns (1907)				
All Business	48.7	7.7	43.6	39
Banking	58.0	4.9	37.1	81
Lumber	43.0	0.0	57.0	7
Newspapers	53.1	18.4	28.6	49
Law	62.5	8.8	28.8	80

from medium cities of 20,000 to 200,000. The largest numbers came from small towns and cities. Small cities of 2500 to 20,000 population contributed 18 per cent (82) of the men, while villages of under 2500 population claimed 33 per cent (155). It proved virtually impossible to distinguish between rural non-farm, estimated at 27 per cent (127) and the farm-born, estimated at 4.5 per cent (only 21 men). Probably more were actually born on farms. Even when the Chicagoans are included, as well as the foreign born, cities of more than 20,000 population were the birthplaces of only 30 per cent of the Chicago elite. In Wichita the small-town bias was even stronger, with 19 per cent of the city's total elite (90 out of 480) born on farms, while another 45 per cent (218) came from towns of under 3000 population, and only 6 per cent (27) from cities of more than 100,000. The metropolitan leadership community was, indeed, bred in the small town, but not necessarily on a farm.

That old-stock, well-educated, rural and small-town bred, white Protestant elites in the Midwestern metropolises were Republicans is not too surprising, but the poor showing of the Democratic party is remarkable. Table 7 shows the breakdown by location. In Chicago, Detroit, and the twin cities, Minneapolis and Saint Paul, the Democrats enrolled a meager 10 per cent of the elite. In

Wichita they did a little better (14 per cent), but only in the border city of
Saint Louis did they enlist a respectable quarter of the elite. The Republicans
included about half the elite everywhere except Saint Louis, where they were
held to a third. A substantial proportion, ranging from 30 per cent in Wichita to
nearly 50 per cent in the larger cities were politically so apathetic that they
listed no major party identification for themselves in the directories. This
included a tiny handful of third party members like the four Socialists and two
Prohibitionists in Chicago, and a few men who specified they were "independent in politics."

The Democratic showing was not much better in the various occupational
groups, except that fewer lawyers were independents and the Democrats picked
up support there. Businessmen in fields that might seem dependent upon
political favoritism, like construction, real estate, and railroads, were no more
politically involved than others. Indeed, railroad managers and owners, and
especially physicians, clergymen, educators, and other professionals clearly
tended to avoid partisanship. Perhaps they considered themselves technical
experts who stood above petty partisanship; or perhaps they moved around so
much that they never acquired firm roots in local politics. In Wichita, 35 per
cent of the 150 men who had lived less than eight years in the city were
non-partisan, in contrast to only 27 per cent of the 327 longer-term residents.
Only in Saint Louis did the Democrats outnumber the Republicans in any
occupational groups, but there the Democratic strength rested primarily on the
large numbers of Southerners and Catholics. If these two groups are excluded,
the Saint Louis Republicans outnumbered Democrats by 3 to 1 or 4 to 1 in
every category. The overall political complexion of the city does not seem to
have been a decisive factor, since Republicans outpolled the Democrats in most
elections in every city except Chicago.

The Republicans fared no better among the richest members of the elite than
among the average members. The "richest" were identified by lists of capitalists,
bankers, corporate directors, and investors in another compendium similar to
the Marquis directories. Table 8 gives the politics of the richest men in Illinois,
Michigan, Minnesota, and Missouri, and, for comparison, Iowa and six states in
the deep South. So few capitalists lived in Kansas City, Missouri, that a few
names had to be taken from Kansas City, Kansas, including one Christian
Balzac Hoffman, one of the wealthiest millers in the country, owner of a chain
of grain elevators in Kansas, and a member of the Socialist party.

The most striking pattern in Table 8 is the heavy partisanship of bankers
outside the large cities. The exception is Minnesota, where partisanship seems to
have become old-fashioned already. The metropolitan capitalists tabulated in
Table 8 represent, beyond doubt, some of the wealthiest and busiest men in the
country. They apparently held so many directorships, presidencies, portfolios,
and country club memberships that they had little time or inclination for
politics (although some held high party or government posts). The evidence
suggests that politics was most salient in the small cities and least relevant to the
metropolitan notables, who, as indicated above, tended themselves to come
from small cities; perhaps much of their remaining partisanship was the
lingering effect of youthful indoctrination.[12]

[12] For opposite results in the 1960's, see Everett Ladd, *Ideology in America*
(Ithaca, 1969).

TABLE 8

PARTISANSHIP BY LOCATION, CAPITALISTS, 1911 *

	Per cent Republican	Per cent Democrat	Per cent None, NA & Other	N
Illinois:				
Chicago	55.6%	8.7%	38.4%	403
Downstate	75.1	18.1	7.0	144
Michigan:				
Detroit	48.3	20.7	31.0	29
Upstate	71.0	21.1	7.9	114
Minnesota:				
Twin Cities	46.4	7.2	46.4	97
Middle-Size	43.2	0.0	56.8	44
Small cities and towns	61.4	8.6	30.0	140
Missouri:				
Saint Louis	38.9	23.1	37.9	203
Kansas City	50.0	25.0	25.0	16
Outstate	37.1	59.1	3.8	159
Iowa	82.8	15.2	2.0	197
Deep South (Ala., Ark., Fla., Ga., La., Miss.)	7.8	83.6	8.6	370

* Based on Leonard, ed., *Who's Who in Finance* (footnote 2).

The few Democrats who entered the elite may have had difficult relations with their peers—only 15 per cent of the Chicago Democrats belonged to one or more of the three leading social clubs (Union League, University, Chicago), in contrast to 34 per cent of the Republicans. One reason may have been their close ties to the notorious Chicago machine of Mayor Carter Henry Harrison (who was listed in the directory). Lawyers accounted for 41 per cent of the Democrats, in contrast to only 15 per cent of the other elite men, and 38 per cent of all the Democrats had already been candidates for public office, in contrast to only 11 per cent of the Republicans. Of course, there were a few men like Robert Hall McCormick of the reaper family, a noted collector of art and member of the best clubs, who were Democrats; McCormick's son was Republican. Only a handful of men in the various samples (just two in Chicago) identified themselves as "progressive Republicans," "insurgent Republicans" or "Progressives." Equally uncommon was the designation "gold" or "Cleveland" Democrat.

Robert Wiebe and Samuel Hays have suggested that a new middle class of businessmen emerged in the metropolis early in the twentieth century who were cosmopolitan rather than localistic in outlook, and for whom professional, technical, and trade associations rather than political parties served as vehicles for relating their expertise to social and political problems.[13] Such a group should show up in the elite sample, and indeed there are traces of them in

[13] Robert Wiebe, *The Search for Order: 1877–1920* (New York, 1967), 129; Samuel P. Hays, "Political Parties and the Community-Society Continuum," in William N. Chambers and Walter Dean Burnham, eds., *The American Party Systems* (New York, 1967), 152–81.

Chicago, as Table 9 suggests. More than 40 per cent of the Republicans and non-partisans mentioned one or more association memberships, in contrast to only 28 per cent of the Democrats, who were still wedded to machine politics. Of the men who listed memberships, one-sixth of the Republicans and Democrats also held leadership positions in them, in contrast to one-third of the non-partisans.[14] Thus, it would appear that professional leadership served as a substitute for political activism, as the hypothesis suggests. The figures are somewhat deceptive, however. Physicians and educators, two highly non-partisan groups, were much more likely to join professional societies than businessmen by the very nature of their work. Only 12.5 per cent of the 64 physicians held no memberships, in contrast to 80 per cent of the men in trade, transportation, and manufacturing. However, the businessmen averaged 2.5 memberships each in social clubs, while the professional men (excluding lawyers) averaged only 1.1 each. Clearly, medical and other professional societies served as substitutes for social clubs in addition to their technical functions.

TABLE 9

TECHNICAL ASSOCIATIONS BY PARTISANSHIP, CHICAGO, 1911

Partisanship	Per cent with membership in technical or professional associations	Per cent of members holding leadership positions	N
Republicans	40.4%	17.0%	334
Democrats	28.4	15.8	67
Nonpartisans	43.0	33.6	312

However, the hypothesis becomes dubious when a specific group, such as physicians, are considered. A sample of 182 elite doctors in Saint Louis disclosed that one-sixth of the Republicans (7 out of 44), and one-sixth of the non-partisans (17 out of 104) held leadership positions in medical affairs, in contrast to fully one-third of the Democrats (11 out of 34), or the reverse of the results of Table 9. In Saint Louis, therefore, Democratic affiliation was associated with professional leadership among physicians; the two roles were mutually reinforcing, not mutually exclusive as the Wiebe-Hays interpretation would suggest. (Only 3 partisan and 12 non-partisan doctors listed no memberships in medical societies, while the solitary Socialist turned out to be an eminent surgeon.)

The use of a computerized research design facilitates the investigation of the basic question of multivariate analysis: how does one variable affect the relationship between two other variables? For example, does the same relationship between occupation and partisanship hold for young, middle-aged, and old men? If different patterns emerge for the different age groups, then the historian must explain the patterns either in terms of the biological effects of aging, or in terms of the different specific historical experiences encountered by each

[14] Leadership positions included the president of a medical society, member of the city or state board of health, editor of a medical journal, dean of a medical school, or delegate to an international conference.

generation in its formative years. Since age seemed the variable most likely to have a multivariate effect, the Chicago elite was divided into three cohorts, "old" (born before 1849), "middle-aged" (born between 1850 and 1869), and "young" (born after 1870), and every pair of variables was examined for each cohort.

An example of the biological effects of aging appeared in the relationship between occupation and recreation. The physicians, educators, clergy, engineers, architects, authors, artists, and scientists in the sample were so busy with technical activities that they enjoyed little leisure time. Only 10 per cent of the 30 young men in these categories specifically mentioned any form of recreation, along with 18 per cent of the 97 middle-aged and 4 per cent of the 24 elderly. What little time was available for recreation came in middle age for these professionals. By contrast, the corresponding rates for businessmen and lawyers were 54 per cent for 107 young men, 46 per cent for 344 middle-aged, and 33 per cent for 108 elderly gentlemen. Unlike the professionals, the businessmen enjoyed their recreation more when they were younger, as would be expected from aging factors. The non-lawyer professionals were also much less likely to be members of lodges (12 per cent of 151, versus 26 per cent for businessmen and lawyers.)

The most intriguing result of the age cohort analysis was the changed relationship between occupation and partisanship. The partisanship patterns for each occupation are roughly the same across the cohorts, except for finance, manufacturing, and law. Table 10 shows the pattern. Financiers and manufacturers born between 1850 and 1869 were 14.8 points more Republican than older and younger men in the same line of work. Lawyers born between 1850 and 1869, however, were 15.4 points more Democratic than other lawyers. The most plausible explanation is in terms of the different political experiences of each generation. Men born in the 1850's and 1860's came of age politically and entered their occupations between about 1874 and 1900, precisely the period when the currency and tariff questions were the most salient issues in national politics, with the Republican party taking positions favored by banking and

TABLE 10

PARTISANSHIP, BY AGE AND OCCUPATION, CHICAGO, 1911

| | Finance & Manufacturing | | All Other Occupations | |
	Middle-age	Young & Old	Middle-age	Young & Old
Per cent Republican	58.4%	45.6%	37.3%	36.7%
Per cent Democrat	9.7	5.4	5.5	5.8
Per cent Other	31.8	48.9	57.1	57.5
N	154	92	217	120

| | Law | |
	Middle-age	Young & Old
Per cent Republican	54.3%	68.4%
Per cent Democrat	29.4	14.0
Per cent Other	16.2	17.5
N	68	57

manufacturing interests. The middle cohort of bankers and manufacturers was, therefore, less independent and more Republican than the other cohorts which came of age when other issues were more salient, and was also more Republican than men in the same cohort but in occupations not so directly affected by monetary and tariff debates. As for the lawyers, it is notable that the only decades in which promising young Democrats could reasonably aspire to high offices in Illinois or on a national level were precisely those during which the middle cohort came of age. Since most lawyers had a bent toward politics, it is not surprising that the law would be especially attractive to ambitious Democrats of the middle cohort, or conversely that the Democratic party was especially attractive to aspiring lawyers in that cohort.

TABLE 11

PARTISANSHIP, BY AGE AND OCCUPATION, SAINT LOUIS, 1912

| | Finance & Manufacturing | | All Other Occupations | |
	Middle-aged	Young & Old	Middle-aged	Young & Old
Republican	35.6%	36.5%	26.6%	41.7%
Democrat	18.4	17.6	18.1	10.7
Independent	46.0	45.9	55.3	47.6
N	87	74	94	84

| | Law | |
	Middle-aged	Young & Old
Republican	46.1%	47.6%
Democrat	46.1	42.9
Independent	7.8	9.5
N	13	21

Before accepting an interpretation of Table 10 based on political generations, it would be well to consider the corresponding patterns for Saint Louis, shown in Table 11. The middle cohorts of financiers and manufacturers there showed the identical partisan distribution as the young and old cohorts, as did the middle cohort of lawyers. For other occupations, however, the middle-aged cohort was significantly less Republican than the young and old cohorts. A revision of the generational hypothesis offered for Chicago applies to both cities (except for lawyers, for whom the Saint Louis sample size is too small to allow reliable conclusions). In Chicago the age cohorts were politically similar except for a Republican bulge among middle-aged financiers and manufacturers. In Saint Louis, the cohorts were also similar, except for a Democratic bulge among the middle-aged in other occupations. In both cities the middle-aged financiers and manufacturers were significantly more Republican, in terms of the combination of age and occupation, than might have been expected by looking at other occupations. Thus, Republican party policy in the 1870's, 1880's, and 1890's seems to have influenced the partisanship of men who were *both* young at that time and engaged in occupations that were affected by national tariff and monetary policies.

This paper has touched on only a few of the questions that can be studied through quantitative collective biography. The relationships between age and mobility, occupation and party, religion and education, partisanship and technical associations, and age-occupation-partisanship-city, which have been discovered are only suggestive of the rich results made possible by computerized research. Of course, collective biography has limitations beyond the biases and omissions that have already been mentioned. The directories were snapshots at one moment in time of lives that were not yet complete. No historian would ever guess from the Chicago data that the Republican party was about to split, or that the world would soon plunge into a great war. What reader of the optimistic autobiographies in the 1929 Wichita directory would guess that the city's economy was about to collapse? And what about the beliefs, attitudes, fears, aspirations, and calculations of the elite? How are they to be discovered, or if found, coded? Party, religion, and memberships provide "hard" data on activities; but are they adequate substitutes for individual attitudes? Clearly the directories cannot answer half the questions the historian can ask about metropolitan elites.

On the other hand, quantitative collective biography promises to answer half the questions that have been unanswerable before, and to free the historian from dependence on the haphazard generalizations of journalists, novelists, and biographers of famous men. Hunches can give way to numerically specific conclusions. Simple tabulations will show who comprised the elite, where they came from, what their family structures, social activities, business connections, political involvements, and recreations were like. Cross-tabulations, multivariate analysis, linkages with earlier and later directories, and comparisons with other cities will reveal patterns that were never even suspected, and provide clues to the explanations of those patterns.

Bibliography

The following is a selected list of published works in the quantitative analysis of American history, drawn largely from the extensive footnotes in the introductory essays of this book. The organization is topical, following the arrangement of the chapter headings. The intent is to provide a convenient listing of the items which, in the opinion of the editor, comprise the major contributions in the field. Readers are referred to the chapter introductions for annotated comments on these works plus many not included here.

I. General: Method and Theory

Berkhofer, Robert F., Jr. *A Behavioral Approach to Historical Analysis.* New York: Free Press, 1969.

Bernstein, Jeremy. *The Analytical Engine: Computers—Past, Present and Future.* New York: Random House, 1963.

Blalock, Hubert M., Jr. *Social Statistics.* New York: McGraw-Hill Book Co., 1960.

Borko, Harold (ed.). *Computer Applications in the Behavioral Sciences.* Englewood Cliffs, N.J.: Prentice-Hall, 1962.

Bowles, Edmund A. (ed.). *Computers in Humanistic Research: Readings and Perspectives.* Englewood Cliffs, N.J.: Prentice-Hall, 1967.

Clubb, Jerome M. "The Inter-University Consortium for Political Research: Progress and Prospects," *Historical Methods Newsletter,* II (June, 1969), 1–5.

Clubb, Jerome M., and Howard W. Allen. "Computers and Historical Studies," *Journal of American History,* LIV (Dec., 1967), 599–607.

Condon, Thomas J. "Goals for Humanistic Research with Computers," *ACLS Newsletter,* XVIII (Apr., 1967), 1–7.

Gottschalk, Louis (ed.). *Generalization in the Writing of History: A Report of the Committee on Historical Analysis of the Social Science Research Council.* Chicago: University of Chicago Press, 1963.

Hexter, Jack H. "Some American Observations [on Quantitative History]," *Journal of Contemporary History,* II (Jan., 1967), 5–23.

Hoover, Dwight W. "Political Behavioralism in American History: A Case Study," Indiana Academy of the Social Sciences, *Proceedings, Third Series,* II (1967), 144–60.

Jensen, Richard, and Charles M. Dollar. *Quantitative Historical Research.* New York: Holt, Rinehart, Winston, 1970.

Key, V. O., Jr. *A Primer of Statistics for Political Scientists.* New York: Thomas Y. Crowell Co., 1966.

Komarovsky, Mirra (ed.). *Common Frontiers of the Social Sciences.* Glencoe, Ill.: Free Press, 1957.

Marczewski, Jean. "Quantitative History," *Journal of Contemporary History,* III (Apr., 1968), 179–91.

Rashevsky Nicholas. *Looking at History Through Mathematics.* Cambridge, Mass.: MIT Press, 1968.

Rosen, Saul. "Electronic Computers: A Historical Survey," *Computing Surveys,* I (Mar., 1969), 7–36.

Rummel, R. J. "Understanding Factor Analysis," *Journal of Conflict Resolution,* XI (Dec., 1967), 455–77.

Saveth, Edward N. (ed.). *American History and the Social Sciences.* Glencoe, Ill.: Free Press, 1964.
Siegal, Sidney. *Nonparametric Statistics for the Behavioral Sciences.* New York: McGraw-Hill Book Co., 1956.
Zemsky, Robert M. "Numbers and History: The Dilemma of Measurement," *Computers and the Humanities,* III (Sept., 1969), 31–40.

II. Content Analysis

Gerbner, George, Ole R. Holsti, Klaus Krippendorff, William J. Paisley, and Philip J. Stone. *The Analysis of Communication Content: Developments in Scientific Theories and Computer Techniques.* New York: John Wiley & Sons, 1969.
Holsti, Ole R. "An Adaptation of the General Inquirer for the Systematic Analysis of Political Documents," *Behavioral Science,* IX (1964), 383–88.
——. *Content Analysis for the Social Sciences and Humanities.* Reading, Mass.: Addison-Wesley Pub. Co., 1969.
Lantz, Herman R., Margaret Britton, Raymond Schmitt, and Eloise C. Snyder. "Pre-Industrial Patterns in the Colonial Family in America: A Content Analysis of Colonial Magazines," *American Sociological Review,* XXXIII (June, 1968), 413–26.
Merritt, Richard L. *Symbols of American Community, 1735–1775.* New Haven, Conn.: Yale University Press, 1966.
Mosteller, Frederick, and David L. Wallace. *Inference and Disputed Authorship: The Federalist.* Reading, Mass.: Addison-Wesley Pub. Co., 1964.
——. "Inference in an Authorship Problem," *Journal of the American Statistical Association,* LVIII (1963), 275–309.
North, Robert C., Ole R. Holsti, M. George Zaninovich, and Dina A. Zinnes. *Content Analysis: A Handbook with Applications for the Study of International Crisis.* Evanston, Ill.: Northwestern University Press, 1963.
Pool, Ithiel de Sola (ed.). *Trends in Content Analysis.* Urbana, Ill.: University of Illinois Press, 1959.
Stone, Philip J., Robert F. Bales, J. Zvi Namenwirth, and Daniel M. Ogilvie. *The General Inquirer: A Computer Approach to Content Analysis in the Behavioral Sciences.* Cambridge, Mass.: MIT Press, 1966.

III. Legislative and Judicial Behavior

Alexander, Thomas B. *Sectional Stress and Party Strength: A Computer Analysis of Roll-Call Voting Patterns in the United States House of Representatives, 1836–1860.* Nashville, Tenn.: Vanderbilt University Press, 1967.
Anderson, Lee F., Meredith W. Watts, Jr., and Allen R. Wilcox. *Legislative Roll-Call Analysis.* Evanston, Ill.: Northwestern University Press, 1966.
Belknap, George M. "A Method for Analyzing Legislative Behavior," *Midwest Journal of Political Science,* II (Nov., 1958), 377–402.
Cherryholmes, Cleo H., and Michael J. Shapiro. *Representatives and Roll-Calls: A Computer Simulation of Voting in the Eighty-Eighth Congress.* Indianapolis, Ind.: Bobbs-Merrill Co., 1969.
Clubb, Jerome M., and Howard W. Allen. "Party Loyalty in the Progressive Years: The Senate, 1909–1915," *Journal of Politics,* XXIX (Aug., 1967), 567–84.
Gambill, Edward L. "Who Were the Senate Radicals," *Civil War History,* XI (Sept. 1965), 237–44.
Grumm, John G. "The Systematic Analysis of Blocs in the Study of Voting Behavior," *Western Political Quarterly,* XVIII (June, 1965), 350–62.
Linden, Glenn M. " 'Radicals' and Economic Policies: The House of Representatives, 1861–1873," *Civil War History,* XIII (Mar., 1967), 51–65.
——. " 'Radicals' and Economic Policies: The Senate, 1861–1873," *Journal of Southern History,* XXXII (May, 1966), 189–199.
MacRae, Duncan, Jr. "A Method for Identifying Issues and Factions from Legislative Votes," *American Political Science Review,* LIX (Dec., 1965), 909–26.
——. *Dimensions of Congressional Voting: A Statistical Study of the House of*

Representatives in the Eighty-first Congress. Berkeley: University of California Press, 1958.

Moore, John R. "The Conservative Coalition in the United States Senate, 1942–1945," *Journal of Southern History,* XXXIII (Aug., 1967), 368–76.

Russett, Bruce M. "Discovering Voting Groups in the United Nations," *American Political Science Review,* LX (June, 1966), 327–39.

Schmidhauser, John R. "Judicial Behavior and the Sectional Crisis of 1837–1860," *Journal of Politics,* XXIII (Nov., 1961), 615–40.

Schubert, Glendon A. *Judicial Behavior: A Reader in Theory and Research.* Chicago: Rand McNally, 1964.

———. *The Judicial Mind: The Attitudes and Ideologies of Supreme Court Justices, 1946–1963.* Evanston, Ill.: Northwestern University Press, 1965.

Shover, John L. "Populism in the Nineteen-Thirties: The Battle for the AAA," *Agricultural History,* XXXIX (Jan., 1965), 17–24.

Silbey, Joel. *The Shrine of Party: Congressional Voting Behavior, 1841–1852.* Pittsburgh: University of Pittsburgh Press, 1967.

Tanenhaus, Joseph. "The Cumulative Scaling of Judicial Decisions," *Harvard Law Review,* LXXIX (June, 1966), 1583–94.

Thelen, David P. "Social Tensions and the Origins of Progressivism," *American Historical Review,* LVI (Sept., 1969), 323–41.

Todd, James E. "An Analysis of Security Council Voting Behavior," *Western Political Quarterly,* XXII (Mar., 1969), 61–78.

Ulmer, S. Sidney. "The Analysis of Behavior Patterns on the United States Supreme Court," *Journal of Politics,* XXII (Nov., 1960), 629–53.

———. "Sub-group Formation in the Constitutional Convention," *Midwest Journal of Political Science,* X (Aug., 1966), 288–303.

Wolff, Gerald. "The Slavocracy and the Homestead Problem of 1854," *Agricultural History,* XL (Apr., 1966), 101–11.

IV. Popular Voting Behavior

Alexander, Thomas B., Peggy Duckworth Elmore, Frank M. Lowery, and Mary Jane Pickens Skinner. "The Basis of Alabama's Ante-Bellum Two-Party System," *Alabama Review,* XIX (Oct., 1966), 243–76.

Benson, Lee. "An Approach to the Scientific Study of Past Public Opinion," *Public Opinion Quarterly,* XXXI (Winter, 1967–1968), 522–67.

Daniels, George. "Immigrant Vote in the 1860 Election: The Case of Iowa," *Mid-America,* XLIV (July, 1963), 142–62.

Formisano, Ronald P. "Analyzing American Voting, 1830–1860: Methods," *Historical Methods Newsletter,* II (Mar., 1969), 1–12.

Hackney, Sheldon. *Populism to Progressivism in Alabama.* Princeton, N.J.: Princeton University Press, 1969.

Hays, Samuel P. "The Social Analysis of American Political History, 1880–1920," *Political Science Quarterly,* LXXX (Sept., 1965), 373–94.

Holt, Michael F. *Forging a Majority: The Formation of the Republican Party in Pittsburgh, 1848–1860.* New Haven, Conn.: Yale University Press, 1969.

Kann, Robert A. "Public Opinion Research: A Contribution to Historical Method," *Political Science Quarterly,* LXXIII (Sept., 1958), 374–96.

Kleppner, Paul. *The Cross of Culture: A Social Analysis of Midwestern Politics, 1850–1900.* New York: Free Press, 1970.

———. "Lincoln and the Immigrant Vote: A Case of Religious Polarization," *Mid-America,* XLVIII (July, 1966), 176–95.

Luebke, Frederick C. *Immigrants and Politics: The Germans of Nebraska, 1880–1900.* Lincoln, Neb.: University of Nebraska Press, 1969.

MacRae, Duncan, Jr., and James A. Meldrum. "Critical Elections in Illinois, 1888–1958," *American Political Science Review,* LIV (Sept., 1960), 669–83.

Parsons, Stanley B. "Who Were the Nebraska Populists?" *Nebraska History,* XLIV (June, 1963), 83–99.

Pomper, Gerald. *Election in America: Control and Influence in Democratic Politics.* New York: Dodd, Mead, 1969.

Robinson, W. S. "Ecological Correlations and the Behavior of Individuals," *American Sociological Review*, XV (June, 1950), 351–57.

Rogin, Michael P. *The Intellectuals and McCarthy: The Radical Specter*. Cambridge, Mass.: MIT Press, 1967.

Stanley, John L. "Majority Tyranny in Tocqueville's America: The Failure of Negro Suffrage in 1846," *Political Science Quarterly*, LXXXIV (Sept., 1969), 412–35.

V. Economic History

Bailyn, Bernard, and Lotte Bailyn. *Massachusetts Shipping, 1697–1714: A Statistical Study*. Cambridge, Mass.: Harvard University Press, 1959.

Bogue, Allan G., and Margaret Beattie Bogue. " 'Profits' and the Frontier Land Speculator," *Journal of Economic History*, XVII (Mar., 1957), 1–24.

Cochran, Thomas C. "Economic History, Old and New," *American Historical Review*, LVI (June, 1969), 1561–72.

Conrad, Alfred H., and John R. Meyer. *The Economics of Slavery and Other Studies in Econometric History*. Chicago: Aldine Pub. Co., 1964.

Davis, Lance E. "Professor Fogel and the New Economic History," *Economic History Review, Second Series*, XIX (Dec., 1966), 652–63.

Davisson, William I. "Essex County Price Trends: Money and Markets in 17th Century Massachusetts," *Essex Institute Historical Collections*, CIII (Apr., 1967), 144–85.

——. "Essex County Wealth Trends: Wealth and Economic Growth in 17th Century Massachusetts," *Essex Institute Historical Collections*, CIII (Oct., 1967), 291–342.

Engerman, Stanley L. "The Effects of Slavery Upon the Southern Economy: A Review of the Recent Debate," *Explorations in Entrepreneurial History, Second Series*, IV (Winter, 1967), 71–97.

Fishlow, Albert. *American Railroads and the Transformation of the Ante-Bellum Economy*. Cambridge, Mass.: Harvard University Press, 1965.

Fogel, Robert W. "The New Economic History, Its Findings and Methods," *Economic History Review, Second Series*, XIX (Dec., 1966), 642–63.

——. *Railroads and American Economic Growth: Essays in Econometric History*. Baltimore, Md.: The Johns Hopkins Press, 1964.

——. "The Reunification of Economic History with Economic Theory," *American Economic Review*, LV (May, 1965), 92–98.

Fogel, Robert W., and Stanley L. Engerman. "A Model for the Explanation of Industrial Expansion During the Nineteenth Century: With an Application to the American Iron Industry," *Journal of Political Economy*, LXXI (June, 1969), 306–28.

Hunt, E. H. "The New Economic History: Professor Fogel's Study of American Railways," *History*, LIII (Feb., 1968), 3–18.

North, Douglass C. *Growth and Welfare in the American Past: A New Economic History*. New York: Prentice-Hall, 1966.

Purdue Faculty Papers in Economic History, 1956–1966 [Herman C. Krannert Graduate School of Industrial Administration, Purdue University Monograph Series, Vol. 4]. Homewood, Ill.: E. D. Irwin Pub. Co., 1967.

Redlich, Fritz. " 'New' and Traditional Approaches to Economic History and Their Interdependence," *Journal of Economic History*, XXV (Dec., 1965), 480–95.

——. "Potentialities and Pitfalls in Economic History," *Explorations in Entrepreneurial History, Second Series*, VI (Fall, 1968), 93–108.

Swierenga, Robert P. *Pioneers and Profits: Land Speculation on the Iowa Frontier*. Ames, Iowa: Iowa State University Press, 1968.

VI. Social and Demographic History

Blumin, Stuart. "The Historical Study of Vertical Mobility," *Historical Methods Newsletter*, I (Sept., 1968), 1–13.

Cahnman, Richard D., and Alvin Boskoff (eds.). *Sociology and History: Theory and Research*. New York: Free Press, 1964.

Curti, Merle E., Robert Daniel, Shaw Livermore, Jr., Joseph Van Hise, and Margaret W. Curti. *The Making of an American Community: A Case Study of Democracy in a Frontier County.* Stanford, Calif.: Stanford University Press, 1959.

Demos, John. "Families in Colonial Bristol, Rhode Island: An Exercise in Historical Demography," *William and Mary Quarterly,* XXV (Jan., 1968), 40–57.

DePillis, Mario S. "Trends in American Social History and the Possibilities of Behavioral Approaches," *Journal of Social History,* I (Fall, 1967), 38–60.

Gatell, Frank Otto. "Money and Power in Jacksonian America: A Quantitative Look at New York City's Men of Quality," *Political Science Quarterly,* LXXXII (June, 1967), 235–52.

Graham, Otis L., Jr. *An Encore for Reform: The Old Progressives and the New Deal.* New York: Oxford University Press, 1967.

Greven, Philip J. "Historical Demography and Colonial America," *William and Mary Quarterly,* XXIV (July, 1967), 438–54.

Harris, P. M. G. "The Social Origins of American Leaders: The Demographic Foundations," *Perspectives in American History,* III (1969), 159–343.

Katz, Michael B. *The Irony of Early School Reform: Educational Innovation in the Mid-Nineteenth Century.* Cambridge, Mass.: Harvard University Press, 1968.

Knights, Peter S. "City Directories as Aids to Ante-Bellum Urban Studies: A Research Note," *Historical Methods Newsletter,* II (Sept., 1969), 1–10.

Lipset, Seymour Martin, and Richard Hofstadter (eds.). *Sociology and History: Methods.* New York: Basic Books, 1968.

Thernstrom, Stephan. "Notes on the Historical Study of Social Mobility," *Comparative Studies in History and Theory,* X (Jan., 1968), 162–72.

———. *Poverty and Progress: Social Mobility in a Nineteenth Century City.* Cambridge, Mass.: Harvard University Press, 1964.

———. "Urbanization, Migration, and Social Mobility in Late Nineteenth Century America," in Barton Bernstein (ed.), *Towards a New Past: Dissenting Essays in American History* (New York: Random House, 1967), 158–75.

Thernstrom, Stephan, and Richard Sennett (eds.). *Nineteenth Century Cities: Essays in the New Urban History.* New Haven, Conn.: Yale University Press, 1969.

Warner, Sam Bass, Jr. *Streetcar Suburbs: The Process of Growth in Boston, 1870–1900.* Cambridge, Mass.: Harvard University Press, 1962.

Wooster, Ralph A. *The People in Power: Courthouse and Statehouse in the Lower South, 1850–1860.* Knoxville, Tenn.: University of Tennessee Press, 1969.

The Contributors

WILLIAM O. AYDELOTTE is a professor of history at the University of Iowa. His special interests are English political history of the nineteenth century and the broader questions of philosophy of history and method. He has published numerous articles.

LEE BENSON, a professor of history at the University of Pennsylvania, is the author of *The Concept of Jacksonian Democracy; Merchants, Farmers and Railroads,* and *Turner and Beard.* He also has published several major articles on historical method.

ALLAN G. BOGUE is Frederick Jackson Turner Professor of American History at the University of Wisconsin. He is a specialist in American frontier history, but his interests are wide-ranging, including social theory, political history, and historical method. He has published *Money at Interest* and *From Prairie to Corn Belt.*

WALTER DEAN BURNHAM is a professor of political science at Washington University at St. Louis. He is interested in American electoral patterns and has published widely.

LANCE E. DAVIS is a professor of economics at the California Institute of Technology at Pasadena. He is the co-author of the textbook *American Economic History,* and of many articles on American capital resources in the nineteenth century.

RODNEY O. DAVIS is a professor of history at Knox College. He is interested in nineteenth-century political history.

WILLIAM I. DAVISSON is a professor of economics at the University of Notre Dame. He has published articles in colonial economic history and has co-authored the textbook *An Introduction to Microeconomic Theory.*

ROBERT R. DYKSTRA is a professor of history at the University of Iowa. He is a specialist in frontier social and political history of the nineteenth century and is the author of *The Cattle Towns* and numerous articles.

ROBERT W. FOGEL is a professor of economics under a joint appointment at the universities of Chicago and Rochester. He has published *The Union Pacific Railroad* and *Railroads and American Economic Growth,* as well as many articles in nineteenth-century economic history.

IVOR S. FRANCIS is a professor of economic and social statistics at the New York School of Industrial and Labor Relations at Cornell University.

SHELDON HACKNEY is a professor of history at Princeton University. He is interested in the New South and has written *Populism to Progressivism in Alabama*.

HARLAN HAHN is a professor of political science at the University of California at Riverside. He is interested in American voting analysis and has published articles in this field.

RICHARD JENSEN is a professor of history at Washington University at St. Louis. He is a co-author of the methodology textbook *Quantitative Historical Research* and author of the forthcoming *Winning of the Midwest*.

RICHARD L. MERRITT is a professor of political science at the University of Illinois. He has written *Symbols of American Community, 1735–1775*, co-authored *Western European Perspectives on International Affairs*, and published many other works in political opinion analysis.

ARTHUR SCHLESINGER, JR., is a professor of history at the City University of New York. He is interested in American political history and has written *The Age of Jackson* and the multivolume *Age of Roosevelt*.

MARSHALL SMELSER is a professor of history at the University of Notre Dame. He has written *The Campaign for the Sugar Islands, 1759; The Congress Founds the Navy, 1787–1789;* and *The Democratic Republic, 1801–1815*.

STEPHAN THERNSTROM is a professor of history at Brandeis University, and is on a visiting appointment at the University of California at Los Angeles for 1969–1970. An urban specialist, he has published *Progress and Poverty: Social Mobility in a Nineteenth-Century City*, numerous articles, and has co-authored *Nineteenth-Century Cities*.

S. SIDNEY ULMER is a professor of political science at the University of Kentucky. He has published many articles in the quantitative anaylsis of judicial behavior.

ROGER E. WYMAN is a professor of history at Rutgers, The State University. He is interested in applying quantitative techniques in American electoral analysis.

Index

Silva, Ruth C., 41
Skinner, B. F., 33
Slavery, profitability of, 16
Smelser, Marshall, xix, 5
Social mobility, 40, 344–45
    definition of, 368–69
    explained, 369
    and geographical mobility, 370–72
    and intergenerational mobility, 383–88
    Newburyport study, 72–73
    and occupational mobility, 374–83
Social saving, 276–78, 294–95, 308
Social Science Research Council, 27, 29, 42, 43, 44, 45
Social science synthesis, 189–90
Social science "unified field theory," 282
Social statistics, *see* Statistics
Stanford Institute, 45
Statistical measures
    Bayes' Theorem, 99, 108–17
    Chi-square, 393–94
    log-odds, 113–15
    negative binomial distribution, 105–07
    Pearson's product-moment correlation coefficient *r, see* Correlation
    Pearson's contingency coefficient C, *see* Correlation
    Poisson model, 104–07, 109
    weight-rate study, 99, 117–18
Statistics, xv
    descriptive, 10–11
    inferential, 10–11
Stigler, George, 284
Stone, Lawrence, 9, 10
Stone, Philip J., 78
Suicide-homicide ratio, 350
Survey Research Center of the University of Michigan, 42, 194–95
Swierenga, Robert P., 270–71
Symbol analysis
    concept of, 83–85
    method of, 85–90
        and American nationalism, 91–95
    value of, 89–91

Temin, Peter, 269, 270, 286–87
Thelen, David P., 130
Thernstrom, Stephan, xiv–xv, 5, 10, 344–45
Thomas, Robert P., 269
Throne, Mildred, 344
Thrupp, Sylvia L., 10
Tilly, Charles, 10, 69
Turner, Frederick Jackson, xiii, 36, 44, 70, 132–33, 151

Ulmer, S. Sidney, xx, 129

"Vanderbilt School," 344
Van Deusen, Glyndon, 150
Von Neumann, John, xi, xvii
Voting behavior, 229–30, 253
    aggregationists, 194
    ethno-cultural factors, 235–37
    ethno-religious conflict, 239 ff
    functional thesis of, 218–25
    and immigrants, 206
    negative-reference group theory, 221–22
    and Negroes, 206, 222, 228–38
    participation
        drop-off, 198–99
        estimated turn-out, 196–201, 232
        mean partisan swing, 196–98
        roll-off, 196–98
        split-ticket voting, 196–98
    and rurality, 208–09
    state-level analysis, 201–16
    studies in, 194–95
    surge and decline model, 216–18
    survey research, 194
    and women suffrage, 206

Wallace, David L., 80, 97–99, 105, 119
Warner, Sam B., Jr., xiv, 10, 13–14
Whitney, William, 279
Wiebe, Robert, 401
Wiener, Norbert, 34–35
Wolff, Gerald, 130
Wyman, Roger E., 190–91

Robert P. Swierenga

Robert P. Swierenga is Associate Professor of History at Kent State University, Kent, Ohio. He received his master's degree from Northwestern University in 1958, and his doctorate from the State University of Iowa in 1965. He is the author of *Pioneers and Profits: Land Speculation on the Iowa Frontier*, and has contributed to numerous journals such as the *Journal of Economic History, Business History Review, Explorations in Economic History, Civil War History,* and *Agricultural History*.

DATE DUE

DISPLAY			
I'' 4-14-88			
GAYLORD			PRINTED IN U.S.A.